The Discourse Reader

Discourse analysis is a vast interdisciplinary movement. This *Reader* steers a clear path through the different areas and demonstrates the centrality of language in all domains of social life.

The Discourse Reader is the first comprehensive and integrative collection of key, original writings on discourse analysis.

The *Reader* is designed as a structured sourcebook for students from introductory undergraduate level upwards. Divided into clear sections, the *Reader* covers the foundations of modern discourse analysis and represents all of its contemporary methods and traditions, including:

- speech art theory;
- conversation analysis and ethnomethodology;
- interactional sociolinguistics;
- narrative analysis;
- critical discourse analysis.

Each section is introduced by the editors. *The Discourse Reader* is an indispensable introduction to theoretical writings and the best examples of discourse analysis. Contributors:

J. Maxwell Atkinson, J.L. Austin, M.M. Bakhtin, Allan Bell, Pierre Bourdieu, Penelope Brown, Carmen Rosa Caldas-Coulthard, Deborah Cameron, Aaron V. Cicourel, Norman Fairclough, Michel Foucault, Elizabeth Frazer, Anthony Giddens, Erving Goffman, Charles Goodwin, H.P. Grice, John J. Gumperz, John Heritage, Janet Holmes, Ian Hutchby, Roman Jakobson, Adam Kendon, Gunther Kress, William Labov, Stephen C. Levinson, Bronislaw Malinowski, Hugh Mehan, Elinor Ochs, Ben Rampton, Kay Richardson, Harvey Sacks, Emanuel A. Schegloff, Deborah Schiffrin, Deborah Tannen, Teun A. van Dijk, Theo van Leeuwen, Cynthia Wallat, Katherine Young.

Adam Jaworski is Senior Lecturer and **Nikolas Coupland** is Professor and Chair, both at the Cardiff Centre for Language and Communication Research at the University of Wales, Cardiff.

The Discourse Reader

Edited by Adam Jaworski
and Nikolas Coupland

Jennifer
Thackaberry

ROUTLEDGE
ROUTLEDGE
Taylor & Francis Group

London and New York

First published 1999
by Routledge
11 New Fetter Lane, London EC4P 4EE

Reprinted in 2000, 2001

Simultaneously published in the USA and Canada
by Routledge
29 West 35th Street, New York, NY 10001

Routledge is an imprint of the Taylor & Francis Group

Typeset in Perpetua by
Florence Production Ltd, Stoodleigh, Devon

Printed and bound in Great Britain by
Biddles Ltd, Guildford and King's Lynn

British Library Cataloguing in Publication Data
A catalogue record for this book is available from the British Library

Library of Congress Cataloguing in Publication Data
The discourse reader/[edited by] Adam Jaworski and
Nikolas Coupland.
p. cm.
ISBN 0-415-19733-3. — ISBN 0-415-129734-1 (pbk.)
1. Discourse analysis. I. Jaworski, Adam, 1957– .
II. Coupland, Nikolas, 1950– .
P302.D564 1999
401′.41—dc21
ISBN 0–415–19734–1 (Pbk)
ISBN 0–415–19733–3 (Hbk)

CONTENTS

FIGURES

PREFACE

THE DISCOURSE READER is an integrated and structured set of original writings, representing the interdisciplinary field of discourse studies, focusing principally on linguistic, interactional, textual, social and cultural issues. The volume is planned for use as a beginners'/intermediate degree-level teaching text, either on its own or as a secondary sourcebook. The readings are organised to provide a graded introduction to discourse theory and practice. For this reason, we have included several different sorts of text:

- influential early papers which laid the ground for the concept of discourse and defined the main priorities for 'discourse analysis';
- discussions of research methods and resources;
- reflexive commentaries by leading theorists, highlighting key differences between sub-traditions of discourse studies;
- papers showing what discourse analysis is able to achieve, applied to different social issues and social settings.

There is, therefore, a general chronological movement through the book from past to present, and from origins through methods to applications.

Since so many disciplines nowadays claim the term 'discourse' as their own, it is inevitably true that we have emphasised some traditions and schools more than others. Whatever discourse is, and however concretely or abstractly the term is used, there will at least be agreement that it has focally to do with language, meaning and context. For this reason we have started with a substantial section of readings on this theme. It is certainly true that discourse is not the privileged domain of linguists and linguists alone. But some appreciation of early ideas in functional linguistics and linguistic philosophy is essential for all students of discourse. Similarly, and although we would resist the idea that discourse analysis is 'a research method' in the conventional sense (see our Introduction to Part Two), it is important to see the broader research enterprise to which discourse analysis contributes. Part Two is therefore a collection of readings on methods and resources for doing discourse analysis. It introduces different traditions of social research and questions of research ethics, linked to practical issues of representing and analysing discourse data, and to forms of language analysis.

Parts Three to Six of the *Reader* then reproduce many of the key articles and book chapters which, over two decades and more, have dealt with specific themes and foci in discourse studies. Despite the need to be selective, we think that a large proportion of the most influential writers and texts are represented. Part Three introduces those approaches most concerned with sequence and discourse structure, tracing links back to ethnomethodology and carried forward in modern conversation analysis (CA) and related research. Part Four deals with social and relational aspects of discourse; Five with identity and subjectivity, as mediated by language; and Six with ideology, power and control and with critical approaches to discourse.

Establishing boundaries around an academic topic is always difficult. One specific problem for us in this case has been to establish a boundary between discourse analysis and those approaches to language and society referred to as 'interactional sociolinguistics'. In many people's view, including our own, there is no meaningful distinction between interactional work in sociolinguistics and discourse analysis applied to social settings and themes. Several of the readings we include in the present volume would be considered important contributions to interactional sociolinguistics. It would be useful, therefore, to consult the collection of articles entitled *Sociolinguistics: A Reader and Coursebook* (Coupland, N. and Jaworski, A. (eds) Macmillan, 1997).

We have reproduced all original papers and chapters as faithfully as we have been able to, given the inevitable restrictions of space and the need to produce a coherent and readable collection. We have, for example, maintained authors' original writing styles and conventions, whether they wrote to British or North American norms. In several cases this policy results in maintaining sexist-pronoun usage (e.g. Grice's and many others' use of 'man' for non-specific gender, where 'person' would be more usual and acceptable today). Where we have had to shorten original material, [. . .] shows that we have omitted a significant amount of original material (usually several sentences or whole sections). Sometimes we have added a short summary of the topic or main points of omitted sections. All our editorial comments are contained in square brackets: [ ].

ACKNOWLEDGEMENTS

The editors are grateful to Justine Coupland, Deborah Cameron, Paul Cobley and Darek Galasiński for their advice and practical help in the preparation of this volume. They would also like to thank staff at Routledge for their support in the preparation of this volume, especially Louisa Semlyen and Miranda Filbee.

The editors and publishers would like to thank the following copyright holders for permission to reprint material:

J. L. Austin, 'How to do things with words', 1975 OUP, by permission of Oxford University Press.

M. M. Bakhtin, 'The problem of speech genres' from *Speech Genres and Other Late Essays* by M. M. Bakhtin, translated by Vern W. McGee, edited by Caryl Emerson and Michael Holquist, Copyright © 1986. By permission of the University of Texas Press.

Allan Bell, 'News stories as narratives', from *The Language of News Media*, reproduced by permission of Blackwell Publishers 1991. Copyright © Allan Bell, 1991.

Pierre Bourdieu, chapter 2 from *Language and Symbolic Power*, by permission of Blackwell Publishers and Harvard University Press.

Penelope Brown and Stephen Levinson, 'Politeness: some universals in language usage', by permission of Cambridge University Press and the authors.

Carmen Rosa Caldas-Coulthard, '"Women who pay for sex. And enjoy it": transgression versus morality in women's magazines', from *Texts and Practices*, edited by Malcolm Coulthard and Carmen Rosa Caldas-Coulthard, 1995. Reproduced by permission of Routledge and Carmen Rosa Caldas-Coulthard.

Deborah Cameron, 'Performing gender identity: young men's talk and the construction of heterosexual masculinity', from *Language and Masculinity*,
edited by Sally Johnson and Ulrike Meinhof. Reproduced by permission
of Blackwell Publishers and Deborah Cameron.

Deborah Cameron, Elizabeth Frazer, Penelope Harvey, Ben Rampton and
Kay Richardson, 'Ethics, advocacy and empowerment', by permission
of Routledge, and Deborah Cameron and Kay Richardson on behalf of
the authors.

Aaron Cicourel, 'Interpretive Processes', reproduced by permission of the
author.

Norman Fairclough, 'Linguistic and intertextual analysis within discourse
analysis', from *Discourse & Society* 3/2. Reprinted by permission of Sage
Publications Ltd and Norman Fairclough.

Michel Foucault, 'The incitement to discourse', from *The History of Sexuality.
Volume 1: An Introduction*. Translation by Robert Hurley (Random House:
New York, 1978). Originally published in French as *La Volonté de savoir*
by Éditions Gallimard, Paris. Copyright © 1976 Éditions Gallimard.
Reprinted by permission of Georges Borchardt, Inc.

Anthony Giddens, 'Modernity and self-identity: tribulations of the self', from
Modernity and Self-Identity by Anthony Giddens with the permission of
the US publishers, Stanford University Press and Blackwell Publishers.
© 1991 Anthony Giddens.

Erving Goffman, 'On Face-work', from Erving Goffman, *Interaction Ritual:
Essays on Face-to-Face Behaviour*, Garden City, NY: Anchor Books, 1967.

Charles Goodwin, 'Practices of color classification in professional discourse',
by permission of Charles Goodwin.

H. P. Grice, 'Logic and conversation' from *Syntax and Semantics*, vol. 3, *Speech
Acts*, 41–58 (1975). Reproduced by permission of the Academic Press.

John J. Gumperz, 'Sociocultural knowledge in conversational inference', from
Linguistics and Anthropology, edited by Muriel Saville Troike, Georgetown
University Round Table on Language and Linguistics, 1977. Reproduced
by permission of Georgetown University Press.

Janet Holmes, 'Women, men and politeness: agreeable and disagreeable
responses', from *Women, Men and Politeness* by Janet Holmes. Reprinted
by permission of Addison Wesley Longman, Ltd.

Ian Hutchby, 'Power in discourse: the case of arguments on a British talk radio
show', from *Discourse & Society* 7/4, published by Sage Publications.
Reprinted by permission of the author and Sage Publications Ltd.

Roman Jakobson, 'Linguistics and poetics', from *Style in Language*, edited
by Thomas A. Sebeok, 1960. Reproduced by permission of the MIT
Press.

J. Maxwell Atkinson and John Heritage, 'Jefferson's transcript notation', from *Structures of Social Action: Studies in Conversation Analysis*, edited by J. Maxwell Atkinson and John Heritage. Reproduced by permission of Cambridge University Press.

Adam Kendon, 'The negotiation of context in face-to-face interaction' from *Rethinking Context* edited by A. Duranti and C. Goodwin. Reproduced by permission of Cambridge University Press and Adam Kendon.

Gunther Kress and Theo van Leeuwen, 'Representation and interaction: designing the position of the viewer', from *Reading Images: A Grammar of Visual Design*, 1996. Reproduced by permission of Routledge, Gunther Kress and Theo van Leeuwen.

William Labov, 'The transformation of experience in narrative', from *Language in the Inner City: Studies in Black English Vernacular* by William Labov. Copyright © 1972 University of Pennsylvania Press. Reprinted by permission of the University of Pennsylvania Press and Blackwell Publishers.

B. Malinowski, 'On phatic communion', from *The Meaning of Meaning*, edited by C. K. Ogden and I. A. Richards. Reproduced by permission of Routledge.

Hugh Mehan, 'Oracular reasoning in a psychiatric exam', from *Conflict Talk*, edited by A. Grimshaw. Reproduced by permission of Cambridge University Press and Hugh Mehan.

Elinor Ochs, 'Transcription as theory', from *Developmental Pragmatics*, edited by Elinor Ochs and Bambi B. Schieffelin, 1979. Reproduced by permission of the Academic Press.

H. Sacks, 'Everyone has to lie', from *Sociocultural Dimensions of Language Use*, edited by Mary Sanches and Ben G. Blount, 1975. Reproduced by permission of the Academic Press and Emanuel A. Schegloff, literary executor for Harvey Sacks.

Emanuel A. Schegloff, 'Reflections on talk and social structure', from *Talk and Social Structure*, edited by Dierdre Boden and Don Zimmerman. Permission granted by the Regents of the University of California and the University of California Press, Blackwell Publishers and Emanuel A. Schegloff. © 1991 Polity Press.

Emanuel A. Schegloff and H. Sacks, 'Opening up Closings' from *Semiotica* 7: 1973. Reproduced by permission of Mouton de Gruyter: A division of Walter de Gruyter GmbH & Co. Publishers, and Emanuel A. Schegloff.

Deborah Schiffrin, '*Oh* as a marker of information management', from *Discourse Markers* by D. Schiffrin. Reproduced by permission of Cambridge University Press and Deborah Schiffrin.

Deborah Tannen, 'New York Jewish conversational style' from the *International Journal of Sociology of Language*: 30, 1981. Reproduced by permission of Mouton de Gruyter and Deborah Tannen.

Deborah Tannen and Cynthia Wallat, 'Interactive frames and knowledge schemas in interaction: examples from a medical examination/interview', from *Social Psychology Quarterly*, June 1987. Reproduced by permission of the American Sociological Association and Deborah Tannen.

Teun A. van Dijk, 'Discourse and the denial of racism', from *Discourse & Society* 3/1. Reprinted by permission of Sage Publications Ltd and Teun A. van Dijk.

Katharine Young, 'Narrative embodiments: enclaves of the self in the realm of medicine', from *Texts of Identity*, edited by J. Shotter and K. J. Gergen, 1989. Reprinted by permission of Sage Publications Ltd.

Every effort has been made to obtain permission to reproduce copyright material. If any proper acknowledgement has not been made, or permission not received, we would invite copyright holders to inform us of the oversight.

Introduction:

PERSPECTIVES ON DISCOURSE ANALYSIS
Adam Jaworski and Nikolas Coupland

Discourse: an interdisciplinary movement

Deborah Schiffrin's (1994) book, *Approaches to Discourse,* compiles and discusses various definitions of discourse. Here are three of them from Schiffrin (pp. 23–43):

> Discourse is: 'language above the sentence or above the clause'.
> (Stubbs 1983:1)

> The study of discourse is the study of *any* aspect of language use.
> (Fasold 1990: 65)

> the analysis of discourse is, necessarily, the analysis of language in use. As such, it cannot be restricted to the description of linguistic forms independent of the purposes or functions which these forms are designed to serve in human affairs.
> (Brown and Yule 1983: 1)

Here are some others:

> with the sentence we leave the domain of language as a system of signs and enter into another universe, that of language as an instrument of communication, whose expression is discourse.
>
> (Benveniste 1971: 110, cited in Mills 1997: 4–5)

> Instead of gradually reducing the rather fluctuating meaning of the word 'discourse', I believe I have in fact added to its meanings: treating it sometimes as the general domain of all statements, some-times as an individualizable group of statements, and sometimes as a regulated practice that accounts for a number of statements.
>
> (Foucault 1972: 80, cited in Mills 1997: 6; see also Chapter 30)

> Fowler says that his programme for literary studies has the aim 'to change or even deconstruct the notion of literature so that a very wide range of discourses is actively used by individuals in their conscious engagements with ideology, experience and social organization'.
>
> (Fowler 1981: 199)

> 'Discourse' is for me more than *just* language use: it is language use, whether speech or writing, seen as a type of social practice.
>
> (Fairclough 1992: 28)

> Discourse *constitutes* the social. Three dimensions of the social are distinguished – knowledge, social relations, and social identity – and these correspond respectively to three major functions of language ... Discourse is shaped by relations of power, and invested with ideologies.
>
> (Fairclough 1992: 8; see also Chapter 11)

> According to Lee, it is an 'uncomfortable fact that the term "discourse" is used to cover a wide range of phenomena ... to cover a wide range of practices from such well documented phenomena as sexist discourse to ways of speaking that are easy to recognise in particular texts but difficult to describe in general terms (competitive discourse, discourse of solidarity, etc.).'
>
> (Lee 1992: 197)

> 'Discourse' . . . refers to language in use, as a process which is
> socially situated. However . . . we may go on to discuss the con-
> structive and dynamic role of either spoken or written discourse
> in structuring areas of knowledge and the social and institutional
> practices which are associated with them. In this sense, discourse
> is a means of talking and writing about and acting upon worlds,
> a means which both constructs and is constructed by a set of
> social practices within these worlds, and in so doing both repro-
> duces and constructs afresh particular social-discursive practices,
> constrained or encouraged by more macro movements in the over-
> arching social formation.
>
> (Candlin 1997: ix)

Other definitions of discourse will appear in the chapters to follow. These, and
the ones above, span a considerable range, although a core set of concerns also
emerges. It is this core, and the best-established deviations from it, that we
intend to unpack in the pages of the *Reader*. The quotations above consistently
emphasise 'language in use'. But there is a large body of opinion (see the later
quotations) that stresses what discourse is *beyond* language in use. Discourse
is language use relative to social, political and cultural formations – it is language reflecting social order but also language shaping social order, and shaping individuals' interaction with society. This is the key factor explaining
why so many academic disciplines entertain the notion of discourse with such
commitment. Discourse falls squarely within the interests not only of linguists,
literary critics, critical theorists and communication scientists, but also of geo-
graphers, philosophers, political scientists, sociologists, anthropologists, social
psychologists, and many others. Despite important differences of emphasis, discourse is an inescapably important concept for understanding society and
human responses to it, as well as for understanding language itself.

Part of the explanation for the upsurge of interest in discourse lies in a
fundamental realignment that has taken place, over the last two decades or so,
in how academic knowledge, and perhaps all knowledge, is assumed to be constituted. To put the negative side of this change, we might describe it as a
weakening of confidence in traditional ways of explaining phenomena and
processes, a radical questioning of how people, including academics, come to
appreciate and interpret their social and cultural environments. The rise in
importance of discourse has coincided with a falling off of intellectual security
in what we know and what it means to know – that is, a shift in epistemology,
in the theorising of knowledge (see Foucault, Chapter 30). The question of

how we build knowledge has come more to the fore, and this is where issues to do with language and linguistic representation come into focus.

Academic study, but in fact all aspects of experience, are based on acts of classification, and the building of knowledge and interpretations is very largely a process of defining boundaries between conceptual classes, and of labelling those classes and the relationships between them. This is one central reason why all intellectual endeavour, and all routine social living, needs to examine language, because it is through language that classification becomes possible (Lee 1992). Seen this way, language ceases to be a neutral medium for the transmission and reception of pre-existing knowledge. It is the key ingredient in the very constitution of knowledge. Many disciplines, more or less simultaneously, have come to see the need for an awareness of language, and of the structuring potential of language, as part of their own investigations. This is the shift often referred to as the 'linguistic turn' in the social sciences, but it is being experienced in academic study more generally.

All the same, it is not as if linguistics, 'the scientific study of language', has always provided the most appropriate means of studying knowledge-making processes and their social implications. Linguistics has tended to be an inward-looking discipline. It has not always appreciated the relevance of language and discourse to people other than linguists. The dominant traditions in linguistics, one could say until at least the 1970s, were particularly narrow, focusing on providing good descriptions of the grammar and pronunciation of utterances at the level of the sentence. Considerations of meaning in general, and particularly of how language, meaning and society interrelate, are still quite recent concerns. Discourse analysis is therefore a relatively new area of importance to linguistics too, which is moving beyond its earlier ambitions to describe sentences and to gain autonomy for itself as a 'scientific' area of academic study. Under the heading of discourse, studies of language have come to be concerned with far wider issues. Discourse linguists analyse, for example, the structure of conversations, stories and various forms of written text, the subtleties of implied meanings, and how language in the form of speech interacts with non-linguistic (e.g. visual or spatial) communication. Under the headings of cohesion and coherence they study how one communicative act or text depends on previous acts or texts, and how people creatively interact in the task of making and inferring meaning. We consider some of these main developments, in linguistics and in other disciplines, in more detail in Part One of the *Reader*.

So discourse has gained importance through at least two different, concurrent developments – a shift in the general theorising of knowledge and a broadening of perspective in linguistics. The *Reader* includes extracts from many of the most influential original writings on discourse, both theoretical and applied, which have brought about and benefited from this confluence of ideas. As individual chapters show, language studied as discourse opens up countless new areas for the critical investigation of social and cultural life – the composition of cultural groups, the management of social relations, the constitution of social institutions, the perpetuation of social prejudices, and so on.

Other general trends too have promoted interest in discourse. One is the growing recognition that contemporary life, at least in the world's most affluent and 'developed' societies, has qualities which distinguish it quite markedly from the 'modern' industrial, pre-World War Two period. One of the most obvious manifestations of what Anthony Giddens has called 'Late' or 'High Modernity' (Giddens 1991; see Chapter 24), and what is more generally referred to as *Postmodernity*, is the shift in advanced capitalist economies from manufacturing to service industries. Norman Fairclough (1992; 1995; Chapter 11) refers to one part of this phenomenon as the *technologisation* of discourse in post-Fordist societies (since the beginning of mass production of motor cars and similar industrial developments). Manufacturing and assembly workers working on production lines, isolated from consumers of the items they are producing, have been largely replaced by teams of workers networked together on communication tasks of different sorts or representing their companies in different kinds of service encounters with clients. In a rather literal sense, language takes on greater significance in the worlds of providing and consuming services, even if only in the promotional language of selling services in the competitive environment of banking, insurance companies or telephone-sales warehouses.

Rapid growth in communications media, such as satellite and digital television and radio, desktop publishing, telecommunications (mobile phone networks, video-conferencing), email, internet-mediated sales and services, information provision and entertainment, has created new media for language use. It is not surprising that language is being more and more closely scrutinised (e.g. within school curricula and by self-styled experts and guardians of so-called 'linguistic standards' – see Milroy and Milroy 1991; Cameron 1995 for detailed discussion of these issues), while simultaneously being shaped and honed (e.g., by advertisers, journalists and broadcasters) in a drive to generate ever-more attention and persuasive impact. Under these circumstances, language itself becomes marketable and a sort of commodity, and its purveyors can market themselves through their skills of linguistic and textual manipulation (see Bourdieu, Chapter 29). Discourse ceases to be 'merely' a function of work; it becomes work, just as it defines various forms of leisure and, for that matter, academic study. The analysis of discourse becomes correspondingly more important − in the first instance for those with direct commercial involvement in the language economies, and second, for those who need to deconstruct these new trends, to understand their force and even to oppose them.

This *critical* or socially engaged perspective on analysing discourse is apparent in several of the quotations above, pp. 1–3 − most obviously those from Christopher Candlin, Norman Fairclough and Roger Fowler. (Part Six of the *Reader* contains several critically orientated texts, but see also Chapters 8, 11 and 23.) If we ask what is the purpose of doing discourse analysis, the answer from critical discourse analysts would go well beyond the description of language in use. Discourse analysis offers a means of exposing or deconstructing the social practices which constitute 'social structure' and what we might call the conventional meaning structures of social life. It is a sort of forensic activity, with a libertarian political slant. The motivation for doing discourse analysis is very often a concern about social inequality and the perpetuation of power relationships, either between individuals or between social groups, difficult though it is to pre-judge moral correctness in many cases.

As this implies, the focus for a particular analysis can be either very local − analysing a particular conversation between two people or a single diary entry − or very global and abstract. In this latter tradition, the theoretical work of Michel Foucault (see Chapter 30) and that of Michel Pêcheux (1982) has been very influential in introducing the link between discourse and ideology. Pêcheux stresses how any one particular discourse or 'discursive formation' stands, at the level of social organisation, in conflict with other discourses. He gives us a theory of how societies are organised through their ideological struggles, and how particular groups (e.g. social class groups or gender groups) will be either more or less privileged in their access to particular discourse networks. Local and global perspectives come together when some type of discourse analysis can show how the pressure of broad social or institutional norms is brought to bear on the identity and classification of individuals (see, for example, Mehan's analysis of a psychiatric interview in Chapter 33).

Let us recap briefly. At the most basic level, discourse is definable as language in use, but many definitions incorporate significantly more than this. Discourse is implicated in expressing people's points of view and value systems, many of which are 'pre-structured' in terms of what is 'normal' or 'appropriate' in particular social and institutional settings. Discourse practices can therefore by seen as the deployment of, and indeed sometimes as acts of resistance to, dominant ideologies. The focus of discourse analysis will usually be the study of particular texts (e.g., conversations, interviews, speeches, etc., or various written documents), although discourses are sometimes held to be abstract value systems which will never surface directly as texts. Texts are specific products which, to varying degrees, will reflect global as well as local discourse practices relevant to their production and reception. Discourse analysis can range from the description and interpretation of meaning-making and meaning-understanding in specific situations through to the critical analysis of ideology and access to meaning-systems and discourse networks. Language and discourse seem to have a particular salience in contemporary, late-modern social arrangements.

From this preliminary overview it is already apparent why the study of discourse is an interdisciplinary project. Most disciplines, and certainly all of the human and social sciences, need to deal with the interrelations between discourse and concepts such as social structure, social relations, conflict, ideology, selfhood, postmodernity and social change.

Multi-modal and multi-voiced discourses

It is worth emphasising that discourse reaches out further than language itself. When we think of discourse in the wider context of communication, we can extend its analysis to include non-linguistic *semiotic systems* (systems for signalling meaning), those of non-verbal and non-vocal communication which accompany or replace speech or writing (see Hodge and Kress 1991 for an overview of social semiotics). Discourse practices include the 'embodied' or more obviously physical systems of representation, for example performance art, sign language or, more generally, what Pierre Bourdieu has called the 'bodily hexis'; see Chapter 29). Other non-verbal discourse modes include painting, sculpture, photography, design, music and film (see Kress and van Leeuwen 1996; Chapter 23; Kress, Leite-Garcia and van Leeuwen 1997; O'Toole 1994).

If discourse is the set of social practices which 'make meaning', then many of the texts produced in this process are *multi-modal*, that is, they make use of more than one semiotic system. For example, a television commercial may combine any of the following elements: spoken and written language, still and moving images, 'live' actors and animation/computer graphics, music, etc. (e.g. Goodman 1996; Graddol 1996). The *Reader* is mainly concerned with discourse as spoken and written linguistic interaction, because this is where the preponderance of research has been done. But we have also included several chapters which explicitly deal with other modalities and semiotic systems, often intimately intertwined with language (see, especially, Kendon, Chapter 22; Kress and van Leeuwen, Chapter 23; Goodwin, Chapter 28; and Bourdieu, Chapter 29).

The idea that discourse is multiply structured has been dominant since the earliest days of discourse analysis and its predecessor in functional linguistics (see our Introduction to Part One). Roman Jakobson (Chapter 1), Michael Halliday and others stressed that language in use realises many functions simultaneously, for example an informational function alongside relational and aesthetic functions. The focus on multi-modal discourse is in one sense a continuation of this traditional view, especially when it can be shown that different semiotic resources or dimensions (e.g., visual images and linguistic text in a school textbook) fulfil different communicative functions. But texts can be multiply structured in other ways, if they *show multiple voicing* or *heteroglossia* (Bakhtin 1981; 1986; Chapter 7). Texts often reflect and recycle different voices, which may be realised through different modalities or indeed a single modality, and addressing one or many audiences. For example, David Graddol's (1996) study of a wine label illustrates how the label, as a 'semiotic space', consists of different sub-texts, realised in different visual fonts and layout. The sub-texts are a description of the type of wine and its qualities, a health warning, and a bar and numerical code. Many of them realise different voices – consumerist, legal, commercial. They address potentially different audiences – consumers, health promoters, retailers – and for different reasons. We might think of these voices as fragments of different discourses – socially organised ways of thinking, talking and writing about wine and food, with value systems built into familiar patterns of expression.

Or to take another example, a hypothetical car TV commercial which may embody a number of 'real' or 'implied' voices, addressing viewers in a multitude of roles – as drivers, passengers, car experts, status-seekers, parents concerned over their children's safety, overseers of family budgets, etc. The different voices to be heard (or seen) in this context can be realised via spoken language, e.g., a matter-of-fact commentary on the merits of the car, such as its safety, its comfort or its favourable price. They may appear through written/visual signs, e.g., the company's logo or the advertisement's small print. Cinematic and musical elements will also be present, e.g., photographs representing selected features of the car's design or its appearance and performance on the road, or a well-known tune with 'fitting' lyrics, and so on.

Some of these voices may be competing with each other or representing conflicting interests or ideologies (e.g., safety vs. speeding). For Mikhail Bakhtin, all discourse is multi-voiced, as all words and utterances echo other words and utterances derived from the historical, cultural and genetic heritage of the speaker and from the ways these words and utterances have been previously interpreted. In a broader sense then, 'voices' can be interpreted as discourses – positions, ideologies or stances that speakers and listeners take in particular instances of co-constructed interaction. Since many and even *most* texts are not 'pure' reflections of single discourses, analysis will have to incorporate a significant element of text-to-text comparison, tracing the influence of one sort or genre of text upon another. This is what Fairclough (Chapter 11) and others have referred to as an *intertextual* approach to discourse analysis. The forensic task of the discourse analysis will be to track how various forms of discourse, and their associated values and assumptions, are incorporated into a particular text, why and with what effects.

The layering of social meaning in discourse

Discourse analysis is an interdisciplinary project for many reasons. Most obviously, as we suggested above, many disciplines are fundamentally engaged with discourse as social and cultural practice. But let us accept, for the moment, the least ambitious definition of discourse analysis from the set of quotations at the head of this Introduction, 'the analysis of language in use'. Even at this level, it is easy enough to demonstrate that discourse is, for example, a thoroughly linguistic *and* social *and* cognitive affair. Consider the following simple instance, reconstructed from a real social event, but with the names of the participants changed. The person called 'Mother' is the mother of the 8-year-old child, called 'Rebecca'. The person called 'Mrs Thomson' is employed as a domestic cleaner by the family in which 'Mother' is the mother; Mrs Thomson's first-name is 'Margaret'. Mrs Thomson has just come in through the front door, having rung the doorbell first, and Mother speaks first, calling downstairs to her daughter:

Extract 1
(*The front door bell rings.*)
Mother: Open the door, darling. Who is it?

Rebecca:	It's only Maggie.
Mother:	(*looking sheepish*) Oh hello, Mrs Thomson.
Mrs Thomson:	(*smiles*) Hello.

Even this short sequence alerts us to the complexities of meaning-making and the range of resources that both we, as observers or analysts, and the participants themselves have to draw on to 'make sense' of what is happening in the sequence, as a piece of situated social interaction. It seems obvious that there is a measure of discomfort in the conversational exchanges here, signalled in our representation of Mother's facial expression as 'sheepish'. 'Sheepish' is, of course, already an interpretation (ours). It is based on a linguistic classification of a possibly complex emotional state. In glossing Mother's expression as 'sheepish', we are appealing to a 'state' that we assume is both recognisable to others (in this case, you, the readers of this text), and reasonably applicable to the facial and perhaps postural configurations that we remember as being adopted by Mother. A video-taped recording would in fact be important in justifying our use of the term 'sheepish', if we needed to. But even then, our interpretation that these face and body features properly represent the category 'sheepishness' would depend on others (such as you) making the same or a similar inference.

So far, we have pointed to one small aspect of the linguistic work of classification that is built into the written record of Extract 1. But of course there are very many other classification processes at work here, for us and for the participants themselves. As readers, you may be asking *why* Mother is uncomfortable, and how the discourse – the totality of meaning-making and meaning-inferring generated through this interaction – produces an impression that this is the probable emotional effect. A likely explanation (and the one that led us to choose this bit of talk as an example) is that Mother is embarrassed by her daughter referring to Mrs Thomson as 'Maggie'. She is probably embarrassed further by the expression *only Maggie*, especially (or maybe *only*?) because Mrs Thompson has overheard Rebecca's utterance referring to her.

A linguistic analysis of the usual circumstances under which we use the word 'only' will get us some distance here, when we realise that 'only' often projects an event as being unimportant or unexceptional. Mother may well be embarrassed that Rebecca considers Mrs Thomson's arrival as an event of the sort that might be called 'only'. She may also be uncomfortable that her daughter, a child, is referring to an adult by an overly familiar expression – using her first name, all of that being witnessed by Mrs Thompson.

We have few problems making these or similar inferences. But it is interesting to consider just *how* we are able to make them. For example, they seem to rely, in part, on there being a social consensus about how children usually do, or ought to, talk to adults. But is this universally true or just a convention in one particular cultural situation? More particularly, some of the social sensitivity in the exchange hinges on the child using a first name not only in reference to an adult, but to an adult employed as a cleaner. There are particularly strong reverberations of social class and economic power behind this exchange, and they certainly make up an element of its 'meaning'. However, bringing these underlying political and economic assumptions to the surface is a social taboo, and it is Rebecca's unwitting breaking of this taboo that probably also causes her mother's embarrassment.

In the other direction, there is an element of 'understanding' suggested in Mrs Thomson's smile, perhaps implying she appreciates that Rebecca is not fully able to judge the social conventions or rules for addressing adults. The smile may be an attempt to mitigate the discomfort Mother is feeling. On the other hand, Mrs Thompson's smile could also be an accommodating reaction to Rebecca's remark. For her to react in a different way and signal indignation would mean breaking another taboo. In any case, note how 'child' and 'cleaner', not to mention 'mother' and 'daughter', are linguistic labels for social categories with predictable social qualities and expectations attached to them. Note that our access to 'the meaning' of the interaction depends on how we hang these labels on individuals, and on people's labelling of others. Note how we have to make inferences about people's intentions, and about how those intentions are perceived and evaluated by others.

Another part of what is achieved as meaning in the interaction depends on rather precise timing and placement, which are not at all captured in the written transcript of what was said. As has been suggested above, Mother's embarrassment may be exacerbated by the fact that, in our reconstruction of it, the *It's only Maggie* utterance is said when all three participants are present together, face to face. *Maggie* might well be the usual way the family has of referring to Mrs Thomson when she is not present. Changing the composition of the group by Mrs Thompson's joining the *participation framework* as an unratified recipient, or 'overhearer' (Goffman 1981: 132), of Rebecca's utterance certainly shifts expectations of what are the 'appropriate' forms of expression. In this regard, we might read a particular significance into Mother's *Oh*, perhaps as a conventional way of expressing a 'change of state' (Heritage 1984a; Schiffrin, Chapter 16). Mother's expectation that she was speaking with her daughter, and only her, is broken when she sees that Mrs Thomson has already entered the house, and Mother signals this in her talk when she uses the particle *Oh*.

There are other, seemingly more mundane, observations to be made about how this interaction is structured, although they are still important from some perspectives. For example, we take it for granted that Mrs Thomson's *Hello* is structurally linked to Mother's *Hello* in the previous turn at talk. That is, it is not coincidental that both speakers do greeting, and do it through the use of the same greeting word. As CA (conversation analysis) has established (see Schegloff and Sacks, Chapter 15 and our Introduction to Part Three), the second *Hello* not only follows the first, but is occasioned by the first; it is the second part of a pair of utterances. Its absence would be a noticeable absence. In more cognitive terms, it is probable that Mrs Thomson feels something of an obligation, however subconsciously, to match Mother's *Hello* which had been offered to her. This is part of what it means to call an exchange of greetings a cultural convention, or a *mini-ritual* of social interaction. Exchanging paired greetings is the predictable or 'unmarked' way of opening social encounters, between either strangers or (as here) people already familiar with each other.

The general point is that, in social interaction, speakers are achieving meaning at many levels. They are exchanging information between them (although very little of the extract under discussion is concerned with trans-mitting 'information' in the usual sense of 'facts' or 'data'), and negotiating particular relationships between them as individuals. But at the same time their talk is filling out and confirming wider patterns of social organisation, for example in running through predictable patterns of turn-taking, and pairing of utterances. We can say that the structured nature of everyday talk (see Goffman's 1983 concept of *the interaction order*) generates and confirms broader patterns of social organisation (*the social order*). One important facet of discourse analysis is therefore, as we saw earlier, to show how micro-level social actions realise and give local form to macro-level social structures.

Rather than pursue this particular example any further, we can at least summarise those dimensions of discourse that we need to attend to if we are to (begin to) understand how it functions as a discourse event. We have, directly or indirectly, already identified the following aspects:

1   The meaning of an event or of a single utterance is only partly accounted for by its formal features (that is, by the 'direct meaning' of the words used). The social significance of discourse, if we define it simply as language in use, lies in the relationship between linguistic meanings and the wider

context (i.e. the social, cultural, economic, demographic and other characteristics of the communicative event) in which interaction takes place.

2   Our interpretation of discourse therefore relates far more to what is
     done by participants than what is said (or written, or drawn, or pointed
     at) by them. That is, a functional analysis of language and other semi-
     otic systems lies at the heart of analysing discourse.

3   It is important to distinguish between meanings (including goals and
     intentions) inferred by observers and meanings (including goals and inten-
     tions) inferred by participants. Analysing discourse is often making infer-
     ences about inferences.

4   All aspects of meaning-making are acts of construction. Attributing
     meaning to discursive acts is never a neutral or value-free process.

5   Social categorisation is central to these acts of construction. Our lan-
     guage presents us with many categories that seem 'natural' or 'obvious',
     although they are very probably so only at a given time and place: they
     may well be culture specific or idiosyncratic (favoured by an individual).

6   We can only access discourse through the textual data which we collect
     by observation, audio or video-recording. This means that the texts we
     analyse are always 'filtered' or 'mediated'; they are in themselves a
     form of social (re)construction.

7   Linguistic expression itself (as speech or writing) often needs to be
     interrelated with other physical, temporal and behavioural aspects of
     the social situation, such as body movement and the synchronisation of
     actions. Discourse is more than (verbal/vocal) language itself.

8   Close attention to and critical reading of particular instances of language
     in use, linked to other aspects of the social context, is a useful way of
     discovering the normal and often unwritten assumptions behind commu-
     nication. Although interpretation will always have elements of subjectiv-
     ity within it, communication is based on linked, subjective interaction
     (*inter-subjectivity*). A more formal approach is likely to miss the creative
     inter-subjectivity of social interaction. (In saying this we do not deny that
     language is a structured phenomenon, or deny the importance of this fact.
     Language and other semiotic systems have recognisable structures and
     the study of these structures as formal systems constitutes an entirely
     viable, but different, research programme.)

9   Discourse analysis provides a way of linking up the analysis of local
     characteristics of communication to the analysis of broader social char-
     acteristics. It can let us see how macro-structures are carried through
     micro-structures.

Traditions of discourse analysis

The *Reader* offers a broad and inclusive perspective on the concept of discourse, which is appropriate in view of how many academic disciplines (as we have explained) now see discourse as an important theoretical and empirical focus for them. At the same time discourse, however we define it, has focally to do with language use. Some approaches remain quite close to the central goals of linguistics, offering better linguistic descriptions of texts, spoken and written. At the other extreme, as we have seen, there are approaches to discourse which assume that the most significant sorts of linguistic organisation are highly abstract, and not directly amenable to textual analysis.

We can use this approximate scale of directness–indirectness as a way to organise a discussion of several different traditions of discourse analysis. All of them are represented in the *Reader*, although the following sub-sections (as many taxonomic or listing frameworks do) probably overstate the degree of difference between approaches. In practice, discourse analysts and the analyses they produce do not fall quite so neatly into these types. It is also true that many researchers have taken an inclusive view of discourse studies, to the extent that their work spans most or all of the traditions we survey below. One clear instance is the work of Teun van Dijk, who has been more responsible than any other person for integrating the field of discourse analysis (see, for example, van Dijk 1977; 1984; 1985; 1988; 1997; also Chapter 32).

Despite these limitations, it should be helpful to approach the various Parts of the *Reader* armed with a mental map of the principal traditions of discourse studies and their main defining qualities. These general overviews should also be helpful in identifying sources for further reading for students new to any of these fields. We have included at the end of this chapter a list of the main academic journals which print new research in discourse and related fields.

Speech act theory and pragmatics

The study of meaning is at the heart of the discipline referred to as pragmatics. Closely related to semantics, which is primarily concerned with the study of word and sentence meaning, pragmatics concerns itself with the meaning of utterances in specific contexts of use. It is one thing to understand a phrase as far as the individual meanings of its words and its referential meaning is concerned, and quite another to know what its intended meaning may be in context. Charles Fillmore illustrates the pitfalls of relying on sentence meaning in interpreting talk and disregarding pragmatic meaning of an utterance by recounting two anecdotes concerning the fixed phrase *I thought you'd never ask*:

> It's a fairly innocent teasing expression in American English, but it could easily be taken as insulting by people who did not know its special status as a routine formula. In one case a European man asked an American woman to join him in the dance, and she, being playful, said, 'I thought you'd never ask'. Her potential dancing partner withdrew his invitation in irritation. In another case a European hostess offered an American guest something to drink, when he, unilaterally assuming a teasing relationship, said, 'I thought you'd never ask'. He was asked to leave the party for having insulted his host.
>
> (Fillmore 1984:129–30)

Jenny Thomas (1995) distinguishes three types of meaning (illustrated here with our own examples):

- *abstract* meaning (the meaning of words and sentences in isolation, e.g., the various meanings of the word *grass*, or the ambiguity of the sentence *I saw her duck*);
- *contextual* or *utterance* meaning (e.g., when two intimate persons hold their faces very near each other and one says to the other *I hate you* while smiling, the utterance 'really' means 'I love you'); and
- utterance *force* (i.e., how the speaker intends his/her utterance to be understood; e.g., when X says to Y *are you hungry?*, X may intend the question as a request for Y to make X a sandwich).

Thomas focuses on utterance meaning and force, which are central to pragmatics, which she defines as the study of 'meaning in interaction' (p. 22) with the special emphasis on the interrelationship between the speaker, hearer, utterance and context.

The notion of force is borrowed directly from J. L. Austin's work on speech act theory (Chapter 2), and his three-fold distinction into the *locution* of a speech act (the actual words used in an utterance), its *illocution* (the force or the intention of the speaker behind the utterance), and its *perlocution* (the effect of the utterance on the listener). Studying the effects of the speaker's utterances on the listener derived from Austin's view of language as a form of *action*. Austin observed that by saying something, we not only communicate ideas, but may also transform the reality. Speech acts which effect such a change through the action of being spoken are called *performative speech acts* (or *performatives*). For example, the act of joining two people in marriage is principally a (performative) speech act involving the formula: *I now/hereby pronounce you husband and wife.* Of course, in order for a performative to realise its perlocutionary force, it has to meet certain social and cultural criteria, or fulfil *felicity conditions*. It is clear, for example, that unauthorised individuals cannot pronounce anyone husband and wife.

Much of speech act theory has been concerned with taxonomising speech acts and defining felicity conditions for different types of speech acts. For example, John Searle (1969; 1979) suggested the following typology of speech acts based on different types of conditions which need to be fulfilled for an act to obtain: 'representatives (e.g., asserting), directives (e.g., requesting), commissives (e.g., promising), expressives (e.g., thanking), and declarations (e.g., appointing)' (quoted after Schiffrin 1994: 57). This taxonomy was one of many, and it soon became clear in speech act theory that a full and detailed classification would be unwieldy given the multitude of illocutionary verbs in English. Stipulating the felicity conditions for all of them appeared to be not only a complex procedure but also an 'essentialising' one – relying too heavily on factors assumed to be essential in each case, when reality shows us that they are variably determined by the precise social context.

An elaboration of speech act theory was offered by Labov and Fanshel (1977) in their examination of a psychiatric interview. Although their prime concern was with the identification of speech acts and specifying the rules governing their successful realisation, they broadened the view that an utterance may only perform one type of speech act at a time. For example, the following utterance by a client in their data, reported to have been said to her mother: *Well, when d'you plan to come home?* may be a request for information, a challenge, or an expression of obligation (cf. Taylor and Cameron 1987).

Like Austin and Searle, Labov and Fanshel explain communication in terms of hearers accurately identifying the intended meaning of the speaker's utterance and responding to it accordingly. However, given the multi-functionality of utterances, we cannot be sure that a hearer alway picks up the 'right' interpretation of an utterance, i.e., the one that was intended by the speaker. In general, the problem of intentionality and variability in people's discourse rules precluded developing a coherent framework for explaining communication, beyond producing an inventory of such rules and speech act types. A different way of explaining communication was proposed by H. P. Grice (Chapter 3), whose work was central in the development of inferential pragmatics and interactional sociolinguistics (on the latter field, see pp. 27–29).

Grice, like Austin and Searle, was a philosopher, whose interest in language stemmed from the investigations of sense, reference, truth, falsity and logic. However, Grice argued that the logic of language (or conversation, as the title of his classic paper has it) is not based on the same principles as formal (mathematical) logic. Instead, he proposed a model of communication based on the notion of the *Cooperative Principle*, i.e. the collaborative efforts of rational participants in directing conversation towards attaining a common goal. In following the Cooperative Principle the participants follow a number of specific maxims (conversational maxims), such as *be informative, be truthful, be relevant* and *be clear*. When the maxims are adhered to, meaning is produced in an unambiguous, direct way. However, most meaning is *implied*, through two kinds of *implicatures*: 'conventional implicatures', which follow from the conventional meanings of words used in utterances, and 'conversational implicatures', which result from the non-observance of one (or more) of the conversational maxims. When participants assume that the Cooperative Principle is being observed but one of the maxims is violated, they seek an indirect interpretation via conversational implicature. To use a well-known example from Grice (see p. 85), if a letter of recommendation appears to be underinformative (violating the maxim *be informative*) and concentrates wholly on, say, the candidate's punctuality and good manners (violating the maxim *be relevant*), assuming the cooperativity of its author, the addressee may infer that the candidate is not suitable for the job.

Grice's impact on pragmatics and discourse analysis in general cannot be overestimated. Although he has been criticised for formulating his Cooperative Principle to suit the conversational conventions of middle-class English speakers, and for not attending to the idea of strategic *non*-cooperation, the guiding principle of inference as a primary source of meaning in interaction remains central in most current approaches to discourse. Two areas in which Grice's influence has been felt most strongly are in the theories of linguistic politeness (see Chapters 19 and 20) and of relevance. We will introduce relevance theory in some detail because it is a significant independent model of discourse processing which we have been unable to cover in its own discrete chapter.

The cognitively orientated approach to communication proposed by Dan Sperber and Deirdre Wilson (1986/1995) makes Grice's maxim of relevance central to explaining how information is processed in discourse. In sharp opposition to the code models of language, *relevance theory* assumes that linguistic communication is based on *ostension* and *inference*, which can be said to be the same process viewed from two different perspectives. The former belongs to the communicator, who is involved in ostension, and the latter to the audience, who is/are involved in inference. Inferential compre- hension of the communicator's ostensive behaviour relies on deductive processing of any new information presented in the context of old information. This derivation of new information is spontaneous, automatic and uncon- scious, and gives rise to certain contextual effects in the cognitive environment of the audience. The occurrence of contextual effects, such as contextual implications, contradictions and strengthening, is a necessary condition for relevance. The relation between contextual effects and relevance is that, other things being equal, 'the greater the contextual effects, the greater the rele- vance' (Sperber and Wilson 1986: 119). In other words, an assumption which has no contextual effects at some particular moment of talk is irrel- evant, because processing this assumption does not change the old context.

A second factor in assessing the degree of relevance of an assumption is the processing effort necessary for the achievement of contextual effects. It is a negative factor, which means that, other things being equal, 'the greater the pro- cessing effort, the lower the relevance' (Sperber and Wilson 1986: 124). The theory holds that, in communication, speaking partners first assume the rele- vance of an assumption and then select a context in which relevance will be max- imised (it is not the case that context is determined first and then the relevance of a stimulus assessed). Sperber and Wilson also say that, of all the assumptions that a phenomenon can make manifest to an individual, only some will actually catch his/her attention. Others will be filtered out at a subattentive level. These phenomena, which have some bearing on the central thought processes, draw the attention of an individual and make assumptions and inferences appear at a conceptual level. Thus, they define the relevance of a phenomenon as follows:

> [A] phenomenon is relevant to an individual to the extent that the contextual effects achieved when it is optimally processed are large . . .
> [A] phenomenon is relevant to an individual to the extent that the effort required to process it optimally is small.
>
> (Sperber and Wilson 1986: 153)

Owing to its cognitive orientation and its initial interest in information processing, relevance theory has been largely concerned with the referential function of language. Due to this methodological and programmatic bias, it has been criticised for being inadequate to account for the socially relevant aspects of discourse, and for insufficient involvement with the interactional aspects of language use. Relevance theory has dismissed such criticisms as misguided, because its primary interest has explicitly *not* been social. Still, in recent revisions, its authors have begun to explain the potential of relevance theory in accounting for social aspects of communication (see Sperber and Wilson 1997).

Conversation analysis

The origins and much of current practice in conversation analysis (CA) reside in the sociological approach to language and communication known as *ethnomethodology* (Garfinkel 1974; Cicourel, Chapter 4). Ethnomethodology means studying the link between what social actors 'do' in interaction and what they 'know' about interaction. Social structure is a form of order, and that order is partly achieved through talk, which is itself structured and orderly. Social actors have common-sense knowledge about what it is they are doing interactionally in performing specific activities and in jointly achieving communicative coherence. Making this knowledge about ordinary, everyday affairs explicit, and in this way finding an understanding of how society is organised and how it functions, is ethnomethodology's main concern (Garfinkel 1967; Turner 1974; Heritage 1984b).

Following this line of inquiry, CA views language as a form of social action and aims, in particular, to discover and describe how the organisation of social interaction makes manifest and reinforces the structures of social organisation and social institutions (see, e.g., papers in Boden and Zimmerman 1991; Drew and Heritage 1992a; Schegloff, Chapter 6; Hutchby and Wooffitt 1998). Hutchby and Wooffitt, who point out that 'talk in interaction' is now commonly preferred to the designation 'conversation', define CA as follows:

> CA is the study of *recorded, naturally occurring talk-in-interaction* ... Principally it is to discover how participants understand and respond to one another in their turns at talk, with a central focus being on how sequences of interaction are generated. To put it

> another way, the objective of CA is to uncover the tacit reasoning
> procedures and sociolinguistic competencies underlying the pro-
> duction and interpretation of talk in organized sequences of
> interaction.
>
> (1998: 14)

As this statement implies, the emphasis in CA in contrast to earlier
ethnomethodological concerns has shifted away from the patterns of 'knowing'
per se towards discovering the *structures of talk* which produce and reproduce patterns of social action. At least, structures of talk are studied as the
best evidence of social actors' practical knowledge about them. (Schegloff,
Ochs and Thompson 1996 give an informative account of the early history
of CA.)

One central CA concept is *preference*, the idea that, at specific points in
conversation, certain types of utterances will be more favoured than others
(e.g. the socially preferred response to an invitation is acceptance, not rejection). Other conversational features which CA has focused on include:

- openings and closings of conversations (see Schegloff and Sacks,
  Chapter 15);
- adjacency pairs (i.e. paired utterances of the type summons-answer,
  greeting-greeting, compliment-compliment response, etc.);
- topic management and topic shift;
- conversational repairs;
- showing agreement and disagreement;
- introducing bad news and processes of troubles-telling;
- (probably most centrally) mechanisms of turn-taking.

In their seminal paper, Sacks, Schegloff and Jefferson (1974) suggested a
list of guiding principles for the organisation of turn-taking in conversation (in
English). They observed that the central principle which speakers follow in
taking turns is to avoid gaps and overlaps in conversation. Although gaps do of
course occur, they are brief. Another common feature of conversational turns
is that, usually, one party speaks at a time. In order to facilitate turn-taking,
speakers observe a number of conventionalised principles. For example, speakers follow well-established scripts, as in service encounters, in which speaker
roles are clearly delineated. They fill in appropriate 'slots' in discourse structure, e.g., second part utterances in adjacency pairs, and they anticipate completion of an utterance on the basis of a perceived completion of a grammatical

unit (a clause or a sentence). Speakers themselves may signal their willingness to give up the floor in favour of another speaker (who can be 'nominated' by current speaker only). They can do this by directing their gaze towards the next speaker and employing characteristic gesturing patterns synchronising with the final words. They may alter pitch, speak more softly, lengthen the last syllable or use stereotyped tags (e.g., *you know* or *that's it*) (see Graddol, Cheshire and Swann 1994 for a summary; also Kendon, Chapter 22).

Turn-taking is additionally facilitated by the fact that it is most likely to take place in highly predictable, recurring moments in conversation, *the transition–relevance places* (Sacks *et al.* 1974). The cues signalling that a turn is about to be terminated (outlined in the preceding paragraph) tend to coincide with the end of various structural units of talk: clauses, sentences, narratives, but they may also be signalled after smaller formal units, such as phrases or single words.

This brief overview does not do justice to CA's contribution to the description of talk in a wide range of private and public settings. Suffice it to say that its insights are valuable to understand patterns of individual relations between interactants, individuals' positions within larger institutional structures (e.g., Mehan, Chapter 33), and overall societal organisation. What is also important is that CA has taken the study of discourse firmly into a more dynamic realm of interaction away from the speaker-centredness of speech act theory (see above).

This is not to say that CA is without its critics. The most contested notion in relation to CA is that of 'context'. Indeed, what CA programmatically assumes to be the sole (and sufficient) source of its analysis is, as John Heritage points out, the organisation of talk itself:

> The initial and most fundamental assumptions of conversation analysis is that all aspects of social action and interaction can be examined in terms of the conventionalized or institutionalized structural organizations which analyzably inform their production. These organizations are to be treated as structures in their own right which, like other social institutions and conventions, stand independently of the psychological or other characteristics of particular participants.
>
> (Heritage 1984b: 1–2)

The ethnographic critique of CA's disregard for the cultural and historical context of interactions is summarised by Alessandro Duranti (1997). Although he does not dismiss CA's methods and goals *a priori*, he also argues that some of the insights and observations about interaction cannot be accessed without attending to the fine ethnographic detail. (See Moerman 1988; Besnier 1989; Ochs 1988 for examples of studies which combine CA with attention to the cultural detail characteristic of the ethnographic approach. We return to aspects of this critique in our Introduction to Part Three of the *Reader*.)

Discursive psychology

An interdisciplinary movement like discourse analysis is likely to spawn new areas of specialist research, at first on the fringes of established disciplines. Discursive psychology (Edwards and Potter 1992 is an integrative overview) has recently established itself as a coherent approach to some traditional research themes in psychology such as the study of attitudes, but strongly opposing the statistical and experimental methods which have come to dominate research in psychology (including social psychology). Jonathan Potter and Margaret Wetherell's (1987) book, *Discourse and Social Psychology: Beyond Attitudes and Behaviour*, was a ground-breaking critique of established methods and assumptions in social psychology.

Discourse analysts' hostility to the notion of linguistic 'behaviour' (referred to in their title) should already be clear from what we have said so far. No approach which treats language as behaviour can come to terms with the strategic complexity and the local and emergent contextualisation of talk, with how talk is co-constructed by social actors, or with how meanings are generated by inference as much as by overt signalling. Potter and Wetherell's position on attitude research is similar. They stress the need to examine contextualised accounts of beliefs, rather than surveying (usually by questionnaire methods) large numbers of people's decontextualised and self-reported attitudes, as social psychologists have tended to do:

> Contextual information gives the researcher a much fuller understanding of the detailed and delicate organization of accounts. In addition, an understanding of this organization clarifies the action orientation of talk and its involvement in acts such as blaming and disclaiming.
>
> (Potter and Wetherell 1987: 54)

Accounts, they go on to argue, can and should focus on variability and even inconsistency, rather than trying to disguise variation in the hope of producing clear and stable patterns. Rather antagonistically, they suggest that variability in discursive accounts of beliefs amounts to 'a considerable embarrassment to traditional attitude theories' (*ibid.*). They also argue that attitude research tends to reify the assumption that attitudes are held about 'an existing out-there-in-the-world group of people' (*ibid.*) when most naturally occurring accounts are directed at specific cases rather than idealised 'objects'. A discursive approach to the psychology of attitudes will bring research back to investigating local and specific discourse representations, which are how we produce and experience 'attitudes' in everyday life.

Discursive psychology is, however, more than the application of concepts and methods from discourse analysis and CA in the traditional realm of social psychology, even though this may have been its origins. Much of the most articulate and insistent theorising of *social constructionism* has emerged from social psychology, for example in John Shotter's (1993) book, *Conversational Realities* (see also Billig 1991; Gergen 1982; 1991). Psychology, studying the interface between individuals, cognition and society, needs to theorise 'reality' — arguably more urgently than other disciplines. Shotter's argument, like that of Potter and Wetherell, is that psychology and most social science has tended to seek out invariance, and ignore the processes by which we come to see the world as stable:

> In our reflective thought, upon the nature of the world in which we live, we can either take what is invariant as its primary subject matter and treat change as problematic, or, activity and flux as primary and treat the achievement of stability as problematic. While almost all previous approaches to psychology and the other social sciences have taken the first of these stances, social constructionism takes the second.
>
> (Shotter 1993: 178)

Shotter and his colleagues are therefore keen to reintroduce a *relativist* perspective into social science (see Cameron *et al.*, Chapter 8 pp. 144–147) and to take very seriously Edward Sapir and Benjamin Lee Whorf's early research on linguistic relativity: the so-called Sapir/Whorf hypothesis (e.g., Whorf 1956; Lucy 1992).

The principle of relativism followed from an early American anthropological tradition (developed mainly by Franz Boas at the beginning of the twentieth century) which argued that languages classify experience, and that each language does so differently. The classification of experience through language was held to be automatic and beyond speakers' awareness. Sapir's and Whorf's comments on social reality are well worth pondering, many decades after publication:

> Language is a guide to 'social reality' . . . Human beings do not live in the objective world alone, nor alone in the world of social activity as ordinarily understood, but are very much at the mercy of the particular language which has become the medium of expression for their society . . . the 'real world' is to a large extent unconsciously built up on the language habits of the group. No two languages are ever sufficiently similar to be considered as representing the same social reality. The worlds in which different societies live are distinct worlds, not merely the same world with different labels attached. . . .
>
> We see and hear and otherwise experience very largely as we do because the language habits of our community predispose certain choices of interpretation . . . From this standpoint we may think of language as the *symbolic guide to culture.*
> (Sapir, originally published in 1929; quoted in Lucy 1992: 22)

> That portion of the whole investigation here to be reported may be summed up in two questions: (1) Are our own concepts of 'time,' 'space,' and 'matter' given in substantially the same form by experience to all men, or are they in part conditioned by the structure of particular languages? (2) Are there traceable affinities between (a) cultural and behavioral norms and (b) large-scale linguistic patterns?
> (Whorf 1956: 138;
> see also Coupland and Jaworski 1997: 446)

One of Whorf's key observations that transfers directly into the domain of discourse analysis is that a language or an utterance form can unite demonstrably different aspects of reality by giving them similar linguistic treatment, what Whorf calls the process of *linguistic analogy.* Linguistic analogy allows or encourages us to treat diverse experience as 'the same'. A famous example in the area of vocabulary is the word 'empty' in the expression *empty gasoline drums.* As Whorf pointed out, the word 'empty' commonly implies a void or absence, and conjures up associations of 'absence of threat' or 'safety'. It is as if this expression steers us into treating 'empty gasoline drums' as lacking danger, when they are in fact unusually dangerous. Language used to shape cognitive structures can therefore be referred to as *the cognitive appropriation of linguistic analogies.*

As Shotter (1993: 115) concludes, 'Whorf forces us to see that the basic "being" of our world is not as basic as we had thought; it can be thought of and talked of in other ways'. More recent studies in discursive psychology have elaborated on this central point and supported Sapir's, Whorf's, Shotter's and others' theorising with textual analysis. Potter (1996), for example, analyses how 'out-there-ness' is discursively constructed in the writing styles of empiricist (experimental, quantitative) scientific researchers (cf. Gilbert and Mulkay 1984). Derek Edwards's (1997) book is a radical reworking of cognitive themes in psychology, for example research on 'ape language' and child language acquisition, and on the psychology of emotions. He attends to the language in which psychologists represent and objectify cognition. It is perhaps the ultimate challenge for a psychologist (even of the discursive kind) to undermine cognitivism, but Edwards writes that 'one of the reasons for pursuing discursive psychology is the requirement to re-conceptualize relations between language and mind, and to find alternative ways of dealing empirically with that "constitutive" relationship' (p. 44).

The ethnography of communication

In the 1960s and 1970s, the Chomsky-inspired formalism in linguistics triggered a concerted reaction from function- and action-orientated researchers of language. Most notably, Noam Chomsky (1965) contrasted the notion of *linguistic competence,* i.e. internalised knowledge of the rules of a language and the defined object of linguistic inquiry, with what he called *linguistic performance,* i.e. the realisation of competence in actual speech. Dell Hymes (1972a) also viewed language as 'knowledge', but extended the object of (socio)linguistic inquiry, or what he called the ethnography of communication, to *communicative competence.* Hymes's definition of the term consisted of four elements:

- whether and to what degree something is grammatical (linguistic competence);
- whether and to what degree something is appropriate (social appropriateness);

- whether and to what degree something is feasible (psycholinguistic limitations);
- whether and to what degree something is done (observing actual language use).

This far broader conceptualisation of language, and indeed of the purpose of language study, imposed a radically different methodology from Chomsky's linguistics, which was based on introspection and intuition. The object of inquiry for Hymes was no longer the structure of isolated sentences, but *rules of speaking* within a community. Consequently, the sentence was replaced as a basic unit of analysis with a three-fold classification of speech communication (Hymes 1972b):

- *speech situations,* such as ceremonies, evenings out, sports events, bus trips, and so on; they are not purely communicative (i.e., not only governed by rules of speaking) but provide a wider context for speaking.
- *speech events* are activities which are *par excellence* communicative and governed by rules of speaking, e.g., conversations, lectures, political debates, ritual insults, and so on. As Duranti (1997: 289) comments, these are activities in which 'speech plays a crucial role in the definition of what is going on – that is, if we eliminate speech, the activity cannot take place'.
- *speech acts* are the smallest units of the set, e.g. orders, jokes, greetings, summonses, compliments, etc.; a speech act may involve more than one move from only one person, e.g., greetings usually involve a sequence of two 'moves'.

Hymes's model was based on a set of *components of speech events,* which provided a descriptive framework for ethnography of communication. These components were arranged into an eight-part mnemonic based on the word *speaking*:

situation (physical, temporal psychological setting defining the speech event);
participants (e.g. speaker, addressee, audience);
ends (outcomes and goals);
act sequence (form and content);
key (manner or spirit of speaking, e.g. mock, serious, perfunctory, painstaking);

*i*nstrumentalities (channels, e.g. spoken, written and forms of
   speech (dialects, codes, varieties and registers);
*n*orms of interaction, e.g. organisation of turn-taking and norm of
   interpretation, i.e. conventionalised ways of drawing inferences;
*g*enres, e.g. casual speech, commercial messages, poems, myths,
   proverbs.

Although the *Reader* does not explicitly address the ethnographic tradition
(we deal with it in greater detail in Coupland and Jaworski 1997, especially
chapters 5, 10, 11, 33, and part VIII; see also Bauman and Scherzer 1974;
Saville-Troike 1989), the impact of the ethnography of communication, its
methodology and attendance to contextual, historical and cultural detail of
interaction is felt across most discourse analytic traditions, especially in interactional sociolinguistics (see, e.g., Rampton 1995; Jaquemet 1996).

Interactional sociolinguistics

This approach to discourse is inextricably linked with the names of the sociologist Erving Goffman (e.g., 1959; 1967; 1974; 1981; Chapter 18) and
Hymes's close associate, the anthropological linguist John Gumperz (e.g.,
1982a; 1982b; Chapter 5). Gumperz aimed 'to develop interpretive sociolinguistic approaches to the analysis of real time processes in face to face
encounters' (1982a: vii), and this aim has been taken up by various sociolinguists and discourse analysts in a wide range of approaches to social
interaction. Many of them are represented in this volume (see Schiffrin,
Chapter 16; Brown and Levinson, Chapter 19; Tannen, Chapter 27). Goffman
summarises his research programme in one of his later papers as being

> to promote acceptance of the . . . face-to-face domain as an analyt-
> ically viable one – a domain which might be titled, for want of
> any happy name, the interaction order – a domain whose preferred
> method of study is microanalysis.
>
> (1983: 2)

Although it is hard to find any contemporary approach to discourse which
does *not* more or less explicitly refer to Goffman's work, we have included
in the *Reader* several papers in which the affinity to Goffman's work is especially clear. Apart from the chapters mentioned above (in relation to

Gumperz's work), see Kendon (Chapter 22), Young (Chapter 25), and Tannen and Wallat (Chapter 21).

Much of Gumperz's research has concentrated on *intercultural interaction* and, especially, on the mechanisms of *miscommunication*. For example, in Chapter 5, he demonstrates how seemingly irrelevant signalling details, such as falling rather than rising intonation on a single word, can trigger complex patterns of interpretation and misinterpretation between members of different cultural groups (see also Roberts *et al.* 1992). These patterns of (mis)interpretation, which he labels *conversational inferencing* (Chapter 5) depend not only on the 'actual' contents of talk, but to a great extent on the processes of perception and evaluation of a number of the signalling mechanisms, based on details of intonation, tempo of speech, rhythm, pausing, phonetic, lexical, and syntactic choices, non-verbal signals, and so on. Gumperz calls such features *contextualisation cues*, and he showed that they

> relate what is said to the contextual knowledge (including knowledge of particular activity types: cf. frames; Goffman 1974 [Tannen and Wallat, Chapter 21, this volume]) that contributes to the presuppositions necessary to the accurate inferencing of what is meant (including, but not limited to, the illocutionary force).
>
> (Schiffrin 1994: 99–100)

Gumperz adapts and extends Hymes's ethnographic framework by examining how interactants from different cultural groups apply different rules of speaking in face-to-face interaction. In his work, he draws heavily on the pragmatic notion of inferential meaning and the ethnomethodological understanding of conversation as joint action.

We have already mentioned the link between Gumperz's contextualisation cues and their role as markers signalling types of speech event, or in Goffman's terms *frames*, which participants engage in. Frames are part of the interpretive means by which participants understand or disambiguate utterances and other forms of communicative behaviour. For example, a person waving his or her arm may be stopping a car, greeting a friend, flicking flies or increasing blood circulation (Goffman 1974). There is a constant interplay between contextualisation cues and what is being said. Framing devices usually form a part of the communicated message but they are used to label or categorise the communicative process itself. Therefore, they also constitute the utterance's *metamessage* (Watzlawick *et al.* 1967; Tannen 1986), or its 'message about its own status as a message'. When we look for ways in which frames are constructed and changed or shifted, we try to identify how participants convey their metamessages through various verbal and non-verbal cues.

Another concept which links Goffman's work with that of Gumperz is *footing*, 'the alignments we take up to ourselves and the others present as expressed in the way we manage the production or reception of an utterance' (Goffman 1981: 128). As Goffman notes, changes in footing depend in part on the use of specific contextualisation cues, for example, switching between language codes or speech styles.

One of the most significant developments in interactional sociolinguistics was the formulation of politeness theory (Brown and Levinson [1978] 1987; Chapter 19). Penelope Brown and Stephen Levinson draw heavily on sociological influences from Goffman, and the inferential model of Grice. They believe that the phenomenon of politeness is responsible for how people, apparently universally, deviate from the maximally efficient modes of communication, as outlined by Grice. In other words, politeness is the reason why people do not always 'say what they mean'. Politeness theory, which aims to provide a universal descriptive and explanatory framework of social relations, is built around Goffman's notion of *face* (Chapter 18), i.e., a person's self-image and projected self onto others, and Grice's model of inferential communication and the assumption that people communicating are rational. Brown and Levinson stress the strategic nature of human communication, which is a radical departure from rule-oriented approaches (e.g. Lakoff's rules of politeness as summarised by Tannen, Chapter 27).

The *Reader* carries several original chapters on face (Goffman, Chapter 18) and politeness (Brown and Levinson, Chapter 19; Holmes, Chapter 20), so we will not present an overview of these interconnected theories here. But it is worth pointing out that, apart from Lakoff's approach to politeness mentioned above, there have been several other alternative attempts to theorise politeness. The best-known example is Leech's (1983) approach, based on Grice's notion of the 'Politeness Principle' (analogous to the Cooperative Principle but never fully developed by Grice himself) and a set of corresponding politeness maxims, such as *tact*, *generosity*, *approbation*, *modesty*, and so on.

Narrative analysis

Telling stories is a human universal of discourse. Stories or narratives are discursive accounts of factual or fictitious events which take, or have taken or will take place at a particular time. We construct narratives as structured representations of events in a particular temporal order. Sometimes, the ordering of events is chronological (e.g. most fairy stories) although some plays, novels or news stories (e.g., Bell 1998; Chapter 13) may move backwards and forwards in time, for particular reasons and effects.

Narratives can be verbal (spoken or written), musical, mimed or pictorial, e.g. in children's picture books. Sometimes a story can be narrated in a single visual image, a painting or a photograph, implying a temporal succession of events (e.g. something has happened or is about to happen). Of course, narratives often combine different modalities and many voices in a single storytelling event. For example, recounting a family holiday may involve several family members presenting their versions of events, to which the participating audience may add questions and comments. It may involve showing souvenirs, photographs or a video, or even sampling foods brought home from the trip. This can turn the narrative into a multi-modal, multi-voiced text, including the gustatory (taste) and olfactory (smell) channels! Sometimes, different voices are introduced into a story by a single narrator, for example by introducing quotations as direct speech, perhaps marked by changes in pitch or body posture.

The functions of storytelling are quite varied. Some stories are primarily informative (e.g., news stories, see Bell, Chapter 13), others are used for self-presentation (e.g., during a medical examination, see Young, Chapter 25), for entertainment (e.g., sex narratives, see Caldas-Coulthard, Chapter 31), for strengthening in-group ties (e.g., gossip), in therapy or problem-solving (e.g., life-stories told in counselling sessions or in problem-sharing among friends), and so on. Although narratives vary greatly in their form (including their length) and function, all verbal narratives share a basic structure (Labov, Chapter 12; Bell, Chapter 13). William Labov's study of oral narratives was based on data he collected in New York City, in response to the interview question 'Were you ever in a situation where you were in a serious danger of being killed' (Labov 1972: 363; Chapter 12). He formulated the following structural features of narratives (as summarised by Ochs 1997: 195), although it is clear that some narratives do not display all of the following properties:

(1) abstract (for example, 'My brother put a knife in my head'),
(2) orientation ('This was just a few days after my father died'),
(3) complicating action ('I twisted his arm up behind him . . .'),
(4) evaluation ('Ain't that a bitch?'), (5) result or resolution

('After all a that I gave the dude the cigarette, after all that'),
and (6) coda ('And that was that').

One element that is common to all narratives is of course the plotline,
or what the story is about. Plot is most commonly associated with narratives found in various literary genres (e.g., novels, ballads, fairy tales) and
its structure has indeed been extensively studied within a sub-branch of
discourse analysis which may be called literary stylistics (e.g., Propp 1968;
Toolan 1988). One example of how this type of work may be applied to the
study of non-literary texts is given by Vestergaard and Schroeder (1985) in
their study of the language of advertising. Following Greimas's (1966)
taxonomy of participants (or as Greimas called them 'actants') in narratives,
Vestergaard and Schroeder distinguished the following six, paired roles:

subject − object
helper − opponent
giver − receiver.

The relationships between those roles can be presented diagrammatically in
the following way:

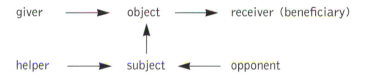

A realisation of this model can be found in many fairy tales. Consider Michael
Toolan's 'generic' summary:

> The subject or hero, perhaps a young man of lowly origin, seeks
> marriage to a beautiful princess (object), in which case the man
> will also be beneficiary (possibly the princess and the country will
> too). In his quest he is helped generously but with limited success
> by a friend or relative (helper), but their combined efforts count
> for little in the struggle against some opponents (wicked uncle of
> the princess, some other eligible but ignoble suitor), until a sender
> (better, a superhelper), such as the king or God, or some individual
> with magical powers for good, intervenes.
>
> (Toolan 1988: 93–4)

Narratives are not at all objective or impartial ways of representing events, even though they might be *objectifying devices* (ways of claiming or constructing an air of factuality). This is immediately clear with regard to narratives which are works of fiction (fairly tales, detective stories, etc.). But even 'factual' narratives are intimately tied to the narrator's point of view, and the events recounted in a narrative are his/her (re)constructions rather than some kind of objective mirror-image of reality. The first instance of the narrator's subjectivity is present in what s/he chooses to narrate, what s/he finds 'tellable' or 'reportable'. Furthermore, as Goffman explains, the meaning of the narrative is jointly constructed by the selectively filtering actions of both speaker and listener:

> A tale or anecdote, that is, a replaying, is not merely any reporting of a past event. In the fullest sense, it is such a statement couched from the personal perspective of an actual or potential participant who is located so that some temporal, dramatic development of the reported event proceeds from that starting point. A replaying will therefore incidentally be something that listeners can empathetically insert themselves into, vicariously re-experiencing what took place. A replaying, in brief, recounts a personal experience, not merely reports on an event.
> (Goffman 1974: 504; quoted in Ochs 1997: 193)

In sum, narrative analysis is an important tradition within discourse analysis. It deals with a pervasive genre of communication through which we enact important aspects of our identities and relations with others. It is partly through narrative discourse that we comprehend the world and present our understanding of it to others.

Critical discourse analysis

In all but its blandest forms, such as when it remains at the level of language description, discourse analysis adopts a 'critical' perspective on language in use. Roger Fowler (1981) is explicit about what 'critical' means for his own research, much of it related to literary texts. He says it does *not* mean 'the flood of writings about texts and authors which calls itself literary criticism', nor the sense of 'intolerant fault-finding' (p. 25):

> I mean a careful analytic interrogation of the ideological cate-
> gories, and the roles and institutions and so on, through which a
> society constitutes and maintains itself and the consciousness of
> its members ... All knowledge, all objects, are constructs: crit-
> icism analyses the processes of construction and, acknowledging
> the artificial quality of the categories concerned, offers the possi-
> bility that we might profitably conceive the world in some
> alternative way.
>
> (Fowler 1981: 25)

There are many elements in Fowler's definition of critical analysis which
we have already met as hallmarks of discourse analysis – notably its questioning of objectivity and its interest in the practices which produce apparent
objectivity, normality and factuality. What we called the forensic goals
of discourse analysis re-surface in Fowler's definition, probing texts and
discourse practices in order to discover hidden meaning and value structures.
His view of society as a set of groups and institutions structured through
discourse is closely reminiscent of Foucault's and Pêcheux's theoretical
writings.

There is a wealth of critical theoretic writing behind these general
perspectives, which we have decided not to represent directly in the *Reader*.
Our thinking is that *critical theory*, while exerting considerable influence on
discourse analysis, remains 'theory'. It is a diverse set of abstract and philosophical writing (for example by Louis Althusser, Roland Barthes, Emile
Benveniste, Jacques Derrida, Umberto Eco and Jacques Lacan) which does
not impinge directly on the analysis of discourse, but is definitely part of the
same intellectual climate. (Belsey 1980 provides a useful overview of critical
theory approaches; Cobley 1996 is an excellent collection of original writings
by several of these theorists.) Those 'theory' chapters we have included
– Bakhtin (Chapter 7), Bourdieu (Chapter 29) and Foucault (Chapter 30)
– are ones where theoretical concepts lead naturally to forms of linguistic/
textual/discourse analysis.

But if Fowler's *critical* perspective is established in all or most discourse
analysis, why does critical discourse analysis need to be distinguished as a separate tradition? One reason is historical. Several early approaches to discourse,
such as the work of the Birmingham school linguists who developed analyses
of classroom discourse (Sinclair and Coulthard 1976), had mainly descriptive
aims. They introduced an elaborate hierarchical framework for coding teachers' and pupils' discourse 'acts', 'moves' and 'transactions' in classroom talk.

The intention was to provide an exhaustive structural model of discourse organisation, from the (highest) category, 'the lesson', down to the (lowest) category of individual speech acts. A critical approach to discourse distances itself from descriptivism of this sort. It foregrounds its concern with social constructionism and with the construction of *ideology* in particular. As Theo van Leeuwen says, 'Critical discourse analysis is, or should be, concerned with . . . discourse as the instrument of the social construction of reality' (1993: 193). Ideological structures are necessarily concerned with the analysis of power relations and social discrimination, for example through demonstrating differential access to discourse networks.

Norman Fairclough gives the clearest account of critical discourse analysis as ideological analysis:

> I view social institutions as containing diverse 'ideological-discursive formations' (IDFs) associated with different groups within the institution. There is usually one IDF which is clearly dominant. . . . Institutional subjects are constructed, in accordance with the norms of an IDF, in subject positions whose ideological underpinnings they may be unaware of. A characteristic of a dominant IDF is the capacity to 'naturalise' ideologies, i.e. to win acceptance for them as non-ideological 'common sense'. It is argued that the orderliness of interactions depends in part upon such naturalised ideologies. To 'denaturalise' them is the objective of a discourse analysis which adopts 'critical' goals. I suggest that denaturalisation involves showing how social structures determine properties of discourse, and how discourse in turn determines social structures.
>
> (Fairclough 1995: 27)

The important point about concepts such as 'naturalisation' and 'denaturalisation' is that they are dynamic processes. They imply a continuing struggle over social arrangements and acts of imposition and resistance. In fact, the critical perspective is oriented to social change, in two different senses. First, critical discourse analysis, particularly in Fairclough's work, sets out to understand social changes in the ideological use of language. We have briefly mentioned Fairclough's arguments about 'technologisation'. Under this heading, he identifies an ongoing cultural 'process of redesigning existing discursive practices and training institutional personnel in the redesigned practices' (Fairclough 1995: 102), brought about partly through so-called 'social skills training'. Fairclough suggests that social skills training is marked by the emergence of 'discourse technologists', the policing of discourse prac- tices, designing context-free discourse techniques and attempts to standardise them (p. 103). He finds examples in the instituting of 'staff development' and 'staff appraisal' schemes in British universities (and of course elsewhere). New forms of discourse (e.g., learning terminology which will impress super- visors or assessors, or learning how to appear efficient, friendly or resourceful) are normalised (made to appear unexceptional) and policed or monitored, with a system of status-related and financial rewards and penalties following on from them. Other discursive shifts that Fairclough has investigated are the conversationalisation of public discourse and the marketisation of public institutions (again, in particular, universities).

The second aspect of change is the critic's own attempt to resist social changes held to curtail liberty. Ideological critique is often characterised by some form of intervention. Notice how Fowler (in the quotation above) mentions 'profitably conceiv[ing] the world in some alternative way'. A critical orientation is not merely 'deconstructive'; it may aim to be 'reconstructive', reconstructing social arrangements. Fowler's use of the term 'profitable' is perhaps unfortunate, although he seems to mean 'more justifiable' or 'more fair'. Fairclough too writes that

> the problematic of language and power is fundamentally a question of democracy. Those affected need to take it on board as a polit- ical issue, as feminists have around the issue of language and gender . . . Critical linguists and discourse analysts have an impor- tant auxiliary role to play here [i.e. secondary to the role of people directly affected] in providing analyses and, importantly, in providing critical educators with resources of what I and my colleagues have called 'critical language awareness'.
> (1995: 221). (A range of perspectives on critical language awareness is provided in Fairclough 1992.)

Critical discourse analysis in this view is a democratic resource to be made available through the education system. Critical discourse analysts need to see themselves as politically engaged, working alongside disenfranchised social groups. This point returns us to issues of method and ethics, of the sort debated by Cameron *et al.* in Chapter 8.

Overview: What discourse analysis can and can not do

It may be useful to end this overview chapter with a brief consideration of the limitations inherent in the discourse perspective and on what discourse analysis *cannot* do. Understandably enough, the readings in this book actively construct the discipline of discourse studies as a vibrant one, alert to social divisions and, in some cases, seeking to resist them. Discourse promotes itself as aware, liberated and liberating, and to us this stance seems generally justified.

Yet there are some basic issues of research methods and interpretation which do not and should not get overlooked in the rush to discourse. Discourse analysis is a committedly *qualitative* orientation to linguistic and social understanding. It inherits both the strengths and the weaknesses associated with qualitative research. As weaknesses, there will always be problems in justifying the selection of materials as research data. It is often difficult to say why a particular stretch of conversation of a particular piece of written text has come under the spotlight of discourse analysis, and why certain of its characteristics are attended to and not others. If discourse analysis is able to generalise, it can normally only generalise about process and not about distribution. This is a significant problem for research projects which assert that there are broad social changes in discourse formations within a community – e.g., Fairclough's claims about increasing technologisation. A claim about change over time – and Fairclough's claims are intuitively convincing – needs to be substantiated with time-sequenced data, linked to some principled method for analysing it, able to demonstrate significant differences. The point is that qualitative, interpretive studies of particular fragments of discourse are not self-sufficient. They need support from other traditions of research, even quantitative surveying. Discourse is therefore not a panacea, and is suited to some types of research question and not others.

Discourse data tend not to lend themselves to distributional surveying. If we emphasise the local contexting of language and the shared construction of meaning, then it follows that we cannot confidently identify recurring instances of 'the same' discourse phenomenon (such as a conversational interruption, a racist reference or an intimate form of address). It is certainly true that a lot of quantitative research has been done inappropriately on discourse data, through gross coding of language forms and expressions which hide significant functional/contextual/inferential differences. But it is also true that discourse analysts often feel the *need* to make distributional claims (e.g. that men interrupt more than women do, that racist discourse is rife in contemporary Britain or that some forms of signalled intimacy redress threats to a person's face) which their data, analysed qualitatively, may not directly support. One common weakness of discourse analysis is therefore that there is a potential mismatch between the analytic method and the interpretation of data in distributional terms. In-depth single-case analyses (e.g., of a particular conversation or written report) are entirely appropriate in discourse analytic research, and have full validity, relative to their aims and objectives (usually to demonstrate meaning-making processes and to build rich interpretations of local discourse events). But they cannot stand as alternatives to larger-scale projects based on sampled instances, designed to answer questions about social differences or social change. Such studies have their own limitations and (as we suggested above) risk essentialising complex local processes. But research is inherently imperfect, and we would support the line of argument that multiple perspectives and methods increase the likelihood of reaching good explanations.

Several strands of discourse analysis, as we have seen, find their vigour in opposing other research trends and assumptions. This is evident in, for example, discursive psychology's antagonism to quantitative social psychology, and in ethnomethodology and CA's resistance to the 'conventional' sociology of social structure. In both these cases, discourse theorists argue for more tentativeness, more context relatedness, more contingency and more tolerance of ambiguity. It is hard to avoid the conclusion that the discourse perspective requires us to scale back our ambition, again particularly in relation to generalising, when it comes to linguistic and social explanation. The nature of research itself as a discourse practice needs to be questioned (see Cameron *et al.*, Chapter 8; Gilbert and Mulkay 1984), but when we question we lose some of the security as well as the hegemony of the research institutions. The discourse analysis perspective is, at the same time, liberating *and* debilitating.

The fundamental positive in discourse is therefore the possibility of a greater clarity of vision, specifically of how language permeates human affairs, offering us opportunities but also constraints. Duranti, as a linguistic anthropologist, has written lucidly about this:

> Having a language is like having access to a very large canvas
> and to hundreds or even thousands of colors. But the canvas and
> the colors come from the past. They are hand-me-downs. As we
> learn to use them, we find out that those around us have strong
> ideas about what can be drawn, in which proportions, in what

combinations, and for what purposes. As any artist knows, there is an ethics of drawing and coloring as well as a market that will react sometimes capriciously, but many times quite predictably to any individual attempts to place a mark in the history or representation or simply readjust the proportions of certain spaces at the margins. . . . Just like art-works, our linguistic products are constantly evaluated, recycled or discarded.

(Duranti 1997: 334)

Duranti's metaphor captures many of the insights that we have anticipated in this Introduction, to be filled out and illustrated in the following chapters. But it also follows that if we can become more aware of the ethics of using language, and of the linguistic market and its practices, we should be better prepared to use language for the purposes we deem valuable. As the 'information revolution' continues to gain new ground, demands will increase on us to acquire new literacies and discourse competences. These competences will include 'technical' literacies, such as the ability to produce and read new media-generated texts (Snyder 1998). But they will also include being able to produce reasoned accounts and interpretations of complex discourse events and situations. The ability to reflect critically on and analyse discourse will increasingly become a basic skill for negotiating social life and for imposing a form of interpretive, critical order on the new discursive universe.

References

Bakhtin, M. M. (1981) *The Dialogic Imagination: Four Essays*, ed. Holquist, M. Trans. McGee, V. W., Austin, Texas: University of Texas Press.
—— (1986) *Speech Genres and Other Late Essays*, trans. McGee, V. W., Austin, Texas: University of Texas Press.
Bauman, R. and Scherzer, J. (eds) (1974) *Explorations in the Ethnography of Speaking*, Cambridge: Cambridge University Press.
Bell, A. (1998) 'The discourse structure of news stories', in Bell, A. and Garrett, P. (eds) *Approaches to Media Discourse*, Oxford: Blackwell, 64–104.
Belsey, C. (1980) *Critical Practice*, London: Methuen.
Benveniste, E. (1971) *Problems in General Linguistics*, Florida: University of Miami Press.
Besnier, N. (1989) 'Information withholding as a manipulative and collusive strategy in Nukulaelae gossip', *Language in Society* 18: 315–41.
Billig, M. (1991) *Ideologies and Beliefs*, London: Sage.

Boden, D. and Zimmerman, D. H. (eds) (1991) *Talk and Social Structure: Studies in Ethnomethodology and Conversation Analysis*, Oxford: Polity Press.

Brown, G. and Yule, G. (1983) *Discourse Analysis*, Cambridge: Cambridge University Press.

Brown, P. and Levinson, S. (1987) *Politeness: Some Universals in Language Usage*, Cambridge: Cambridge University Press. (Originally published in 1978 in Goody, E. N. (ed.) *Questions and Politeness*, Cambridge: Cambridge University Press.)

Cameron, D. (1995) *Verbal Hygiene*, London: Routledge.

Candlin, C. N. (1997) 'General editor's preface', in Gunnarsson, B.-L., Linell, P. and Nordberg, B. (eds) *The Construction of Professional Discourse*, London: Longman, ix–xiv.

Chomsky, N. (1965) *Aspects of the Theory of Syntax*, Cambridge, MA: MIT Press.

Cobley, P. (ed.) (1996) *The Communication Theory Reader*, London: Routledge.

Coupland, N. and Jaworski, A. (eds) (1997) *Sociolinguistics: A Reader and Coursebook*, London: Macmillan.

Drew, P. and Heritage, J. (eds) (1992a) *Talk at Work: Interaction in Institutional Settings*, Cambridge: Cambridge University Press.

—— (1992b) 'Analyzing talk at work: an introduction', in Drew, P. and Heritage, J. (eds) *Talk at Work: Interaction in Institutional Settings*, Cambridge: Cambridge University Press, 3–65.

Duranti, A. (1997) *Linguistic Anthropology*, Cambridge: Cambridge University Press.

Edwards, D. (1997) *Discourse and Cognition*, London: Sage.

Edwards, D. and Potter, J. (1992) *Discursive Psychology*, London: Sage.

Fairclough, N. (1992) 'Introduction', in Fairclough, N. (ed.) *Critical Language Awareness*, London: Longman.

—— (1995) *Critical Discourse Analysis: The Critical Study of Language*, London: Longman.

Fasold, R. (1990) *Sociolinguistics of Language*, Oxford: Blackwell.

Fillmore, C. (1984) 'Remarks on contrastive pragmatics', in Fisiak, J. (ed.) *Contrastive Linguistics: Prospects and Problems*, Berlin: Mouton, 119–41.

Foucault, M. (1972) *The Archaeology of Knowledge,* Trans. Smith, S., London: Tavistock.

Fowler, R. (1981) *Literature as Social Discourse: The Practice of Linguistic Criticism,* London: Batsford Academic.

Garfinkel, H. (1967) *Studies in Ethnomethodology*, Englewood Cliffs, NJ: Prentice Hall.

—— (1974) 'On the origins of the term "ethnomethodology"', in Turner, R. (ed.) *Ethnomethodology*, Harmondsworth, Middlesex: Penguin, 15–18.

Gergen, K. J. (1982) *Toward Transformation in Social Knowledge*, New York: Springer.
—— (1991) *The Saturated Self: Dilemmas of Identity in Contemporary Life*, New York: Basic Books.
Giddens, A. (1991) *Modernity and Self-Identity: Self and Society in the Late Modern Age,* Cambridge: Polity Press.
Gilbert, G. N. and Mulkay, M. (1984) *Opening Pandora's Box: A Sociological Analysis of Scientists' Discourse*, Cambridge: Cambridge University Press.
Goffman, E. (1959) *The Presentation of Self in Everyday Life*, New York: Doubleday Anchor.
—— (1967) *Interaction Ritual: Essays on Face-to-Face Behavior*, New York: Doubleday Anchor.
—— (1974) *Frame Analysis: An Essay on the Organization of Experience,* New York: Harper and Row.
—— (1981) 'Footing', in Goffman, E. *Forms of Talk*, Philadelphia: University of Pennsylvania Press, 124–59. (First published in *Semiotica* 25, 1979: 1–29.)
—— (1983) 'The interaction order', *American Sociological Review* 48: 1–17.
Goodman, S. (1996) 'Visual English', in Goodman, S. and Graddol, D. (eds) *Redesigning English: New Texts, New Identities,* London: Routledge in association with The Open University, 38–72.
Graddol, D. (1996) 'The semiotics of a wine label', in Goodman, S. and Graddol, D. (eds) *Redesigning English: New Texts, New Identities,* London: Routledge in association with The Open University, 73–81.
Graddol, D., Cheshire, J. and Swann, J. (1994) *Describing Language,* 2nd edn, Buckingham: Open University Press.
Greimas, A. (1966) *Semantique Structurale*, Paris: Larousse.
Gumperz, J. J. (1982a) *Discourse Strategies*, Cambridge: Cambridge University Press.
—— (ed.) (1982b) *Language and Social Identity*, Cambridge: Cambridge University Press.
Heritage, J. (1984a) 'A change-of-state token and aspects of its sequential place-ment', in Atkinson, J. and Heritage, J. (eds) *Structures of Social Action: Studies in Conversation Analysis*, Cambridge: Cambridge University Press, 299–345.
—— (1984b) *Garfinkel and Ethnomethodology*, Oxford: Blackwell.
Hodge, R. and Kress, G. (1991) *Social Semiotics*, Cambridge: Polity.
Hutchby, I. and Wooffitt, R. (1998) *Conversation Analysis,* Cambridge: Polity Press.
Hymes, D. (1972a) 'On communicative competence', in Pride, J. B. and Holmes, J. (eds) *Sociolinguistics*, Harmondsworth, Middlesex: Penguin, 269–93 (origi-nally published in 1971).

—— (1972b) 'Models of the interaction of language and social life', in Gumperz, J. J. and Hymes, D. (eds) *Directions in Sociolinguistics,* New York: Holt, Rinehart & Winston and Oxford: Blackwell, 35–71.

Jacquemet, M. (1996) *Credibility in Court: Communicative Practices in the Camorra Trials,* Cambridge: Cambridge University Press.

Kress, G., Leite-Garcia, R. and van Leeuwen, T. (1997) 'Discourse semiotics', in van Dijk, T.A. (ed.) *Discourse Studies: A Multidisciplinary Introduction. Vol. 1. Discourse as Structure and Process,* London: Sage, 257–91.

Kress, G. and van Leeuwen, T. (1996) *Reading Images: The Grammar of Visual Design,* London: Routledge.

Labov, W. (1972) 'The transformation of experience in narrative syntax', in Labov, W. *Language in the Inner City,* Philadelphia: University of Philadelphia Press and Oxford: Blackwell, 354–96.

Labov, W. and Fanshel, D. (1977) *Therapeutic Discourse: Psychotherapy as Conversation,* New York: Academic Press.

Lee, D. (1992) *Competing Discourses,* London: Longman.

Leech, G. (1983) *Principles of Pragmatics,* London: Longman.

Lucy, L. (1992) *Language Diversity and Thought: A Reformulation of the Linguistic Relativity Hypothesis,* Cambridge: Cambridge University Press.

Mills, S. (1997) *Discourse,* London: Routledge.

Milroy, J. and Milroy, L. (1991) *Authority in Language: Investigating Language Prescription and Standardisation,* 2nd edn, London: Routledge.

Moerman, M. (1988) *Talking Culture: Ethnography and Conversation Analysis,* Philadelphia: University of Pennsylvania Press.

Ochs, E. (1988) *Culture and Language Development: Language Acquisition and Language Socialization in a Samoan Village,* Cambridge: Cambridge University Press.

—— (1997) 'Narrative', in van Dijk, T. A. (ed.) *Discourse Studies: A Multidisciplinary Introduction. Vol. 1: Discourse as Structure and Process,* London: Sage, 185–207.

Ochs, E., Schegloff, E. A. and Thompson, S. A. (eds) (1996) *Interaction and Grammar,* Cambridge: Cambridge University Press.

O'Toole, M. (1994) *The Language of Displayed Art,* London: Leicester University Press.

Pêcheux, M. (1982) *Language, Semantics and Ideology,* Basingstoke: Macmillan.

Potter, J. (1996) *Representing Reality,* London: Sage.

Potter, J. and Wetherell, M. (1987) *Discourse and Social Psychology: Beyond Attitudes and Behaviour,* London: Sage.

Propp, V. (1968) *Morphology of Folk Tale,* Austin, Texas: University of Texas Press (First published in Russian, 1928.)

Rampton, B. (1995) *Crossing: Language and Ethnicity among Adolescents,* London: Longman.

Roberts, C., Davies, E. and Jupp, T. (1992) *Language and Discrimination: A Study of Communication in Multi-ethnic Workplaces*, London: Longman.

Sacks, H., Schegloff, E. and Jefferson G. (1974) 'A simplest systematics for the organisation of turn-taking for conversation', *Language* 50: 696–735.

Saville-Troike, M. (1989) *The Ethnography of Communication: An Introduction*, 2nd edn, Oxford: Blackwell.

Schegloff, E. A., Ochs, E. and Thompson, S. A. (1996) 'Introduction', in Ochs, E., Schegloff, E. A. and Thompson, S. A. (eds) *Interaction and Grammar*, Cambridge: Cambridge University Press.

Schiffrin, D. (1994) *Approaches to Discourse*, Oxford: Blackwell.

Searle, J. R. (1969) *Speech Acts: An Essay in the Philosophy of Language*, Cambridge: Cambridge University Press, 1–51.

—— (1979) 'The classification of illocutionary acts', *Language in Society* 8: 137–51.

Shotter, J. (1993) *Conversational Realities*, London: Sage.

Sinclair, J. McH. and Coulthard, M. (1975) *Towards an Analysis of Discourse: The English Used by Teachers and Pupils*, Oxford: Oxford University Press.

Snyder, I. (ed.) (1998) *Page to Screen: Taking Literacy into the Electronic Era*, London: Routledge.

Sperber, D. and Wilson, D. (1986) *Relevance: Communication & Cognition*, Oxford: Blackwell (2nd edn 1995).

—— (1997) 'Remarks on relevance theory and the social sciences', *Multilingua* 16: 145–52.

Stubbs, M. (1983) *Discourse Analysis*, Chicago: University of Chicago Press.

Tannen, D. (1986) *That's Not What I Meant! How Conversational Style Makes or Breaks your Relations with Others*, New York: William Morrow, Ballantine.

Taylor, T. and Cameron, D. (1987) *Analysing Conversation: Rules and Units in the Structure of Talk*, Oxford: Pergamon.

Thomas, J. (1995) *Meaning in Interaction: An Introduction to Pragmatics*, London: Longman.

Toolan, M. J. (1988) *Narrative: A Critical Linguistic Introduction*, London: Routledge.

Turner, R. (1974) *Ethnomethodology*. Harmondsworth, Middlesex: Penguin.

Van Dijk, T. (1977) *Text and Context*, London: Longman.

—— (1984) *Prejudice in Discourse*, Amsterdam: Benjamins.

—— (ed.) (1985) *Handbook of Discourse Analysis*, 4 vols, New York: Academic Press.

—— (1988) *News Analysis: Case Studies of International and National News in the Press*, Hillsdale, NJ: Lawrence Erlbaum.

—— (ed.) (1997) *Discourse as Social Interaction*, London: Sage.

Van Leeuwen, T. (1993) 'Genre and field in critical discourse analysis', *Discourse & Society* 4/2: 193–225.

Vestergaard, T. and Schroeder, K. (1985) *The Language of Advertising*, Oxford: Blackwell.

Watzlawick, P., Beavin-Bavelas, J. and Jackson, D. (1967) *The Pragmatics of Human Communication*, New York: Norton.

Whorf, B. L. (1956) *Language, Thought and Reality: Selected Writings of Benjamin Lee Whorf*, (ed.) Carroll, J. B., Cambridge, MA: MIT Press.

Journals

The following is a list of journals publishing discourse research.

Discourse Processes (subtitled 'a multidisciplinary journal'), published by Ablex. Publishes descriptive linguistic and cognitive as well as interpretive studies of discourse.

Discourse and Society, published by Sage. Specialises in critical discourse analysis.

Discourse Studies, published by Sage. A new journal, open to all traditions of discourse analysis.

Human Communication Research, published by and for the International Communication Association. Publishes a wide range of quantitative and some qualitative research on communication.

International Journal of Applied Linguistics, published by Novus. Very broad based, including applied linguistics, sociolinguistics and some discourse studies.

Journal of Communication, published by the International Communication Association. Deals mostly with mass-media communication and other social semiotic approaches to communication.

Journal of Language and Social Psychology, published by Sage. Covers quantitative and experimental research, but is increasingly open to qualitative discourse research on themes relevant to social psychology.

Journal of Multilingual and Multicultural Development, published by Multilingual Matters. Publishes primarily quantitative and qualitative research on intercultural communication and language and ethnicity.

Journal of Pragmatics, published by Elsevier. Focuses mainly on linguistic aspects of pragmatics and discourse, but increasingly open to socially and culturally inclined studies.

Journal of Sociolinguistics, published by Blackwell. Both editors of this *Reader* are involved editorially, along with Allan Bell. It covers the whole interdisciplinary field of sociolinguistics and discourse studies and is open to innovative approaches.

Language Awareness, published by Multilingual Matters. Promotes varied approaches, including critical and applied approaches, to language and discourse.

Language and Communication, published by Pergamon/Elsevier. Another very broad-based journal, publishing theoretical as well as empirical studies.

Language and Discourse, published by the Department of English Language and Literature, University of Liverpool, UK.

Language and Literature, published by SAGE for the Poetics and Linguistics Association. Publishes research on stylistics, critical theory, pragmatics and discourse analysis of literary texts.

Language in Society, published by Cambridge University Press. An established sociolinguistics journal, open to discourse analytic research with a strong anthropologic/ethnographic bias.

Multilingua, published by Mouton de Gruyter. Originally exploring the interface between language, culture and second-language acquisition, now open to all current research in sociolinguistics and discourse analysis.

Pragmatics, published by and for the International Pragmatics Association. Wide ranging, including culturally focused, linguistic and critical approaches to discourse.

Research on Language and Social Interaction, published by Lawrence Erlbaum. Specialises in talk-in-interaction/conversation analytic research.

Semiotica, published by Mouton de Gruyter. Interdisciplinary and orientated towards the analysis of different semiotic systems and multimodality; notable for many review articles of books in all areas of semiotic research.

Text (subtitled 'an interdisciplinary journal for the study of discourse'), published by Mouton de Gruyter. Another broad-based, established journal, open to all traditions of discourse analysis.

Discourse: meaning and context

Editors' Introduction to Part One

IN THE GENERAL INTRODUCTION we characterised discourse analysis as a reaching out beyond the visible or audible forms of language into social context, and as exploring the interplay between language and social processes. Construing language as discourse involves orientating to language as a form of social action, as a functioning form of social action embedded in the totality of social processes. In this Part of the *Reader* we represent many of the key writers and texts who, influentially, argued the case for a functional approach to language, initially within their various disciplines – linguistics (Jakobson, Bakhtin), philosophy (Austin, Grice), linguistic anthropology/sociolinguistics (Gumperz) and sociology (Cicourel, Sacks). What is important here is not so much the disciplinary origins, even though these clearly influence individuals' ways of theorising and writing. Rather, it is the cumulative perspective that develops out of their work – pressure towards a notion of discourse (whether so labelled or not) and towards new theoretical frameworks for explaining meaning-making and sense-making as contextual processes.

Roman Jakobson's text introduces what he saw as the six basic functions of verbal communication: *referential, emotive, conative, phatic, metalingual* and *poetic.* Although it focuses specifically on the link between linguistics and poetics, Jakobson's article clearly demonstrates how, as early as 1960, European linguists were committed to a multifunctional view of language. Such a perspective was to become the foundation of Michael Halliday's functional linguistics, influenced heavily by the functionalism of J. R. Firth which is itself a strong contemporary influence on social semiotic and critical linguistic approaches to discourse. But the mainstream of descriptive and theoretical linguistics did not follow this line. It came to be dominated by structuralist models, culminating in Chomsky's formal and cognitivist theory of language. We can therefore see modern discourse studies as a reimposition of some early priorities in functional linguistics, and this is why Jakobson's work remains an important foundational source.

Jakobson challenges the view that using language is a simple exchange of referential information. What he called the conative function attends to relationships between speakers and what communication achieves in this social dimension. The phatic function is realised in aspects of socially organised, ritualised communication; the emotive function relates to the expressive and subjective dimension of talk; the metalinguistic function identifies those ways in which language can be turned in on itself, used self-reflexively. All these concepts recur in the *Reader*, many of them developed as major traditions of discourse analysis (reflected in the *Reader*'s sectional structure). Exploring the poetic function of language, as much of this particular Jakobson text does, is particularly stimulating for discourse analysis, for example Jakobson's suggestion that 'virtually any poetic message is a quasi-quoted discourse' (p. 60). The poetic function of language, as Jakobson points out, is not restricted to poetry alone. It surfaces whenever discourse achieves playfulness, self-awareness or creativity, and when we respond to language in these terms. For example, Tannen (Chapter 27) comments on the pleasure which interactants derive from sharing a conversational style (in this case, the ethnic style of New Yorkers of Jewish origin) as an emotional and aesthetic experience. The use of formal conversational features (such as fast tempo of speech, frequent asking of questions, reciprocal interruption, and so on) go beyond serving the referential function of language. These are recognised and 'safe' elements of the linguistic palette for the co-construction of an exhilarating performance. Likewise, Cameron (Chapter 26) demonstrates how five young men's informal talk, ranging between gossip about other men and verbal duelling, is full of imaginative and humorous, even if sometimes offensive language. Finally, as we are all aware, everyday, spontaneous narratives not only recount personal experiences and series of events but can be arresting (Young, Chapter 25) and entertaining stories (Caldas-Coulthard, Chapter 31).

The same concern with communicative function dominates J. L. Austin's famous series of lectures, delivered at Harvard University in 1955, entitled 'How to do things with words' (Chapter 2). In this case, the backdrop is linguistic philosophy and his concern for a 'true' account of what utterances achieve. Austin's method, working with single instances of fabricated utterances seems to suggest little concern for social context. But his argument is precisely that the function of an utterance (e.g., making a promise or, famously, naming a ship) is partly constituted by the social circumstances in which it is uttered. He shows that utterances have to have 'felicitous' conditions for their function to be fulfilled, and that utterance meaning lies in the interplay between social circumstances and utterances themselves.

There are some important questions for discourse analysis embedded in this text. The question, 'Can saying make it so?' is one. This is the social constructionist stance (see Cameron *et al*. Chapter 8), developed in detail and with a much heavier theoretical loading in the ethnomethodological tradition (Cicourel, Chapter 4) and in critical discourse analytic research (Fairclough, Chapter 11; Part Six). The exploration of the nature of implied meaning is another central concern of Austin's text, and the distinction between the explicit and implicit functioning of utterances. This perspective again opens up a territory beyond mainstream linguistics, taken up, for example, in Gumperz's sociolinguistic theory of conversational inferencing (Chapter 5). Another important early observation is Austin's insight that 'function' includes far more than what is achieved '*in* the act of uttering', but also what is achieved *through* utterances. As Austin writes, 'saying something will often, or even normally, produce certain consequential effects upon the feelings, thoughts or actions of the audience, or of the speaker, or of other persons: and it may be done with design, intention or purpose of producing them' (p. 70). Language is aligned to social action generally, and to communicative goals and strategies, and their social effects.

H. P. Grice's perspective on language and implied meaning, very much in the same philosophical tradition as Austin, was also first developed in a series of lectures at Harvard, this time in 1967. Grice takes many of the emphases we see in Austin's work as his own starting point – that discourse is driven by speakers fulfilling specific goals and purposes, that much of the significant meaning of talk is implicit and needing to be reconstructed by inference, and that talk is essentially a form of collaborative social action. Grice points to the specific importance of the medium of conversation as a resource for making sense of what speakers say. Certain generalities follow from being able to assume, for example, that conversation is a cooperative medium – not in the sense that people are always supportive or compliant but in that they jointly collaborate in the production of meanings and inferences. Talk is a matter of sharing in meaning-making procedures, the starting point for conversation analysis (CA) (e.g., Chapters 6 and 15).

Austin wanted to see talking as a special case or variety of purposive, indeed rational, behaviour. His approach to discourse is actually,
then, a specification of social action and of the conditions under which
human communicators can mutually generate meanings and interpret them.
Grice's maxims are an attempt to specify some of these conditions, as regular
assumptions about communicative intention that permit inferences to
be drawn. According to this view, we are only able to draw useful and appropriate inferences as to what speakers mean if we presuppose a set of
principles according to which conversation takes place (see our general
Introduction).

Not surprisingly, many of the chapters in this first Part of the *Reader*
are attempts to generalise about 'normal' or 'unexceptional' discourse
processes. Jakobson, Austin and Grice are mainly interested in detailing the
character of talk between individuals in the most general possible of terms.
This reflects the fact that the earliest important contributions to discourse
analysis needed to argue against the dominant traditions in linguistics, in
linguistic semantics and in the philosophy of language. They needed to make
the case that context is theoretically central to the understanding of language
in use, and, initially, this took priority over more local studies of discourse
in particular settings.

The work we have discussed so far originated in different disciplines
(linguistics, philosophy, logic) but none of these functional approaches to
discourse came to be recognised as an established tradition of research. A
more distinct tradition of work, which has been (and rightly continues to be)
highly influential in all fields of discourse analysis, originated in the USA in
the 1960s as an offshoot of sociology. It consolidated around the label
ethnomethodology (see our general Introduction pp. 19–22). Aaron Cicourel
is one of the main disseminators of ethnomethodology, interpreting and
explaining the scintillating but challenging theoretical writings of Harold
Garfinkel. In Chapter 4, Cicourel offers us a definition of ethnomethodology
as 'the study of interpretive procedures and surface rules in everyday social
practices and scientific activities' (p. 89). Ethnomethodologists opposed what
they saw as the glib and uncritical assumptions made by academics (including
social scientists) about how society is structured. They embarked on a radical
critique of the methods of scientific enquiry, and of how specific practices
and assumptions are naturalised and rendered invisible (see Cameron *et al*.
Chapter 8). Through a critique of language and discourse, ethnomethodology
tried to show that social facts and a sense of orderliness in social practices
(including research) are generated within those practices themselves.

Ethnomethodology is therefore the origin of radical social relativism and social constructionism and its influence is still strongly apparent in many strands of discourse analysis (especially critical discourse analysis and discursive psychology).

Cicourel writes about 'interpretive procedures' since they are the filter through which social organisation is perceived and constructed. In a few pages, Cicourel runs through several of the implicit assumptions, embedded in the practice of talk, which make social reality perceivable (illusorily, he suggests) as stable and meaningful. These include the assumptions communicators make about their reciprocal alignment to each other (e.g. that the world looks the same from each viewpoint); suspending their problems of interpretation and 'letting pass' uninterpretable aspects of communication; trusting and acquiescing in the 'normality' of talk itself; deferring their interpretations of what others are saying; etc. (This last 'etc.' is of course highly salient!) The implication is that social interaction is designed to hide incongruity and interpretive uncertainty. For science and social science, the further implication is that interpretive practices are self-regularising, hiding an actual interpretive void. Ethnomethodology need not be as nihilistic, however, as this suggests (although again see Cameron *et al.* Chapter 8, for the opposite view). It is most productive when it functions as a radically cynical perspective on how and why claims about social structure are made, and when it displays the constructional processes at work in specific instances of discourse. It flourishes in Harvey Sacks's detailed analyses of conversation structure and constructions, and then in many contemporary contributions to CA (see Chapters 6, 14 and 15).

John Gumperz explicitly acknowledges his debt to ethnomethodology before outlining his theory of conversational inferencing (Chapter 5), although he glosses ethnomethodology simply (in a less loaded way) as 'sociological analysis of verbal interaction' (p. 99). Gumperz's principal interests in discourse and conversation, represented in several major theoretical and empirical collections (see the general Introduction for references) have been specifically linked to cultural diversity and inter-ethnic communication. Chapter 5 gives a clear overview of his theoretical framework and examples of conversational moments when participants make social judgements about people and situations based on small details of linguistic or interactional style. The political imperative in Gumperz's work is that, often, culturally influenced styles of talk (even if only in small details of pronunciation or intonation) can trigger prejudicial stereotypes and inferences about 'personality' or 'intention'. In addition to the links between Gumperz's work and that of Goffman and Hymes pointed out in our general Introduction, we should see this strand of discourse analysis as building on ethnomethodology's theorising of interpretive procedures, but building constructively on its critical insights.

Emanuel Schegloff's work is one of the true cornerstones of CA. His paper with Harvey Sacks on the structuring of conversation closings is reprinted as Chapter 15. We have chosen to include Schegloff's theoretical article, 'Talk and social structure' in this first Part of the *Reader* because it argues a controversial but challenging position on the link between language and context. There is wide agreement, in the other articles we have discussed so far, that meaning is 'located' not so much in language itself as in the interaction between language used and the circumstances of use. This is a core claim of discourse analysis and one that Schegloff would not contest. But he is keen to identify the limits to what we can claim about the role of social context in specifying the meaning of talk. His arguments are largely about methods, and specifically about how, as discourse analysts and conversation analysts, we can infer meaning from our knowledge of context. We might have included this reading in Part Two for this reason, the Part on methods in discourse analysis. But Schegloff's arguments are fundamental to how we theorise discourse itself, or what conversation analysts prefer to call talk-in-interaction.

Carrying forward a fundamental sociological line of inquiry, Schegloff does not deny that social structure – in the classical sociological sense of, say, social status or professional role or social situation – is relevant to interactants. He is arguing that there is a need to *demonstrate* the relevance and 'procedural consequentiality' of any potential social contextual classification to interactants at the moment of interaction. His position is the one we see in Cicourel's reading of ethnomethodology, that social reality is only achieved in specific actors' occasioned (localised) orientations to it. Social reality is only what social actors see as relevant to their actions at any given point.

A contrary position, briefly considered in the next Part by Cameron *et al.* (Chapter 8) is that this extreme relativism is untenable and altogether too destructive. Also, it is not entirely clear why there needs to be demonstrable evidence – and evidence in the flow of talk itself – of the relevance and consequentiality of the social categories, as Schegloff insists there must be. It is unlikely that interactants will often make clear which aspects of social context they are in fact 'orienting to' (where orientation will presumably include tacit cognitive processing of the sort usually called 'attending', 'evaluating' and 'attributing'). Nor is it clear what this evidence would look like. Schegloff's examples are specific patterns of turn-taking in, for instance, legal encounters, but 'evidence' could presumably include many other markers of selective attention or perceived salience. It is only a commitedly empiricist and anti-cognitivist stance that would insist on behavioural marking of relevance, in the name of 'evidencing' or 'warranting'. Interestingly enough, Schegloff mentions in a footnote to the Chapter 6 paper (which we have not included) that he and Harvey Sacks had resisted representing the data for their 'Opening up closings' paper, which we reproduce as Chapter 15, 'as contextually specific to American culture'.

In the very approximate time-ordering of Part One of the *Reader*, M. M. Bakhtin's Chapter (7), 'The problem of speech genres', written in the 1930s, is clearly out of sequence. We have placed it at the end of this foundational part of the *Reader* because, in his highly unique way, Bakhtin manages to be highly contemporary. His work, whose origins and even precise authorship are still mysterious, is probably more widely cited now than at any previous time. The text tends to be repetitive, and we have edited it heavily. It is sometimes obscure, partly because of the difficulty in translating his terminology from Russian into English. For example, a key term like 'utterances' seems to equate to all language use or discourse; 'the national language' sometimes appears to refer to the standard language code of a community, and at other times to any group-based variety of language. Bakhtin's arguments tend to be highly abstract, but they set an agenda for modern perspectives on discourse.

The view of all language as organised into specific genres is a case in point. Bakhtin presents a highly dynamic view of speech genres, inter-penetrating and 're-accentuating' each other and being continually renewed as they are used. These claims are the basis for an intertextual perspective on discourse, seeing discourse as the recontextualising of already existing forms and meanings, one text echoing and partially replaying the forms, meanings and values of another (what Bakhtin calls the 'organized chain of other utterances' (p. 124; see Fairclough, Chapter 11). Bakhtin stresses the active role of the listener and the co-construction of meaning ('the listener becomes the speaker', p. 124), which is now a standard assumption about conversational practice. He is interested in the shifting boundary between the individual and the social structure, anticipating much recent research on selfhood and subjectivity (see Part Five). In a chapter where virtually every sentence is 'a quotable', Bakhtin's text invites us to reconsider what is new and what is actually of long-standing theoretical importance at the interface of language, society, ideology and selfhood.

Chapter 1

Roman Jakobson

LINGUISTICS AND POETICS

[. . .]

Language must be investigated in all the variety of its functions. [. . .] An outline of these functions demands a concise survey of the constitutive factors in any speech event, in any act of verbal communication. The ADDRESSER sends a MESSAGE to the ADDRESSEE. To be operative the message requires a CONTEXT referred to, seizable by the addressee, and either verbal or capable of being verbalized; a CODE fully, or at least partially, common to the addresser and addressee (or in other words, to the encoder and decoder of the message); and, finally, a CONTACT, a physical channel and psychological connection between the addresser and the addressee, enabling both of them to enter and stay in communication. All these factors inalienably involved in verbal communication may be schematized as follows:

```
                        CONTEXT
                        MESSAGE
ADDRESSER ------------------------------------------------- ADDRESSEE
                        CONTACT
                        CODE
```

Each of these six factors determines a different function of language. Although we distinguish six basic aspects of language, we could, however,

Source: Roman Jakobson, 'Closing statement: linguistics and poetics; in Thomas A. Sebook (ed.) *Style in Language*, Cambridge, Mass: the MIT Press, 1960: 350–77.

hardly find verbal messages that would fulfill only one function. The diversity lies not in a monopoly of some one of these several functions but in a different hierarchical order of functions. The verbal structure of a message depends primarily on the predominant function. But even though a set (*Einstellung*) toward the referent, an orientation toward the CONTEXT – briefly the so-called REFERENTIAL, "denotative," "cognitive" function – is the leading task of numerous messages, the accessory participation of the other functions in such messages must be taken into account by the observant linguist.

The so-called EMOTIVE or "expressive" function, focused on the ADDRESSER, aims a direct expression of the speaker's attitude toward what he is speaking about. It tends to produce an impression of a certain emotion whether true or feigned; therefore, the term "emotive" [. . .] has proved to be preferable to "emotional." The purely emotive stratum on language is presented by the interjections. They differ from the means of referential language both by their sound pattern (peculiar sound sequences or even sounds elsewhere unusual) and by their syntactic role (they are not components but equivalents of sentences). "*Tut! Tut!* said McGinty": the complete utterance of Conan Doyle's character consists of two suction clicks. The emotive function, laid bare in the interjections, flavors to some extent all our utterances, on their phonic, grammatical, and lexical level. If we analyze language from the standpoint of the information it carries, we cannot restrict the notion of information to the cognitive aspect of language. A man, using expressive features to indicate his angry or ironic attitude, conveys ostensible information, and evidently this verbal behavior cannot be likened to such nonsemiotic, nutritive activities as "eating grapefruit" [. . .] The difference between [big] and the emphatic prolongation of the vowel [bi:g] is a conventional, coded linguistic feature like the difference between the short and long vowel in such Czech pairs as [vi] 'you' and [vi:] 'knows,' but in the latter pair the differential information is phonemic and in the former emotive. As long as we are interested in phonemic invariants, the English /i/ and /i:/ appear to be mere variants of one and the same phoneme, but if we are concerned with emotive units, the relation between the invariant and variants is reversed: length and shortness are invariants implemented by variable phonemes.[. . .]

Orientation toward the ADDRESSEE, the CONATIVE function, finds its purest grammatical expression in the vocative and imperative, which syntactically, morphologically, and often even phonemically deviate from other nominal and verbal categories. The imperative sentences cardinally differ from declarative sentences: the latter are and the former are not liable to a truth test. When in O'Neill's play *The Fountain*, Nano, "(in a fierce tone of command)," says "Drink!" – the imperative cannot be challenged by the question "is it true or not?" which may be, however, perfectly well asked after such sentences as "one drank," "one will drink," "one would drink." In contradistinction to the imperative sentences, the declarative sentences are convertible into interrogative sentences: "did one drink?" "will one drink?" "would one drink?" "will one drink?" "would one drink?"

The traditional model of language as elucidated particularly by Bühler (1933) was confined to these three functions – emotive, conative, and referential – and the three apexes of this model – the first person of the addresser, the second person of the addressee, and the "third person," properly – someone or something spoken of. Certain additional verbal functions can be easily inferred from this triadic model. Thus the magic, incantatory function is chiefly some kind of conversion of an absent or inanimate "third person" into an addressee of a conative message. For example, "May this sty dry up, *tfu, tfu, tfu, tfu*" (Lithuanian spell); "Water queen river, daybreak! Send grief beyond the blue sea, to the sea-bottom, like a grey stone never to rise from the sea-bottom, may grief never come to burden the light heart of God's servant, may grief be removed and sink away." (North Russian incantation); "Sun, stand thou still upon Gibeon; and thou, Moon, in the valley of Aj-a-lon. And the sun stood still, and the moon stayed . . ." (Josh. 10.12). We observe, however, three further constitutive factors of verbal communication and three corresponding functions of language.

There are messages primarily serving to establish, to prolong, or to discontinue communication, to check whether the channel works ("Hello, do you hear me?") , to attract the attention of the interlocutor or to confirm his continued attention ("Are you listening?" or in Shakespearean diction, "Lend me your ears!" – and on the other end of the wire "Um-hum!"). This set for CONTACT, or in Malinowski's terms PHATIC function (1953; Chapter 17) may be displayed by a profuse exchange of ritualized formulas, by entire dialogues with the mere purport of prolonging communication. Dorothy Parker caught eloquent examples: " 'Well!' the young man said. 'Well!' she said. 'Well, here we are,' he said. 'Here we are,' she said, 'Aren't we?' 'I should say we were,' he said, 'Eeyop! Here we are.' 'Well!' she said. 'Well!' he said, 'well.'" The endeavor to start and sustain communication is typical of talking birds; thus the phatic function of language is the only one they share with human beings. It is also the first verbal function acquired by infants; they are prone to communicate before being able to send or receive informative communication.

A distinction has been made in modern logic between two levels of language, "object language" speaking of objects and "metalanguage" speaking of language. But metalanguage is not only a necessary scientific tool utilized by logicians and linguists; it plays also an important role in our everyday language. Like Molière's Jourdain who used prose without knowing it, we practice metalanguage without realizing the metalingual character of our operations. Whenever the addresser and/or the addressee need to check up whether they use the same code, speech is focused on the CODE: it performs a METALINGUAL (i.e., glossing) function. "I don't follow you – what do you mean?" asks the addressee, or in Shakespearean diction, "What is't thou say'st?" And the addresser in anticipation of such recapturing questions inquires: "Do you know what I mean?" Imagine such an exasperating dialogue: "The sophomore was plucked." "But what is *plucked?*" "*Plucked* means the same as *flunked*." "And *flunked?*" "To be *flunked* is to *fail in an exam*." "And what is *sophomore?*" persists the interrogator innocent of school vocabulary. "A *sophomore* is (or means) a *second-year student*." All these equational sentences convey information merely about the lexical code of English; their function is strictly metalingual. Any process of language learning, in particular child acquisition of the mother tongue, makes wide use of such metalingual operations; and aphasia may often be defined as a loss of ability for metalingual operations.

We have brought up all the six factors involved in verbal communication except the message itself. The set (*Einstellung*) toward the MESSAGE as such, focus on the message for its own sake, is the POETIC function of language. This function cannot be productively studied out of touch with the general problems of language, and, on the other hand, the scrutiny of language requires a thorough consideration of its poetic function. Any attempt to reduce the sphere of poetic function to poetry or to confine poetry to poetic function would be a delusive oversimplification. Poetic function is not the sole function of verbal art but only its dominant, determining function, whereas in all other verbal activities it acts as a subsidiary, accessory constituent. This function, by promoting the palpability of signs, deepens the fundamental dichotomy of signs and objects. Hence, when dealing with poetic function, linguistics cannot limit itself to the field of poetry.

"Why do you always say *Joan and Margery*, yet never *Margery and Joan?* Do you prefer Joan to her twin sister?" "Not at all, it just sounds smoother." In a sequence of two coordinate names, as far as no rank problems interfere, the precedence of the shorter name suits the speaker, unaccountably for him, as a well-ordered shape of the message.

A girl used to talk about "the horrible Harry." "Why horrible?" "Because I hate him." "But why not *dreadful, terrible, frightful, disgusting?*" "I don't know why, but *horrible* fits him better." Without realizing it, she clung to the poetic device of paronomasia.

The political slogan "I like Ike" /ay layk ayk/, succinctly structured, consists of three monosyllables and counts three diphthongs /ay/, each of them symmetrically followed by one consonantal phoneme, / . . l . . k . . k/. The make-up of the three words presents a variation: no consonantal phonemes in the first word, two around the diphthong in the second, and one final consonant in the third. A similar dominant nucleus /ay/ was noticed by Hymes in some of the sonnets of Keats. Both cola of the trisyllabic formula "I like /Ike" rhyme with each other, and the second of the two rhyming words is fully included in the first one (echo rhyme), /layk/ – /ayk/, a paronomastic image of a feeling which totally envelops its object. Both cola alliterate with each other, and the first of the two alliterating words is included in the second: /ay/ – /ayk/, a paronomastic image of the loving subject enveloped by the beloved object. The secondary, poetic function of this electional catchphrase reinforces its impressiveness and efficacy.

As we said, the linguistic study of the poetic function must overstep the limits of poetry, and, on the other hand, the linguistic scrutiny of poetry cannot limit itself to the poetic function. The particularities of diverse poetic genres imply a differently ranked participation of the other verbal functions along with the dominant poetic function. Epic poetry, focused on the third, strongly involves the referential function of language; the lyric, oriented toward the first person, is intimately linked with the emotive function; poetry of the second person is imbued with the conative function and is either supplicatory or exhortative, depending on whether the first person is subordinated to the second one or the second to the first.

Now that our cursory description of the six basic functions of verbal communication is more or less complete, we may complement our scheme of the fundamental factors by a corresponding scheme of the functions:

REFERENTIAL

POETIC

EMOTIVE   PHATIC   CONATIVE

METALINGUAL

What is the empirical linguistic criterion of the poetic function? In particular, what is the indispensable feature inherent in any piece of poetry? To answer this question we must recall the two basic modes of arrangement used in verbal behavior, *selection* and *combination*. If "child" is the topic of the message, the speaker selects one among the extant, more or less similar, nouns like child, kid, youngster, tot, all of them equivalent in a certain respect, and then, to comment on this topic, he may select one of the semantically cognate verbs – sleeps, dozes, nods, naps. Both chosen words combine in the speech chain. The selection is produced on the base of equivalence, similarity and dissimilarity, synonymity and antonymity, while the combination, the build up of the sequence, is based on contiguity. *The poetic function projects the principle of equivalence from the axis of selection into the axis of combination*. Equivalence is promoted to the constitutive device of the sequence. In poetry one syllable is equalized with any other syllable of the same sequence; word stress is assumed to equal word stress, as unstress equals unstress; prosodic long is matched with long, and short with short; word boundary equals word boundary, no boundary equals no boundary; syntactic pause equals syntactic pause, no pause equals no pause. Syllables are converted into units of measure, and so are morae or stresses.

[. . .]

In poetry, and to a certain extent in latent manifestations of poetic function, sequences delimited by word boundaries become commensurable whether they are sensed as isochronic or graded. "Joan and Margery" showed us the poetic principle of syllable gradation, the same principle which in the closes of Serbian folk epics has been raised to a compulsory law. Without its two dactylic words the combination "*innocent* by*stander*" would hardly have become a hackneyed phrase. The symmetry of three disyllabic verbs with an identical initial consonant and identical final vowel added splendor to the laconic victory message of Caesar: "*Veni, vidi, vici*."

Measure of sequences is a device which, outside of poetic function, finds no application in language. Only in poetry with its regular reiteration of equivalent units is the time of the speech flow experienced, as it is – to cite another semiotic pattern – with musical time. Gerard Manley Hopkins, an outstanding searcher in the science of poetic language, defined verse as "speech wholly or partially repeating the same figure of sound" (1959). Hopkins's subsequent question, "but is all verse poetry?" can be definitely answered as soon as poetic function ceases to be arbitrarily confined to the domain of poetry. Mnemonic lines cited by Hopkins (like "Thirty days hath September"), modern advertising jingles, and versified medieval laws, mentioned by Lotz, or finally Sanscrit scientific treatises in verse which in Indic tradition are strictly distinguished from true poetry (*kāvya*) – all these metrical texts make use of poetic function without, however, assigning to this function the coercing, determining role it carries in poetry. Thus verse actually exceeds the limits of poetry, but at the same time verse always implies poetic function. And apparently no human culture ignores verse-making, whereas there are many cultural patterns without "applied" verse; and even in such cultures which possess both pure and applied verses, the latter appear to be a secondary, unquestionably derived phenomenon. The adaptation of poetic means for some heterogeneous purpose does not conceal their primary essence, just as elements of emotive language, when utilized in poetry, still maintain their emotive tinge. A filibusterer may recite *Hiawatha* because it is long, yet poeticalness still remains the primary intent of this text itself. Self-evidently, the existence of versified, musical, and pictorial commercials does not separate the questions of verse or of musical and pictorial form from the study of poetry, music, and fine arts.

To sum up, the analysis of verse is entirely within the competence of poetics, and the latter may be defined as that part of linguistics which treats the poetic function in its relationship to the other functions of language. Poetics in the wider sense of the word deals with the poetic function not only in poetry, where this function is superimposed upon the other functions of language, but also outside of poetry, when some other function is super-imposed upon the poetic function.

[. . .]

Ambiguity is an intrinsic, inalienable character of any self-focused message, briefly a corollary feature of poetry. Let us repeat with Empson (1955): "The machinations of ambiguity are among the very roots of poetry." Not only the message itself but also its addresser and addressee become ambiguous. Besides the author and the reader, there is the "I" of the lyrical hero or of the fictitious storyteller and the "you" or "thou" of the alleged addressee of dramatic mono-logues, supplications, and epistles. For instance the poem "Wrestling Jacob" is addressed by its title hero to the Saviour and simultaneously acts as a subjective message of the poet Charles Wesley to his readers. Virtually any poetic message is a quasi-quoted discourse with all those peculiar, intricate problems which "speech within speech" offers to the linguist.

The supremacy of poetic function over referential function does not oblit-erate the reference but makes it ambiguous. The double-sensed message finds correspondence in a split addresser, in a split addressee, and besides in a split reference, as it is cogently exposed in the preambles to fairy tales of various peoples, for instance, in the usual exordium of the Majorca storytellers: "Aixo era y no era" (It was and it was not). The repetitiveness effected by imparting the equivalence principle to the sequence makes reiterable not only the con-stituent sequences of the poetic message but the whole message as well. This capacity for reiteration whether immediate or delayed, this reification of a poetic message and its constituents, this conversion of a message into an endur-ing thing, indeed all this represents an inherent and effective property of poetry.

[. . .]

In poetry the internal form of a name, that is, the semantic load of its con-stituents, regains its pertinence. The "Cocktails" may resume their obliterated kinship with plumage. Their colors are vivified in Mac Hammond's lines "The ghost of a Bronx pink lady // With orange blossoms afloat in her hair," and the etymological metaphor attains its realization: "O, Bloody Mary, // The cocktails have crowded not the cocks!" ("At an Old Fashion Bar in Manhattan"). Wallace Stevens's poem "An Ordinary Evening in New Haven" revives the head word of the city name first through a discreet allusion to heaven and then through a direct pun-like confrontation similar to Hopkins's "Heaven-Haven."

> The dry eucalyptus *seeks god in the rainy cloud.*
> Professor Eucalyptus of New Haven *seeks him in New Haven* . . .
> The instinct *for heaven* had its counterpart:
> The instinct for earth, *for New Haven,* for his room . . .

The adjective "New" of the city name is laid bare through the concatenation of opposites:

> The oldest-newest day is the newest alone.
> The oldest-newest night does not creak by . . .

When in 1919 the Moscow Linguistic Circle discussed how to define and delimit the range of *epitheta ornantia,* the poet Majakovskij rebuked us by saying that for him any adjective while in poetry was thereby a poetic epithet, even "great" in the *Great Bear* or "big" and "little" in such names of Moscow streets as *Bol'shaja Presnja* and *Malaja Presnja.* In other words, poet-icalness is not a supplementation of discourse with rhetorical adornment but a total re-evaluation of the discourse and of all its components whatsoever.

A missionary blamed his African flock for walking undressed. "And what about yourself?" they pointed to his visage, "are not you, too, somewhere naked?" "Well, but that is my face." "Yet in us," retorted the natives, "every-where it is face." So in poetry any verbal element is converted into a figure of poetic speech.

My attempt to vindicate the right and duty of linguistics to direct the investigation of verbal art in all its compass and extent can come to a conclu-sion with the same burden which summarized my report to the 1953 conference at Indiana University: "Linguista sum; linguistici nihil a me alienum puto." If the poet Ransom is right (and he is right) that "poetry is a kind of language," the linguist whose field is any kind of language may and must include poetry in his study. [. . .]

References

Bühler, K. (1933) "Die Axiomatik der Sprachwissenschaft," *Kant-Studien* 38: 19–90.
Empson, W. (1955) *Seven Types of Ambiguity*, New York: Chatto & Windus, 3rd edition.
Hopkins, G. M. (1959) *The Journals and Papers*, H. House (ed.), London.
Malinowski, B. (1953) "The problem of meaning in primitive languages," in C. K. Ogden and I. A. Richards, *The Meaning of Meaning*, 9th edition, New York and London: Routledge & Kegan Paul, 296–336.

Chapter 2

J. L. Austin

HOW TO DO THINGS WITH WORDS

WHAT I SHALL HAVE to say here is neither difficult nor contentious; the only merit I should like to claim for it is that of being true, at least in parts. The phenomenon to be discussed is very widespread and obvious, and it cannot fail to have been already noticed, at least here and there, by others. Yet I have not found attention paid to it specifically.

It was for too long the assumption of philosophers that the business of a 'statement' can only be to 'describe' some state of affairs, or to 'state some fact', which it must do either truly or falsely. Grammarians, indeed, have regularly pointed out that not all 'sentences' are (used in making) statements:[1] there are, traditionally, besides (grammarians') statements, also questions and exclamations, and sentences expressing commands or wishes or concessions. And doubtless philosophers have not intended to deny this, despite some loose use of 'sentence' for 'statement'. Doubtless, too, both grammarians and philosophers have been aware that it is by no means easy to distinguish even questions, commands, and so on from statements by means of the few and jejune grammatical marks available, such as word order, mood, and the like: though perhaps it has not been usual to dwell on the difficulties which this fact obviously raises. For how do we decide which is which? What are the limits and definitions of each?

But now in recent years, many things which would once have been accepted without question as 'statements' by both philosophers and grammarians have been scrutinized with new care. [. . .] It has come to be commonly held that many utterances which look like statements are either

Source: J.L. Austin, *How to do Things with Words*, Oxford: Oxford University Press, 1962.

not intended at all, or only intended in part, to record or impart straight-forward information about the facts: for example, 'ethical propositions' are perhaps intended, solely or partly, to evince emotion or to prescribe conduct or to influence it in special ways. [. . .] We very often also use utterances in ways beyond the scope at least of traditional grammar. It has come to be seen that many specially perplexing words embedded in apparently descriptive statements do not serve to indicate some specially odd additional feature in the reality reported, but to indicate (not to report) the circumstances in which the statement is made or reservations to which it is subject or the way in which it is to be taken and the like. To overlook these possibilities in the way once common is called the 'descriptive' fallacy; but perhaps this is not a good name, as 'descriptive' itself is special. Not all true or false statements are descriptions, and for this reason I prefer to use the word 'Constative' [. . .]

Utterances can be found [. . .] such that:

A   they do not 'describe' or 'report' or constate anything at all, are not 'true or false'; and
B   the uttering of the sentence is, or is a part of, the doing of an action, which again would not *normally* be described as, or as 'just', saying something . . .

[. . .]

Examples:

(a)   'I do (sc. take this woman to be my lawful wedded wife)' – as uttered in the course of the marriage ceremony.
(b)   'I name this ship the *Queen Elizabeth*' – as uttered when smashing the bottle against the stem.
(c)   'I give and bequeath my watch to my brother' – as occurring in a will.
(d)   'I bet you sixpence it will rain tomorrow.'

In these examples it seems clear that to utter the sentence (in, of course, the appropriate circumstances) is not to *describe* my doing of what I should be said in so uttering to be doing or to state that I am doing it: it is to do it. None of the utterances cited is either true or false: I assert this as obvious and do not argue it. It needs argument no more than that 'damn' is not true or false: it may be that the utterance 'serves to inform you' – but that is quite different. To name the ship *is* to say (in the appropriate circumstances) the words 'I name, etc.'. When I say, before the registrar or altar, 'I do', I am not reporting on a marriage: I am indulging in it.

What are we to call a sentence or an utterance of this type? I propose to call it a *performative sentence* or a performative utterance, or, for short, 'a performative'. The term 'performative' will be used in a variety of cognate ways and constructions, much as the term 'imperative' is. The name is derived, of course, from 'perform', the usual verb with the noun 'action': it indicates that the issuing of the utterance is the performing of an action – it is not normally thought of as just saying something.

[. . .]

Are we then to say things like this:

'To marry is to say a few words', or
'Betting is simply saying something'?

Such a doctrine sounds odd or even flippant at first, but with sufficient safe-guards it may become not odd at all.

[. . .]

The uttering of the words is, indeed, usually a, or even *the*, leading incident in the performance of the act (of betting or what not), the perfor-mance of which is also the object of the utterance, but it is far from being usually, even if it is ever, the *sole* thing necessary if the act is to be deemed to have been performed. Speaking generally, it is always necessary that the *circumstances* in which the words are uttered should be in some way, or ways, *appropriate*, and it is very commonly necessary that either the speaker himself or other persons should *also* perform certain *other* actions, whether 'phys-ical' or 'mental' actions or even acts of uttering further words. Thus, for naming the ship, it is essential that I should be the person appointed to name her; for (Christian) marrying, it is essential that I should not be already married with a wife living, sane and undivorced, and so on; for a bet to have been made, it is generally necessary for the offer of the bet to have been accepted by a taker (who must have done something, such as to say 'Done'); and it is hardly a gift if I *say* 'I give it you' but never hand it over.

[. . .] But we may, in objecting, have something totally different, and this time quite mistaken, in mind, especially when we think of some of the more awe-inspiring performatives such as 'I promise to . . .'. Surely the words must be spoken 'seriously' and so as to be taken 'seriously'? This is, though vague, true enough in general – it is an important commonplace in discussing the purport of any utterance whatsoever. I must not be joking, for example, nor writing a poem. [. . .]

[. . .] Well we shall next consider what we actually do say about the utterance concerned when one or another of its normal concomitants is *absent*. In no case do we say that the utterance was false but rather that the utterance – or rather the *act*, e.g., the promise – was void, or given in bad faith, or not implemented, or the like. In the particular case of promising, as with many other performatives, it is appropriate that the person uttering the promise should have a certain intention, viz. here to keep his word: and perhaps of all concomitants this looks the most suitable to be that which 'I promise' does describe or record. Do we not actually, when such intention is absent, speak of a 'false' promise? Yet so to speak is *not* to say that the utterance 'I promise that . . .' is false, in the sense that though he states that he does he doesn't, or that though he describes he misdescribes – misreports. For he *does* promise: the promise here is not even *void*, though it is given *in bad faith*. His utterance is perhaps misleading, probably deceitful and doubtless wrong, but it is not a lie or a misstatement. At most we might make out a case for saying that it implies or insinuates a falsehood or a misstatement (to the effect that he does intend to do something): but that is a very different matter. Moreover, we do not speak of a false bet or a false christening; and that we *do* speak of a false promise need commit us no more than the fact that we speak of a false move. 'False' is not necessarily used of statements only.

[. . .]

Besides the uttering of the words of so-called performative, a good many other things have as a general rule to be right and to go right if we are to be said to have happily brought off our action. What these are we may hope to discover by looking at and classifying types of case in which something *goes wrong* and the act – marrying, betting, bequeathing, christening, or what not – is therefore at least to some extent a failure: the utterance is then, we may say, not indeed false but in general *unhappy*. And for this reason we call the doctrine of *the things that can be and go wrong* on the occasion of such utterances, the doctrine of the *Infelicities*.

Suppose we try first to state schematically – and I do not wish to claim any sort of finality for this scheme – some at least of the things which are necessary for the smooth or 'happy' functioning of a performative (or at least of a highly developed explicit performative, such as we have hitherto been alone concerned with), and then give examples of infelicities and their effects. [. . .]

A.1   There must exist an accepted conventional procedure having a certain conventional effect, that procedure to include the uttering of certain words by certain persons in certain circumstances, and further,

A.2   the particular persons and circumstances in a given case must be appropriate for the invocation of the particular procedure invoked.

B.1   The procedure must be executed by all participants both correctly and

B.2   completely.

C.1   Where, as often, the procedure is designed for use by persons having certain thoughts or feelings, or for the inauguration of certain consequential conduct on the part of any participant, then a person participating in and so invoking the procedure must in fact have those thoughts or feelings, and the participants must intend so to conduct themselves, and further

C.2   must actually so conduct themselves subsequently.

Now if we sin against any one (or more) of these six rules, our performative utterance will be (in one way or another) unhappy. But, of course, there are considerable differences between these 'ways' of being unhappy – ways which are intended to be brought out by the letter–numerals selected for each heading.

The first big distinction is between all the four rules A and B taken together, as opposed to the two rules C [. . .]. If we offend against any of the former rules (As or Bs) – that is, if we, say, utter the formula incorrectly, or if, say, we are not in a position to do the act because we are, say, married already, or it is the purser and not the captain who is conducting the ceremony, then the act in question, e.g., marrying, is not successfully performed at all, does not come off, is not achieved. Whereas in the two C cases the act *is* achieved, although to achieve it in such circumstances, as when we are, say, insincere, is an abuse of the procedure. Thus, when I say 'I promise' and have no intention of keeping it, I have promised but . . . We need names for referring to this general distinction, so we shall call in general those infelicities A.1–B.2 which are such that the act for the performing of which, and in the performing of which, the verbal formula in question is designed, is not achieved, by the name MISFIRES: and on the other hand we may christen those infelicities where the act *is* achieved ABUSES. [. . .] When the utterance is a misfire, the procedure which we purport to invoke is disallowed or is botched: and our act (marrying, etc.) is void or without effect, etc. We speak of our act as a purported act, or perhaps an attempt – or we use such an expression as 'went through a form of marriage' by contrast with 'married'. On the ther hand, in the C cases, we speak of our infelicitous act as 'professed' or 'hollow' rather than 'purported' or 'empty', and as not implemented, or not consummated, rather than as void or without effect. But let me hasten to add that these distinctions are not hard and fast, and more especially that such words as 'purported' and 'professed' will not bear very much stressing. Two final words about being void or without effect. This does not mean, of course, to say that we won't have done anything: lots of things will have been done – we shall most interestingly have committed the act of bigamy – but we shall *not* have done the purported act, viz. marrying. Because despite the name, you do not when bigamous marry twice.[. . .] Further, 'without effect' does not here mean 'without consequences, results, effects'.

[. . .]

The performative utterances I have taken as examples are all of them highly developed affairs, of the kind that we shall call *explicit* performatives, by contrast with merely *implicit* performatives. That is to say, they (all) begin with or include some highly significant and unambiguous expression such as 'I bet', 'I promise', 'I bequeath' – an expression very commonly also used in naming the act which, in making such an utterance, I am performing – for example betting, promising, bequeathing, etc. But, of course, it is both obvious and important that we can on occasion use the utterance 'go' to achieve practically the same as we achieve by the utterance 'I order you to go': and we should say cheerfully in either case, describing subsequently what someone did, that he ordered me to go. It may, however, be uncertain in fact, and, so far as the mere utterance is concerned, is always left uncertain when we use so inexplicit a formula as the mere imperative 'go', whether the utterer is ordering (or is purporting to order) me to go or merely advising, entreating, or what not me to go. Similarly 'There is a bull in the field' may or may not be a warning, for I *might* just be describing the scenery, and 'I shall be there' may or may not be a promise. Here we have primitive as distinct from explicit performatives; and there may be nothing in the circumstances by which we can decide whether or not the utterance is performative at all. Anyway, in a given situation it can be open to me to take it as *either* one or the other. It was a performative formula – *perhaps* – but the procedure in question was not sufficiently explicitly invoked. Perhaps I did not *take it as* an order or was not anyway *bound* to take it as an order. The person did not *take it as* a promise: i.e., in the particular circumstance he did not accept the procedure, on the ground that the ritual was incompletely carried out by the original speaker.

[. . .]

We shall next consider three of the many ways in which a statement implies the truth of certain other statements. One of those that I shall mention has been long known. The others have been discovered quite recently. We shall not put the matter too technically, though this can be done. I refer to the discovery that the ways we can do wrong, speak outrageously, in uttering conjunctions of 'factual' statements, are more numerous than merely by contradiction [. . .]

1   *Entails*: 'All men blush' entails 'some men blush'. We cannot say 'All men blush but not any men blush', or 'the cat is under the mat and the cat is on top of the mat' or 'the cat is on the mat and the cat is not on the mat', since in each case the first clause entails the contradictory of the second.

2   *Implies*: My saying 'the cat is on the mat' implies that I believe it is [. . .] We cannot say 'the cat is on the mat but I do not believe it is'. (This is actually not the ordinary use of 'implies': 'implies' is really weaker: as when we say 'He implied that I did not know it' or 'You implied you knew it' (as distinct from believing it.)

3   *Presupposes*: 'All Jack's children are bald' presupposes that Jack has some children. We cannot say 'All Jack's children are bald but Jack has no children', or 'Jack has no children and all his children are bald'.

      There is a common feeling of outrage in all these cases. But we must not use some blanket term, 'implies' or 'contradiction', because there are very great differences. There are more ways of killing a cat than drowning it in butter; but this is the sort of thing (as the proverb indicates) we overlook: there are more ways of outraging speech than contradiction merely [. . .]

The act of 'saying something' in the full normal sense I call, i.e., dub, the performance of a locutionary act, and the study of utterances thus far and in these respects the study of locutions, or of the full units of speech. Our interest in the locutionary act is, of course, principally to make quite plain what it is, in order to distinguish it from other acts with which we are primarily concerned [. . .]

To perform a locutionary act is in general, we may say, also and *eo ipso* to perform an *illocutionary* act, as I propose to call it. Thus in performing a locutionary act we shall also be performing such an act as:

   asking or answering a question;
   giving some information or an assurance or a warning;
   announcing a verdict or an intention;
   pronouncing sentence;
   making an appointment or an appeal or a criticism;
   making an identification or giving a description;

and the numerous like. (I am not suggesting that this is a clearly defined class by any means.) [. . .] When we perform a locutionary act, we use speech: but in what way precisely are we using it on this occasion? For there are very numerous functions of or ways in which we use speech and it makes a great difference to our act in some sense – in which way and which *sense* we were on this occasion 'using' it. It makes a great difference whether we were advising, or merely suggesting, or actually ordering, whether we were strictly promising or only announcing a vague intention, and so forth. These issues penetrate a little but not without confusion into grammar, but we constantly do debate them, in such terms as whether certain words (a certain locution) *had the force of* a question, or *ought to have been taken as* an estimate and so on.

I explained the performance of an act in this new and second sense as the performance of an 'illocutionary' act, i.e. performance of an act *in* saying something as opposed to performance of an act *of* saying something; I call the act performed an 'illocution' and shall refer to the doctrine of the different types of function of language here in question as the doctrine of 'illocutionary forces'.

[. . .]

There is yet a further sense in which to perform a locutionary act, and therein an illocutionary act, may also be to perform an act of another kind. Saying something will often, or even normally, produce certain consequential effects upon the feelings, thoughts, or actions of the audience, or of the speaker, or of other persons: and it may be done with the design, intention or purpose of producing them; and we may then say, thinking of this, that the speaker has performed an act in the nomenclature of which reference is made either (a), only obliquely, or even (b), not at all, to the performance of the locutionary or illocutionary act. We shall call the performance of an act of this kind the performance of a 'perlocutionary' act, and the act performed, where suitable – essentially in cases falling under (a) – a 'perlocution' [. . .]

Acts of all our three kinds [locutionary, illocutionary and perlocutionary] necessitate, since they are the performing of actions, allowance being made for the ills that all action is heir to. We must systematically be prepared to distinguish between 'the act of doing *x*', i.e., achieving *x*, and 'the act of attempting to do *x*'.

In the case of illocutions we must be ready to draw the necessary distinction, not noticed by ordinary language except in exceptional cases, between:

(a)   the act of attempting or purporting (or affecting or professing or claiming or setting up or setting out) to perform a certain illocutionary act, and

(b)   the act of successfully achieving or consummating or bringing off such an act.

This distinction is, or should be, a commonplace of the theory of our language about 'action' in general. But attention has been drawn earlier to its special importance in connexion with performatives: it is always possible, for example, to try to thank or inform somebody yet in different ways to fail, because he doesn't listen, or takes it as ironical, or wasn't responsible for whatever it was, and so on. This distinction will arise, as over any act, over locutionary acts too; but failures here will not be unhappiness as there, but rather failures to get the words out, to express ourselves clearly, etc.

Since our acts are actions, we must always remember the distinction between producing effects or consequences which are intended or unintended; and (i) when the speaker intends to produce an effect it may nevertheless not occur, and (ii) when he does not intend to produce it or intends not to produce it it may nevertheless occur. To cope with complication (i) we invoke as before the distinction between attempt and achievement; to cope with complication (ii) we invoke the normal linguistic devices of disclaiming (adverbs like 'unintentionally' and so on) which we hold ready for general use in all cases of doing actions.

[. . .]

The perlocutionary act may be either the achievement of a perlocutionary object (convince, persuade) or the production of a perlocutionary sequel. Thus the act of warning may achieve its perlocutionary object of alerting and also have the perlocutionary sequel of alarming, and an argument against a view may fail to achieve its object but have the perlocutionary sequel of convincing our opponent of its truth ('I only succeeded in convincing him'). What is the perlocutionary object of one illocution may be the sequel of another. For example, warning may produce the sequel of deterring and saying 'Don't', whose object is to deter, may produce the sequel of alerting or even alarming. Some perlocutionary acts are always the producing of a sequel, namely those where there is no illocutionary formula: thus I may surprise you or upset you or humiliate you by a locution, though there is no illocutionary formula 'I surprise you by . . .', 'I upset you by . . .', 'I humiliate you by . . .'

It is characteristic of perlocutionary acts that the response achieved, or the sequel, can be achieved additionally or entirely by non-locutionary means: thus intimidation may be achieved by waving a stick or pointing a gun. Even in the cases of convincing, persuading, getting to obey and getting to believe, we may achieve the response non-verbally; but if there is no illocutionary act, it is doubtful whether this language characteristic of perlocutionary objects should be used. Compare the use of 'got him to' with that of 'got him to obey'. However, this alone is not enough to distinguish illocutionary acts, since we can for example warn or order or appoint or give or protest or apologize by non-verbal means and these are illocutionary acts. Thus we may cock a snook or hurl a tomato by way of protest.

[. . .]

When we originally contrasted the performative with the constative utterance we said that

1   the performative should be doing something as opposed to just saying something; and
2   the performative is happy or unhappy as opposed to true or false.

Were these distinctions really sound? Our subsequent discussion of doing and saying certainly seems to point to the conclusion that whenever I 'say' anything (except perhaps a mere exclamation like 'damn' or 'ouch') I shall be performing both locutionary and illocutionary acts, and these two kinds of acts seem to be the very things which we tried to use, under the names of 'doing' and 'saying', as a means of distinguishing performatives from constatives. If we are in general always doing both things, how can our distinction survive?

Let us first reconsider the contrast from the side of constative utterances: of these, we were content to refer to 'statements' as the typical or paradigm case. Would it be correct to say that when we state something

1   we are doing something as well as and distinct from just saying something, and
2   our utterance is liable to be happy or unhappy (as well as, if you will, true or false)?

Surely to state is every bit as much to perform an illocutionary act as, say, to want or to pronounce. Of course it is not to perform an act in some specially physically way, other than in so far as it involves, when verbal, the making of movements of vocal organs; but then nor, as we have seen, is to warn, to protest, to promise or to name. 'Stating' seems to meet all the criteria we had for distinguishing the illocutionary act. Consider such an unexceptionable remark as the following:

In saying that it was raining, I was not betting or arguing or warning: I was simply stating it as a fact.

Here 'stating' is put absolutely on a level with arguing, betting, and warning [. . .]

Moreover, although the utterance 'He did not do it' is often issued as a statement, and is then undoubtedly true or false (*this* is if anything is), it does not seem possible to say that it differs from 'I state that he did not do it' in this respect. If someone says 'I state that he did not do it', we investigate the truth of his statement in just the same way as if he had said 'He did not do it' [. . .]

Moreover, if we think of the alleged contrast, according to which performatives are happy or unhappy and statements true or false, again from the side of supposed constative utterances, notably statements, we find that statements *are* liable to every kind of infelicity to which performatives are liable. Let us look back again and consider whether statements are not liable to precisely the same disabilities as, say, warnings by way of what we called 'infelicities' – that is various disabilities which make an utterance unhappy without, however, making it true or false.

We have already noted that sense in which saying, as equivalent to stating, 'The cat is on the mat' implies that I believe that the cat is on the mat. This is parallel to the sense – is the same sense – as that in which 'I promise to be there' implies that I intend to be there and that I believe I shall be able to be there. So the statement is liable to the *insincerity* form of infelicity; and even to the *breach* form of infelicity in this sense, that saying or stating that the cat is on the mat commits me to saying or stating 'The mat is underneath the cat' just as much as the performative 'I define X as Y' (in the *fiat* sense say) commits me to using those terms in special ways in future discourse, and we can see how this is connected with such acts as promising. This means that statements can give rise to infelicities of our two C kinds.

Now what about infelicities of the A and B kinds, which rendered the act – warning, undertaking, etc. – null and void? Can a thing that looks like a statement be null and void just as much as a putative contract? The answer seems to be Yes, importantly. The first cases are A.1 and A.2, where there is no convention (or not an accepted convention) or where the circumstances are not appropriate for its invocation by the speaker. Many infelicities of just this type do infect statements.

We have already noticed the case of a putative statement *presupposing* (as it is called) the existence of that which it refers to; if no such thing exists, 'the statement' is not about anything. Now some say that in these circumstances, if, for example, someone asserts that the present King of France is bald, 'the question whether he is bald does not arise'; but it is better to say that the putative statement is null and void, exactly as when I say that I sell you something but it is not mine or (having been burnt) is not any longer in existence. Contracts often are void because the objects they are about do not exist, which involves a breakdown of reference.

But it is important to notice also that 'statements' too are liable to infelicity of this kind in other ways also parallel to contracts, promises, warnings, etc. Just as we often say, for example, 'You cannot order me', in the sense 'You have not the right to order me', which is equivalent to saying that you are not in the appropriate position to do so: so often there are things you cannot state – have no right to state – are not in a position to state. You *cannot* now state how many people there are in the next room; if you say 'There are fifty people in the next room', I can only regard you as guessing or conjecturing (just as sometimes you are not ordering me, which would be inconceivable, but possibly asking me to rather impolitely, so here you are 'hazarding a guess' rather oddly). Here there is something you might, in other circumstances, be in a position to state; but what about statements about other persons' feelings or about the future? Is a forecast or even a prediction about, say, persons' behaviour really a statement? It is important to take the speech-situation as a whole.

[. . .]

Once we realize that what we have to study is *not* the sentence but the issuing of an utterance in a speech situation, there can hardly be any longer a possibility of not seeing that stating is performing an act [. . .]

What then finally is left of the distinction of the performative and constative utterance? Really we may say that what we had in mind here was this:

(a)   With the constative utterance, we abstract from the illocutionary (let alone the perlocutionary) aspects of the speech act, and we concentrate on the locutionary: moreover, we use an oversimplified notion of correspondence with the facts – oversimplified because essentially it brings in the illocutionary aspect. This is the ideal of what would be right to say in all circumstances, for any purpose, to any audience, etc. Perhaps it is sometimes realized.

(b)   With the performative utterance, we attend as much as possible to the illocutionary force of the utterance, and abstract from the dimension of correspondence with facts.

Perhaps neither of these abstractions is so very expedient: perhaps we have here not really two poles, but rather a historical development. Now in certain cases, perhaps with mathematical formulas in physics books as examples of constatives, or with the issuing of simple executive orders or the giving of simple names, say, as examples of performatives, we approximate in real life to finding such things. It was examples of this kind, like 'I apologize', and 'The cat is on the mat', said for no conceivable reason, extreme marginal cases, that gave rise to the idea of two distinct utterances. But the real conclusion must surely be that we need (1) to distinguish between locutionary and illocutionary acts, and (2) specially and critically to establish with respect to each kind of illocutionary act – warnings, estimates, verdicts, statements, and descriptions – what if any is the specific way in which they are intended, first to be in order or not in order, and second, to be 'right' or 'wrong'; what terms of appraisal and disappraisal are used for each and what they mean. This is a wide field and certainly will not lead to a simple distinction of 'true' and 'false'; nor will it lead to a distinction of statements from the rest, for stating is only one among very numerous speech acts of the illocutionary class.

Furthermore, in general the locutionary act as much as the illocutionary is an abstraction only: every genuine speech act is both.

[. . .]

Note

1   It is, of course, not really correct that a sentence ever *is* a statement: rather, it is *used* in *making a statement*, and the statement itself is a 'logical construction' out of the makings of statements.

Chapter 3

H. P. Grice

LOGIC AND CONVERSATION

[. . .]

Suppose that A and B are talking about a mutual friend, C, who is now
working in a bank. A asks B how C is getting on in his job, and B replies,
Oh quite well, I think; he likes his colleagues, and he hasn't been to prison yet. At
this point, A might well inquire what B was implying, what he was suggesting,
or even what he meant by saying that C had not yet been to prison. The
answer might be any one of such things as that C is the sort of person likely
to yield to the temptation provided by his occupation, that C's colleagues
are really very unpleasant and treacherous people, and so forth. It might, of
course, be quite unnecessary for A to make such an inquiry of B, the answer
to it being, in the context, clear in advance. I think it is clear that whatever
B implied, suggested, meant, etc., in this example, is distinct from what B
said, which was simply that C had not been to prison yet. I wish to introduce, as terms of art, the verb *implicate* and the related nouns *implicature* (cf.
implying) and *implicatum* (cf. *what is implied*). The point of this maneuver is
to avoid having, on each occasion, to choose between this or that member
of the family of verbs for which *implicate* is to do general duty. I shall, for
the time being at least, have to assume to a considerable extent an intuitive
understanding of the meaning of *say* in such contexts, and an ability to recognize particular verbs as members of the family with which *implicate* is
associated. I can, however, make one or two remarks that may help to clarify

Source: H. P. Grice, 'Logic and conversation', in Peter Cole and Jerry L. Morgan (eds) *Syntax
and Semantics*, Volume 3: *Speech Arts*, New York: Academic Press, 41–58.

the more problematic of these assumptions, namely, that connected with the meaning of the word *say*.

In the sense in which I am using the word *say*, I intend what someone has said to be closely related to the conventional meaning of the words (the sentence) he has uttered. Suppose someone to have uttered the sentence *He is in the grip of a vice*. Given a knowledge of the English language, but no knowledge of the circumstances of the utterance, one would know something about what the speaker had said, on the assumption that he was speaking standard English, and speaking literally. One would know that he had said, about some particular male person or animal *x*, that at the time of the utterance (whatever that was), either (1) *x* was unable to rid himself of a certain kind of bad character trait or (2) some part of *x*'s person was caught in a certain kind of tool or instrument (approximate account, of course). But for a full identification of what the speaker had said, one would need to know (a) the identity of *x*, (b) the time of utterance, and (c) the meaning, on the particular occasion of utterance, of the phrase *in the grip of a vice* (a decision between (1) and (2)). This brief indication of my use of *say* leaves it open whether a man who says (today) *Harold Wilson is a great man* and another who says (also today) *The British Prime Minister is a great man* would, if each knew that the two singular terms had the same reference, have said the same thing. But whatever decision is made about this question, the apparatus that I am about to provide will be capable of accounting for any implicatures that might depend on the presence of one rather than another of these singular terms in the sentence uttered. Such implicatures would merely be related to different maxims.

In some cases the conventional meaning of the words used will determine what is implicated, besides helping to determine what is said. If I say (smugly), *He is an Englishman; he is, therefore, brave*, I have certainly committed myself, by virtue of the meaning of my words, to its being the case that his being brave is a consequence of (follows from) his being an Englishman. But while I have said that he is an Englishman, and said that he is brave, I do not want to say that I have SAID (in the favored sense) that it follows from his being an Englishman that he is brave, though I have certainly indicated, and so implicated, that this is so. I do not want to say that my utterance of this sentence would be, STRICTLY SPEAKING, false should the consequence in question fail to hold. So SOME implicatures are conventional, unlike the one with which I introduced this discussion of implicature.

I wish to represent a certain subclass of nonconventional implicatures, which I shall call CONVERSATIONAL implicatures, as being essentially connected with certain general features of discourse; so my next step is to try to say what these features are.

The following may provide a first approximation to a general principle. Our talk exchanges do not normally consist of a succession of disconnected remarks, and would not be rational if they did. They are characteristically, to some degree at least, cooperative efforts; and each participant recognizes in them, to some extent, a common purpose or set of purposes, or at least a mutually accepted direction. This purpose or direction may be fixed from the start (e.g., by an initial proposal of a question for discussion), or it may evolve during the exchange; it may be fairly definite, or it may be so indefinite as to leave very considerable latitude to the participants (as in a casual conversation). But at each stage, SOME possible conversational moves would be excluded as conversationally unsuitable. We might then formulate a rough general principle which participants will be expected, other things being equal, to observe, namely: make your conversational contribution such as is required, at the stage at which it occurs, by the accepted purpose or direction of the talk exchange in which you are engaged. One might label this the Cooperative Principle [Grice later refers to this as the CP].

On the assumption that some such general principle as this is acceptable, one may perhaps distinguish four categories under one or another of which will fall certain more specific maxims and sub-maxims, the following of which will, in general, yield results in accordance with the Cooperative Principle. Echoing Kant, I call these categories Quantity, Quality, Relation, and Manner. The category of Quantity relates to the quantity of information to be provided, and under it fall the following maxims:

1   Make your contribution as informative as is required (for the current purposes of the exchange).
2   Do not make your contribution more informative than is required.

(The second maxim is disputable; it might be said that to be overinformative is not a transgression of the CP but merely a waste of time. However, it might be answered that such overinformativeness may be confusing in that it is liable to raise side issues; and there may also be an indirect effect, in that the hearers may be misled as a result of thinking that there is some particular POINT in the provision of the excess of information. However this may be, there is perhaps a different reason for doubt about the admission of this second maxim, namely, that its effect will be secured by a later maxim, which concerns relevance.)

Under the category of Quality falls a supermaxim – 'Try to make your contribution one that is true' – and two more specific maxims:

1   Do not say what you believe to be false.
2   Do not say that for which you lack adequate evidence.

Under the category of Relation I place a single maxim, namely, 'Be relevant.' Though the maxim itself is terse, its formulation conceals a number of problems that exercise me a good deal: questions about what different kinds and focuses of relevance there may be, how these shift in the course of a talk exchange, how to allow for the fact that subjects of conversation are legitimately changed, and so on. I find the treatment of such questions exceedingly difficult, and I hope to revert to them in a later work.

Finally, under the category of Manner, which I understand as relating not (like the previous categories) to what is said but, rather, to HOW what is said is to be said, I include the supermaxim – 'Be perspicuous' – and various maxims such as:

1   Avoid obscurity of expression.
2   Avoid ambiguity.
3   Be brief (avoid unnecessary prolixity).
4   Be orderly.

And one might need others.

It is obvious that the observance of some of these maxims is a matter of less urgency than is the observance of others; a man who has expressed himself with undue prolixity would, in general, be open to milder comment than would a man who has said something he believes to be false. Indeed, it might be felt that the importance of at least the first maxim of Quality is such that it should not be included in a scheme of the kind I am constructing; other maxims come into operation only on the assumption that this maxim of Quality is satisfied. While this may be correct, so far as the generation of implicatures is concerned it seems to play a role not totally different from the other maxims, and it will be convenient, for the present at least to treat it as a member of the list of maxims.

There are, of course, all sorts of other maxims (aesthetic. social, or moral in character), such as 'Be polite', that are also normally observed by participants in talk exchanges, and these may also generate nonconventional implicatures. The conversational maxims, however, and the conversational implicatures connected with them, are specially connected (I hope) with the particular purposes that talk (and so, talk exchange) is adapted to serve and is primarily employed to serve. I have stated my maxims as if this purpose were a maximally effective exchange of information; this specification is, of course, too narrow, and the scheme needs to be generalized to allow for such general purposes as influencing or directing the actions of others.

As one of my avowed aims is to see talking as a special case or variety of purposive, indeed rational, behavior, it may be worth noting that the specific expectations or presumptions connected with at least some of the foregoing maxims have their analogues in the sphere of transactions that are not talk exchanges. I list briefly one such analog for each conversational category.

1   Quantity. If you are assisting me to mend a car, I expect your contribution to be neither more nor less than is required; if, for example, at a particular stage I need four screws, I expect you to hand me four, rather than two or six.
2   Quality. I expect your contributions to be genuine and not spurious. If I need sugar as an ingredient in the cake you are assisting me to make, I do not expect you to hand me salt; if I need a spoon, I do not expect a trick spoon made of rubber.
3   Relation. I expect a partner's contribution to be appropriate to immediate needs at each stage of the transaction; if I am mixing ingredients for a cake, I do not expect to be handed a good book, or even an oven cloth (though this might be an appropriate contribution at a later stage).
4   Manner. I expect a partner to make it clear what contribution he is making, and to execute his performance with reasonable dispatch.

These analogies are relevant to what I regard as a fundamental question about the CP and its attendant maxims, namely, what the basis is for the assumption which we seem to make, and on which (I hope) it will appear that a great range of implicatures depend, that talkers will in general (other things being equal and in the absence of indications to the contrary) proceed in the manner that these principles prescribe. A dull but, no doubt at a certain level, adequate answer is that it is just a well-recognized empirical fact that people DO behave in these ways; they have learned to do so in childhood and not lost the habit of doing so; and, indeed, it would involve a good deal of effort to make a radical departure from the habit. It is much easier, for example, to tell the truth than to invent lies.

I am, however, enough of a rationalist to want to find a basis that underlies these facts, undeniable though they may be; I would like to be able to think of the standard type of conversational practice not merely as something that all or most do IN FACT follow but as something that it is REASONABLE for us to follow, that we SHOULD NOT abandon. For a time, I was attracted by the idea that observance of the CP and the maxims, in a talk exchange, could be thought of as a quasi-contractual matter, with parallels outside the realm of discourse. If you pass by when I am struggling with my stranded car, I no doubt have some degree of expectation that you will offer help, but once you join me in tinkering under the hood, my expectations become stronger and take more specific forms (in the absence of indications that you are merely an incompetent meddler); and talk exchanges seemed to me to exhibit, characteristically, certain features that jointly distinguish cooperative transactions:

1   The participants have some common immediate aim, like getting a car mended; their ultimate aims may, of course, be independent and even in conflict – each may want to get the car mended in order to drive off, leaving the other stranded. In characteristic talk exchanges, there is a common aim even if, as in an over-the-wall chat, it is a second-order one, namely, that each party should, for the time being, identify himself with the transitory conversational interests of the other.
2   The contributions of the participants should be dovetailed mutually dependent.
3   There is some sort of understanding (which may be explicit but which is often tacit) that, other things being equal, the transaction should continue in appropriate style unless both parties are agreeable that it should terminate. You do not just shove off or start doing something else.

But while some such quasi-contractual basis as this may apply to some cases, there are too many types of exchange, like quarrelling and letter writing, that it fails to fit comfortably. In any case, one feels that the talker who is irrelevant or obscure has primarily let down not his audience but himself. So I would like to be able to show that observance of the CP and maxims is reasonable (rational) along the following lines: that anyone who cares about goals that are central to conversation/communication (e.g. giving and receiving information, influencing and being influenced by others) must be expected to have an interest, given suitable circumstances, in participation in talk exchanges that will be profitable only on the assumption that they are conducted in general accordance with the CP and the maxims. Whether any such conclusion can be reached, I am uncertain; in any case, I am fairly sure that I cannot reach it until I am a good deal clearer about the nature of relevance and of the circumstances in which it is required.

It is now time to show the connection between the CP and maxims, on the one hand, and conversational implicature on the other.

A participant in a talk exchange may fail to fulfill a maxim in various ways, which include the following:

1   He may quietly and unostentatiously VIOLATE a maxim; if so, in some cases he will be liable to mislead.
2   He may OPT OUT from the operation both of the maxim and of the CP; he may say, indicate, or allow it to become plain that he is unwilling

to cooperate in the way the maxim requires. He may say, for example,
I cannot say more; my lips are sealed.

3   He may be faced by a CLASH: He may be unable, for example, to fulfill
the first maxim of Quantity (Be as informative as is required) without
violating the second maxim of Quality (Have adequate evidence for
what you say).

4   He may FLOUT a maxim; that is, he may BLATANTLY fail to fulfill it.
On the assumption that the speaker is able to fulfill the maxim and to
do so without violating another maxim (because of a clash), is not
opting out, and is not, in view of the blatancy of his performance,
trying to mislead, the hearer is faced with a minor problem: How can
his saying what he did say be reconciled with the supposition that he
is observing the overall CP? This situation is one that characteristically
gives rise to a conversational implicature; and when a conversational
implicature is generated in this way, I shall say that a maxim is being
EXPLOITED.

   I am now in a position to characterize the notion of conversational implicature. A man who, by (in, when) saying (or making as if to say) that p has
implicated that q, may be said to have conversationally implicated that q,
PROVIDED THAT (1) he is to be presumed to be observing the conversational
maxims, or at least the cooperative principle; (2) the supposition that he is
aware that, or thinks that, q is required in order to make his saying or making
as if to say p (or doing so in THOSE terms) consistent with this presumption; and (3) the speaker thinks (and would expect the hearer to think that
the speaker thinks) that it is within the competence of the hearer to work
out, or grasp intuitively, that the supposition mentioned in (2) IS required.
Apply this to my initial example, to B's remark that C has not yet been to
prison. In a suitable setting A might reason as follows: '(1) B has apparently
violated the maxim "Be relevant" and so may be regarded as having flouted
one of the maxims conjoining perspicuity, yet I have no reason to suppose
that he is opting out from the operation of the CP; (2) given the circumstances, I can regard his irrelevance as only apparent if, and only if, I suppose
him to think that C is potentially dishonest; (3) B knows that I am capable
of working out step (2). So B implicates that C is potentially dishonest.'

   The presence of a conversational implicature must be capable of being
worked out; for even if it can in fact be intuitively grasped, unless the intuition is replaceable by an argument, the implicature (if present at all) will
not count as a CONVERSATIONAL implicature; it will be a CONVENTIONAL
implicature. To work out that a particular conversational implicature is
present, the hearer will rely on the following data:

1   the conventional meaning of the words used, together with the identity of any references that may be involved;
2   the CP and its maxims;
3   the context, linguistic or otherwise, of the utterance;
4   other items of background knowledge; and
5   the fact (or supposed fact) that all relevant items falling under the previous headings are available to both participants and both participants know or assume this to be the case.

A general pattern for the working out of a conventional implicature might be given as follows: 'He has said that p; there is no reason to suppose that he is not observing the maxims, or at least the CP; he could not be doing this unless he thought that q; he knows (and knows that I know that he knows) that I can see that the supposition that he thinks that q IS required; he has done nothing to stop me thinking that q; he intends me to think, or is at least willing to allow me to think, that q; and so he has implicated that q.'

I shall now offer a number of examples, which I shall divide into three groups.

Group A

Examples in which no maxim is violated, or at least in which it is not clear that any maxim is violated

A is standing by an obviously immobilized car and is approached by B; the following exchange takes place:

(1)   A: I am out of petrol.
         B: There is a garage round the corner.

(Gloss: B would be infringing the maxim 'Be relevant' unless he thinks, or thinks it possible, that the garage is open, and has petrol to sell; so he implicates that the garage is, or at least may be open, etc.)

In this example, unlike the case of the remark *He hasn't been to prison yet*, the unstated connection between B's remark and A's remark is so obvious that, even if one interprets the supermaxim of Manner, 'Be perspicious,' as applying not only to the expression of what is said but also to the connection of what is said with adjacent remarks, there seems to be no case for regarding that supermaxim as infringed in this example. The next example is perhaps a little less clear in this respect:

(2)   A: Smith doesn't seem to have a girlfriend these days.
       B: He has been paying a lot of visits to New York lately.

B implicates that Smith has, or may have, a girlfriend in New York. (A gloss is unnecessary in view of that given for the previous example.)

In both examples, the speaker implicates that which he must be assumed to believe in order to preserve the assumption that he is observing the maxim of relation.

Group B

An example in which a maxim is violated, but its violation is to be explained by the supposition of a clash with another maxim

A is planning with B an itinerary for a holiday in France. Both know that A wants to see his friend C, if to do so would not involve too great a prolongation of his journey:

(3)   A: Where does C live?
       B: Somewhere in the south of France.

(Gloss: There is no reason to suppose that B is opting out; his answer is, as he well knows, less informative than is required to meet A's needs. This infringement of the first maxim of Quantity can be explained only by the supposition that B is aware that to be more informative would be to say something that infringed the maxim of Quality, 'Don't say what you lack adequate evidence for', so B implicates that he does not know in which town C lives.)

Group C

Examples that involve exploitation, that is, a procedure by which a maxim is flouted for the purpose of getting in a conversational implicature by means of something of the nature of a figure of speech

In these examples, though some maxim is violated at the level of what is said, the hearer is entitled to assume that that maxim, or at least the overall Cooperative Principle, is observed at the level of what is implicated.

A flouting of the first maxim of Quantity

(4) A is writing a testimonial about a pupil who is a candidate for a philosophy job, and his letter reads as follows: Dear Sir, Mr X's command of English is excellent, and his attendance at tutorials has been regular. Yours, etc.' (Gloss: A cannot be opting out, since if he wished to be uncooperative, why write at all? He cannot be unable, through ignorance, to say more, since the man is his pupil; moreover, he knows that more information than this is wanted. He must, therefore, be wishing to impart information that he is reluctant to write down. This supposition is tenable only on the assumption that he thinks Mr X is no good at philosophy. This, then, is what he is implicating.)

Extreme examples of a flouting of the first maxim of Quantity are provided by utterances of patent tautologies like *Women are women* and *War is war*. I would wish to maintain that at the level of what is said, in my favored sense, such remarks are totally noninformative and so, at that level, cannot but infringe the first maxim of Quantity in any conversational context. They are, of course, informative at the level of what is implicated, and the hearer's identification of their informative content at this level is dependent on his ability to explain the speaker's selection of this PARTICULAR patent tautology.

[. . .]

Examples in which the first maxim of Quality is flouted

(5) *Irony.* X, with whom A has been on close terms until now, has betrayed a secret of A's to a business rival. A and his audience both know this. A says 'X is a fine friend.' (Gloss: It is perfectly obvious to A and his audience that what A has said or has made as if to say is something he does not believe, and the audience knows that A knows that this is obvious to the audience. So, unless A's utterance is entirely pointless, A must be trying to get across some other proposition than the one he purports to be putting forward. This must be some obviously related proposition; the most obviously related proposition is the contradictory of the one he purports to be putting forward.)

(6) *Metaphor.* Examples like *You are the cream in my coffee* characteristically involve categorical falsity, so the contradictory of what the speaker has made as if to say will, strictly speaking, be a truism; so it cannot be THAT that such a speaker is trying to get across. The most likely supposition is that the speaker is attributing to his audience some feature or features in respect of which the audience resembles (more or less fancifully) the mentioned substance.

It is possible to combine metaphor and irony by imposing on the hearer two stages of interpretation. I say *You are the cream in my coffee*, intending the hearer to reach first the metaphor interpretant 'You are my pride and joy' and then the irony interpretant 'You are my bane.'

(7) *Meiosis.* Of a man known to have broken up all the furniture one says *He was a little intoxicated.*

(8) *Hyperbole. Every nice girl loves a sailor.*

Examples in which the second maxim of Quality, 'Do not say that for which you lack adequate evidence', *is flouted* are perhaps not easy to find, but the following seems to be a specimen.

(9) I say of X's wife, *She is probably deceiving him this evening.* In a suitable context, or with a suitable gesture or tone or voice, it may be clear that I have no adequate reason for supposing this to be the case. My partner, to preserve the assumption that the conversational game is still being played, assumes that I am getting at some related proposition for the acceptance of which I DO have a reasonable basis. The related proposition might well be that she is given to deceiving her husband, or possibly that she is the sort of person who would not stop short of such conduct.

Examples in which an implicature is achieved by real, as distinct from apparent, violation of the maxim of Relation are perhaps rare, but the following seems to be a good candidate.

(10) At a genteel tea party, A says *Mrs X is an old bag.* There is a moment of appalled silence, and then B says *The weather has been quite delightful this summer, hasn't it?* B has blatantly refused to make what HE says relevant to A's preceding remark. He thereby indicates that A's remark should not be discussed and, perhaps more specifically, that A has committed a social gaffe.

[. . .]

I have so far considered only cases of what I might call particularized conversational implicature – that is to say, cases in which an implicature is carried by saying that *p* on a particular occasion in virtue of special features of the context, cases in which there is no room for the idea that an implicature of this sort is NORMALLY carried by saying that *p*. But there are cases of generalized conversational implicature. Sometimes one can say that the use of a certain form of words in an utterance would normally (in the ABSENCE of special circumstances) carry such-and-such an implicature or type of implicature. Noncontroversial examples are perhaps hard to find, since it is all too easy to treat a generalized conversational implicature as if it were a conventional implicature. I offer an example that I hope may be fairly noncontroversial.

(11) Anyone who uses a sentence of the form *X is meeting a woman this evening* would normally implicate that the person to be met was someone other than X's wife, mother, sister, or perhaps even close platonic friend. Similarly, if I were to say *X went into a house yesterday and found a tortoise inside the front door*, my hearer would normally be surprised if some time later I revealed

that the house was X's own. I could produce similar linguistic phenomena involving the expressions *a garden, a car, a college*, and so on.

[. . .]

When someone, by using the form of expression *an X*, implicates that the X does not belong to or is not otherwise closely connected with some identifiable person, the implicature is present because the speaker has failed to be specific in a way in which he might have been expected to be specific, with the consequence that it is likely to be assumed that he is not in a position to be specific. This is a familiar implicature situation and is classifiable as a failure, for one reason or another, to fulfill the first maxim of Quantity. The only difficult question is why it should, in certain cases, be presumed, independently of information about particular contexts of utterance, that specification of the closeness or remoteness of the connection between a particular person or object and a further person who is mentioned or indicated by the utterance should be likely to be of interest. The answer must lie in the following region: transactions between a person and other persons or things closely connected with him are liable to be very different as regards their concomitants and results from the same sort of transactions involving only remotely connected persons or things; the concomitants and results, for instance, of my finding a hole in MY roof are likely to be very different from the concomitants and results of finding a hole in someone else's roof. Information, like money, is often given without the giver's knowing to just what use the recipient will want to put it. If someone to whom a transaction is mentioned gives it further consideration, he is likely to find himself wanting the answers to further questions that the speaker may not be able to identify in advance; if the appropriate specification will be likely to enable the hearer to answer a considerable variety of such questions for himself, then there is a presumption that the speaker should include it in his remark; if not, then there is no such presumption.

Finally, we can now show that, conversational implicature being what it is, it must possess certain features:

1   Since, to assume the presence of a conversational implicature, we have to assume that at least the Cooperative Principle is being observed, and since it is possible to opt out of the observation of this principle, it follows that a generalized conversational implicature can be cancelled in a particular case. It may be explicitly cancelled, by the addition of a clause that states or implies that the speaker has opted out, or it may be contextually cancelled, if the form of utterance that usually carries it is used in a context that makes it clear that the speaker IS opting out.

2   Insofar as the calculation that a particular conversational implicature is present requires, besides contextual and background information, only a knowledge of what has been said (or of the conventional commitment of the utterance), and insofar as the manner of expression plays no role in the calculation, it will not be possible to find another way of saying the same thing, which simply lacks the implicature in question, except where some special feature of the substituted version is itself relevant to the determination of an implicature (in virtue of one of the maxims of Manner). If we call this feature NONDETACHABILITY, one may expect a generalized conversational implicature that is carried by a familiar, non-special locution to have a high degree of nondetachability.

3   To speak approximately, since the calculation of the presence of a conversationsal implicature presupposes an initial knowledge of the conventional force of the expression the utterance of which carries the implicature, a conversational implicatum will be a condition that is not included in the original specification of the expression's conventional force. Though it may not be impossible for what starts life, so to speak, as a conversational implicature to become conventionalized, to suppose that this is so in a given case would require special justification. So, initially at least, conversational implicata are not part of the meaning of the expressions to the employment of which they attach.

4   Since the truth of a conversational implicatum is not required by the truth of what is said (what is said may be true – what is implicated may be false), the implicature is not carried by what is said, but only by the saying of what is said, or by 'putting it that way.'

5   Since, to calculate a conversational implicature is to calculate what has to be supposed in order to preserve the supposition that the Cooperative Principle is being observed, and since there may be various possible specific explanations, a list of which may be open, the conversational implicatum in such cases will be disjunction of such specific explanations; and if the list of these is open, the implicatum will have just the kind of indeterminacy that many actual implicata do in fact seem to possess.

Chapter 4

Aaron V. Cicourel

INTERPRETIVE PROCEDURES

[. . .]

The use of the term 'rules' (or legal and extra-legal norms) in everyday life usually means various prescriptive and proscriptive norms (Morris 1956; Bierstedt 1957; Williams 1960; Gibbs 1966). I have labelled such norms surface rules. In this paper I shall treat norms in everyday life and scientific rules of procedure as legal and extra-legal surface rules governing everyday conduct and scientific inquiry, in keeping with recent work in ethnomethodology (Garfinkel 1967). By ethnomethodology I mean the study of interpretive procedures and surface rules in everyday social practices and scientific activities. Hence a concern with everyday practical reasoning becomes a study in how members employ interpretive procedures to recognize the relevance of surface rules and convert them into practised and enforced behaviour. Scientific research has its ideal or normative conceptions of how inquiry is conducted as well as implicit or intuitive strategies followed by individual researchers and promoted by different 'schools'. Paradigms of 'normal science' (Kuhn 1962) emerge in different fields to define temporally enforceable strategies of research and bodies of acceptable propositions. As Michael Polanyi (1958) has argued, the scientist's success in his research relies heavily upon 'tacit knowledge' or unstated knowledge that cannot be articulated into surface rules.

Interpretive procedures in everyday life and scientific research, however, are not 'rules' in the sense of such general policies or practices like

Source: Aaron V. Cicourel, Cognitive Sociology: Language and Meaning in Social Interaction, Harmondsworth; Penguin Education.

operational definitions or legal and extra-legal norms, where a sense of a 'right' and 'wrong' pre- or proscriptive norm or practice is at issue. Instead they are part of all inquiry yet exhibit empirically defensible properties that 'advise' the member about an infinite collection of behavioural displays, and provide him with a sense of social structure (or, in the case of scientific activity, provide an intuitive orientation to an area of inquiry). I assume that interpretive and surface rules govern normal science in the same sense in which everyday social behaviour requires that members generate and use 'acceptable' descriptive accounts about their environments; scientists seek accounts that can be viewed and accepted as recognizable and intelligible displays of social reality. Scientific procedures orientate the researcher's conception of normal science surface rules in normative or actual practice.

The child cannot be taught to understand and use surface rules unless he acquires a sense of social structure, a basis for assigning meaning to his environment. The acquisition of language rules is like the acquisition of norms; they both presuppose interpretive procedures. The child must learn to articulate a general rule or policy (a norm) with a particular event or case said to fall under the general rule (Rawls 1955). There are no surface rules for instructing the child (or adult) on how the articulation is to be made.

[. . .]

Our present knowledge of the nature of interpretive procedures is sparse. I do not want to suggest or claim the existence of a 'complete' list (or of any 'list') but will simply describe a few properties to facilitate further discussion.

The reciprocity of perspectives. Schutz (1953; 1955) describes this property as consisting of

(a)   the member's idealization of the interchangeability of standpoints whereby the speaker and hearer both take for granted that each (A assumes it of B and assumes B assumes it of A, and vice versa) would probably have the same experiences of the immediate scene if they were to change places, and

(b)   that until further notice (the emergence of counter-evidence) the speaker and hearer both assume that each can disregard, for the purpose at hand, any differences originating in their personal ways of assigning meaning to, and deciding the relevance of, everyday life activities, such that each can interpret the environment of objects they are both attending in an essentially identical manner for the practical action in question. A corollary of this property is that members assume, and assume others assume it of them, that their descriptive accounts or utterances will be intelligible and recognizable features of a world

known in common and taken for granted. The speaker assumes the
hearer will expect him to emit utterances that are recognisable and
intelligible, and the speaker also assumes that his descriptive accounts
are acceptable products and will be so received by the hearer. Finally,
the hearer assumes that the speaker has assumed this property for the
hearer, and expects to comply with the tacit but sanctioned behaviour
of appearing to 'understand' what is being discussed.

The et cetera assumption. To suggest that speakers and hearers sanction the
simulated 'understanding' of each other implies something more than a reciprocity of perspectives. Garfinkel (1964: 247–8) suggests the understanding
requires that a speaker and hearer 'fill in' or assume the existence of common
understandings or relevances of what is being said on occasions when the
descriptive accounts are seen as 'obvious' and even when not immediately
obvious. The tolerance for utterances viewed as not obvious or not meaningful depends upon further properties and their reflexive features. The et
cetera assumption serves the important function of allowing things to pass
despite their ambiguity or vagueness, or allowing the treatment of particular
instances as sufficiently relevant or understandable to permit viewing descriptive elements as 'appropriate'. What is critical about the et cetera assumption
is its reliance upon particular elements of language itself (lexical items,
phrases, idiomatic expressions or *double entendres*, for example) and paralinguistic features of exchanges for 'indexing' (Garfinkel 1967) the course
and meaning of the conversation. But notice that neither the reciprocity of
perspectives nor the et cetera assumption imply that consensus exists or is
necessary; rather, they indicate that a presumed 'agreement' to begin, sustain,
and terminate interaction will occur despite the lack of conventional notions
about the existence of substantive consensus to explain concerted action.

Normal forms. Reference to a reciprocity of perspectives and the et cetera
assumption presumes the existence of certain normal forms of acceptable talk
and appearances upon which members rely for assigning sense to their environments. Thus, on occasions when the reciprocity of perspectives is in doubt
(when the appearance of the speaker or hearer, or the talk itself, is not viewed
as recognizable and intelligible such that the et cetera assumption cannot
overcome discrepancies or ambiguities) efforts will be made by both speaker
and hearer to normalize the presumed discrepancies (this is similar in sense to
the reduction of dissonance or incongruity, cf. Festinger 1957; Brown 1962;
1965). But, unlike the social psychologist's interest in dissonance, the anthropologist–sociologist's attention must be directed to the recognition and
description of normal forms, and to how members' linguistic and paralinguistic behaviour reveals the ways in which interpretive procedures and surface

rules are called into question and the ways in which the social scene is sustained as dissonant or is restored to some sense of normality. Competent members (those who can expect to manage their affairs without interference and be treated as 'acceptable types') recognize and employ normal forms in daily interaction under the assumption that all communication is embedded within a body of common knowledge or 'what everyone knows' (Garfinkel 1964: 237–8).

Retrospective–prospective sense of occurrence. Routine conversation depends upon speakers and hearers waiting for later utterances to decide what was intended before. Speakers and hearers both assume that what each says to the other has, or will have at some subsequent moment, the effect of clarifying a presently ambiguous utterance or a descriptive account with promissory overtones. This property of interpretive procedures enables the speaker and hearer to maintain a sense of social structure despite deliberate or presumed vagueness on the part of the participants in an exchange. Waiting for later utterances (that may never come) to clarify present descriptive accounts, or 'discovering' that earlier remarks or incidents now clarify a present utterance, provide continuity to everyday communication.

The properties of interpretive procedures have been ignored because sociologists have taken them for granted when pursuing their own research, particularly research in their own society. Hence the sociologist invokes the properties of interpretive rules as a necessary part of making sense of the activities and environment of members he studies, and his use of these properties is derived from his own membership in the society, not from his professional training or from knowledge gained from research. Members use the properties of interpretive procedures to clarify and make routine sense of their own environments, and sociologists must view such activities (and their own work) as practical methods for constructing and sustaining social order.

Garfinkel (1966) has suggested that the properties of practical reasoning (what I am calling interpretive procedures) be viewed as a collection of instructions to members by members, and as a sort of continual (reflexive) feedback whereby members assign meaning to their environment. The interpretive procedures, therefore, have reflexive features linking their properties to actual scenes such that appropriate surface rules are seen as relevant for immediate or future inference and action. The reflexive features of talk can be viewed as saying that the properties of interpretive procedures, as a collection, are reflexive because they are necessary for members to orient themselves

(a)   In the presence of, but not in contact with (for example, driving a car alone), other members.
(b)   During face-to-face or telephone exchanges.
(c)   In the absence of actual contact with others.

The properties of interpretive procedures provide members with a sense of social order during periods of solitary living, and they are integral to actual contact with others (though the contact may vary from walking alone in a crowded street, to sitting on a bus but not conversing, to actual exchanges with others). Within talk and in the absence of talk, reflexive features of interpretive procedures operate to provide a continuous feedback to members about the routine sense of what is happening. Hence physical features of the ecological scene, the members' presence or absence, the existence or absence, of conversation and features of talk within conversation, all provide the participants with continuous 'instructions' for orienting themselves to their environment and deciding appropriate inferences and action.

Talk itself as reflexive. Talk is reflexive to participants because it is seen as fundamental to 'normal' scenes. I am not referring to the content of talk but simply its presence during speech and the expectation that particular forms of speech will give a setting the appearance of something recognisable and intelligible. The timing of speech (as opposed to deliberate or random hesitation and alterations of normal-form intonational contours) and the timing of periods of silence or such occasional reminders of normal speech like the 'uh huh', 'I see', 'ah', 'oh', reflexively guide both speaker and hearer throughout exchanges. The observer must also make use of reflexive features to assign normal-form significance to a scene or sequence of scenes as a condition for deciding the content of talk. Talk provides members with information about the appropriateness of occasions. Garfinkel notes that talk is a constituent feature of all settings because members count on its presence as an indication that 'all is well', and members also use talk as a built-in feature of some arrangement of activities to produce a descriptive account of those same arrangements. Thus the member's accounting of some arrangement relies upon the talk itself as a necessary way of communicating the recognizable and intelligible elements of the scene. Talk is continuously folded back upon itself so that the presence of 'proper' talk and further talk provide both a sense of 'all is well' and a basis for members to describe the arrangement successfully to each other.

Descriptive vocabularies as indexical expressions. In recommending further reflexive features of the properties of interpretive procedures I draw upon Garfinkel's discussion of how members take for granted their reliance upon the existence and use of descriptive vocabularies for handling bodies of information and activities, where the vocabularies themselves are constituent features of the experiences being described. The vocabularies are an index of the experience. But the experiences, in the course of being generated or transformed, acquire elements of the vocabularies as part of the generative process and permit the retrieval of information indexed by selected elements of the original

vocabularies. Garfinkel uses catalogues in libraries as an example of this reflexive feature of practical reasoning. The titles used to index reports to facilitate a
search for something, are invariably part of the vocabulary that went into the
terminologies or vocabularies of the very experiences they describe. The catalogues are terminologies or vocabularies of the experiences they describe.
Several years ago Bar-Hillel (1954) noted the necessity of indexical expressions
in ordinary language, stating that context is essential but that different sentences
might require knowing different common knowledge or presumed common
knowledge to give them some kind of interpretation. Thus it might be necessary to know where the utterance was made, who made it, and its temporal
character. The significance of conversational or written indexical expressions,
however, cannot be stated as merely a problem in pragmatic context; rather it
requires some reference to the role of 'what everyone knows' in deciding the
indexicality of the utterance or some part of the utterance. The significance of
descriptive vocabularies as indexical expressions lies in their providing both
members and researchers with 'instructions' for recovering or retrieving the
'full' relevance of an utterance; suggesting what anyone must presume or 'fill
in' in order to capture the fidelity of a truncated or indexical expression whose
sense requires a specification of common assumptions about context (the time
or occasion of the expression, who the speaker was, where the utterance was
made, and the like). Brown and Bellugi (1964: 146–7) suggest elements of this
problem in discussing parental expansions of children's speech:

> How does a mother decide on the correct expansion of one of
> her child's utterances? Consider the utterance 'Eve lunch'. So far
> as grammar is concerned this utterance could be appropriately
> expanded in any one of a number of ways: 'Eve is having lunch';
> 'Eve had lunch'; 'Eve will have lunch'; 'Eve's lunch', and so
> forth. On the occasion when Eve produced the utterance,
> however, one expansion seemed more appropriate than any other.
> It was then the noon hour, Eve was sitting at the table with a
> plate of food before her and her spoon and fingers were busy. In
> these circumstances 'Eve lunch' had to mean 'Eve is having lunch'.
> A little later when the plate had been stacked in the sink and Eve
> was getting down from her chair the utterance 'Eve lunch' would
> have suggested the expansion 'Eve has had her lunch'. Most expan-
> sions are responsive not only to the child's words but also to the
> circumstances attending their utterance.

Brown and Bellugi are concerned with how the mother decides the appropriateness of expansions under situational constraints. But there are several

problems here: the child's telegraphic utterance viewed as a reflection of a simple grammar of less complexity than adult grammar, thus endowing the child with limited competence; the adult expansion that encodes elements of social organization not coded by the child's telegraphic utterance; the child's utterance as indexical to children's grammar; and the adult's various expansions decided according to the indexicality deemed appropriate to the situational constraints or context. We should not confuse children's normal forms and the child's ability to recognize and use indexical expressions with the adult's stock of normal forms and typical usage of indexical expressions for encoding broader conceptions of social organization than those possessed by the child. When Brown and Bellugi (1964: 147–8) suggest that a mother's expansion of a child's speech is more than teaching grammar, that it is providing the child with elements of a word-view, there is the presumption of a developmental acquisition of social structure. Hence the child's creation of social meanings not provided by an adult model would parallel the creation of children's grammar not based exclusively upon a model provided by an adult but generated by innovative elements of the child's deep-structure grammar. The child's creative attempts at constructing social reality or social structure and grammar can be viewed as generated by a simple conception of indexicality stemming from developmental stages in the acquisition of the properties of interpretive procedures and deep-structure grammatical rules. The acquisition of interpretive procedures would parallel the acquisition of language, with the child's interpretive procedures gradually replaced or displaced by adult interpretive procedures.

A necessary condition of animal and human socialization, therefore, is the acquisition of interpretive procedures. Sufficient conditions for appropriate use of language and interpretive rules in actual settings include:

1   The acquisition of childhood rules (gradually transformed into adult surface rules).
2   Interpretive procedures and their reflexive features as instructions for negotiating social scenes over time.

Hence members are continually giving each other instructions (verbal and nonverbal cues and content) as to their intentions, social character, biographies, and the like. *The interpretive procedures and their reflexive features provide continuous instructions to participants such that members can be said to be programming each other's actions as the scene unfolds.* Whatever is built into the members as part of their normal socialization is activated by social scenes, but there is no automatic programming; the participants' interpretive procedures and reflexive features become instructions by processing the behavioural scene of appearances, physical movements, objects, gestures, sounds, into inferences that permit action. The progressive acquisition of interpretive procedures and surface rules is reflected in how children and adults interact, or how children interact with other children. Children continually rehearse their acquisition of social structure (and language) in ways reminiscent of adults rehearsing for a play or translating a written play into a live production. But in the latter cases the interpretive procedures and surface rules are already built-in elements of the actors, while in children it is possible to observe different stages of complexity over time. For example, the child's ability to learn surface rules governing a game follows a developmental sequence, and his ability to decide the relevance and applicability of surface rules is always a function of the development of interpretive procedures.

The child's conception of 'fairness' in games, play or family settings cannot be specified by reference to surface rules. Nor will any conception of norms now available in the sociological literature provide a basis for explaining how the child learns eventually to distinguish between games and their normal forms, and everyday life activities and their normal forms. What seems plausible despite little or no empirical evidence is that children acquire interpretive procedures prior to their use of language, and that they develop normal forms of voice intonation and expect their usage by others. Children are able to recognize and insist upon normal-form spacing in speech and to develop their own indexical expressions.

The child's acquisition of social structure, therefore, begins with a simple conception of interpretive procedures and surface rules, and his stock of common knowledge is expressed initially in the form of single lexemes whose meaning by parents is usually judged by reference to imputations of childhood competence and adult meanings. Inasmuch as our knowledge of adult recognition and usage of meanings is unclear, a word about this problem is in order before going on to strategies for the semantic analysis of adult speech that could be useful for following the development of meaning in children.

References

Bar-Hillel, Y. (1954) 'Indexical expressions', *Mind*, 63: 359–79.
Bierstedt, R. (1957) '*The Social Order*, New York: McGraw-Hill.
Brown, R. (1962) 'Models of attitude change', in Brown R. *et al.*, *New Directions in Psychology*, New York: Holt, Rinehart & Winston, 1–85.
—— (1965) *Social Psychology*, New York: Free Press.

Brown, R., and Bellugi, U. (1964) 'Three processes in the child's acquisition of syntax', in Lenneberg, E. (ed.), *New Directions in the Study of Language*, Cambridge, MA: MIT Press.

Festinger, L. (1957) *A Theory of Cognitive Dissonance*, Row: Peterson.

Garfinkel, H. (1964) 'Studies of the routine grounds of everyday activities', *Social Problems*, 11: 220–50.

—— (1966), Dittoed transcriptions of lectures.

—— (1967), *Studies in Ethnomethodology*, New York: Prentice-Hall.

Gibbs, J. (1966) 'The sociology of law and normative phenomena', *Amer. Soc. Rev.* 31: 315–25.

Kuhn, T.S. (1962) *The Structure of Scientific Revolutions*, Chicago: University of Chicago Press.

Morris, R. T. (1956) 'Typology of norms', *Amer. Sociol, Rev.* 7: 610–13.

Polanyi, M. (1958) *Personal Knowledge: Towards a Post-Critical Philosophy*, Chicago: University of Chicago Press.

Rawls, J. (1955) 'Two concepts of rules', *Phil. Rev.,* 64: 3–32.

Schutz, A. (1953) 'Common-sense and scientific interpretation of human action', *Phil. Phenomenol. Res.,* 14: 1—38.

—— (1955), 'Symbol, reality and society', in L. Bryson, L. Finkelstein, H. Hoagland and R. M. MacIver (eds), *Symbols and Society*, New York: Harper, 135–203.

Williams, R. M. (1960) *American Society*, (rev. edn), New York: Knopf.

Chapter 5

John J. Gumperz

SOCIOCULTURAL KNOWLEDGE IN CONVERSATIONAL INFERENCE[1]

'CONVERSATIONAL INFERENCE', as I use the term, is the 'situated' or context-bound process of interpretation, by means of which participants in a conversation assess others' intentions, and on which they base their responses. Conversational inference is ultimately a semantic process, but it is distinguished from linguists' assignment of meaning to utterances or classification of speech acts, as well as from the social scientists' measurement of attitudes. Both conventional linguistic analysis and social science measurement involve the labeling of utterances by other utterances, more often than not after the fact. Conversational inference, by contrast, is, part of the very act of conversing. One indirectly or implicitly illustrates one's understanding of what is said through verbal and nonverbal responses, by the way one builds on what one hears to participate in a conversation, rather than through talking about it in abstract terms. It follows that analysis of such processes requires different and perhaps more indirect methods of study which examine meaning as a function of the dynamic pattern of utterances and responses as they occur in conversation.

Recent studies of conversation from a variety of linguistic, psychological, anthropological, and sociological perspectives, have shed light upon a number of issues important to the study of conversational inference. It is generally agreed that grammatical knowledge is only one of several factors in the interpretation process. Aside from physical setting, participants' personal background knowledge, and their attitudes toward each other, sociocultural

Source: John J. Gumperz, 'Sociocultural knowledge in conversational inference', in Muriel Saville-Troike (ed.) *Linguistics and Anthropology*, Georgetown University Round Table on Languages and Linguistics 1977, Washington D.C.: Georgetown University Press, 1977, 191–211.

assumptions concerning role and status relationships, as well as social values associated with various message components, also play an important role. So far, however, treatment of such contextual factors has been primarily descriptive. The procedure has been to identify or list what can potentially affect interpretation. With rare exceptions, there have been no systematic attempts to show how social knowledge is used in situated interpretation. Yet we know that social presuppositions and attitudes change in the course of interaction, often without a change in extralinguistic context. Therefore, the social input to conversation is not entirely constant. Assumptions about role and status relationships vary as the conversation progresses, and these changes are signalled through speech itself (Gumperz and Cook-Gumperz 1976). The signals by which this is accomplished can be regarded as a metalanguage or a meta-signalling system. So far, however, we know very little about this metalanguage. In this paper I want to suggest at least the outlines of a theory which deals with the question of how social knowledge is stored in the mind, how it is retrieved from memory, and how it is integrated with grammatical knowledge in the act of conversing.

[. . .]

Ethnomethodologists have gone a long way toward producing a theory which treats conversation as a cooperative endeavor, subject to systematic constraints. However, a number of important questions still remain to be answered. A social view of language such as the one ethnomethodologists advocate must be able to account for interspeaker difference, yet, so far, only the pan-cultural aspects of conversational control mechanisms have been dealt with. A sociolinguist needs to know how speakers use verbal skills to create contextual conditions that reflect particular culturally realistic scenes. Furthermore, how is speakers' grammatical and phonological knowledge employed in carrying out these strategies? For example, if regular speaker change is to take place, participants must be able to scan phrases to predict when an utterance is about to end. They must be able to distinguish between rhetorical pauses and turn-relinquishing pauses. Although speaker overlap is an integral part of interaction, conversational cooperation requires that speakers not be interrupted at random. To follow the thematic progression of an argument, moreover, and to make one's contribution relevant, one must be able to recognize culturally possible lines of reasoning. To account for all these phenomena, it is necessary to show how the ethnomethodologists' control mechanisms are integrated into other aspects of speakers' linguistic knowledge.

To this end, we will look at two examples of actual conversation. [. . .] We will analyze two sequences which occurred in public situations.

They are representative of a much larger body of data we have collected, both by chance, as in these examples, and in connection with systematic programs. The first interaction is one which any native speaker of English would be able to interpret. The second constitutes an interethnic encounter, and we will show how habitual conversational inferences led to a misinterpretation of intent.

The first incident occurred when I was sitting in an aisle seat on an airplane bound for Miami, Florida. I noticed two middle-aged women walking towards the rear of the plane. Suddenly, I heard from behind, 'Tickets, please! Tickets, please!' At first I was startled and began to wonder why someone would be asking for tickets so long after the start of the flight. Then one of the women smiled toward the other and said, 'I TOLD you to leave him at home'. I looked up and saw a man passing the two women, saying, 'STEP to the rear of the bus, please'.

Americans will have no difficulty identifying this interchange as a joke, and hypothesizing that the three individuals concerned were probably traveling together and were perhaps tourists setting off on a pleasure trip. What we want to investigate is what linguistic knowledge forms the basis for such inferences, and to what extent this knowledge is culturally specific.

The initial utterance, 'Tickets, please', was repeated without pause and was spoken in higher than normal pitch, more than usual loudness, and staccato rhythm. For this reason it sounded like an announcement, or like a stock phrase associated with travel situations. My first inkling that what I heard was a joke came with the woman's statement to her friend, 'I TOLD you to leave him at home'. Although I had no way of knowing if the participants were looking at each other, the fact that the woman's statement was perfectly timed to follow the man's utterance was a cue that she was responding to him, even though her comment was addressed to a third party. Furthermore, the stress on *told* functioned to mark her statement as another stock utterance, contributing to the hypothesis that she and he were engaging in a similar activity. If the statement of the man or the woman had been uttered in normal pitch and conversational intonation, the connection between them might not have been clear. Only after I was able to hypothesize that the participants were joking, could I interpret their utterances. My hypothesis was then confirmed by the man's next statement, 'Step to the rear of the bus, please'. This was also uttered in announcement pitch, loudness, and intonation. In retrospect, we may note that both of the man's utterances were formulaic in nature, and thus culturally specific and context bound. He was exploiting the association between walking down an aisle in a plane and the similar walk performed by a conductor on a train or a bus. In identifying the interaction as a joke, I was drawing on the same situational-association knowledge, as well as on my awareness of the likelihood of joking among travelers bound for Miami.

Thus, suprasegmental and other surface features of speech are crucial to understanding the nature of an interaction. Such features have been extensively discussed in the linguistic literature, but treatments have dealt with the referential meaning of individual sentences. When seen in isolation, sentences can have many intonation and paralinguistic contours, without change in referential meaning. The prevalent view is that these features add expressive overtones to sentences. Moreover, the signs by which listeners recognize these overtones tend to be seen as language independent. If, however, we look at conversational inference rather than referential meaning, we see that paralinguistic and intonation contours play an important role in the identification of interpretative frames.

This identification of specific conversational exchanges as representative of socioculturally familiar activities is the crucial process I call 'contextualization'. It is the process by which we evaluate message meaning and sequencing patterns in relation to aspects of the surface structure of the message, called 'contextualization cues'. The linguistic basis for this matching procedure resides in 'co-occurrence expectations', which are learned in the course of previous interactive experience and form part of our habitual and instinctive linguistic knowledge. Co-occurrence expectations enable us to associate styles of speaking with contextual presuppositions. We regularly rely upon these matching processes in everyday conversation, but they are rarely talked about. In fact, they tend to be noticed only when things go wrong, and even then, the conclusions drawn are more likely to be about the other person's attitudes than about differences in linguistic conventions. Yet, as our next example shows, contextualization expectations are highly culturally specific; that is, they are dependent upon interactants' ethnic or communicative background.

The second incident I am going to relate took place in London, England, on a bus driven by a West Indian driver–conductor. The bus was standing at a stop, and passengers were filing in. The driver announced periodically, 'Exact change, please', as London bus drivers often do. When passengers who had been standing close by either did not have money ready or tried to give him a large bill, the driver repeated, 'Exact change, please'. The second time around, he said 'please' with extra loudness, high pitch, and falling intonation, and he seemed to pause before 'please'. One passenger so addressed, as well as others following him, walked down the bus aisle exchanging angry looks and obviously annoyed, muttering, 'Why do these people have to be so rude and threatening about it?' Was the bus driver really annoyed? Did he intend to be rude, or is the passengers' interpretation a case of cross-cultural misunderstanding?

To understand what happened here and why it happened, it is necessary to go into some more detail about the nature of contextualization cues and their function in conversation. The term 'contextualization cue' refers to any aspect of the surface form of utterances which, when mapped onto message content, can be shown to be functional in the signalling of interpretative frames. In the examples given in this paper, the cues are largely prosodic and paralinguistic, but many other signalling mechanisms can function as contextualization cues, including lexical or phonological choice; use of idiomatic or formulaic expressions such as greetings, openers, interjections, or frozen sequences; or code-switching (Gumperz 1976; Gumperz and Cook-Gumperz 1976). In the present discussion, however, we concentrate on prosody (i.e., intonation and stress) and paralinguistics (pitch register, rhythm, loudness, etc.) since some aspects of these features are always involved in conversation.

[. . .]

Prosody consists of three basic signalling mechanisms: tone grouping; tonic or nucleus placement within a tone group; and tune, the direction of the tonal change which characterizes the nucleus. Paralinguistic features include, among others, pitch register, loudness, rhythm, and tempo, and apply to the tone group as a whole, rather than to parts thereof.

Among prosodic cues, tone grouping refers to the use of intonation and stress to chunk larger stretches of speech into separable bits of information that are to be processed as single units. Our example:

Exact change please //

could be uttered as a single chunk, as it was the first time the driver said it, or as two chunks:

Exact change / please //

as he said it the second time. To treat *please* as a separate bit of information implies that it is worthy of separate attention. We recognize two types of tone group boundaries: minor tone group, (/) which suggests that the preceding message portion is semantically related to others within a larger whole, and a major tone group, (//) which suggests finality.

The second element of prosody, tonic or nucleus placement, refers to the selection of one or another of the stressed syllables in a tone of group as the nucleus, or the part on which the tonal shift occurs. Nucleus placement is predictable in many types of sentences. Normally, it identifies that portion of the message that is to be regarded as new, as compared to what can be assumed to be shared or given. Note, however, that this is not merely a matter of syntax or lexicon but also a matter of culturally specific practice. If I say

> I'm giving my paper //

it is the object, *paper*, which is assumed to carry the new information. In

> I'm cancelling my paper //

the verb is normally stressed, since *cancelling*, in our culture, is not a customary activity in relation to paper giving.

The third prosodic mechanism, tune, refers to the fall and rises in tone such as are associated with the intonational contrast between questions and answers. We furthermore distinguish two levels on which the fall or rise can occur: high or low.

> Please //
> please //

A shift to high level generally calls special attention to the segments so marked; a shift to low level often indicates that an item of information is known or expected.

Note that in English, tune is also important in signalling thematic progression. It is used, for example, to show the distinction between dependent and independent clauses.

> Because I'm busy / I don't want to be interrupted //

If *busy* were spoken with a fall rather than a rise, this sentence would sound odd.

Paralinguistic cues, finally, are the relative pitch level or loudness of an entire tone group, rather than part of the group as in nucleus placement, and the rhythm or tempo of the utterance. In English, these cues usually signal special discourse functions, such as distinctions in degree of formality; they can also mark quotes, interjections or asides, or indicate, for example, announcing style as in *Tickets, please*.

To be understood at all, all sentences must carry some kind of tone grouping, nucleus placement and tune. When these are in keeping with expectations based on content, no additional meanings are signalled. However, there are also certain optional uses of prosody to highlight unexpected information which function to suggest indirect inferences. For example, isolating an utterance segment as part of a separate tone group, as the bus driver did in my second example, assigns it special importance and invites the listener to infer the reason. Note, however, that in British as well as in American English, tone grouping options are constrained by pragmatic rules. Of the following examples, (1), (2), and (3) are all possible.

1   See that chair over there in the corner. //
2   See that chair / Over there in the corner. //
3   Put that chair over there in the corner, //
4   Put that chair / Over there in the corner. //

Example (4) seems odd, however, since *over there* is semantically a part of the predicate, rather than part of a separate adverbial complement.

Optional nucleus placement on an item which under ordinary conditions would count as given, is unexpected. The hearer's attempt to understand the speaker's motivation constitutes the conversational inference. The woman plane passenger in my first example uses this device in saying 'I told you to leave him at home' and, given our knowledge of similar situations and of the extralinguistic setting, we use this information to identify her utterance as formulaic.

Similarly, the use of high rise or fall when low rise or fall is expected can serve to signal special emphasis. I use the term 'normal information flow' to indicate uses of prosody which are expected and signal no indirect inferences. The term 'contrastiveness', on the other hand, refers to those cases where deviations from expected patterns are exploited conversationally.

Note that while short utterances need not show contrastiveness, longer utterances involving complex, connected discourse employ contrastiveness as an essential part of the signalling process. Only through contrastiveness can we scan utterances to determine the relative importance of various bits of information in longer messages.

[. . .]

In contrast to prosody, paralinguistic cues are somewhat more optional in English. Nevertheless, they are a regular feature of everyday conversation. In fact, as already suggested, they are our primary means of distinguishing various degrees of formality of talk and degrees of interspeaker involvement, of signalling topic changes, and distinguishing between asides and main parts of the argument. In our first example, the paralinguistic cues enabled us to identify *Tickets, please* as an announcement.

Let us now return to the second example:

Exact change, please.

As previously noted, the West Indian bus driver said this sentence twice, using different contextualization cues in each case. A speaker of British English in repeating this utterance, could optionally (a) place the nucleus on *change* or (b) split the sentence into two tone groups with two nuclei: *change* and *please*. In (a), the normal interpretation would be, 'I said, "change".' In (b), the separation of *please* would emphasize that word and call attention to the fact that a request has been made. Note that in (b) *please* must carry rising time, to suggest tentativeness and avoid excessive directness, which would seem rude. The bus driver in our example said *please* with falling intonation as well as increased pitch and loudness. Hence, for speakers using British English contextualization conventions, the conclusion of rudeness is natural.

In order to determine whether the interpretation of rudeness corresponds to West Indian contextualization conventions, we want to look at how prosodic and paralinguistic cues normally function in West Indian conversation. Examination of the contextualization conventions employed in our tapes of West Indian Londoners talking to each other, suggests that their use of prosody and paralinguistics is significantly different from that of British English or American English speakers. For example, syntactic constraints on the placement of tone group boundaries differ. West Indians can split a sentence into much smaller tone group units than British English speakers can. Furthermore, their use of rising tone to indicate intersentence connections is much more restricted. Moreover, once a tone group boundary has been established, nucleus placement within such a tone group must be on the last content word of that tone group, regardless of meaning. In contrast to other forms of English, therefore, nucleus placement is syntactically rather than semantically constrained. Finally, pitch and loudness differences serve as a major means of signalling contrastiveness rather than expressiveness. They are regularly used to indicate emphasis without any connotation of excitement or other emotional overtones. To give only one example, in the course of an ordinary, calm discussion, one speaker said,

He was selected/ MAINLY/ because he had a degree//.

The word *mainly* was separated by tone group boundaries and set off from the rest of the sentence by increased pitch and loudness. The context shows that the word *mainly* was used contrastively within a line of reasoning which argued that having practical experience was as important as formal

education. Our conclusion is that the West Indian bus driver's *Exact change
/ please //* was his normal way of emphasizing the word *please*, corresponding
to the British English option (b). Therefore, his intention was, if anything,
to be polite.

To summarize, then, we conclude that conversational inference processes
such as we have discussed involve several distinct elements. On the one hand is
the perception of prosodic and paralinguistic cues. On the other is the problem
of interpreting them. Interpretation in turn requires, first of all, judgments of
expectedness and then a search for an interpretation that makes sense in terms
of what we know and what we have perceived. We can never be certain of the
ultimate meaning of any message, but by looking at systematic patterns in
the relationship of perception of surface cues to interpretation, we can gather
strong evidence for the social basis of contextualization conventions.

[. . .]

Note

1   Work on this paper was supported in part by NIMH grant MN26831–03.
Many of the ideas expressed here were developed in discussion with Jenny
Cook-Gumperz. I am grateful to Denise Gubbay and other staff members
of the National Center for Industrial Language Training, Southall,
Middlesex, England, for cooperation in field work and for sharing with
me their many insights into problems of interethnic communication.
Deborah Tannen assisted in the preparation and organization of the manu-
script and provided many helpful suggestions.

References

Gumperz, J. (1976) 'Language communication and public negotiation', in
Sanday, P. (ed.) *Anthropology and the Public Interest*, New York: Academic
Press.
Gumperz, J. and Cook-Gumperz, J. (1976) Papers on language and context.
Working Papers No. 46, Language Behavior Research Laboratory,
University of California, Berkeley.

Chapter 6

Emanuel A. Schegloff

TALK AND SOCIAL STRUCTURE[1]

W HETHER STARTING FROM A programmatic address to the structure of face-to-face interaction or from a programmatic concern with
the constitutive practices of the mundane world, whether in pursuit of
language, culture or action, a range of inquiries in several social science disciplines (most relevantly anthropology, sociology and linguistics) have over the
past 25 to 30 years[2] brought special attention to bear on talk-in-interaction.
It is not unfair to say that one of the most focused precipitates of this broad
interest has been that family of studies grouped under the rubric "conversation analysis." It is, in any case, with such studies of "talk" that I will be
concerned in reflecting on "talk and social structure."

Although itself understandable as a sustained exploration of what is entailed
in giving an analytic account of "a context" (as in the phrase "in the context of
ordinary conversation"), various aspects of inquiry in this tradition of work have
prompted an interest in neighboring disciplines in relating features of talk-in-
interaction to "contexts" of a more traditional sort – linguistic contexts, cultural
contexts, and institutional and social structural contexts. At the same time,
investigators working along conversation analytic lines began to deal with talk
with properties which were seemingly related to its production by participants
oriented to a special "institutional" context; and, wishing to address those
distinctive properties rather than ones held in common with other forms of talk
(as Sacks had done in some of his earliest work based on group-therapy sessions),
these investigators faced the analytic problems posed by such an undertaking.

Source: Emanuel A. Schegloff, 'Reflections on talk and social structure', in Deirdre Boden and Don
H. Zimmerman (eds) *Talk and Social Structure: Studies in Ethnomethodology and Conversation
Analysis*, Cambridge: Polity Press in association with Blackwell, 1991, 44–70.

The interest in the theme "talk and social structure" comes, then, from several directions – the most prominent being technical concerns in the analysis of certain forms of talk on the one hand, and an impulse to effectuate a *rapprochement* with the concerns of classical sociology, and to do so by relating work on talk-in-interaction to those social formations which get referred to as "social structures," or generically as "social structure," on the other hand. My reflections will have this latter impulse as their point of departure, but will quickly seek to engage it by formulating and confronting the analytic problems which it poses.

Of course, a term like "social structure" is used in many different ways. In recent years, to cite but a few cases, Peter Blau (1977) has used the term to refer to the distribution of a population on various parameters asserted to be pertinent to interaction, claiming a derivation from Simmel and his notion of intersecting social circles. Many others have in mind a structure of statuses and/or roles, ordinarily thereby building in an inescapable normative component, of just the sort Blau wishes to avoid. Yet others intend by this term a structured distribution of scarce resources and desirables, such as property, wealth, productive capacity, status, knowledge, privilege, power, the capacity to enforce and preserve privilege, etc. Still others, have in mind stably patterned sets of social relations, whether formalized in organizations or more loosely stabilized in networks.

The sense of "social structure" intended in the thematic concern with "talk and social structure" does not range across all these usages. But almost certainly it includes a concern with power and status and its distribution among social formations such as classes, ethnic groups, age grade groups, gender, and professional relations. It is this sense which has animated, for example, the work by West (1979) and Zimmerman and West (1975) on gender and interruption, and West's work (1984) on doctor/patient interaction. And it includes as well a concern with the structured social relations which comprise organizations and occupational practice and the institutional sectors with which they are regularly identified (as, for example, in Atkinson and Drew's treatment of the courts (1979), in the work of Zimmerman and his associates on the police (for instance, Zimmerman 1984; Whalen and Zimmerman 1987), Maynard's work (1984) on the legal system, that of Heritage (1985) on mass-media news, or Boden's (1994) on organization.

[. . .]

Whatever substantive gains there are to be had from focusing on the relationship between talk and social structure in the traditional sense, this focus is not needed in order to supply conversation analysis with its sociological credentials. The work which is focused on the organization of talk-in-interaction in its own right – work on the organization of turn-taking, or on the organization of sequences, work addressed to the actions being done in turns and the formats through which they are done, work on the organization of repair, and work directed to the many discrete practices of talking and acting through talk which do not converge into domains of organization – this work is itself dealing with social organization and social structures, albeit of a different sort than in the received uses of those terms, and is no less sociological in impulse and relevance (Schegloff 1987).

For some, the fact that conversation analysis (henceforth, CA) concerns itself with the details of talking has meant that it is a form of linguistics. Perhaps so, but certainly not exclusively so. If it is not a distinctive discipline of its own (which it may well turn out to be), CA is at a point where linguistics and sociology (and several other disciplines, anthropology and psychology among them) meet. For the target of its inquiries stands where talk amounts to action, where action projects consequences in a structure and texture of interaction which the talk is itself progressively embodying and realizing, and where the particulars of the talk inform what actions are being done and what sort of social scene is being constituted. Now, from the start, one central preoccupation of sociology and social theory has been with the character of social action and what drives it (reason, passion, interest, utility) – this is familiar enough. Another concern has been with the character of interaction in which action is embedded, for it is observations about some aspects of the character of interaction that motivated such hoary old distinctions as those between *Gemeinschaft* and *Gesellschaft*, between status and contract, and the like. "Action in interaction" is, then, a longstanding theme of social analysis.

CA's enterprise, concerned as it is with (among other things) the detailed analysis of how talk-in-interaction is conducted as an activity in its own right and as the instrument for the full range of social action and practice, is then addressed to one of the classic themes of sociology, although to be sure in a distinctive way. Of the several ways in which CA shows its deep preoccupation with root themes of social science and sociology in particular, these standing conversation analytic preoccupations resonate more with the title of the Atkinson/Heritage collection (1984): they are concerned with "structures of social action" – structures of single actions and of series and sequences of them. Atkinson and Heritage's title is, of course, a thoroughly unveiled allusion to the title of Talcott Parsons's first major work, *The Structure of Social Action* (1937), the work which launched the enterprise of Parsonian action theory. The difference between Parsons's title and the Atkinson/Heritage allusion, "*The Structure* of Social Action" versus "*Structures* of Social Action," may suggest some of the distinctiveness.

Parsons's tack was conceptual and global. For him there was "the structure," and it was arrived at by theoretic stipulation of the necessary components of an analytical unit – the "unit act," components such as "ends," "means," "conditions." This was a thoroughly conceptual enterprise on a thoroughly analytic object. The Atkinson/Heritage "structures of" suggests not only multiplicity of structures, but the empirical nature of the enterprise. The units are concrete activities, and the search for their "components" involves examination and description of empirical instances.

But with all the differences in conception, mode of working, etc., there is a common enterprise here, and it has long been a central one for sociology and the social sciences more generally – to try to get at the character of social action and social interaction. In CA's addressing of this theme and the varied problems and analytic tasks to which it gives rise, it is itself engaged in – "*echt*" sociology, even without the introduction of traditional sociological concerns such as "social structure." But the claim that the problems which have preoccupied conversation analysis are sociological in impulse and import is without prejudice to our engagement with the work which tries to relate talk to more traditional conceptions of social structure. That engagement is already underway.

The reasons for thinking about the relationships of talk and social structure are ready to hand. Both our casual and our studied examination of interaction and talk-in-interaction provide a lively sense of the occasions on which who the parties are relative to one another seems to matter, and matter to *them*. And these include senses of "who they are" that connect directly to what is ordinarily meant by "social structure" – their relative status, the power they differentially can command, the group affiliations they display or can readily have attributed to them such as their racial or ethnic memberships, their gender and age-grade status, their occupational status and its general standing and immediate interactional significance, and the other categories of membership in the society which can matter to the participants and which fall under the traditional sociological rubric "social structure."

The issue I mean to address is not: is there such a thing as gender/class/power/status/organization/etc.? Or: does it affect anything in the world? Rather, the question is: whatever observations we initially make about how such features of social organization as these work and bear on interaction, how do we translate them into defensible, empirically based analyses that help us to get access to previously unnoticed particular details of talk-in-interaction, and appreciate their significance. For the lively sense we may all share of the relevance of social structure along the lines I have mentioned needs to be converted into the hard currency (if you'll pardon the cash nexus) of defensible analysis – analysis which departs from, and can always be referred to and grounded in, the details of actual occurrences of conduct in interaction.

Again, I do not mean to be addressing myself to two apparently neigh-boring stances, although there may well be implications for them. I am not centrally concerned with those investigators whose primary analytic commit-ment is to social structure in the received senses of that term, and who mean to incorporate examination of talk into their inquiries because of the role attributable to it in the "production" of social structure. And I do not take up the position (apparently embraced in Goffman 1983) in which the prima-facie relevance of social structure to the organization of interaction is in principle to be disputed (although I do suggest that some received notions may not be sustainable when required to come to terms with the details of actual occurrences). Rather, I mean to formulate and explore the challenges faced by those attracted to the interaction/social structure nexus. A solution must be found to the analytic problems which obstruct the conversion of intuition, casual (however well-informed) observation, or theoretically moti-vated observation into demonstrable analysis. For without solutions to these problems, we are left with "a sense of how the world works," but without its detailed explication.

My discussion will be organized around three issues: the problem of relevance, the issue of "procedural consequentiality," and a concern for the competing attentional and analytic claims of conversational structures and "social structure" respectively in the analysis of the data of talk-in-interaction.

The problem of relevance

First, *relevance* [. . .]

The original focus of the work by Sacks which I mean to recall was the way in which persons engaged in talk-in-interaction did their talk, specifi-cally with respect to reference to persons. Sacks noted that members refer to persons by various category terms – as man/woman, protestant/catholic/jew, doctor/patient, white/black/chicano, first baseman/second baseman/shortstop, and the like. He remarked that these category terms come in collections. In presenting them above, they are inscribed in groups: [man/woman], [protestant/catholic/jew]; and so on; and that is the correct way to present them. It is not [man/woman/protestant], [catholic/jew]. This is what is being noted in the observation that the category terms are organized in *collections*.

Some of these collections Sacks called "Pn adequate;" they were adequate to characterize or categorize any member of any population, however speci-fied, whether or not it had been specified (for example, counted, character-ized or bounded) in some fashion (Sacks 1972: 32–3). Other collections were not Pn adequate. [Male/female] *is* Pn adequate; [first baseman/second baseman/shortstop . . .] is *not* Pn adequate, because the latter is only usable on populations already specified or characterized as "baseball teams," whereas the former is not subject to such restrictions.

One of Sacks's main points was that there demonstrably are many Pn- adequate category collections. The collection of category terms for gender/ sex and age are the most obvious ones, and these two alone serve to allow the posing of the problem of relevance. The point is that since everyone who is an instance of some category in one of those collections is necessarily (for that is the import of Pn adequacy) also an instance of some category in the other, or *an* other, the fact that someone *is* male, or *is* middle aged, or *is* white, or *is* Jewish is, by itself, no warrant for so referring to them, for the warrant of "correctness" would provide for use of any of the other reference forms as well. Some principle of relevance must underlie use of a reference form, and has to be adduced in order to provide for one rather than another of those ways of characterizing or categorizing some member. That is the problem of relevance: not just the descriptive adequacy of the terms used to characterize the objects being referred to, but the relevance that one has to provide if one means to account for the use of some term – the relevance of that term relative to the alternative terms that are demonstrably available.

Now, this problem was developed by Sacks initially in describing how members talk about members. It showed the inadequacy of an account of a conversationalist's reference to another as a "cousin" by reference to the other "actually being a cousin." But, once raised, the point is directly relevant to the enterprise of professional analysts as well. Once we recognize that whoever can be characterized as "male" or as "protestant," or as "president" or whatever, can be characterized or categorized in other ways as well, our scholarly/ professional/scientific account cannot 'naively' rely on such characterizations, that is, cannot rely on them with no justification or warrant of their relevance.

Roughly speaking, there are two types of solution to this problem in the methodology of professional analysis. One type of solution can be characterized as the "positivist" stance, in one of the many senses in which that term is currently used. In this view, the way to warrant one, as compared to another, characterization of the participants (for example, in interaction) is the "success" of that way of characterizing them in producing a professionally acceptable account of the data being addressed. "Success" is measured by some "technology" – by statistical significance, a preponderance of historical evidence, and so forth. Sometimes there is an additional requirement that the characterization which produces "successful" analysis be theoretically interpretable; that is, that the selection of descriptive terms for the participants converge with the terms of a professional/scientific theory relevant to the object of description. In this type of solution, which I am calling "positivistic," it does not matter whether or not the terms that are used to characterize the participants in some domain of action, and which have yielded "significant" results, are otherwise demonstrably orientated to or not by the participants being described. That is what makes this solution of the problem "positivist."

The alternative type of solution insists on something else, and that is that professional characterizations of the participants be grounded in aspects of what is going on that are demonstrably relevant to the participants, and at that moment − at the moment that whatever we are trying to provide an account of occurs. Not, then, just that we see them to be characterizeable as "president/assistant," as "chicano/black," as "professor/student," etc. But that for them, at that moment, those are terms relevant for producing and interpreting conduct in the interaction.

This issue should be of concern when we try to bring the kind of traditional sociological analysis that is implied by the term "social structure" to bear on talk-in-interaction. Much of what is meant by "social structure" in the traditional sense directly implicates such characterizations or categorizations of the participants as Sacks was examining. If the sense of social structure we are dealing with is the one that turns on the differential distribution of valued resources in society, whether status or power or money or any of the other "goods" whose distribution can be used to characterize social structure, then that implies a characterization or categorization of the participants on that occasion as one relevantly to be selected from that set of terms. But then the problem presents itself of the relevance of those terms to the participants for what they are doing. Without a show of that warrant, we are back to a "positivistic" stance, even though the animating concerns may be drawn from quite anti-positivistic theoretical sources or commitments.

Now let us be clear about what is and what is not being said here. The point is not that persons are somehow not male or female, upper or lower class, with or without power, professors and/or students. They may be, on some occasion, demonstrably members of one or another of those categories. Nor is the issue that those aspects of the society do not matter, or did not matter on that occasion. We may share a lively sense that indeed they do matter, and that they mattered on that occasion, and mattered for just that aspect of some interaction on which we are focusing. There is still the problem of *showing from the details of the talk or other conduct in the materials* that we are analyzing that those aspects of the scene are what the parties are oriented to. For *that is to show how the parties are embodying for one another the relevancies of the interaction and are thereby producing the social structure.*

The point here is not only methodological but substantive. It is not just to add a methodological apparatus supporting analyses already in hand. It is rather to add to, and potentially to transform, the analysis of the talk and other conduct itself by enriching our account of it with additional detail; and to show that, and how, "social structure" in the traditional sense enters into the production and interpretation of determinate facets of conduct, and is thereby confirmed, reproduced, modulated, neutralized or incrementally transformed in that actual conduct to which it must finally be referred.

This is not, to my mind, an issue of preferring or rejecting some line of analysis, some research program or agenda. It is a problem of analysis to be worked at: how to examine the data so as to be able to show that the parties were, with and for one another, demonstrably orientated to those aspects of who they are, and those aspects of their context, which are respectively implicated in the "social structures" which we may wish to relate to the talk. If we treat this as a problem of analytic craft, we can use it as leverage to enhance the possibility of learning something about how talk-in-interaction is done, for it requires us to return again to the details of the talk to make the demonstration.

Procedural consequentiality

The issue just discussed with respect to the characterization of the participants in some talk-in-interaction also is relevant to a characterization of "the context" in which they talk and interact. "Context" can be as much a part of what traditionally has been meant by "social structure" as attributes of the participants are. So, for example, remarking that some talk is being conducted "in the context of a bureaucracy, in a classroom," "on a city street," etc. is part of what is sometimes intended by incorporating the relevance of social structure.

Such characterizations invoke particular aspects of the setting and not others. They involve selections among alternatives, and among subalternatives. For example, one type of formulation of context characterizes it by "place," and this is an alternative to various other sorts of context characterization. But within that context type, various forms of place formulation are available, all of which can be correct (Schegloff 1972). So, although the details of the argument have not been fully and formally worked out for the characterization of context or setting in the way that Sacks worked them out for the characterization of participants, it appears likely that the issue of relevance can be posed in much the same way for context as it has been for person reference.

What I want to do here is add something to this relevance problem for contexts. It concerns what I am calling the "procedural consequentiality" of contexts.

Even if we can show by analysis of the details of the interaction that some characterization of the context or the setting in which the talk is going on (such as "in the hospital") is relevant for the parties, that they are oriented to the setting so characterized, there remains another problem, and that is to show how the context or the setting (the local social structure), in that aspect, is procedurally consequential to the talk.

How does the fact that the talk is being conducted in some setting (say, "the hospital") issue in any consequences for the shape, form, trajectory, content, or character of the interaction that the parties conduct? And *what is the mechanism by which the context-so-understood has determinate consequences for the talk?*

This is a real problem, it seems to me, because without a specification of such a linkage we can end up with characterizations of context or setting which, however demonstrably relevant to the parties, do little in helping us to analyze, to explain, to understand, to give an account of how the interaction proceeded in the way in which it did, how it came to have the trajectory, the direction, the shape that it ended up having. When a formulation of the context is proposed, it is *ipso facto* taken to be somehow relevant and consequential for what occurs in the context. It is the analyst's responsibility either to deliver analytic specifics of that consequentiality or to abjure that characterization of the context. Otherwise, the analysis exploits a tacit feature of its own discursive format, but evades the corresponding analytic onus. A sense of understanding and grasp is conveyed to, and elicited from, the reader, but is not earned by the elucidation of new observations about the talk.

So, this is an open question, somewhat less formally stated than the other: how shall we find formulations of context or setting that will allow us (a) to connect to the theme that many want to connect to – social structure in the traditional sense, but (b) that will do so in a way that takes into account not only the demonstrable orientation of the participants, but, further, (c) that will allow us to make a direct "procedural" connection between the context so formulated and what actually happens in the talk. Otherwise we have a characterization that "hovers around" the interaction, so to speak, but is not shown actually to inform the production and grasp of the details of its conduct.

As with the issue of "relevance," I am here putting forward not principled objections to the invocation of social structure as context, but jobs to be taken on by those concerned with the intersection of talk and familiar senses of social structure. They challenge us to be alert to possible ways of showing such connections.

[. . .]

Consider, for example, the case of the courtroom in session (cf. Atkinson and Drew 1979; my remarks here rest on a much looser, vernacular and unstudied sense of the setting). To focus just on the turn-taking organization, it *is* the "courtroom-ness" of courtrooms in session which seems in fact to organize the way in which the talk is distributed among the persons present, among the *categories* of persons present, in the physical setting. So, for example, onlookers (members of the "audience") *are* not potential next speakers, as the official proceedings go on. And among the others who *are* potential next speakers at various points – the judge, the attorneys, the witness and the like, there are socially organized procedures for determining when they can talk, what they can do in their talk, and the like. It could be argued, then, that to characterize some setting of talk-in-interaction as in a court-in-session characterizes it with a formulation of context which can not only be claimed to connect to the general concern for "social structure" (for it certainly relates to institutional context), but can be shown to be procedurally consequential as well. Insofar as members of the audience sitting behind the bar never get up and talk but rather whisper to one another in asides, whereas the ones in front of the bar talk in defined and regular ways, by the very form of their conduct they show themselves to be oriented to the particular identities that are legally provided by that setting and show themselves to be oriented to "the-court-in-session" as a context.

[. . .]

Social structure or conversational structure?

The third concern mobilized by the present theme is for the balance between the focus on social structure and the focus on conversational structure in studying talk-in-interaction. These two thematic focuses (we would like to think) are potentially complementary. But are they really? We must figure out how to make them complementary, because they can also be alternatives in a more competitive sense. Each makes its own claims in organizing observation and analysis of the data, and one can pre-empt the other. In particular, the more familiar concerns with social structure can pre-empt new findings about conversational phenomena.

Let me offer some illustrations of this tension, and exemplify them from a recent paper of Zimmerman's, "Talk and its occasion" (1984), whose object of interest is "calls to the police" (an object with which I have also had some experience, cf. Schegloff 1967). The paper's enterprise appears directed specifically to attending both to the concerns of social structure and to the concerns of conversational structure. It offers a full account of this type of talk-in-interaction, and it does so with a sensitivity not only to the social structure involved, but also to the conversational structure of these occurrences. For example, the paper begins with an account of the kind of overall structural organization of the calls, and then focuses on the particular sequence type that makes up most of the calls, namely, an extended request or complaint sequence.

Despite this commitment to both concerns, it seems to me, there is a tendency for the formulated social-structural context to "absorb" and "naturalize" various details of talk. These features of the talk are thereby made unavailable, in practice if not in principle, for notice and analysis as accountable details of the talk. Their character as aspects of the talk produced by reference to some conversational or interactional organization is vulnerable to being slighted, in favor of assimilation to some social-structural, institutional, or vernacularly contextual source. How to balance these competing claims on our attention, when the competition takes this form, will be a matter to which analysts who are concerned with the thematics of talk-and-social structure will have to remain sensitive. [. . .]

A methodological canon is suggested: establishing relevance and establishing procedural consequentiality should not be "threshold" issues, in the sense that once you have done "enough" to show it, you are finished. Rather they are questions for continuing analysis. And not necessarily in the "loaded" form of "how are they now doing 'calling the police'?", but in "open" form – "what does the form of the talk show about recipient design considerations and about orientation to context (institutional, social-structural, sequential, or whatever)." Because we "know" that not everything said *in* some context (institutional or other) is relevantly oriented to that context.

If the focus of inquiry is the organization of conduct, the details of action, the practices of talk, then every opportunity should be pressed to enhance our understanding of any available detail about those topics. Invoking social structure at the outset can systematically distract from, even blind us to, details of those domains of event in the world.

If the goal of inquiry is the elucidation of *social structure*, one might think that quite a different stance would be warranted, and one would want to give freer play to the effective scope of social structure, and to do so free of the constraints I have been discussing. Though this stance has much to recommend it, it could as well be argued that one does not best serve the understanding of social structure by attributing to it properties which are better understood as the products of other aspects of organized social life, such as interactional structure, or by failing to explicate how social structure is accomplished *in* the conduct. In any case, the understanding of social structure will be enhanced if we explicate how its embodiment in particular contexts on particular occasions permeates the "membrane" (Goffman 1961) surrounding episodes of interaction to register its stamp within them.

[. . .]

Conclusion

These then are three sorts of issues mobilized, or remobilized, for me when the talk turns to "talk and social structure." However lively our intuitions, in general or with respect to specific details, that it matters that some participants in data we are examining are police, or female, or deciding matters which are specifically constrained by the law or by economic or organizational contingencies, however insistent our sense of the reality and decisive bearing of such features of "social structure" in the traditional sense, the challenge posed is to find a way to show these claims, and show them from the data in three respects:

1   That what is so loomingly relevant for us (as competent members of the society or as professional social scientists) was relevant for the parties to the interaction we are examining, and thereby arguably implicated in their production of the details of that interaction.

2   That what seems inescapably relevant, both to us and to the participants, about the "context" of the interaction is demonstrably consequential for some specifiable aspect of that interaction.

3   That an adequate account for some specifiable features of the interaction cannot be fashioned from the details of the talk and other conduct of the participants as the vehicle by which *they* display the relevance of social-structural context for the character of the talk, but rather that this must be otherwise invoked by the analyst, who furthermore has developed defensible arguments for doing so.

In brief, the issue is how to convert insistent intuition, however correct, into empirically detailed analysis.

This is a heavy burden to impose. Meeting it may well lead to exciting new results. But if it is not to be met in one or more respects, arguments will have to be put forward that the concerns I have discussed are no longer in point, are superseded by other considerations, or must yield to the new sorts of findings that are possible if one holds them in abeyance. Simple invocation of the burden of the sociological past will not suffice.

With respect to social structure, then, as with respect to other notions from social science's past such as "intention," the stance we might well consider is treating them as programmatically relevant for the parties, and hence for us. In principle, some one or more aspects of who the parties are and where/when they are talking may be indispensably relevant for producing and grasping the talk, but these are not decisively knowable a priori. It is not for us to *know* what about context is crucial, but to *discover* it, and to discover *new sorts* of such things. Not, then, to privilege sociology's concerns under the rubric "social structure," but to discover them in the members' worlds, if they are there.

[. . .]

Notes

1   My thanks to Jennifer Mandelbaum for contributions of tact and clarity in the preparation of this chapter. I am also indebted to Deirdre Boden, Paul Drew, Douglas Maynard and especially Jack Whalen, whose reactions to an earlier draft, or to the reactions of others to the earlier draft, helped in my efforts to arrive at a text which might be understood as I meant it.
2   Editors' note: this article was published in 1991.

References

Atkinson, J. M. and Drew, P. (1979): *Order in Court: The Organisation of Verbal Interaction in Judicial Settings*, London: Macmillan.
Atkinson, J. M. and Heritage, J. (eds) (1984) *Structures of Social Action: Studies in Conversation Analysis*, Cambridge: Cambridge University Press.
Blau, P. M. (1977) *Inequality and Heterogeneity: A Primitive Theory of Social Structure*, New York: Free Press/Macmillan.
Boden, D. (1994) *The Business of Talk: Organizations in Action*, Cambridge: Polity Press.
Goffman, E. (1961) *Encounters*, Indianapolis: Bobbs-Merrill Educational.
—— (1983) 'The interaction order', *American Sociological Review* 48: 1–17.
Heritage, J. (1985) 'Analyzing news interviews: aspects of the production of talk for an "overhearing" audience', in van Dijk, T. (ed.) *Handbook of Discourse Analysis*, vol. 3: *Discourse and Dialogue*, London: Academic Press, 95–119.
Maynard, D. W. (1984) *Inside Plea Bargaining*, New York: Plenum.
Parsons, T. (1937) *The Structure of Social Action*, New York: McGraw-Hill.
Sacks, H. (1972) 'An initial investigation of the usability of conversational data for doing sociology', in Sudnow, D. (ed.) *Studies in Social Interaction*, New York: Free Press, 31–74.
Schegloff, E. (1967) 'The first five seconds: the order of conversational openings', unpublished Ph.D. dissertation, Department of Sociology, University of California, Berkeley.

—— (1972) 'Notes on a conversational practice: formulating place', in Sudnow, D. (ed.) *Studies in Social Interaction*, New York: Macmillan/Free Press, 75–119.

—— (1987) 'Analyzing single episodes of interaction: an exercise in conversation analysis', *Social Psychological Quarterly* 50: 101–14.

West, C. (1979) 'Against our will: male interruptions of females in cross-sex conversations', *Annals of the New York Academy of Science* 327: 81–97.

—— (1984) *Routine Complications: Troubles in Talk Between Doctors and Patients*, Bloomington, IN: Indiana University Press.

Whalen, M. R. and Zimmerman, D. H. (1987) 'Sequential and institutional contexts in calls for help', *Social Psychology Quarterly* 50: 172–85.

Zimmerman, D. H. (1984) 'Talk and its occasion: the case of calling the police', in Schiffrin, D. (ed.) *Meaning, Form, and Use in Context: Linguistic Applications*, Georgetown University Roundtable on Language and Linguistics, Washington, DC: Georgetown University Press, 210–28.

Zimmerman, D. and West, C. (1975) 'Sex roles, interruptions and silences in conversations', in Thorne, B. and Henley, N. (eds) *Language and Sex: Difference and Dominance*, Rowley, MA: Newbury House, 105–29.

Chapter 7

M.M. Bakhtin

THE PROBLEM OF SPEECH GENRES

ALL THE DIVERSE AREAS of human activity involve the use of language. Quite understandably, the nature and forms of this use are just as diverse as are the areas of human activity. This, of course, in no way disaffirms the national unity of language. Language is realized in the form of individual concrete utterances (oral and written) by participants in the various areas of human activity. These utterances reflect the specific conditions and goals of each such area not only through their content (thematic) and linguistic style, that is, the selection of the lexical, phraseological, and grammatical resources of the language, but above all through their compositional structure. All three of these aspects — thematic content, style, and compositional structure — are inseparably linked to the *whole* of the utterance and are equally determined by the specific nature of the particular sphere of communication. Each separate utterance is individual, of course, but each sphere in which language is used develops its own *relatively stable types* of these utterances. These we may call *speech genres.*

The wealth and diversity of speech genres are boundless because the various possibilities of human activity are inexhaustible, and because each sphere of activity contains an entire repertoire of speech genres that differentiate and grow as the particular sphere develops and becomes more complex. Special emphasis should be placed on the extreme *heterogeneity* of speech genres (oral and written). In fact, the category of speech genres should include short rejoinders of daily dialogue (and these are extremely varied

Source: M. M. Bakhtin, *Speech Genres and Other Late Essays*, translated by Vern W. McGee, edited by Caryl Emerson and Michael Holquist, Austin: University of Texas Press, 1986.

depending on the subject matter, situation, and participants), everyday narration, writing (in all its various forms), the brief standard military command, the elaborate and detailed order, the fairly variegated repertoire of business documents (for the most part standard), and the diverse world of commentary (in the broad sense of the word: social, political). And we must also include here the diverse forms of scientific statements and all literary genres (from the proverb to the multivolume novel). It might seem that speech genres are so heterogeneous that they do not have and cannot have a single common level at which they can be studied. [. . .] One might think that such functional heterogeneity makes the common features of speech genres excessively abstract and empty. This probably explains why the general problem of speech genres has never really been raised. Literary genres have been studies more than anything else. But from antiquity to the present, they have been studied in terms of their specific literary and artistic features, in terms of the differences that distinguish one from the other (within the realm of literature), and not as specific types of utterances distinct from other types, but sharing with them a common *verbal* (language) nature. The general linguistic problem of the utterance and its types has hardly been considered at all. [. . .]

A clear idea of the nature of the utterance in general and of the peculiarities of the various types of utterances (primary and secondary), that is, of various speech genres, is necessary, we think, for research in any special area. To ignore the nature of the utterance or to fail to consider the peculiarities of generic subcategories of speech in any area of linguistic study leads to perfunctoriness and excessive abstractness, distorts the historicity of the research, and weakens the link between language and life. After all, language enters life through concrete utterances (which manifest language) and life enters language through concrete utterances as well. The utterance is an exceptionally important node of problems.

Any style is inseparably related to the utterance and to typical forms of utterances, that is, speech genres. Any utterance – oral or written, primary or secondary, and in any sphere of communication – is individual and therefore can reflect the individuality of the speaker (or writer); that is, it possesses individual style. But not all genres are equally conducive to reflecting the individuality of the speaker in the language of the utterance, that is, to an individual style. The most conducive genres are those of artistic literature: here the individual style enters directly into the very task of the utterance, and this is one of its main goals (but even within artistic literature various genres offer different possibilities for expressing individuality in language and various aspects of individuality). The least favorable conditions for reflecting individuality in language obtain in speech genres that require a standard form, for example, many kinds of business documents, military commands, verbal signals in industry, and so on. Here one can reflect only the most superficial, almost biological aspects of individuality (mainly in the oral manifestation of these standard types of utterances). In the vast majority of speech genres (except for literary-artistic ones), the individual style does not enter into the intent of the utterance, does not serve as its only goal, but is, as it were, an epiphenomenon of the utterance, one of its by-products. Various genres can reveal various layers and facets of the individual personality, and individual style can be found in various interrelations with the national language. The very problem of the national and the individual in language is basically the problem of the utterance (after all, only here, in the utterance, is the national language embodied in individual form). The very determination of style in general, and individual style in particular, requires deeper study of both the nature of the utterance and the diversity of speech genres.

[. . .]

It is especially harmful to separate style from genre when elaborating historical problems. Historical changes in language styles are inseparably linked to changes in speech genres. Literary language is a complex, dynamic system of linguistic styles. The proportions and interrelations of these styles in the system of literary language are constantly changing. Literary language, which also includes nonliterary styles, is an even more complex system, and it is organized on different bases. In order to puzzle out the complex histor- ical dynamics of these systems and move from a simple (and, in the majority of cases, superficial) description of styles, which are always in evidence and alternating with one another, to a historical explanation of these changes, one must develop a special history of speech genres (and not only secondary, but also primary ones) that reflects more directly, clearly, and flexibly all the changes taking place in social life. Utterances and their types, that is, speech genres, are the drive belts from the history of society to the history of language. There is not a single new pheomenon (phonetic, lexical, or grammatical) that can enter the system of language without having traversed the long and complicated path of generic–stylistic testing and modification.

In each epoch, certain speech genres set the tone or the development of literary language. And these speech genres are not only secondary (literary, commentarial, and scientific), but also primary (certain types of oral dialogue – of the salon, of one's own circle, and other types as well, such as familiar, family – everyday, sociopolitical, philosophical, and so on). Any expansion of the literary language that results from drawing on various extraliterary strata of the national language inevitably entails some degree of penetration into all genres of written language (literary, scientific, commentarial, conversational, and so forth) to a greater or lesser degree, and entails new generic devices for the construction of the speech whole, its finalization, the accommodation of the listener or partner, and so forth. This leads to a more or less fundamental restructuring and renewal of speech genres.

[. . .]

Still current in linguistics are such *fictions* as the "listener" and "understander" (partners of the "speaker"), the "unified speech flow," and so on. These fictions produce a completely distorted idea of the complex and multifaceted process of active speech communication. Courses in general linguistics (even serious ones like Saussure's) frequently present graphic-schematic depictions of the two partners in speech communication – the speaker and the listener (who perceives the speech) – and provide diagrams of the active speech processes of the speaker and the corresponding passive processes of the listener's perception and understanding of the speech. One cannot say that these diagrams are false or that they do not correspond to certain aspects of reality. But when they are put forth as the actual whole of speech communication, they become a scientific fiction. The fact is that when the listener perceives and understands the meaning (the language meaning) of speech, he simultaneously takes an active, responsive attitude toward it. He either agrees or disagrees with it (completely or partially), augments it, applies it, prepares for its execution, and so on. And the listener adopts this responsive attitude for the entire duration of the process of listening and understanding, from the very beginning – sometimes literally from the speaker's first word. Any understanding of live speech, a live utterance, is inherently responsive, although the degree of this activity varies extremely. Any understanding is imbued with response and necessarily elicits it in one form or another: the listener becomes the speaker.[. . .]

Moreover, any speaker is himself a respondent to a greater or lesser degree. He is not, after all, the first speaker, the one who disturbs the eternal silence of the universe. And he presupposes not only the existence of the language system he is using, but also the existence of preceding utterances – his own and others' – with which his given utterance enters into one kind of relation or another (builds on them, polemicizes with them, or simply presumes that they are already known to the listener). Any utterance is a link in a very complexly organized chain of other utterances.

[. . .]

The boundaries of each concrete utterance as a unit of speech communication are determined by a *change of speaking subjects*, that is, a change of speakers. Any utterance – from a short (single-word) rejoinder in everyday dialogue to the large novel or scientific treatise – has, so to speak, an absolute beginning and an absolute end: its beginning is preceded by the utterances of others, and its end is followed by the responsive utterances of others (or, although it may be silent, others' active responsive understanding, or, finally, a responsive action based on this understanding). The speaker ends his utterance in order to relinquish the floor to the other or to make room for the other's active responsive understanding. The utterance is not a conventional unit, but a real unit, clearly delimited by the change of speaking subjects, which ends by relinquishing the floor to the other, as if with a silient, *dixi*, perceived by the listeners (as a sign) that the speaker has finished.

This change of speaking subjects, which creates clear-cut boundaries of the utterance, varies in nature and acquires different forms in the heterogeneous spheres of human activity and life, depending on the functions of language and on the conditions and situations of communication. One observes this change of speaking subjects most simply and clearly in actual dialogue where the utterances of the interlocutors or partners in dialogue (which we shall call rejoinders) alternate. Because of its simplicity and clarity, dialogue is a classic form of speech communication. Each rejoinder, regardless of how brief and abrupt, has a specific quality of completion that expresses a particular position of the speaker, to which one may respond or may assume, with respect to it, a responsive position. But at the same time rejoinders are all linked to one another. And the sort of relations that exist among rejoinders of dialogue – relations between question and answer, assertion and objection, assertion and agreement, suggestion and acceptance, order and execution, and so forth – are impossible among units of language (words and sentences), either in the system of language (in the vertical cross section) or within the utterance (on the horizontal plane). These specific relations among rejoinders in a dialogue are only subcategories of specific relations among whole utterances in the process of speech communication. These relations are possible only among utterances of different speech subjects; they presuppose *other* (with respect to the speaker) participants in speech communication. The relations among whole utterances cannot be treated grammatically since, we repeat, such relations are impossible among units of language, and not only in the system of language, but within the utterance as well.

[. . .]

Complexly structured and specialized works of various scientific and artistic genres, in spite of all the ways in which they differ from rejoinders in dialogue, are by nature the same kind of units of speech communication.

They, too, are clearly demarcated by a change of speaking subjects, and these boundaries, while retaining their *external* clarity, acquire here a special internal aspect because the speaking subject – in this case, the *author* of the work – manifests his own individuality in his style, his world-view, and in all aspects of the design of his work. This imprint of individuality marking the work also creates special internal boundaries that distinguish this work from other works connected with it in the overall processes of speech communication in that particular cultural sphere: from the works of predecessors on whom the author relies, from other works of the same school, from the works of opposing schools with which the author is contending, and so on.

The work, like the rejoinder in dialogue, is oriented toward the response of the other (others), toward his active responsive understanding, which can assume various forms: educational influence on the readers, persuasion of them, critical responses, influence on followers and successors, and so on. It can determine others' responsive positions under the complex conditions of speech communication in a particular cultural sphere. The work is a link in the chain of a speech communion. Like the rejoinder in a dialogue, it is related to other work-utterances: both those to which it responds and those that respond to it. At the same time, like the rejoinder in a dialogue, it is separated from them by the absolute boundaries created by a change of speaking subjects.

[. . .]

The speaker's speech will is manifested primarily in the *choice of a particular speech genre*. This choice is determined by the specific nature of the given sphere of speech communication, semantic (thematic) considerations, the concrete situation of the speech communication, the personal composition of its participants, and so on. And when the speaker's speech plan with all its individuality and subjectivity is applied and adapted to a chosen genre, it is shaped and developed within a certain generic form. Such genres exist above all in the great and multifarious sphere of everyday oral communication, including the most familiar and the most intimate.

We speak only in definite speech genres, that is, all our utterances have definite and relatively stable typical *forms of construction of the whole*. Our repertoire of oral (and written) speech genres is rich. We use them confidently and skillfully *in practice,* and it is quite possible for us not even to suspect their existence *in theory*. Like Molière's Monsieur Jourdain who, when speaking in prose, had no idea that was what he was doing; we speak in diverse genres without suspecting that they exist. Even in the most free, the most unconstrained conversation, we cast our speech in definite generic forms, sometimes rigid and trite ones, sometimes more flexible, plastic, and creative ones (everyday communication also has creative genres at its disposal). We are given these speech genres in almost the same way that we are given our native language, which we master fluently long before we begin to study grammar. We know our native language — its lexical composition and grammatical structure — not from dictionaries and grammars but from concrete utterances that we hear and that we ourselves reproduce in live speech communication with people around us. We assimilate forms of language only in forms of utterances and in conjunction with these forms. The forms of language and the typical forms of utterances, that is, speech genres, enter our experience and our consciousness together, and in close connection with one another. To learn to speak means to learn to construct utterances (because we speak in utterances and not in individual sentences, and, of course, not in individual words). Speech genres organize our speech in almost the same way as grammatical (syntactical) forms do.

[. . .]

The generic forms in which we cast our speech, of course, differ essentially from language forms. The latter are stable and compulsory (normative) for the speaker, while generic forms are much more flexible, plastic, and free. Speech genres are very diverse in this respect. A large number of genres that are widespread in everyday life are so standard that the speaker's individual speech will is manifested only in its choice of a particular genre, and, perhaps, in its expressive intonation. Such, for example, are the various everyday genres of greetings, farewells, congratulations, all kinds of wishes, information about health, business, and so forth. These genres are so diverse because they differ depending on the situation, social position, and personal interrelations of the participants in the communication. These genres have high, strictly official, respectful forms as well as familiar ones. And there are forms with varying degrees of familiarity, as well as intimate forms (which differ from familiar ones). These genres also require a certain tone; their structure includes a certain expressive intonation. These genres, particularly the high and official ones, are compulsory and extremely stable. The speech will is usually limited here to a choice of a particular genre. And only slight nuances of expressive intonation (one can take a drier or more respectful tone, a colder or warmer one; one can introduce the intonation of joy, and so forth) can express the speaker's individuality (his emotional speech intent). But even here it is to re-accentuate genres. This is typical of speech communication: thus, for example, the generic form of greeting can move from the official sphere into the sphere of familiar communication, that is, it can be used with parodic-ironic re-accentuation. To a similar end, one can deliberately mix genres from various spheres.

In addition to these standard genres, of course, freer and more creative genres of oral speech communication have existed and still exist: genres of salon conversations about everyday, social, aesthetic, and other subjects, genres of table conversation, intimate conversations among friends, intimate conversations within the family, and so on. (No list of oral speech genres yet exists, or even a principle on which such a list might be based.) The majority of these genres are subject to free creative reformulation (like artistic genres, and some, perhaps, to a greater degree). But to use a genre freely and creatively is not the same as to create a genre from the beginning; genres must be fully mastered in order to be manipulated freely.

[. . .]

Any utterance is a link in the chain of speech communion. It is the active position of the speaker in one referentially semantic sphere or another. Therefore, each utterance is characterized primarily by a particular referentially semantic content. The choice of linguistic means and speech genre is determined primarily by the referentially semantic assignments (plan) of the speech subject (or author). This is the first aspect of the utterance that determines its compositional and stylistic features.

The second aspect of the utterance that determines its composition and style is the *expressive* aspect, that is, the speaker's subjective emotional evaluation of the referentially semantic content of his utterance. The expressive aspect has varying significance and varying degrees of force in various spheres of speech communication, but it exists everywhere. There can be no such thing as an absolutely neutral utterance. The speaker's evaluative attitude toward the subject of his speech (regardless of what his subject may be) also determines the choice of lexical, grammatical, and compositional means of the utterance. The individual style of the utterance is determined primarily by its expressive aspect. This is generally recognized in the area of stylistics. Certain investigators even reduce style directly to the emotionally evaluative aspect of speech.

[. . .]

When selecting words, we proceed from the planned whole of our utterance, and this whole that we have planned and created is always expressive. The utterance is what radiates its expression (rather, our expression) to the word we have selected, which is to say, invests the word with the expression of the whole. And we select the word because of its meaning, which is not in itself expressive but which can accommodate or not accommodate our expressive goals in combination with other words, that is, in combination with the whole of our utterance. The neutral meaning of the word applied to a particular actual reality under particular real conditions of speech communication creates a spark of expression. And, after all, this is precisely what takes place in the process of creating an utterance.[. . .]

A speech genre is not a form of language, but a typical form of utterance; as such the genre also includes a certain typical kind of expression that inheres in it. In the genre, the word acquires a particular typical expression. Genres correspond to typical situations of speech communication, typical themes, and, consequently, also to particular contacts between the *meanings* of words and actual concrete reality under certain typical circumstances. Hence also the possibility of typical expressions that seem to adhere to words. This typical expression (and the typical intonation that corresponds to it) does not have that force of compulsoriness that language forms have. [. . .] Speech genres in general submit fairly easily to re-accentuation, the sad can be made jocular and gay, but as a result something new is achieved (for example, the genre of comical epitaphs).

[. . .]

The words of a language belong to nobody, but still we hear those words only in particular individual utterances, we read them in particular individual works, and in such cases the words already have not only a typical, but also (depending on the genre) a more or less clearly reflected individual expression, which is determined by the unrepeatable individual context of the utterance.

Neutral dictionary meanings of the words of a language ensure their common features and guarantee that all speakers of a given language will understand one another, but the use of words in live speech communication is always individual and contextual in nature. Therefore, one can say that any word exists for the speaker in three aspects: as a neutral word of a language, belonging to nobody; as an *others'* word, which belongs to another person and is filled with echoes of the other's utterance; and, finally, as *my* word, for, since I am dealing with it in a particular situation, with a particular speech plan, it is already imbued with my expression. In both of the latter aspects, the word is expressive, but, we repeat, this expression does not inhere in the word itself. It originates at the point of contact between the word and actual reality, under the conditions of that real situation articulated by the individual utterance. In this case the word appears as an expression of some evaluative position of an individual person (authority, writer, scientist, father, mother, friend, teacher, and so forth), as an abbreviation of the utterance.

In each epoch, in each social circle, in each small world of family, friends, acquaintances, and comrades in which a human being grows and lives, there are always authoritative utterances that set the tone – artistic, scientific, and journalistic works on which one relies, to which one refers, which are cited, imitated, and followed. In each epoch, in all areas of life and activity, there are particular traditions that are expressed and retained in verbal vestments: in written works, in utterances, in sayings, and so forth. There are always some verbally expressed leading ideas of the "masters of thought" of a given epoch, some basic tasks, slogans, and so forth.

[. . .]

This is why the unique speech experience of each individual is shaped and developed in continuous and constant interaction with others' individual utterances. This experience can be characterized to some degree as the process of *assimilation* – more or less creative – of others' words (and not the words of a language). Our speech, that is, all our utterances (including creative works), is filled with others' words, varying degrees of otherness or varying degrees of "our-own-ness," varying degrees of awareness and detachment. These words of others carry with them their own expression, their own evaluative tone, which we assimilate, rework, and re-accentuate.

[. . .]

Utterances are not indifferent to one another, and are not self-sufficient; they are aware of and mutually reflect one another. These mutual reflections determine their character. Each utterance is filled with echoes and reverberations of other utterances to which it is related by the communality of the sphere of speech communication. Every utterance must be regarded primarily as a *response* to preceding utterances of the given sphere (we understand the word "response" here in the broadest sense). Each utterance refutes, affirms, supplements, and relies on the others, presupposes them to be known, and somehow takes them into account. After all, as regards a given question, in a given matter, and so forth, the utterance occupies a particular *definite* position in a given sphere of communication. It is impossible to determine its position without correlating it with other positions. Therefore, each utterance is filled with various kinds of responsive reactions to other utterances of the given sphere of speech communication. These reactions take various forms: others' utterances can be introduced directly into the utterance, or one may introduce words or sentences, which then act as representatives of the whole utterance. Both whole utterances and individual words can retain their alien expression, but they can also be re-accentuated (ironically, indignantly, reverently, and so forth). Others' utterances can be repeated with varying degrees of reinterpretation. They can be referred to as though the interlocutor were already well aware of them; they can be silently presupposed; or one's responsive reaction to them can be reflected only in the expression of one's own speech – in the selection of language means and intonations that are determined not by the topic of one's own speech but by the others' utterances concerning the same topic. [. . .] The utterance is filled with *dialogic overtones*, and they must be taken into account in order to understand fully the style of the utterance. After all, our thought itself – philosophical, scientific, and artistic – is born and shaped in the process of interaction and struggle with others' thought, and this cannot but be reflected in the forms that verbally express our thought as well.

[. . .]

Any utterance, when it is studied in greater depth under the concrete conditions of speech communication, reveals to us many half-concealed or completely concealed words of others with varying degrees of foreignness. Therefore, the utterance appears to be furrowed with distant and barely audible echoes of changes of speech subjects and dialogic overtones, greatly weakened utterance boundaries that are completely permeable to the author's expression. The utterance proves to be a very complex and multiplanar phenomenon if considered not in isolation and with respect to its author (the speaker) only, but as a link in the chain of speech communication and with respect to other, related utterances (these relations are usually disclosed not on the verbal – compositional and stylistic – plane, but only on the referentially semantic plane).

[. . .]

The topic of the speaker's speech, regardless of what this topic may be, does not become the object of speech for the first time in any given utterance; a given speaker is not the first to speak about it. The object, as it were, has already been articulated, disputed, elucidated, and evaluated in various ways. Various viewpoints, world-views, and trends cross, converge, and diverge in it. The speaker is not the biblical Adam, dealing only with virgin and still unnamed objects, giving them names for the first time. [. . .] The utterance is addressed not only to its own object, but also to others' speech about it. But still, even the slightest allusion to another's utterance gives the speech a dialogical turn that cannot be produced by any purely referential theme with its own object. The attitude toward another's word is in principle distinct from the attitude toward a referential object, but the former always accompanies the latter. We repeat, an utterance is a link in the chain of speech communication, and it cannot be broken off from the preceding links that determine it both from within and from without, giving rise within it to unmediated responsive reactions and dialogic reverberations.[. . .]

We have already said that the role of these others, for whom my thought becomes actual thought for the first time (and thus also for my own self as well) is not that of passive listeners, but of active participants in speech communication. From the very beginning, the speaker expects a response from them, an active responsive understanding. The entire utterance is constructed, as it were, in anticipation of encountering this response.

An essential (constitutive) marker of the utterance is its quality of being directed to someone, its *addressivity*. As distinct from the signifying units of a language – words and sentences – that are impersonal, belonging to nobody and addressed to nobody, the utterance has both an author (and, consequently, expression, which we have already discussed) and an addressee. This addressee can be an immediate participant-interlocutor in an everyday dialogue, a differentiated collective of specialists in some particular area of cultural communication, a more or less differentiated public, ethnic group, contemporaries, like-minded people, opponents and enemies, a subordinate, a superior, someone who is lower, higher, familiar, foreign, and so forth. And it can also be an indefinite, unconcretized *other* (with various kinds of monological utterances of an emotional type). All these varieties and conceptions of the addressee are determined by that area of human activity and everyday life to which the given utterance is related. Both the composition and, particularly, the style of the utterance depend on those to whom the utterance is addressed, how the speaker (or writer) senses and imagines his addressees, and the force of their effect on the utterance. Each speech genre in each area of speech communication has its own typical conception of the addressee, and this defines it as a genre.

[. . .]

Methods and resources for analysing discourse

Editors' Introduction to Part Two

IN PREPARING THIS BOOK we at first resisted the suggestion of including a section of methods for the study of discourse. Discourse analysis, we wanted to argue, is not a method, and its basic assumptions about the local and emergent construction of meaning and value would be obscured if we incorporated readings (and some do exist; see also Chapter 11, p. 185) which offered set rules and procedures for discourse analysts to follow. It is important to hold on to this objection. At the same time, studying language as discourse *does* mean adopting a certain perspective on the asking and answering of study questions, on treating language as 'data', on representing language, and on interacting with language users. The concept of discourse brings with it an agenda of theoretical issues that are related to how research is and can be done, and these are the themes we want to pick up in this Part of the book.

First we should make it clear that there are some senses of the term discourse which are too abstract to make any detailed, direct empirical procedure for studying discourses feasible. In relation, for example, to Fairclough's sense of discourse (see Chapter 11), it is not conceivable that any one 'discourse' will offer itself directly for inspection or analysis. This very definition of 'discourse' (similar to Foucault's sense — see the Introduction to Part Six) requires it to be an elusive and veiled phenomenon. Similarly, if we consider Fairclough's sense of the term 'discourse community', we cannot expect to identify a community of language users, in the classic sociolinguistic sense of William Labov's research (1972). But even according to Fairclough's theoretical approach, discourses *are* systematically linked to texts, which are potential sites for empirical investigation. This means that, as in most approaches to discourse, we do need to engage in empirical linguistic study of some sort, and to establish principles according to which empirical investigation may proceed.

The chapter by Deborah Cameron, Elizabeth Frazer, Penelope Harvey, Ben Rampton and Kay Richardson (Chapter 8) is a wide-ranging and stimulating discussion not only of some practical aspects of linguistic research but also of its theoretical grounding. Cameron *et al.* begin with clear outlines of three general orientations in social research: *positivism*, *relativism* and *realism*. Their arguments lead them to dismiss the positivist orientation; they say that 'the limits of positivism are severe and restrictive' (p. 151) for the study of language use, even though it is widely seen by others as *the* scientific approach. As Cameron and her colleagues argue, studying the local contextualisation of meaning is incompatible with a formal, measurement-based, distributional, empiricist, scientistic orientation to 'language behaviour'. Discourse theory itself rules out certain research methods.

Cameron and colleagues then consider relativist research approaches, and specifically the radical ethnomethodological arguments we met in Part One of the *Reader* about the interactional construction of social reality. Their line is that language research, like their own, which addresses various sorts of social inequality cannot avoid the 'reality' of social structures, having an existence outside of language and interaction. They are therefore committed to what one might call a 'mild', or 'less-than-radical' social relativism, and take this forward into their discussion of relationships between researchers and the people they research – which is the main thrust of the chapter. Cameron *et al.* then sketch out three idealised patterns of relationship, *ethical*, *advocacy* and *empowerment* relationships, arguing that the third is the morally, and indeed theoretically, required option. It should be valuable to bear these ideal types in mind when reading the particular studies of discourse reported in later parts of the *Reader*. At that point, the empowerment stance will probably appear to be not only idealised but unattainable in its full form. We might ask whether the phenomenon called 'academic research' is in fact able to encompass the ideal of 'researching on, for and with' researched populations, as part of a process of empowering them. Cameron and colleagues acknowledge this in their own discussion, but this does not prevent the chapter being a compelling discussion of the moral and socio-political framing of research, and of how discourse analysis should position itself as a research practice.

At a more mundane level, where this is spoken language, then any research approach which helps to record the 'data' – e.g., electronic audio-recording or audio-visual recording – will be a practical necessity. We have not included a chapter which advises on these techniques, but Duranti (1997) provides an excellent overview. Further detail on methods in sociolinguistics, which overlap with those used in many studies of spoken discourse (e.g., interviewing procedures, sampling of spontaneous uses of language, issues of 'naturalness', and methods in observational research) can be found in Coupland and Jaworski (1997, Chapters 8–11).

One specific facet of qualitative research on language texts, again with theoretical implications, is the practice of transcribing verbal interaction into a written form. Conversation analysts and discourse analysts have developed very sophisticated means of representing speech in writing, many going well beyond normal writing or *orthographic* conventions. We include two readings on transcription in this Part, one detailing what has become near to a standard form of transcript notation in discourse studies – the one originally developed by Gail Jefferson in her research on conversation. The other reading is a reflexive discussion by Elinor Ochs of how any transcribing practice must reflect the interests and priorities of researchers using it. Ochs also presents a system – a modified version of the Jefferson conventions – appropriate to her own research on child-language development.

In many ways, Jefferson's transcript conventions are an attempt to construct, from scratch, a new set of resources to representing those aspects of speech production and delivery that, in linguistics, have been called paralinguistic (e.g., voice quality) and prosodic features (e.g., rate of speaking, pitch movement and stress – these last two usually referred to as intonation features). It is certainly true that linguistic studies of prosody have not produced a simple, uniform system for representing such features. There is no recognised system for showing non-vocal features like gaze direction (where a speaker's eyes are focused at any one point – in fact it is a difficult assessment to make, even with the use of video-recordings. Outside of Jefferson's system there is no regular way, for example, of representing laughter, even though it is a crucial and hardly rare aspect of the affective functioning of talk. Some of Jefferson's conventions are inherited from phonetics, and in particular from the International Phonetic Association's (IPA) transcript notation – e.g., a single dot to represent vowel-lengthening. The principle behind Jefferson's transcript is to use commonplace, orthographic English spelling as far as possible to show phonetic and prosodic/paralinguistic characteristics. The broader ambition is to capture, in a reasonably readable format, all or most of the features of spoken delivery that speakers and listeners are likely to attend to and respond to.

The Jefferson conventions have, as we said above, gained widespread acceptance in Conversation Analysis and beyond, so it is important to become familiar with them. It is nevertheless true that the system raises several theoretical and descriptive dilemmas, for example in its means of representing vowel qualities, where it stops well short of the IPA level of phonetic detail. Several particular problems come to mind. In the examples given in Chapter 9, it is difficult to justify representing 'just' as 'ju::ss', when other stop consonants likely to have been de-emphasised are not deleted from the transcript. Again, placing the length-marking colons after the 'e' in 're::ally' rather than after the 'a' seems arbitrary, unless the claim is that it is the first part of the diphthongal vowel in that word which is the prolonged segment (and many accents have monophthongs in this position). It is not clear why vowel reduction – of 'your' to 'yih' – should be represented and not other reduced vowels, which are commonplace in most varieties of spoken English. Which dialects are represented in the transcripts and how do we know which features would be salient? Why show some elided items with inverted comma (e.g., 's'pose') and not others? The underlining conventions show very little sensitivity to syllable structure (see Jefferson's implied suggestion that a single consonant, e.g. in *way*, can bear emphasis; the 'w' consonant may be prolonged, but emphasis would inevitably be carried through the whole syllable). In these and potentially many other ways, the system is wayward in its representation of phonetic and phonemic processes, so we should think of it as, at best, a semi-formal device, although it is undeniably a useful and common one.

Ochs's discussion of transcription (Chapter 10) as theory provides a very valuable reflection on transcribing in general and on Jefferson's conventions in particular. Ochs starts with the basic question of what 'data' are for discourse analysis and how transcripts cannot avoid being *selective* representations of them. Orthography is itself one form of selectivity. The form of a transcript encourages readers to use it in different ways, and reflects cultural biases. Ochs's chapter is in fact a mix of theoretical discussion and practical hints, including a detailed list of possible conventions, more detailed and in many ways better rationalised than Jefferson's in its coverage of nonverbal features. It is very useful as a general resource for analytic projects involving transcription, although Ochs's general stance is that there is and can be no perfect transcription – only a transcription that meets particular needs and is systematically linked to one's goals and theoretical assumptions about language meaning and context.

Clearly, in every instance of empirically grounded work on discourse, researchers face making decisions about how best to transcribe their data to suit their own theoretical and practical goals. At the same time, it is important to make transcripts clear and informative enough to their readers, unacquainted with the original recordings. Not surprisingly, this leads to a considerable variation in the use of transcription conventions (even though many stem from the same source), as is evidenced in the keys to transcription provided by the authors of studies included in this *Reader*.

As the final chapter in this short Part we have reprinted almost the whole text of Norman Fairclough's review article, first published in 1992 in the journal *Discourse & Society*. Fairclough begins with a useful section in which he clearly defines terms which he recognises are 'slippery' – including the term *discourse* itself (see his first note). For Fairclough, discourse is 'a practice of signifying a domain of knowledge of experience from a particular perspective'. He defines *intertextual analysis* as 'draw[ing] attention to the dependence of texts upon history and society in the form of the resources made available within the order of discourse (genres, discourses, etc.)' (p. 208). As we commented earlier, there are very strong echoes of Bakhtin here (Chapter 7). Like Bakhtin, Fairclough conceives of texts as ad-mixtures of pre-existing genres and texts, which in turn are informed by (in his sense) different discourses. One important goal of discourse analysis, richly illustrated in this reading, is to deconstruct how particular texts have come to be structured as they are, and with what social and political implications.

The chapter is useful for the many ways in which it suggests refining *linguistic* analyses as part of the broader discourse analysis and intertextual analysis of social and institutional affairs. Many practical lines of analysis are suggested, including how we recognise the infusion of one genre (e.g., a counselling genre) into another (e.g., the medical interview); or the blending of the time-referenced, humourless public-sphere voice and the more contemporary voice of casual conversation. A term which has become increasingly important in critical studies of discourse is *hybridity*, pointing to the absence of fixed boundaries between styles and genres of language, and people's fusing of multiple styles and registers when they communicate. We have an excellent further instance of the hybridity of texts and discourses in Fairclough's re-analysis of how military and religious discourses are intertwined in a published account of government and religious leaders' comments on nuclear deterrence. We should also notice the breadth of Fairclough's appeal in this chapter. He argues that discourse analysis should become 'part of the methodological armoury of social science' (p. 203). Fairclough is one of the leading theorists and practitioners of critical discourse analysis (see the general Introduction, pp. 32–35). Chapter 11 also serves as a very useful map to Fairclough's main publications prior to 1992.

References

Coupland, N. and Jaworski, A. (eds) (1997) *Sociolinguistics: A Reader and Coursebook*, London: Macmillan.

Duranti, A. (1997) *Linguistic Anthropology*, Cambridge: Cambridge University Press.

Labov, W. (1972) *Sociolinguistic Patterns*, Philadelphia: University of Pennsylvania Press and Oxford: Blackwell.

Deborah Cameron, Elizabeth Frazer, Penelope Harvey, Ben Rampton and Kay Richardson

POWER/KNOWLEDGE: THE POLITICS OF SOCIAL SCIENCE

A S MANY COMMENTATORS HAVE pointed out – perhaps the fullest and most insistent statement can be found in the various works of Michel Foucault [see Chapter 30] – social science is not and has never been a neutral enquiry into human behaviour and institutions. It is strongly implicated in the project of social control, whether by the state or by other agencies that ultimately serve the interests of a dominant group.

As a very obvious illustration, we may notice what an enormous proportion of all social research is conducted on populations of relatively powerless people. It is factory workers, criminals and juvenile delinquents as opposed to their bosses or victims who fill the pages of social science texts. Doubtless this is partly because members of powerful elites often refuse to submit to the probing of researchers – their time is valuable, their privacy jealously guarded. But it is also because a lot of social research is directly inspired by the need to understand and sometimes even to contain 'social problems' – the threats (such as crime or industrial disruption) that powerless groups are felt to pose to powerful ones.

Foucault observes, putting a new spin on the familiar saying 'knowledge is power', that the citizens of modern democracies are controlled less by naked violence or the economic power of the boss and the landlord than by the pronouncements of expert discourse, organised in what he calls

Source: Deborah Cameron, Elizabeth Frazer, Penelope Harvey, M. B. H. Rampton and Kay Richardson, *Researching Language: Issues of Power and Method*, London: Routledge, 1992.

'regimes of truth' — sets of understandings which legitimate particular social attitudes and practices. Evidently, programmes of social scientific research on such subjects as 'criminality' or 'sexual deviance' or 'teenage motherhood' have contributed to 'regimes of truth'. In studying and presenting the 'facts' about these phenomena, they have both helped to construct particular people ('criminals', 'deviants', 'teenage mothers') as targets for social control and influenced the form the control itself will take.

We could consider, for example, the medico-legal discourses interpreting but also, crucially, regulating the behaviour of women. Recently, some acts of aggression by women have been explained as a consequence of hormonal disturbance ('pre-menstrual syndrome'); conversely, some instances of women drinking while pregnant have been explained (and indeed punished) as acts of conscious negligence (since they may lead to problems for the newborn, most seriously 'foetal alcohol syndrome'). There are two things to note here. One is that although the categories 'pre-menstrual syndrome' and 'foetal alcohol syndrome' are presented as objective and value-free scientific discoveries, it is clear that these new pieces of knowledge function as forms of social control over women. The other is that although they may seem to contradict one another (since one makes women less responsible for damage they cause while the other makes them more responsible than in the past) they nevertheless complement each other at a higher level of analysis: they fit and reinforce the logic of that broader control discourse feminists call 'sexism'.

This interplay of power and knowledge (Foucaultians write 'power/ knowledge') and the historical link between social science and social control pose obvious dilemmas for the radical social scientist. We have to recognise that we are inevitably part of a tradition of knowledge, one which we may criticise, certainly, but which we cannot entirely escape. Even the most iconoclastic scholar is always in dialogue with those who went before. Our own disciplines, anthropology, sociology and linguistics, have problematic histories. Scholars of language and society may be less powerful than lawyers and doctors, but we have certainly contributed to 'regimes of truth' and regulatory practices which are hard to defend.

[. . .]

It would be quite irresponsible to deny the real effects of research in our disciplines or to play down the contribution they have made to maintaining and legitimating unequal social arrangements. And in this light, our hopes of 'empowering' the subjects of linguistic research might start to look at best naïve. Perhaps it would be better to stop doing social science research altogether?

The questions of how 'empowering' social research can hope to be, and whether in the end certain kinds of research should be undertaken at all are certainly serious ones. [. . .] For us, though, the starting point was that we had done research in situations of inequality, and we felt a need to reappraise critically the ways we had gone about it, making explicit issues of method that were not necessarily foregrounded at the time.

Linguistic interaction is social interaction, and therefore the study of language use is fundamental to our understanding of how oppressive social relations are created and reproduced. If, as we believed, the politics of language is real politics, it is at least worth considering whether knowledge about it could be framed in a way that research subjects themselves would find relevant and useful.

Theoretical issues: the status of academic knowledge

Our early discussions of how research on language might empower its subjects raised general theoretical questions in two main areas: one was the status of academic knowledge itself and the other concerned the relation between researcher and researched in the making of knowledge. [. . .]

We will go on to distinguish a number of approaches or 'isms', which differ in their conceptions of reality, the object of knowledge, and therefore in their opinions about how it can be described and explained. Initially we will distinguish two broad categories among scientists and social scientists: those who subscribe to *positivism* and those who do not. Among the non-positivists we will further distinguish between *relativist* and *realist* approaches.

It must be acknowledged that positivism, relativism and realism are complex positions whose definition is contested rather than fixed. Our presentation of them will simplify the picture by describing a sort of 'ideal-typical' position rather than the nuances of any specific theorist's actual position. [. . .]

Positivism

Positivism entails a commitment to study of the frequency, distribution and patterning of observable phenomena, and the description, in law-like general terms, of the relationship between those phenomena. [. . .] Positivism is strongly averse to postulating the reality of entities, forces or mechanisms that human observers cannot see. Such things are myths, mere theoretical inventions which enable us to predict and explain observable events but cannot be seen as the stuff of reality itself. At the same time, positivism is strongly committed to the obviousness and unproblematic status of what we *can* observe: observations procured in a scientific manner have the status of value-free facts.

This distinction between fact and value is important. Though confident that there are methods which can provide a clear view of reality, positivism is very much aware of the potential for observation to be value laden, especially in the social as opposed to natural sciences. Indeed, for many it is a mark of 'pseudoscientific' theories like Marxism and psychoanalysis that their adherents will see what they want, or what the theory dictates they should; such theories are shot through with political bias. Nor can you set up a controlled experiment to test Marx's hypothesis that the class in society which owns the means of production will also have control of political and cultural institutions by virtue of their economic dominance. It might well be true that there are no known counterexamples to Marx's statement, but we still cannot say that the statement itself holds up. It would be difficult to set out to falsify this statement, as positivism requires, because so many variables are involved and there seems to be no way of isolating and manipulating the relevant one. Because it does not provide us with hypotheses that can be in principle falsified, Marxism for strict positivists is a pseudoscience rather than a science.

[. . .]

Challenges to positivism

Positivism is the 'hegemonic' position, the one scientists have generally been taught to regard not as a scientific method but as *the* scientific method. That is why we have grouped alternative positions as 'challenges to positivism': however different they may be from one another, they are obliged to define themselves first and foremost in opposition to positivism, the dominant 'common sense' of modern science. As this section makes clear, though, the two main challenges we identify – relativism and realism – are by no means 'the same thing'.

Relativism

Relativism does not recognise the observer's paradox (see p. 150) as a problem because relativism does not recognise the fact/value distinction. Reality for a relativist is not a fixed entity independent of our perceptions of it. Our perceptions in turn depend on (are relative to) the concepts and theories we are working with whenever we observe. We invariably have some preconceived notion of what is there to be seen, and it affects what we actually see. Thus someone training as a doctor, say, has to learn to see in a different way: the 'reality' she sees in a chest X-ray is different from what she saw before she did her training, and different again from what a traditional healer from a non-allopathic perspective would see. The history of ideas and the sociology of knowledge provide many examples of scientific theories having close links with the oral and cultural values of their time and place.

Dale Spender (1980) cites a good example of how language plays a part in linking scientific theories with social assumptions. Psychologists investigating people's visual perception discovered two ways of responding to a figure on a ground: abstracting it from its context (the ground) or relating it to its context. These responses were labelled 'field independence' and 'field dependence' respectively. They were also associated with the behaviour of male subjects ('field independence') and female subjects ('field dependence'). Spender's point is that it is not a coincidence that the male-associated strategy was given a label implying a more positive evaluation – 'independence' is conceived as both a positive and a male characteristic. The female tendency could have been called 'context awareness' and the male tendency 'context unawareness'. That this alternative did not occur to the scientist has nothing to do with the nature of his findings about visual perception, and everything to do with his social preconceptions (i.e. he took it for granted that the positive term must be accorded to what men do).

Relativism in the social sciences particularly addresses the role of language in shaping an actor's social reality, as opposed to merely reflecting or expressing some pre-existent, non-linguistic order. The 'Sapir-Whorf hypothesis of linguistic relativity' has inspired a great deal of discussion on the language dependence of social reality. As Sapir argued:

> The fact of the matter is that the 'real world' is to a large extent unconsciously built up on the language habits of the group. No two languages are ever sufficiently similar to be considered as representing the same social reality. The worlds in which different societies live are different worlds, not the same world with different labels attached.
>
> (Sapir 1949: 162)

Subsequently, many social theorists and philosophers in the phenomenological tradition have stressed that social order exists *only* as a product of human activity. For some, this can even mean that there is no social reality, no facts, other than the actor's subjective experience.

Ethnomethodology [see Chapters 4, 6] is a development of this tradition which illustrates both the strengths and the weaknesses of relativism. Ethnomethodology takes very seriously indeed the actor's subjective experience of a situation, to the point of denying any other reality. In particular, it is hostile to the Marxist notion of historical forces determining actors' lives, and to the structuralist postulation of social structures which coerce people into social roles and hierarchical relations. In this view, a social researcher is just like anyone else, an actor experiencing a situation: all research can really ever amount to is the reporting of one's experience. Clearly, this is an extreme anti-positivist position.

The problem here, though, is that in their zeal to emphasise the actor's own role in constructing a social world, ethnomethodologists have left us with a picture which implies that social actors could in principle construct the world exactly as they pleased. More precisely, they have given no account of why we cannot do this.

What makes this problematic? Very crudely, you might say it is a variant of not being able to see the wood for the trees. Indeed, since they deny the existence of higher-level social structures or social forces that the individual actor is unaware of, ethnomethodologists must be sceptical of the idea that the trees in any sense add up to a wood. For them there is no 'big picture' into which the study of some particular phenomenon like a tree must be fitted.

We can put the point a bit more technically. Ethnomethodology is one of those approaches that emphasise the 'micro' level of social organisation – a single interaction between two people, say – over the 'macro' level of institutions and classes, and so forth. In contrast to positivists, who conceive of explanation as stating general statistical regularities, ethnomethodologists give explanatory weight to the subject's account of herself. This means that if a woman says something like 'being a woman has made no difference to my life', the ethnomethodologist has no theoretical warrant for invoking the macro-category of gender. Here the ethnomethodologist is reacting against the Marxist idea of 'false consciousness', which implies that people are entirely deluded about the circumstances of their lives and that nothing a subject says should be taken at face value. Ethnomethodologists find this too deterministic (as well as condescending). For them, the way things are is the way subjects say they are.

For us, though we do not necessarily embrace the idea of false consciousness, this absolute faith in the subject's own account poses very serious problems. We do want to pay attention to actors' own understandings, but do we want to give them the last word in every case? We would prefer to say that whatever they say, people are not completely free to do what they want to do, be what they want to be. For we would want to claim that on the contrary, social actors are schooled and corrected, they come under pressure to take up certain roles and occupations, they are born into relations of class, race, gender, generation, they occupy specific cultural positions, negotiate particular value systems, conceptual frameworks and social institutions, have more or less wealth and opportunity . . . and so on, *ad infinitum*. As Berger and Luckmann say (1967), social reality may be a human product but it faces humans like a coercive force. It is a grave weakness of ethnomethodology, and more generally of relativism, that it offers no convincing account of that fact.

This critical view of relativism brings us closer to a 'realist' position, arguing that there is indeed a social reality for actors and researchers to study and understand.

Realism

Realism, like relativism, accepts the theory ladenness of observation [see Chapter 10, this volume] but not the theory-dependent nature of reality itself. Realism posits a reality existing outside and independent of the observer, but also stresses that this reality may be impossible to observe or to describe definitively.

Realism parts company with positivism on the question of reality being only what we can observe. Neither the social order nor gravity can be observed, and therefore in positivist terms neither is 'real' (strictly speaking, only the observable effects of a gravitational field are real; the gravitational field for positivists is an artificial theoretical construct). Realism, as its name suggests, is committed to the notion that things like gravity *are* real, though at any time an observer might describe them incorrectly and so give a misleading or mistaken account of their real character. It follows, too, that for realism explanation is more than just stating regularities or predicting outcomes (the positivist model). When a realist describes the workings of gravity she believes she is giving an account of how the world works and not just stating what would be likely to happen if you conducted a particular operation in the world.

In the philosophical project of deciding what counts as 'real' – atoms and molecules, tables and chairs, rainbows, societies, classes and genders – there is still everything to play for. The area is full of ambiguities: for example, does the Sapir-Whorf hypothesis imply that reality itself is linguistically determined or that actors' experience of it, their 'mental reality', is? Commentators have expressed differing opinions on this. And does a 'mental reality' count as 'real'? These are hard questions, and philosophers have not resolved them.

What is hard to dispute, though, is the proposition that whatever the ultimate status of 'social reality', it is, partly at least, a *human* product. The continuing existence of such phenomena as social rules, behavioural rituals, institutions e.g., marriage and government, is dependent on human action. Human action maintains these phenomena, and they are therefore suscep-tible to change and transformation by human beings.

The study of social reality

The challenges to positivism we have just considered have implications for the study of social reality. For if the experience of social actors is language and culture dependent, and if we grant that there are many languages and cultures, a number of problems for social science present themselves at once.

To begin with, and whether or not she believes it has an independent objec-tive reality, the social researcher cannot take it for granted that she knows or recognises exactly what a social phenomenon or event is when she sees it. A woman turning over the earth in a flower bed with a spade might immediately be understood by an observer to be 'digging the garden'. In fact, though, the digger's own understandings and intentions would be an important part of the reality – she might not be gardening, but preparing to bury the budgie. Even if she were gardening, the observer who simply recorded this might miss some very important aspects of the scene: the gardener might be letting off steam after a row with her children, relaxing after a hard day at the office or worshipping the Goddess Earth by cultivating her. These meanings are properly a part of the real-ity being observed; the question 'what is going on here' cannot be answered without reference to the agent's own understanding of what she is doing.

If there are problems discovering exactly what is going on in one's own backyard, so to speak, if the objective and non-interactive observation assumed by positivism as the ideal is impossible or useless even so close to home, the problems for social scientists who study cultures and social groups not their own are even more acute. There are two main problems: the exis-tence of differing and shifting conceptual frameworks, and the difficulty of translating from one to another. Can the researcher situate herself within the conceptual framework of the researched and thereby understand what is going on? And can she give an account of this 'otherness' for an audience of readers who can relate to her (original) conceptual framework but not the frame-work of her subjects? We might be alive to the dangers of ethnocentrism, but in the end, can anything be done about it?

Some influential philosophers have replied in the negative, arguing that there are no universally valid standards by which to judge the rightness or wrongness of belief systems; conceptual frameworks cannot validly be compared. This is a strongly relativist position. It has also been strongly opposed by those who argue that there is in fact a fundamental level of shared human experience and concepts. We are all sentient, rational beings who inhabit a world of solid objects: we must all have an understanding of the continued existence of objects in time and space, of cause and effect, and so on. Given such a 'bridgehead' between different human societies it is not so hard to see how we come to understand that some-one else can have a different idea from ours of what causes rain, for instance. In other words, it is at least arguable that even radically unfamiliar conceptual frameworks can come to make sense to the observer.

But whether or not one holds an extreme relativist position, this debate highlights the problem that social reality is not just transparent to the observer. The social scientist must validate her understandings and interpre-tations with the community of researchers of which she is part (thus again raising the issue of theory-dependence in social scientific observation), but also and crucially she must validate her observations with the actors being observed. Asking what people are doing and why, as social scientists must, makes interaction with them inescapable.

You cannot validate a particular observation simply by repeating it. However many questionnaires you give out or interviews you conduct, it is impossible to be sure that all respondents who gave the 'same' answer meant the same thing by it, and that their responses are a direct representation of the truth. Furthermore, since persons are social actors the researcher cannot treat descriptions of their behaviour as chains of cause and effect, in the way one might describe the motion of billiard balls. To be sure, there are regularities to be discovered in the social world, but they are there because of people's habits, intentions, understandings and learning. Social scientists have to be concerned with what produces regularities as well as with the regularities themselves; and once again, this implies interaction with the researched.

[. . .]

The relations between researcher and researched: ethics, advocacy and empowerment

[. . .]

In this section we will distinguish three positions researchers may take up *vis-à-vis* their subjects: ethics, advocacy and empowerment. We will argue that ethics and advocacy are linked to positivist assumptions, while the more radical project of empowerment comes out of relativist and realist understandings.

Ethics

The potentially exploitative and damaging effects of being researched on have long been recognised by social scientists. We touched earlier on one important source of potential damage, the way social science is used within regimes of truth, or directly for social control. Even when you do not work for a government agency, and whatever your own political views, it is always necessary to think long and hard about the uses to which findings might be put, or the effects they might have contrary to the interests of subjects. If a researcher observes, for example, that the average attainment of some group of schoolchildren is less than might be anticipated, that can colour the expectations of teachers and contribute to the repetition of underachievement by the same group in future. That might be very far from what the researcher intended, but an ethically aware social scientist will see the possible dangers and perhaps try to forestall them.

A second worry is that the researcher might exploit subjects during the research process. One controversy here concerns the acceptability of covert research, in which subjects cannot give full informed consent because the researcher is deliberately misleading them as to the nature and purpose of the research, or perhaps concealing the fact that research is going on at all. For instance, a great deal of research in social psychology relies on subjects thinking the experimenter is looking for one thing when she is really looking for something else. Some sociological studies have involved the researcher 'passing' as a community member; and some sociolinguists have used the technique of getting subjects to recount traumatic experiences because the surge of powerful emotions stops them from being self-conscious about their pronunciation, circumventing the observer's paradox. In cases like these one wonders how far the end justifies the means. Even when the deception is on the face of it innocuous, it raises ethical problems because it is a deception.

[. . .]

Apart from preventing the abuse of subjects, an ethical researcher will be advised to ensure that their privacy is protected (e.g. by the use of pseudonyms when the findings are published) and where appropriate to compensate them for inconvenience or discomfort (whether in cash, as commonly happens in psychology, or in gifts, as from anthropologists to a community, or in services rendered, as with many sociolinguistic studies).

In ethical research, then, there is a wholly proper concern to minimise damage and offset inconvenience to the researched, and to acknowledge their contribution (even where they are unpaid, they will probably be thanked in the researcher's book or article). But the underlying model is one of 'research *on'* social subjects. Human subjects deserve special ethical consideration, but they no more set the researcher's agenda than the bottle of sulphuric acid sets the chemist's agenda. This position follows, of course, from the positivist emphasis on distance to avoid interference or bias. However, it is also open to positivistically inclined researchers to go beyond this idea of ethics and make themselves more directly accountable to the researched. They may move, in other words, to an *advocacy* position.

Advocacy

What we are calling the 'advocacy position' is characerised by a commitment on the part of the researcher not just to do research *on* subjects but research *on and for* subjects. Such a commitment formalises what is actually a rather common development in field situations, where a researcher is asked to use her skills or her authority as an 'expert' to defend subjects' interests, getting involved in their campaigns for healthcare or education, cultural autonomy or political and land rights, and speaking on their behalf.

[. . .]

Labov (1982) suggests two principles. One is the principle of 'error correction': if we as researchers know that people hold erroneous views on something, we have a responsibility to attempt to correct those views. (This, incidentally, is a clear example of 'commitment' and 'objectivity' serving the exact same ends; Labov believes in or is committed to putting truth in place of error.) The second principle is that of 'the debt incurred'. When a community has enabled linguists to gain important knowledge, the linguist incurs a debt which must be repaid by using the said knowledge on the community's behalf when they need it. This is clearly an advocacy position.

Labov further stresses that the advocate serves the community, and that political direction is the community's responsibility. As an outsider, Labov accepts – and counsels others to accept – an auxiliary role. 'They [linguists] don't claim for themselves the right to speak for the community or make the decision on what forms of language should be used' (Labov 1982: 27).

[. . .] The important point we want to make is that while Labov's position is in some ways extremely radical, it is so *within a positivist framework*. That framework sets limits on Labov's advocacy, and without underestimating the usefulness and sincerity of what he says and what he has done, we have to add that in our view the limits of positivism are severe and restrictive.

Labov's positivism is clearly visible in his uneasy juxtaposition of 'objectivity' and 'commitment'. Obviously he is worried that a researcher's advocacy might undermine the validity of her findings (the 'bias' or 'pseudoscience' problem). He gets around the problem by claiming that [in the specific case of the Ann Arbor 'Black English' trial], the one reinforced or enhanced the other. It was the work of African American linguists, many motivated at least partly by social and political considerations, that resolved the disagreements, anomalies, distortions and errors of previous work on 'Black English'. The field became better, more objective and more scientific as a result of these linguists' commitment.

This is a powerful and effective argument if one is inclined to place emphasis on notions of factual truth, error, bias, etc. – in other words, it is a positivistic argument. For a non-positivist it concedes too much – the absolute fact/value distinction for example, and the notion that there is one true account that we will ultimately be able to agree on. [. . .]

Empowerment

So far we have spoken of 'empowerment' and 'empowering research' as if the meaning of those expressions were self-evident. It will surprise no one if we now admit that they are not transparent or straightforward terms. As soon as we have dealt with the positivist objection that 'empowering research' is biased and invalid, we are likely to face more sophisticated questions from more radical quarters, in particular, 'what do you mean by power and what is empowerment?', followed swiftly by 'and how do you know who needs or wants to be "empowered"?' [. . .]

Our own position on power draws on both Foucaultian and non-Foucaultian understandings. We do treat power metaphorically as a property which some people in some contexts can have more of than others – that is, we cannot follow Foucault all the way in his rejection of the 'economic' metaphor. On the other hand we follow him in understanding it as a multiple relation (not something that has a single source, as in Marxism or Maoism); in emphasising its connection with knowledge and 'regimes of truth'; and in recognising the links between power and resistance.

Our decision to retain some notion of people or groups being more or less powerful exposes us to a further challenge, however. A sceptic might well ask how the would-be empowering researcher recognises who has more and who has less power: are we implying that the powerful and the powerless are recognisable to researchers as the poor and the wealthy are recognisable to economists? Obviously, if we were Marxists or Maoists who took economic ownership or gun-holding as straight forward indicators of power we could answer 'yes' to the sceptic's question. Since we find these views simplistic we are obliged to answer more thoughtfully. For if the 'real' centre of power is impossible to locate and we cannot identify who has power and who has not, how can we talk blithely about 'empowering research' as if it were easy to see where power lies and to alter its distribution?

We think this question lends weight to our argument that people's own definitions and experiences have to be considered. But consulting those involved, though it tells us something about how they perceive the question of power, does not automatically solve the problem: once again, we encounter the issue we discussed in relation to ethnomethodology, whether the actor's subjective account is the ultimate or only truth. Is, say, the happy slave's account of her experience the final account of it? To that we have to respond that the spectre of moral relativism is a frightening one. We would not want to be in a position where we could not assert, for instance, that slavery is wrong, or that extremes of wealth and poverty are unjust and undesirable.

The sceptic who thinks our notion of power simplistic, and challenges us to identify these 'powerless' people whom we propose to empower, has perhaps oversimplified the notion of empowerment. We must return here to the principle that power is not monolithic – the population does not divide neatly into two groups, the powerful and the powerless – from which it follows that 'empowering' cannot be a simple matter of transferring power from one group to the other, or giving people power when before they had none. Precisely because power operates across so many social divisions, any individual must have a complex and multiple identity: the person becomes an intricate mosaic of differing power potentials in different social relations. And we should not forget a further complication, that those who are domi-nated in particular social relations can and do develop powerful oppositional discourses of resistance – feminism, Black power, gay pride, for example – to which, again, people respond in complex ways. Importantly, though, the extent to which oppositional discourses and groupings are organised or alter-native meanings generated varies: some groups are more cohesive and more effective in resistance than others. [. . .]

Empowering research

[. . .]

We have characterised 'ethical research' as *research on* and 'advocacy research' as *research on and for*. We understand 'empowering research' as *research on, for and with*. One of the things we take that additional 'with' to imply is the use of interactive or dialogic research methods, as opposed to the distancing or objectifying strategies positivists are constrained to use. It is the centrality of interaction 'with' the researched that enables research to be empowering in our sense; though we understand this as a necessary rather than a suffi-cient condition.

We should also point out that we do not think of empowerment as an absolute requirement on all research projects. There are instances where one would not wish to empower research subjects: though arguably there is polit-ical value in researching on powerful groups, such an enterprise might well be one instance where 'research on' would be the more appropriate model. But if we are going to raise the possibility of 'research on, for and with' as an appropriate goal in some contexts, we must also acknowledge that the standards and constraints of positivist 'research on' – objectivity, disinter-estedness, non-interaction – will not be appropriate in those contexts. This raises the question: what alternative standards would be appropriate?

Whatever standards we propose at this stage can only be provisional: much more discussion is needed. [. . .]

The three main issues we will take up in this provisional way are (a) the use of interactive methods; (b) the importance of subjects' own agendas; and (c) the question of 'feedback' and sharing knowledge. On each of these points we will begin with a programmatic statement and then pose various ques-tions in relation to it.

(a)   'Persons are not objects and should not be treated as objects.'
The point of this statement is not one that needs to be laboured, since we believe most researchers would find it wholly uncontentious that persons are not objects, and are entitled to respectful treatment. What is more contentious is how strictly we define 'treating persons as objects', and whether if we make the definition a strict one we can avoid objectification and still do good ('valid') research.

We have raised the question of whether 'ethical research' permits methods (e.g., concealment of the researcher's purpose) that might be regarded as objectifying. Indeed, we have asked whether non-interactive methods are by definition objectifying, and thus inappropriate for empowering research. If empowering research is research done 'with' subjects as well as 'on' them it must seek their active co-operation, which requires disclosure of the researcher's goals, assumptions and procedures.

On the question of whether this kind of openness undermines the quality or validity of the research, it will already be clear what we are suggesting. We have devoted a great deal of space in this chapter to the argument that interaction *enhances* our understanding of what we observe, while the claims made for non-interaction as a guarantee of objectivity and validity are philosophically naïve.

The question before us, then, is how we can make our research methods more open, interactive and dialogic. This is not a simple matter, particularly in situations of inequality.

(b)   'Subjects have their own agendas and research should try to address them.' One of the ways in which researchers are powerful is that they set the agenda for any given project: what it will be about, what activities it will involve, and so on. But from our insistence that 'persons are not objects' it obviously follows that researched persons may have agendas of their own, things they would like the researcher to address. If we are researching 'with' them as well as 'on and for' them, do we have a responsibility to acknowledge their agendas and deal with them in addition to our own?

This might involve only fairly minor adjustments to research procedures: making it clear, for instance, that asking questions and introducing topics is not the sole prerogative of the researcher. While traditional handbooks for positivist research warn against addressing questions subjects might ask, interactive methods oblige the researcher not only to listen but also, if called upon, to respond. But making space for subjects' agendas might mean rather more than this. It might mean allowing the researched to select focus for joint work, or serving as a resource or facilitator for research they undertake themselves. [. . .]

Activities that are 'added on' in order to meet subjects' needs may turn out to generate new insights into the activities the researcher defined: in other words, 'our' agenda and 'theirs' may sometimes intertwine.

(c)   'If knowledge is worth having, it is worth sharing.' This is perhaps the most complicated of the issues we are raising here. Is it, or should it be, part of the researcher's brief to 'empower' people in an educational sense, by giving them access to expert knowledge, including the knowledge a research project itself has generated?

First, let us backtrack: what is this 'expert knowledge'? For, to a very substantial degree, social researchers' knowledge is and must be constructed out of subjects' own knowledge; if this is made explicit (as arguably it should be) the effect might be to demystify 'expert knowledge' as a category. Such a blurring of the boundary between what 'we' know and what 'they' know, brought about by making explicit the processes whereby knowledge acquires its authority and prestige, might itself be empowering. But it does complicate the picture of 'sharing knowledge', suggesting that there are different sorts of knowledge to be shared and different ways of sharing.

[. . .]

Most research, even when it is precisely concerned with finding out what subjects think, does not provide opportunities for reinterpretation [allowing informants to gain new perspective on what they know or believe]. Indeed, for the positivist researcher such intervention would be anathema, since a cardinal rule is to leave your subjects' beliefs as far as possible undistributed. Needless to say, we are not greatly upset if our practice separates us from positivist researchers. But it might also seem to separate us from the many researchers who, sincerely and properly concerned about the imbalance of power between themselves and their subjects, follow the apparently very different practice of 'letting subjects speak for themselves'. There is a convention in some contemporary research of reproducing subjects' own words on the page unmediated by authorial comment, in order to give the subject a voice of her own and validate her opinions. This *non*-intervention might also be claimed as an empowering move.

In assessing these two strategies, intervention versus 'giving a voice', one might want to distinguish between what is empowering in the context of *representing* subjects (that is, in a text such as an article, a book or a film) and what is empowering in the context of *interacting* with them. In the former context we see that there may be value in non-intervention (though see Bhavnani (1988), who criticises some instances for perpetuating stereotypes and reproducing disinformation). But in the latter context we have our doubts whether subjects are most empowered by a principled refusal to intervene in their discourse. Discourse after all is a historical construct: whether or not intervention changes someone's opinions, it is arguable that they gain by knowing where those opinions have 'come from' and how they might be challenged or more powerfully formulated. Clearly, it is a principle we use when we teach: not only do we engage with students' views, we engage with them *critically*. The question we are raising, then, is whether there is some merit in extending that practice from the context of the classroom to the context of research.

Even if we decide to answer this question in the affirmative, other questions remain as to how knowledge can be shared, and what the effects might be. There is also the question of how to integrate educational or knowledge-sharing aims into the broader scope of a researched project. [. . .]

References

Berger, P. and Luckmann, T. (1967) *The Social Construction of Reality*, Harmondsworth: Penguin.

Bhavnani, K. (1988) 'Empowerment and social research: some comments', *Text* 81 (2): 41–50.

Labov, W. (1982) 'Objectivity and commitment in linguistic science: the case of the Black English trial in Ann Arbor', *Language in Society* 11: 165–201.

Sapir, E. (1949) *Selected Writings in Language, Culture and Personality*, Mandelbaum, D. (ed.) Berkeley: University of California Press.

Spender, D. (1980) *Man Made Language*, London: Routledge & Kegan Paul.

Chapter 9

J. Maxwell Atkinson and John Heritage

JEFFERSON'S TRANSCRIPT NOTATION

T HE TRANSCRIPT NOTATION often used in conversation analytic research, has been developed by Gail Jefferson. It is a system that continues to evolve in response to current research interests. Sometimes it has been necessary to incorporate symbols for representing various non-vocal activities, such as gaze, gestures, and applause.

Previous experience suggests that it is useful to group symbols with reference to the phenomena they represent.

Simultaneous utterances

Utterances starting simultaneously are linked together with either double or single left-hand brackets:

> [[Tom: [[I used to smoke a lot when I was young
> Bob: [[I used to smoke Camels

Overlapping utterances

When overlapping utterances do not start simultaneously, the point at which an ongoing utterance is joined by another is marked with a single left-hand

Source: J. Maxwell Atkinson and John Heritage (eds) *Structures of Social Action: Studies in Conversation Analysis*, Cambridge: Cambridge University Press, 1984.

bracket, linking an ongoing with an overlapping utterance at the point where overlap begins:

[
    Tom: I used to smoke [a lot
    Bob: [He thinks he's real tough

The point where overlapping utterances stop overlapping is marked with a single right-hand bracket:

]
    Tom: I used to smoke [a lot] more than this
    Bob: [I see]

Contiguous utterances

When there is no interval between adjacent utterances, the second being latched immediately to the first (without overlapping it), the utterances are linked together with equal signs:

=
    Tom: I used to smoke a lot=
    Bob: =He thinks he's real tough

The equal signs are also used to link different parts of a single speaker's utterance when those parts constitute a continuous flow of speech that has been carried over to another line, by transcript design, to accommodate an intervening interruption:

    Tom: I used to smoke [a lot more than this=
    Bob: [You used to smoke
    Tom: =but I never inhaled the smoke

Sometimes more than one speaker latches directly onto a just-completed utterance, and a case of this sort is marked with a combination of equal signs and double left-hand brackets:

        Tom: I used to smoke a lot=
=[[Bob: =[[He thinks he's tough
        Ann: [[So did I

When overlapping utterances end simultaneously and are latched onto by a subsequent utterance, the link is marked by a single right-handed bracket and equal signs:

```
         Tom: I used to smoke  a lot
]  =     Bob:                 [I see ]=
         Ann: =So did I
```

Intervals within and between utterances

When intervals in the stream of talk occur, they are timed in tenths of a second and inserted within parentheses, either within an utterance:

(0.0)   Lil: When I was (0.6) oh nine or ten

or between utterances:

Hal: step right up
       (1.3)
Hal: I said step right up
       (0.8)
Joe: Are you talking to me

A short untimed pause within an utterance is indicated by a dash:

–   Dee: Umm – my mother will be right in

Unlimited intervals heard between utterances are described within double parentheses and inserted where they occur:

((pause))   Rex: Are you ready to order
                   ((pause))
            Pam: Yes thank you we are

Characteristics of speech delivery

In these transcripts, punctuation is used to mark not conventional grammatical units but, rather, attempts to capture characteristics of speech delivery. For example, a colon indicates an extension of the sound or syllable it follows:

co:lon   Ron: What ha:ppened to you

and more colons prolong the stretch:

co :: lons   Mae: I ju::ss can't come
              Tim: I'm so:::sorry re:::ally I am

The other punctuation marks are used as follows:

- .   A period indicates a stopping fall in tone, not necessarily the end of a sentence.
- ,   A comma indicates a continuing intonation, not necessarily between clauses of sentences.
- ?   A question mark indicates a rising inflection, not necessarily a question.
- ?   A combined question mark/comma indicates a rising intonation weaker than that indicated by a question mark.
- !   An exclamation point indicates an animated tone, not necessarily an exclamation.
- —   A single dash indicates a halting, abrupt cutoff, or, when multiple dashes hyphenate the syllables of a word or connect strings of words, the stream of talk so marked has a stammering quality.

Marked rising and falling shifts in intonation are indicated by upward and downward pointing arrows immediately prior to the rise or fall:

↓↑   Thatcher: I am however (0.2) very ↓fortunate (0.4) in
                   having (0.6) ↑mar:vlous dep↓uty

Emphasis is indicated by underlining:

Ann: It happens to be <u>mine</u>

Capital letters are used to indicate an utterance, or part thereof, that is spoken much louder than the surrounding talk:

Announcer: an the winner: ↓iz:s (1.4) RACHEL ROBERTS for
           Y↑ANKS

A degree sign is used to indicate a passage of talk which is quieter than the surrounding talk:

°°   M: ·hhhh (.)°U<u>m</u> ::°'Ow is yih <u>m</u>other by: th'<u>wa</u>:y.h

Audible aspirations (hhh) and inhalations (·hhh) are inserted in the speech where they occur:

> hhh   Pam: An thi(hh)s is for you hhh
> ·hhh   Don: ·hhhh O(hh) tha(h)nk you rea(hh)lly

A 'gh' placed within a word indicates gutturalness:

> gh   J: Ohgh(h)h hhuh <u>huh</u> <u>huh</u> ·huh

A subscribed dot is used as a "hardener." In this capacity it can indicate, for example, an especially dentalized "t":

> dọt   J: Was it ↑ la:s' nighṭ.

Double parentheses are used to enclose a description of some phenomenon with which the transcriptionist does not want to wrestle.

These can be vocalizations that are not, for example, spelled gracefully or recognizably:

> (( ))   Tom: I used to ((cough)) smoke a lot
>   Bob: ((sniff)) He thinks he's tough
>   Ann: ((snorts))

or other details of the conversational scene:

> Jan: This is just delicious
>   ((telephone rings))
> Kim: I'll get it

or various characterizations of the talk:

> Ron: ((in falsetto)) I can do it now
> Max: ((whispered)) He'll never do it

When part of an utterance is delivered at a pace quicker than the surrounding talk, it is indicated by being enclosed between "less than" signs:

> ><   Steel: the Gua<u>r</u>:dian <u>new</u>spaper <u>loo</u>ked through >the
>   manifestoes< la:<u>st</u> ↑week

Transcriptionist doubt

In addition to the timings of intervals and inserted aspirations and inhalations, items enclosed within single parentheses are in doubt, as in:

>   ( )   Ted: I ('spose I'm not)
>   (Ben):   We all (t–   )

Here "spose I'm not," the identity of the second speaker, and "t–" represent different varieties of transcriptionist doubt.

Sometimes multiple possibilities are indicated:

> Ted: I ₁ (spoke to Mark)
>   ('spose I'm not)
>
> Ben: We all try to figure a (tough angle) for it
>   (stuffing girl)

When single parentheses are empty, no hearing could be achieved for the string of talk or item in question:

>   Todd: My (   ) catching
>   (   ):   In the highest (   )

Here the middle of Todd's utterance, the speaker of the subsequent utterance, and the end of the subsequent utterance could not be recovered.

Gaze direction

The gaze of the speaker is marked above an utterance, and that of the addressee below it. A line indicates that the party marked is gazing toward the other. The absence of a line indicates lack of gaze. Dots mark the transition movement from nongaze to gaze, and the point where the gaze reaches the other is marked with an X:

>   Beth: . . . .   ₁X_____
>   Terry –   ['Jerry's fa ₁ scinated with elephants
>   Don: . . . . .   [X_____

Here Beth moves her gaze toward Don while saying "Terry"; Don's gaze shifts toward and reaches hers just after she starts to say "fascinated."

If gaze arrives within a pause each tenth of a second within the pause is marked with a dash:

Ann: . . . ⌈X_____
         Well (--- -) We coulda used ⌊a liddle, marijuana.=
Beth: ⌈X_____

Here Beth's gaze reaches Ann three-tenths of a second after she has said "Well-" and one-tenth of a second before she continues with "We coulda used . . . "

Commas are used to indicate the dropping of gaze:

Ann: _____
         Karen has this new hou:se. en it's got all this
Beth: _____ , , ,

Here Beth's gaze starts to drop away as Ann begins to say "new."

Movements like head nodding are marked at points in the talk where they occur:

Ann: _____
         Karen has this new hou:se. en it's got all this
Beth: _____ , , ,   ((Nod))

Here Beth, who is no longer gazing at Ann, nods as the latter says "got."

Asterisks are used in a more ad hoc fashion to indicate particular phenomena discussed in the text. In the following fragment, for example, Goodwin uses them to indicate the position where Beth puts food in her mouth:

Ann: _____
         =like–(0.2) ssilvery: :g–go : ld wwa:llpaper.
Beth: ****** [. .] ⌊X_____

Applause

Strings of *X*'s are used to indicate applause, with lower- and uppercase letters marking quiet and loud applause respectively:

Audience: xxXXXXXXXXXXXXXXxxx

Here applause amplitude increases and then decreases.

An isolated single clap is indicated by dashes on each side of the x:

Audience: −x−

Spasmodic or hesitant clapping is indicated by a chain punctuated by dashes:

Audience: −x−x−x

A line broken by numbers in parentheses indicates the duration of applause from the point of onset (or prior object) to the nearest tenth of a second. The number of X's does *not* indicate applause duration except where it over-laps with talk, as in the second of the following examples:

Speaker: I beg >to supp↓ort the m↓otion<=
            ┝————————— (8.0) ——————————┥
Audience: =xx−xxXXXXXXXXXXXXXxxxx−x
Speaker: THIS ↓WEEK SO >THAT YOU CAN STILL MAKE ⌐=
Audience: ⌊xx−XXXXXXXXXXXXXXXXXXXX ⌐=
Speaker: =⌈⌈YER MINDS UP<
Audience: =⌈⌈XXXXXXXXXXXXXXXXXX ((edited cut))

Other transcript symbols

The left-hand margin of the transcript is sometimes used to point to a feature of interest to the analyst at the time the fragment is introduced in the text. Lines in the transcript where the phenomenon of interest occurs are frequently indicated by arrows in the left-hand margin. For example, if the analyst had been involved in a discussion of continuations and introduced the following fragment:

          Don: I like that blue one very much
    →   Sam: And I'll bet your wife would like it
          Don: If I had the money I'd get one for her
    →   Sam: And one for your mother too I'll bet

the arrows in the margin would call attention to Sam's utterances as instances of continuations.

Horizontal ellipses indicate that an utterance is being reported only in part, with additional speech coming before, in the middle of, or after the reported fragment, depending on the location of the ellipses. Thus, in the following example, the parts of Don's utterance between "said" and "y'know" are omitted:

Don: But I said . . . y' know

Vertical ellipses indicate that intervening turns at talking have been omitted from the fragment:

Bob: Well I always say give it your all
.
.
.
Bob: And I always say give it everything

Codes that identify fragments being quoted designate parts of the chapter authors' own tape collections.

Chapter 10

Elinor Ochs

TRANSCRIPTION AS THEORY

Naturalistic speech as a database

[. . .]

A pervasive sentiment among those who draw from performance data is that the data they utilize are more accurate than intuition data: their data constitute the real world – what *is* as opposed to what *ought* to be. There are many issues that could be entertained concerning this orientation. Here I would like to address the problem of what in fact are the performance data for such researchers: even here the internal issues are manifold. There is the issue of data collection: the means of observing and recording, the conditions (setting, time, etc.) under which the data are collected, and so on. The influence of the observer on *the* observed is, of course, a classic concern within the philosophy of science (Borger and Cioffi 1970; Popper 1959).

The utilization of mechanical means of recording may appear to eliminate some of these problems. An audiotape recorder registers a wide range of sounds and a video-tape recorder registers visual behavior falling within its scope. (We are ignoring for now the problem of camera placement; use of zoom versus wide-angle lens, and so on.) A stand taken in this chapter is that the problems of selective observation are not eliminated with the use of recording equipment. They are simply *delayed* until the moment at which the researcher sits down to transcribe the material from the audio- or video-tape. At this point, many of the classic problems just emerge.

Source: Elinor Ochs, 'Transcription as theory', in Elinor Ochs and Bambi B. Schiefflen (eds) *Developmental Pragmatics*, New York: Academic Press, 1979, 43–72.

A major intention of this chapter is to consider with some care the transcription process. We consider this process (a) because for nearly all studies
based on performance, *the transcriptions are the researcher's data*; (b) because
transcription is a selective process reflecting theoretical goals and definitions; and (c)
because, with the exception of conversational analysis (Sacks, Schegloff and
Jefferson 1974), *the process of transcription has not been foregrounded in empirical
studies of verbal behavior.* The focus of this discussion will be on the nature of
transcription for child language behavior. [. . .]

One of the important features of a transcript is that it should not have
too much information. A transcript that is too detailed is difficult to follow
and assess. A more useful transcript is a more selective one. Selectivity, then,
is to be encouraged. But selectivity should not be random and implicit.
Rather, the transcriber should be conscious of the filtering process. The basis
for the selective transcription should be clear. It should reflect what is known
about children's communicative behavior. For example, it should draw on
existing studies of children's cognitive, linguistic, and social development.
Furthermore, the transcript should reflect the particular interests – the
hypotheses to be examined – of the researcher.

One of the consequences of ignoring transcription procedure is that
researchers rarely produce a transcript that does reflect their research goals
and the state of the field. Furthermore, developmental psycholinguists
are unable to read from one another's transcripts the underlying theoretical
assumptions.

Yet, these skills are critical in understanding and assessing the generalizations reached in a particular study. As already noted, the transcriptions
are the researcher's data. What is on a transcript will influence and constrain what generalizations emerge. For example, the use of standard
orthography rather than phonetic representation of sounds will influence
the researcher's understanding of the child's verbal behavior. One area
of behavior that is 'masked' by the use of standard orthography is sound
play (Keenan 1974). The use of standard orthography forces a literal
interpretation on utterances that otherwise may be simply objects of
phonological manipulation. The use of standard orthography is based on
the assumption that utterances are pieces of information, and this, in
turn, assumes that language is used to express ideas. In sound play, the
shape rather than the content of utterances is foregrounded and the
function of language is playful and phatic (in the case of sound-play dialogue)
rather than informative: where the researcher uses standard orthography,
not all instances of sound play can be easily seen. This assumes importance
when a case of sound play is reported in the literature, as in my own
situation. It is difficult to assess whether its rare appearance in the literature

reflects the nature of children's verbal behavior or the nature of psycholinguistic transcription procedures.

[. . .]

Page layout

A first item to attend to in organizing and appraising a transcript is the way in which the data are physically displayed on each page. As members of a culture, we, the transcribers, bring into the transcription process a biased spatial organization. We display our data with the cultural expectation that certain items will be noticed before *others* and that certain items will be seen as part of particular units and categories (e.g., utterances, turns at talk).

Top-to-bottom biases

Across many cultures, there is a convention whereby written language is decoded from the top to the bottom of each inscription. The reading of conversational transcripts takes no exception to this norm, and, generally, the history of a discourse is unfolded in a downward direction. Utterances that appear below other utterances are treated as occurring later in time.

As our eyes move from top to bottom of a page of transcription, we interpret each utterance in light of the verbal and nonverbal behavior that has been previously displayed. In examining adult-adult conversation, overwhelmingly we treat utterances as *contingent* on the behavioral history of episode. For example, unless marked by a topic shifter (Sacks and Schegloff 1974), the contents of a speaker's turn are usually treated as in some way *relevant* to the immediately prior to turn. The expectation of the reader matches the expectation of adult speakers [see Grice, Chapter 3], and by and large inferences based on contingency are correct. These expectations and assumptions are reflected in the format in which adult conversations are typically displayed. Speaker's turns are placed below one another, as in dramatic script (from *Love's Labor's Lost,* I. xxi):

ARMADO: Boy, what sign is it when a man of great spirit grows melancholy?

MOTH: A great sign, sir, that he will look sad.

Here, for example, Moth's utterance is interpreted with respect to Armado's previous utterance. The reader makes such links as his eyes move

line by line down the page. If the reader misses a reading or has not understood an utterance, he frequently looks back to the immediately preceding
line (above). Practices such as linking back (above) and linking forward
(below) again reflect expectations of turn-by-turn relevance.

When we examine the verbal and nonverbal behavior of young children,
important differences emerge with respect to adult communicative norms.
In particular, the expectation that a speaker usually makes utterances contingent on prior talk does not match that for adult speakers. This is particularly the case in interactive situations involving a child and one or more conversational partners. Young children frequently "tune out" the utterances of
their partner, because they are otherwise absorbed or because their attention span has been exhausted, or because they are bored, confused, or
uncooperative.

We cannot necessarily count on an immediately prior utterance, particularly that of another speaker, to disambiguate a child's verbal act. We
also cannot count on the child to signal noncontingency in a conventional
manner. This means that we cannot even be certain that an utterance of a
child that follows an immediately prior question is necessarily a response to
that question. [. . .]

The connection between this discussion and the transcription process is
that the format of a transcript influences the interpretation process carried
out by the reader (researcher). Certain formats encourage the reader to link
adjacent utterances and turns, whereas others encourage the reader to treat
verbal acts more independently. For example, the standard "script" format
described earlier tends to impose a contingent relation between immediately
adjacent utterances of different speakers. Such an imposition is appropriate
to the extent that it matches the conventional behavior of the speakers themselves. Such a transcript is thus far more appropriate to adult western speech
than to the speech of language-acquiring children.

[. . .]

Left-to-right biases

The European culture of literacy socializes its members to encode ideas not
only from top to bottom, but from left to right of the writing surface. For
a page of transcription, this directionality means that within each line utterances to the left of other utterances have been produced earlier. Similarly,
words to the left of other words on the same line have been uttered earlier.
Leftness is linked with priority and also with inception of a statement or
entire discourse.

Very close to its association with priority and inception is the link between leftness and prominence in written expression. This is clearest within the sentence in English, where subjects or topics normally appear to the left of their predicates in the declarative modality. Topics constitute the major arguments of a proposition, and subjects control verb agreement and a number of other syntactic processes.

These associations may influence the overall organization of a transcription in at least two ways. Most studies of child language involve the child interacting with just one other individual, usually an adult. In this situation, the transcriber who has opted for parallel placement of speaker turns has to decide which speaker is to be assigned to the leftmost speaker column and which to the right.

A brief review of the adult-child interaction literature indicates that, with some exception, the overwhelming tendency is for researchers to place the adult's speaker column to the left of the child's speaker column. I would like to point out here that this tendency may not be arbitrary. Rather, it may reflect perceived notions of dominance and control. That is, the researcher may be quite subtly influenced by an adult's status as caretaker or competent speaker in letting this figure assume the predominant location on the page of transcription.

The placement of the adult in the leftmost position may not only reflect but actually *reinforce* the idea of the adult as a controlling figure. How could this reinforcement come about? Recall that leftness is associated not only with prominence (e.g., placement of subject in English standard active declarative sentences), but with *temporal priority* in English-language transcripts. Each line of transcription starts at the left margin and moves towards the right. The decoding of each line as well is affected by this directionality. If the reader wants to look back at prior talk, then the eyes are orientated to the left. If the reader wants to locate the starting point of an utterance, the eyes move left until they locate the initiation of talk following a pause, interruption or final interactional boundary.

These expectations concerning where talk initiates could very well affect judgements concerning the initiation of a *sequence* of talk. A tendency for the western reader may be to turn to the left to locate such initiation points in a verbal interaction. In particular, readers may turn to talk in the leftmost speaker column as a "natural" location for opening up an interactional sequence. Looking to the right-hand column of talk, is, in this sense, a less "natural" move in the pursuit of an interactional opening.

This means that whichever speaker is assigned to the leftmost column has a better than average probability of being an initiator of a sequence of talk. In transcripts in which the adult is assigned to this speaker column, the adult becomes the more probable occupant of the initiator role.

[. . .]

Placement of nonverbal and verbal behavior

In studies of child-language development, there is an overwhelming preference for foregrounding verbal over nonverbal behavior. This is due to at least
three sources:

The first and most obvious is the *goal* of the research at hand. The researcher
is, after all, concerned primarily with language. Nonverbal context is usually
considered to the extent that it directly relates to the utterance produced.

A second source is the *method of recording* child behavior. Child-language
studies have relied upon three basic means of obtaining data: diary method,
audiotape recording plus notetaking and video-tape recording. While the use
of video-tape allows a relatively detailed view of nonverbal behavior and
environment, it is still a relatively restricted mode of documentation within
developmental psycholinguistics. [. . .]

A third source of verbal foregrounding stems from using *analyses of adult
communicative behavior as models*. In nearly all linguistic, sociological, and psychological treatments of adult–adult speech behavior, nonverbal considerations
in the immediate situation are minimized or ignored. Where nonverbal behavior is attended to [for example, see Kendon, Chapter 22], such behavior
tends to be treated as a set of variables that co-occur with language
but do not necessarily constitute part of the idea conveyed. By and large, the
message content is considered to be conveyed through language.

One of the major advances within child language in the past decade has
been the understanding of the communicative import of nonverbal behavior
among young children. There are now numerous documents of the communicative skills of children before language emerges. These studies show that
nonverbal behavior may be an *alternative* rather than an accompaniment to
verbal behavior. Children are able to employ gesture, body orientation and
eye gaze to perform a variety of communicative acts (e.g., pointing out the
existence of some object, requesting some future action from the intended
addressee, offering, demonstrating, etc.). The emergence of language is
understood as a move away from a primary reliance on nonverbal means
towards greater reliance on verbal means to convey an intention. In the
course of this process, verbal means are employed conjointly with nonverbal
means and *together* they convey the child's intentions.

[. . .]

A practical fact to be reckoned with is that it takes more space to
represent nonverbal behavior than to represent verbal behavior. This might
be minimized by a well-developed system of notation for nonverbal features.
However, there are just so many features that one would want to symbolize

in code-like fashion. In the typical transcript, utterances would be surrounded by notes on nonverbal context, and the researcher would be faced with sorting out the forest from the trees in many of the analyses to be carried out.

An above or below representation of nonverbal and verbal behavior becomes increasingly unfeasible the greater the amount of nonverbal information there is to report. We should consider, before going on, the extent to which we need to deal with quantities of nonverbal data. One could argue, for example, that only in the very early stages of communication development is the detailed recording of nonverbal context critical to assessing intentionality. In looking over a great many transcripts, I see that while reliance on the immediate context lessens over developmental time, it is still the case that children continue to rely heavily on the immediate setting well into the multiworld stage. This generalization holds more for certain physical and social conditions than for others. For example, where a child is talking in bed at night or in the semi-darkness of early morning, nonverbal considerations are minimized. Where a child is carrying out some activity other than talking, for example, eating, playing, in a daylight setting, nonverbal considerations take on a greater importance. Not only setting but also co-participants seem to affect the extent to which here and now is communicatively significant for the child. Whereas an adult may lead the child into discussions of past and future events, child–child interaction is rooted in the here and now. [. . .]

To understand the role of eye gaze, gesture, action and setting in peer interaction, consider the following scene, involving Toby and David Keenan at age three years and five months. While earlier months of recording involved the children interacting in their bedroom in near darkness between 6 a.m. and 7 a.m., at this time of the year, the morning light was considerably brighter. The children made greater use of stuffed animals and blankets and played in a number of locations within the room. The piece of recording which we are examining shows Toby and David sitting face to face on Toby's bed. David is sucking his thumb, holding a toy rabbit and security blanket. Toby holds a monkey wrapped inside his security blanket. Prior to the moment at hand, Toby had announced that his blanket was a *steamroller* and David had agreed. Both Toby and David are looking down at Toby's blanket. At this moment, David begins to hum, where upon Toby interrupts, saying *yeah Im gonna make car/*.

In the course of his utterance, Toby performs a series of actions. In the course of *Im gonna make* he moves his blanket and monkey to his right side. (His blanket unfolds in the process.) Between *make* and *car* there is a slight pause (a 'beat'), and in this pause, Toby begins pushing his blanket into a ball, completing the process as he utters the word *car*. Following this sequence of actions, Toby says *heres here thats handle/*. In the course of this utterance, yet another series of actions is performed. Immediately following *heres,* Toby picks up a section of the blanket, holding it in the air for one 'beat' between *thats* and *handle.* While uttering *handle,* he pushes the section down to the bed. Immediately he says *and thats people,* picking up another section of the blanket in the space of a beat between *thats* and *people.* Following the uttering of *people,* Toby drops that section of the blanket. Actions and utterances of similar character follow.

This description indicates the amount of nonverbal data that needs to be recorded to assess the nature of reference and other speech acts carried out by the child. For example, without indicating accompanying nonverbal behavior, we would not know if *steamroller* and *car* named the same referent, and we would not know the referents for the deictic terms *heres, here,* and *thats.* The detailed recording of accompanying movements and eye gaze is, then, not superfluous to an analysis of communicative competence.

This description as well indicates the difficulties of integrating verbal and nonverbal behavior. It indicates the amount of nonverbal data that needs to be reported for a small number of utterances. (In the preceding description, four utterances are examined.) While the situation is reported in "prose style", it indicates the difficulties in following exactly what is happening across both nonverbal and verbal modalities when both are reported in the same descriptive space.

The situation just examined illustrates yet a further feature of nonverbal and verbal behavior that is not captured in any of the transcripts written for or by developmental psycholinguists. This feature is that of *interoccurrence.* Verbal behavior may occur one or more times in the course of some other action carried out by a participant. Alternatively, nonverbal actions may be carried out one or several times in the course of any one single utterance. [. . .] Careful observation shows that typically utterances and actions do not start at the same point in time. An utterance usually precedes or follows the initiation of some nonverbal act. For example, in the situation reported above, the action of picking up a section of the blanket overlaps but *precedes* the utterance of *here thats handle.* Alternatively, the same action occurs in the *middle* of the subsequent utterance *and thats people.*

The initiation points of utterances and actions provide clues concerning the organization of a communicative act. For example, in the utterances treated above, the relation of verbal and nonverbal behavior differs. In the first case (*here thats handle*), verbal behavior makes reference to and predicates something about an object that is already a focus of attention. The verbal act identified an object previously indicated through nonverbal means. In the second case (*and thats people*), reference is expressed initially through verbal means and only subsequently through nonverbal means. Here nonverbal means clarify what object is being referred to by the lexical item *that*. In these two utterances, then, nonverbal and verbal behavior may carry out different types of communicative work. [. . .]

Ideally, we want our transcript to meet practical as well as theoretical considerations. We want our transcript to express the relation between nonverbal and verbal behavior as accurately as possible: we want it to encode not only prior and subsequent behaviors, but co-occurrent and interoccurrent behaviors as well. We do not want a transcript that discourages the reader from integrating verbal and nonverbal acts. On the other hand, we want a readable transcript, one that displays clearly and systematically utterances and contexts.

One possible solution to these demands is to display verbal and nonverbal data in separate locations but to use *superscripts* to locate where verbal and nonverbal acts occur. In so doing, utterances and nonverbal information would be distinguishable, yet, through superscripting, would be integrated. Where children are young, where the setting is light (daytime), where actions are varied and frequent, nonverbal information should be given prominence. In these situations, nonverbal behavior should be reported to the *left* of a participant's verbal behavior. Both nonverbal and verbal behavior of a participant are placed within that participant's behavior column.

Table 10.1 illustrates the use of superscripting with a re-reporting of the situation outlined earlier. Certain symbols will be used to describe nonverbal actions and frames, as well as matters of timing. These symbols are explained in the following section.

Transcription symbols for verbal and nonverbal behavior

The orthographic representation of utterances will vary according to the goals of the research undertaken. Scollon's work (1976) indicates that utterances at the single-word stage should be transcribed phonetically. As the child's pronunciation approaches adult norms, use of phonetic representation should be less critical. However, there are situations in which the speech of older participants is best represented phonetically. These include instances of sound play (Keenan 1974) and instances of unintelligible speech. Furthermore, strictly standard orthography should be avoided. Rather, a modified orthography such as that adopted by Sacks *et al.* (1974) [see Chapter 9] should be employed. A modified orthography captures roughly the way in which a lexical item is pronounced versus the way in which it is written. For example,

Table 10.1 Numbered actions are explained in the nonverbal column

David		Toby	
Nonverbal	*Verbal*	*Nonverbal*	*Verbal*
[1]sucks thumb ⇓ Toby's blanket	(1.2)[1] mm//mm	[2]moves blanket & monkey towards rt., >	//yeah][2] Im gonna make, (³) car[4]
		[3]blanket, blanket reaches rest loc. [4]pushes blanket into ball [5]picks up part of blanket [6]holds part, ⇓ part [7]pushes part down [8]picks up another part, holds it [9]releases part	heres/ [5]here thats? (⁶) [7]handle≠ and thats, (⁸) people≠[9]

modified orthography includes such items as *gonna, wanna, whazat, yah see?, lemme see it*, and the like.

The conventions will be presented in the form of detailed tables (see Tables 10.2 and 10.3). In these tables, three types of information will be provided. First, the tables will present each behavioral property to be represented in the transcript. Second, the convention for representing each of the properties will be displayed, along with an illustration of its use. Third, the tables will briefly point out the motivation for marking this property, its significance in an assessment of communicative competence.

Do our data have a future?

The discussion of transcription and theory presented here is to be taken as a first venture into a vast wilderness of research concerns. Many issues have not been addressed. Furthermore, certain transcription conventions invite modification by others with expertise in the field. [. . .]

Table 10.2   Verbal transcription

What to Mark	How to Mark	Why
1 Utterance boundary	/placed at end of utterance example: *don't make ears funny/he cry/like that/*	Utterance = basic unit in assessing and measuring communicative development.
2 No gap (latching)	=placed between utterances with no time gap example: *look ≠ look ≠ look ≠ look*	Utterances should have a single intonation contour and single breath group, but there are cases in which more than one intonational contour appears in single breath unit. Each contour may correspond to an informational unit. To mark contours linked in this way (no gap), we use "latch marks" (=).
3 Pause length	(.3) placed before utterance; utterances separated by significant pauses should be placed on separate lines example: *and/lettuce/man's eating lettuce/* (5) *one day/was little rabbit/called Lucy/* (.) indicates very slight pause example: *gonna (.) throwit (.) fields/*	a partly defines utterance boundary b partly define "turn" (turn = utterance bounded by significant pause or by utterance of other participant) c number of utterances per turn may be measure of control d may signal end of topic sequence or propositional sequence e may signal leavetaking of floor, elicit feedback from next speaker f may signal distress (cognitive, linguistic, disagreement)

Table 10.2   continued

What to Mark	How to Mark	Why

4 Overlap	//placed at beginning of overlap,
	] placed at end of overlapped utterances overlapped utterances go on same line example:
	    A
	    steamroller's stuck
	    //now]/
	    B
	    oh dear] dear /
		a like pause length, indicates sensitivity to turn and utterance units; may show child or caretaker sensitivity to informational units
		b frequency and placement of overlap may be variable in caretaker speech
		c may be important in assessing cultural differences in language socialization

5 Self-interruption	– placed at point of interruption example: *want some – all of it /*	a may reflect trouble spots in interaction (see 3); trouble can be cognitive, sociological, etc., e.g., can't get reference established, can't get attention of addressee b extent to which speaker can reformulate utterance indicates ability to (1) self-correct, (2) paraphrase

6 Intonation prosodic quality	, marks low rise
	? marks high rise
	. marks low fall (only use in adult speech)
	! marks exclamatory utterance
	place, ?.! at end of utterance
	
	capital letters mark increased volume:
	example:
	    YOU SILLY/
	    _____ marks stress
		a may mark new information
		b may mark hearer selection (e.g., self or other, human versus toy, etc.)
		c may mark communicative act
		d may mark utterance boundary

Table 10.2   continued

What to Mark	How to Mark	Why

	example:
	   I want that one/.
	: : : marks lengthened
	syllable (each : = one
	"beat")
	example:
	   hello::/
	(( )) marks other
	voice qualities, e.g.,
	((LF)) laugh
	((WH)) whisper
	((CR)) cry
	((WM)) whimper
	((WN)) whine
	((GR)) grunt
		e : : : may be tied to marking of
		aspect

7 Audible breathing	-h marks in-breath h marks out-breath (h) marks laughter	a may indicate utterance boundary b hesitation marker
8 Metatrans- cription marks	( ) unclear reading, no hearing achieved (cow) tentative reading X/repetition of prior utterance, e.g., *no/X/X/*	

Table 10.3   Nonverbal transcription

What to Mark	How to Mark	Why
1. Changes in gross motor activity	Bloom *et al.* (unpublished manuscript 1974) suggest using present progressive tense to describe action simultaneous with utterance. Use simple present tense to describe action prior or subsequent to utterance. Put action prior to utterance on line above, simultaneous action on same line, and subsequent action on line below utterance (in nonverbal column). If using videotape, mark precise overlap of action and utterance with a superscripted number above point in utterance. example: [*want^{1}cow/^{1}grabs cow* If superscripts are used, use only present tense to describe action, as simultaneity is otherwise marked.	a aids in determining reference and predication b aids in interpretation of communicative act (self-description, refusal, etc.) c aids in interpretation of interactional sequence (nonverbal means of accomplishing 1st or 2nd part of a sequential pair d provides information linking utterance to change of state or change of object. e indicates child's understanding of or ability to express tense of aspect.

Table 10.3   continued

What to Mark	How to Mark	Why

2 Eye gaze	⇑ looks up (+target: +name)
	⇓ looks down (+target: +name)
	example:
	   ⇑M (use initial for person)
	   ⇓ car
	   > towards right
	   < towards left
	   ▽ facing camera
	   △ back of head to camera
	example:
	   >⇓ M (looks down towards right of monitor screen at mother)
		a indicates intended addressee, referent
		b indicates extent to which child attending
		c indicates extent to which speech is planned

3 Gestures	PT pointing R reaching HD holding up TG tugging OF offer	a primary means of reference b indicates communi-cative act (e.g., summons, offer, description)
4 Body orientation	⊂ marks direction of pelvis (bird's eye view) example: A (A and B are facing ∩ each other; A's body ∪ is facing camera, B's B back is to camera)	a provides social "frame" for talk and action b indicates extent to which participants engaged in focused interaction

A greater awareness of transcription form can move the field in productive directions. Not only will we able to read much more off our own transcripts, we will be better equipped to read the transcriptions of others. This, in turn, should better equip us to evaluate particular interpretations of data (i.e., transcribed behavior).

Our data may have a future if we give them the attention they deserve.

References

Bloom, L., Lightbrown, P. M. and Hood, L (1974) 'Conventions for transcription of child language recordings', unpublished manuscript, Teachers College, Columbia University.

Borger, R. and Cioffi, F. (1970) *Explanation in the Behavioural Sciences: Confrontations*, Cambridge: Cambridge University Press.

Keenan, E. Ochs (1974) 'Conversational competence in children', *Journal of Child Language* 1: 163–85.

Popper, K. (1959) *The Logic of Scientific Discovery*, New York: Science Editions, Inc.

Sacks, H. and Schegloff, E. (1974) 'Two preferences in the organization of reference of persons in conversation and their interaction' in Avison, N. H. and Wilson, R. J. (eds) *Ethnomethodology: Labelling Theory and Deviant Behavior*, London: Routledge & Kegan Paul.

Scollon, R. (1976) *Conversations with a One Year Old*, Honolulu: University of Hawaii Press.

Chapter 11

Norman Fairclough

LINGUISTIC AND INTERTEXTUAL ANALYSIS WITHIN DISCOURSE ANALYSIS

THIS PAPER IS ABOUT the analysis of text as a part of discourse analysis. It is premised on the need for discourse analysis to map systematic analyses of spoken or written texts onto systematic analyses of social contexts (my version of this position is given in Fairclough 1989; 1991). The main objective of the paper is to try to stimulate a dialogue amongst discourse analysts about the nature and value of textual analysis. I endeavour to do this by arguing that detailed textual analysis will always strengthen discourse analysis, notwithstanding the considerable range of objectives and theories and methods in the field, and the diversity of the academic disciplines which draw upon it and contribute to it.

Specifically, I show how more systematic and detailed textual analysis can add to a variety of current approaches to discourse analysis, without of course wishing to minimize what these approaches achieve without it. Closer attention to texts sometimes helps to give firmer grounding to the conclusions arrived at without it, sometimes suggests how they might be elaborated or modified, and occasionally suggests that they are misguided. I have taken as a sample of current approaches to discourse analysis the twenty papers which appeared in the first four numbers of [the Journal, *Discourse & Society* (*D&S*)] – 1(1), 1(2), 2(1) and 2(2), 1990–1.

Textual analysis is distinguished in this instance from other ways of treating texts, some of which are exemplified in the *D&S* papers. For example, in some papers (e.g., West 1990) textual samples are adduced to illustrate

Source: Norman Fairclough, 'Discourse and text: linguistic and intertextual analysis within discourse analysis', *Discourse & Society* 3(2): 193–217.

a pre-established coding system, while in other papers (e.g., Hacker *et al.* 1991) there is commentary on the content of textual samples but not on their form. I understand textual analysis to necessarily involve analysis of the form or organization of texts – of what one might call, after Halliday and Hasan (1976), their 'texture'. This is not simply analysis of form as opposed to analysis of content or meaning: I would argue that one cannot properly analyse content without simultaneously analysing form, because contents are always necessarily realized in forms, and different contents entail different forms and vice versa. In brief, form is a part of content. I elaborate and illustrate this claim below.

I regard textual analysis as subsuming two complementary types of analysis: linguistic analysis and intertextual analysis. And I understand linguistic analysis in an extended sense to cover not only the traditional levels of analysis within linguistics (phonology, grammar up to the level of the sentence, and vocabulary and semantics) but also analysis of textual organization above the sentence, including intersentential cohesion and various aspects of the structure of texts which have been investigated by discourse analysts and conversation analysts (including properties of dialogue such as the organization of turn-taking [see Part Three]).

Whereas linguistic analysis shows how texts selectively draw upon linguistic systems (again, in an extended sense), intertextual analysis shows how texts selectively draw upon *orders of discourse* – the particular configurations of conventionalized practices (genres, discourses, narratives, etc.)[1] which are available to text producers and interpreters in particular social circumstances (on orders of discourse in this sense, see Fairclough 1989; 1991). Bakhtin's writings on text and genre (see especially Bakhtin [Chapter 7]) contain a sustained argument for intertextual analysis as a necessary complement to linguistic analysis, and that argument has recently been vigorously supported by, amongst others, social semioticians such as Kress and Threadgold (1988) and Thibault (1991). Intertextual analysis draws attention to the dependence of texts upon society and history in the form of the resources made available within the order of discourse (genres, discourses, etc.); genres according to Bakhtin are 'the drive belts from the history of society to the history of language' [Chapter 7, p. 123]. Intertextual analysis consequently presupposes accounts of individual genres and types of discourse (e.g., the accounts of conversation which have been produced by conversation analysts, or accounts of what are sometimes called 'registers', such as scientific German or the English of advertising). But intertextual analysis as it is dynamically and dialectically conceived by Bakhtin also draws attention to how texts may transform these social and historical resources, how texts may 're-accentuate' genres, how genres (discourses, narratives, registers) may be mixed in texts. In the words of

Kristeva, it is a matter of 'the insertion of history (society) into a text and of this text into history' (1986: 39). From this perspective, accounts of individual genres and discourse types appear to be largely accounts of ideal types, for actual texts are generally to a greater or lesser degree constituted through mixing these types. I also argue, in the final section of the paper, that intertextual analysis crucially mediates the connection between language and social context, and facilitates more satisfactory bridging of the gap between texts and contexts, referring to my three-dimensional framework for discourse analysis in which intertextual analysis occupies this mediating position (Fairclough 1989; 1991).

The intertextual properties of a text are realized in its linguistic features. Given the dynamic view of genre above, according to which a particular text may draw upon a plurality of genres, discourses or narratives, there is an expectation that texts may be linguistically heterogeneous, i.e. made up of elements which have varying and sometimes contradictory stylistic and semantic values (see Maingueneau 1987; Kress and Threadgold 1988; Fairclough 1991). This contrasts with a common assumption in textual analysis that texts are (normally) linguistically homogeneous. In fact, real text may be relatively homogeneous or relatively heterogeneous, and I would wish to historicize claims about the linguistic and intertextual heterogeneity of texts: it is a particular feature of periods and areas of intense social and cultural change, which perhaps accounts for the current popularity of theories stressing intertextuality and heterogeneity (see Fairclough 1990).[2]

What has moved me to write this paper is the feeling that if discourse analysis is to establish itself as a method in social scientific research it must move beyond a situation of multidisciplinarity and pluralism towards interdisciplinarity, which entails a higher level of debate between proponents of different approaches, methods and theories. The aim is not of course uniformity of practice, but a roughly common agenda – the establishment of at least some consensus over what are the main theoretical and methodological issues in the field. The nature of texts and textual analysis should surely be one significant cluster of issues of common concern.

Of the 20 papers in the four issues of D&S, 15 include substantial textual samples and therefore fall within the scope of this paper. Of these, 7 analyse a specific discourse event or linked series of events (e.g., a political speech, two contrasting medical interviews, contributions to a public dialogue over US nuclear weapons policy), 4 analyse a corpus of collected data, and 4 analyse interviews generated in the course of the research. In 3 of the 15 papers (West 1990; WAUDAG 1990; Yankah 1991), textual samples are mainly used to illustrate coding categories rather than being subjected to detailed textual analysis.

The papers can roughly be divided into five groups on the basis of what properties of discourse are the main focus of systematic analysis. Four papers focus upon linguistic features of texts (Fisher 1991; West 1990; WAUDAG 1990; Yankah 1991); 2 focus upon discourse strategies in dialogue between institutions or nations (Chilton 1990; Mehan *et al.* 1990); and 2 upon a version of what I call intertextual analysis (Michael 1991; Seidel 1990); 3 analyse narrative structures (Billig 1990; Downing 1990; Sorensen 1991); and finally 4 analyse argumentation (Hacker *et al.* 1991; Liebes and Ribak 1991; Ullah 1990; Wodak 1991). Beyond these differences of emphasis, there is quite a lot of common ground. Thus most of the papers include some textual analysis, and indeed some (e.g., Chilton 1990) include a great deal, though in most cases analysis is neither systematic nor detailed. I refer in some detail to 5 papers (in order of discussion: Fisher 1991; Downing 1990; Hacker *et al.* 1991; Mehan *et al.* 1990; Ullah 1990), and more briefly to 4 others (Billig 1990; Chilton 1990; Liebes and Ribak 1991; Wodak 1991), using and reanalysing textual samples from them all.

One source of difficulty for textual analysis is the use of translated data (as in Chilton 1990; Wodak 1991; Yankah 1991). To include textual analysis of translated data as part of the analysis of the discursive event, as these papers do, strikes me as a procedure which is open to serious objections. What light can analysis of the researcher's English translation of a Gorbachev speech cast upon the political and discursive analysis of a Soviet, and Russian-language, discursive event? In my opinion, discourse analysis papers should reproduce and analyse textual samples in the original language, despite the added difficulty for readers.

Linguistic analysis in search of intertextual analysis

The first paper, Fisher (1991), contains a great deal of linguistic analysis, but no intertextual analysis. I argue that the latter would enhance Fisher's analysis of the data, and I extend that argument to Billig (1990). Carrying out intertextual analysis also entails further linguistic analysis, as I show.

Fisher's paper is a comparison between two medical interviews, one conducted by a doctor, and another by a 'nurse practitioner', a new category of health professional in the USA characterized by an emphasis on 'adding caring to curing' and on prevention and education. Fisher's analysis focuses upon the organization of interaction: differences in how the two types of medical staff control patients' contributions to the interaction. Thus, for example, the doctor asks closed questions which permit patient accounts, whereas the nurse practitioner asks open questions which encourage them;

and the doctor filters patient responses to focus upon medical issues, whereas the nurse practitioner follows up clues in the patient's responses about her social circumstances and style of life. This counts as linguistic analysis in terms of the distinctions I set up above; more specifically, it is what many linguists would see as discourse analysis.

According to Fisher, one difference between the doctor and nurse practitioners is that the latter 'supports' the patient and 'legitimizes her explanation' (p. 170). For example (p. 167), the patient in the nurse practitioner interview (Prudence) gives an account of her day from early morning to evening, concluding her description as follows:

> You know, just the normal things that I've always been doing. I don't know. I'm just tired. I don't know if I need vitamins or what?

and the nurse practitioner (Katherine) responds:

> And then you fall face forward on the floor.

The response 'legitimizes the patient's experience', according to Fisher, and she describes Katherine's responses in the exchange below in the same terms (p. 169):

Prudence: I've always been a mother, a wife and a housecleaner. I want to do something else [laughs]. You know?
Katherine: You know that's absolutely understandable. That's, that doesn't (P.: Good, laughs) make you a bad person.
Prudence: Good [laughs] that's one reason I went out and got a job in September cause I couldn't handle it being home all the time, you know, I was, just no adult conversation . . .
Katherine: You know that's a real growth step for you, to realize those needs and then to go take some action, to do something about them. Do you see that as a growth step?

And, again, when Prudence says (p. 167):

> He thinks his sex life is crazy. He thinks 'what do you want to read books', when you know it . . .

Her voice trails off and Katherine 'finishes her sentence':

When you could be having sex.

Fisher describes her analysis as a search for 'recurrent patterns in form – the discourse structure – and content' (p. 161). Whereas some of the earlier comparisons between the discourse of the doctor and that of the nurse practitioner are comparisons of form, the way Katherine 'legitimizes the patient's experience' in these extracts is dealt with as a matter of content. I want to suggest that it is also a matter of the texture of her texts, and therefore of form: in particular, Katherine's contributions repay an intertextual analysis. Her way of conducting interviews seems to be a mixture of medical interview genre and counselling interview genre. One feature of counselling interview genre is that the interviewer sometimes shows empathy with the interviewee by completing or capping her contributions (see Fairclough 1989: 222–5, for an example). This happens when Katherine 'finishes Prudence's sentence', and is realized linguistically by Katherine's turn consisting only of a grammatically subordinate clause (a temporal adverbial clause). It also happens in the first extract above where Katherine's turn (*And then you fall face forward on the floor*) completes Prudence's story of a normal day with a sort of punch line, the completive function of the turn being linguistically marked by the cohesive element *and then*. (Notice how intertextual analysis in these cases leads into additional linguistic analysis.)

Another element of counselling interview genre is that the speech-exchange system is in part conversational rather than simply that of the canonical interview. In the four-turn interaction reproduced above, for example, Katherine and Prudence are engaged in what is recognizably a conversational exchange, responding to and building upon each other's contributions in a symmetrical way: Katherine's first turn is a comment on and evaluation of Prudence's first turn (*that* refers anaphorically to Prudence's statement that she wants to do something else), Prudence's second turn begins with an acknowledgement of Katherine's evaluation (*Good*), and then elaborates the statements of her first turn with a brief personal narrative, which Katherine then evaluates (and classifies, as 'a growth step'), again using *that* anaphorically to refer to Prudence's account. Responses are also elicited, most clearly by *you know* at the end of Prudence's first turn, presumably with question intonation, but *you know* arguably has a more covert eliciting function in all the turns. *You know* can be interpreted in these terms as a marker of conversational style, but it perhaps also points to a third feature of this genre: accommodation by the nurse practitioner to the communicative style of the patient, both of whose turns include *you know*. It would be interesting to listen to the recording for phonetic or prosodic evidence of accommodation. In addition to elements of counselling interview genre, Katherine's contributions also feature a counselling *discourse* (see note 1 on the distinction between discourse and genre), specifically the signification of individual biography in terms of personal 'growth'. The discourse is linguistically realized in a distinctive lexicalization of the self, exemplified and evoked here by the collocation *growth step*.

The focus for systematic analysis in Billig's (1990) paper, in contrast with Fisher's, is narrative structures, but the two have in common relatively close attention to linguistic features of texts which can be enhanced by intertextual analysis. Billig's paper is a study of a *Souvenir Royal Album* published by the *Sun* in 1988 to mark the birth of the daughter of the Duke and Duchess of York, compared with a similar series of 'cigarette cards' on the Kings and Queens of England published by John Player in 1935.

Billig notes that the two differ in their representations of historical time, and that in particular the *Sun's Royal Album* 'expresses an assumption about the essential role of personality in the diachronic movement of history' (p. 28). He also notes that the *Album* is in keeping with the daily style of its parent newspaper in certain respects. Taking these two observations together, an intertextual analysis of Billig's textual samples does, I think, point to a development of his analysis of them. Here is one of them:

Charles I
(1600–1649) was a sickly child who had difficulty walking. He became a short, shy, lonely man with a stammer and high voice. He was a good husband and father and loved beautiful things, but he had no sense of humour and was pig-headed. He was not afraid to die, and when his head was cut off the assembled crowd gave a groan of despair.

Much of this portrait is very similar to portraits in the John Player series and belongs, as Billig points out, to a common historical culture which those of my generation in the UK easily recognize. But I suspect that one clause *(he had no sense of humour and was pig-headed)* contains a new element, belonging to a different culture and a different discourse. Whereas the common historical culture Billig identifies is a culture of the public sphere associated with the written language, lacking a sense of humour and being pig-headed are standard personality attributions in the private sphere, and in casual conversation. What we have is not, I think, as Billig suggests, a text which is 'internally consistent', 'smooth' and 'undilemmatic' (pp. 18–19), but a text which shows the sort of intertextual and linguistic heterogeneity which is typical of the journalism of the *Sun* and similar newspapers, being a hybridiza-tion of public, written discourse and private, conversational discourse (Fowler 1991; Fairclough 1991). The development of Billig's analysis which the example suggests is that the personalities which play such an essential role in the *Sun's* representation of history are partly drawn from models in the (predominantly private sphere) world of common experience, the 'lifeworld' in the sense of Habermas, the world of 'more or less diffuse, always unprob-lematic, background convictions' (1984: 70), which increase their potency. It is noteworthy that the heterogeneity of the text is linguistically realized through a conjunctive 'listing' structure in which the clause I have mentioned is conjoined with a discursively contrasting clause (*He was a good husband and father and loved beautiful things*). Notice that the clauses have parallel internal structures involving conjunction of predicates. See Fairclough (1989 chapter 7) for a further example of listing structures as vehicles for creating config-urations of contrasting discourses.

Scripts in search of textual analysis

Downing (1990) is concerned with the role of media in the constitution of 'political memory' and their effect upon public participation in the formation of US foreign policy on South Africa in the post-Second World War period. The media help build up 'mnemonic frameworks of definition' in terms of which news stories are subsequently interpreted. These frameworks comprise (fol-lowing van Dijk 1988) 'frames', 'scripts' and 'situation models'. The paper traces how these frameworks are drawn upon and developed, what they exclude as well as what they include, in articles published in *Time* and *Newsweek* over the period. The paper actually includes quite a lot of textual analysis, specifically linguistic analysis. However, there is a gap between the textual analysis and the identification of constructs such as scripts. I want to suggest that the gap could be filled by more detailed textual analysis including intertextual analysis. Here is one of the textual samples from the paper (Downing 1990: 56):

> Exactly how and why a student protest became a killer riot may not
> be known until the conclusion of an elaborate inquiry that will be
> carried out by Justice Petrus Cillie, Judge President of the Transvaal.

and Downing's analysis of it:

> The text does not pronounce on the reason for this proclaimed
> transition from student protest to 'killer riot', but it is implied

that the most sombre aspect of the event is to be found here, not in the behaviour of the regime's police and army in rioting against unarmed schoolchildren. 'African barbarism' seems to be lurking in the wings once more. Nothing, moreover, underpinned a 'law and order' definition of the situation more strongly than the bestowal of judicial authority, supreme in its impartiality, on Mr Cillie, Judge President of the Transvaal. Somehow *Time's* writers could not disentangle themselves from the assumption that a judge in a legal system cannot but be detached from prejudice and bias. The character of the regime's legal system and the policies of most of the judges prepared to work within it posed a very serious question-mark against this glib inference.

Downing's reference to a 'proclaimed transition' from student protest to 'killer riot' hint at the ambivalence of voice[3] in this extract without actually going into that issue. Whose formulation (Heritage and Watson 1979) of events *is* 'a student protest became a killer riot'? There is a weak implication that this is the formulation which defines the scope of the legal inquiry, but there is no clear legal authority behind the formulation. The proposition is presupposed (Levinson 1983) rather than asserted, and therefore taken as 'given' and in principle attributable, but it is not possible to identify (at least from this short extract) other external voices to attribute it to. So is this the voice of the journal(ist) masquerading, through presupposition, as the voice of some unspecified external authority? These issues of speech reportage and multiplicity of voice in texts are a concern for intertextual analysis (see Fairclough 1991; Thibault 1991).

The key expression is, of course, *killer riot*. Since what Downing calls our 'mnemonic frameworks of definition' tell us that police and army don't riot but students do, *riot* implicitly puts the responsibility onto the students. But how is it that the script of 'African barbarism' seems to be 'lurking in the wings', as Downing puts it? If it is lurking in the wings, that is because it is evoked by some feature of the text, and textual analysis should attempt to specify what it is that evokes this script. It is, I think, the unusual collocation of *killer* + *riot*. *Riot*, as I have suggested, places the responsibility on the students, and *killer* implies not just the production of fatalities on this occasion (*fatal riot* would have done that), but the involvement in the riot (and therefore the existence among the students) of those whose nature is to kill (which is the reputation of 'killer whales' and which is implied in locutions like 'he's a killer', 'killer on the loose').[4] Linguistic analysis identifies a creative collocation, and intertextual analysis points to the provenance of its elements in different discourses of race and the social, indicating how readers might be pointed in an interpretative direction which evokes the 'African barbarism' script.

A further point to make about this example is that the 'bestowal of judicial authority' which Downing notes emerges more clearly with a little closer linguistic analysis. Passivization places *Justice Petrus Cillie, Judge President of the Transvaal* in the informationally salient final position (as 'information focus', see Halliday 1985*)*. This is enhanced by the weight of the identifying expression (it consists of two nominal groups), and the unusual nominal compound structure of *Judge President* which dignifies the status of the judge.

Closer linguistic analysis again supports Downing's comments on the following extract from *Newsweek's* report of the Sharpeville massacre (1990: 53), but also suggests that they could be developed:

> Frightened and perhaps in very real danger of their lives, the police simply leveled their carbines and Sten guns and fired at point-blank range . . .

Downing notes that police fear is strongly emphasized, which 'could not but mitigate the regime's responsibility'. The emphasis on police fear is achieved textually by topicalizing *frightened*, i.e. putting it at the beginning of the sentence as one of a pair of 'minor' clauses without finite verbs. The other minor clause, *perhaps in very real danger of their lives*, is striking in its modality: there are two contradictory reporter assessments of the danger, *perhaps* constructing it as no more than a possibility, whereas *very real* in effect cancels out this nod in the direction of journalistic circumspection. (On topicalization, minor clauses and modality, see Halliday 1985.) This indicates how, in mitigating the regime's responsibility, the report manages to nevertheless appear to be cautious and circumspect. A third linguistic feature worth noting is the word *simply,* a 'hedge' which implies absence of malicious intent or premeditation, and comprehensible human error. What, indeed, is the significance of choosing *the police simply leveled their carbines and Sten guns and fired at point-blank range* rather than the semantically adequate *the police fired at point-blank range?* It strikes me that the former, along with the initial minor clauses, embeds the shooting in a police-centred narrative, which mitigates it.

Interactional analysis in studies of media reception

Hacker *et al.* (1991) is an analysis of deconstruction of news (i.e. the identification and criticism of ideology in news) by television viewers in cognitive response and interview data collected by the authors. The method employed is, according to the authors, 'content analysis'. The following extract illustrates again my claim earlier in the paper that form is a part of content, and that textual analysis is a part of content analysis:

> Barb: There was one on, there was that story about the Muslims and about how they were holding neighbourhood watches or something . . . and people do that all the time and they're telling about how these people, they turn violent, but they're really stressing that these people are Muslim, and it was like because these people are Muslim they were doing this and I don't know, I didn't see the connection about, like, what liberty do they have in making the connection that these people were violent because they were Muslim? Or that these people are wrong because they are Muslim.
>
> Res: Okay, did you see the news making that connection?
>
> Barb: Yeah.
>
> Res: Okay, how were they making that connection?
>
> Barb: Well, it was like in, every time they referred to these people, and what they did it was because they were, it was just like, Muslim, and these Muslim people live in, it just seemed like they were making that connection. Like between that people group, and the, everyone that, is like that act that way.

According to Hacker *et al.*, this extract illustrates that although viewers could often identify news bias, they 'had difficulty' in explaining on what basis they arrive at a judgement of bias. But what Hacker *et al.* do not show is that the 'difficulty' Barb experiences is manifest in the text: her reply to the researcher's last question is noticeably disfluent, with a number of anacolutha (grammatical constructions abandoned before completion in favour of other grammatical constructions), in contrast to the greater fluency of her first turn in the extract. The following are some of the incomplete constructions: *it was like in, these Muslim people live in, between that people group, and the.* The 'difficulty' is part of the content *and the form* of what Barb says.

However, what I want to focus on in the case of this paper is what intertextual analysis has to contribute specifically to studies of media reception. Here is another textual sample from the paper (p. 194), which occurred in an interview just after the researcher had given the interviewee (Beth) an account of media economics:

> *Beth:* Well, they would have to, there probably'd be some rela-
> tionship between the two because they have a responsibility
> to the companies that are backing them. And if something's
> going on with a company in another country, you know
> it, you can't, they wouldn't be able to show the bad side.
> I wouldn't think. Because that company'd yell, like loud.
> You know, pull away their backing.
>
> *Res:* So you think there could be some sort of relationship there.
>
> *Beth:* Mmmm hmmm.
>
> *Res:* Between who owns the news companies and perhaps what
> they do with the content.
>
> *Beth:* Yeah, it's almost like the company owns the news, so like
> they're the boss and you have to follow what the boss says.
> That's kind of a general way to put it.

Hacker *et al.* comment as follows on this sample (p. 195):

> The viewer does not elaborate on her bias statement until the
> researcher clarifies for her what she might, in effect, be stating.
> Beth's clarification in this case may or may not be a result of her
> own deconstruction of the news. It is arguable, of course, that
> she may be adjusting her discourse to the researcher. On the other
> hand, it may be that Beth has perceived some form of ideology
> in the news, but has never had this type of context for articu-
> lating these perceptions.

Intertextual analysis helps, I think, to shed light on whether Beth's deconstruction of the news is indeed her own, or an adjustment to the discourse
of the researcher. Specifically, Beth draws for the deconstructive statements
upon a range of lifeworld discourses, that is, discourses which circulate in
the commonplace interactions of the private domain rather than in public,
institutional spheres. *You can't, they wouldn't be able to show the bad side* draws
upon a popular discourse of bias and equity according to which equity means
'showing all sides' (an expression used by Beth in another textual sample);
the rewording of *you can't* as *they wouldn't* seems to index the process of
shifting this discourse from a matrix of experiential lifeworld talk to a matrix
of analytical public talk (*you* as an indefinite pronoun being predominantly a
lifeworld form). *That company'd yell, like loud* assimilates inter-institutional
relations to the discourse of interpersonal relations; notice, however, that
Beth reformulates it in public domain discourse (*you know, pull away their
backing*), as if she were providing the researcher with a translation. *So like*

they're the boss and you have to follow what the boss says assimilates the position of the media organization in relation to the media corporation to the position of the worker in relation to the boss, in the discourse of work relations. Notice again the presence of the lifeworld indefinite pronoun *you*. There is no evidence that Beth is adjusting her discourse to the researcher if that means using the researcher as a model in her deconstructive statements (though there is the instance where she adjusts in the sense of offering the researcher a translation of lifeworld discourse). On the contrary, she is drawing upon her own resources, her own discursive experience.

Here is another of the textual samples discussed by Hacker *et al.* (p. 195):

> I guess my view is that the way I view is, deconstruction is to look at the issue and think about it from your own perspective. And I, that's what I like to do anyways. I like to watch a story and, and just kind of take in what's broadcast and what's told to me and then just to kind of think about it. And come up with my own viewpoints. And I think that's how I would, in general, relate to deconstruction.

Hacker *et al.* see this extract in terms of a modification by the viewer of their definition of deconstruction. The viewer does indeed give an explicit definition in the first sentence, but I think a more fruitful way of interpreting the extract is in intertextual terms. The viewer is appropriating the concept of deconstruction through a lifeworld narrative of media use and opinion formation. The viewer tells a story about his own viewing practices: he watches and assimilates a news story, then thinks about it. This is by no means just his own account of the viewing process; it is a widely used, and ideologically potent, social narrative.

What intertextual analysis offers media reception studies is a textual basis for answering questions about what social resources and experiences are drawn upon in the reception and interpretation of media, and what other domains of life media messages are linked or assimilated to in interpretation. Such an approach would seem to be a helpful one in the context of recent arguments that media reception studies should extend their concerns beyond the moment of reception to consider how media messages are taken up, used and transformed in various spheres of life — the family, work, political activities, leisure activities, religion, etc. According to Thompson (1990), such investigations should involve studies of the 'discursive elaboration' of media messages, of how they figure and how they are transformed in a variety of discursive practices and across a variety of orders of discourse. Intertextual analysis would clearly be an important resource for such studies.

The same case for intertextual analysis applies to the other media reception paper (Liebes and Ribak 1991), which is a study of different decoding strategies, on the part of political 'hawks' and 'doves' within the same family, for Israeli television news reports about the Palestinian *intifada*. The authors point out, for instance, that whereas the hawkish daughter of the family draws upon 'social scientific terms' in asserting that television represents the dominant reality, the mother, a 'dove', criticizes television coverage in the light of her own experience. This indication of the establishment in reception of contrasting connections between the media message and other domains of social practice (social science on the one hand, lifeworld experience on the other) can again be strengthened through intertextual analysis. Thus a striking feature of the mother's discourse is the extent to which it draws upon oral narrative genre, constantly telling stories to support a critical reading of the news. The following sample (p. 214), for instance, is made up almost entirely of a complex tissue of stories (I have numbered the lines of the transcription for ease of reference below):

> As I was saying, no Arab ever threw a stone at me, but some Jew did. On
> a *Shabbat* I got hit by a stone, on my car, and they threw a garbage bin at
> me, and they almost jumped at us; she's [i.e. the daughter] my witness;
> here, just next to the house. I believe more in the Arabs than in the
> 5   religious Jews. I am more afraid of them. I don't know, this is my opinion.
> In the morning I sit in the kitchen and I hear under my window, *'shabbes!'*
> [Sabbath!] and *'pritzes!'* [whoring!]; here under this window is the prob-
> lematic street Yam Suf, and they want to close it [to traffic on Saturdays].
> If I got into my car I don't know what they would do to me. They would
> 10   come in the tens and hundreds, and would anybody pay attention? So they
> arrest them, and in the evening they let them go. On *Lag Ba'omer* [a
> holiday when bonfires are lit]: I was at a friend's today, and she told me
> that she went to see a bonfire in the center of town, not in Mea She'arim,
> not Mea She'arim but closer to the center of town, and she said that the
> 15   religious started a bonfire there, and burned the Israeli flag.

The passage contains different types of narrative which are closely integrated with the non-narrative sections of the passage, which argue that the 'religious Jews' are more reprehensible than the Arabs. Line 1 sets up the contrast between Arabs and Jews in terms of the mother's personal experience of violence, and pre-formulates the story of lines 2–3, which is a personal experience narrative. Notice the rhetorical structure of this story, in particular how the outrageous nature of the incident is underscored through the double locative adverbial of *here, just next to the house*, and the positioning of it after *she's my witness* as a post-completion to the story. This strikes me as very much a form of conversational narrative rhetoric. Like the other stories in the passage, this one has the primarily indexical function (Barthes 1977: 91–7) of connoting the character of the 'religious Jews', which is the basis for coherent linkage between the story and the main argumentative part of the passage in lines 4–5: the former provides a reason for the latter, though their logical relationship is left implicit. The same relationship exists between the argument of lines 4–5 and the next story, in lines 5–8, which is also a narrative of personal experience but of a different type, what one might call a narrative of ritual personal experience (the mother's story of what she regularly hears). This is followed immediately by a thematically linked hypothetical narrative in lines 9–10, about what would happen if she drove her car in Yam Suf street on a Saturday. Within the same sentence, from the middle of line 10, there is an interpolated argument (to the effect that nobody controls the violence of the 'religious Jews') which is itself implicitly grounded in the non-personal ritual narrative of lines 10–11. Finally, in lines 11–15 there is another personal experience narrative about the mother's visit to a friend into which is embedded the friend's personal experience narrative about the burning of the Israeli flag (lines 13–15). The brevity and pointedness of these narratives is striking. They are typical of the conversational narratives which constitute an important element of the social repertoires of the lifeworld, and the way in which they are knitted together for purposes of argument here is typically conversational. What I think is potentially useful in this sort of analysis for studies of media reception is that it can show in some detail how conversational resources are mobilized in the reception of media, and how therefore the practices and experience of the lifeworld come to be integrated with the mass media.

Discourse strategies and intertextual analysis

Mehan *et al.* suggest that 'the relations between voices in public political discourse take the form of a conversation' (1990: 135), a dialogue, in which discourse strategies or moves on the part of one organization (government, churches, other governments, etc.) provoke responses from others. This perspective is applied to the evolution of the 'nuclear conversation', discourse appertaining to nuclear arms policy, in the USA in the 1980s. The authors see this conversation in terms of a loss of control by the Reagan Administration of the discourse system associated with deterrence, and the consequential opening up of a new discourse space which domestic and foreign opponents of the regime used to undermine deterrence. Discourse strategies were identified through a content analysis of texts. I want to suggest that intertextual and linguistic analysis of texts provides a solid and more tangible analytical grounding for the identification of moves and strategies.

Let me briefly review the moves and counter-moves identified by the authors within the nuclear conversation. The first move is talk on the part of the Reagan Administration about the need for a war-winning capacity, a significant departure from the discourse system of deterrence which assumed that the deployment of nuclear weapons was about avoiding rather than winning wars. This provoked many responses, including one from the National Council of Catholic Bishops, whose discourse strategy was to shift the argument from technical to moral ground. This in turn sparked off a battle for control of the moral highground involving supporters of deterrence and of the Reagan Administration, other protest groups, etc. A further move was the proposal for a nuclear freeze, which involved a 'populist appeal' (p. 148) for wider participation in the debate, provoking further counter-moves which effectively buried the freeze proposal. A dramatic new move was the Reagan Administration's proposal for the Strategic Defense Initiative (popularly known as 'Star Wars'), which 'began as a way to silence moral voices and the nuclear forces of the peace movement' by seizing the moral ground, but 'achieved success . . . at the cost of further undermining the conventions of deterrence' (p. 152). When the Strategic Defense Initiative began to run into trouble, Gorbachev 'entered the American strategic conversation by proposing the elimination of nuclear weapons' (pp. 156–7).

Implicit in the authors' account of the nuclear conversation is a series of shifting articulations between the technical/strategic, political and moral public domains, and the private domain of the lifeworld. The authors' formulations also suggest a struggle to produce configurations of these domains capable of dominating the discursive field. What is missing, however, is detailed analysis of how the strategic moves within this struggle are textually enacted. This is where intertextual analysis can be of help. Let me illustrate this for two of the moves in the conversation.

The bishop's response to the Reagan Administration's initial move took the form of a pastoral letter addressed to the Catholic faithful. Here is an extract (pp. 139–40):

> Under no circumstances may nuclear weapons or other instruments of mass slaughter be used for purposes of destroying population or other predominantly civilian targets. We also cannot reconcile our principles with the use of any weapons aimed at military targets, however defined, where the targets lie so close to concentrations of populations that destruction of the targets would likely devastate those nearby populations . . . No Christian

can carry out orders or policies deliberately aimed at killing non-combatants.

What is striking about this extract from an intertextual point of view is the hybridization of military/strategic discourse and theological discourse, the latter involving both the regulative ('edict enunciating') genre of the first and last sentences (both of which are categorical prohibitions realized linguistically by the placement of negative particles not on their modal verbs but in their initial prepositional and nominal phrases) and the genre of moral debate and analysis in the second. This hybridization is most starkly illustrated in another sentence which the authors quote, by the sharp transition from the strategic discourse of the grammatical subject to the moral discourse of the predicate complement: 'the deterrence relationship between the United States, the Soviet Union and other powers is an objectively sinful situation' (p. 140). Metaphor is used here as a vehicle for achieving reclassification (deterrence is reclassified as a form of sin, with the simple present tense form of the verb (*is*) giving the new classificatory relationship the modal status of categorical fact: on the relationship between tense and modality, see Kress and Hodge 1979; Halliday 1985). The bishops would need to choose between alternative means of making their intervention, and the choice of a pastoral letter genre is significant: because of the ostensibly 'internal' nature of the document (i.e. internal to the Church) they can draw upon an authoritative and unmitigated moral discourse which might be difficult for them to use if they were overtly addressing themselves to the outside (including the government).

The nuclear freeze proposal was the focus for a political movement, and included a critique of institutionalized expertise and a call for wider popular participation in the nuclear conversation. This populism is manifest in textual samples in the presence of elements from the discursive repertoires of the lifeworld (e.g., p. 148):

> The real problem is that our governments have gone insane world-wide and the people are the only ones who have the sense that they're crazy. The governments don't think so. And so somehow or other we've got to find a way to get through to governments to say 'we know what's going on and what's going on is you're crazy'.

People talking to governments is represented in the direct speech at the end of the extract on the model of how you might talk to a troublesome neighbour. Moreover, not only is insanity lexicalized in a lifeworld way as *crazy*, *you're crazy* also has a meaning which belongs to lifeworld discourse: it is an accusation of departure from good sense, not a judgement about mental health. Again, the following explanation of 'mutual assured deterrence' is not just, as Mehan *et al.* say, 'a folksy metaphor' (p. 149), but a lifeworld way of making an argumentative point by telling a story:

> I see this as two old adversaries locked in a room knee-deep in gasoline. One has nine matches and the other has seven matches, and it really does not matter who strikes the first match because the consequence for both would be the same – total annihilation.

In both these cases, and more generally, the intertextual constitution of texts is connected with audience. As the authors point out, the bishops' pastoral letter 'was heard by multiple audiences simultaneously' (p. 144). We can also assume that it was designed in anticipation of multiple audiences: that, as I suggested above, a consideration in the choice of pastoral genre would be its effectiveness as a vehicle for directing moral discourse and the bishops' moral authority at the wider governmental, protest group and other audiences in the public sphere; and that in producing a hybridization of theological/moral and strategic discourses, the bishops would be sensitive to the need to come across as plausible in both, given their multiple intended audiences. The fit between intertextuality and audience is not always a matter of such conscious design as it tends to be in the hands of sophisticated politicians (in the wider sense), but the question of audience anticipation is always relevant to intertextuality.

That question is a focus in Chilton's paper (1990), which analyses the politeness strategies used in speeches by Gorbachev and Reagan in their efforts to address multiple audiences in ways which build consensus, play down 'face-threatening' acts, and so forth. Chilton's analysis of Reagan's 1986 State of the Union Address includes observations on the intertextuality of the text, specifically the mixing of religious and political discourse, as a positive politeness strategy. In this case, the strategy is designed to unify a diverse national audience around the supposed common ground of religion. I would argue, however, for systematic recourse to intertextual analysis, rather than intertextuality just being treated as one of a highly diverse set of means for being positively polite. Indeed, since genres are pragmatically variable, a pragmatic analysis would seem to presuppose an intertextual analysis.

A multifunctional view of text

Ullah (1990) writes within a social psychological approach to discourse analysis about the rhetoric of self-categorization, the arguments used by children born in England of Irish parents in identifying themselves as Irish or English, and the effects of context upon these arguments. I shall suggest that the focus upon argumentation entails a monofunctional orientation to texts, while there are good reasons for adopting a multifunctional orientation to texts, especially when dealing with questions of social identity.

The following extract (pp. 179–80) is taken to illustrate how two different 'interpretative repertoires' can be applied to the political conflict in Northern Ireland by the same person on the same occasion without any sense of inconsistency:

> P. U.:   You know the Wolf Tones, and bands like that who sing about the Troubles . . . .
> Boy: They put their views over in their songs.
> P. U.:   And so, do you find you sympathize with the Irish cause?
> Boy: Oh yes, you do. You're up there and you're banging the tables, you know.
> P. U.:   Do you believe in it generally, or is it just when you hear the songs that you feel like that?
> Boy: No, not even when you hear the songs. I never believe it when I hear the songs, but . . . I don't mind singing. You've had a few pints and someone says 'Up the IRA!' and you say 'Yes, up the IRA!' You're never bothered really . . . and then like, you know, someone will say to you, like, 'Oh, isn't it great what they're doing?' and I just turn around and say 'No I think it's terrible'.

Ullah's comment that 'this boy saw no inconsistency in first claiming that the music made him feel sympathetic with the Irish cause and then denying that it ever did so' strikes me as misleading. First, it ignores the difference between *sympathize with* and *believe in* in the interviewer's (P.U.'s) questions, and the fact that the 'boy' says *I never believe in it* and not *I never sympathize with it*. This is not at all inconsistent if one assumes that the boy differentiates between sympathy and belief.

Second, Ullah's comment does not take account of the intertextual properties of the interaction. The two interpretative repertoires cannot, I think, be reduced, as Ullah suggests, to two 'vocabularies' (on the model of *terrorists* versus *rebels* as terms for the IRA). There is no contrast of vocabularies in this case, but rather a contrast of narratives: the 'boy's' answers include elements of a narrative about having a good time at a gig, and elements of a narrative about a political conversation. He is evoking two distinct discursive practices occurring within the one social setting, and *Up the IRA* is acceptable in one but not in the other. It's not just a matter of it having two different meanings, as Ullah suggests.

Moreover, and this is my main point, a closer textual analysis suggests that there is more than argumentation at issue in the process of self identification in this extract. Notice that in reply to the interviewer's second turn, the boy uses not the first-person pronoun but indefinite *you:* 'Oh yes, *you* do. *You're* up there and *you're* banging the tables . . .' (p. 180, emphasis added). *You* coincides with the first of the two types of narrative, *I* with the second *(I think it's terrible).* *You* deindividualizes the boy's answer: he answers as one of a group, not as an individual. And the form of his answer is cast in terms of the habitual practices and common experiences of a group, using preconstructed meanings and expressions (the meanings are inseparable from the expressions) associated with 'a good night out' from the first type of narrative (e.g. 'you're banging the tables', 'you're never bothered'). All this is germane to the self-identification process, for the boy is here constructing his own identity on the stereotypical model of the group. But it is nothing to do with argumentation or indeed with the 'ideational' function of language (language in the construction of knowledge and experience) which subsumes argumentation. This is the 'interpersonal' function of language, involving what I have called elsewhere the 'relational' and 'identity' subfunctions (Fairclough 1991): language in the construction of social relationships and language in the construction of social identity. (On 'ideational' and 'interpersonal' functions, see Halliday 1978.) A fuller analysis of these functions could be made on the basis of a more detailed account and transcription of the data: for example, the total communicative style including phonetic, prosodic and paralinguistic properties of the mode of utterance, and other semiotic modalities such as the kinesic, are relevant to the construction of social identity. The general point is that issues of social identification in texts cannot be fully addressed without a multifunctional view of language such as Halliday's.

A focus on argumentation can of course be very productive, but argumentative strategies themselves are not purely ideational in character, they necessarily go along with the interpersonal 'work' of the text and depend upon it for their effectiveness. The following is an extract from Wodak's analysis of argumentative strategies in antisemitic discourse in an Austrian news broadcast (1991: 74–5):

> *Kreisky:*   First of all, I knew nothing about any of the things being asserted about Dr Waldheim as a person. However, if I had known, I would certainly not have withheld my recommendation in this case uh uh, because it all happened a long, long time ago. And

he was a young man . . . But that is not what it is all about. The point is, that certain groups, albeit very small ones, are interfering in the Austrian campaign . . . with both candidates in an improper way in my opinion. I am not prepared to tolerate this. But these groups have been fighting me for decades . . .

Interviewer: Dr Kreisky, your party argues that, it is said, that to a certain extent he admits that he was there, that he did not say that from the beginning. How do you see this?

Kreisky: Yes, well, that is none of my business. I don't want to have anything to do with it. Oh, it is all very unpleasant, and I don't want to have anything to do with it.

Commenting on the last turn of Kreisky (the former Austrian chancellor), Wodak says that he employs a 'macro-strategy of justification . . . he simply cuts off the discussion'. Applying a strategy label to the turn actually captures little of what appears to be going on. The translation gives the impression of a shift in genre and voice which carries a shift in interpersonal meanings: Kreisky shifts from political argument to what comes across in the English as a petulant emotional outburst.[5] The accomplishment of the argumentative strategy in this case is clearly dependent upon, and inseparable from, the generic and interpersonal shift.

Textual analysis in social scientific research

There is a need for linguists and others committed to textual analysis to convince not only the diverse community of discourse analysts but also the wider communities of social scientists that textual analysis has an important role to play in social scientific research. This is not an easy thing to do, despite the widely acclaimed 'linguistic turn' in social science. Many social scientists have concerns and objectives which on the face of it lie in quite different directions, and textual analysis can easily be seen as an irrelevance or a formalist diversion. I shall suggest four reasons why textual analysis ought to be more widely recognized, within a framework for discourse analysis, as part of the methodological armoury of social science: a theoretical reason, a methodological reason, a historical reason and a political reason (see also Thibault 1991). These arguments need to be taken in conjunction with my contention in the main part of the paper that, if one is dealing with texts, it is always worth analysing them in a serious way.

The theoretical reason is that the social structures which are the focus of attention for many social scientists with 'macro' social interests are in a dialectical relationship with social action (the concern of 'micro' social analysis), such that the former are both conditions and resources for the latter, and constituted by the latter (Giddens 1984; Callinicos 1987). Texts constitute one important form of social action. As a consequence, even social scientists who have such apparently macro interests as class relations or gender relations cannot justify entirely ignoring texts. In practice, they necessarily base their analyses upon texts, but often do not acknowledge doing so.

A further important point is that language is widely misperceived as transparent, so that the social and ideological 'work' that language does in producing, reproducing or transforming social structures, relations and identities is routinely 'overlooked'. Social analysts not uncommonly share the misperception of language as transparent, not recognizing that social analysis of discourse entails going beyond this natural attitude towards language in order to reveal the precise mechanisms and modalities of the social and ideological work of language.

The methodological reason is that texts constitute a major source of evidence for grounding claims about social structures, relations and processes. The evidence we have for these constructs comes from the various material forms of social action, including texts. There is, for example, a growing recognition that analysis of ideology must be answerable to the detailed properties of texts (Thompson 1984; 1990).

The historical reason is that texts are sensitive barometers of social processes, movement and diversity, and textual analysis can provide particularly good indicators of social change. This relates to my comments at the beginning of the paper about how a Bakhtinian form of generic analysis (intertextual analysis in my sense) highlights the role of texts in making history, and moreover links this to generic and linguistic heterogeneity. Texts provide evidence of ongoing processes such as the redefinition of social relationships between professionals and publics, the reconstitution of social identities and forms of self, or the reconstitution of knowledge and ideology (see Fairclough 1994; Selden 1991; for examples). Textual analysis can therefore act as a counter-balance to overly rigid and schematizing social analyses, and is a valuable method in studies of social and cultural change. For example, there is an absence of textual analysis in Foucault's influential historical studies of discourse [see Chapter 30] which I would link to some of the criticisms which have been made of the schematism of his work and its failure to specify detailed mechanisms of change (see Taylor 1986; Fairclough 1991, Chapter 2).

The political reason relates specifically to social science with critical objectives. It is increasingly through texts (notably but by no means only those of the media) that social control and social domination are exercised (and indeed negotiated and resisted). Textual analysis, as a part of critical discourse analysis, can therefore be an important political resource, for example in connection with efforts to establish *critical language awareness* (Clark *et al.* 1990; Fairclough 1992) as an indispensable element in language education.

The reluctance of social scientists hitherto to recognize the value of textual analysis is, however, comprehensible given the paucity of usable analytical frameworks. Discourse analysis can help fill this gap. But there is a continuing problem with linguistic analysis because linguistics is still dominated by a formalism which has little time for integrating linguistic analysis into interdisciplinary frameworks. There is a real need for relevant models of language: for frameworks which turn the insights of linguists into comprehensible and usable forms. My own feeling is that the systemic–functional theory of language is particularly helpful in this regard (Halliday 1978; 1985; Hodge and Kress 1988; Thibault 1991), both because its approach to studying grammar and other aspects of language form is a functional one (a property it shares with other approaches such as that of Givón 1979), and because it is systematically orientated to studying the relationship between the texture of texts and their social contexts.

Systemic–functional linguistics also has a view of texts which is a potentially powerful basis not only for analysis of what is in texts, but also for analysis of what is absent or omitted from texts, which is a major concern for a number of the papers in *D&S* (e.g., Downing 1990). Textual analysis is often exclusively concerned with what is in the text and has little to say about what is excluded. The systemic view of texts emphasizes choice, the selection of options from systems constituting meaning potentials (and lexicogrammatical potentials and phonic potentials). Choice entails exclusion as well as inclusion. This view of text has already been applied critically in 'critical linguistics' (e.g., Fowler *et al.* 1979), which highlights, for instance, the potential ideological significance of opting for agentless passive constructions and thereby excluding other constructions in which agents are explicitly present. My discussion of intertextual analysis in this paper suggests a view of text as choice at a different level of analysis, involving selection amongst options within what one might call the intertextual potential of an order of discourse (i.e. available repertoires of genres, discourses and narratives). And the same view of text can usefully be extended to the identification of 'absences' as well as presences at other levels suggested in some of the papers.

Another and even more serious obstacle to social scientists recognizing the value of textual analysis is that analysis of text is perceived as frequently proceeding with scant attention to context. This is a fair criticism of much textual analysis that goes on in linguistics. The emphasis in my own publications in the field (see the References) has been upon bringing a stronger orientation to context into textual analysis. This paper has in a sense reversed that emphasis by arguing that discourse analysts with a commitment to social and cultural aspects of discursive practice would benefit from a stronger orientation to textual analysis. This is in no sense a change of position, or an abandonment of the project of making textual analysis more socially relevant and meaningful: discourse analysis needs a developed sense of and systematic approach to *both* context *and* text.

As I indicated earlier, I believe that intertextual analysis has an important mediating role in linking text to context. What intertextual analysis draws attention to is the discursive processes of text producers and interpreters, how they draw upon the repertoires of genres and discourses available within orders of discourse, generating variable configurations of these resources which are realized in the forms of texts. How texts are produced and interpreted, and therefore how genres and discourses are drawn upon and combined, depends upon the nature of the social context. Thus a relatively stable social domain and set of social relations and identities would tend to predict relatively normative ways of drawing upon orders of discourse, i.e. ways which entail sticking quite closely (and 'appropriately') to the conventions of particular genres and discourse types; whereas, for example, the highly unstable cross-gender practices and relations of various social domains in modern European and American societies are associated with creative and innovatory ways of drawing upon orders of discourse, conventional models of interaction between women and men having become problematized. And while the former scenario manifests itself in texts which are relatively semantically homogeneous, the latter manifests itself in texts which are relatively heterogeneous. (See Fairclough 1989; 1991 for detailed accounts of this position.)

Let me briefly illustrate how this three-dimensional view of discourse and discourse analysis (analysis of context, analysis of processes of text production and interpretation, analysis of text) can help strengthen the linkage of text to context in the case of one of the analyses discussed above, Fisher's analysis of doctor–patient and nurse practitioner–patient medical interviews. I argued that intertextual analysis helps to show how the nurse practitioner, in contrast to the doctor, legitimizes the patient's experiences, suggesting that nurse practitioner interviews are constituted through a mixture of medical interview genre and counselling interview genre, the latter entailing elements of conversational style. In fact the tension between traditional forms of medical interview and forms of conversationalized interview, often drawing upon counselling models, is a pervasive feature of contemporary interaction between medical practitioners and patients (Davis 1988; Mishler 1984; Fairclough 1991), and an important characteristic of discourse production and interpretation in that domain. On the one hand, this property of discourse production and interpretation is one dimension of the social and cultural flux which characterizes this and other spheres of professional–client relations – the problematization of traditional models of professional practice, pressures towards greater individual autonomy and more democracy in relations between professionals and clients, the impact of marketization and models of consumer choice on the professions, and so forth. Structures and relations have become more unstable, and practices more diverse and open to nego-tiation, such that there are many hybridizations of traditional medical, counselling, conversational, managerial and marketing genres and discourses. This diversity is manifested in the variability and heterogeneity of texts: it is impossible to arrive at a unitary characterization of the language or register of 'the medical interview' in contemporary social and discursive conditions.

Let me now make a few comments about this paper by way of conclu-sion. A general observation on linguistic analysis in the *D&S* papers is that it is often conceived in rather narrow terms as analysis of vocabulary and perhaps metaphor with an occasional grammatical example. I have tended to focus upon the case for intertextual analysis, so I have not done as much as I might have done to correct that emphasis. In fact linguistics, especially with more recent enhancements from pragmatics, discourse analysis and conversation analysis, offers a rich array of types of analysis, though much of the richness is tucked away in forbidding technical literature.

As regards intertextual analysis, I have tried to show that its use along-side linguistic analysis can help to break down the 'form versus content' distinction. Constructs such as 'frame', 'script', 'move', 'strategy' and 'argu-ment' can be deployed in discourse analysis without textual analysis, and indeed are so deployed in the papers I have referred to with some inter-esting results. But I have suggested that the results can be more firmly grounded and further insights can be added if their deployment is tied to textual analysis. Let me put the point more forcefully: the signifier (form) and signified (content) constitute a dialectical and hence inseparable unity in the sign, so that one-sided attention to the signified is blind to the essential material side of meaning, and one-sided attention to the signifier (as in much linguistics) is blind to the essential meaningfulness of forms.

Finally, the position I have taken has its own problems. For example, the identification of configurations of genres and discourses in a text is obviously an interpretative exercise which depends upon the analyst's experience of and sensitivity to relevant orders of discourse, as well as the analyst's interpreta-tive and strategic biases. There are problems in justifying such analysis which are not made easier by the slipperiness of constructs such as genre and discourse, the difficulty sometimes of keeping them apart, and the need to assume a relatively well defined repertoire of discourses and genres in order to use the constructs in analysis. Reanalysis of others' data must have an especially tentative character given that one's knowledge of relevant orders of discourse is likely to be considerably less than that of the authors of the papers, and one might not have chosen for purposes of textual analysis the samples which authors include. What all this amounts to is an acknowledgement that the intertextual analyses which I have suggested for fragments of texts can no more than hint at the potential I have identified for analysis of processes of discourse production and interpretation to establish mediating links between text and context: one really needs to engage in social and ethnographic research over significant periods of time in particular institutional settings, gathering and analysing textual samples and information on social and cognitive aspects of their production and interpretation as a part of this more broadly defined research. This is not to backtrack on my claims about the importance of textual analysis in social research, merely to insist upon the need to frame it adequately.

Notes

I am grateful to the following for their helpful comments on an earlier draft of the paper: Paul Chilton, Geoffrey Leech, Günther Kress, Teun van Dijk.

1   There is unfortunately no agreement about terms for analytical categories in intertextual analysis. I use 'genre' for a socially ratified type of linguistic activity with specified positions for subjects (e.g., interview, television news), 'discourse' for a practice of signifying a domain of knowledge or experience from a particular perspective (e.g., Marxist political discourse, feminist discourse) and 'narrative' for a socially ratified story type. See further Kress and Threadgold (1988), Fairclough (1991).

2   The distinction between linguistic and intertextual analysis does not clarify the position of pragmatics. See Fairclough (1989) for a proposal that pragmatics and intertextual analysis should be grouped together with 'text interpretation', while linguistic analysis falls within 'text description'.

3   'Voice' is adapted from its use in Bakhtin's writings (see, for example, Bakhtin 1986) to focus specifically upon subject positions associated with particular genres or discourses. For other uses of the terms see Mishler (1984) and Thibault (1991).

4   An examination of collocation of *killer* + lexical item in three million words of computerized corpus data available at Lancaster University (the

Lancaster–Oslo–Bergen corpus, the Brown corpus and the Associated Press corpus) seems to bear this out, though the numbers are surprisingly small with only seven collocations in all. There are two instances of *killer dust,* one each of *killer earthquake, killer hurricane, killer rabbit* and *killer sub.* All of these involve the notion of that whose nature or function is to kill. There is also one instance of *killer instinct.* I am grateful to Geoffrey Leech for supplying me with these data.

5   Kreisky's last turn in the original German is: *Ja, also, das geht mir nichts an. Ich will damit nichts zu tun haben. Ah, das ist alles sehr unerfreulich, und ich will damit nichts zu tun haben.* The shift in genre and voice to a petulant emotional outburst seems to be there in the original (notice sentence initial *Ah,* and the repetition of *ich will damit nichts zu tun haben.* The full German text appears in Wodak *et al.* (1990: Ch. 7). I am grateful to Ruth Wodak for providing me with a copy.

References

Bakhtin, M. (1986) *Speech Genres and Other Late Essays,* Austin: University of Texas Press.

Barthes, R. (1977) 'Introduction to the structural analysis of narratives', *Image, Music, Text,* Selected and trans., Heath, S., London: Fontana.

Billig, M. (1990) 'Stacking the cards of ideology: the history of the *Sun Souvenir Royal Album*', *Discourse & Society* 1(1): 17–37.

Callinicos, A. (1987) *Making History,* Cambridge: Polity Press.

Chilton, P. (1990) 'Politeness, politics and diplomacy', *Discourse & Society* 1(2): 201–24.

Clark, R., Fairclough, N., Ivanic, R. and Martin-Jones, M. (1990) 'Critical language awareness part 1: a critical review of three current approaches to language awareness', *Language and Education* 4: 249–609.

—— (1991) 'Critical language awareness part 2: towards critical alternatives', *Language and Education* 5: 41–54.

Davis, K. (1988) *Power Under the Microscope: Toward a Grounded Theory of Gender Relations in Medical Encounters,* Dordrecht: Foris.

Downing, J. (1990) 'US media discourse on South Africa: the development of a situation model', *Discourse & Society* 1(1): 39–60.

Fairclough, N. (1989) *Language and Power,* London: Longman.

—— (1990) 'Critical linguistics, "new times", and language education', in R. Clark *et al.* (eds) *Language and Power: Papers from 22 annual Meeting of the British Association of Applied Linguistics,* London: CILT.

—— (1991) *Discourse and Social Change,* Cambridge: Polity Press.

—— (1992) *Critical Language Awareness,* London: Longman.

—— (1994) 'Discoursal and social change: a conflictual view', in Tollefson, J. (ed.) *Language, Power and Inequality*, New York: Cambridge University Press.

Fisher, S. (1991) 'A discourse of the social: medical talk/power talk/oppositional talk?', *Discourse & Society* 2(2): 157–82.

Fowler, R. (1991) *Language in the News*, London: Routledge.

Fowler, R., Hodge, B., Kress, G. and Trew, T. (1979) *Language and Control*, London: Routledge.

Giddens, A. (1984) *The Constitution of Society*, Cambridge: Polity Press.

Givón, T. (1979) *On Understanding Grammar*, New York: Academic Press.

Habermas, J. (1984) *The Theory of Communicative Action. Volume 1: Reason and the Rationalization of Society*, trans. McCarthy, T., London: Heinemann.

Hacker, K., Coste, T. G., Kamm, D. F. and Bybee, C. R. (1991) 'Oppositional readings of network television news: viewer deconstruction', *Discourse & Society* 2(2): 183–202.

Halliday, M. A. K. (1978) *Language as Social Semiotic*, London: Edward Arnold.

Halliday, M. A. K. (1985) *Introduction to Functional Grammar*, London: Edward Arnold.

Halliday, M. A. K. and Hasan, R. (1976) *Cohesion in English*, London: Longman.

Heritage, J. C. and Watson, D. R. (1979) 'Formulations as conversational objects', in Psathas, G. (ed.) *Everyday Language: Studies in Ethnomethodology*, New York: Irvington.

Hodge, B. and Kress, G. (1988) *Social Semiotics*, Cambridge: Polity Press.

Kress, G. and Hodge, B. (1979) *Language as Ideology*, London: Routledge.

Kress, G. and Threadgold, T. (1988) 'Towards a social theory of genre', *Southern Review* 21: 215–43.

Kristeva, J. (1986) 'Word, dialogue and novel', in Moi, T. (ed.) *The Kristeva Reader*, Oxford: Blackwell.

Levinson, S. (1983) *Pragmatics*, Cambridge: Cambridge University Press.

Liebes, T. and Ribak, R. (1991) 'A mother's battle against TV news: a case study of political socialization', *Discourse & Society* 2(2): 203–22.

Maingueneau, D. (1987) *Nouvelles tendances en analyse du discours*, Paris: Hachette.

Mehan, H., Nathanson, C. and Skelly, J. (1990) 'Nuclear discourse in the 1980s: the unravelling conventions of the cold war', *Discourse & Society* 1(2): 134–65.

Michael, M. (1991) 'Discourse of danger and dangerous discourses: patrolling the borders of science, nature and society', *Discourse & Society* 2(1): 5–28.

Mishler, E. (1984) *The Discourse of Medicine: Dialectics of Medical Interviews*, Norwood, NJ: Ablex.

Seidel, G. (1990) ' "Thank God I said no to Aids": on the changing discourse of Aids in Uganda', *Discourse & Society* 1(1): 61–84.

Selden, R. (1991) 'The rhetoric of enterprise', in Keat, R. and Abercrombie, N. (eds) *Enterprise Culture*, London: Routledge.

Sorensen, J. (1991) 'Mass media and discourse of famine in the Horn of Africa', *Discourse & Society* 2(2): 223–42.

Taylor, C. (1986) 'Foucault on discourse and truth', in Hoy, D. C. (ed.) *Foucault: A Critical Reader*, Oxford: Blackwell.

Thibault, P. (1991) *Social Semiotics as Praxis*, Minneapolis: University of Minnesota Press.

Thompson, J. (1984) *Studies in the Theory of Ideology*, Cambridge: Polity Press.

Thompson, J. (1990) *Ideology and Modern Culture*, Cambridge: Polity Press.

Ullah, P. (1990) 'Rhetoric and ideology in social identification: the case of second generation Irish youths', *Discourse & Society* 1(2): 167–88.

Van Dijk, T. (1988) *News as Discourse*, Hillsdale, NJ: Erlbaum.

Van Dijk, T. (1990) '*Discourse & Society*: a new journal for a new research focus', *Discourse & Society* 1(1): 5–16.

WAUDAG (1990) 'The rhetorical construction of a president', *Discourse & Society* 1(2): 189–200.

West, C. (1990) 'Not just "doctor's orders": directive-response sequences in patients' visits to women and men physicians', *Discourse & Society* 1(1): 83–112.

Wodak, R. (1991) 'Turning the tables: anti-semitic discourse in post-war Austria', *Discourse & Society* 2(1): 65–83.

Wodak, R., et al. (1990) '*Wir Sind Alle Unschuldige Tater*', *Diskurshistorische Studien zum Nachkriegsantisemitismus*, Frankfurt-am-Main: Suhrkamp.

Yankah, K. (1991) 'Oratory in Akan society', *Discourse & Society* 2(1): 47–64.

Sequence and structure

Editors' Introduction to Part Three

W E H A V E S E E N T H A T sequence and structure are the focal concerns of conversation analysis (CA). Many other approaches to discourse emphasise how texts and discourses are organised as patterned entities. To some extent this reflects the long-standing concerns of linguistics with matters of composition and structure, but there are more important reasons which we have come across in previous Parts. If, as Bakhtin suggests, we need to see language in use as organised into various generic types, and, more generally, if discourses (in Fairclough's definition) are organised sets of ideological meanings and values, then discovering patterns in discourse is a primary objective. The patterning of discourse is in fact the construction of social structures and ideologies. In CA terms, the sorts of structuring that interactants submit to and reproduce in their talk form a core dimension of social structure and of what Giddens (cf. Chapter 24) has called 'structuration' (see also Schegloff, Chapter 6). Therefore, as we have said before, there is a direct link between conversational production of the interaction order and production of the social order. Here we see one of the main ways in which discourse analysis is able to use micro-level (linguistic, textual, intertextual) commentary to explain macro-level (societal, cultural, ideological) processes. (Papers collected in Coupland *et al.* 1999 treat this question in more depth; it is briefly discussed by Cameron *et al.*, Chapter 8)

In Labov and Waletzky's (1967) structural analysis of the stories told by street-gang youngsters, summarised in William Labov's single-authored paper (Chapter 12), we are introduced to some core concepts for the analysis of narrative which have been used productively in many other social settings. As another case study, Bell's analysis of newspaper 'stories' in Chapter 13, builds directly on Labov's narrative categories. Labov's structural analysis is in itself very valuable. But it is worth emphasising the title of Labov's text – the 'transformation of experience in narrative'. Labov shows how the structuring of the narrative genre not only recounts but refashions experience. This is most apparent in the 'evaluation' component of narrative – the means by which a narrator explains the purpose and 'so what' of a story. Stories, for example among young street-gang members, function to establish social status for the narrator–protagonist, in both dimensions of context – the story context and the story-telling context. This is why we find features in narratives that Labov calls 'intensifiers'. These include non-verbal gestures, expressive phonology and repetition. Similarly, 'comparators' compare events which did occur with those that did not; 'correlatives' combine events into single accounts; 'explicatives' explain complications inherent in the narrative for listeners. These are sets of syntactic and pragmatic devices that Labov considers in the source article (not included in the excerpted text). They are some of the means by which experience, in the telling of it, is transformed and, in the spoken stories of street-gang members that Labov describes, animated and performed.

The mass media are the primary contemporary means of disseminating accounts of events and reactions, and in journalistic news reports 'story-telling' takes on new characteristics and emphases. Allan Bell's analyses of two newspaper stories in Chapter 13 shows that Labov's structural model is an extremely robust general framework. But 'evaluation' relates here to 'newsworthiness' and the marketability of the news media (reflected in newspaper sales or radio news listening statistics). Bell explains the technical systems by which news stories are produced and the editorial processes they are subject to, and how these factors result in modified story forms. The sequencing of events in news stories, for example, is often complex and not fully resolved. Teun van Dijk's research is another key resource for the analysis of media discourse (e.g., van Dijk 1985; 1988; his research on racist discourse is exemplified in Chapter 32); see also Young, Chapter 25; Caldas-Coulthard, Chapter 31).

Harvey Sacks's essay, Chapter 14, may on first reading seem an unusual choice for this Part of the *Reader*. At one level, it is concerned with the truth of the statement in its title, 'Everyone has to lie'. This might not appear to be a matter of discourse structure in any sense. But Sacks works towards his theme of 'lying' through an ethnomethodologist's concern with how we contextualise statements and how we incorporate knowledge into talk. As he says, the claim that 'everyone has to lie' may look like 'a thing one could monitor the world with' (p. 253). But he argues we need to examine the claim in relation to how statements like this one are used by people in everyday talk, and how they are contextualised. By this standard, Sacks demonstrates that some forms of 'lying' are not only conventional practices but practices written into the rules of social interaction. And this is the connection with discourse structure and social structure.

The specific interactional moment Sacks analyses is the 'How are you?' exchange in conversational greetings. In a closely argued analysis of (mainly hypothetical) cases, Sacks shows that people responding to a 'How are you?' enquiry must make judgements about the fitness of their addressee to deal with accounts of personal troubles that will predictably follow on from an answer like 'Lousy!'. The element of lying lies in the speaker's strategic response to 'How are you?' (which is often other than true), in anticipation of the consequences of his or her own response to the question. (More recent studies of the 'How are you?' exchange include Coupland and Coupland 1992 and Coupland, Robinson and Coupland 1994. See also J. Coupland 1999.)

So the key concept in Sacks's text is 'regulation', not only the sequencing rules for conversational greetings but the monitoring and regulating of what can be said in conversation, relative to predictable social outcomes with specific groups of people. Sacks's essay is in fact a brilliant exposition of why CA has invested so heavily in matters of sequence and structure. The version we have printed is heavily edited, and even if the remaining text is dense and in places highly abstract – reminiscent of a logician's syllogistic argument – it is far less so than the original! It is tempting to see a wilful and even playful formalism in Sacks's own lecturing style (remembering that this text is a transcript of Sacks's original lecture notes). The result is an intriguing admixture of mundane data from everyday talk and multiply embedded syntax and arcane expression. In fact, it would lend itself to a Faircloughian analysis of intertextuality (see Chapter 11). One line of inter-pretation might be that Sacks is parodying serious and self-aware academic styles of argument, while generating highly original and perceptive insights. Meaning, says Sacks, turns on the utterance and the occasion of its use. This clearly foreshadows Schegloff's stance, as expressed in Chapter 6. It shows a radical commitment to understanding language as locally produced. Questions, including research questions, can only be addressed once we know the contexts which make their asking relevant. There is a profound relativity in Sacks's assumptions about meaning – the ethnomethodologists' relativism discussed by Cameron *et al.* (Chapter 8)

'Opening up closings', by Emanuel Schegloff and Harvey Sacks (Chapter 15), is one of the truly classic papers in CA. We can read it for its richly detailed insights into the structural arrangements speakers deploy in closing conversations. But it is probably more important to read it as an agenda-setting statement for the discipline of CA and an outline of its principles and methodological priorities. To this extent it follows on directly from the Sacks chapter and confirms many of its central points. Schegloff and Sacks are very explicit, early in the chapter, about the 'technical' nature of CA, and this term resurfaces at several points. They refer to CA as striving to be 'a naturalistic observational discipline' able to 'deal with the details of social action(s) rigorously, empirically and formally' (p. 263). We can make sense of these claims when we see the emphasis CA places on 'actual data' and when we remember the interpretive restrictions that Schegloff argued (in Chapter 6, which is in fact a later development of ideas that are expressed in this chapter) should apply in how analysts use contextual information. There is certainly a sort of 'formality' in CA and certainly its transcribing conventions (see Chapter 9) suggests a particular form of rigour in the representation of data. At the same time, terms like 'formal' and 'empirical' run counter to the priorities, linguists and philosophers have brought to the study of discourse – as evidenced in Part One of the *Reader*. For them, discourse deals in function not form, and reaches out to social context to build its analyses rather than ruling some aspects of social context out of bounds. This is why there are enduring tensions between CA and DA, despite their many shared ambitions and insights. There is an irony in sociologists (in the name of CA) striving for naturalism and empiricism in their dealings with discourse, while linguists are very largely striving to shake off the formalism and empiricism of early versions of linguistics. (These issues are debated in more detail in Coupland and Jaworski 1997.)

In Deborah Schiffrin's work we see how CA's passion for analysing structure can usefully be developed into close analysis of individual discourse particles – in the case Schiffrin considers in Chapter 16 the particle *oh*. It is through discourse analysis that many of linguistic features excluded from most traditional accounts of sentence structure and meaning come to prominence. As Schiffrin says, it is difficult to attribute much semantic or grammatical meaning to *oh*, yet it makes an important regular contribution to discourse structure – particularly through marking how listeners receive new and newly salient information from speakers, and how this changes their knowledge states. The initial motivation for using *oh* is therefore primarily a cognitive one. To put it another way, *oh* is the linguistic reflex of cognitive realignment. We may well be able to experience cognitive realignment to information without any audible marking. But the fact of marking these realignments, in all of the many sub-contexts Schiffrin illustrates, does conversational work in the relational dimension too. *Oh* can mark a speaker's occupancy of a 'listener' or 'supportive listener' role. It can signal that a consensus of understanding has been achieved, at a particular moment in talk. Alternatively, it can signal disjunction and a listener's surprise at not sharing a point of view or a knowledge state.

So the general view of discourse functioning that Schiffrin's analysis gives us is the same multi-functional one we saw in many of the introductory chapters in Part One. Talk realises and fulfils multiple communicative goals and functions simultaneously – ideational (or information related), relational (or interpersonal) and identity related. It does these simultaneously and in a multi-layered fashion. In Schiffrin's study of *oh* we can see how ideational structures in discourse also, and in themselves, function at the level of social relationships.

References

Coupland, J. (ed.) (1999) *Small Talk*, London: A W Longman.

Coupland, J. and Coupland, N. (1992) ' "How are you?": negotiating phatic communion', *Language in Society* 21: 207–30.

Coupland, J., Robinson, J. D. and Coupland, N. (1994) 'Frame negotiation in doctor–elderly patient consultations', *Discourse & Society* 5/1: 89–124.

Coupland, N. and Jaworski, A. (1997) 'Relevance, accommodation and conversation: modelling the social dimension of communication', *Multilingua* 16: 233–58.

Coupland, N., Sarangi, S. and Candlin, C. (eds) (1999) *Sociolinguistics and Social Theory*, London: A W Longman.

Labov, W. and Waletzky, J. (1967) 'Narrative analysis: oral versions of personal experience', in Helm, J. (ed.), *Essays on the Verbal and Visual Arts: Proceedings and the 1966 Annual Spring Meeting of the American Ethnological Society*, Seattle: University of Washington Press, 12–44. (Reprinted in *Journal of Narrative and Life History* 7/1–4. Special issue: *Oral Versions of Personal Experience: Three Decades of Narrative Analysis*, Bamberg, M. G. W. (ed.), 3–38.)

Van Dijk, T. (ed.) (1985) *Handbook of Discourse Analysis*, 4 vols, New York: Academic Press.
—— (1988) *News Analysis: Case Studies of International and National News in the Press*, Hillsdale, NJ.: Lawrence Erlbaum.

Chapter 12

William Labov

THE TRANSFORMATION OF EXPERIENCE IN NARRATIVE

[. . .]

In a previous study we have presented a general framework for the analysis of narrative which shows how verbal skills are used to evaluate experience (Labov and Waletzky 1967). In this chapter we examine the narratives we obtained in our study of south-central Harlem from preadolescents (9 to 13 years old), adolescents (14 to 19), and adults to see what linguistic techniques are used to evaluate experience within the black English [BE] vernacular culture [. . .]

It will be helpful for the reader to be acquainted with the general character and impact of narratives in black vernacular style. We will cite here in full three fight narratives from leaders of vernacular peer groups in south-central Harlem who are widely recognized for their verbal skills and refer to these throughout the discussion to illustrate the structural feature of narrative. The first is by Boot.[1]

Extract 1
(Something Calvin did that was really wild?)
Yeah.
a   It was on a Sunday
b   and we didn't have nothin' to do after I — after we
        came from church.

Source: William Labov, *Language in the Inner City: Studies in the Black English Vernacular*, Philadelphia: University of Pennsylvania Press and Oxford: Blackwell.

c   Then we ain't had nothin' to do.
d   So I say, "Calvin, let's go get our – out our dirty clothes
        on
        and play in the dirt."
e   And so Calvin say, "Let's have a rock – a rock war."
f   And I say, "All right."
g   So Calvin had a rock.
h   And we as – you know, here go a wall
i   and a far away here go a wall.
j   Calvin th'ew a rock.
k   I was lookin' and – uh –
l   And Calvin th'ew a rock.
m   It oh – it almost hit me
n   And so I looked down to get another rock;
o   Say "Ssh!"
p   An' it pass me.
q   I say, "Calvin, I'm bust your head for that!"
r   Calvin stuck his head out.
s   I th'ew the rock
t   An' the rock went up,
u   I mean – went up –
v   came down
w   an' say [slap!]
x   an' smacked him in the head
y   an' his head busted.

The second narrative is by Larry H., a core member of the Jets gang. This is one of three fight stories told by Larry which match in verbal skill his outstanding performance in argument, ritual insults, and other speech events of the black vernacular culture.

Extract 2
a   An' then, three weeks ago I had a fight with this
        other dude outside
b   He got mad
        'cause I wouldn't give him a cigarette.
c   Ain't that a bitch?
        (Oh yeah?)
d   Yeah, you know, I was sittin' on the corner an' shit,
        smokin' my cigarette, you know
e   I was high, an' shit.

f	He walked over to me,
g	"Can I have a cigarette?"
h	He was a little taller than me,
	but not that much.
i	I said, "I ain't got no more, man,"
j	'cause, you know, all I had was one left.
k	An' I ain't gon' give up my last cigarette unless I got some more.
l	So I said, "I don't have no more, man."
m	So he, you know, dug on the pack,
	'cause the pack was in my pocket.
n	So he said, "Eh man, I can't get a cigarette, man?
o	I mean – I mean we supposed to be brothers, an' shit,"
p	So I say, "Yeah, well, you know, man, all I got is one, you dig it?"
q	An' I won't give up my las' one to nobody.
r	So you know, the dude, he looks at me,
s	An' he – I 'on' know –
	he jus' thought he gon' rough that
	motherfucker up.
t	He said, "I can't get a cigarette."
u	I said, "Tha's what I said, my man".
v	You know, so he said, "What you supposed to be *bad*, an' shit?
w	What, you think you *bad* an' shit?"
x	So I said, "Look here, my man,
y	I don't think I'm bad, you understand?
z	But I mean, you know, if I had it,
	you could git it
aa	I like to see you with it, you dig it?
bb	But the sad part about it,
cc	You got to do without it.
dd	That's all, my man."
ee	So the dude, he 'on' to pushin' me, man.
	(Oh he pushed you?)
ff	An' why he do that?
gg	*Everytime somebody fuck with me,*
	why they do it?
hh	I put that cigarette down,
ii	An' boy, let me tell you,
	I beat the shit outa that motherfucker.

jj   I tried to *kill* 'im – over one cigarette"

kk   I tried to *kill* 'im. Square business!

ll   After I got through stompin' him in the face, man,

mm   You know, all of a sudden I went crazy!

nn   I jus' went crazy.

oo   An' I jus' wouldn't stop hittin the motherfucker.

pp   Dig it, I couldn't stop hittin' 'im, man,
      till the teacher pulled me off o' him.

qq   An' guess what? After all that I gave the dude the cigarette,
      after all that.

rr   Ain't that a bitch?
      (How come you gave 'im a cigarette?)

ss   I 'on' know.

tt   I jus' gave it to him.

uu   An' he smoked it, too!

Among the young adults we interviewed in our preliminary exploration of south-central Harlem, John L. struck us immediately as a gifted story teller; the following is one of many narratives that have been highly regarded by many listeners.

Extract 3

(What was the most important fight that you remember, one that sticks in your mind . . .)

a   Well, one (I think) was with a girl.

b   Like I was a kid, you know,

c   And she was the baddest girl, *the baddest girl in
      the neighborhood.*

d   If you didn't bring her candy to school,
      she would punch you in the mouth;

e   And you had to kiss her
      when she'd tell you.

f   This girl was only about 12 years old, man,

g   but she was a killer.

h   She didn't take no junk;

i   She whupped all her brothers.

j   And I came to school one day

k   and I didn't have no money.

l   My ma wouldn't give me no money.

m   And I played hookies one day,

n   (She) put something on me.[2]

o   I played hookies, man,

p   so I said, you know, I'm not gonna play hookies no
        more
        'cause I don't wanna get a whupping

q   So I go to school

r   and this girl says, "Where's the candy?"

s   I said, "I don't have it."

t   She says, powww!

u   So I says to myself, "There's gonna be times
        my mother won't give me money
        because (we're) a poor family

v   And I can't take this all, you know, every time she
        don't give me any money."

w   So I say, "Well, I just gotta fight this girl.

x   She gonna hafta whup me.

y   I hope she don't whup me."

z   And I hit the girl: powwww!

aa   and I put something on it.

bb   I win the fight.

cc   That was one of the most important.

This discussion will first review briefly the general definition of narrative and its overall structure. [. . .] The main body of narratives cited are from our work in south-central Harlem, but references will be made to materials drawn from other urban and rural areas, from both white and black subjects.

Definition of narrative

We define narrative as one method of recapitulating past experience by matching a verbal sequence of clauses to the sequence of events which (it is inferred) actually occurred. For example, a pre-adolescent narrative:

Extract 4
a This boy punched me
b and I punched him
c and the teacher came in
d and stopped the fight.

An adult narrative:

Extract 5
a Well this person had a little too much to drink
b and he attacked me
c and the friend came in
d and she stopped it.

In each case we have four independent clauses which match the order of the inferred events. It is important to note that other means of recapitulating these experiences are available which do not follow the same sequence; syntactic embedding can be used:

Extract 6
a A friend of mine came in just
   in time to stop
   this person who had a little too much to drink
   from attacking me.

Or else the past perfect can be used to reverse the order:

Extract 7
a The teacher stopped the fight.
b She had just come in.
c I had punched this boy.
d He had punched me.

Narrative, then, is only one way of recapitulating this past experience: the clauses are characteristically ordered in temporal sequence; if narrative clauses are reversed, the inferred temporal sequence of the original semantic interpretation is altered: *I punched this boy/ and he punched me* instead of *This boy punched me/ and I punched him.*

With this conception of narrative, we can define a *minimal narrative* as a sequence of two clauses which are *temporally ordered*: that is, a change in their order will result in a change in the temporal sequence of the original semantic interpretation. In alternative terminology, there is temporal juncture between the two clauses, and a minimal narrative is defined as one containing a single temporal juncture.

The skeleton of a narrative then consists of a series of temporally ordered clauses which we may call *narrative clauses*. A narrative such as 4 or 5 consists entirely of narrative clauses. Here is a minimal narrative which contains only two:

Extract 8
a   I know a boy named Harry.
b   Another boy threw a bottle at him right in the head
c   and he had to get seven stitches.

This narrative contains three clauses, but only two are narrative clauses. The first has no temporal juncture, and might be placed after *b* or after *c* without disturbing temporal order. It is equally true at the end and at the beginning that the narrator knows a boy named Harry. Clause *a* may be called a *free clause* since it is not confined by any temporal juncture. [. . .]

It is only independent clauses which can function as narrative clauses – and as we will see below, only particular kinds of independent clauses. In the representation of narratives in this section, we will list each clause on a separate line, but letter only the independent clauses. [. . .]

The overall structure of narrative

Some narratives, like 4, contain only narrative clauses; they are complete in the sense that they have a beginning, a middle, and an end. But there are other elements of narrative structure found in more fully developed types. Briefly, a fully-formed narrative may show the following:

Extract 9
1   Abstract.
2   Orientation.
3   Complicating action.
4   Evaluation.
5   Result or resolution.
6   Coda.

Of course there are complex chainings and embeddings of these elements, but here we are dealing with the simpler forms. Complicating action has been characterized above, and the result may be regarded for the moment as the termination of that series of events. We will consider briefly the nature and function of the abstract, orientation, coda, and evaluation.

The abstract

It is not uncommon for narrators to begin with one or two clauses summarizing the whole story.

Extract 10

(Were you ever in a situation where you thought you were in
   serious danger of being killed?)
I talked a man out of – Old Doc Simon I talked him out of pulling
   the trigger.

When this story is heard, it can be seen that the abstract does encapsulate
the point of the story. In 11 there is a sequence of two such abstracts.

Extract 11

(Were you ever in a situation where you were in serious danger
   of being killed?)
a My brother put a knife in my head.
   (How'd that happen?)
b Like kids, you get into a fight
c and I twisted his arm up behind him.
d This was just a few days after my father died . . .

Here the speaker gives one abstract and follows it with another after the
interviewer's question. Then without further prompting, he begins the narrative proper. The narrative might just as well have begun with the free clause
d; b and *c* in this sense are not absolutely required, since they cover the same
ground as the narrative as a whole. Larry's narrative (see Extract 2) is the
third of a series of three, and there is no question just before the narrative
itself, but there is a well-formed abstract:

a An' then, three weeks ago I had a fight with this other
      dude outside.
b He got mad
      'cause I wouldn't give him a cigarette.
c Ain't that a bitch?

Larry does not give the abstract in *place* of the story; he has no intention of
stopping there, but goes on to give the full account.
   What then is the function of the abstract? It is not an advertisement or
a warning: the narrator does not wait for the listener to say, "I've heard
about that," or "Don't tell me that now." If the abstract covers the same
ground as the story, what does it add? We will consider this problem further
in discussing the evaluation section below.

Orientation

At the outset, it is necessary to identify in some way the time, place, persons, and their activity or the situation. This can be done in the course of the first several narrative clauses, but more commonly there is an orientation section composed of free clauses. In Boot's narrative (Extract 1), clause *a* sets the time (*Sunday*); clause *b* the persons (*we*), the situation (*nothin' to do*) and further specification of the time (*after we come from church*); the first narrative clause follows. In Larry's narrative (Extract 2), some information is already available in the abstract (the time – *three weeks ago*; the place – *outside of school*); and the persons – *this other dude and Larry*). The orientation section then begins with a detailed picture of the situation – *Larry sittin' on the corner, high*.

Many of John L.'s narratives begin with an elaborate portrait of the main character – in this case, clauses *a–i* are all devoted to *the baddest girl in the neighborhood*, and the first narrative clause brings John L. and the girl face to face in the schoolyard.

The orientation section has some interesting syntactic properties; it is quite common to find a great many past progressive clauses in the orientation section – sketching the kind of thing that was going on before the first event of the narrative occurred or during the entire episode. But the most interesting thing about orientation is its *placement*. It is theoretically possible for all free orientation clauses to be placed at the beginning of the narrative, but in practice, we find much of this material is placed at strategic points later on, for reasons to be examined below.

The Coda

There are also free clauses to be found at the ends of narratives; for example, John L.'s narrative ends:

cc. That was one of the most important

This clause forms the *coda*. It is one of the many options open to the narrator for signalling that the narrative is finished. We find many similar forms.

Extract 12
And that was that.
Extract 13
And that – that was it, you know.

Codas may also contain general observations or show the effects of the events of the narrator. At the end of one fight narrative, we have

Extract 14
I was given the rest of the day off.
  And ever since then I haven't seen the guy
    'cause I quit.
    I quit, you know.
  No more problems.

Some codas which strike us as particularly skillful are strangely disconnected from the main narrative. One New Jersey woman told a story about how, as a little girl, she thought she was drowning, until a man came along and stood her on her feet – the water was only four-feet deep.

Extract 15
And you know that man who picked me out of the water?
He's a detective in Union City
And I see him every now and again.

These codas (14, 15) have the property of bridging the gap between the moment of time at the end of the narrative proper and the present. They bring the narrator and the listener back to the point at which they entered the narrative. There are many ways of doing this: in 15, the other main actor is brought up to the present: in 14, the narrator. But there is a more general function of codas which subsumes both the examples of 14, 15 and the simpler forms of 12, 13. Codas close off the sequence of complicating actions and indicate that none of the events that followed were important to the narrative. A chain of actions may be thought of as successive answers to the question "Then what happened?"; "And then what happened?" After a coda such as *That was that*, the question "Then what happened?" is properly answered, "Nothing; I just told you what happened." It is even more obvious after the more complex codas of 14 and 15; the time reference of the discourse has been reshifted to the present, so that "what happened then?" can only be interpreted as a question about the present; the answer is "Nothing; here I am." Thus the "Disjunctive" codas of 14 and 15 forestall further questions about the narrative itself: the narrative events are pushed away and sealed off.[3]

Evaluation

Beginnings, middles, and ends of narratives have been analyzed in many accounts of folklore or narrative. But there is one important aspect of narrative which has not been discussed – perhaps the most important element in addition to the basic narrative clause. That is what we term the *evaluation* of the narrative: the means used by the narrator to indicate the point of the narrative, its *raison d'être*: why it was told, and what the narrator is getting at. There are many ways to tell the same story, to make very different points, or to make no point at all. Pointless stories are met (in English) with the withering rejoinder, "So what?" Every good narrator is continually warding off this question; when his narrative is over, it should be unthinkable for a bystander to say, "So what?" Instead, the appropriate remark would be, "He did?" or similar means of registering the reportable character of the events of the narrative.

The difference between evaluated and unevaluated narrative appears most clearly when we examine narrative of vicarious experience. In our first series of interviews with preadolescents in south-central Harlem, we asked for accounts of favorite television programs; the most popular at the time was "The Man from U.N.C.L.E."

Extract 16
a   This kid – Napoleon got shot
b   and he had to go on a mission,
c   And so this kid, he went with Solo.
d   So they went
e   And this guy – they went through the window,
f   and they caught him.
g   And then he beat up them other people.
h   And they went
i   and then he said
    that this old lady was his mother
j   and then he – and at the end he say
    that he was the guy's friend.

This is typical of many such narratives of vicarious experience that we collected. We begin in the middle of things without any orientation section; pronominal reference in many ways ambiguous and obscure throughout. But the meaningless and disorientated effect of 16 has deeper roots. None of the remarkable events that occur *is evaluated*. We may compare 16 with a narrative of personal experience told by Norris W., eleven years old:

Extract 17
a   When I was in fourth grade –
    no, it was in third grade –
b   This boy he stole my glove.
c   He took my glove

d and said that his father found it downtown on the
   ground
   (And you fight him?)
e I told him that it was impossible for him to find
   downtown
      'cause all those people were walking by
      and just the father was the only one
      that found it?
f So he got all (mad).
g Then I fought him.
h I knocked him all out in the street.
i So he say he give.
j and I kept on hitting him.
k Then he started crying
l and ran home to his father.
m And the father told him
n that he ain't find no glove.

This narrative is diametrically opposed to 16 in its degree of evaluation. Every line and almost every element of the syntax contributes to the point, and that point is self-aggrandizement. Each element of the narrative is designed to make Norris look good and "this boy" look bad. Norris knew that this boy stole his glove – had the nerve to just walk off with it and then make up a big story to claim that it was his. Norris didn't lose his cool and started swinging; first he destroyed this boy's fabrication by logic, so that everyone could see how phony the kid was. Then this boy lost his head and got mad and started fighting. Norris beat him up, and was so outraged at the phony way he had acted that he didn't stop when the kid surrendered – he "went crazy" and kept on hitting him. Then this punk started crying, and ran home to his father like a baby. Then his father – his *very own father* told him that his story wasn't true.

Norris's story follows the characteristic two-part structure of fight narratives in the BE vernacular; each part shows a different side of his ideal character. In the account of the verbal exchange that led up to the fight, Norris is cool, logical, good with his mouth, and strong in insisting on his own right. In the second part, dealing with the action, he appears as the most dangerous kind of fighter, who "just goes crazy" and "doesn't know what he did." On the other hand, his opponent is shown as dishonest, clumsy in argument, unable to control his temper, a punk, a lame, and a coward. Though Norris does not display the same degree of verbal skill that Larry shows in 2, there is an exact point-by-point match in the structure and evaluative features of the two narratives. No one listening to Norris's story within the framework of the vernacular value system will say "So what?" The narrative makes its point and effectively bars this question.

If we were to look for an evaluation section in 17 concentrating upon clause ordering as in Labov and Waletzky (1967), we would have to point to *d–e*, in which the action is suspended while elaborate arguments are developed. This is indeed the major point of the argument, as shown again in the dramatic coda *m–n*. But it would be a mistake to limit the evaluation of 17 to *d–e*,

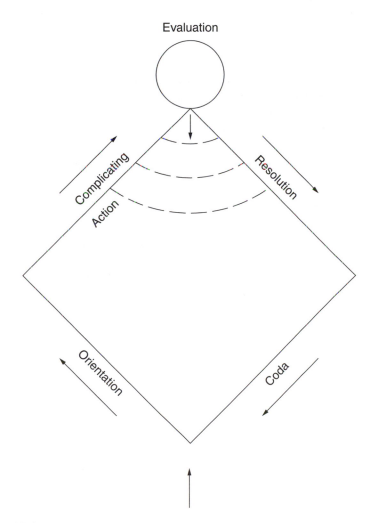

Figure 12.1 Narrative structure

since evaluative devices are distributed throughout the narrative. We must therefore modify the scheme of Labov and Waletzky (1967) by indicating E as the focus of waves of evaluation that penetrate the narrative as in Figure 12.1.

A complete narrative begins with an orientation, proceeds to the complicating action, is suspended at the focus of evaluation before the resolution, concludes with the resolution, and returns the listener to the present time with the coda. The evaluation of the narrative forms a secondary structure which is concentrated in the evaluation section but may be found in various forms throughout the narrative. [. . .]

We can also look at narrative as a series of answers to underlying questions:

a Abstract: what was this about?
b Orientation: who, when, what, where?
c Complicating action: then what happened?
d Evaluation: so what?
e Result: what finally happened?

Only c, the complicating action, is essential if we are to recognize a narrative, as pointed out above. The abstract, the orientation, the resolution, and the evaluation answer questions which relate to the function of effective narrative: the first three to clarify referential functions, the last to answer the functional question d – why the story was told in the first place. But the reference of the abstract is broader than the orientation and complicating action: it includes these and the evaluation so that the abstract not only states what the narrative is about, but why it was told. The coda is not given in answer to any of these five questions, and it is accordingly found less frequently than any other element of the narrative. The coda *puts off* a question – it signals that questions c and d are no longer relevant.

[. . .]

Notes

1   Remarks in parentheses are by the interviewer. The initial questions asked by the interviewer are also given to help clarify the evaluative focus of the narrative.
2   To *put something on someone* means to 'hit him hard'. See also aa, *I put something on it* 'I hit hard'.
3   The coda can thus be seen as one means of solving the problem of indicating the end of a "turn" at speaking. As Harvey Sacks has pointed out,

a sentence is an optimal unit for the utterance, in that the listener's syntactic competence is employed in a double sense – to let him know when the sentence is complete and also when it is his turn to talk. Narratives require other means for the narrator to signal the fact that he is beginning a long series of sentences which will form one "turn" and to mark the end of that sequence. Many of the devices we have been discussing here are best understood in terms of how the speaker and the listener let each other know whose turn it is to talk. Traditional folk tales and fairy tales have fixed formulas which do this at the beginning and the end, but these are not available for personal narratives. It can also be said that a good coda provides more than a mechanical solution for the sequencing problem: it leaves the listener with a feeling of satisfaction and completeness that matters have been rounded off and accounted for.

Reference

Labov, W. and Waletzky, J. (1967) 'Narrative analysis' in *Essays on the Verbal and Visual Arts*, Helm, J. (ed.), Seattle: University of Washington Press, 12–44.

Chapter 13

Allan Bell

NEWS STORIES AS NARRATIVES

JOURNALISTS DO NOT WRITE ARTICLES. They write stories. A story has structure, direction, point, viewpoint. An article may lack these. Stories come in many kinds and are known in all cultures of the world. They include fairy tales, fables, parables, gospels, legends, epics and sagas. Stories are embedded in all sorts of language use, from face-to-face conversation to public addresses. The role of the storyteller is a significant one both in language behaviour and in society at large. Much of humanity's most important experience has been embodied in stories.

Journalists are professional storytellers of our age. The fairy tale starts: 'Once upon a time.' The news story begins: 'Fifteen people were injured today when a bus plunged . . .' The journalist's work is focused on the getting and writing of stories. This is reflected in the snatches of phrases in which newsroom business is conducted. A good journalist 'gets good stories' or 'knows a good story'. A critical news editor asks: 'Is this really a story?' 'Where's the story in this?'

[. . .]

News stories and personal narratives

As a first approach to the nature of the news story, I will compare news with another kind of story which has been researched in recent decades:

Source: Allan Bell, *The Language of News Media*, Oxford: Blackwell, 1991.

narratives of personal experience told in face-to-face conversation. The similarities and differences between these two kinds of stories will illuminate what news has in common with other storytelling, and where it differs. Labov and Waletzky (1967) and Labov [Chapter 12] have analysed the structure of such narratives into six elements:

1   The abstract summarizes the central action and main point of the narrative. A storyteller uses it at the outset to pre-empt the questions, what is this about, why is this story being told?
2   The orientation sets the scene; the who, when, where, and initial situation or activity of the story.
3   The complicating action is the central part of the story proper answering the question, what happened (then)?
4   The evaluation addresses the question, so what? A directionless sequence of clauses is not a narrative. Narrative has point, and it is narrators' prime intention to justify the value of the story they are telling, to demonstrate why these events are reportable.
5   The resolution is what finally happened to conclude the sequence of events.
6   Finally, many narratives end with a coda – 'and that was that.' This wraps up the action, and returns the conversation from the time of the narrative to the present.

These six elements occur in the above order, although evaluation can be dispersed throughout the other elements. Only the complicating action, and some degree of evaluation, are obligatory components of the personal narrative. To what extent do news stories follow this pattern, and where do they depart from it? [. . .]

The examples I use in this chapter are from the press. Because press stories are generally longer and carry much more detail than broadcast news, the structure of press stories is more complex. A framework which handles press news is likely to be adequate for the text of broadcast stories. Even long broadcast stories such as those carried by Britain's *Channel Four News* or *World at One*, with their multiple inputs, are shorter and less complex than many press stories. The use of the newsmaker's actual voice in broadcast news is in principle no different from direct quotation in printed news. For television news one would require additional apparatus to relate voiceover commentary to the visuals. This is less of a problem than it seems. The Glasgow University Media Group's analysis (see, for instance, 1976: 125) indicates that despite television newsworkers' efforts and beliefs to the contrary, the written text remains paramount and the visual subsidiary. In practice, news pictures are often tangential to the spoken text of a story, because it is impossible for cameras to be regularly in the right place at the right time. There are differences between printed and broadcast news styles, which we will touch on below, but the differences are less than the similarities.

Figure 13.1 displays a hard news story typical of those which appear daily on the international pages of any newspaper. The international news agencies are the chief suppliers of hard news and custodians of its style (as, for example, in Cappon's *Associated Press Guide to Good News Writing* (1982)).

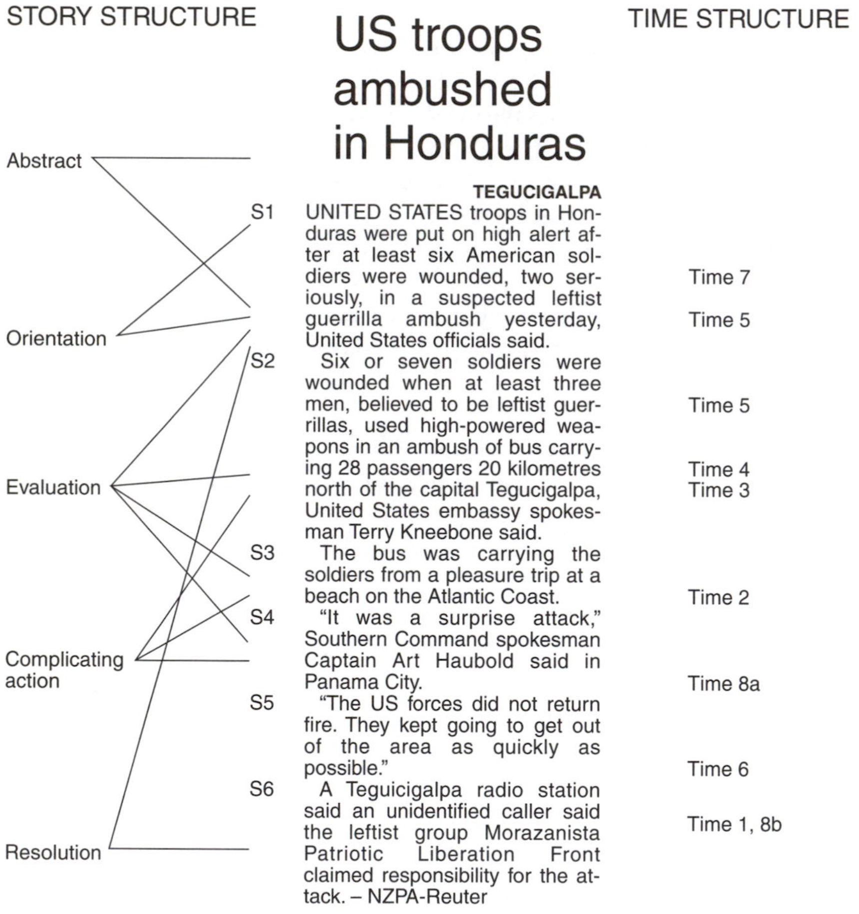

STORY STRUCTURE   US troops ambushed in Honduras   TIME STRUCTURE

Abstract

S1 TEGUCIGALPA
UNITED STATES troops in Honduras were put on high alert after at least six American soldiers were wounded, two seriously, in a suspected leftist guerrilla ambush yesterday, United States officials said.   Time 7

Time 5

Orientation

S2 Six or seven soldiers were wounded when at least three men, believed to be leftist guerrillas, used high-powered weapons in an ambush of bus carrying 28 passengers 20 kilometres north of the capital Tegucigalpa, United States embassy spokesman Terry Kneebone said.   Time 5

Time 4
Time 3

Evaluation

S3 The bus was carrying the soldiers from a pleasure trip at a beach on the Atlantic Coast.   Time 2

S4 "It was a surprise attack," Southern Command spokesman Captain Art Haubold said in Panama City.   Time 8a

Complicating action

S5 "The US forces did not return fire. They kept going to get out of the area as quickly as possible."   Time 6

S6 A Teguicigalpa radio station said an unidentified caller said the leftist group Morazanista Patriotic Liberation Front claimed responsibility for the attack. – NZPA-Reuter   Time 1, 8b

Resolution

Figure 13.1   Narrative structure and time structure of international spot news story

Source: The Dominion, Wellington, 2 April 1990

We can expect such stories to embody the core components of news discourse. Our example story contains some but not all of the elements of the personal narrative, and their order and importance are different.

Abstract

The importance of the lead or first paragraph in establishing the main point of a news story is clear. The lead has precisely the same function in news as the abstract in personal narrative. It summarizes the central action and establishes the point of the story. For major news stories, the lead paragraph is often set off from the remainder of the story in larger type or across several columns of the body copy.

In Figure 13.1, the first paragraph presents two main actions – the wounding of the US soldiers, and the consequent alert for US troops in Honduras. The story has a double abstract, a feature which can also occur in personal narratives. The consequence is treated as the prior point, with the violent incident second. The lead as summary or abstract is obligatory in hard news, where in personal narrative it remains optional. The lead is the device by which copy editor or audience can get the main point of a story from reading a single opening sentence, and on that basis decide whether to continue.

Press news has headlines as well as lead paragraphs. The headline is an abstract of the abstract. The lead pares the story back to its essential point, and the headline abstracts the lead itself. In Figure 13.1 the headline highlights the ambush, even though the lead begins with the consequent military alert. The lead paragraph is the journalist's primary abstract of a story. While to the reader the headline appears as first abstract in the printed story, in fact headlines are absent from broadcast news and even in press news are a last-minute addition. Broadcast news has no headlines, except in so far as stories are summarized at the beginning and/or end of a news bulletin. There are no headlines in news agency copy, from which most published news derives. Nor do journalists put headlines on their own stories: that is the work of subeditors. For journalists and news agencies, stories are identified by the ultimate in abstracts – a one-word catchline or slugline, unique to the story.

Orientation

In personal narrative, orientation sets the scene: who are the actors, where and when did the events take place, what is the initial situation? In news stories, such orientation is obligatory. For journalists *who*, *what*, *when* and *where* are the basic facts which concentrate at the beginning of a story, but may be expanded further down. The lead in Figure 13.1 crams in no less than five sets of people: United States troops in Honduras, the six wounded soldiers, the two seriously wounded, leftist guerrillas and US officials.

International agency stories as received off the wire are 'datelined' at the top for time and place origin, with the deictics *here* and *today* used in the lead paragraph.[1] In this story the time of the ambush is given as *yesterday*. The time of the alert is unspecified (but in fact was also *yesterday* because this was published in the morning paper, and Honduras is some 18 hours behind New Zealand time). The dateline specifies the location from which the journalist 'filed' the story to the news agency. Here as in many newspapers, the dateline is carried below the headline and above the lead. The lead paragraph names Honduras, the second sentence (S2) specifies the exact site of the ambush and identifies the capital city, a necessary detail for news about a country whose geography will not be well known to the readers. Further detail of place is given in S3. In S4 there is a change of country with a regional command spokesperson outside Honduras quoted. This may indicate that the story has been combined by agency copy editors from separate despatches from both Tegucigalpa and Panama City.

Evaluation

Evaluation is the means by which the significance of a story is established. In personal narrative, evaluation is what distinguishes a directionless sequence of sentences from a story with point and meaning. In the case of the fight stories studied by Labov, the point is often the self-aggrandizement of the narrator. Evaluation pre-empts the question, so what? It gives the reason why the narrator is claiming the floor and the audience's attention.

News stories also require evaluation, and in their case its function is identical to that in personal narrative: to establish the significance of what is being told, to focus the events, and to justify claiming the audience's attention. The story in Figure 13.1 stresses repeatedly the importance of what has happened. *High alert*, *at least six* wounded, *two seriously* in the lead paragraph all stake claims on the reader to take these events, quite literally, seriously. The claims continue in the remaining paragraphs, but with diminishing frequency and force: *at least three men*, *high-powered weapons* (S2), *surprise attack* (S4), *as quickly as possible* (S5).

The lead paragraph is a nucleus of evaluation, because the function of the lead is not merely to summarize the main action. The lead focuses the story in a particular direction. It forms the lens through which the remainder of the story is viewed. This function is even more obvious for the headline, especially when it appears to pick up on a minor point of the story. Focusing a story is a prime preoccupation of the journalist. Until a journalist finds what to lead a story with, the story remains unfocused. It is an article but not a story, and may be rejected or rewritten by editors on those grounds. On the other hand, once the journalist decides what the lead is, the rest of the story often falls into place below it. If no good lead can be found, the material may be rejected altogether as a non-story.

In personal narrative, evaluative devices may occur throughout the narrative but are typically concentrated near the end, just before the resolution of the events. In the news story, evaluation focuses in the lead. Its function is to make the contents of the story sound *as X as possible*, where *X* is big, recent, important, unusual, new; in a word – newsworthy. The events and news actors will be given the maximum status for the sake of the story. In the same fashion, narrators of fight stories are at pains to enhance the scale of their adversary – 'the baddest girl in the neighborhood' – and hence the magnitude of their own eventual victory [Labov, Chapter 12].

Action

At the heart of a personal narrative is the sequence of events which occurred. In Labov's analysis, a defining characteristic of narrative as a form is the temporal sequence of its sentences. That is, the action is invariably told in the order in which it happened. News stories, by contrast, are seldom if ever told in chronological order. Even within the lead paragraph of Figure 13.1, result (the military alert) precedes cause (the ambush). Down in the story proper, the time sequence is also reversed. The sequence of events as one of the participants might have told it is:

> About 30 of us went by bus for a day at the beach.
> On the way back we got to 20 kilometres north of Tegucigalpa.
> There some guerrillas ambushed us and shot up the bus with high
>   powered rifles.
> They wounded six or seven of the soldiers.

Figure 13.1 shows the time structure of events in the story. S2 and S3 of the news story run these events in precisely the reverse order to which they happened. The result is placed before the action which caused it. This is a common principle of news writing, that it is not the action or the process which takes priority but the outcome. Indeed, it is this principle which enables news stories to be updated day after day or hour by hour. If there is a new outcome to lead with, the previous action can drop down in the story. Our example shows traces of just such an origin in the dual abstract of its lead paragraph, which reads like an updating story from the international wires. A previous story probably carried news of the ambush, and Figure 13.1 is a follow-up which leads with the more recent information of the military alert.

The time structure of the story is very complex. In S1 the latest occurring event is presented first, followed by its antecedent. S2 and S3 pick up the action at that antecedent point in time and trace it backwards as described above. S4 shifts the story into another setting and timeframe for commentary on what happened, and S5 describes the final action of the main incident, namely the bus's escape from the ambush. The last paragraph moves into a third setting and presents what is in fact temporally the beginning of the events, the group (possibly) responsible for the ambush.

Where chronological order defines the structure of personal narrative, a completely different force is driving the presentation of the news story. Perceived news value overturns temporal sequence and imposes an order completely at odds with the linear narrative point. It moves backwards and forwards in time, picking out different actions on each cycle. In one case, at the start of S2, it even repeats an action – *six or seven soldiers were wounded* – from the previous sentence. This wilful violation of our expectations that narratives usually proceed in temporal succession is distinctive of news stories. It may also have repercussions for how well audiences understand news stories.

Resolution

The personal narrative moves to a resolution: the fight is won, the accident survived. News stories often do not present such clearcut results. When they do, as noted above, the result will be in the lead rather than at the end of the story. In Figure 13.1, the nearest thing to a resolution is the general military alert. But this, of course, is only the latest step in a continuing saga. The news is more like a serial than a short story. The criminal was arrested, but the trial is in the future. The accident occurred, but the victims are still in hospital. One kind of news does follow the chronology of the personal narrative more closely: sports reporting. Sport makes good news just because there is always a result. A sports story will lead in standard news fashion with the result of the game and a few notable incidents, but then settle down to chronological reporting of the course of the game.

News stories are not rounded off. They finish in mid-air. The news story consists of instalments of information of perceived decreasing importance. It is not temporally structured, or turned in a finished fashion. One very good reason for this is that the journalist does not know how much of her story will be retained by copy editors for publication. Stories are regularly cut from the bottom up, which is a great incentive to get what you believe to be the main points in early.

Coda

Nor is there a coda to the news story. The reason lies in the function which the coda performs in personal narrative. It serves as an optional conclusion to the story, to mark its finish, to return the floor to other conversational partners, and to return the tense from narrative time to the present. None of these functions is necessary in the newspaper, where the floor is not open, and where the next contribution is another story. But the coda does have some parallel in broadcast news. The end of a news bulletin or programme – but not of individual news stories – will usually be explicitly signalled by 'that is the end of the news' or a similar formula. Between broadcast stories there is no discourse marker to mark one off from the other, although intonation or (on television) visual means will be used to flag the change of topic.

Our first approach to the structure of news stories indicates interesting similarities and differences to personal narrative. In news, the abstract is obligatory not optional. Orientating and evaluative material occurs in a similar fashion to personal narrative, but tends to concentrate in the first sentence. The central action of the news story is told in non-chronological order, with result presented first followed by a complex recycling through various time zones down through the story. One characteristic which news and personal narrative share is a penchant for direct quotation. The flavour of the eyewitness and colour of direct involvement is important to both forms.

The Honduras example story also points up four features which are typical of news stories but alien to the face-to-face narrative. First, the personal narrative is just that – *personal*. It relates the narrator's own experience, while the news story reports on others' experiences. The reporter has usually not witnessed these, and first person presentation is conventionally excluded from standard news reporting. Second, and consequently, where the personal narrative is told from one viewpoint – the narrator's – in news a range of sources is often cited. In Figure 13.1 at least four separate sources are named in the space of six paragraphs. Third, the news revels in giving numbers with a precision which is foreign to conversational stories. In the Honduras story, six sets of figures counting the guerrillas, passengers, casualties, distance to the location occur in the first two paragraphs. Fourth, the syntax of personal narratives is simple, with mostly main clauses and little subordination. The syntax of news stories can be complex, as S1 and S2 show (although these are unusually long sentences for hard news). [. . .]

> [Bell goes on to review previous studies of the discourse struc-
> ture of news reports, including Teun van Dijk's 1988 analysis of
> topic-based 'macropropositions' and his 1985 analysis of 'news
> schemata'.]

Analysing a political news story's structure

In figure 13.1 we looked at a spot news story from the international news agencies. Figure 13.2 displays a typical example of the other predominant product of the same agencies, diplomatic and political news. The possible component categories of the story's structure are annotated alongside the copy. In Figure 13.3, that linear structure is redisplayed as a tree diagram, which reunites the components of different events from where they are scattered throughout the story. The structure as diagrammed in Figure 13.3 looks complex, and so it is, but in fact I have here telescoped levels and omitted nodes in order to simplify the presentation as much as possible. The complexity is a true reflection of the structure of such international diplomatic/political stories.

The news text consists of abstract, attribution and the story proper (Figure 13.3). The attribution is outside the body copy of the story, and indicates place at the top (*Moscow*, Figure 13.2) and source at the bottom (*NZPA–Reuter*). In many papers all three constituents of the attribution would conventionally be presented at the start of the lead paragraph: *Moscow, 31 March, NZPA-Reuter*. Here the time is not stated in attribution, headline or lead, but is explicit within the story – *yesterday* (S2, S12). The NZPA-Reuter attribution means that the story originates from one of the principal international agencies, channelled through London, New York or Paris, and finally Sydney and Wellington. Although most of the action takes place in Lithuania, the story is datelined Moscow. This may indicate a reporter working from Lithuania through a Moscow office. More likely the reporting is in fact being done from Moscow itself. Such off-the-spot reporting is completely standard in international news. Within the story other media are named as sources of specific information – Vilnius radio (S15) and Tass (S19) for Events 5 and 2 respectively. Unusually, and in contrast to the Honduras story, no non-media sources of information are credited.

Troops take over Lithuanian office

HEADLINE

Event 1

ATTRIBUTION

Place

LEAD

Evaluation S1

Event 1

Event 2

EVENT 3 S2

Previous episodes S3

EVENT 1 S4

EVENT 4 S5

Action S6

EVENT 1

Context S7

Previous episodes

Context S8

Reaction S9

S10

S11

Action S12

S13

Action

S14 Evaluation

Attribution

S15 EVENT 5

S16 EVENT 6

S17

S18

EVENT 2

S19

Attribution

ATTRIBUTION

MOSCOW

S1 STEPPING up the pressure on rebel Lithuania, Soviet troops seized a government office in the capital – and neighbouring Byelorussia threatened to claim a slice of the republic if it secedes from the Soviet Union.

S2 The parliament in Lithuania's sister Baltic republic of Estonia, meanwhile announced yesterday it wanted to break with Moscow too, declaring the beginning of a transitional period that would end in full independence.

S3 Moscow has refused to recognise Lithuania's March 11 declaration of independence.

S4 Instead it has waged what Lithuanians call a war of nerves, with soldiers occupying public buildings and arresting Lithuanian military deserters.

S5 United States President George Bush sent Soviet President Mikhail Gorbachev a note urging peaceful settlement of the dispute.

S6 A few hours later, Interior Ministry troops moved into the public prosecutor's office in the Lithuanian capital Vilnius.

S7 It was the first Lithuanian building to be occupied by Soviet troops since Wednesday, when the Communist Party headquarters was seized.

S8 It was also the first to be taken over from the government as opposed to the party.

S9 Lithuanian President Vytautas Landsbergis went on television yesterday to denounce the move, saying it would bring shame on Moscow.

S10 "We have endured all these years . . . we will this time as well," he said.

"What the USSR is doing now will bring only shame in the eyes of all the world."

S12 Earlier yesterday, deputy Soviet prosecutor Alexei Vasilyev told staff at the prosecutor's office that Moscow had relieved their boss, Alturas Paulauskas, from his post.

S13 In his place Mr Vasilyev announced Moscow had appointed Antanas Petrauskas, who quickly told journalists he did not recognise Lithuanian independence.

S14 Control of the prosecutor's office is considered crucial for Moscow to enforce Soviet law which it says still holds sway in Lithuania, including penalties for army desertion.

S15 Vilnius Radio said, Interior Ministry troops had also taken over the history institute of the Lithuanian Communist Party.

S16 Chief military prosecutor Alexander Katusev said yesterday a defence ministry amnesty announced on Friday for any Lithuanian deserters who returned to their units was invalid.

S17 They would be considered on a case-by-case basis, he said.

S18 Lithuanian was also set upon by its neighbour Byelorussia, where the parliamentary leadership said it would lay claim to Vilnius and six other districts if Lithuania seceded.

S19 "We shall be obliged to insist on the return of Byelorussian land to the Byelorussian Soviet Socialist Republic," the presidium of the republic's Supreme Soviet, or parliament said, according to the official news agency Tass. – NZPA-Reuter.

Figure 13.2 Components of an international news agency story (capitals represent major categories, lower-case labels are subordinate categories)

Source: *Dominion Sunday Times*, Wellington, 1 April 1990

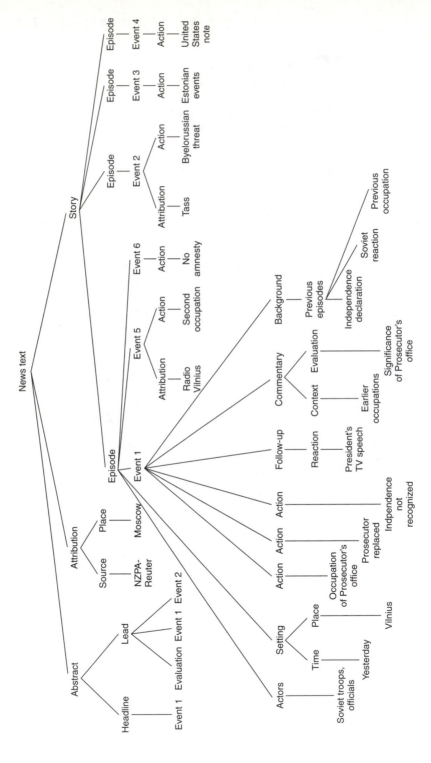

Figure 13.3 Structure of Lithuania story from Figure 13.2

The abstract breaks down into headline and lead. The headline covers only Event 1, the occupation – the subeditor gratefully picking out the only hard action from a generally verbal story. The lead covers the occupation plus event 2, the Byelorussian threat, as well as evaluating their effect on the situation. The evaluative clause *stepping up the pressure on rebel Lithuania* generalizes on the significance of the two separate events reported in the lead. This kind of explicit evaluation is a common device for drawing together the often disparate threads of such a story. There is no expansion or justification of the evaluation within the body of the story.

The story itself covers no fewer than six events:

1   Occupation of the prosecutor's office (S1, S3–4, S6–14);
2   Byelorussian threat to claim territory (S1, S18–19);
3   Estonia's announcement of desired independence (S2);
4   Bush's note to Gorbachev (S5);
5   Occupation of the Communist Party history institute (S15);
6   Withdrawal of deserter amnesty (S16–17).

In Figure 13.3 I subsume events 1, 5 and 6 under a single episode. They share a common setting of place (Vilnius) as well as principal actors (Soviet troops and officials). However, it is not clear from the story how related these happenings are, and further information might lead us to treat them as separate episodes. Events 2 and 4 are related to the main episode only through the general theme of the Lithuanian independence issue. Event 3 is even more remote, drawing parallels between happenings in Estonia and Lithuania. The story as published bears all the hallmarks of a shotgun marriage by the news agency of up to four originally separate stories covering the occupation, the Byelorussian threat, Bush's note, and the Estonian situation.

Events 3–6 are picked up and dropped within a paragraph or so each (Figure 13.2). In the diagram I have not specified all the categories required in the analysis. For example, each event implies actors and setting as well as action. Although events 1 and 2 are treated at greater length, they are delivered by instalments in a manner characteristic of news narrative. A number of devices are used to bring cohesion out of these diverse components. The inclusion of event 3 is justified (S2) by describing Estonia as *Lithuania's sister Baltic republic*, together with the use of *meanwhile* – a sure signal that a journalist is about to draw a tenuous connection between disparate events (cf. Glasgow University Media Group 1976: 118). Event 4, Bush's note, is said to deal with *the dispute* (S5), the label under which everything is here subsumed. (In fact, the Bush note was covered in an adjacent story in the newspaper.) A time relationship is specified (S6), linking Bush's note with the occupation which occurred *a few hours later*. The juxtaposition seems to imply not just a temporal but a causal or at least concessive relationship. The occupation is interpreted as taking place in disregard of Bush's plea for a peaceful settlement. *Also* is used both to tie event 5 in to the main occupation (S15), and when event 2 – mentioned in the lead then dropped – reappears in S18.

The actors, time and place structure are as complicated as the action. News narrative, as Manoff (1987) notes, is a means of knitting diverse events together. The story ranges across several locations. Each event belongs to a different place, principally the Lithuanian capital Vilnius (several sites), Byelorussia, Estonia, Washington and Moscow. As well as the complex interleaving of other events between the two main events, the time structure of the main events themselves is presented non-chronologically. Event 2 is included in the lead by the rather clumsy punctuation device of the dash, and surfaces again only at the end of the story. Event 1 consists of three actions (Figure 13.3), plus follow-up, commentary and background. The event moves from the occupation itself (S1), back in time to previous episodes which form the broad background to it (S3–4). It then presents detail about the occupation (S6) plus background about previous occupation events (S7–8), moves forward in time to Lithuanian verbal reaction to the occupation (S9–11), and returns to the occupation again (S12–13) plus evaluative background on its significance (S14). Such a to-and-fro time structure is completely standard for this kind of story – which does not make it any easier for the reader to keep track of. As van Dijk (1988: 65) says, getting coherence out of the discontinuous nature of news can be a demanding comprehension task. The analysis of a standard fire story from the *Baltimore Sun* undertaken by Pollard-Gott *et al.* (1979) shows how the same kind of non-chronological presentation, cycling through different actions, consequences and causes, occurs in a local spot news item.

[. . .]

The structure of news stories

We are now in a position to draw some general conclusions about the categories and structure of news discourse. Most of the categories which van Dijk has identified in news discourse – and others in other story types – are needed, with a few relabellings and additions. A news text will normally consist of an abstract, attribution and the story proper (Figure 13.4). Attribution of where the story came from is not always explicit. It can include agency credit and/or journalist's byline, optionally plus place and time.

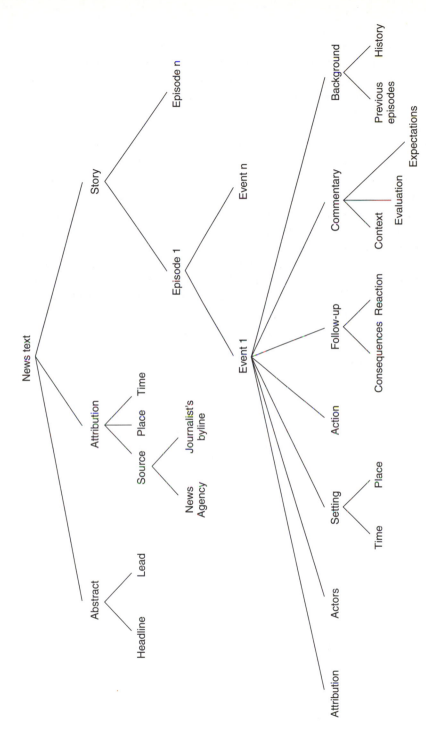

Figure 13.4 Outline model structure of news texts. There can be a number of Events or Episodes. Follow-up and Background Categories can have Episodes embedded into them. Headline and Lead pick-up components from the Story itself. Categories such as Attribution or Setting can be components of either an Event or an Episode

The abstract consists of the lead and, for press news, a headline. The lead will include the main event, and possibly a second event. This necessarily entails giving some information on actors and setting involved in the event. The lead may also incorporate attribution (as in the Honduras story), and supplementary categories such as evaluation (see the Lithuania story).

A story consists of one or more episodes, which in turn consist of one or more events. Events must contain actors and action, usually express setting, and may have explicit attribution. The categories of attribution, actors and setting (time and place) need to be recognized as part of the structure of news stories. They perform the orientation which Labov [Chapter 12] found in narratives, as well as embedding all or part of a story as information given by a particular source. These are also part of the journalist's mental analysis of what goes in a story: who, when, where, who said?

As well as those elements which present the central action, we recognize three additional categories that can contribute to an event: *follow-up*, *commentary* and *background* (Figure 13.4). The Lithuanian story contained all three of these, and all but three of the lower categories of which they can be composed: consequences, expectations, and history.

Follow up covers any action subsequent to the main action of an event. It can include verbal reaction, as in the Lithuania story, or non-verbal consequences – for example, if the upshot of the occupation had been demonstrations in Vilnius instead of a presidential speech. Because it covers action occurring after what a story has treated as the main action, follow-up is a prime source of subsequent updating stories – themselves called 'follow-ups'. We can easily imagine a subsequent story where the lead reads *Lithuanian President Vytautas Landsbergis has gone on television to condemn Soviet occupation of* . . . . If the follow-up action had in fact been a demonstration, that would certainly have claimed the lead on a later agency story.

Commentary provides the journalist's or news actors' observations on the action. It may be represented by context, such as the S7–8 information comparing this occupation with previous ones. It may be by explicit evaluation, as in the S14 presentation of the significance of occupying the prosecutor's office. Third, and not exemplified in the Lithuania story, it may express expectations held by the journalist or a news actor on how the situation could develop next.

The category of background covers any events prior to the current action. These are classed as 'previous episodes' if they are comparatively recent. They probably figured as news stories in their own right at an earlier stage of the situation. If the background goes beyond the near past, it is classed as 'history'. Information on the relationship of Lithuania to the Soviet Union during the Second World War was included in stories on other events around this time.

Follow-up and background can have the character of episodes in their own right. That is, episode is a recursive category and can be embedded under consequences, reaction, history or background. If the previous episodes outlined in S3–4 of the Lithuanian story had been more fully expanded, they could easily have incorporated the apparatus of a full episode within them, including categories such as context or evaluation. Similarly, follow-up reaction or consequences can be complex. These are by nature categories which were full stories in their own right at a previous time, or may become so tomorrow.

[. . .]

Note

1   In the days of wire despatches both the place and date were carried on the dateline. Most of the elements surrounding news copy are named after the line above the body copy of which they traditionally occurred – head-line, catch-line, date-line, by-line. 'Datelined Moscow' means the story was 'filed' – written and supplied to the news agency – from Moscow. The slugline is named for the 'slugs' of hard metal type used in the orig-inal letterpress technology before the advent of offset printing and computer typesetting.

References

Cappon, R. J. (1982) *The Word: An Associated Press Guide to Good News Writing*, New York: Associated Press.

Glasgow University Media Group (1976) *Bad News*, London: Routledge & Kegan Paul.

Labov, W. and Waletzky, J. (1967) 'Narrative analysis: oral versions of personal experience', in Helm, J. (ed.) *Essays on the Verbal and Visual Arts (Proceedings of the 1966 Annual Spring Meeting of the American Ethnological Society)*, Seattle: University of Washington Press, 12–44.

Manoff, R. (1987) 'Writing the news (by telling the "story")', in Manoff, R. K. and Schudson, M. (eds) *Reading the News*, New York: Pantheon, 197–229.

Pollard-Gott, L., McCloskey, M. and Todres, A. K. (1979). 'Subjective story structure', *Discourse Processes* 2(4): 251–81.

Van Dijk, T. A. (1988) *News as Discourse*, Hillsdale, NJ: Lawrence Erlbaum.

Van Dijk, T. A. (1985) 'Structures of news in the press', in Van Dijk, T. A. (ed.) *Discourse and Communication: New Approaches to the Analysis of Mass Media Discourse and Communication*, Berlin: de Gruyter, 69–93.

Chapter 14

Harvey Sacks

EVERYONE HAS TO LIE

THIS CHAPTER REPORTS an attempt to develop an experience for the problem: what should an analysis look like that has as its aim proposing that something that a member says about the social world is true? I will proceed by seeking to show that a particular commonplace statement that members make, *Everyone has to lie*, is true.

[. . .]

First of all, that it is a commonplace, proverbial expression suggests the possibility that its reference might be something quite general, that the experiences it reflects are, and are perceived by their user to be, common and thereby, for a sociologist, possibly organizationally based.

[. . .]

As we shall see, it is not at all obvious that a statement with the subject term *everyone* names a larger population than a statement with, e.g., the subject term *doctors* or *men*, etc. Second, what may be crucial for a statement's truth is *how it is that a population is formulated*, i.e., what identificatory term is used. In saying this, what I want to notice is that, given a same-population in the sense of some bunch of people of whom something is to be predicated, the acceptability as correct of a statement saying something about them may turn on which of some set of correct identifications are used in the statement. [. . .]

Source: Harvey Sacks, 'Everyone has to lie', in Mary Sanches and Ben G. Blount (eds) *Sociocultural Dimensions of Language Use*, New York: Academic Press, 1975.

At least some – perhaps many – of the statements that have these "more limited" identificatory terms as their subjects seem to have the occasion of their correct characterization of some circumstance. The consequence of this is that although one might treat such a statement as a thing one could monitor the world with, it does not turn out to be so used. And therefore, on occasions when it might appear to be usable to find that it is incorrect, such occasions might be characterized by another term than its subject term. So, e.g., the statement *women are fickle* might be used only on some occasion when someone who happens to be a woman was fickle. On some occasion when someone who could be so characterized was faithful, she might be otherwise characterized, as, for example, by saying *Older people are faithful*. It is not – at least for the researcher – obvious what is involved in selecting an identification that is used on some occasion. [. . .]

A virtue of the statement *Everyone has to lie*, for having its truth determined, is, in a sentence, this: For that statement it appears that you can state some ways that the contrast class true–false is relevant on that statement's occurrence.

[. . .]

The statement *Everyone has to lie* **can** be made either as a complaint or as an excuse – of course, other things also. When it is either of these, assertions about truth or falsity would thereby be sequentially relevant; and thereby, then, for some occasions of the utterance *Everyone has to lie*, its truth or falsity would be sequentially relevant [. . .]

For the actual case in which the utterance was used, it appears that *Everyone has to lie* was offered as a complaint, that is, as "Everyone has to lie and isn't that terrible," "Everyone has to lie and I can't do it," "Everyone has to lie and I hate to do it." What we may then be heard to have said is that the fact that members assert a statement in the doing of some activity can be informative for us of the status of that item in their corpus of knowledge. That they take it that the statement is true is evidenced by its use for doing some class of actions such as, for example, complaining.

[. . .]

I have noted that some of the categorical identificatory terms do not appear to be regularly used in the sense that, for them to be correct, each person they could characterize needs to have what is predicated of them true of them. And perhaps *everyone* is a sort of categorical term. If so, what sort might it be? "Everyone" is used for various category collections. For example, I have seen an advertisement that goes: *Something for everyone: An X for Dad, a Y for Mom, a Z for Brother, a T for Sister*. Here, *everyone* refers to the category collection "family." Now, what that suggests is that the size of the population being referred to by "everyone" can be quite small. That is to say, "everyone" could, intentionally, understandably, refer to "all the members of some family" or "all the persons playing some bridge game." If, now, "everyone" were used for reference to some family's members, while it may have a summative intention – be intended to hold for each – it would nonetheless be holding for what might be a rather small group. And then, too, if it held for a category, it might not have a summative intention to it.

In short, when "everyone" is used summatively it might not have a very large set-population intended; and when it is used where it might have a rather large population intended, it might not be used in such a way as to have *each* of that population intended. Consider such uses as *Everyone's going, can I go?* This is not – though it might be so construed – a paradox. "Everyone" here is apparently being used in a programatically relevant fashion.

The upshot of this last discussion is: it may be the case that a determination of what "everyone" refers to turns on the utterance and the occasion of its use. Some readings were suggested – such as that "everyone" can be used programatically, can be used for a rather small set-population, can be used for categories. By use of these, an approach that seeks, as ours does, to find how the statement might be possibly true seems not necessarily burdened with what might appear to be a more attractive approach – that is, to find that it could not be true (i.e. to formulate such a sense of "everyone" as permits the ready location of falsifying evidence). Such an approach might simply not be terribly informative about the *uses* of *everyone*, or about its social organizational aspects.

With these considerations in hand, let us turn to another body of material, the use of which will set up our detailed analysis.

Several years ago I was working on a study of "greetings" – things like *Hi–Hi, Hello–Hello*, etc. I had acquired various small points, and finding them not overly interesting, sought – as a way of increasing their interest – to see if some of those results could be incorporated into a more extended investigation that would involve, by its turning on them, a way of developing some of their interest. That rather independent study of greetings turned out to have use for the consideration of the truth of the statement *Everyone has to lie*, which I was also studying.

We will proceed with some points about greetings. First, two small points: (1) greetings are ahistorically relevant, and (2) when they occur they properly occur at the beginning of a conversation. To say that greetings are ahistorically relevant as compared to, say, "introductions" (which, having been gone through once or perhaps twice, or erroneously three times or five times, are no longer appropriate) intends that in the case of greetings as between any two people, without regard to how long they have been acquainted, there is no rule that says "On some $N + K$ conversation, no longer begin conversations with greetings." Instead, every conversation those two people have – they could have been married 30 years – can begin with some greetings. Not only that; their first conversation can also begin with greetings. This is not to say that every conversation must begin with greetings, but that there is no exclusion rule for greetings.

With respect to the placing of greetings, there is a technical relevance to the fact that greetings properly occur at the beginning of conversations. This relevance concerns the technical issues of an analyst's being in the position to say that something did not happen, that it was absent. Now, saying that something was absent and thereby making some point is not, obviously, a simple task. For to say simply that any event T was absent, that T did not occur, potentially allows indefinitely extending the list of things that did not occur, and insofar as T is thereby a member of an indefinitely large class, the point that some particular T did not occur is made trivial. It is not discriminable from the rest of the things that also can be said to have not occurred.

However, insofar as there is a rule that says "If greetings do occur, they ought to occur at the beginning of a conversation," and insofar as there is a further rule that says "Greetings may occur at the beginning of any conversation," i.e., there is no exclusion rule for greetings, then there is a place to look to see where greetings should be found, such that if they are not there, they can be said to be absent in a way that other things cannot be said to be absent.

[. . .]

Greetings are, however, asserted to be absent, and they are asserted to be absent when they do not occur at the beginning of a conversation, as in Extract 1:

Extract 1
Operator: *Mister Savage is gonna pick up an' talk to* [*yuh*
Lerhoff: *All right*
          (Approx. 50 seconds intervening)
Operator: *Did Mr Savage ever pick up?*
Lerhoff: *If he did, he didn't say "Hello."*
Operator: *Oh, all right* [*sma(hh)rty, just hold on.*
Lerhoff: *heh heh heh heh heh*
Operator: *heh!*

With these two facts in hand – greetings are ahistorically relevant and greetings properly occur at the beginning of a conversation – we proceed to construct some classes of conversationalists. We will establish a class of "proper conversationalists" and construct subclasses of that class. Let us call the first subclass, subclass A. We will say about subclass A that what is definitive of it is that its co-members may engage in something we will call a "minimal proper conversation" and no more.

There is, of course, at least one other subclass, subclass B, about which we will say, for now, that what is definitive of it is that its co-members can properly mutually engage in a minimal proper conversation and more. [. . .]

If we can say that a "minimal proper conversation" can consist of an exchange of greetings, then in the first instance we know – or at least have so far asserted – that subclass A can do that. Co-members may be able to do no more, properly, than exchange greetings, but they can do that.

It is worth noting in this regard that there are people who do engage in conversations who are not co-members of a subclass of proper conversationalists but are, instead, "improper conversationalists." [. . .] It may be seen that when people who are not proper conversationalists engage in conversation, they do so, or begin to do so at least, often in special ways. Thus, for example, if a person seeking to engage another in conversation, and not being a proper conversationalist for that other person, is to bring off a conversation with that other person, then one sort of thing he may do – and does – is to begin not with greetings but by using an utterance, which we call a "ticket," that indicates the reason he is starting to talk with that other person. He may, for example, say *Excuse me, I'm lost*, and [say this], in particular, without greetings. [. . .]

If the various subclasses other than subclass A are somehow ranked by reference to intimacy, status relations, and the like, it nonetheless appears that even the most intimate of such people can on some occasion make only an exchange of greetings, without one party of such a pair feeling wronged. A couple married 30 years may, in passing on the dance floor, at a party, or elsewhere, just exchange greetings. And neither feels that the other has, by not otherwise talking, done an improper act.

[. . .]

There are two issues for our consideration. The first – the placing of greetings – has been discussed. The second matter – that on a first greeting a second should follow – is evidenced not only by the fact that that does happen but also by the fact that when it does not happen it is notable. So, for example, a child may be told, *Didn't you hear A say **hi** to you?*, which is itself an interesting way to inform the child that he or she should also have said **hi**. Also, when a first greeting is offered and not returned, a repetition may occur (Schegloff 1968). Since the exchange of greetings proceeds according to the sequencing rules of conversation, the exchange of greetings is at least part of a conversation. Insofar as the exchange of greetings is not required to be followed by more talk, the exchange of greetings is, thus, a minimal proper conversation.

I want now to introduce something I call a "greeting substitute." The particular sort of greeting substitute we shall be most interested in is such a thing as *How are you?* Let me state some features of the class. First, a greeting substitute may be used as a greeting. Instead of using *Hi*, one may use *How are you?*. You might ask, since *how are you?* can go where greetings can go, why not call it a greeting? Why call it a greeting substitute? A first reason [. . .] is that greetings are not repeatably used. [. . .] That is, a pair of people should not, after saying *Hi–Hi*, say *Hi–Hi* again. There is an exception to this: in the case of telephone calls, in which *Hello* is the appropriate utterance of the first speaker, i.e., the one who answers the phone, the answerer regularly does not know who it is he is saying *Hello* to; and while *Hello* is then returnable when on an exchange of *Hellos* the initial speaker discovers from the second *Hello*, by recognition of the voice, to whom he is speaking, he may then say *Hi*, and the other may then also return *Hi*. In the case of telephone calls, then, one does get *Hello–Hello*, *Hi–Hi*. But that is a special situation. [. . .]

But greeting substitutes can be used in combination with greetings. That is to say, one can have:

> A: *Hi.*
> B: *Hi.*
> A: *How are you?*
> B: *Fine, how are you?*

Furthermore, if greetings and greeting substitutes are combined, and both occur, they occur in a fixed order. Greetings precede greeting substitutes. But – and this is the point we want to retain – speakers can choose to use greeting substitutes when they do not use greetings, and a greeting will not be absent. In that regard, then, what I have said about greetings holds for greeting substitutes; that is, an exchange of greeting substitutes can constitute a minimal proper conversation. [. . .]

Two more classes are needed. One of them I call "personal states," which consist of things like *mood*, *appetite*, *sleep*, etc.; the other I call "value states," which consist of terms like *good*, *lousy*, *great*, *rotten*, *wonderful*, etc. The latter terms are organized into three subsets, which I will denote by the symbols

[–], [0], [+]. [. . .] Any of the value states can describe some personal state for some person at some time. *How's your appetite? Great!* (or *Rotten!*). Prototypical terms: for [–], *lousy*, for [0], *ok*, for [+], *great*. The organization of the terms into subsets involves mutual exclusion as between subsets. If a term belongs to one, it does not properly belong to another.

Now, *How are you?* has its proper answers among the value state descriptors. So if you ask somebody *How are you?*, he or she should pick a term from among those.

[. . .]

Given the occurrence of an answer from subset [0], e.g., *ok, fine*, etc., no further inquiries are appropriate. Given the occurrence of an answer from the [–] subset, a sequence is appropriately launched, directly, to determining "what's the matter." For example, that question or *Why?* should be used when, e.g., the answer to *How are you?* has been *Lousy!* (In the case of the [+] subset, some "comment" like *Great!* may follow the answer *Wonderful!* or an inquiry might also be launched via things like, e.g., *What happened?*) The sequence launched on the occurrence of an answer from the [–] subset, e.g., *Lousy!* to the question *How are you?* (launched, e.g., by the question *Why?* or *What's the matter?*) I call a "diagnostic sequence," and it has at one point in it the offering of such an account as explains how it is that the answerer is in the [–] subset. [. . .]

Regulations that exist concern such matters as what it is that should be held within the family, what should be told only to your doctor or a priest, and the like. Furthermore, such regulations not only hold to exclude some people from hearing some items of information, but even for those who may hear such information there are appropriate sequences whereby they should be told, such that some people should not hear before others. Information varies as to whom it may be given to. Some matters may be told to a neighbor, others not; some to a best friend, others, while they may be told to a best friend, may only be told to a best friend after another has been told, e.g., a spouse.

[. . .]

We may say that the presentation of an answer to the question *How are you?* proceeds in two steps. A first step I call "monitoring" and a second step "selecting a term." The first step involves selecting a subset. The second step, given the selection of a subset, involves selecting a term from that subset. There are ways in which it would appear that the notion "monitoring" is artificial. Let me attempt to indicate what I intend by the use of that term. I intend to notice a difference between the way two different sorts of statements are dealt with. For the first, if, e.g., a little girl comes home and says to her mother, *Mama, I'm pretty* or *Mama, I'm smart*, the mother could say "Who told you that?." For the second, if someone says *I'm tired* or *I feel lousy*, etc., no such thing is asked. One is responsible for knowing some things on one's own behalf, in contrast to the situation in which one is treated as likely to be repeating what another has told him about himself. We have data to that effect: *You keep saying you're insane. Has somebody been telling you that recently?.* The notion, then, of "monitoring" attempts to come to terms with the difference between things that are heard as things you know on your own behalf and things that are heard as things you know by virtue of another's having told you. The answers to *How are you?* are things you know on your own behalf.

We will proceed, then, to the notion "lying". Lying, we will say, consists of announcing in your answer a term that is excluded by the monitoring operation. So if the monitoring operation comes up with [+], then one uses a term from [0]; if the monitoring operation comes up with [−], then one uses a term from [+] or [0], etc. With that in hand we can return to the regulation of information on "troubles" and to the question: How is it that, given the regulation of information about troubles, conformity to the rules that regulate that information is achieved? We will turn, also, to a newer question: Given the formulation of lying, why should anyone lie?

How, then, are the regulations about information transmission enforced? [. . .]

It is certainly imaginable that regulation of information (about, e.g., troubles) transmission is achieved by having a potential elicitor of such information, one who might ask *How are you?* and thereby potentially engender a diagnostic sequence, be constrained from asking that question if he is not in a position to receive the sort of information he might receive. [. . .] Such a system of regulations does not seem to be workable. In any event, it is not used. [. . .] If such a set of regulations were operative, *How are you?* would be an almost unaskable question, but *How are you?* is not an unaskable question. It is, instead, the most askable of questions. The system of regulations involves not a potential asker's determination of whether he could handle any information but, instead, an answerer's determination of whether a given asker can receive the particular information or handle it now. That is, it is the business of one who is asked *How are you?* to determine whether the asker can handle that information, and to control his answer by reference to that determination. If such information as is not giveable to the asker obtains, and occasions that the monitoring product is [−], then the procedure for not getting into the diagnostic sequence is: Do not offer such an answer as generates the diagnostic sequence. Answer, e.g., *Ok* or *Fine*.

[. . .]

What we have arrived at is that any person feeling lousy and having some trouble as the explanation of feeling lousy, if asked how he is feeling by someone who ought not to hear that trouble or hear it now, may control that one's access to that information by avoiding the diagnostic sequence, and the diagnostic sequence is avoided by choosing a term from a subset other than the subset the monitoring operation comes up with; that is, he may lie.

Now for a brief remark on the term *has to*. It might be said that while somebody in that situation might lie, we really should not say *He has to lie*. On the contrary, however, it is the case that such a situation is properly characterized by the term *has to*, for conforming to a violable rule is something one can say one *has to do*. People say, for example, *Everyone has to pay their taxes*. You do not have to pay your taxes, you can take your chances on going to jail. "Has to" apparently can properly be used where there is some rule that says "you ought to" and that rule has sanctions. The foregoing seems to leave us in a situation in which we can say that it is at least conceivable that anyone might be in a position in which such "need" to lie would be present. This does not say that anyone *will* be in such a position. [. . .]

It happens to be the case that the particular occurrence of *Everyone has to lie* that occasioned the research I am here reporting on was asserted complainingly by one who had as part of her troubles that not only did she feel seriously lousy but also that others were routinely asking her *How are you?* while sometimes being quite uninterested in being recipients of a report of troubles and sometimes being distinctly improper recipients. Then, it is not unreasonable to suppose that she could see how the arrangement of conversation was a source of her troubles, or the part of them that focused on their being raised as potentially tellable to be then rejected for actually being told, and that such troubles were not at all hers in particular.

What we have seen about what we have called "lying" with respect to the *How are you?* situation is that lying involves the selection of a known incorrect answer to the question: Which of the value states is correct for you?, where what the possible answers are is known. We have, then, a situation in which the selection of a known-to-be-false answer can occur by virtue of its offerer's orientation to the sequential implications of alternative answers. This notion of "lying" is directly generalizable and, as generalized, seems to capture a correct sense of lying.

In circumstances in which alternative answers to a question are known, and the alternative answers have alternative consequences for that conversation or for other events, then one way in which people are known to attempt to control those alternative consequences is to select answers by reference to their intended selection of a consequence. If children are asked some question, one of whose alternative answers may occasion a rebuke and another not, then apparently they learn, and apparently it is learned that they have learned, to produce answers that are directed to avoiding the rebuke, which answer production can involve them in lying [. . .]

Some final remarks about "everyone" will suggest some further extensions of these phenomena. In returning to "everyone" we may proceed by considering the following conversation:

Extract 2
A: *Why do you want to kill yourself?*
B: *For the same reason everyone does.*
A: *What's that?*
B   *You just want to know if anyone cares.*

Now, in this extract there is a rather characteristic use of "everyone." It seems to be something we might put as "for the same reason as anyone in such a situation." If "everyone" can mean "anyone in such a situation as I" or "anyone in such a situation where what that situation is is characterizable," then a rather important shift may be made with respect to the issue of what people "everyone" characterizes. At least for some uses, "everyone" characterizes no people at all. This is not to say that it characterizes nothing. Instead, however, of "everyone" being another way of referring to, e.g., a designated person or to a category or a collection of categories, or to the incumbents of a collection of categories, "everyone" may also refer to what Garfinkel (personal communication) has characterized as "the sociologist's person, ideally," that is to say, a "course of action" person. Let me elucidate this concept.

There are uses of "everyone" that seem to be noting that the people so identified are sufficiently identified if the situation they are in is stated. That is, for whomever is in that situation, the specification of that situation constitutes a sufficient account of what they may be expected to do, how they may be expected to feel, or how they may be expected to behave.

Let it be noted that such uses of "everyone" are not at all infrequent. And, among other things, it appears that what such uses of "everyone" accomplish is that having specified a situation – and again, this is so only, apparently, for some situations and members – no addition of identificatory references gives, for example, motivational gains or explanatory gains with respect to formulating an account of what it is that that one did or will do, or why, or how. Such a use of "everyone" has as its specific import (not merely making irrelevant any numerical identifier or categorial identifier) that it is *productively* usable. By "productively" I mean the following. What is relevant for things that are known in such a way that "everyone" – properly used in the sense I have stated — is appropriate is not whether in the course of his life each person in fact finds himself in such a circumstance, or is found in such a circumstance, but that "anyone might." These matters, formulated situationally for such situations, seem not to be the specific troubles of "men, women or children," "professional people," "members of various sects," and the like. Instead, they are known as matters that can happen to whomsoever and are, in any event, not excludable by some history one has had that may be formulated in terms of, e.g., one's categorical memberships.

Given the foregoing extension of "everyone," it now becomes unnecessary to find that some situation can be found for each categorizable population or each nameable person in which the organization of conversation, the rules of information regulation, and their personal circumstances converge to lead them to feel that they "have to lie." What is instead involved is that the statement is true if the organization of conversation is such that any next conversation can formally produce the problem of having to deal with some such sequentially implicative question as *How are you?* where the question is asked by one with whom the respondent, by reference to other rules, e.g., of information transmissal, is placed in a situation that he sees involves either getting into a sequence in this conversation that he should not get into or lying so as to avoid that sequence. The organization of conversation being such, the statement is *true*.

Reference

Schegloff, E. (1968) 'Sequencing in conversational openings', *American Anthropologist* 70: 1075–95.

Chapter 15

Emanuel A. Schegloff
and Harvey Sacks

OPENING UP CLOSINGS

O UR AIM IN THIS PAPER is to report in a preliminary fashion on
analyses we have been developing of closings of conversation. Although
it may be apparent to intuition that the unit 'a single conversation' does not
simply end, but is brought to a close, our initial task is to develop a technical basis for a closing problem. This we try to derive from a consideration
of some features of the most basic sequential organization of conversation
we know of – the organization of speaker turns. [. . .]

This project is part of a program of work undertaken several years ago
[this paper was first delivered to the American Sociological Association in
1969] to explore the possibility of achieving a naturalistic observational discipline that could deal with the details of social action(s) rigorously, empirically,
and formally. For a variety of reasons that need not be spelled out here, our
attention has focused on conversational materials; suffice it to say that this is
not because of a special interest in language, or any theoretical primacy we
accord conversation. Nonetheless, the character of our materials as conversational has attracted our attention to the study of conversation as an activity in
its own right, and thereby to the ways in which any actions accomplished in
conversation require reference to the properties and organization of conversation for their understanding and analysis, both by participants and by professional investigators. This last phrase requires emphasis and explication.

We have proceeded under the assumption (an assumption borne out by our
research) that insofar as the materials we worked with exhibited orderliness,

Source: Emanuel A. Schegloff and Harvey Sacks, 'Opening up closings', *Semiotica* 7: 289–327.

they did so not only for us, indeed not in the first place for us, but for the co-participants who had produced them. If the materials (records of natural conversations) were orderly, they were so because they had been methodically produced by members of the society for one another, and it was a feature of the conversations that we treated as data that they were produced so as to allow the display by the coparticipants to each other of their orderliness, and to allow the participants to display to each other their analysis, appreciation, and use of that orderliness. Accordingly, our analysis has sought to explicate the ways in which the materials are produced by members in orderly ways that exhibit their orderliness, have their orderliness appreciated and used, and have that appreciation displayed and treated as the basis for subsequent action.

In the ensuing discussion, therefore, it should be clearly understood that the 'closing problem' we are discussing is proposed as a problem for conversationalists; we are not interested in it as a problem for analysts except insofar as, and in the ways, it is a problem for participants. (By 'problem' we do not intend puzzle, in the sense that participants need to ponder the matter of how to close a conversation. We mean that closings are to be seen as achievements, as solutions to certain problems of conversational organization.) [. . .]

The materials with which we have worked are audiotapes and transcripts of naturally occurring interactions (i.e., ones not produced by research intervention such as experiment or interview) with differing numbers of participants and different combinations or participant attributes. There is a danger attending this way of characterizing our materials, namely, that we be heard as proposing the assured relevance of numbers, attributes of participants, etc., to the way the data are produced, interpreted, or analyzed by investigators or by the participants themselves. Such a view carries considerable plausibility, but for precisely that reason it should be treated with extreme caution, and be introduced only where warrant can be offered for the relevance of such characterizations of the data from the data themselves.

[. . .]

It seems useful to begin by formulating the problem of closing technically in terms of the more fundamental order of organization, that of turns. Two basic features of conversation are proposed to be: (1) at least, and no more than, one party speaks at a time in a single conversation; and (2) speaker change recurs. The achievement of these features singly, and especially the achievement of their co-occurrence, is accomplished by co-conversationalists through the use of a 'machinery' for ordering speaker turns sequentially in conversation. The turn-taking machinery includes as one component a set of procedures for organizing the selection of 'next speakers', and, as another, a set of procedures for locating the occasions on which transition to a next speaker may or should occur. The turn-taking machinery operates utterance by utterance. That is to say [. . .] it is within any current utterance that possible next speaker selection is accomplished, and upon possible completion of any current utterance that such selection takes effect and transition to a next speaker becomes relevant. We shall speak of this as the 'transition relevance' of possible utterance completion. [. . .] Whereas these basic features [. . .] deal with a conversation's ongoing orderliness, they make no provision for the closing of conversation. A machinery that includes the transition relevance of possible utterance completion recurrently for any utterance in the conversation generates an indefinitely extendable string of turns to talk. Then, an initial problem concerning closings may be formulated: HOW TO ORGANIZE THE SIMULTANEOUS ARRIVAL OF THE CO-CONVERSATION-ALISTS AT A POINT WHERE ONE SPEAKER'S COMPLETION WILL NOT OCCASION ANOTHER SPEAKER'S TALK, AND THAT WILL NOT BE HEARD AS SOME SPEAKER'S SILENCE. The last qualification is necessary to differentiate closings from other places in conversation where one speaker's completion is not followed by a possible next speaker's talk, but where, given the continuing relevance of the basic features and the turn-taking machinery, what is heard is not termination but attributable silence, a pause in the last speaker's utterance, etc. It should suggest why simply to stop talking is not a solution to the closing problem: any first prospective speaker to do so would be hearable as 'being silent' in terms of the turn-taking machinery, rather than as having suspended its relevance. [. . .]

How is the transition relevance of possible utterance completion lifted? A proximate solution involves the use of a 'terminal exchange' composed of conventional parts, e.g., an exchange of 'good-byes'. [. . .] We note first that the terminal exchange is a case of a class of utterance sequences which we have been studying for some years, namely, the utterance pair, or, as we shall refer to it, the adjacency pair. [. . .] Briefly, adjacency pairs consist of sequences which properly have the following features: (1) two utterance length, (2) adjacent positioning of component utterances, (3) different speakers producing each utterance. The component utterances of such sequences have an achieved relatedness beyond that which may otherwise obtain between adjacent utterances. That relatedness is partially the product of the operation of a typology in the speakers' production of the sequences. The typology operates in two ways: it partitions utterance types into 'first pair parts' (i.e., first parts of pairs) and second pair parts; and it affiliates a first pair part and a second pair part to form a 'pair type'. 'Question-answer', 'greeting-greeting,' 'offer-acceptance/refusal' are instances of pair types. [. . .] Adjacency pair sequences, then, exhibit the further features (4) relative ordering of parts (i.e. first pair parts precede second pair parts) and

(5) discriminative relations (i.e., the pair type of which a first pair part is a member is relevant to the selection among second pair parts). [. . .]

In the case of that type of organization which we are calling 'overall structural organization', it may be noted that at least initial sequences (e.g., greeting exchanges), and ending sequences (i.e., terminal exchanges) employ adjacency pair formats. It is the recurrent, institutionalized use of adjacency pairs for such types of organization problems that suggests that these problems have, in part, a common character, and that adjacency pair organization [. . .] is specially fitted to the solution of problems of that character. [. . .]

But it may be wondered, why are two utterances required for either opening or closing? [. . .] What two utterances produced by different speakers can do that one utterance cannot do it: by an adjacently positioned second, a speaker can show that he understood what a prior aimed at, and that he is willing to go along with that. Also, by virtue of the occurrence of an adjacently produced second, the doer of a first can see that what he intended was indeed understood, and that it was or was not accepted. [. . .]

We are then proposing: If WHERE transition relevance is to be lifted is a systematic problem, an adjacency pair solution can work because: by providing that transition relevance is to be lifted after the second pair part's occurrence, the occurrence of the second pair part can then reveal an appreciation of, and agreement to, the intention of closing NOW which a first part of a terminal exchange reveals its speaker to propose. Given the institutionalization of that solution, a range of ways of assuring that it be employed have been developed, which make drastic difference between one party saying "good-bye" and not leaving a slot for the other to reply, and one party saying "good-bye" and leaving a slot for the other to reply. The former becomes a distinct sort of activity, expressing anger, brusqueness, and the like, and available to such a use by contrast with the latter. it is this consequentiality of alternatives that is the hallmark of an institutionalized solution. [. . .]

In referring to the components of terminal exchanges, we have so far employed "good-bye" as an exclusive instance. But, it plainly is not exclusively used. Such other components as "ok", "see you", "thank you", "you're welcome", and the like are also used. Since the latter items are used in other ways as well, the mere fact of their use does not mark them as unequivocal parts of terminal exchanges. [. . .]

The adjacency pair is one kind of 'local', i.e., utterance, organization. It does NOT appear that FIRST parts of terminal exchanges are placed by reference to that order of organization. While they, of course, occur after some utterance, they are not placed by reference to a location that might be formulated as 'next' after some 'last' utterance or class of utterances. Rather, their placement seems to be organized by reference to a properly initiated closing SECTION.

The [relevant] aspect of overall conversational organization concerns the organization of topic talk. [. . .] If we may refer to what gets talked about in a conversation as 'mentionables', then we can note that there are considerations relevant for conversationalists in ordering and distributing their talk about mentionables in a single conversation. There is, for example, a position in a single conversation for 'first topic'. We intend to mark by this term not the simple serial fact that some topic gets talked about temporally prior to others, for some temporally prior topics such as, for example, ones prefaced by "First, I just want to say . . .", or topics that are minor developments by the receiver of the conversational opening of "how are you" inquiries, are not heard or treated as 'first topic' is to accord it to a certain special status in the conversation. Thus, for example, to make a topic 'first topic' may provide for its analyzability (by coparticipants) as 'the reason for' the conversation, that being, furthermore, a preservable and reportable feature of the conversation. In addition, making a topic 'first topic' may accord it a special importance on the part of its initiator [. . .].

These features of 'first topics' may pose a problem for conversationalists who may not wish to have special importance accorded some 'mentionable', and who may not want it preserved as 'the reason for the conversation'. It is by reference to such problems affiliated with the use of first topic position that we may appreciate such exchanges at the beginnings of conversations in which news is later reported, as:

    A: What's up.
    B: Not much. What's up with you?
    A: Nothing.

Conversationalists, then, can have mentionables they do not want to put in first topic position, and there are ways of talking past first topic position without putting them in.

A further feature of the organization of topic talk seems to involve 'fitting' as a preferred procedure. That is, it appears that a preferred way of getting mentionables mentioned is to employ the resources of the local organization of utterances in the course of the conversation. That involves holding off the mention of a mentionable until it can 'occur naturally', that is, until it can be fitted to another conversationalist's prior utterance [. . .]

There is, however, no guarantee that the course of the conversation will provide the occasion for any particular mentionable to 'come up naturally'.

This being the case, it would appear that an important virtue for a closing structure designed for this kind of topical structure would involve the provision for placement of hitherto unmentioned mentionables. The terminal

exchange by itself makes no such provision. By exploiting the close organization resource of adjacency pairs, it provides for an immediate (i.e., next
turn) closing of the conversation. That this close-ordering technique for terminating not exclude the possibility of inserting unmentioned mentionables can
be achieved by placement restrictions on the first part of terminal exchanges,
for example, by requiring 'advance note' or some form of foreshadowing.

[. . .]

The first proper way of initiating a closing section that we will discuss is one
kind of (what we will call) 'pre-closing'. The kind of pre-closing we have in
mind takes one of the following forms, "We-ell . . .", "O.K . . .", "So-oo", etc.
(with downward intonation contours), these forms constituting the entire
utterance. These pre-closings should properly be called 'POSSIBLE pre-closing',
because providing the relevance of the initiation of a closing section is only one
of the uses they have. One feature of their operation is that they occupy the floor
for a speaker's turn without using it to produce either a topically coherent utterance or the initiation of a new topic. With them a speaker takes a turn whose
business seems to be to 'pass,' i.e., to indicate that he has not now anything
more or new to say, and also to give a 'free' turn to the next, who, because such
an utterance can be treated as having broken with any prior topic, can without
violating topical coherence take the occasion to introduce a new topic [. . .]
When this opportunity is exploited [. . .] then the local organization otherwise
operative in conversation, including the fitting of topical talk, allows the same
possibilities which obtain in any topical talk. The opening [. . .] may thus result
in much more ensuing talk than the initial mentionable that is inserted [. . .] The
extendability of conversation to great lengths past a possible preclosing is not a
sign of the latter's defects with respect to initiating closings, but of its virtues
in providing opportunities for further topic talk that is fitted to the topical
structure of conversation.

[. . .]The other possibility is that coconversationalists decline an opportunity to insert unmentioned mentionables. In that circumstance, the pre-closing
may be answered with an acknowledgement, a return 'pass' yielding a
sequence such as:

A: O.K.
B: O.K.

thereby setting up the relevance of further collaborating on a closing section.
When the possible pre-closing is responded to in this manner, it may constitute the first part of the closing section.

[. . .]

Clearly, utterances such as "O.K.", "We-ell", etc. (where those forms are the whole of the utterance), occur in conversation in capacities other than that of 'pre-closing'. It is only on some occasions of use that these utterances are treated as pre-closings. [. . .]

[They] operate as possible pre-closings when placed at the analyzable (once again, TO PARTICIPANTS) end of a topic.

[. . .] Not all topics have an analyzable end. One procedure whereby talk moves off a topic might be called 'topic shading', in that it involves no specific attention to ending a topic at all, but rather the fitting of differently focused but related talk to some last utterance in a topic's development. But co-conversationalists may specifically attend to accomplishing a topic boundary, and there are various mechanisms for doing so; these may yield 'analyzable ends,' their analyzability to participants being displayed in the effective collaboration required to achieve them.

For example, there is a technique for 'closing down a topic' that seems to be a formal technique for a class of topic types, in the sense that for topics that are of the types that are members of the class, the technique operates without regard to what the particular topic is. [. . .] We have in mind such exchanges as:

A: Okay?
B: Alright

Such an exchange can serve, if completed, to accomplish a collaboration on the shutting down of a topic, and may thus mark the next slot in the conversational sequence as one in which, if an utterance of the form "We-ell", "O.K.", etc. should occur, it may be heard as a possible pre-closing.

Another 'topic-bounding' technique involves one party's offering of a proverbial or aphoristic formulation of conventional wisdom which can be heard as the 'moral' or 'lesson' of the topic being thereby possibly closed. Such formulations are 'agreeable with'. When such a formulation is offered by one party and agreed to by another, a topic may be seen (by them) to have been brought to a close. Again, an immediately following "We-ell" or "O.K." may be analyzed by its placement as doing the alternative tasks a possible pre-closing can do.

Dorrinne: Uh-you know, it's just like bringin the– blood up.
Theresa: Yeah well, THINGS UH ALWAYS WORK OUT FOR THE // BEST
Dorrinne: Oh certainly. Alright //Tess.

(1) *Theresa:*   Oh huh,
    Theresa: Okay,
    Dorrinne: G'bye.
    Theresa: Goodnight,

(2) *Johnson:*   . . . and uh, uh we're gonna see if we can't uh tie in our plans a little better.
    Baldwin: Okay // fine.
    Johnson: ALRIGHT?
    Baldwin: RIGHT.
    Johnson: Okay boy,
    Baldwin: Okay
    Johnson: Bye // bye
    Baldwin: G'night

[. . .]

What the preceding discussion suggests is that a closing section is initiated, i.e., turns out to have begun, when none of the parties to a conversation care or choose to continue it. Now that is a WARRANT for closing the conversation, and we may now be in a position to appreciate that the issue of placement, for the initiation of closing sections as for terminal exchanges, is the issue of warranting the placement of such items as will initiate the closing at some 'here and now' in the conversation. The kind of possible pre-closing we have been discussing – "O.K.", "We-ell", etc. – is a way of establishing one kind of warrant for undertaking to close a conversation. Its effectiveness can be seen in the feature noted above, that if the floor offering is declined, if the "O.K." is answered by another, then together these two utterances can constitute not a possible, but an actual first exchange of the closing section. The pre-closing ceases to be 'pre-' if accepted, for the acceptance establishes the warrant for undertaking a closing of the conversation at some 'here'.

We may now examine other kinds of pre-closings and the kinds of warrants they may invoke for initiating the beginning of a closing section. The floor-offering-exchange device [above] is one that can be initiated by any party to a conversation. In contrast to this, there are some [. . .] devices whose use is restricted to particular parties. We can offer some observations about telephone contacts, where the formulation of the parties can be specified in terms of the specific conversation, i.e., caller – called. What we find is that there are, so to speak, 'caller's techniques' and 'called's techniques' for inviting the initiation of closing sections. [. . .]

One feature that many of them have in common [is] that they employ as their warrant for initiating the closing the interests of the other party. It is in the specification of those interests that the techniques become assigned to one or another party. Thus, the following invitation to a closing is caller-specific and makes reference to the interests of the other.

> A discussion about a possible luncheon has been proceeding:
> A: Uhm livers 'n an gizzards 'n stuff like that makes it real yummy. Makes it too rich for *me* but: makes it yummy.
> A: *Well* I'll letchu go. I don't wanna tie up your phone.

And, on the other hand, there are such called-specific techniques, also making reference to the other's interests, as

> A: This is costing you a lot of money.

There are, of course, devices usable by either party which do not make reference to the other's interests, most familiarly, "I gotta go".
> [. . .]

The 'routine' questions employed at the beginnings of conversations, e.g., "what are you doing?", "where are you going?", "how are you feeling?", etc., can elicit those kinds of materials that will have a use at the ending of the conversation in warranting its closing, e.g., "Well, I'll let you get back to your books", "why don't you lie down and take a nap?", etc. By contrast with our earlier discussion of such possible pre-closings as "O.K." or "We-ell", which may be said to accomplish or embody a warrant for closing, these may be said to announce it. That they do so may be related to the possible places in which they may be used.
> [. . .]

It is the import of some of the preceding discussion that there are slots in conversation 'ripe' for the initiation of closing, such that utterances inserted there may be inspected for their closing relevance. To cite an example, "why don't you lie down and take a nap" properly placed will be heard as an initiation of a closing section, not as a question to be answered with a "Because [. . .]" (although, of course, a coparticipant can seek to decline the closing offering by treating it as a question). To cite actual data:

> B has called to invite C, but has been told C is going out to dinner:
> B: Yeah. Well get on your clothes and get out and collect some of that free food and we'll make it some other time Judy then.
> C: Okay then Jack

B: Bye bye
C: Bye bye

While B's initial utterance in this excerpt might be grammatically characterized as an imperative or a command, and C's "Okay" as a submission or
accession to it, in no sense but a technical syntactic one would those be
anything but whimsical characterizations. While B's utterance has certain
imperative aspects in its language form, those are not ones that count; his
utterance is a closing initiation; and C's utterance agrees not to a command
to get dressed (nor would she be inconsistent if she failed to get dressed
after the conversation), but to an invitation to close the conversation. The
point is that no analysis – grammatical, semantic, pragmatic, etc. – of these
utterances taken singly and out of sequence, will yield their import in use,
will show what coparticipants might make of them and do about them. That
B's utterance here accomplishes a form of closing initiation, and C's accepts
the closing form and not what seems to be proposed in it, turns on the placement of these utterances in the conversation. Investigations which fail to
attend to such considerations are bound to be misled. [Schegloff and Sacks
go on to discuss 'pre-topic closing offerings', utterances like "Did I wake
you up?", which offer listeners a means of moving into a closing section.]

[. . .]

Once properly initiated, a closing section may contain nothing but a
terminal exchange and accomplish a proper closing thereby. Thus, a proper
closing can be accomplished by:

A: *O*.K.
B: O.K.
A: Bye Bye
B: Bye

Closing sections may, however, include much more. There is a collection of
possible component parts for closing sections which we cannot describe in the
space available here. Among others, closings may include 'making arrangements', with varieties such as giving directions, arranging later meetings, invitations, and the like; reinvocation of certain sorts of materials talked of earlier
in the conversation, in particular, reinvocations of earlier-made arrangements
(e.g., "See you Wednesday") and reinvocations of the reason for initiating
the conversation (e.g., "Well, I just wanted to find out how Bob was"), not
to repeat here the earlier discussion of materials from earlier parts of the

conversation to do possible pre-closings; and components that seem to give a 'signature' of sorts to the type of conversation, using the closing section as a place where recognition of the type of conversation can be displayed (e.g., "Thank you"). Collections of these and other components can be combined to yield extended closing sections, of which the following is but a modest example:

> B: Well that's why I *said* "I'm not gonna say anything, I'm not making *any* *comments* // about anybody"
> C: Hmh
> C: Ehyeah
> B: Yeah
> C: Yeah
> B: *Al*righty. Well *I'll* give you a call before we decide to come down. O.K.?
> C: O.K.
> B: *Al*righty
> C: O.K.
> B: We'll *see* you then
> C: O.K.
> B: *Bye* bye
> C: Bye

However extensive the collection of components that are introduced, the two crucial components (FOR THE ACHIEVEMENT OF PROPER CLOSING; other components may be important for other reasons, but not for closing *per se*) are the terminal exchange which achieves the collaborative termination of the transition rule, and the proper initiation of the closing section which warrants the undertaking of the routine whose termination in the terminal exchange properly closes the conversation.

[. . .]

To capture the phenomenon of closings, one cannot treat it as the natural history of some particular conversation; one cannot treat it as a routine to be run through, inevitable in its course once initiated. Rather, it must be viewed, as much conversation as a whole, as a set of prospective possibilities opening up at various points in the conversation's course; there are possibilities throughout a closing, including the moments after a 'final' goodbye, for reopening the conversation. Getting to a termination, therefore, involves work at various points in the course of the conversation and of the closing section; it requires accomplishing. For the analyst, it requires a description of the prospects and possibilities available at the various points, how they work, what the resources are, etc., from which the participants produce what turns out to be the finally accomplished closing.

[. . .]

Symbols used in transcriptions

/	— indicates upward intonation
//	— indicates point at which following line interrupts
(n.0)	— indicates pause of n.0 seconds
( )	— indicates something said but not transcribable
(word)	— indicates probable, but not certain, transcription
but	— indicates accent
emPLOYee	— indicates heavy accent
DO	— indicates very heavy accent
: : : :	— indicates stretching of sound immediately preceding, in proportion to number of colons inserted
becau-	— indicates broken word

Chapter 16

Deborah Schiffrin

OH AS A MARKER OF INFORMATION MANAGEMENT

U NDERSTANDING DISCOURSE MARKERS requires separating the contribution made by the marker itself from the contribution made by characteristics of the discourse slot in which the marker occurs. We must pose the following questions. Does an item used as a marker have semantic meaning and/or grammatical status which contributes to its discourse function? And how does such meaning interact with a sequential context of the marker to influence production and interpretation?

I examine [a] discourse marker in this chapter – *oh* – whose uses are not clearly based on semantic meaning or grammatical status. [. . .] *Oh* is traditionally viewed as an exclamation or interjection. When used alone, without the syntactic support of a sentence, *oh* is said to indicate emotional states, e.g. surprise, fear, or pain (*Oxford English Dictionary* 1971, Fries 1952). (1) and (2) illustrate *oh* as exclamation:

(1) *Jack:*   Was that a serious picture?
      Freda: **Oh**:! Gosh yes!
(2) *Jack:*   Like I'd say, 'What d'y'mean you don't like classical
              music?'
      Freda: '**Oh**! I can't stand it! It's draggy.'

Oh can also initiate utterances, either followed by a brief pause:

(3) *Freda:*   **Oh**, well they came when they were a year.

Source: Deborah Schiffrin, *Discourse Markers*, Cambridge: Cambridge University Press.

or with no pause preceding the rest of the tone unit:

(4) *Jack:*   Does he like opera? **Oh** maybe he's too young.

We will see, regardless of its syntactic status or intonational contour, that *oh* occurs as speakers shift their orientation to information. (A very similar view of *oh* is Heritage (1984: 299), who views *oh* as a particle 'used to propose that its producer has undergone some kind of change in his or her locally current state of knowledge, information, orientation or aware- ness'.) We will see that speakers shift orientation during a conversation not only as they respond affectively to what is said (e.g., as they exclaim with surprise as in 1 and 2), but as they replace one information unit with another, as they recognize old information which has become conversation- ally relevant, and as they receive new information to integrate into an already present knowledge base. All of these are **information management tasks** in which *oh* has a role: *oh* pulls from the flow of information in dis- course a temporary focus of attention which is the target of self and/or other management.

[. . .]

Oh in repairs

Repair is a speech activity during which speakers locate and replace a prior information unit. Because they focus on prior information, repairs achieve information transitions anaphorically – forcing speakers to adjust their orien- tation to what has been said before they respond to it in upcoming talk.

Almost anything that anyone says is a candidate for repair either by the speaker him/herself or by a listener. Once an utterance actually is subjected to repair, however, the method by which it is repaired is more restricted than its initial selection: although both repair initiation and completion can be performed by a listener (other-initiation, other-completion), speakers are more likely to participate in their own repairs either by initiating (self- initiation) or completing (self-completion) the repair. (Schegloff, Jefferson and Sacks 1977 speak of this tendency as the preference for self-repair.)

Oh in repair initiation

Oh prefaces self-initiated and other-initiated repairs. Example 5 shows *oh* at self-initiated repairs. In (5), Freda is answering a question about whether she believes in extra-sensory perception (ESP) by describing her husband Jack's abilities to predict future political events.

> (5) I mean . . . he can almost foresee: . . . eh : : for instance with Nixon . . . . . . He said . . . now he's not in a medical field my husband. He said coagulating his blood, . . . uh thinning his – Nixon's blood . . . will not be good for him, if he should be operated on. **Oh** maybe it's just knowledge. I don't know if that's ESP or not in that c– in this case.

Freda recategorizes a particular description from an instance of ESP to an instance of knowledge: this self-repair is initiated with *oh*. Another self-repair from *coagulating* to *thinning* is marked with *uh*. Two other self-repairs, the addition of background information following *he said*, and replacement of *that c–* by *this case*, are not marked.

[. . .]

Not all self-initiated repairs are actual replacements of one unit of information with another: in some, speakers search for information to fill a temporary gap in recall. In (6), for example, Jack interrupts a story to provide background information about his age at the time of the reported experience – which he cannot then remember precisely. *Oh* fills the slot between his self-interruption and his first attempt at specifying his age.

> (6) There was a whole bunch of oth– I was about– **oh**: younger than Robert. I was about uh . . . maybe Joe's age. Sixteen.

Note that *uh* seems to serve the same general function as *oh* in this example: both are place-holders for Jack as he searches for information. But *oh* initiates the repair (it is preceded by a self-interruption), whereas *uh* continues the repair.

Example (7) illustrates other-initiated repairs. (Differentiating other-initiated repairs from disagreements often requires interpretation of speaker intent, especially when the same phrases are used, e.g., *what do you mean X?*. Because it is not always possible (from either an analyst's or participant's viewpoint) to know whether it is one's information output that is being corrected (repair), or one's knowledge of information that is being assessed (disagreement), I am including any replacement by one speaker of what another has said as other-repair. Note that this ambiguity may be one reason why other-repairs are marked forms of repair.) In (7), I am explaining what I mean by 'ethnic group'.

(7) *Debby:*   By ethnic group I meant nationality. Okay like um
              Irish or:– I guess there aren't

too many Irish Jews but   ] =
I see! Yeh yeh. **Oh** yes =

Jack:
Debby: = Italian:
Jack: = there is!

Jack's *I see* acknowledges my description of ethnic group. His *Oh yes there is!*
is an other-initiated repair to my assertion about Irish Jews.

[. . .]

Oh in repair completion

Repairs are completed when the repairable is replaced by a new item; additional completion can be provided through confirmation of the replacement.
When the replacement is issued by the same speaker who had issued the
repairable, we can speak of self completion; when the repairable is replaced
by another speaker, of other completion. *Oh* prefaces both self and other-
completions. [. . .] Example (7) showed combinations of other-initiated and
other-completed repairs. [. . .]

 Oh also occurs when one party completes a repair initiated by the other
– when other-initiated repairs are self-completed, and when self-initiated
repairs are other-completed. In 8, for example, Zelda and Henry are
answering my questions about who they visit.

(8) *Henry:*   Ah: who can [answer that,] the kids. We have nobody =
    Zelda: [Our kids.   ]
    Henry: = else.   **Oh** yeh we– my sister =
    Zelda: Yeh, you have a sister.
    Zelda: = we see in the summertime a lot.

Henry forgets to mention his sister: thus, Zelda other-initiates a repair to
this effect. Henry then self-completes the repair by replacing his earlier
answer with one which includes his sister as someone whom he visits.

[. . .]

 In sum, that self and other participate in both initiation and completion
of repair shows a speaker/hearer division of responsibility for information
management. Self-initiation and completion of repair show speakers' sensitivity to their own **production** of discourse: by locating and replacing an

item from an outgoing utterance, speakers display their productive efforts. Other-initiation and completion of repair show hearers' sensitivity to their **reception** of discourse: by locating and replacing an item from an incoming utterance, hearers display their pursual of understanding and their effort to interpret what is being said as it is being received. Thus, jointly managed repairs are evidence of a participation framework in which both producer and recipient of talk replace information units and publicly redistribute knowledge about them.

[We omit a detailed section where Schiffrin considers *oh* in repairs achieved through clarification sequences]

Oh in question/answer/acknowledgement sequences

Another speech activity which explicitly manages and distributes information is the three-part sequence of question, answer, and acknowledgement. Question/answer pairs complete a proposition, which may then be verbally acknowledged by the questioner – the individual who first opened the proposition for completion. The conditions under which *oh* prefaces questions, answers, and acknowledgements are sensitive to the different information management tasks accomplished in these turns.

Question/answer pairs

Question/answer pairs are adjacency pairs, i.e., sequentially constrained pairs in which the occurrence of a first-pair-part creates a slot for the occurrence of a second-pair-part (a conditional relevance), such that the non-occurrence of that second-pair-part is heard as officially absent [see Chapter 15]. One reason why questions constrain the next conversational slot is semantic: WH-questions are incomplete propositions; yes–no questions are propositions whose polarity is unspecified (e.g., Carlson 1983). Completion of the proposition is up to the recipient of the question, who either fills in the WH-information or fixes the polarity. This semantic completion allows a speaker/hearer re-orientation toward an information unit, i.e., redistribution of knowledge about a proposition.

Oh with questions
Question/answer pairs are rarely couplets which are totally disconnected from their containing discourse. In fact, some questions are quite explicitly connected to immediately prior utterances: for example, requests for clarification

are often formulated as syntactic questions. Other questions are used to request elaboration of what has just been said. Example (9) shows that like requests for clarification, requests for elaboration may also be prefaced by *oh*.

(9) *Val:*   Is it safe?
     Freda: Uh: we found a safe way! But it's the long way!
     Val: **Oh** it's a special way?

Elaboration requests are similar to clarification requests because they, too, focus on prior information. There are two differences, however. First, clarification requests indicate a reception problem which will be resolved through upcoming clarification; elaboration requests acknowledge receipt of information which has been sufficiently interpreted to allow the receiver to prompt its further development. Second, compliance with a clarification request is the amendment of **old** information; compliance with an elaboration request is provision of **new** information.

Despite these differences, both clarification and elaboration requests can be prefaced by *oh* because both display speakers' receipt of information (partial or complete) at the same time that they solicit further information. The only other questions prefaced by *oh* are those which are suddenly remembered by a speaker as previously intended. Prior to (10), for example, I had been checking my interview schedule, when I saw a question that I had not yet asked.

(10) *Debby:*   **Oh** listen, I forgot to ask you what your father did
                 when you were growing up.

Like requests for clarification and elaboration, the suddenly remembered question in (10) displays the questioner's receipt of information – although here, the just-received information may not be presented by an interlocutor, but may be recalled by the speaker him/herself. In short, questions through which speakers only solicit information are not prefaced by *oh*; it is only questions which are evoked by the reception of information which may be prefaced by *oh*.

Oh with answers
Answers to questions are prefaced with *oh* when a question forces an answerer to reorientate him/herself to information – that is, when the question makes clear that information presumed to be shared is not so, or that a similar orientation toward information was wrongly assumed. At the same time, answers with *oh* make explicit to the questioner the violation of a prior expectation about information.

Such re-orientations may be caused by a mismatch between the information that the questioner assumed to be shared: the questioner may have assumed too much or too little to be shared, or the questioner may have made a wrong assumption. Consider (11). I have told Irene that I am a student at a local university.

> (11) *Irene:*   How can I get an appointment t'go down there t'bring my son on a tour?
>
> *Debby:*   **Oh** I didn't even know they gave tours! I'm not the one t'ask about it.

Irene's son is interested in attending the university, and she assumes that I would know (as a student) that the university gives tours to prospective students. But since I had no knowledge of the tours, Irene's question had assumed more shared information than was warranted: my *oh* shows both my receipt of this new information and alerts Irene to her misguided expectation as to what information we had shared.

[. . .]

Oh with acknowledgement of answers

Question/answer pairs are often followed by the questioner's response to the informational content of the answer which had been elicited. Such responses may vary from evaluations of the answer (endorsements, challenges) to re-solicitations of the answer (as accomplished through requests for clarification). (That certain registers, such as teacher talk, use a three-part question/answer/evaluation format is well known. See e.g., Mehan 1979.) Another possible response is acknowledgement of the answer, i.e., the questioner's display of receipt of the answer.

Consider, however, that exactly **what** is acknowledged varies depending upon whether the questioner finds that the answer to his/her question contains anticipated information. [. . .]

In (12), for example, Irene's answer does not conform to the expectations encoded through my question:

> (12) *Debby:*   So what, you have *three* kids?
> *Irene:*   I have *four.* ⎡Three boys⎤ and a girl.
> *Debby:*   ⎣*Four* kids. ⎦   **Oh** I didn't know that.

Note that I am not distinguishing old from new information: both anticipated and unanticipated answers provide **new** information. But new information

which has been anticipated creates less of a reorientation than does new information which has not been anticipated. [. . .]

Oh and the status of information

Thus far we have focused on speech activities whose goal is the management of information and whose exchange structure helps accomplish that
goal. We have seen that *oh* marks different tasks involved in this management: the production and reception of information, the replacement and
redistribution of information, the receipt of solicited, but unanticipated,
information. *Oh* is more likely to be used when locally provided information
does not correspond to a speaker's prior expectations: in repairs, questions,
answers, and acknowledgements, *oh* marks a shift in speaker's orientation to
information.

Use of *oh* is hardly confined to speech activities whose exchange structure is focused on information management. In this section, I examine *oh*
first, as a marker of recognition of familiar information – more specifically,
old information which has become newly relevant – and second, as a marker
of new information receipt.

Oh as recognition display

Recognition of familiar information is often conversationally triggered. In the
following examples, one speaker prompts another into recall, which is then
explicitly marked not only with *oh*, but with confirmation of the correctness
of the prompt, and/or provision of information testifying to the speaker's
prior knowledge.

In (13), I prompt Zelda and Henry through use of *do you know X?*

> (13) *Debby:*   No this–d'you–d'you know um: I was talkin' to the
> Kramers, down, 4500.
> *Zelda:*   **Oh** yeh, Freda?
> *Debby:*   ⎡ Yeh. ⎤
> *Henry:*   ⎣ **Oh** ⎦ yeh. Jack?

Both Zelda and Henry mark their recognition with *oh* and with elaboration
of the topic which I have evoked (the Kramers' first names). [. . .] Recognition
of familiar information may also result from the speaker's own cognitive
search for a particular piece of known information. In (14), for example,

Zelda and Henry are telling me about their favorite restuarants; Henry has just said that they have been eating out more than ever.

> (14) *Zelda:*   And uh– **Oh!** We– when we go to the kids, we
> always eat out.
> We eat at the F1– Blue Fountain.

It sounds as if Zelda is about to add another restaurant to her list of favorites (because of her initial *and*). But she switches to a reason for the frequency with which they have been dining out (*when we go to the kids, we always eat out*), and then mentions another restaurant (*Blue Fountain*). The reason seems to be a sudden recall, and it is the reason that is marked by *oh*.

[. . .]

Oh as information receipt

Oh also marks a speaker's receipt of new information. In (15), for example, Zelda doesn't know prior to Irene's telling her that Irene's husband Ken had been fixing their back door. Note how Irene prompts Zelda's realization by introducing the news discourse topic with *y'know*.[. . .]

> (15) *Irene:*   You know who was bangin' out there for twenty
> minutes. Ken.   He didn't know where I
> was. =
> *Zelda:*   **Oh**
> *Irene:*   ⎡ = He was fixin' the back ⎤ door.
> *Zelda:*   ⎣ **Oh** I didn't hear him! ⎦

Speakers also introduce new discourse topics by tying them to information they assume their hearers will find familiar. Henry and Zelda know that my parents own a house near their summer home. In (16), they are trying to find a location with which I am familiar in order to locate their summer home for me.

> (16) *Debby:* Where are you? Which– ⎡ which street? ⎤
> *Henry:*   ⎣ We're on   ⎦ Arkansas.
>   Right from– across from the bank.
> *Zelda:* D'y'know where the Montclair is? And the Sea View?
>   D'you ever ride down the:– ⎡ uh ⎤   The =
> *Debby:*   ⎣ The ⎦ motels? There?

Zelda: = motels. On the boardwalk. ⌈ D'you go bike riding?   ⌉
Henry: ⌊ Do you know where Abe's ⌋
        is?   ⌉ Right across the =
Debby: Yeh I know where Abe's is. ⌋
Henry: = street.
Debby: **Oh** it's that way.

When I finally do acknowledge a familiar location (*where Abe's is*), Henry locates his home in relation to that place. I then acknowledge receipt of this new piece of information.

[. . .]

Oh and shifts in subjective orientation

Speaker orientation to information is not just a matter of recognition and receipt of the informational content of ongoing discourse. Orientation also involves the **evaluation** of information: speakers respond affectively and subjectively to what is said, what they are thinking of, and what happens around them. Just as speakers display shifts in objective orientation, so too, do they display shifts in subjective orientation. And not surprisingly, *oh* can be used when speakers display shifts in expressive orientation.

One such subjective orientation is **intensity**: a speaker is so committed to the truth of a proposition that future estimates of his or her character hinge on that truth (Labov 1984). In (17), for example, I have unintentionally provoked a disagreement between Freda and Jack about something for which they both display strong feelings: girls' high schools. Note Freda's repetition, meta-talk, and contrastive stress on *do* – all expressions of intensity commonly used in argument (Schiffrin 1982: Chapter 8).

(17a) *Debby:* Well I think there's a lot of competition between
                girls.
                In an *all* girls school. More than well– more acad-
                emically ⌈ anyway.   ⌉
      Freda: ⌊ **Oh**   ⌋ yes. **Oh** yes. They're better
                students I *do* believe that.

Later in the argument, Freda responds to Jack's accusation that the girls' high school which she and I both attended is no longer academically respected. Her defense intensifies when Jack adds to his accusation the demise of the local boys' high school.

(17b) *Jack:*   In fact it had lost its popularity, didn't it.

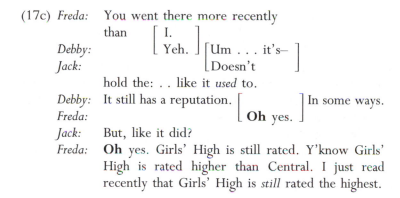

She later solicits endorsement of her position from me. Note her use of *oh yes* upon receipt of my endorsement, and, as preface to her response to Jack's question – a response which intensifies her position about the academic quality of Girls' High still further.

Thus, in (17), *oh* accompanies Freda's increasingly intensive orientation toward her position. The cumulative interactional effect of these progressive shifts in Freda's own commitment in her position is increased distance from Jack's position.

[. . .]

Why *oh?*

We have seen that *oh* marks different tasks of information management in discourse. These productive and receptive tasks, however, are hardly dependent on *oh*: speakers are certainly able to replace, recognize, receive, and re-evaluate information without verbalization through *oh*. Why, then, does *oh* occur?

Since the overall role of *oh* is in information state transitions, let us begin with this component of talk. One of the basic goals of talk is the exchange of information. This goal can be realized because speakers and hearers redistribute knowledge about entities, events, states, situations, and so on – whatever real world knowledge is being represented through talk. Furthermore, because discourse involves the **exchange** of information, knowledge and meta-knowledge are constantly in flux, as are degrees of certainty about, and salience of, information. Another way of saying this is that information states are constantly evolving over the course of a conversation: what speakers and hearers can reasonably expect one another to know, what they can expect about the other's knowledge of what they know, how certain they can expect one another to be about that knowledge, and how salient they can expect the other to find that knowledge are all constantly changing. In short, information states are dynamic processes which change as each one of their contributing factors changes.

Oh has a role in information state transitions because *oh* marks a focus of speaker's attention which then also becomes a candidate for hearer's attention. This creation of a joint focus of attention not only allows transitions in information state, but it marks information as more salient with a possible increase in speaker/hearer certainty as to shared knowledge and meta-knowledge. So it is by verbally marking a cognitive task, and opening an individual processing task to a hearer, that *oh* initiates an information state transition.

But suggesting that *oh* has a pragmatic effect – the creation of a joint focus – does not really answer the question of **why** *oh* has this pragmatic effect. To try to answer this question, let us consider in more detail how *oh* is situated in social interaction.

First, *oh* makes evident a very general and pervasive property of participation frameworks: the division of conversational labor between speaker and hearer. Back-channel *oh*, for example, ratifies the current participation structure of the conversation: speaker remains speaker, and hearer remains hearer. Thus, *oh* as back-channel not only marks information receipt, and marks an individual as an occupant of a specific participation status (active recipient), but it also ratifies the current division of turn-taking responsibilities in the exchange structure.

Second, *oh* displays individuals in specific participation statuses and frameworks. Because *oh* displays one's own ongoing management of information, its user is temporarily displayed as an individual active in the role of utterance reception. Recall that *oh* is used not only as a back-channel response, but to incorporate requested clarifications and unanticipated answers into talk. These uses display a hearer as an active recipient of information who acknowledges and integrates information as it is provided. This functional capacity is complementary to the speaker's capacity as animator (Goffman 1981: 144): both display individuals as occupants of mechanically defined nodes in a system of information transmission.

Oh displays still another aspect of participation frameworks: speaker/ hearer alignment toward each other. We have seen that individuals evaluate each other's orientations: what one defines as an appropriate level of commitment to a proposition, another may define as inappropriate. Different speaker/hearer alignments can be characterized in part by whether individuals share subjective orientations toward a proposition. For example, we might characterize an argument as an alignment in which Speaker A is committed to the truth of a proposition to which B is not similarly committed, and Speaker B is committed to the truth of another proposition to which A is not similarly committed. When *oh* marks a speaker's realization of the other's unshared commitment, then, it may serve as a signal of a potentially argumentative stance. Thus, it is because *oh* makes accessible speaker/hearer assumptions about each others' subjective orientations toward information, that it can display speaker/hearer alignments toward each other.

And, finally, consider that conversation requires a delicate balance between the satisfaction of one's own needs and the satisfaction of others' needs. Included is not only an individual cognitive need – individuals need time (no matter how short) to transform the content that they have in mind into talk – but a reciprocal social need: individuals need to receive appreciation for self and show deference to others (Goffman 1967 [Chapter 18]; Lakoff 1973; Tannen 1984). *Oh* may help service individuals' cognitive needs by providing time to focus on informational tasks – while still displaying one's interactional presence in deference to the satisfaction of social needs.

In sum, although *oh* is a marker of information management tasks which are essentially cognitive, the fact that it verbalizes speakers' handling of those tasks has interactional consequences. Thus, use of *oh* may very well be cognitively motivated. But once an expression makes cognitive work accessible to another during the course of a conversation, it is open for pragmatic interpretation and effect – and such interpretations may become conventionally associated with the markers of that work. Intended interactional effects and meanings may thus account for the use of *oh* as readily as the initial cognitive motivation. Such conventionalized effects may further explain why speakers verbally mark information management tasks with *oh*.

References

Carlson, L. (1983) *Dialogue Games*, Dordrecht: Reidel.

Fries, C. (1952) *The Structure of English*, London: Longman.

Goffman, E. (1967) 'The nature of deference and demeanor' in *Interaction Ritual*, New York: Anchor Books, 49–95.

—— (1981) 'Footing', in *Forms of talk*, 124–57, Philadelphia: University of Pennsylvania Press. (Originally published 1979 in *Semiotica* 25: 1–29.)

Heritage, J. (1984) 'A change-of-state token and aspects of its sequential place-
    ment', in Atkinson, J. M. and Heritage, J. (eds) *Structures of Social Action:
    Studies in Conversation Analysis*, Cambridge: Cambridge University Press,
    299–345.
Labov, W. (1984) 'Intensity', in Schiffrin, D. (ed.) *Meaning, Form and Use in
    Context: Linguistic Applications*, Georgetown University Round Table on
    Languages and Linguistics 1984, Washington, DC: Georgetown University
    Press, 43–70.
Lakoff, R. (1973) 'The logic of politeness, or minding your p's and q's', *Papers
    from the 9th Regional Meeting, Chicago Linguistic Society*, Chicago: Linguistics
    Department, University of Chicago, 292–305.
Mehan, H. (1979) *Learning Lessons: Social Organization in the Classroom*, Cambridge,
    MA: Harvard University Press.
Oxford English Dictionary (1971), Oxford: Oxford University Press.
Schegloff, E., Jefferson, G. and Sacks, H. (1977) 'The preference for self-correc-
    tion in the organization of repair in conversation', *Language* 53: 361–82.
Schiffrin, D. (1982) 'Discourse markers: semantic resources for the construc-
    tion of conversation', Ph.D. dissertation, University of Pennsylvania.
Tannen, D. (1984) *Conversational Style: Analyzing Talk Among Friends*, Norwood,
    NJ: Ablex.

PART FOUR

Negotiating social relationships

Editors' Introduction to Part Four

DESPITE ARGUMENTS THAT LANGUAGE in use is multi-functional (see Part One), the fact that discourse is not only used for exchanging information but is also equally functional in shaping interpersonal and inter-group relations comes as news to some people. In a self-report study of under-graduate students' 'language awareness' (Jaworski 1995), the relational (or 'conative' in Jakobson's term, Chapter 1) dimension of language was the one students said they were least aware of, before they engaged with the field of discourse studies. But studies of relational aspects of communication are very well established in social and cultural anthropology.

The opening chapter in this Part is a classic by the anthropologist Bronislaw Malinowski, first published in 1923. The original date of publication is important for two reasons. First, it indicates Malinowski's pioneering theo-retical work, establishing the basic theme of this Part of the *Reader* – how language achieves closeness and intimacy between people, what he referred to as *phatic communion*. Second, it explains the rather dated rhetoric of the paper, which, like most other writings of Malinowski's, is based on his work in the Pacific. Certainly, references by a white, middle-class anthropologist to the 'savage tribes' or to 'the primitive mind . . . among savages or our own un-educated classes' (p. 303) are the voice of colonialism and class prejudice today. But regardless of these limitations, which can be explained by history and the shifting ideological frameworks of social research, Malinowski's placing of language (and more specifically *talk*) at the centre of social relations is highly significant. Phatic communion, 'a type of speech in which ties of union are created by a mere exchange of words' (p. 303), has become a prototypical manifestation of sociability through discourse.

One of the important aspects of phatic communion which drew analysts' interest was its ritualistic character. It was mainly John Laver's (1974; 1981) work which first refined the ideas put forward by Malinowski, and Laver pointed out that phatic communion is ritualised usage in at least two senses. First, phatic communion, like much of everyday conversation (Cheepen 1988), is highly predictable. Like other ritualistic behaviour, phatic communion proceeds according to well-established patterns, or scripts. Anyone who has been to more than one drinks party can attest that 'all' conversations s/he has had there 'were exactly the same'. But there is a good reason for this apparent repetitiveness of phatic communion, and that brings us to the second understanding of its ritualistic aspect. This time, more in line with the cultural anthropological approach to communication (e.g., Leach 1976), the term 'ritual' refers to the wide range of activities in which people engage during transitional or *liminal* moments in social time and space: ceremonies such as baptisms, weddings, funerals, initiation rites, birthdays (especially those marking 'significant' ages, e.g. 18, 21, and all the 'round-number' birthdays at decade boundaries). In other words, all our *rites of passage*, big or small, are marked by rituals. Verbal and non-verbal ritualistic activities help social actors in these situations to overcome the unusually significant face-threat associated with the uncertainty of the situation (moving from one state to another) and often being in the centre of attention. Having a script to follow makes such occasions (e.g., weddings) bearable and manageable by giving all the participants clear and predefined 'roles' to play.

However, social rituals are enacted more often than this. Meeting new people, starting and closing conversations, or just having a chat while taking time off work in an office are, according to Laver, all marginal phases of interaction which resemble other rites of passage, and they place social actors in liminal spaces. Phatic communion, then, offers us scripts to pass through these moments in a non-threatening and socially acceptable way.

Malinowski's original definition of phatic communion, and Laver's (1974: 220; 1981: 301) elaboration of it, centre on its use to 'defuse the potential hostility of silence in situations where speech is conventionally anticipated'. This, again, requires a brief comment. On the one hand, such an approach relegates phatic communion to the realm of trivial and unimportant talk. It may make the participants in a speech event comfortable, but in itself the talk is seemingly dismissed as a filler for silence: we might call it 'small talk', 'gossip' or 'chit-chat'. Coupland, Coupland and Robinson (1992) and J. Coupland (1999) re-examine this relative negativity in the folk and analytic metalanguage about phatic communion. They show that 'phaticity' is an important and intricate discursive practice, co-constructed by all participants in delicate negotiations of face and social distance. Besides, silence need not always be a signal of interpersonal unease.

It appears that small talk and silence (construed by Malinowski and his followers as antonyms or opposites) are in fact complementary in their distribution. Nessa Wolfson's (1988) bulge theory suggests that (among American, white, middle-class people) rules for spoken discourse are quite similar between intimates, status unequals and strangers, as opposed to between nonintimates, status unequal friends, co-workers and acquaintances:

> [W]hen we examine the ways in which different speech acts are realized in actual everyday speech, and when we compare these behaviors in terms of the social relationships of the interlocutors, we find again and again that the two extremes of social distance – minimum and maximum – seem to call forth very similar behavior, while relationships which are more toward the center show marked differences.
>
> (Wolfson, 1988: 32)

Thinking of phaticity as the type of communicative behavior which foregrounds positive relational goals (Coupland and Coupland 1992), we may observe a 'bulge' pattern in the distribution of phatic talk and silence. Other things being equal, relationships 'toward the centre' (casual friends and acquaintances) will be marked by a more frequent use of phatic talk than those at the extreme ends of the social distance: intimacy and detachment (see Jaworski 1999).

This discussion of the sociable nature of talk and treating everyday encounters as mini performances or rituals was developed with great insight by the American sociologist, Erving Goffman, whose chapter on *face-work* is reproduced in this Part (Chapter 18). We have already mentioned Goffman in our general Introduction but his influence on the discourse analytic research of sociability is so great that we need to devote more space here to his contribution. Goffman takes us further to a more localised perspective on communication, mainly because his analyses were grounded in his own informal observation of North American social and interactional styles of communication. The subtitle of the book from which we have excerpted Chapter 18 is 'Essays on face-to-face behavior' (first published in 1967), and we have selected a famous essay dealing with the ritualised nature of talk and with the intriguing concept of 'face'. Face has become a major theme in discourse studies, most notably developed in Brown and Levinson's research on 'politeness' (see Chapter 19). Goffman uses face to analyse how a person's standing and integrity are 'managed' in everyday interaction, how people are attentive to their own and others' faces, and how they deal with moments that threaten esteem and credibility.

The metaphor which dominates Goffman's analyses is that of the theatre, and when he uses the term 'actor' (often in preference to 'speaker' or 'listener') and 'performance' (often instead of 'talk' or 'behaviour') he is deliberately invoking the theatrical senses of these terms. The idea of 'pose' (self-control) and that of face itself suggest stage 'masks' that people carefully select and 'wear' to conjure up specific images and effects. Goffman strips away the levels of control and self-management that produce conventionalised social behaviour in public. He leaves us recognising these traits – in ourselves and others – but perhaps also feeling rather like voyeurs of social processes. Goffman picks up what is most ordinary in social interaction and, brilliantly, identifies the goals, strategies and conceits that are interwoven into everyday face-to-face communication.

Not surprisingly, very many aspects of Goffman's work have left a deep imprint on the methods and assumptions of discourse analysis. We could list some of them:

- the view of language in use as social action, and, as we have just mentioned, seeing people as social actors;
- the assumption that discourse does not merely happen but is achieved, as part of strategic performances;
- the role of discourse in the construction and management of individuals and 'selfhood';
- studying how individual people's language is coordinated with other people's, so that social interaction is a delicately collaborative achievement;
- discourse as, in many regards, pre-structured, predictable and ritualistic;
- the orderliness of talk (e.g., 'the little ceremonies of greeting and farewell' (p. 318)) being explicable in terms of speakers' concerns for protecting and extending their relationships (see Schegloff and Sacks, Chapter 15);
- building a sociological 'map' of social norms and customs through analysis of local patterns of talk ('the traffic rules of social interaction' (p. 309)).

Goffman's writings are clearly contributions to sociological analysis. His writing is peppered with phrases like 'in our society' and comments on potentially different practices and norms for interaction in different cultural groups. Most obviously he is a sociologist mapping out the sociology of human relationships. Goffman does not give us examples of specific utterances, and his analyses are therefore largely built around general categories of utterance (e.g. 'employing courtesies', 'making a belittling demand' or 'providing explanations') or of non-verbal behaviour ('avoidance' or 'leave-taking'). But these categories, the building blocks of Goffman's interactional analysis which he sometimes calls 'moves', are of course speech-act types of the sort Austin (Chapter 2) and Grice (Chapter 3) were (more formally) discussing. They are functional and pragmatic units which Watzlawick *et al.* (1967) saw as the architecture of relational communication. Despite their widely differing origins, we again see a confluence of ideas and interests in these foundational texts – in studying the discursive basis of everyday communication.

A combination of Goffman's work on face and interaction and Grice's perspective on conversational cooperativity left Penelope Brown and Stephen Levinson two main legacies in formulating their politeness theory (Chapter 19). Grice in fact recognises politeness as a specific dimension of talk where it is possible to formulate general maxims, and this is largely what Brown and Levinson have done, building a model of the normal expectations communicators make about how to 'save face'. The extract we reproduce here comes from their original work (first published as an extended paper in 1978, and later reprinted in book form in 1987), and it gives an outline of the theory. Due to limited space we cannot reproduce their elaborate taxonomy of politeness strategies, which Brown and Levinson illustrate in their original text with numerous examples, mainly from English, Tamil and Tzeltal. But we have provided a short appendix, summarising these strategies (pp. 334–35).

Politeness Theory has at its heart Goffman's notion of face. Face has two aspects: a want to be liked and appreciated by others, *positive face*, and a want to be left free of imposition, *negative face*. Both positive and negative face can be damaged or threatened in contact with others, when a *face-threatening act* (FTA) of some sort is performed. Thus, individuals adopt various politeness strategies to mitigate or avoid the face-threat associated with such acts as criticisms and accusations (threatening to positive face), or requests and orders (threatening to negative face). Mitigation strategies in discourse then take the form of either *indirectness* (in the sense of violating Grice's Cooperative Principle), or they can be *direct with a mitigating comment* before an FTA is performed. An example of this second case is when a criticism is preceded by a compliment, or when an accusation is accompanied by giving an account or a justification.

Politeness theory has become an enormously influential paradigm in discourse analysis. It has spawned a large body of literature on politeness strategies and face in different context, social and cultural groups (see Kasper 1997 for a catalogue of these studies). It has offered a comprehensive system for describing and explaining the communicative behaviour of individuals across a wide range of speech events. However, some claims made by politeness theory have been criticised and we need to summarise this critique briefly.

Politeness theory purports to be universal. That is, it assumes that the principles of social interaction it describes are common to (rational) individuals in all societies. However, some authors have questioned the universality of Brown and Levinson's categories. Some of the main observations made are that:

- the notion of face, built around the wants of an individual, does not fully apply in societies where the identity and well-being of an in-group seems to override an individual's concerns of self-presentation (e.g., Gu 1990);
- the claim that some speech acts are intrinsically face threatening is problematic, as different acts (such as requests, for example) may be perceived as an imposition in one group but as an expression of camaraderie in another (Sifianou 1992);
- the way the model is formulated by Brown and Levinson, and the way their examples of politeness strategies are listed, suggests that each FTA is normally mitigated by only one type of strategy; however, as Brown and Gilman (1989) observe, politeness strategies of different sorts are typically merged in a single utterance;
- although Brown and Levinson's data come from naturally occurring discourse in three different (genetically unrelated) languages, their examples are mostly single utterances taken out of their wider context; Coupland et al. (1988) argue that the specific social situations (for example talk between people of different generations, in contexts of care) radically affects our interpretations of utterances as being, for example, 'positively polite'; high-intimacy talk to older people is often construed as patronising and even ageist;
- Brown and Levinson's classification of different strategies of politeness ranks non-performance of an FTA as the most polite option; they do

not engage in any discussion of this strategy because, for them, it produces no interesting linguistic reflexes; however, silence can of course be very face-threatening, and it can also be used as a positive or a negative politeness strategy (see Jaworski 1993; Sifianou 1997).

Despite these criticisms, politeness theory provides an excellent theoretical basis for continuing work on how individuals achieve sociability in face-to-face interaction, particularly if more sensitivity to social and cultural contexts can be incorporated into analyses. The criticisms we have listed have led to modifications of the theory to account for greater subtleties in polite (and impolite) usage. Janet Holmes's chapter (Chapter 20) is an example of a study which documents the differences in politeness strategies among men and women. In the book on gender and politeness from which this chapter is extracted, Holmes (1995) defines politeness as a way of making one's interlocutor feel good. In her detailed, qualitative and quantitative examination of ethnographically collected data (coming predominantly from middle-class, white New Zealand English speakers), Holmes demonstrates consistently how, other things being equal, women rather than men use strategies typically associated with showing greater concern for the other. (This finding seems to be corroborated by a number of other studies of gender and language in other communities.)

Questions of interpretation are extremely important here. We obviously need to ask ourselves whether we interpret certain strategies used predominantly by women as 'polite' *because* they are used by women. Holmes suggests that some instances of stereotypical male talk (e.g., verbal aggression) which appear to be offensive and impolite, may actually signal in-group rapport and camaraderie, not unlike Brown and Levinson's positive politeness. In other words, men and women may, at times, be *equally* polite in their own terms, but achieve this in dramatically different ways, not always acceptable to the other group.

Such a view may be easily challenged from positions assuming unequal power relations between the sexes by arguing that if women 'do' politeness by showing less aggression than men, it is because they are in a powerless position, which does not allow them to use conventionalised aggression as much as (powerful) men do. However, in her review of male–female differences in speech, Milroy (1992) questions this view of politeness as too stereotyped. For example, she argues that men in powerful jobs (say, top executives of large companies) are likely to follow the stereotypically female patterns of politeness (e.g., hedging their requests or using indirectness) precisely because they are powerful. *You wouldn't have time to type this letter for me?* may be a sufficiently explicit and 'more effective' request from a male boss to a female secretary than *Type this letter, now!* In Part Five, Cameron (Chapter 26) goes even further in questioning the explanations of 'typical' linguistic behaviour in men and women. She says they too often conform to our stereotypes of what is 'normal', predictable and accepted behaviour by men and women.

The next two chapters by Tannen and Wallat (Chapter 21) and Kendon (Chapter 22) are concerned with a different aspect of interpersonal communication: framing. Drawing on linguistic, sociological and cognitive work, Deborah Tannen and Cynthia Wallat start with a helpful summary of related concepts such as 'frame', 'footing' and 'knowledge schema'. They apply these terms to an analysis of a paediatric consultation, in which the doctor shifts *register* (style of speaking), signalling how the speech event is restructured from moment to moment. Style shifts mark changes in the type of activity she is engaged in (medical examination of the child, giving explanations to the mother, giving explanations to students, recording diagnosis), and changes in the 'participation framework' (speaking to the child, or mother, or student). This chapter shows also how frames are established interactively, or part of a negotiative process and through conversational work. The doctor alternates between the interactive frames of 'examination' and 'consultation' on the one hand, and 'social encounter' on the other, thus showing sensitivity to the mother, for whom unmitigated, matter-of-fact talk about her child's impairment could be emotionally difficult to cope with. Thus, to ease the mother's emotional burden, the doctor

> blunts the effect of the information she imparts by using circum-
> locutions and repetitions; pausing and hesitating; and minimizing
> the significant danger of the arteriovenous malformation by using
> the word 'only' ('only danger') by using the conditional tense
> ('that would be the danger'), and by stressing what sounds posi-
> tive, that they're not going to get worse.
>
> (p. 358)

These framing devices, not unlike Gumperz's contextualization cues (see the general Introduction, p. 28) perform the dual role of signalling what kind of frame is being established in interaction at the moment of speaking, and forming part of the message communicated within this frame, too.

In this chapter, Adam Kendon elaborates on the concept of framing by developing Goffman's notion of 'attentional tracks' and distinguishes *main-line* or *story-line track* (i.e., actions at the centre of attention), *directional track* (i.e., actions providing organisation for main-line track) and *disattend track* (i.e., activities which go on simultaneously with main-line track but are treated as irrelevant to it). Kendon offers a compelling overview of verbal and, even more importantly, non-verbal means which allow social actors to negotiate and establish recognised frameworks of interaction. In the process of what Kendon calls *frame-attunement*, even the most superfluous, 'disattended' activities (e.g., body posture) *are* in fact registered by communicators which allows them to communicate intended actions before they are actually performed. Kendon (1990) illustrates this process with an example of a daughter showing off her yo-yo tricks to her father sitting in his chair, reading a newspaper. The show-ing off of yo-yo tricks is a co-constructed activity in which the child assumes a body orientation and posture suitable for her 'performance' (e.g., orientat-ing her front to the father), and the father puts down his paper and looks up at her. The performance is the main-track dimension, and the non-verbal attunement establishes a joint focus, anticipating the beginning of the perfor-mance. Thus, frame attunement requires participants' knowledge of which actions contribute to the main-line activities, and which aspects of behaviour are responsible for the signalling of prior, parallel or subsequent activities.

There is an affinity between Kendon's work (1990; Chapter 22) and Charles Goodwin's (Chapter 28) in Part Five, as they both demonstrate the interplay between the verbal and non-verbal synchrony in performing joint actions. Kendon focuses on sociable interaction (including phatic communion, cf. Malinowski, Chapter 17), and Goodwin deals with professional discourse and the negotiating of a factually important piece of evidence in archaeo-logical discourse (colour of excavated dirt). But they both show the amount of complex relational work which participants must do in attuning their orien-tations to even the simplest of interactional events. Once again Kendon's chapter (not unlike the others in this Part of the *Reader*) demonstrates that meaning making in discourse has to do with adopting interactional stances and orientations *vis-à-vis* other participants and that social relationships are subject to negotiation and joint production.

This Part ends with an example of a study of relational issues in a medium other than language – visual communication. Gunther Kress and Theo van Leeuwen's study (Chapter 23) of the meaning of visual images as a semiotic system is a multidisciplinary project which draws on history of art, semiotics and linguistics. The authors argue that language is only one of the represen-tational and communicative systems and can no longer be considered as central to human communication. For them, the *semiotic landscape* (the world of meaning) in which we live has undergone a transformation and is now dominated by *multi-modality*, or diversity of media (see our general Introduction). As far as visual images are concerned, they pose a challenge: we can see them and (in most cases) be sure what they 'show', but the processes of visual representation are far more subtle than being able to say what a picture shows. In their analysis of the structural relationships of elements within images and their compositional arrangements, Kress and van Leeuwen give us the basis for an understanding of how these images are constructed; a key to *visual literacy*.

In the chapter we have extracted here, Kress and van Leeuwen demonstrate what type of interpersonal relationships can be established between the (human) subject of an image and its viewer. They examine three dimensions of interpersonal relations which are typically associated with discursive patterns of communication: distance, rapport and power, and link them to three formal aspects of image making: closeness of the shot, frontal/oblique angle, and high/low angle. Kress and van Leeuwen propose that these relationships are patterned in the following way: close shot – intimate/personal, medium shot – social, long shot – impersonal; frontal angle – involvement, oblique angle – detachment; high angle – viewer power, eye-level angle – equality, low angle – represented participant power.

References

Brown, P. and Levinson, S. C. (1987) *Politeness: Some Universals in Language Usage*, Cambridge: Cambridge University Press. (Originally published in Goody, E. (ed.) (1978) *Questions and Politeness* Cambridge: Cambridge University Press.)

Brown, R. and Gilman, A. (1989) 'Politeness theory and Shakespeare's four major tragedies', *Language in Society* 18: 159–212.

Cheepen, C. (1988) *The Predictability of Everyday Conversation*, London: Pinter.

Coupland, J. 'Introduction', in Coupland, J. (ed.) *Small Talk*, London: A W Longman.

Coupland, J., Coupland, N. and Robinson, J. D. (1992) ' "How are you?": negotiating phatic communion', *Language in Society* 21: 207–30.

Coupland, N., Grainger, K. and Coupland, J. (1988) 'Politeness in context: intergenerational issues', Review article of Brown, P. and Levinson, S. C. (1987), *Language in Society* 17: 253–62.

Gu, Y. (1990) 'Politeness phenomena in modern Chinese', *Journal of Pragmatics* 14: 237–57.

Holmes, J. (1995) *Women, Men and Politeness*, London: Longman.

Jaworski, A. (1993) *The Power of Silence: Social and Pragmatic Perspectives*, Newbury Park, CA: Sage.

—— (1995) 'Language awareness in applied linguistics students: evidence from "Linguistic and Cultural Heritage Essays"', in Alatis, J. E., Straehle, C. A., Gallenberger, B. and Ronkin, M. (eds) *Georgetown University Round Table on Languages and Linguistics 1995*, Washington, DC: Georgetown University Press, 213–29.

—— (1999) 'Silence and small talk', in Coupland, J. (ed.) *Small Talk*, London: A W Longman.

Kasper, G. (1997) 'Linguistic etiquette', in Coulmas, F. (ed.) *The Handbook of Sociolinguistics*, Oxford: Blackwell, 374–85.

Kendon, A. (1990) 'Behavioral foundations for process of frame-attunement in fact-to-face interaction', in Kendon, A. *Conducting Interaction: Patterns of Behavior in Focused Encounters*, Cambridge: Cambridge University Press, 239–62.

Laver, J. (1974) 'Communicative functions of phatic communion', in Kendon, A., Harris, R. M. and Ritche Key, M. (eds) *Organization of Behavior in Face-to-face Interaction*, The Hague: Mouton, 215–38.

—— (1981) 'Linguistic routines and politeness in greeting and parting', in Coulmas, F. (ed.) *Conversational Routine: Explorations in Standardized Communication Situations and Prepatterned Speech*, The Hague: Mouton, 289–304.

Leach, E. R. (1976) *Culture and Communication: The Logic by which Symbols are Connected. An Introduction to the Use of Structuralist Analysis in Social Anthropology*, Cambridge: Cambridge University Press.

Milroy, L. (1992) 'New perspectives in the analysis of sex differentiation in language', in Bolton, K. and Kwok, H. (eds) *Sociolinguistics Today: International Perspectives*, London: Routledge, 163–79.

Sifianou, M. (1992) *Politeness Phenomena in England and Greece: A Cross-Cultural Perspective*, Oxford: Clarendon Press.

—— (1997) 'Silence and politeness', in Jaworski, A. (ed.) *Silence: Interdisciplinary Perspectives*, Berlin: Mouton de Gruyter, 63–84.

Watzlawick, P., Beavin-Bavelas, J. and Jackson, D. (1967) *The Pragmatics of Human Communication*, New York: Norton.

Wolfson, N. (1988) 'The bulge: a theory of speech behavior and social distance', in Fine, J. (ed.) *Second Language Discourse: A Textbook of Current Research*, Norwood, NJ: Ablex, 21–38.

Chapter 17

Bronislaw Malinowski

ON PHATIC COMMUNION

[. . .]

The case of language used in free, aimless, social intercourse requires special consideration. When a number of people sit together at a village fire, after all the daily tasks are over, or when they chat, resting from work, or when they accompany some mere manual work by gossip quite unconnected with what they are doing – it is clear that here we have to do with another mode of using language, with another type of speech function. Language here is not dependent upon what happens at that moment, it seems to be even deprived of any context of situation. The meaning of any utterance cannot be connected with the speaker's or hearer's behaviour, with the purpose of what they are doing.

A mere phrase of politeness, in use as much among savage tribes as in a European drawing-room, fulfils a function to which the meaning of its words is almost completely irrelevant. Inquiries about health, comments on weather, affirmations of some supremely obvious state of things – all such are exchanged, not in order to inform, not in this case to connect people in action, certainly not in order to express any thought. It would be even incorrect, I think, to say that such words serve the purpose of establishing a common sentiment, for this is usually absent from such current phrases of intercourse; and where it purports to exist, as in expressions of sympathy, it is avowedly spurious on one side. What is the *raison d'être*, therefore, of

Source: Bronislaw Malinowski, 'The problem of meaning in primitive languages' in C. K. Ogden and I. A. Richards (eds) *The Meaning of Meaning*, London: Routledge & Kegan Paul, 1923, 296–336.

such phrases as 'How do you do?' 'Ah, here you are,' 'Where do you come from?' 'Nice day to-day' — all of which serve in one society or another as formulae of greeting or approach?

I think that, in discussing the function of speech in mere sociabilities we come to one of the bedrock aspects of man's nature in society. There is in all human beings the well-known tendency to congregate, to be together, to enjoy each other's company. Many instincts and innate trends, such as fear or pugnacity, all the types of social sentiments such as ambition, vanity, passion for power and wealth, are dependent upon and associated with the fundamental tendency which makes the mere presence of others a necessity for man.

Now speech is the intimate correlate of this tendency, for, to a natural man, another man's silence is not a reassuring factor, but, on the contrary, something alarming and dangerous. The stranger who cannot speak the language is to all savage tribesmen a natural enemy. To the primitive mind, whether among savages or our own uneducated classes, taciturnity means not only unfriendliness but directly a bad character. This no doubt varies greatly with the national character but remains true as a general rule. The breaking of silence, the communion of words is the first act to establish links of fellowship, which is consummated only by the breaking of bread and the communion of food. The modern English expression, 'Nice day to-day' or the Melanesian phrase, 'Whence comest thou?' are needed to get over the strange and unpleasant tension which men feel when facing each other in silence.

After the first formula, there comes a flow of language, purposeless expressions of preference or aversion, accounts of irrelevant happenings, comments on what is perfectly obvious. Such gossip, as found in primitive societies, differs only a little from our own. Always the same emphasis of affirmation and consent, mixed perhaps with an incidental disagreement which creates the bonds of antipathy. Or personal accounts of the speaker's views and life history, to which the hearer listens under some restraint and with slightly veiled impatience, waiting till his own turn arrives to speak. For in this use of speech the bonds created between hearer and speaker are not quite symmetrical, the man linguistically active receiving the greater share of social pleasure and self-enhancement. But though the hearing given to such utterances is as a rule not as intense as the speaker's own share, it is quite essential for his pleasure, and the reciprocity is established by the change of roles.

There can be no doubt that we have here a new type of linguistic use — *phatic communion* I am tempted to call it, actuated by the demon of terminological invention — a type of speech in which ties of union are created by a mere exchange of words. Let us look at it from the special point of view with which we are here concerned; let us ask what light it throws on the function or nature of language. Are words in phatic communion used primarily to convey meaning, the meaning which is symbolically theirs? Certainly not! They fulfil a social function and that is their principal aim, but they are neither the result of intellectual reflection, nor do they necessarily arouse reflection in the listener. Once again we may say that language does not function here as a means of transmission of thought.

But can we regard it as a mode of action? And in what relation does it stand to our crucial conception of context of situation? It is obvious that the outer situation does not enter directly into the technique of speaking. But what can be considered as *situation* when a number of people aimlessly gossip together? It consists in just this atmosphere of sociability and in the fact of the personal communion of these people. But this is in fact achieved by speech, and the situation in all such cases is created by the exchange of words, by the specific feelings which form convivial gregariousness, by the give and take of utterances which make up ordinary gossip. The whole situation consists in what happens linguistically. Each utterance is an act serving the direct aim of binding hearer to speaker by a tie of some social sentiment or other. Once more language appears to us in this function not as an instrument of reflection but as a mode of action.

I should like to add at once that though the examples discussed were taken from savage life, we could find among ourselves exact parallels to every type of linguistic use so far discussed. The binding tissue of words which unites the crew of a ship in bad weather, the verbal concomitants of a company of soldiers in action, the technical language running parallel to some practical work or sporting pursuit – all these resemble essentially the primitive uses of speech by man in action and our discussion could have been equally well conducted on a modern example. I have chosen the above from a savage community, because I wanted to emphasize that such and no other is the nature of *primitive* speech.

Again in pure sociabilities and gossip we use language exactly as savages do and our talk becomes the 'phatic communion' analysed above, which serves to establish bonds of personal union between people brought together by the mere need of companionship and does not serve any purpose of communicating ideas. [. . .] Indeed there need not or perhaps even there must not be anything to communicate. As long as there are words to exchange, phatic communion brings savage and civilized alike into the pleasant atmosphere of polite, social intercourse.

It is only in certain very special uses among a civilized community and only in its highest uses that language is employed to frame and express thoughts. In poetic and literary production, language is made to embody human feelings and passions, to render in a subtle and convincing manner certain inner states and processes of mind. In works of science and philosophy, highly developed types of speech are used to control ideas and to make them common property of civilized mankind.

Even in this function, however, it is not correct to regard language as a mere residuum of reflective thought. And the conception of speech as serving to translate the inner processes of the speaker to the hearer is one-sided and gives us, even with regard to the most highly developed and specialized uses of speech, only a partial and certainly not the most relevant view.

To restate the main position arrived at in this section we can say that language in its primitive function and original form has an essentially pragmatic character; that it is a mode of behaviour, an indispensable element of concerted human action. And negatively: that to regard it as a means for the embodiment or expression of thought is to take a one-sided view of one of its most derivate and specialized functions.

[. . .]

Chapter 18

Erving Goffman

ON FACE-WORK: AN ANALYSIS OF RITUAL ELEMENTS IN SOCIAL INTERACTION

EVERY PERSON LIVES IN A WORLD of social encounters, involving him either in face-to-face or mediated contact with other participants. In each of these contacts, he tends to act out what is sometimes called a *line* – that is, a pattern of verbal and nonverbal acts by which he expresses his view of the situation and through this his evaluation of the participants, especially himself. Regardless of whether a person intends to take a line, he will find that he has done so in effect. The other participants will assume that he has more or less willfully taken a stand, so that if he is to deal with their response to him he must take into consideration the impression they have possibly formed of him.

The term *face* may be defined as the positive social value a person effectively claims for himself by the line others assume he has taken during a particular contact. Face is an image of self delineated in terms of approved social attributes – albeit an image that others may share, as when a person makes a good showing for his profession or religion by making a good showing for himself.

A person tends to experience an immediate emotional response to the face which a contact with others allows him; he cathects his face; his "feelings" become attached to it. If the encounter sustains an image of him that he has long taken for granted, he probably will have few feelings about the matter. If events establish a face for him that is better than he might have expected, he is likely to "feel good"; if his ordinary expectations are not fulfilled, one expects that he will "feel bad" or "feel hurt." In general, a

Source: Erving Goffman, *Interaction Ritual: Essays on Face-to-Face Behavior*, Garolen City, N.Y.: Anchor/Doubleday, 1967.

person's attachment to a particular face, coupled with the ease with which disconfirming information can be conveyed by himself and others, provides one reason why he finds that participation in any contact with others is a commitment. A person will also have feelings about the face sustained for the other participants, and while these feelings may differ in quantity and direction from those he has for his own face, they constitute an involvement in the face of others that is as immediate and spontaneous as the involvement he has in his own face. One's own face and the face of others are constructs of the same order; it is the rules of the group and the definition of the situation which determine how much feeling one is to have for face and how this feeling is to be distributed among the faces involved.

A person may be said to *have*, or *be in*, or *maintain* face when the line he effectively takes presents an image of him that is internally consistent, that is supported by judgements and evidence conveyed by other participants, and that is confirmed by evidence conveyed through impersonal agencies in the situation. At such times the person's face clearly is something that is not lodged in or on his body, but rather something that is diffusely located in the flow of events in the encounter and becomes manifest only when these events are read and interpreted for the appraisals expressed in them.

[. . .]

A person may be said to *be in wrong face* when information is brought forth in some way about his social worth which cannot be integrated, even with effort, into the line that is being sustained for him. A person may be said to *be out of face* when he participates in a contact with others without having ready a line of the kind participants in such situations are expected to take. The intent of many pranks is to lead a person into showing a wrong face or no face, but there will also be serious occasions, of course, when he will find himself expressively out of touch with the situation.

When a person senses that he is in face, he typically responds with feelings of confidence and assurance. Firm in the line he is taking, he feels that he can hold his head up and openly present himself to others. He feels some security and some relief – as he also can when the others feel he is in wrong face but successfully hide these feelings from him.

[. . .]

Following common usage, I shall employ the term *poise* to refer to the capacity to suppress and conceal any tendency to become shamefaced during encounters with others.

In our Anglo-American society, as in some others, the phrase "to lose face" seems to mean to be in wrong face, to be out of face, or to be shamefaced.

The phrase "to save one's face" appears to refer to the process by which the person sustains an impression for others that he has not lost face. Following Chinese usage, one can say that "to give face" is to arrange for another to take a better line than he might otherwise have been able to take, the other thereby gets face given him, this being one way in which he can gain face.

As an aspect of the social code of any social circle, one may expect to find an understanding as to how far a person should go to save his face. Once he takes on a self-image expressed through face he will be expected to live up to it. In different ways in different societies he will be required to show self-respect, abjuring certain actions because they are above or beneath him, while forcing himself to perform others even though they cost him dearly. By entering a situation in which he is given a face to maintain, a person takes on the responsibility of standing guard over the flow of events as they pass before him. He must ensure that a particular *expressive order* is sustained – an order that regulates the flow of events, large or small, so that anything that appears to be expressed by them will be consistent with his face. [. . .]

Just as the member of any group is expected to have self-respect, so also he is expected to sustain a standard of considerateness; he is expected to go to certain lengths to save the feelings and the face of others present, and he is expected to do this willingly and spontaneously because of emotional identification with the others and with their feelings. In consequence, he is disinclined to witness the defacement of others. The person who can witness another's humiliation and unfeelingly retain a cool countenance himself is said in our society to be "heartless," just as he who can unfeelingly participate in his own defacement is thought to be "shameless."

The combined effect of the rule of self-respect and the rule of considerateness is that the person tends to conduct himself during an encounter so as to maintain both his own face and the face of the other participants. This means that the line taken by each participant is usually allowed to prevail, and each participant is allowed to carry off the role he appears to have chosen for himself. A state where everyone temporarily accepts everyone else's line is established. This kind of mutual acceptance seems to be a basic structural feature of interaction, especially the interaction of face-to-face talk. It is typically a "working" acceptance, not a "real" one, since it tends to be based not on agreement of candidly expressed heart-felt evaluations, but upon a willingness to give temporary lip service to judgements with which the participants do not really agree.

The mutual acceptance of lines has an important conservative effect upon encounters. Once the person initially presents a line, he and the others tend to build their later responses upon it, and in a sense become stuck with it. Should the person radically alter his line, or should it become discredited, then confusion results, for the participants will have prepared and committed themselves for actions that are now unsuitable.

Ordinarily, maintenance of face is a condition of interaction, not its objective. Usual objectives, such as gaining face for oneself, giving free expression to one's true beliefs, introducing depreciating information about the others, or solving problems and performing tasks, are typically pursued in such a way as to be consistent with the maintenance of face. To study face-saving is to study the traffic rules of social interaction; one learns about the code the person adheres to in his movement across the paths and designs of others, but not where he is going, or why he wants to get there. One does not even learn why he *is* ready to follow the code, for a large number of different motives can equally lead him to do so. He may want to save his own face because of his emotional attachment to the image of self which it expresses, because of his pride or honor, because of the power his presumed status allows him to exert over the other participants, and so on. He may want to save the others' face because of his emotional attachment to an image of them, or because he feels that his coparticipants have a moral right to this protection, or because he wants to avoid the hostility that may be directed toward him if they lose their face. He may feel that an assumption has been made that he is the sort of person who shows compassion and sympathy toward others, so that to retain his own face, he may feel obliged to be considerate of the line taken by the other participants.

By *face-work* I mean to designate the actions taken by a person to make whatever he is doing consistent with face. Face-work serves to counteract "incidents" – that is, events whose effective symbolic implications threaten face. Thus poise is one important type of face-work, for through poise the person controls his embarrassment and hence the embarrassment that he and others might have over his embarrassment. Whether or not the full consequences of face-saving actions are known to the person who employs them, they often become habitual and standardized practices; they are like traditional plays in a game or traditional steps in a dance. Each person, subculture, and society seems to have its own characteristic repertoire of face-saving practices. It is to this repertoire that people partly refer when they ask what a person or culture is "really" like. And yet the particular set of practices stressed by particular persons or groups seems to be drawn from a single logically coherent framework of possible practices. It is as if face, by its very nature, can be saved only in a certain number of ways, and as if each social grouping must make its selections from this single matrix of possibilities.

The members of every social circle may be expected to have some knowledge of face-work and some experience in its use. In our society, this kind of capacity is sometimes called tact, *savoir-faire*, diplomacy, or social skill.

Variation in social skill pertains more to the efficacy of face-work than to the frequency of its application, for almost all acts involving others are modified, prescriptively or proscriptively, by considerations of face.

If a person is to employ his repertoire of face-saving practices, obviously he must first become aware of the interpretations that others may have placed upon his acts and the interpretations that he ought perhaps to place upon theirs. In other words, he must exercise perceptiveness. [. . .]

I have already said that the person will have two points of view – a defensive orientation toward saving his own face and a protective orientation toward saving the others' face. Some practices will be primarily defensive and others primarily protective, although in general one may expect these two perspectives to be taken at the same time. In trying to save the face of others, the person must choose a tack that will not lead to loss of his own; in trying to save his own face, he must consider the loss of face that his action may entail for others.

[. . .]

The basic kinds of face-work

The avoidance process

The surest way for a person to prevent threats to his face is to avoid contacts in which these threats are likely to occur. In all societies one can observe this in the avoidance relationship and in the tendency for certain delicate transactions to be conducted by go-betweens. Similarly, in many societies, members know the value of voluntarily making a gracious withdrawal before an anticipated threat to face has had a chance to occur.

Once the person does chance an encounter, other kinds of avoidance practices come into play. As defensive measures, he keeps off topics and away from activities that would lead to the expression of information that is inconsistent with the line he is maintaining. At opportune moments he will change the topic of conversation or the direction of activity. He will often present initially a front of diffidence and composure, suppressing any show of feeling until he has found out what kind of line the others will be ready to support for him. Any claims regarding self may be made with belittling modesty, with strong qualifications, or with a note of unseriousness; by hedging in these ways he will have prepared a self for himself that will not be discredited by exposure, personal failure, or the unanticipated acts of others. And if he does not hedge his claims about self, he will at least attempt to be realistic about them, knowing that otherwise events may discredit him and make him lose face.

Certain protective maneuvers are as common as these defensive ones. The person shows respect and politeness, making sure to extend to others any ceremonial treatment that might be their due. He employs discretion; he leaves unstated facts that might implicitly or explicitly contradict and embarrass the positive claims made by others. He employs circumlocutions and deception, phrasing his replies with careful ambiguity so that the others' face is preserved even if their welfare is not. He employs courtesies, making slight modifications of his demands on or appraisals of the others so that they will be able to define the situation as one in which their self-respect is not threatened. In making a belittling demand upon the others, or in imputing uncomplimentary attributes to them, he may employ a joking manner, allowing them to take the line that they are good sports, able to relax from their ordinary standards of pride and honor. And before engaging in a potentially offensive act, he may provide explanations as to why the others ought not to be affronted by it. For example, if he knows that it will be necessary to withdraw from the encounter before it has terminated, he may tell the others in advance that it is necessary for him to leave, so that they will have faces that are prepared for it. But neutralizing the potentially offensive act need not be done verbally; he may wait for a propitious moment or natural break – for example, in conversation, a momentary lull when no one speaker can be affronted – and then leave, in this way using the context instead of his words as a guarantee of inoffensiveness.

When a person fails to prevent an incident, he can still attempt to maintain the fiction that no threat to face has occurred. The most blatant example of this is found where the person acts as if an event that contains a threatening expression has not occurred at all. He may apply this studied nonobservance to his own acts – as when he does not by outward sign admit that his stomach is rumbling – or to the acts of others, as when he does not "see" that another has stumbled. Social life in mental hospitals owes much to this process; patients employ it in regard to their own peculiarities, and visitors employ it, often with tenuous desperation, in regard to patients. In general, tactful blindness of this kind is applied only to events that, if perceived at all, could be perceived and interpreted only as threats to face.

A more important, less spectacular kind of tactful overlooking is practiced when a person openly acknowledges an incident as an event that has occurred, but not as an event that contains a threatening expression. If he is not the one who is responsible for the incident, then his blindness will have to be supported by his forbearance; if he is the doer of the threatening deed, then his blindness will have to be supported by his willingness to seek a way of dealing with the matter, which leaves him dangerously dependent upon the cooperative forbearance of the others.

Another kind of avoidance occurs when a person loses control of his expressions during an encounter. At such times he may try not so much to overlook the incident as to hide or conceal his activity in some way, thus making it possible for the others to avoid some of the difficulties created by a participant who has not maintained face. Correspondingly, when a person is caught out of face because he had not expected to be thrust into inter-action, or because strong feelings have disrupted his expressive mask, the others may protectively turn away from him or his activity for a moment, to give him time to assemble himself.

The corrective process

When the participants in an undertaking or encounter fail to prevent the occur-rence of an event that is expressively incompatible with the judgements of social worth that are being maintained, and when the event is of the kind that is difficult to overlook, then the participants are likely to give it accredited sta-tus as an incident – to ratify it as a threat that deserves direct official attention – and to proceed to try to correct for its effects. At this point one or more participants find themselves in an established state of ritual disequilibrium or disgrace, and an attempt must be made to re-establish a satisfactory ritual state for them. I use the term *ritual* because I am dealing with acts through whose symbolic component the actor shows how worthy he is of respect or how worthy he feels others are of it. The imagery of equilibrium is apt here because the length and intensity of the corrective effort is nicely adapted to the per-sistence and intensity of the threat. One's face, then, is a sacred thing, and the expressive order required to sustain it is therefore a ritual one.

The sequence of acts set in motion by an acknowledged threat to face, and terminating in the re-establishment of ritual equilibrium, I shall call an *interchange*. Defining a message or move as everything conveyed by an actor during a turn at taking action, one can say that an interchange will involve two or more moves and two or more participants. Obvious examples in our society may be found in the sequence of "Excuse me" and "Certainly," and in the exchange of presents or visits. The interchange seems to be a basic concrete unit of social activity and provides one natural empirical way to study interaction of all kinds. Face-saving practices can be usefully classified according to their position in the natural sequence of moves that comprise this unit. Aside from the event which introduces the need for a corrective interchange, four classic moves seem to be involved.

There is, first, the *challenge*, by which participants take on the respon-sibility of calling attention to the misconduct; by implication they suggest that the threatened claims are to stand firm and that the threatening event itself will have to be brought back into line.

The second move consists of the *offering*, whereby a participant, typically the offender, is given a chance to correct for the offense and re-establish the expressive order. Some classic ways of making this move are available. On the one hand, an attempt can be made to show that what admittedly appeared to be a threatening expression is really a meaningless event, or an unintentional act, or a joke not meant to be taken seriously, or an unavoidable, "understandable" product of extenuating circumstances. On the other hand, the meaning of the event may be granted and effort concentrated on the creator of it. Information may be provided to show that the creator was under the influence of something and not himself, or that he was under the command of somebody else and not acting for himself. When a person claims that an act was meant in jest, he may go on and claim that the self that seemed to lie behind the act was also projected as a joke. When a person suddenly finds that he has demonstrably failed in capacities that the others assumed him to have and to claim for himself – such as the capacity to spell, to perform minor tasks, to talk without malapropisms, and so on – he may quickly add, in a serious or unserious way, that he claims these incapacities as part of his self. The meaning of the threatening incident thus stands, but it can now be incorporated smoothly into the flow of expressive events.

[. . .]

After the challenge and the offering have been made, the third move can occur: the persons to whom the offering is made can *accept* it as a satisfactory means of re-establishing the expressive order and the faces supported by this order. Only then can the offender cease the major part of his ritual offering.

In the terminal move of the interchange, the forgiven person conveys a sign of *gratitude* to those who have given him the indulgence of forgiveness.

The phases of the corrective process – challenge, offering, acceptance, and thanks – provide a model for interpersonal ritual behavior, but a model that may be departed from in significant ways. For example, the offended parties may give the offender a chance to initiate the offering on his own before a challenge is made and before they ratify the offense as an incident. This is a common courtesy, extended on the assumption that the recipient will introduce a self-challenge. Further, when the offended persons accept the corrective offering, the offender may suspect that this has been grudgingly done from tact, and so he may volunteer additional corrective offerings, not allowing the matter to rest until he has received a second or third acceptance of his repeated apology. Or the offended persons may tactfully take over the role of the offender and volunteer excuses for him that will, perforce, be acceptable to the offended persons.

An important departure from the standard corrective cycle occurs when a challenged offender patently refuses to heed the warning and continues with his offending behavior, instead of setting the activity to rights. This move shifts the play back to the challengers. If they countenance the refusal to meet their demands, then it will be plain that their challenge was a bluff and that the bluff has been called. This is an untenable position; a face for themselves cannot be derived from it, and they are left to bluster. To avoid this fate, some classic moves are open to them. For instance, they can resort to tactless, violent retaliation, destroying either themselves or the person who had refused to heed their warning. Or they can withdraw from the undertaking in a visible huff – righteously indignant, outraged, but confident of ultimate vindication. Both tacks provide a way of denying the offender his status as an interactant, and hence denying the reality of the offensive judgment he has made. Both strategies are ways of salvaging face, but for all concerned the costs are usually high. It is partly to forestall such scenes that an offender is usually quick to offer apologies; he does not want the affronted persons to trap themselves into the obligation to resort to desperate measures.

It is plain that emotions play a part in these cycles of response, as when anguish is expressed because of what one has done to another's face, or anger because of what has been done to one's own. I want to stress that these emotions function as moves, and fit so precisely into the logic of the ritual game that it would seem difficult to understand them without it. In fact, spontaneously expressed feelings are likely to fit into the formal pattern of the ritual interchange more elegantly than consciously designed ones.

Making points – the aggressive use of face-work

Every face-saving practice which is allowed to neutralize a particular threat opens up the possibility that the threat will be willfully introduced for what can be safely gained by it. If a person knows that his modesty will be answered by others' praise of him, he can fish for compliments. If his own appraisal of self will be checked against incidental events, then he can arrange for favorable incidental events to appear. If others are prepared to overlook an affront to them and act forbearantly, or to accept apologies, then he can rely on this as a basis for safely offending them. He can attempt by sudden withdrawal to force the others into a ritually unsatisfactory state, leaving them to flounder in an interchange that cannot readily be completed. Finally, at some expense to himself, he can arrange for the others to hurt his feelings, thus forcing them to feel guilt, remorse, and sustained ritual disequilibrium.

When a person treats face-work not as something he need be prepared to perform, but rather as something that others can be counted on to perform or to accept, then an encounter or an undertaking becomes less a scene of mutual considerateness than an arena in which a contest or match is held. The purpose of the game is to preserve everyone's line from an inexcusable contradiction, while scoring as many points as possible against one's adversaries and making as many gains as possible for oneself. An audience to the struggle is almost a necessity. The general method is for the person to introduce favorable facts about himself and unfavorable facts about the others in such a way that the only reply the others will be able to think up will be one that terminates the interchange in a grumble, a meager excuse, a face-saving I-can-take-a-joke laugh, or an empty stereotyped comeback of the "Oh yeah?" or "That's what you think" variety. The losers in such cases will have to cut their losses, tacitly grant the loss of a point, and attempt to do better in the next interchange. Points made by allusion to social class status are sometimes called snubs; those made by allusions to moral respectability are sometimes called digs; in either case one deals with a capacity at what is sometimes called "bitchiness."

[. . .]

Cooperation in face-work

When a face has been threatened, face-work must be done, but whether this is initiated and primarily carried through by the person whose face is threatened, or by the offender, or by a mere witness, is often of secondary importance. Lack of effort on the part of one person induces compensative effort from others; a contribution by one person relieves the others of the task. In fact, there are many minor incidents in which the offender and the offended simultaneously attempt to initiate an apology. Resolution of the situation to everyone's apparent satisfaction is the first requirement; correct apportionment of blame is typically a secondary consideration. Hence terms such as tact and *savoir-faire* fail to distinguish whether it is the person's own face that his diplomacy saves or the face of the others. Similarly, terms such as *gaffe* and *faux pas* fail to specify whether it is the actor's own face he has threatened or the face of other participants. [. . .] Tact in regard to face-work often relies for its operation on a tacit agreement to do business through the language of hint – the language of innuendo, ambiguities, well-placed pauses, carefully worded jokes, and so on. The rule regarding this official kind of communication is that the sender ought not to act as if he had officially conveyed the message he has hinted at, while the recipients have the right and the obligation to act as if they have not officially received the message contained in the hint. Hinted communication, then, is deniable communication; it need not be faced up to. It provides a means by which the person can be warned that his current line or the current situation is leading to loss of face, without this warning itself becoming an incident.

Another form of tacit cooperation, and one that seems to be much used in many societies, is reciprocal self-denial. Often the person does not have a clear idea of what would be a just or acceptable apportionment of judgements during the occasions, and so he voluntarily deprives or depreciates himself while indulging and complimenting the others, in both cases carrying the judgements safely past what is likely to be just. The favorable judgements about himself he allows to come from the others; the unfavorable judgements of himself are his own contributions. This "after you, Alphonse" technique works, of course, because in depriving himself he can reliably anticipate that the others will compliment or indulge him. Whatever allocation of favors is eventually established, all participants are first given a chance to show that they are not bound or constrained by their own desires and expectations, that they have a properly modest view of themselves, and that they can be counted upon to support the ritual code. Negative bargaining, through which each participant tries to make the terms of the trade more favorable to the other side, is another instance; as a form of exchange perhaps it is more widespread than the economist's kind.

A person's performance of face-work, extended by his tacit agreement to help others perform theirs, represents his willingness to abide by the ground rules of social interaction. Here is the hallmark of his socialization as an interactant. If he and the others were not socialized in this way, interaction in most societies and most situations would be a much more hazardous thing for feelings and faces. The person would find it impractical to be orientated to symbolically conveyed appraisals of social worth, or to be possessed of feelings – that is, it would be impractical for him to be a ritually delicate object. And as I shall suggest, if the person were not a ritually delicate object, occasions of talk could not be organized in the way they usually are. It is no wonder that trouble is caused by a person who cannot be relied upon to play the face-saving game.

The ritual roles of the self

So far I have implicitly been using a double definition of self: the self as an image pieced together from the expressive implications of the full flow of events in an undertaking; and the self as a kind of player in a ritual game who copes honorably or dishonorably, diplomatically or undiplomatically, with the judgemental contingencies of the situation. [. . .]

Once the two roles of the self have been separated, one can look to the ritual code implicit in face-work to learn how the two roles are related. When a person is responsible for introducing a threat to another's face, he apparently has a right, within limits, to wriggle out of the difficulty by means of self-abasement. When performed voluntarily these indignities do not seem to profane his own image. It is as if he had the right of insulation and could castigate himself qua actor without injuring himself qua object of ultimate worth. By token of the same insulation he can belittle himself and modestly underplay his positive qualities, with the understanding that no one will take his statements as a fair representation of his sacred self. On the other hand, if he is forced against his will to treat himself in these ways, his face, his pride, and his honor will be seriously threatened. Thus, in terms of the ritual code, the person seems to have a special license to accept mistreatment at his own hands that he does not have the right to accept from others. Perhaps this is a safe arrangement because he is not likely to carry this license too far, whereas the others, were they given this privilege, might be more likely to abuse it.

Further, within limits the person has a right to forgive other participants for affronts to his sacred image. He can forbearantly overlook minor slurs upon his face, and in regard to somewhat greater injuries he is the one person who is in a position to accept apologies on behalf of his sacred self. This is a relatively safe prerogative for the person to have in regard to himself, for it is one that is exercised in the interests of the others or of the undertaking. Interestingly enough, when the person commits a *gaffe* against himself, it is not he who has the license to forgive the event; only the others have that prerogative, and it is a safe prerogative for them to have because they can exercise it only in his interests or in the interests of the undertaking. One finds, then, a system of checks and balances by which each participant tends to be given the right to handle only those matters which he will have little motivation for mishandling. In short, the rights and obligations of an inter-actant are designed to prevent him from abusing his role as an object of sacred value.

[. . .]

Face and social relationships

When a person begins a mediated or immediate encounter, he already stands in some kind of social relationship to the others concerned, and expects to stand in a given relationship to them after the particular encounter ends. This, of course, is one of the ways in which social contacts are geared into the wider society. Much of the activity occurring during an encounter can be understood as an effort on everyone's part to get through the occasion and all the unanticipated and unintentional events that can cast participants in an undesirable light, without disrupting the relationships of the participants. And if relationships are in the process of change, the object will be to bring the encounter to a satisfactory close without altering the expected course of development. This perspective nicely accounts, for example, for the little ceremonies of greeting and farewell which occur when people begin a conversational encounter or depart from one. Greetings provide a way of showing that a relationship is still what it was at the termination of the previous coparticipation, and, typically, that this relationship involves sufficient suppression of hostility for the participants temporarily to drop their guards and talk. Farewells sum up the effect of the encounter upon the relationship and show what the participants may expect of one another when they next meet. The enthusiasm of greetings compensates for the weakening of the relationship caused by the absence just terminated, while the enthusiasm of farewells compensates the relationship for the harm that is about to be done to it by separation. Greetings, of course, serve to clarify and fix the roles that the participants will take during the occasion of talk and to commit participants to these roles, while farewells provide a way of unambiguously terminating the encounter. Greetings and farewells may also be used to state, and apologize for, extenuating circumstances – in the case of greetings for circumstances that have kept the participants from interacting until now, and in the case of farewells for circumstances that prevent the participants from continuing their display of solidarity. These apologies allow the impression to be maintained that the participants are more warmly related socially than may be the case. This positive stress, in turn, assures that they will act more ready to enter into contacts than they perhaps really feel inclined to do, thus guaranteeing that diffuse channels for potential communication will be kept open in the society.

   It seems to be a characteristic obligation of many social relationships that each of the members guarantees to support a given face for the other members in given situations. To prevent disruption of these relationships, it is therefore necessary for each member to avoid destroying the others' face. [. . .] Furthermore, in many relationships, the members come to share a face, so that in the presence of third parties an improper act on the part of one member becomes a source of acute embarrassment to the other members. A social relationship, then, can be seen as a way in which the person is more than ordinarily forced to trust his self-image and face to the tact and good conduct of others.

The nature of the ritual order

[. . .]

Throughout this paper it has been implied that underneath their differences in culture, people everywhere are the same. If persons have a universal human nature, they themselves are not to be looked to for an explanation of it. One must look rather to the fact that societies everywhere, if they are to be societies, must mobilize their members as self-regulating participants in social encounters. One way of mobilizing the individual for this purpose is through ritual; he is taught to be perceptive, to have feelings attached to self and a self expressed through face, to have pride, honor, and dignity, to have considerateness, to have tact and a certain amount of poise. These are some of the elements of behavior which must be built into the person if practical use is to be made of him as an interactant, and it is these elements that are referred to in part when one speaks of universal human nature.

Universal human nature is not a very human thing. By acquiring it, the person becomes a kind of construct, built up not from inner psychic propensities but from moral rules that are impressed upon him from without. These rules, when followed, determine the evaluation he will make of himself and of his fellow-participants in the encounter, the distribution of his feelings, and the kinds of practices he will employ to maintain a specified and obligatory kind of ritual equilibrium. The general capacity to be bound by moral rules may well belong to the individual, but the particular set of rules which transforms him into a human being derives from requirements established in the ritual organization of social encounters. And if a particular person or group or society seems to have a unique character all its own, it is because its standard set of human-nature elements is pitched and combined in a particular way. Instead of much pride, there may be little. Instead of abiding by the rules, there may be much effort to break them safely. But if an encounter or undertaking is to be sustained as a viable system of interaction organized on ritual principles, then these variations must be held within certain bounds and nicely counterbalanced by corresponding modifications in some of the

other rules and understandings. Similarly, the human nature of a particular
set of persons may be specially designed for the special kind of undertakings
in which they participate, but still each of these persons must have within
him something of the balance of characteristics required of a usable participant in any ritually organized system of social activity.

Chapter 19

Penelope Brown and Stephen C. Levinson

POLITENESS: SOME UNIVERSALS IN LANGUAGE USAGE

Assumptions: properties of interactants

We make the following assumptions: that all competent adult members of a society have (and know each other to have):

1   'Face', the public self-image that every member wants to claim for himself, consisting in two related aspects:
    (a) negative face: the basic claim to territories, personal preserves, rights to non-distraction – i.e., to freedom of action and freedom from imposition
    (b) positive face: the positive consistent self-image or 'personality' (crucially including the desire that this self-image be appreciated and approved of) claimed by interactants.
2   Certain rational capacities, in particular consistent modes of reasoning from ends to the means that will achieve those ends.

Face

Our notion of 'face' is derived from that of Goffman (1967; [see Chapter 18]) and from the English folk term, which ties face up with notions of being embarrassed or humiliated, or 'losing face'. Thus face is something that is

Source: Penelope Brown and Stephen C. Levinson, *Politeness: Some Universals in Language Usage*, Cambridge: Cambridge University Press, 1987.

emotionally invested, and that can be lost, maintained, or enhanced, and must be constantly attended to in interaction. In general, people cooperate (and assume each other's cooperation) in maintaining face in interaction, such cooperation being based on the mutual vulnerability of face. That is, normally everyone's face depends on everyone else's being maintained, and since people can be expected to defend their faces if threatened, and in defending their own to threaten others' faces, it is in general in every participant's best interest to maintain each other's face, that is to act in ways that assure the other participants that the agent is heedful of the assumptions concerning face given under (1) above. [. . .]

Furthermore, while the content of face will differ in different cultures (what the exact limits are to personal territories, and what the publicly relevant content of personality consists in), we are assuming that the mutual knowledge of members' public self-image or face, and the social necessity to orient oneself to it in interaction, are universal.

Face as wants

[. . .] We treat the aspects of face as basic wants, which every member knows every other member desires, and which in general it is in the interests of every member to partially satisfy. In other words, we take in Weberian terms the more strongly rational *zweckrational* model of individual action, because the *wertrational* model (which would treat face respect as an unquestionable value or norm) fails to account for the fact that face respect is not an unequivocal right. In particular, a mere bow to face acts like a diplomatic declaration of good intentions; it is not in general required that an actor fully satisfy another's face wants. Second, face can be, and routinely is, ignored, not just in cases of social breakdown (affrontery) but also in cases of urgent cooperation, or in the interests of efficiency.

Therefore, the components of face given above may be restated as follows. We define:

> **negative face**: the want of every 'competent adult member' that his actions be unimpeded by others;
> **positive face**: the want of every member that his wants be desirable to at least some others.

Negative face, with its derivative politeness of non-imposition, is familiar as the formal politeness that the notion 'politeness' immediately conjures up. But positive face, and its derivative forms of positive politeness, are less obvious. The reduction of a person's public self-image or personality to a want that one's wants be desirable to at least some others can be justified in this way. The most salient aspect of a person's personality in interaction is what that personality requires of other interactants – in particular, it includes the desire to be ratified, understood, approved of, liked or admired. The next step is to represent this desire as the want to have one's goals thought of as desirable. In the special sense of 'wanting' that we develop, we can then arrive at positive face as here defined. To give this some intuitive flesh, consider an example. Mrs B is a fervent gardener. Much of her time and effort are expended on her roses. She is proud of her roses, and she likes others to admire them. She is gratified when visitors say 'What lovely roses; I wish ours looked like that! How do you do it?', implying that they want just what she has wanted and achieved.

[. . .]

Rationality

We here define 'rationality' as the application of a specific mode of reasoning [. . .] which guarantees inferences from ends or goals to means that will satisfy those ends. Just as standard logics have a consequence relation that will take us from one proposition to another while preserving truth, a system of practical reasoning must allow one to pass from ends to means and further means while preserving the 'satisfactoriness' of those means. [. . .]

Intrinsic FTAs

Given these assumptions of the universality of face and rationality, it is intuitively the case that certain kinds of acts intrinsically threaten face, namely those acts that by their nature run contrary to the face wants of the addressee and/or of the speaker. By 'act' we have in mind what is intended to be done by a verbal or non-verbal communication, just as one or more 'speech acts' can be assigned to an utterance.

First distinction: kinds of face threatened

We may make a first distinction between acts that threaten negative face and those that threaten positive face.

Those acts that primarily threaten the addressee's (H's) negative-face want, by indicating (potentially) that the speaker (S) does not intend to avoid impeding H's freedom of action, include:

1   Those acts that predicate some future act A of H, and in so doing put some pressure on H to do (or refrain from doing) the act A:
   (a) orders and requests (S indicates that he wants H to do, or refrain from doing, some act A)
   (b) suggestions, advice (S indicates that he thinks H ought to (perhaps) do some act A)
   (c) remindings (S indicates that H should remember to do some A)
   (d) threats, warnings, dares (S indicates that he – or someone, or something – will instigate sanctions against H unless he does A)
2   Those acts that predicate some positive future act of S toward H, and in so doing put some pressure on H to accept or reject them, and possibly to incur a debt:
   (a) offers (S indicates that he wants H to commit himself to whether or not he wants S to do some act for H, with H thereby incurring a possible debt)
   (b) promises (S commits himself to a future act for H's benefit)
3   Those acts that predicate some desire of S toward H or H's goods, giving H reason to think that he may have to take action to protect the object of S's desire, or give it to S:
   (a) compliments, expressions of envy or admiration (S indicates that he likes or would like something of H's)
   (b) expression of strong (negative) emotions toward H – e.g., hatred, anger, lust (S indicates possible motivation for harming H or H's goods)

Those acts that threaten the positive-face want, by indicating (potentially) that the speaker does not care about the addressee's feelings, wants, etc. – that in some important respect he doesn't want H's wants – include:

1   Those that show that S has a negative evaluation of some aspect of H's positive face:
   (a) expressions of disapproval, criticism, contempt or ridicule, complaints and reprimands, accusations, insults (S indicates that he doesn't like/want one or more of H's wants, acts, personal characteristics, goods, beliefs or values)
   (b) contradictions or disagreements, challenges (S indicates that he thinks H is wrong or misguided or unreasonable about some issue, such wrongness being associated with disapproval)

2   Those that show that S doesn't care about (or is indifferent to) H's
     positive face:
     (a) expressions of violent (out-of-control) emotions (S gives H possible
         reason to fear him or be embarrassed by him)
     (b) irreverence, mention of taboo topics, including those that are inap-
         propriate in the context (S indicates that he doesn't value H's values
         and doesn't fear H's fears)
     (c) bringing of bad news about H, or good news (boasting) about S (S
         indicates that he is willing to cause distress to H, and/or doesn't
         care about H's feelings)
     (d) raising of dangerously emotional or divisive topics, e.g., politics,
         race, religion, women's liberation (S raises the possibility or like-
         lihood of face-threatening acts (such as the above) occurring; i.e.,
         S creates a dangerous-to-face atmosphere)
     (e) blatant non-cooperation in an activity – e.g., disruptively interrupt-
         ing H's talk, making non-sequiturs or showing non-attention (S indi-
         cates that he doesn't care about H's negative- or positive-face wants)
     (f) use of address terms and other status-marked identifications in initial
         encounters (S may misidentify H in an offensive or embarrassing
         way, intentionally or accidentally)

Note that there is an overlap in this classification of FTAs, because some
FTAs intrinsically threaten both negative and positive face (e.g., complaints,
interruptions, threats, strong expressions of emotion, requests for personal
information).

Second distinction: threats to H's face versus threats to S's

Second, we may distinguish between acts that primarily threaten *H's* face (as
in the above list) and those that threaten primarily *S's* face. To the extent
that S and H are cooperating to maintain face, the latter FTAs also potentially
threaten H's face. FTAs that are threatening to S include:

1   Those that offend S's negative face:
     (a) expressing thanks (S accepts a debt, humbles his own face)
     (b) acceptance of H's thanks or H's apology (S may feel constrained
         to minimize H's debt or transgression, as in 'It was nothing, don't
         mention it.')
     (c) excuses (S indicates that he thinks he had good reason to do, or
         fail to do, an act which H has just criticized; this may constitute

in turn a criticism of H, or at least cause a confrontation between H's view of things and S's view)

(d) acceptance of offers (S is constrained to accept a debt, and to encroach upon H's negative face)

(e) responses to H's *faux pas* (if S visibly notices a prior *faux pas*, he may cause embarrassment to H; if he pretends not to, he may be discomfited himself)

(f) unwilling promises and offers (S commits himself to some future action although he doesn't want to; therefore, if his unwillingness shows, he may also offend H's positive face)

2   Those that directly damage S's positive face:

(a) apologies (S indicates that he regrets doing a prior FTA, thereby damaging his own face to some degree – especially if the apology is at the same time a confession with H learning about the transgression through it, and the FTA thus conveys bad news)

(b) acceptance of a compliment (S may feel constrained to denigrate the object of H's prior compliment, thus damaging his own face; or he may feel constrained to compliment H in turn)

(c) breakdown of physical control over body, bodily leakage, stumbling or falling down, etc.

(d) self-humiliation, shuffling or cowering, acting stupid, self-contradicting

(e) confessions, admissions of guilt or responsibility – e.g., for having done or not done an act, or for ignorance of something that S is expected to know

(f) emotion leakage, non-control of laughter or tears

These two ways of classifying FTAs (by whether S's face or H's face is mainly threatened, or by whether it is mainly positive face or negative face that is at stake) give rise to a four-way grid which offers the possibility of cross-classifying at least some of the above FTAs. However, such a cross-classification has a complex relation to the ways in which FTAs are handled.

Strategies for doing FTAs

In the context of the mutual vulnerability of face, any rational agent will seek to avoid these face-threatening acts, or will employ certain strategies to minimize the threat. In other words, he will take into consideration the relative weightings of (at least) three wants: (a) the want to communicate the content of the FTA x, (b) the want to be efficient or urgent, and (c) the want to maintain H's face to any degree. Unless (b) is greater than (c), S will want to minimize the threat of his FTA.

The possible sets of strategies may be schematized exhaustively as in Figure 19.1 in this schema, we have in mind the following definitions.

An actor goes **on record** in doing an act A if it is clear to participants what communicative intention led the actor to do A (i.e., there is just one unambiguously attributable intention with which witnesses would concur). For instance, if I say 'I (hereby) promise to come tomorrow' and if participants would concur that, in saying that, I did unambiguously express the intention of committing myself to that future act, then in our terminology I went 'on record' as promising to do so.

In contrast, if an actor goes **off record** in doing A, then there is more than one unambiguously attributable intention so that the actor cannot be held to have committed himself to one particular intent. So, for instance, if I say 'Damn, I'm out of cash, I forgot to go to the bank today', I may be intending to get you to lend me some cash, but I cannot be held to have committed myself to that intent (as you would discover were you to challenge me with 'This is the seventeenth time you've asked me to lend you money'). Linguistic realizations of off-record strategies include metaphor and irony, rhetorical questions, understatement, tautologies, all kinds of hints as to what a speaker wants or means to communicate, without doing so directly, so that the meaning is to some degree negotiable.

Doing an act **baldly**, **without redress**, involves doing it in the most direct, clear, unambiguous and concise way possible (for example, for a request, saying 'Do X!'). This we shall identify roughly with following the specifications of Grice's maxims of cooperation [Chapter 3]. Normally, an FTA will be done in this way only if the speaker does not fear retribution from the addressee, for example in circumstances where (a) S and H both

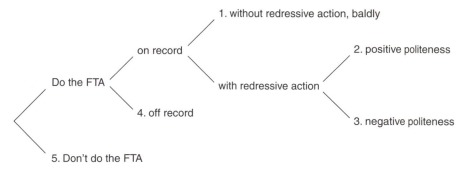

Figure 19.1   Possible strategies for doing FTAs

tacitly agree that the relevance of face demands may be suspended in the interests of urgency or efficiency; (b) where the danger to H's face is *very* small, as in offers, requests, suggestions that are clearly in H's interest and do not require great sacrifices of S (e.g., 'Come in' or 'Do sit down'); and (c) where S is vastly superior in power H, or can enlist audience support to destroy H's face without losing his own.

By **redressive action** we mean action that 'gives face' to the addressee, that is, that attempts to counteract the potential face damage of the FTA by doing it in such a way, or with such modifications or additions, that indicate clearly that no such face threat is intended or desired, and that S in general recognizes H's face wants and himself wants them to be achieved. Such redressive action takes one of two forms, depending on which aspect of face (negative or positive) is being stressed.

Positive politeness is orientated toward the positive face of H, the positive self-image that he claims for himself. Positive politeness is approach-based; it 'anoints' the face of the addressee by indicating that in some respects, S wants H's wants (e.g., by treating him as a member of an in-group, a friend, a person whose wants and personality traits are known and liked). The potential face threat of an act is minimized in this case by the assurance that in general S wants at least some of H's wants; for example, that S considers H to be in important respects, 'the same' as he, with in-group rights and duties and expectations of reciprocity, or by the implication that S likes H so that the FTA doesn't mean a negative evaluation in general of H's face.

Negative politeness, on the other hand, is orientated mainly toward partially satisfying (redressing) H's negative face, his basic want to maintain claims of territory and self-determination. Negative politeness, thus, is essentially avoidance based, and realizations of negative-politeness strategies consist in assurances that the speaker recognizes and respects the addressee's negative-face wants and will not (or will only minimally) interfere with the addressee's freedom of action. Hence negative politeness is characterized by self-effacement, formality and restraint, with attention to very restricted aspects of H's self-image, centring on his want to be unimpeded. Face-threatening acts are redressed with apologies for interfering or transgressing, with linguistic and non-linguistic deference, with hedges on the illocutionary force of the act, with impersonalizing mechanisms (such as passives) that distance S and H from the act, and with other softening mechanisms that give the addressee an 'out', a face-saving line of escape, permitting him to feel that his response is not coerced.

There is a natural tension in negative politeness, however, between (a) the desire to go on record as a prerequisite to being seen to pay face, and

(b) the desire to go off record to avoid imposing. A compromise is reached in **conventionalized indirectness**, for whatever the indirect mechanism used to do an FTA, once fully conventionalized as a way of doing that FTA it is no longer off record. Thus many indirect requests, for example, are fully conventionalized in English so that they are on record (e.g., 'Can you pass the salt?' would be read as a request by all participants; there is no longer a viable alternative interpretation of the utterance except in very special circumstances). And between any two (or more) individuals, any utterance may become conventionalized and therefore on record, as is the case with passwords and codes.

A purely conventional 'out' works as redressive action in negative politeness because it pays a token bow to the negative-face wants of the addressee. That is, the fact that the speaker bothers to phrase his FTA in a conventionally indirect way shows that he is aware of and honours the negative-face wants of H.

Factors influencing the choice of strategies

[. . .] In this section we argue that any rational agent will tend to choose the same genus of strategy under the same conditions – that is, make the same moves as any other would make under the circumstances. This is by virtue of the fact that the particular strategies intrinsically afford certain payoffs or advantages, and the relevant circumstances are those in which one of these payoffs would be more advantageous than any other.

We consider these in turn – first the intrinsic payoffs and then the relevant circumstances – and then relate the two.

The payoffs: *a priori* considerations

Here we present a fairly complete list of the payoffs associated with each of the strategies, derived on *a priori* grounds.

By going *on record*, a speaker can potentially get any of the following advantages: he can enlist public pressure against the addressee or in support of himself; he can get credit for honesty, for indicating that he trusts the addressee; he can get credit for outspokenness, avoiding the danger of being seen to be a manipulator; he can avoid the danger of being misunderstood; and he can have the opportunity to pay back in face whatever he potentially takes away by the FTA.

By going *off record*, on the other hand, a speaker can profit in the following ways: he can get credit for being tactful, non-coercive; he can run less risk of his act entering the 'gossip biography' that others keep of him; and he can avoid responsibility for the potentially face-damaging interpretation. Furthermore, he can give (non-overtly) the addressee an opportunity to be seen to care for S (and thus he can test H's feelings towards him). In this latter case, if H chooses to pick up and respond to the potentially threatening interpretation of the act, he can give a 'gift' to the original speaker. Thus, if I say 'It's hot in here' and you say 'Oh, I'll open the window then!', you may get credit for being generous and cooperative, and I avoid the potential threat of ordering you around.

For going on record with *positive politeness*, a speaker can minimize the face-threatening aspects of an act by assuring the addressee that S considers himself to be 'of the same kind', that he likes him and wants his wants. Thus a criticism, with the assertion of mutual friendship, may lose much of its sting – indeed, in the assumption of a friendly context it often becomes a game and possibly even a compliment (as between opposite-sexed teenagers). Another possible payoff is that S can avoid or minimize the debt implications of FTAs such as requests and offers, either by referring (indirectly) to the reciprocity and on-going relationship between the addressee and himself (as in the reference to a pseudo prior agreement with *then* in 'How about a cookie, then') or by including the addressee and himself equally as participants in or as benefitors from the request or offer (for example, with an inclusive 'we', as in 'Let's get on with dinner' from the husband glued to the TV).

For going on record with *negative politeness*, a speaker can benefit in the following ways: he can pay respect, deference, to the addressee in return for the FTA, and can thereby avoid incurring (or can thereby lessen) a future debt; he can maintain social distance, and avoid the threat (or the potential face loss) of advancing familiarity towards the addressee; he can give a real 'out' to the addressee (for example, with a request or an offer, by making it clear that he doesn't really expect H to say 'Yes' unless he wants to, thereby minimizing the mutual face loss incurred if H has to say 'No'); and he can give conventional 'outs' to the addressee as opposed to real 'outs', that is, pretend to offer an escape route without really doing so, thereby indicating that he has the other person's face wants in mind.

Finally, the payoff for the fifth strategic choice, 'Don't do the FTA', is simply that S avoids offending H at all with this particular FTA. Of course S also fails to achieve his desired communication, and as there are naturally no interesting linguistic reflexes of this last-ditch strategy, we will ignore it in our discussion henceforth.

For our purpose, these payoffs may be simplified to the following summary:

On-record payoffs:

(a)   clarity, perspicuousness
(b)   demonstrable non-manipulativeness

Bald-on-record (non-redressed) payoff:

efficiency (S can claim that other things are more important than face, or that the act is not an FTA at all)

Plus-redress payoff: S has the opportunity to give face

(a)   positive politeness – to satisfy H's positive face, in some respect
(b)   negative politeness – to satisfy H's negative face, to some degree

Off-record payoffs:

(a)   S can satisfy negative face to a degree greater than that afforded by the negative-politeness strategy
(b)   S can avoid the inescapable accountability, the responsibility for his action, that on-record strategies entail.

[. . .]

The circumstances: sociological variables

In this section we argue that the assessment of the seriousness of an FTA (that is, the calculations that members actually seem to make) involves the following factors in many and perhaps all cultures:

1   The 'social distance' (D) of S and H (a symmetric relation).
2   The relative 'power' (P) of S and H (an asymmetric relation).
3   The absolute ranking (R) of impositions in the particular culture.

An immediate clarification is in order. We are interested in D, P, and R only to the extent that the actors think it is mutual knowledge between them that these variables have some particular values. Thus these are not intended as *sociologists'* ratings of *actual* power, distance, etc., but only as *actors'* assumptions of such ratings, assumed to be mutually assumed, at least within certain limits.

Our argument here has an empirical basis, and we make the argument in as strong a form as our ethnographic data will allow.

Computing the weightiness of an FTA

For each FTA, the seriousness or weightiness of a particular FTA x is compounded of both risk to S's face and risk to H's face, in a proportion relative to the nature of the FTA. Thus apologies and confessions are essentially threats to S's face (as we have seen), and advice and orders are basically threats to H's face, while requests and offers are likely to threaten the face of both participants. However, the way in which the seriousness of a particular FTA is weighed seems to be neutral as to whether it is S's or H's face that is threatened, or in what proportion. So let us say that the weightiness of an FTA is calculated thus:

$$W_x = D(S,H) + P(H,S) + R_x$$

where W_x is the numerical value that measures the weightiness of the FTA x, $D(S,H)$ is the value that measures the social distance between S and H, $P(H,S)$ is a measure of the power that H has over S, and R_x is a value that measures the degree to which the FTA x is rated an imposition in that culture. We assume that each of these values can be measured on a scale of 1 to n, where n is some small number. Our formula assumes that the function that assigns a value to W_x on the basis of the three social parameters does so on a simple summative basis. Such an assumption seems to work surprisingly well, but we allow that in fact some more complex composition of values may be involved. In any case, the function must capture the fact that all three dimensions P, D, and R contribute to the seriousness of an FTA, and thus to a determination of the level of politeness with which, other things being equal, an FTA will be communicated.

First, we must clarify our intent. By D and P we intend very general pan-cultural social dimensions which nevertheless probably have 'emic' correlates. We are not here interested in what factors are compounded to estimate these complex parameters; such factors are certainly culture-specific. For instance, $P(H,S)$ may be assessed as being great because H is eloquent and influential, or is a prince, a witch, a thug, or a priest; $D(S,H)$ as great because H speaks another dialect or language, or lives in the next valley, or is not a kinsman. More specifically, we can describe these factors as follows.

D is a symmetric social dimension of similarity/difference within which S and H stand for the purposes of this act. In many cases (but not all), it is based on an assessment of the frequency of interaction and the kinds of material or non-material goods (including face) exchanged between S and H (or parties representing S or H, or for whom S and H are representatives). An important part of the assessment of D will usually be measures of social distance based on stable social attributes. The reflex of social closeness is, generally, the reciprocal giving and receiving of positive face.

P is an asymmetric social dimension of relative power, roughly in Weber's sense. That is, P(H,S) is the degree to which H can impose his own plans and his own self-evaluation (face) at the expense of S's plans and self-evaluation. In general there are two sources of P, either of which may be authorized or unauthorized – material control (over economic distribution and physical force) and metaphysical control (over the actions of others, by virtue of metaphysical forces subscribed to by those others). In most cases an individual's power is drawn from both these sources, or is thought to overlap them. The reflex of a great P differential is perhaps archetypally 'deference', as discussed below.

R is a culturally and situationally defined ranking of impositions by the degree to which they are considered to interfere with an agent's wants of self-determination or of approval (his negative- and positive-face wants). In general there are probably two such scales or ranks that are emically identifiable for negative-face FTAs: a ranking of impositions in proportion to the expenditure (a) of services (including the provision of time) and (b) of goods (including non-material goods like information, as well as the expression of regard and other face payments). These intra-culturally defined costings of impositions on an individual's preserve are in general constant only in their rank order from one situation to another. However, even the rank order is subject to a set of operations that shuffles the impositions according to whether actors have specific rights or obligations to perform the act, whether they have specific reasons (ritual or physical) for not performing them, and whether actors are known to actually *enjoy* being imposed upon in some way.

So an outline of the rankings of negative-face impositions for a particular domain of FTAs in a particular culture involves a complex description like the following:

1   (a) rank order of impositions requiring services
     (b) rank order of impositions requiring goods

2   Functions on (1):
     (a) the lessening of certain impositions on a given actor determined by the obligation (legally, morally, by virtue of employment, etc.) to do the act A; and also by the enjoyment that the actor gets out of performing the required act
     (b) the increasing of certain impositions determined by reasons why the actor *shouldn't* do them, and reasons why the actor *couldn't* (easily) do them

For FTAs against positive face, the ranking involves an assessment of the amount of 'pain' given to H's face, based on the discrepancy between H's own desired self-image and that presented (blatantly or tacitly) in the FTA. There will be cultural rankings of aspects of positive face (for example, 'success', 'niceness', 'beauty', 'generosity'), which can be re-ranked in particular circumstances, just as can negative-face rankings. And there are personal (idiosyncratic) functions on these rankings; some people object to certain kinds of FTAs more than others. A person who is skilled at assessing such rankings, and the circumstances in which they vary, is considered to be graced with 'tact', 'charm', or 'poise'.

We associate with each of these variables D, P, and R, a value from 1 to *n* assigned by an actor in particular circumstances. No special substantial claim is intended; the valuation simply represents the way in which (for instance) as S's power over H increases, the weightiness of the FTA diminishes. One interesting side effect of this numerical representation is that it can describe these intuitive facts: the threshold value of risk which triggers the choice of another strategy is a constant, independent of the way in which the value is composed and assessed. Thus one goes off record where an imposition is small but relative S–H distance and H's power are great, and also where H is an intimate equal of S's but the imposition is very great.

[. . .]

Editors' appendix: list of politeness strategies

Positive politeness strategies:

Notice, attend to H (his/her interests, wants, needs, goods)
Exaggerate (interest, approval, sympathy with H)
Intensify interest to H
Use in-group identity markers
Seek agreement
Avoid disagreement
Presuppose/raise/assert common ground
Joke
Assert or presuppose S's knowledge of and concern for H's wants
Offer, promise
Be optimistic
Include both S and H in the activity
Give (or ask for) reasons
Assume or assert reciprocity
Give gifts to H (goods, sympathy, understanding, cooperation)

Negative politeness strategies:

Be direct/conventionally indirect
Question, hedge
Be pessimistic
Minimise the size of imposition on H
Give deference
Apologise
Impersonalise S and H: avoid pronouns 'I' and 'you'
State the FTA as a general rule
Nominalise
Go on record as incurring a debt, or as not indebting H

Off-record strategies:

Those violating Grice's conversational maxims, see Chapter 3.

Violate maxim of Relevance
Give hints/clues
Give association clues
Presuppose

Violate maxim of Quality
Understate
Overstate
Use tautologies
Use contradictions
Be ironic
Use metaphors
Use rhetorical questions

Violate maxim of Manner
Be ambiguous
Be vague
Over-generalise
Displace H
Be incomplete, use ellipsis

Reference

Goffman, E. (1967) *Interaction Ritual*, New York: Anchor Books.

Chapter 20

Janet Holmes

WOMEN, MEN AND POLITENESS: AGREEABLE AND DISAGREEABLE RESPONSES

Example 1
Two thirteen year-olds discussing a schoolteacher.

David: He's a real dickhead he just bawls you out without
listening at all

Oliver: yeah what an ass-hole/ I can't stand him he's always
raving raving on

The discussion of interactive features such as interruption and minimal responses makes it very clear that the crucial aspects of these features from the point of view of politeness is their function in relation to the on-going discourse (Holmes 1995). Do they disrupt or support the talk of others? Do they threaten to take over the floor or do they encourage the current speaker to continue?

Extending the analysis further in this direction, it is obvious that the content of responses to the talk of others is another aspect of politeness behaviour. Agreeing with others, confirming their opinions and assertions, as illustrated by Oliver in example 1 and Sal and Pat in example 2 is supportive and positively polite behaviour (Brown and Levinson 1987: 112; [Chapter 19]).

Source: Janet Holmes, *Women, Men and Politeness*, London: Longman, 1995.

Example 2

Two young women watching TV together.

Sal: in that *Our House* um . . . she's the mother of teenage kids
      ⌈and she

Pat: ⌊oh yeah that's an awful program isn't it

Sal: mmmm

Pat: it's got that dick who's in the Cocoon film

Sal: oh god he's insufferable!

Pat: and he's so fucking wise ⌈and so so FUCKING American

Sal: ⌊yeah

Sal: and everybody else is always WRONG

Pat: yes and he's always right . . .

                                        (Pilkington 1992: 45)

This example illustrates that [. . .] overlapping and simultaneous talk can be supportive in effect. It also illustrates another pattern, namely, the tendency for women to agree with each other where possible. There is a great deal of evidence that in informal and casual interaction women tend to adopt the strategy of seeking agreement to a greater extent than men do, both in single-sex and mixed-sex contexts [. . .] Coates (1989: 118), for example, comments on the ways in which the women in the discussions she taped work together and collaborate with each other 'to produce shared meanings'. Participants build on each other's contributions, complete each other's utterances, and affirm each other's opinions giving an overall impression of talk as a very cooperative enterprise. Eckert (1990: 122) reports similar patterns among a group of adolescent girls, commenting that 'not one topic is allowed to conclude without an expression of consensus'. (It is interesting to note that this is also a pattern which is typical of more formal Maori interaction, suggesting that cross-cultural contrasts may mirror the gender contrasts observable in middle-class western society.)

A small but very interesting New Zealand study provides further evidence of this pattern. Jane Pilkington (1992) recorded the interactions between a group of women and a group of men working on different nights in a bakery. Her data for the women shows the same supportive and cooperative patterns in New Zealand women's speech as those described by Coates (1989) in the speech of the British women she recorded. The women developed each other's contributions, collaborating 'to produce a text by adding to what the previous speaker has just said', and they provided each other with a great deal of positive encouraging feedback. Facilitative tags were frequent as they encouraged others to comment and contribute. The women completed each other's utterances and agreed frequently. The impression is one of verbal cooperation and conversational sharing.

Example 3

Two young women working together in bakery.

Sal: perhaps next time I see Brian I'll PUMP him for
        ⌈information/ Brian tells me
May: ⌊   the goss
Sal: ⌈I know it's about six years old but
May: ⌊   [*laugh*] but
        I'd forgotten it

(Pilkington 1992: 46)

The men's interactions were very different. There were very few explicitly agreeing responses. Where a woman would have been likely to agree or at least respond, there were often long pauses between speakers. Indeed, Pilkington describes the male talk as typically combative, a kind of verbal sparring, a point which will be discussed further below. This study, then, though small, provides support for the view of New Zealand women as more positively polite than New Zealand men.

Both Gilbert and Stubbe examined the kinds of responses produced by New Zealand school pupils in the discussions they analysed. In the groups of fifteen year-olds (Gilbert 1990), the girls in the single-sex group used more agreeing positive responses than pupils in any other group (74 per cent), while the boys in the single-sex group used the fewest (54 per cent). In mixed-sex groups there were no gender differences in the overall proportion of positive responses; 63 per cent of both girls' and boys' responses were positive. Here is further evidence that the norms of interaction for each group are rather different, and again when girls and boys interact with each other, there is evidence of accommodation since these differences are reduced.

Maria Stubbe (1991) examined the relative numbers of agreeing and disagreeing responses produced by the eleven and twelve year-old children in the pairs she recorded. She found no significant differences in the proportions of agreeing responses produced by girls or boys in single-sex and mixed-sex pairs. There was an overwhelming preference for agreement in all pairs, so that agreeing responses outnumber disagreeing responses by 2:1. With these younger speakers, then, the differences between male and female pairs, in terms of the proportion of agreeing responses, disappeared.

The really interesting pattern that this analysis revealed, however, was in the types of disagreement responses preferred by the girls and boys.

Overall, the boys tended to use more 'bald' disagreements than the girls, especially in discussion with another boy.

Example 4
Two eleven year-olds discussing a problem.
Ray: I think I'd tell my friend
Rees: no that's stupid

The girls, by contrast, tended to modify or qualify their disagreeing responses, so that they were not so confrontational. Such responses allowed for, and indeed encouraged, further discussion of the point of difference between the speakers.

Example 5
Two eleven year-olds discussing a problem.
Pam: I think she should go with her mum
Hanna: but she'd really rather stay um/with her father though wouldn't she

The pattern that Stubbe identified is summarised in Figure 20.1.

It has been suggested that in many contexts being polite means maximising areas of agreement and minimising disagreement (e.g., Brown and Levinson 1987; Leech 1983). Yet clearly people do not always agree, and it is interesting to note that when this happens, women and men tend to approach the problem posed for politeness differently. What polite options are there if one does not agree with the views expressed by a conversational partner? One can change the topic, or keep silent, but both these involve a high risk of offence if they are not skilfully managed (see West and García 1988). Softening the disagreeing response is perhaps the most obvious strategy for a twelve year-old. The girls in Stubbe's study adopted this polite disagreement strategy almost twice as often as the boys.

The boys were much more willing to contradict overtly others or 'baldly' disagree with their conversational partners – a response that is certainly regarded in many contexts as very face threatening (Brown and Levinson 1987 [Chapter 19]). In fact the boys were six times more likely than the girls to respond with a bald disagreement. This again suggests that there may be different norms for females and males, or different levels of tolerance of overt disagreement.

These results are consistent with those of others. Jenkins and Cheshire (1990: 284) conclude their analysis of the interactions between young teenagers with a comment which aptly sums up the research in this area in a number of different countries. They say that

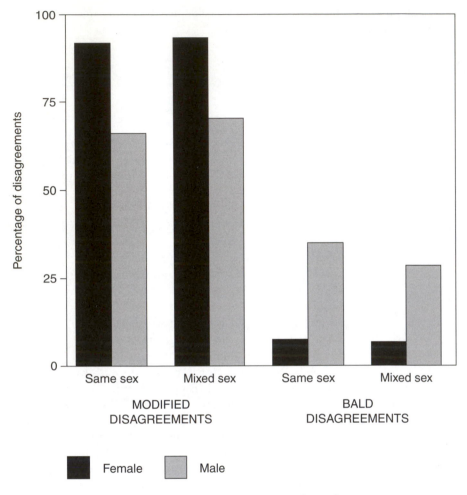

Figure 20.1   Modified and bald disagreements and gender
Source: Stubbe (1991: 88)

on the whole, the girls were careful, sensitive listeners who knew
when to speak and what kind of comment it is appropriate to
make . . . the conversational style of the girls, overall, can be
described as cooperative, generous and designed to allow the
participation of everybody on equal terms.

They also comment that the boys in their study were not so much competitive as unskilled in cooperative interaction. In a study of nine and twelve

year-old Dutch children, van Alphen (1987) reported that the girls' groups avoided disagreement, while the boys, when they did not ignore the comments of others, tended explicitly to challenge or dispute them. Tannen (1990) notes in a study of 'best friends' talk' that the girls were more concerned than the boys to avoid explicit disagreement. Goodwin (1980) noted similar patterns among African-American school-age children in the United States: the girls did not generally use bald challenges or threats, while these were frequent in the boys' interactions. And Sheldon's research (1990; 1992a; 1992b) suggests girls develop such skill at an early age. She describes the 'verbal conflict mediation skills' of preschool girls who effectively used mitigating strategies to disagree without aggressive confrontation.

Similar patterns have been reported for adults (Maltz and Borker 1982). Women tend to soften their disagreeing utterances more often than men. In the United States, for example, Marjorie Swacker (1979) found that women used more modified disagreements than men in the question sessions at the end of conference papers. And in an Australian study of the patterns used by language learners, Munro (1987) reported that the women used more 'softened' dis-agreements than the men. Men, on the other hand, seemed more willing than women to disagree baldly. This was also apparent in the study discussed above of the different ways in which women and men used elicitations in New Zealand seminars. The men were twice as likely as the women to use antagonistic elicitations. In a detailed analysis of the interactions of a group of female and male business managers, Susan Schick Case (1988: 52) reported that 'the mas-culine style was an assertively aggressive one that proposed, opposed, com-peted'. And in her study of the interactions between New Zealand males working in a bakery, Jane Pilkington found that the men tended to challenge and disagree with each other more explicitly and overtly than the women.

Example 6
Young men working together in bakery.
Ben: . . . and ah they're very smart
Dan: well then how come they keep getting caught all the time?
Sam: maybe that's why they ⌈(. . . . . .)
Ben: ⌊they don't Dan / you've got to
          be really clever to pull one you know
                                                    (Pilkington 1992: 52)

The men provided conflicting accounts of the same event, argued about a range of topics such as whether apples were kept in cases or crates, and criticised each other constantly for apparently minor differences of approach to things. Their strategies for amusing each other were often to ridicule the previous speaker's utterance, to put them down or to insult them, as illustrated in Example 7.

Example 7

Young men working in bakery discussing what apples are packed in.

Ray: crate!

Sam: case!

Ray: what

Sam: they come in cases Ray not crates

Ray: oh same thing if you must be picky over every one thing

Sam: just shut your fucking head Ray!

Ray: don't tell me to fuck off fuck (. . . .)

Sam: I'll come over and shut yo

Jim: *(Laughingly using a thick sounding voice)* yeah I'll have a crate of apples thanks

Ray: no fuck off Jim

Jim: a dozen . . .

Dan: *(amused)* shitpicker!

(Pilkington 1992: 53)

Listening to these interactions, it is very clear that the talk of the young men contrasts quite starkly with the cooperative, agreeing, mutually supportive talk of the women (illustrated in Example 3) in exactly the same context – working in the bakery – on a different night.

Women and men appear once again to be operating according to different rules of interaction. For the women, being negatively polite involves avoiding disagreement. Being positively polite is being friendly, and this involves confirming, agreeing and encouraging the contributions of others. But these politeness strategies are not typical of the interchanges described above between males. These young New Zealand men, like the young boys in the classroom discussion groups, are quite prepared to disagree baldly and to challenge the statements of others overtly. Indeed for this group, insults and abuse appear to be strategies for expressing solidarity and mateship, or ways of maintaining and reinforcing social relationships.

This kind of verbal sparring is reported by others who have examined all-male interaction (e.g. Dundes *et al.* 1972; Labov 1972). Labov (1972) described the ritual insults which occurred in the speech of New York adolescent gang members. In New Zealand, an analysis of the exchanges in a rugby changing room before a match demonstrated that the verbal interaction consisted almost entirely of insults – predominantly of a sexually humiliating kind (Kuiper 1991). People of both genders may use swear words to indicate their group membership (see, for example Hughes 1992), but Kuiper's study identifies insults which appear to serve as coercive devices to maintain solidarity and discipline between team members.

It appears, then, that at least in some contexts, female and male interactive norms contrast quite dramatically. The overall impression from the various studies discussed here is that male interaction is typically more competitive, aggressive and argumentative than female. For females, being negatively polite involves avoiding, minimising or mitigating disagreements; being positively polite involves agreeing with others, encouraging them to talk, expressing support verbally and ensuring they get a fair share of the talking time. For males, different norms appear to prevail. They can disagree baldly, challenge others' statements, interrupt and compete for the floor without intending to cause offence. In some contexts, aggressive and competitive verbal behaviour appears to be experienced as thoroughly enjoyable, and mutual insults may even serve as expressions of positive politeness and solidarity.

[. . .]

Transcription conventions

I have generally transcribed utterances as simply as possible. Normal punctuation is used for examples which were noted down, but not recorded on tape or video. For recorded examples, no punctuation is imposed on the transcription, but I have used the following conventions to record features relevant to the particular examples.

Pause length is indicated by slashes: / indicates a short pause and / /a slightly longer pause.

Emphatic stress is indicated by capitals: e.g. CRAZY.

Turns: the relationship between speakers' turns is indicated visually: e.g. minimal feedback is placed at the point it occurs. Nell's *mm* occurs in the pause between Max's words *them* and *she's*.

    Max: I mean I have no idea what story Pat had told them / /
    Nell: mm
    Max: she's got a vivid imagination

Simultaneous speech is indicated with brackets:

Nell: mm/tricky/ did ⌈you ask her   ⌉
Max: ⌊I didn't know   ⌋ what to say

Unclear speech is indicated as follows: (. . . . . .).

References

Brown, P. and Levinson, S. (1987) *Politeness: Some Universals in Language Usage*, Cambridge: Cambridge University Press.

Coates, J. (1989) 'Gossip revisited: language in all-female groups', in Coates, J. and Cameron, D. (eds) *Women in their Speech Communities*, London: Longman, 94–121.

Dundes, A., Leach, J. W. and Özkök, B. (1972) 'The strategy of Turkish boys' verbal dueling rhymes', in Gumperz, J. J. and Hymes, D. (eds) *Directions in Sociolinguistics*, New York: Holt Rinehart and Winston, 130–60.

Eckert, P. (1990) 'Cooperative competition in adolescent "girl talk" ', *Discourse Processes* 13: 91–122.

Gilbert, J. (1990) 'Secondary school students talking about science: language functions, gender and interactions in small group discussions', MA thesis, Wellington: Victoria University.

Goodwin, M. H. (1980) 'Directive-response speech sequences in girls' and boys' task activities', in McConnell-Ginet, S., Borker, R. and Furman, N. (eds) *Women and Language in Literature and Society*, New York: Praeger, 157–73.

Holmes, J. (1995) *Women, Men and Politeness*, London: Longman.

Hughes, S. E. (1992) 'Expletives of lower working-class women', *Language in Society* 21 (2): 291–303.

Jenkins, N. and Cheshire, J. (1990) 'Gender issues in the GCSE oral English examination: part 1', *Language and Education* 4: 261–92.

Kuiper, K. (1991) 'Sporting formulae in New Zealand English; two models of male solidarity', in Cheshire, J. (ed.) *English Around the World: Sociolinguistic Perspectives*, Cambridge: Cambridge University Press, 200–9.

Labov, W. (1972) 'Rules for ritual insults', in Kochman, T. (ed.), *Rappin' and Stylin' Out*, Chicago, IL: University of Illinois Press, 265–314. [Reprinted in Coupland, N. and Jaworski, A. (eds) (1997) *Sociolinguistic: A Reader and Coursebook*, London: Macmillan, 473–86.]

Leech, G. N. (1983) *Principles of Pragmatics*, London: Longman.

Maltz, D. N. and Borker, R. A. (1982) 'A cultural approach to male–female miscommunication', in Gumperz, J. J. (ed.) *Language and Social Identity*, Cambridge: Cambridge University Press, 196–216.

Munro, F. (1987) 'Female and male participation in small-group interaction in the ESOL classroom', unpublished term's project, graduate diploma in TESOL, Sydney: Sydney College of Advanced Education.

Pilkington, J. (1992) ' "Don't try to make out that I'm nice!": the different strategies women and men use when gossiping', *Wellington Working Papers in Linguistics* 5: 37–60.

Schick Case, S. (1988) 'Cultural differences, not deficiencies: an analysis of managerial women's language', in Rose, S. and Larwood, L. (eds) *Women's Careers: Pathways and Pitfalls*, New York: Praeger, 41–63.

Sheldon, A. (1990) 'Pickle fights: gendered talk in preschool disputes', *Discourse Processes* 13: 5–31.

—— (1992a) 'Conflict talk: sociolinguistic challenges to self-assertion and how young girls meet them', *Merrill-Palmer Quarterly* 38 (1): 95–117.

—— (1992b) 'Preschool girls' discourse competence: managing conflict', in Hall, K., Bucholtz, M. and Moonwomon, B. (eds) *Locating Power*, Proceedings of the Second Berkeley Women and Language Conference, 4–5 April 1992, vol. 2, Berkeley, CA: Berkeley Women and Language Group, University of California, 528–39.

Stubbe, M. (1991) 'Talking at cross-purposes: the effect of gender on New Zealand primary schoolchildren's interaction strategies in pair discussions', MA thesis, Wellington: Victoria University.

Swacker, M. (1979) 'Women's verbal behaviour at learned and professional conferences', in Dubois, B.-L. and Crouch, I. (eds) *The Sociology of the Languages of American Women*, San Antonio, TX: Trinity University, 155–60.

Tannen, D. (1990) 'Gender differences in topical coherence: creating involvement in best friends' talk', *Discourse Processes* 13: 73–90.

van Alphen, I. (1987) 'Learning from your peers: the acquisition of gender-specific speech styles', in Dédé Brouwer and Dorian De Haan (eds), *Women's Language, Socialisation and Self-image*, Dordrecht: Foris, 58–75.

West, C. and García, A. (1988) 'Conversational shift work: a study of topical transitions between women and men', *Social Problems* 35 (5): 551–75.

Chapter 21

Deborah Tannen and Cynthia Wallat

INTERACTIVE FRAMES AND KNOWLEDGE SCHEMAS IN INTERACTION: EXAMPLES FROM A MEDICAL EXAMINATION/INTERVIEW[1]

Introduction

Goffman (1981a) introduced the term "footing" as "another way of talking about a change in our frame for events," "a change in the alignment we take up to ourselves and the others present as expressed in the way we manage the production or reception of an utterance" (p. 128). He describes the ability to shift footing within an interaction as "the capacity of a dexterous speaker to jump back and forth, keeping different circles in play" (p. 156). Goffman asserts that "linguistics provides us with the cues and markers through which such footings become manifest, helping us to find our way to a structural basis for analyzing them" (p. 157). Using linguistic "cues and markers" as a "structural basis for analyzing" talk in a pediatric interaction, we show that a mismatch of knowledge schemas can trigger frame switches which constitute a significant burden on the pediatrician when she conducts her examination of a child in the mother's presence. Combining the perspectives of a social psychologist (Wallat) and a linguist (Tannen), we thus examine the specifics of talk in interaction in a particular setting to provide a basis for understanding talk in terms of shifting frames.

Source: Deborah Tannen and Cynthia Wallat, 'Interactive frames and knowledge schemas in interaction: examples from a medical examination/interview', *Social Psychology Quarterly* 5O(2): 205–16, 1987.

Like many of our colleagues, we make use of video-tape to analyze inter-action which is evanescent in nature. In his description of the theoretical and methodological complexity of making informed use of filmed records in social psychological research, Kendon (1979) cautions that micro-analytic analysis must be based on a theoretical perspective involving "context analysis." He sees context analysis as a conceptual framework which presumes that partic-ipants are not isolated senders and receivers of messages. When people are in each other's presence, all their verbal and nonverbal behaviors are poten-tial sources of communication, and their actions and meanings can be understood only in relation to the immediate context, including what preceded and may follow it. Thus, interaction can be understood only in context: a specific context. We have chosen the pediatric setting as an exem-plary context of interaction. Understanding how communication works in this context provides a model which can be applied in other contexts as well.

In examining talk in a pediatric setting, we are interested in the duality of what emerges in interaction: the stability of what occurs as a consequence of the social context, and the variability of particular interactions which results from the emergent nature of discourse. On one hand, meanings emerge which are not given in advance; on the other, meanings which are shaped by the doctor's or patient's prior assumptions (as we will argue, their knowl-edge schemas) may be resistant to change by the interlocutor's talk.

As Cicourel (1975) cautioned over a decade ago, when social scientists create a database for addressing the issues involved in integrating structure and process in the study of participants in medical settings, their textual material should "reflect the complexities of the different modalities and emer-gent contextual knowledge inherent in social interaction" (p. 34). One important way that Cicourel, and after him Richard Frankel (1989), sought to observe such complexities has been to compare discourse produced in spoken and written modalities. We have adopted this practice and have also developed a method of analyzing video-tapes of participants in more than one setting.

[. . .]

Frames and schemas

The term "frame," and related terms such as "script," "schema," "prototype," "speech activity," "template," and "module," have been variously used in linguistics, artificial intelligence, anthropology and psychology. Tannen (1979) reviews this literature and suggests that all these concepts reflect the notion of structures of expectation. Yet that early treatment of a variety of concepts of frames and schemas in the disciplines of linguistics, cognitive psychology and artificial intelligence said little about the type of frames that Goffman (1974) so exhaustively analyzed, as he himself observed (Goffman 1981b). The present paper broadens the discussion of frames to encompass and integrate the anthropological/sociological sense of the term.

The various uses of "frame" and related terms fall into two categories. One is interactive "frames of interpretation" which characterize the work of anthropologists and sociologists. We refer to these "frames," following Bateson (1972), who introduced the term, as well as most of those who have built on his work, including scholars in the fields of anthropology (Frake 1977), sociology (Goffman 1974) and linguistic anthropology (Gumperz 1982; Hymes 1974). The other category is knowledge structures, which we refer to as "schemas," but which have been variously labeled in work in artificial intelligence (Minsky 1975; Schank and Abelson 1977), cognitive psychology (Rumelhart 1975), and linguistic semantics (Chafe 1977; Fillmore 1975; 1976).

Interactive frames

The interactive notion of frame refers to a definition of what is going on in interaction, without which no utterance (or movement or gesture) could be interpreted. To use Bateson's classic example, a monkey needs to know whether a bite from another monkey is intended within the frame of play or the frame of fighting. People are continually confronted with the same interpretative task. In order to comprehend any utterance, a listener (and a speaker) must know within which frame it is intended: for example, is this joking? Is it fighting? Something intended as a joke but interpreted as an insult (it could of course be both) can trigger a fight.

Goffman (1974) sketched the theoretical foundations of frame analysis in the work of William James, Alfred Schutz and Harold Garfinkel to investigate the socially constructed nature of reality. Building on their work, as well as that of linguistic philosophers John Austin and Ludwig Wittgenstein, Goffman developed a complex system of terms and concepts to illustrate how people use multiple frameworks to make sense of events even as they construct those events. Exploring in more detail the linguistic basis of such frameworks, Goffman (1981a) introduced the term "footing" to describe how, at the same time that participants frame events, they negotiate the interpersonal relationships, or "alignments," that constitute those events.

The interactive notion of frame, then, refers to a sense of what activity is being engaged in, how speakers mean what they say. As Ortega y Gasset (1959: 3), a student of Heidegger, puts it, "Before understanding any concrete statement, it is necessary to perceive clearly 'what it is all about' in this statement and 'what game is being played.' "[2] Since this sense is gleaned from the way participants behave in interaction, frames emerge in and are constituted by verbal and nonverbal interaction.

Knowledge schemas

We use the term "knowledge schema" to refer to participants' expectations about people, objects, events and settings in the world, as distinguished from alignments being negotiated in a particular interaction. Linguistic semanticists have been interested in this phenomenon, as they have observed that even the literal meaning of an utterance can be understood only by reference to a pattern of prior knowledge. This is fundamental to the writing of Heidegger (for example, 1962: 199), as in his often quoted argument (p. 196) that the word "hammer" can have no meaning to someone who has never seen a hammer used. To borrow an example from Fillmore (1976), the difference between the phrases "on land" and "on the ground" can be understood only by reference to an expected sequence of actions associated with travel on water and in the air, respectively. Moreover, the only way anyone can understand any discourse is by filling in unstated information which is known from prior experience in the world. This became clear to researchers in artificial intelligence as soon as they tried to get computers to understand even the simplest discourse – hence, for example, the need for Schank and Abelson's (1977) restaurant script to account for the use of the definite article "the" in a minimal discourse such as, "John went into a restaurant; he asked the waitress for a menu."

Researchers in the area of medical sociology and anthropology such as Kleinman (1980) and Mishler (1984) have observed the problem of doctors' and patients' divergent knowledge schemas, although they may not have used this terminology. Cicourel (1983), for example, describes the effects of differing "structures of belief" in a gynecological case. The contribution of our analysis is to show the distinction and interaction between knowledge schemas and interactive frames.

At an earlier stage of this study, we referred to an interactive notion of frame as "dynamic" and the knowledge structure notion of schema as "static," but we now realize that all types of structures of expectations are dynamic, as Bartlett (1932), whose work underlies much of present-day schema theory, pointed out, and as others (for example, Frake 1977) have emphasized. That is, expectations about objects, people, settings, ways to interact, and anything else in the world are continually checked against experience and revised.

The interaction of frames and schemas

We demonstrate here a particular relationship between interactive frames and knowledge schemas by which a mismatch in schemas triggers a shifting of frames. Before proceeding to demonstrate this by reference to detailed analysis of pediatric interaction, we will illustrate briefly with reference to an example of a trivial, fleeting and mundane interchange that was part of a telephone conversation.

One author (Tannen) was talking to a friend on the telephone, when he suddenly yelled, "YOU STOP THAT!" She knew from the way he uttered this command that it was addressed to a dog and not her. She remarked on the fact that when he addressed the dog, he spoke in something approximating a southern accent. The friend explained that this was because the dog had learned to respond to commands in that accent, and, to give another example, he illustrated the way he plays with the dog: "I say, 'GO GIT THAT BALL!' " Hearing this, the dog began running about the room looking for something to fetch. The dog recognized the frame "play" in the tone of the command; he could not, however, understand the words that identified an outer frame, "*referring* to playing with the dog," and mistook the reference for a literal invitation to play.

This example illustrates, as well, that people (and dogs) identify frames in interaction by association with linguistic and paralinguistic cues – the way words are uttered – in addition to what they say. That is, the way the speaker uttered "You stop that!" was associated with the frame "disciplining a pet" rather than "chatting with a friend." Tannen drew on her familiarity with the use of linguistic cues to signal frames when she identified her friend's interjection "You stop that!" as addressed to a dog, not her. But she also drew on the knowledge that her friend was taking care of someone's dog. This was part of her knowledge schema about her friend. Had her schema included the information that he had a small child and was allergic to dogs, she might have interpreted the same linguistic cues as signaling the related frame, "disciplining a misbehaving child." Furthermore, her expectations about how any speaker might express orders or emotions, i.e. frame such expressions, were brought to bear in this instance in conjunction with her expectations about how this particular friend is likely to speak to her, to a dog and to a child; that is, a schema for this friend's personal style. Thus frames and schemas interacted in her comprehension of the specific utterance.

The remainder of this paper illustrates frames and schemas in a video-taped interaction in a medical setting: the examination of a child by a pediatrician in the presence of the mother. It demonstrates that an understanding of interactive frames accounts for conflicting demands on the pediatrician. In addition to communicative demands arising from multiple interactive frames, much of the talk in the pediatric encounter can be understood as resulting from differing knowledge schemas of the mother and the pediatrician. This will be illustrated with reference to their schemas for health and cerebral palsy. Finally, it is the mismatch in knowledge structure schemas that prompts the mother to ask questions which require the doctor to switch frames.

Background of the study

The video-tapes on which our analysis is based were obtained from the Child Development Center of the Georgetown University Medical School, following our presentation of a proposal to the Center's Interdisciplinary Research Committee. The video-tapes had been made as raw material for a demonstration tape giving an overview of the Center's services, and therefore documented all the encounters involving a single family and Center staff, which took place over three weeks.

The primary goal of the Center is to provide interdisciplinary training to future professionals in serving developmentally disabled children and their families. Staff members work in interdisciplinary teams which include an audiologist, speech pathologist, pediatrician, social worker, nutritionist, dentist, nurses and an occupational, an educational and a physical therapist. Each professional meets with the child and, in some cases, other family members; then all meet to pool the results of their evaluations, which are presented to the parents in a group meeting.

The parents of Jody, the 8-year-old cerebral palsied child in this study, were referred to the Center by the parents of another child. Their chief concern was Jody's public school placement in a class for mentally retarded children. Their objective, which was met, was to have a Center representative meet with the supervisor of special education in their district and have Jody placed in a class for the orthopedically rather than mentally handicapped.

In addition to the spastic cerebral palsy (paralysis resulting from damage to the brain before or during birth), Jody was diagnosed as having a seizure disorder; a potentially lethal arteriovenous malformation in her brain (this was subsequently, and happily, rediagnosed as a less dangerous malformation involving veins only, rather than both arteries and veins); facial hemangiomas (red spots composed of blood-filled capillaries); and slight scoliosis (curvature of the spine).

We began our analysis by focusing on the pediatrician's examination/interview, which took place with the mother present. As part of our analysis, we met, separately, with the doctor and the mother, first talking with them and then reviewing segments of the tape. The mother expressed the opinion that this doctor "was great," in explicit contrast with others who "cut you off and make you feel stupid" and deliver devastating information (for example, "she'd be a vegetable") in an offhand manner.

Interactive frames in the pediatric examination

The goal of this paper is to show that examining Jody in her mother's presence constituted a significant burden on the pediatrician, which can be attributed to a conflict in framing resulting from mismatched schemas. To demonstrate this interaction between frames and schemas, we will first show what framing is and how it works, beginning with the crucial linguistic component of register.

Linguistic registers

A key element in framing is the use of identifiable linguistic registers. Register, as Ferguson (1985) defines it, is simply "variation conditioned by use:" conventionalized lexical, syntactic and prosodic choices deemed appropriate for the setting and audience. [. . .]

In addressing the child, the pediatrician uses "motherese": a teasing register characterized by exaggerated shifts in pitch, marked prosody (long pauses followed by bursts of vocalization), and drawn out vowel sounds, accompanied by smiling. For example, while examining Jody's ears with an ophthalmoscope (ear light), the pediatrician pretends to be looking for various creatures, and Jody responds with delighted laughter:

> Doctor: Let me look in your ear. Do you have a monkey in your ear?
> Child: [laughing] No::::.
> Doctor: No:::? . . . Let's see. . . . I . . see . . . . . . a birdie!
> Child: ⌈[laughing] No:::.
> Doctor: ⌊[smiling] No.

In stark contrast to this intonationally exaggerated register, the pediatrician uses a markedly flat intonation to give a running account of the findings of her examination, addressed to no present party, but designed for the benefit of pediatric residents who might later view the video-tape in the teaching facility. We call this "reporting register." For example, looking in Jody's throat, the doctor says, with only slight stumbling:

> Doctor: Her canals are are fine, they're open, um her tympanic
> membrane was thin, and light,

Finally, in addressing the mother, the pediatrician uses conventional conversational register, as for example:

> Doctor: As you know, the important thing is that she does have
> difficulty with the use of her muscles.

Register shifting

Throughout the examination the doctor moves among these registers. Sometimes she shifts from one to another in very short spaces of time, as in the following example in which she moves smoothly from teasing the child while examining her throat, to reporting her findings, to explaining to the mother what she is looking for and how this relates to the mother's expressed concern with the child's breathing at night.

> [Teasing register]
>
> Doctor: Let's see. Can you open up like this, Jody. Look.
> [Doctor opens her own mouth]
> Child: Aaaaaaaaaaaaah.
> Doctor: ⌈Good. That's good.
> Child: ⌊Aaaaaaaaaaaah
>
> [Reporting register]
>
> Doctor: /Seeing/ for the palate, she⌈has a high arched palate →
> Child: ⌊Aaaaaaaaaaaaaaaaaaaaaaaaaah
> Doctor: but there's no cleft,
> [maneuvers to grasp child's jaw]
>
> [Conversational register]
>
> . . . what we'd want to look for is to see how she . . .
> moves her palate. . . . Which may be some of the difficulty with breathing that we're talking about.

The pediatrician's shifts from one register to another are sometimes abrupt (for example, when she turns to the child and begins teasing) and sometimes gradual (for example, her reporting register in "high arched palate" begins to fade into conversational register with "but there's no cleft," and come to rest firmly in conversational register with "what we'd want to look for . . . "). In the following example, she shifts from entertaining Jody to reporting findings and back to managing Jody in a teasing tone:

[Teasing register]

Doctor: That's my light.
Child: /This goes up there./
Doctor: It goes up there. That's right.

[Reporting register]

> Now while we're examining her head we're feeling for lymph nodes in her neck . . . or for any masses . . . okay . . . also you palpate the midline for thyroid, for goiter . . . if there's any.

[Teasing register]

> Now let us look in your mouth. Okay? With my light. Can you open up real big? . . . Oh, bigger. . . . Oh bigger. . . . Bigger.

Frame shifting

Although register shifting is one way of accomplishing frame shifts, it is not the only way. Frames are more complex than register. Whereas each audience is associated with an identifiable register, the pediatrician shifts footings with each audience. In other words, she not only talks differently to the mother, the child and the future video audience, but she also deals with each of these audiences in different ways, depending upon the frame in which she is operating.

The three most important frames in this interaction are the social encounter, examination of the child and a related outer frame of its video-taping, and consultation with the mother. Each of the three frames entails addressing each of the three audiences in different ways. For example, the social encounter requires that the doctor entertain the child, establish rapport with the mother and ignore the video camera and crew. The examination frame requires that she ignore the mother, make sure the video crew is ready and then ignore them, examine the child, and explain what she is doing for the future video audience of pediatric residents. The consultation frame requires that she talk to the mother and ignore the crew and the child – or, rather, keep the child "on hold," to use Goffman's term, while she answers the mother's questions. These frames are balanced nonverbally as well as verbally. Thus the pediatrician keeps one arm outstretched to rest her hand on the child while she turns away to talk to the mother, palpably keeping the child "on hold."

Juggling frames

Often these frames must be served simultaneously, such as when the pediatrician entertains the child and examines her at the same time, as seen in the example where she looks in her ear and teases Jody that she is looking for a monkey. The pediatrician's reporting register reveals what she was actually looking at (Jody's ear canals and tympanic membrane). But balancing frames is an extra cognitive burden, as seen when the doctor accidentally mixes the vocabulary of her diagnostic report into her teasing while examining Jody's stomach:

[Teasing register]

Doctor: Okay. All right. Now let me /?/ let me see what I
can find in there. Is there peanut butter and jelly?
Wait a minute.
Child: No
Doctor: No peanut butter and jelly in there?
Child: No.

[Conversational register]

Doctor: Bend your legs up a little bit. . . . That's right.

[Teasing register]

Okay? Okay. Any peanut butter and jelly in here?
Child: No
Doctor: No.
No. There's nothing in there. Is your spleen palpable over
there?
Child: No.

The pediatrician says the last line, "Is your spleen palpable over there?" in the same teasing register she was using for peanut butter and jelly, and Jody responds with the same delighted giggling "No" with which she responded to the teasing questions about peanut butter and jelly. The power of the paralinguistic cues with which the doctor signals the frame "teasing" is greater than that of the words spoken, which in this case leak out of the examination frame into the teasing register.

In other words, for the pediatrician, each interactive frame, that is, each identifiable activity that she is engaged in within the interaction, entails her establishing a distinct footing with respect to the other participants.

The interactive production of frames

Our analysis focuses on the pediatrician's speech because our goal is to show that the mismatch of schemas triggers the frame switches which make this interaction burdensome for her. Similar analyses could be performed for any participant in any interaction. Furthermore, all participants in any interaction collaborate in the negotiation of all frames operative within that interaction. Thus, the mother and child collaborate in the negotiation of frames which are seen in the pediatrician's speech and behavior.

For example, consider the examination frame as evidence in the pediatrician's running report of her procedures and findings for the benefit of the video audience. Although the mother interrupts with questions at many points in the examination, she does not do so when the pediatrician is reporting her findings in what we have called reporting register.[3] Her silence contributes to the maintenance of this frame. Furthermore, on the three of seventeen occasions of reporting register when the mother does offer a contribution, she does so in keeping with the physician's style: Her utterances have a comparable clipped style.

The homonymy of behaviors

Activities which appear the same on the surface can have very different meanings and consequences for the participants if they are understood as associated with different frames. For example, the pediatrician examines various parts of the child's body in accordance with what she describes at the start as a "standard pediatric evaluation." At times she asks the mother for information relevant to the child's condition, still adhering to the sequence of foci of attention prescribed by the pediatric evaluation. At one point, the mother asks about a skin condition behind the child's right ear, causing the doctor to examine that part of Jody's body. What on the surface appears to be the same activity – examining the child – is really very different. In the first case the doctor is adhering to a preset sequence of procedures in the examination, and in the second she is interrupting that sequence to focus on something else, following which she will have to recover her place in the standard sequence.

Conflicting frames

Each frame entails ways of behaving that potentially conflict with the demands of other frames. For example, consulting with the mother entails not only interrupting the examination sequence but also taking extra time to answer her questions, and this means that the child will get more restless and more difficult to manage as the examination proceeds. Reporting findings to the video audience may upset the mother, necessitating more explanation in the consultation frame. Perhaps that is the reason the pediatrician frequently explains to the mother what she is doing and finding and why.

Another example will illustrate that the demands associated with the consultation frame can conflict with those of the examination frame, and that these frames and associated demands are seen in linguistic evidence, in this case by contrasting the pediatrician's discourse to the mother in the examination setting with her report to the staff of the Child Development Center about the same problem. Having recently learned that Jody has an arteriovenous malformation in her brain, the mother asks the doctor during the examination how dangerous this condition is. The doctor responds in a way that balances the demands of several frames:

> Mother: I often worry about the danger involved too. →
> Doctor: ⌐Yes.
>   Cause she's well I mean like right now, . . . uh . . . in
>   her present condition. →
> Doctor: ⌐mhm
> Mother: I've often wondered about how dangerous they they are
>   to her right now.
> Doctor: We:ll . . . um . . . the only danger would be from
>   bleeding. . . . Fróm them. If there was any rupture, or
>   anything like that. Which CAN happen. . . . um . . .
>   that would be the danger.
> Mother: ⌐mhm

> Doctor: . . . Fór that. But they're . . . . . . mm . . . nót going
>   to be something that will get worse as time goes on.
> Mother: Oh I see.
> Doctor: But they're just thére. Okay?

The mother's question invoked the consultation frame, requiring the doctor to give the mother the information based on her medical knowledge, plus take into account the effect on the mother of the information that the child's life is in danger. However, the considerable time that would normally be required for such a task is limited because of the conflicting demands of the examination frame: the child is "on hold" for the exam to proceed. (Notice that it is admirable sensitivity of this doctor that makes her aware of the needs of both frames. According to this mother, many doctors have informed her in matter-of-fact tones of potentially devastating information about her child's condition, without showing any sign of awareness that such information will have emotional impact on the parent. In our terms, such doctors acknowledge only one frame – examination – in order to avoid the demands of conflicting frames – consultation and social encounter. Observing the burden on this pediatrician, who successfully balances the demands of multiple frames, makes it easy to understand why others might avoid this.)

The pediatrician blunts the effect of the information she imparts by using circumlocutions and repetitions; pausing and hesitating; and minimizing the significant danger of the arteriovenous malformation by using the word "only" ("only danger"), by using the conditional tense ("that would be the danger"), and by stressing what sounds positive, that they're not going to get worse. She further creates a reassuring effect by smiling, nodding and using a soothing tone of voice. In reviewing the video-tape with us several years after the taping, the pediatrician was surprised to see that she had expressed the prognosis in this way, and furthermore that the mother seemed to be reassured by what was in fact distressing information. The reason she did so, we suggest, is that she was responding to the immediate and conflicting demands of the two frames she was operating in: consulting with the mother in the context of the examination.

Evidence that this doctor indeed felt great concern for the seriousness of the child's condition is seen in her report to the staff regarding the same issue:

> Doctor: . . . uh: I'm not sure how much counseling has been
>   dóne, . . . wíth these parents, . . . around . . . the issue
>   . . . of the a-v malformation. Mother asked me ques-
>   tions, . . . about the operability, inoperability of it, . . .

> u:m . . . which I was not able to answer. She was told
> it was inoperable, and I had to say well yes some of
> them are and some of them aren't. . . . And I think that
> this is a . . . a . . . an important point. Because I don't
> know whether . . . the possibility of sudden death, intra-
> cranial hemorrhage, if any of this has ever been discússed
> with these parents.

Here the pediatrician speaks faster, with fluency and without hesitation or circumlocution. Her tone of voice conveys a sense of urgency and grave concern. Whereas the construction used with the mother, "only danger," seemed to minimize the danger, the listing construction used with the staff ("sudden death, intracranial hemorrhage"), which actually refers to a single possible event, gives the impression that even more dangers are present than those listed.

Thus the demands on the pediatrician associated with consultation with the mother; those associated with examining the child and reporting her findings to the video audience; and those associated with managing the interaction as a social encounter are potentially in conflict and result in competing demands on the doctor's cognitive and social capacities.

Knowledge schemas in the pediatric interaction

Just as ways of talking (that is, of expressing and establishing footing) at any point in interaction reflect the operation of multiple frames, similarly, what individuals choose to say in an interaction grows out of multiple knowledge schemas regarding the issues under discussion, the participants, the setting, and so on. We have seen that conflicts can arise when participants are orientated toward different interactive frames, or have different expectations associated with frames. Topics that the mother introduces in the consultation frame sometimes interfere with the doctor's conducting the examination, and time the doctor spends examining Jody in areas in which she has had no problems does not help the mother in terms of what prompted her to take Jody to the Child Development Center: a concern that she was regressing rather than improving in skills. Similarly, when participants have different schemas, the result can be confusion and talking at cross-purposes, and, frequently, the triggering of switches in interactive frames. We will demonstrate this with examples from the pediatrician's and mother's discussions of a number of issues related to the child's health and her cerebral palsy.

Mismatched schemas

Before examining Jody, the pediatrician conducts a medical interview in which she fills out a form by asking the mother a series of questions about Jody's health history and current health condition. After receiving negative answers to a series of questions concerning such potential conditions as bowel problems, bronchitis, pneumonia and ear infections, the pediatrician summarizes her perception of the information the mother has just given her. However, the mother does not concur with this paraphrase:

> Doctor: Okay. And so her general overall health has been good.
> Mother: . . . . . . [sighs] Not really. . . . uh: . . . back . . . uh
>   . . . after she had her last seizure, . . . uh . . . uh . . .
>   it was pretty cold during this . . . that time . . . a:nd
>   uh . . . it seemed that she just didn't have much
>   energy,⌐
> Doctor: └mm
> Mother: . . . and she uh . . . her uh . . . . . . motor abilities at
>   the time didn't seem . . . very good. . . . She kept
>   bumping into walls, . . . and falling, and . . . uh

The mother's schema for health is a comprehensive one, including the child's total physical well-being. The child's motor abilities have not been good; therefore her health has not been good. In contrast, the pediatrician does not consider motor abilities to be included in a schema of health. Moreover, the pediatrician has a schema for cerebral palsy (cp): she knows what a child with cp can be expected to do or not do, i.e. what is "normal" for a child with cp. In contrast, as emerged in discussion during a staff meeting, the mother has little experience with other cp children, so she can only compare Jody's condition and development to those of non-cp children.

Throughout our tapes of interaction between Jody's mother and the pediatrician, questions are asked and much talk is generated because of unreconciled differences between the mother's and doctor's knowledge schemas regarding health and cerebral palsy, resulting from the doctor's experience and training and the mother's differing experience and personal involvement.

Mismatches based on the cp schema account for numerous interruptions of the examination frame by the mother invoking the consultation frame. For example, as briefly mentioned earlier, the mother interrupts the doctor's examination to ask about a skin eruption behind the child's ear. The mother goes on to ask whether there is a connection between the cerebral palsy and the skin condition because both afflict Jody's right side. The doctor explains that there is no connection. The mother's schema for cp does not include the knowledge that it would not cause drying and breaking of skin. Rather, for her, the skin condition and the cp become linked in a "right-sided weakness" schema.

Similar knowledge schema mismatches account for extensive demands on the pediatrician to switch from the examination to the consultation frame. When Jody sleeps, her breathing sounds noisy, as if she were gasping for air. The mother is very concerned that the child might not be getting enough oxygen. When the doctor finishes examining the child's throat and moves on to examine her ears, the mother takes the opportunity to interrupt and state her concern. The doctor halts the examination, turns to the mother and switches to the consultation frame, explaining that the muscle weakness entailed in cp also affects the muscles used in breathing; therefore Jody's breathing sounds "coarse" or "floppy." However, this does not mean that she is having trouble breathing.

Doctor: Jody? . . . I want to look in your ears. . . . Jody?
Mother: This problem that she hás, . . . is not . . . interfering with her breathing, is it?
Child: /Hello/ [spoken into ophthalmoscope]
Doctor: No.
Mother: It just appears that way?
Doctor: Yes. It's very . . . it's . . . really . . . it's like flóppy you know that that's why it sounds the way it is.
Mother: She worries me at night.
Doctor: Yes
Mother: Because uh . . . when she's asleep I keep checking on hér so she doesn't⌐
Doctor: └ As you know the important⌐
Mother: └ I   keep thinking she's not breathing properly. [spoken while chuckling]
Doctor: As you know, the impórtant thing is that she dóes have difficulty with the use of her muscles.⌐
Mother: └ mhm
Doctor: So she has difficulty with the use of muscles, . . . as far as the muscles of her chest, that are used with breathing. Y'know as well as the drooling, the muscles with swallowing, and all that ⌐ so all her muscles

Mother: —Is there some exercise
    /to strengthen or help that/.

The mother's schemas for health and cerebral palsy do not give her the
expectation that the child's breathing should sound noisy. Rather, for her,
noisy breathing is "wheezing," which fits into a schema for ill health: noisy
breathing is associated with difficulty breathing. In fact, the parents, in the
initial medical interview at the Child Development Center, characterize Jody
as having difficulty breathing, and this is entered into the written record of
the interview.

These schemas are not easily altered. The pediatrician's assurance that
Jody is not having trouble breathing goes on for some time, yet the mother
brings it up again when the doctor is listening to Jody's chest through a
stethoscope. Again the doctor shifts from the examination frame to the consultation frame to reassure her at length that the child is not having trouble
breathing, that these sounds are "normal" for a child with cerebral palsy.

Doctor: Now I want you to listen, Jody. We're going to listen
        to you breathe. Can you? Look at me. Can you go like
        this? [inhales] Good. Oh you know how to do all this.
        You've been to a lot of doctors. [Jody inhales] Good.
        Good. Once . . . good. Okay. Once more. Oh you have
        a lot of extra noise on this side. Go ahead. Do it once
        more. ⌜Once more.
Mother: ⌞That's the particular noise she makes when she
        sleeps. [chuckle]
Doctor: Once more. Yeah I hear all that. One more. One more.
        [laughs] Once more. Okay. That's good. She has very
        coarse breath sounds um . . . and you can hear a lot of
        the noises you hear when she breathes you can hear when
        you listen. But there's nothing that's⌝
Mother: ⌞That's the kind
        of noise I hear when she's sleeping at night.
Doctor: ⌞Yes,⌟
        Yes. There's nothing really as far as a pneumonia is
        concerned or as far as any um anything here. There's
        no wheezing um which would suggest a tightness or a
        constriction of the thing. There's no wheezing at all.
        What it is is mainly very coarse due to the . . . the wide
        open kind of flopping.

Nonetheless, during the session in which the staff report their findings to the parents, when the pediatrician makes her report, the mother again voices her concern that the child is having trouble breathing and refers to the sound of Jody's breathing as "wheezing." At this point the doctor adamantly reasserts that there is no wheezing. What for the mother is a general descriptive term for the sound of noisy breathing is for the doctor a technical term denoting a condition by which the throat passages are constricted.

An understanding of the mother's schemas accounts for the resilience of her concern about the child's breathing, despite the doctor's repeated and lengthy reassurances. Our point here is that the mismatch in schemas – that is, the mother's association of noisy breathing with difficulty breathing and the doctor's dissociation of these two conditions and her emphasis on the medical definition of "wheezing" (irrelevant to the mother) – creates a mismatch in expectations about what counts as adequate reassurance. This mismatch causes the mother to ask questions which require the doctor to shift frames from examination to consultation.

Summary and conclusion

We have used the term "frame" to refer to the anthropological/sociological notion of a frame, as developed by Bateson and Goffman, and as Gumperz (1982) uses the term "speech activity." It refers to participants' sense of what is being done, and reflects Goffman's notion of footing: the alignment participants take up to themselves and others in the situation. We use the term "schema" to refer to patterns of knowledge such as those discussed in cognitive psychology and artificial intelligence. These are patterns of expectations and assumptions about the world, its inhabitants and objects.

We have shown how frames and schemas together account for interaction in a pediatric interview/examination, and how linguistic cues, or ways of talking, evidence and signal the shifting frames and schemas. An understanding of frames accounts for the exceedingly complex, indeed burdensome nature of the pediatrician's task in examining a child in the mother's presence. An understanding of schemas accounts for many of the doctor's lengthy explanations, as well as the mother's apparent discomfort and hedging when her schemas lead her to contradict those of the doctor. Moreover, and most significantly, it is the mismatch of schemas that frequently occasions the mother's recurrent questions which, in their turn, require the doctor to interrupt the examination frame and switch to a consultation frame.

The usefulness of such an analysis for those concerned with medical interaction is significant. On a global level, this approach begins to answer the call by physicians (for example, Brody 1980 and Lipp 1980) for deeper understanding of the use of language in order to improve services in their profession. On a local level, the pediatrician, on hearing our analysis, was pleased to see a theoretical basis for what she had instinctively sensed. Indeed, she had developed the method in her private practice of having parents observe examinations, paper in hand, from behind a one-way mirror, rather than examining children in the parents' presence.

The significance of the study, however, goes beyond the disciplinary limits of medical settings. There is every reason to believe that frames and schemas operate in similar ways in all face-to-face interaction, although the particular frames and schemas will necessarily differ in different settings. We may also expect, and must further investigate, individual and social differences both in frames and schemas and in the linguistic as well as nonverbal cues and markers by which they are identified and created.

Transcription conventions

[Brackets linking two lines show overlap:
Two voices heard at once
Reversed-flap brackets shows latching⌐
⌐No pause
between lines
/words/ in slashes reflect uncertain transcription
/?/ indicates inaudible words
? indicates rising intonation, not grammatical question
. indicates falling intonation, not grammatical sentence
: following vowels indicates elongation of sound
. . Two dots indicate brief pause, less than half second
. . . three dots indicate pause of at least half second; more dots indicate longer pauses
→ Arrow at left highlights key line in example
Arrow at right means talk continues without interruption→
on succeeding lines of text
'Accent mark indicates primary stress
CAPS indicate emphatic stress

Notes

1   This chapter [. . .] is a final synthesis of a long-term project analyzing videotapes made at Georgetown University's Child Development Center.

We are grateful to the Center administrators and staff who gave us permission to use the tapes, and to the pediatrician, the mother, and the parent coordinator for permission to use the tapes and for taking the time to view and discuss them with us. We thank Dell Hymes for his observations on how our work blends social psychological and sociolinguistic concerns. Tannen is grateful to Lambros Comitas and the Department of Philosophy and the Social Sciences of Teachers College Columbia University for providing affiliation during her sabbatical leave which made possible the revision of the manuscript. We thank Douglas Maynard for incisive editorial suggestions. [. . .]

2   Thanks to A. L. Becker for the reference to Ortega y Gasset. For a discussion on framing based on numerous examples from everyday life, see chapter 5, "Framing and Reframing," in Tannen (1986).

3   The notion of "reporting register" accounts for a similar phenomenon described by Cicourel (1975) in an analysis of a medical interview.

References

Bartlett, F. C. (1932) *Remembering*, Cambridge: Cambridge University Press.

Bateson, G. (1972) *Steps to an Ecology of Mind*, New York: Ballantine.

Brody, D. S. (1980) 'Feedback from patients as a means of teaching non-technological aspects of medical care', *Journal of Medical Education* 55: 34–41.

Chafe, W. (1977) 'Creativity in verbalization and its implications for the nature of stored knowledge', in Freedle, R. (ed.) *Discourse Production and Comprehension*, Norwood, NJ: Ablex, 41–55.

Cicourel, A. V. (1975) 'Discourse and text: cognitive and linguistic processes in studies of social structure', *Versus* 12: 33–84.

—— (1983) 'Language and the structure of belief in medical communication', in Fisher, S. and Dundas Todd, A. (eds) *The Social Organization of Doctor–Patient Communication*, Washington, DC: Center for Applied Linguistics, 221–39.

Ferguson, C. A. (1985) Editor's introduction. Special language registers, Special issue of *Discourse Processes* 8: 391–94.

Fillmore, C. J. (1976) 'The need for a frame semantics within linguistics', *Statistical Methods in Linguistics*, 5–29, Stockholm: Skriptor.

Frake, C. O. (1977) 'Plying frames can be dangerous: some reflections on methodology in cognitive anthropology', *The Quarterly Newsletter of the Institute for Comparative Human Cognition* 1: 1–7.

Frankel, R. M. (1989) ' "I was wondering – could Raid affect the brain permanently d'y'know?": Some observations on the intersection of speaking and writing in calls to a poison control center', *Western Journal of Speech Communication* 53: 195–226.

Goffman, E. (1974) *Frame Analysis*, New York, Harper & Row.

—— (1981a) *Forms of Talk*, Philadelphia: University of Pennsylvania Press.

—— (1981b) 'Reply to review of frame analysis by Norma Denzin', *Contemporary Sociology* 10: 60–8.

Gumperz, J. J. (1982) *Discourse Strategies*, Cambridge: Cambridge University Press.

Heidegger, M. (1962) *Being and Time*, New York: Harper & Row.

Hymes, D. (1974) 'Ways of speaking', in Bauman, R. and Sherzer, J. (eds) *Explorations in the Ethnography of Speaking*, Cambridge: Cambridge University Press, 433–510.

Kendon, A. (1979) 'Some theoretical and methodological aspects of the use of film in the study of social interaction', in Ginsburg, G. P. (ed.) *Emerging Strategies in Social Psychological Research*, New York: Wiley, 67–94.

Kleinman, A. (1980) *Patients and Healers in the Context of Culture: An Exploration of the Borderland Between Anthropology, Medicine and Psychiatry*, Berkeley, CA: University of California Press.

Lipp, M. R. (1980) *The Bitter Pill: Doctors, Patients and Failed Expectations*, New York: Harper & Row.

Minsky, M. (1975) 'A framework for representing knowledge', in Winston, P. H. (ed.) *The Psychology of Computer Vision*, New York: McGraw Hill, 211–77.

Mishler, E. (1984) *The Discourse of Medicine: Dialectics of Medical Interviews*, Norwood, NJ: Ablex.

Ortega y Gasset, J. (1959) 'The difficulty of reading', *Diogenes* 28: 1–17.

Rumelhart, D. E. (1975) 'Notes on a schema for stories', in Bobrow, D. G. and Collins, A. (eds) *Representation and Understanding*, New York: Academic Press, 211–36.

Schank, R. C. and Abelson, R. P. (1977) *Scripts, Plans, Goals, and Understanding: An Inquiry into Human Knowledge Structures*, Hillsdale, NJ: Erlbaum.

Tannen, D. (1979) 'What's in a frame? Surface evidence for underlying expectations', in Freedle, R. (ed.) *New Directions in Discourse Processing*, Norwood, NJ: Ablex.

Tannen, D. (1986) *That's Not What I Meant!: How Conversational Style Makes or Breaks your Relations with Others*, New York: William Morrow.

Chapter 22

Adam Kendon

THE NEGOTIATION OF CONTEXT IN FACE-TO-FACE INTERACTION

Erving Goffman (1963) distinguished as "focused interaction" those occasions when two or more individuals openly join together to sustain a single common focus of concern. This is done, most characteristically, perhaps, in occasions of talk, but a single focus of concern must likewise be openly entered into when people play games together, dance together or engage in some cooperative task activity such as moving a piano or performing a surgical operation (Goffman 1961b). Goffman pointed out that in any focused encounter a particular "definition of the situation" comes to be shared by the participants. This serves to define what will be considered, for the time being, as irrelevant, as well as what is relevant. A *frame* comes to be placed around the actions and utterances of the participants which provides for the sense in which they are to be taken (Goffman 1961a; 1974).

The ease with which people can adopt a common frame for the interpretation of events may be illustrated by considering games. When we observe game players, as Goffman pointed out, we may see how readily "participants are willing to forswear for the duration of the play any apparent interest in the esthetic, sentimental, or monetary value of the equipment employed, adhering to what might be called *rules of irrelevance*" (Goffman 1961a: 19). For instance, as Goffman points out, it does not matter whether the game of checkers is played with bottle tops on a piece of squared linoleum, or with pennies and dimes on a chalked-out set of squares, gold figurines on inlaid marble, or with uniformed men standing on colored flagstones. Insofar

Source: Adam Kendon, 'The negotiation of context in face-to-face interaction', in Alessandro Duranti and Charles Goodwin (eds), *Rethinking Context: Language as an Interactive Phenomenon*, Cambridge: Cambridge University Press, 1992, 323–34.

as the two players have agreed to play checkers, these items will be treated in exactly the same way. If one of the players were to deal with the pennies or dimes as money, however, or to start a conversation with one of the men on the colored flagstones, he would be breaking the "frame" that had been agreed upon, and he would place in jeopardy the continuance of the game.

While Goffman showed us in a number of ways that such a common frame must be presupposed if the process of focused interaction is to be understood, he did not really discuss the question of *how* such framing is achieved, except in quite general terms. By what means, through what kinds of overt acts, do people come to be able to assume that their co-interactants share with them the same perspective in the situation as they do themselves?

A quick answer to this has been to point out that many interactions are so routine that anyone entering them will know sufficient of what to expect and can count on others to know what to expect also. Thus each can assume that others understand the situation and no negotiation of understanding is needed. Yet, in most situations of daily interaction, where everyone is as well versed in its rules as everyone else, there remains considerable room for uncertainty. For instance, consider the question of how occasions of focused interaction are brought to an end. In maintaining themselves as participants in a focused interaction, participants must have negotiated a common perspective of relevance for each other's actions. In a conversation, for instance, a "topic" comes to be established, together with a "tone" in terms of which it is to be approached (whether it is to be treated seriously or lightly, for example). At any given point within the frame of the topic, participants must organize their utterances so that they will be relevant to the topic in some way. If the topic is to be changed or the whole conversation to be brought to an end, if confusion is to be avoided, it is necessary for all participants to agree to the change or termination before it actually occurs (cf. Schegloff and Sacks [Chapter 15]). If such an agreement is not reached, then any action of P's that, from his own perspective, belongs to a new frame of interpretation, will be interpreted by the other participants in terms of the currently prevailing frame and, accordingly, will be perceived as irrelevant, inconsistent, or in some other way disjunctive. If we are in the midst of a conversation about how to grow roses, for instance, and a comment is expected of me on some point regarding this, but I use my turn-slot to tell of the new car I have just bought, this is likely to produce disorientation in my co-participants. For new actions to be perceived and responded to as meaningful, the shared understanding concerning what we are talking about, i.e. the frame of interpretation all participants are applying in common to what each other says and does, must be changed first. Thus for changes of topic or terminations of conversations to be accomplished in a well-managed fashion, participants must be able to communicate with one another about their intentions to change or terminate before they actually do so (Kendon 1976). The question is, how is this accomplished?

The processes by which participants are able to negotiate the frame or working consensus of an interaction depend to an important degree upon the willingness of participants to allow that only certain aspects of behavior count as "action" (Kendon 1985). Evidently, participants treat only certain aspects of each other's behavior as if they are something fully intended and to be responded to directly. If I clear my throat in the midst of an utterance this is not treated as part of what I am "saying." If I uncross my legs, take a drag on my cigarette or sip my coffee while another is speaking, such actions are not attended to by the other participants as if they are contributions to the conversation. Overt acts of attention to activities of this sort are generally not made at all. Whereas spoken utterances and bodily movements, if perceived as gestures, are regarded as vehicles of explicitly intended messages, directly relevant to the business of the conversation, other aspects of behavior are not regarded in this light. As we shall see in a moment, these "non-relevant" aspects of each other's behavior nevertheless can play an important role in the process by which participants regulate one another's attention and provide information to one another about their level and focus of involvement in the interaction. However, it is the tacit agreement sustained by participants to maintain this distinction between "relevant action" and "non-relevant action" that makes it possible for people to embark upon lines of action in respect to one another, and to observe each other's modes of dealing with those lines of action without, as it were, officially doing so. By making this distinction, by regarding only some aspects of behavior as "explicit" or "official," whereas other aspects are regarded as "unofficial," participants make it possible for themselves to explore one another's interpretive perspectives. They thereby can negotiate some measure of agreement before either of them needs to address the other with any explicit action.

Goffman (1974) has drawn attention to this differentiation in the treatment participants in interaction accord various aspects of each other's behavior by his concept of *attentional tracks*. He suggests that in any social encounter there is always an aspect of the activity going forward that is treated as being within a *main-line* or *story-line track*. A domain of action is delineated as being relevant to the main business of the encounter, and it is oriented to as such and dealt with accordingly. Other aspects of activity are not included, but this does not mean that they have no part to play. Thus Goffman suggested we may also distinguish a *directional track*. Here, in Goffman's words, there is "a stream of signs which is itself excluded from the content of activity but which serves as a means of regulating it, bounding, articulating and qualifying its various components and phrases" (Goffman 1974: 210). One may speak, too, of a *disattend track*, to which are assigned a whole variety of actions that are not counted as being part of the interaction at all. Goffman mentioned here, in particular, various "creature comfort releases" – scratching, postural adjustments, smoking, and so forth – that are, so to speak, allowable deviations from the behavioral discipline to which all participants in a focused encounter are expected to conform. As Goffman himself made clear, and as a moment's reflection reminds us, it is not, of course, that the actions treated as being in the disattend track are not cognized and responded to by participants. On the contrary, they often play an important part in the very process of negotiating common perspectives that, as we have seen, is an essential part of what makes focused interaction possible. What I wish to suggest here, however, is that unless this kind of differential–attentional treatment is engaged in, the process by which participants negotiate the working consensus of the interaction would not be possible.

To illustrate the way in which participants may make use of "unofficial" or non-"main-track" aspects of each other's behavior in frame negotiation, consider the spatial–orientational organization of focused encounters. Participants in focused encounters typically enter into and maintain a distinct spatial and orientational arrangement. By doing so, it seems, participants can provide one another with evidence that they are prepared to sustain a common orientational perspective. By arranging themselves into a particular spatial–orientational pattern, they thereby display each to the other that they are governed by the same set of general considerations. By cooperating with one another to sustain a given spatial–orientational arrangement, they can display a commonality of readiness (Kendon 1973; 1977).

To understand how this can be so, we must first consider how the spatial and orientational position of an individual provides information about his or her attention. In the first place, it may be noted that *any* kind of activity involves the use of space and an orientation to a particular segment of the environment. If I sit at a desk to write, I command a certain space on the desk for this purpose. If I sit and think, closing my eyes to do so, I withdraw from active use of space around me perhaps, yet at the same time, to do this, I am likely to seek out a space that is not in use by others. In either case I can be said to be making use of a segment of the environment, although, in each case, in a very different way.

The segment of space that a person takes up in virtue of the line of activity he or she is pursuing I have called his or her *transactional segment* (Kendon 1977: 181). When two or more persons join to do something together, they come to have a *joint* transactional segment. Persons jointly have an access that is different from others. We may use the term *formation* for any instance where two or more persons sustain through time a spatial–orientational arrangement of some sort – persons standing on a line are participating in a formation, for example. We may distinguish as an *F-formation*, however, instances where two or more individuals position themselves in such a way as to maintain an overlapping or joint transactional segment. Thus whenever two or more individuals are placed close to each other, orientating their bodies in such a way that each of them has an easy, direct and equal access to every other participant's transactional segment, and agree to maintain such an arrangement, they can be said to create an F-formation. The system of spatial and postural behaviors by which people create and sustain this joint transactional space is referred to as an F-formation *system* (Scheflen and Ashcraft 1976; Kendon 1977).

It is noted that by establishing such a system of spatial and orientational relations, individuals create for themselves a context within which preferential access to the other's actions is established. Furthermore, such a system of spatial and orientational relations provides for a visually perceivable arrangement by which participants in a given focused encounter are delineated from those who are outsiders. Indeed, it seems that the kind of arrangements that arise in the F-formation provide a means of clearly demarcating the "world" of the encounter from the rest of the "world" around. Entering into an F-formation, thus, is an excellent means by which interactional and therefore social and psychological "withness" may be established.

F-formations vary in the actual shapes that they have. A roughly circular shape is common in free-standing groups of three or more people where all are participating in the same conversation, but it is by no means the only kind of arrangement. How persons arrange themselves in relation to one another and the environment will have consequences for the kinds of access each has to the others. Hall (1966) pointed out that at different interpersonal distances different kinds of information about the other are available and that this has consequences for the kinds of actions that can be used in interaction. Close up, one may whisper, further off, louder voicings are needed, but at quite large distances the small feedback gestures upon which interactants rely as they organize turn-taking become difficult to detect. As a result, there is a shift in the way the turn-taking system is managed. Such changes in the conditions of interaction have consequences for the kinds of transactions that are possible. Thus to adopt a space of a certain sort can be a way of adopting a "frame" of a certain sort. In this way what is possible becomes delimited but, by the same token, expectations about what is possible can be set up.

From the few studies that have been carried out on this point, it is apparent that there is, as one might expect, a systematic relationship between spatial arrangement and mode of interaction (Batchelor and Goethals 1972;

Kendon 1973). This means that people will not only tend to adopt particular arrangements for particular kinds of interaction but, by adopting a given spatial arrangement or by moving to a position and orientation that might suggest a spatial arrangement of a particular sort, a person can thereby propose an interactive relationship of a particular sort. Spatial positioning is thus available as an expressive resource for interactants. Yet spacing and orientation are generally treated as "background" and belong to the "not counted" part of the stream of action. Spatial and orientational positioning can thus serve well as a device by which expectation and intention can be conveyed and hence negotiated.

Within the course of an ongoing interactional episode, the arrangement adopted within an F-formation may change. Observations by several different investigators show that such changes can occur in conjunction with changes in other aspects of interaction, such as a change from salutation to topical conversation, or a change in conversational topic, suggesting that this is one way in which frame changes within an interaction may be marked in overt behavior (Scheflen 1964; Scheflen and Ashcraft 1976; Kendon and Ferber 1973; Ciolek and Kendon 1980; McDermott, Gospodinoff and Aron 1978; Streeck 1984). This allows us to see how participants may employ spatial and orientational manoeuvres as a means of testing out each other's alignments to a given interpretive frame or as a means of finding out if the other is willing to change to a new one. A participant wishing to change to a new frame may precede any actual change by small manoeuvres in the direction of the new position that would, if completed, constitute a position suitable for a different kind of interaction. If the co-participants are willing to follow the participant's lead, they will make complementary moves, rather than moves that would compensate for them and so maintain the status quo. Such preframe change negotiations can be observed especially when the closing of an encounter is being negotiated. Thus one may observe how one or other of the participants in a standing conversational group may begin to step back, increasing the distance between him- or herself and others. Such a move may be taken as an announcement of a wish for closure. Step-backs by the other participants may follow, and these serve to acknowledge the closure bid, thus making it possible for all of the participants to move into the closing phase of the conversation together (cf. Lockard, Allen, Schiele and Wierner 1978).

By entering into and maintaining an F-formation, participants are able to keep each other continuously informed that they are attending to the current occasion. Furthermore, as we have just seen, by showing themselves responsive to each other's adjustments in spatial–orientational positioning, participants can show whether they are ready or not for alterations in the frame of the situation. However, spatial–orientational positioning, or postural arrangements, as may be observed in seated groups, does not itself constitute the action of interaction. It is for this reason that it can serve so well in the process of frame attunement.

The "action" of the interaction is accomplished through actions, such as utterances, either spoken or gestural, or manipulative actions directed at the other, that are regarded by the participants themselves as moves of some sort in the interactive process they are engaged in. However, except perhaps in two-person encounters, and I think even here, there remains the question as to how participants are to know for whom a given act is meant and hence who is the one from whom the next move is expected. Interactionally explicit acts, as I shall call them, always have an address. Within the frame embodied in the F-formation, thus, sub-frames must be established within which given interchanges of explicit acts occur.

A number of studies have now been published which include detailed analyses of how utterance exchange systems are established and maintained (Kendon 1970; 1973; 1985; Goodwin 1981). It emerges from these analyses that participants in utterance exchange systems interrelate their behavior in a number of ways that are distinctive for them and different from the way their behavior is related to other participants in the gathering. Typically both speaker and direct recipient orient their bodies at least partially toward one another so that one might say of them that they have established a sub-segment of their transactional segments in mutual overlap. They repeatedly focus their eyes upon one another and, from time to time, their eyes meet. The orientation of the body, especially of the head, is toward one another, but it is the intermittent aiming of the eyes at another that is one of the principal ways by which the utterer in an utterance exchange system indicates to whom his or her actions are addressed; and the orienting of the eyes to the utterer is one of the principal ways in which a person can indicate that he or she is a recipient. Indeed, one of the ways in which a recipient of an utterance may redirect the speaker to another is by looking away from the speaker and towards another member of the gathering. If the utterer, then, can begin marking the address of an utterance by patterning his or her gaze in such a way that his or her eyes are aimed repeatedly at the addressee, the recipient must cooperate by maintaining an appropriate patterning on his or her part.

Recipients, furthermore, are commonly observed to display a heightened congruency of posture with that of the speaker, and they also tend to exhibit a particular set of gestures, such as headnods and changes in facial expression, that are patterned in a systematic relation with the organization of the speaker's speech. If the recipient ceases to display these actions and, in particular, if he or she alters the target of his or her eyes to that of another member of the gathering, the utterance exchange system will alter in who it includes or it will come to an end. Since only those within a current exchange system have rights as "next speaker" within that system, if it changes its membership midstream, this also has implications for who may follow as next speaker.

A further feature of the relationship between participants in an utterance exchange system is that the flow of action of speaker and recipient is often rhythmically coordinated and this also can become a means by which persons may attune their expectations to one another. (Pelose 1987 provides a recent comprehensive review.) This is demonstrated by studies of how participants become established as co-participants in an explicit interchange. Micro-analyses of film records of several different episodes of interaction have shown how an individual can announce his or her readiness to be a recipient for another's address by moving into synchrony with him or her. To initiate an explicit exchange with another is always somewhat risky, since there is the possibility that the other party may not wish to reciprocate. By picking up on the rhythm of another person's movements one can establish a "connection" with them which, at the same time, does not commit one to an explicit initiation. If, after having joined the rhythm of another, no reciprocal move is made, it is possible to continue as if no attempt has been made to initiate an "axis" (Kendon and Ferber 1973).

We may see, then, that there are various ways in which aspects of behavior that participants never report on and do not attend to as if they were officially "meant" are nevertheless relied upon for providing the kind of advance information that any one proposing to interact with another must have. I have suggested that, in a number of different ways, persons can make manifest their intentions, they can reveal how they are interpreting the situation without doing anything that would count as making a definite move in an interactional sequence. For this to be possible, there must be a tacit understanding that certain forms of behavior are not to be counted as "moves" even though all those present are fully able to control much of their own behavior that is treated in this way and are fully aware that the information it may make available can be deliberately provided. I believe that it is the willingness and ability of each of us to treat our own and others' behavior in this differential fashion that makes possible much of the process by which the "frame" or "working consensus" of an encounter can be established, maintained or changed in a coordinate fashion. Without this, orderly face-to-face interaction would not be possible.

References

Batchelor, J. P. and Goethals, G. R. (1972) 'Spatial arrangements in freely formed groups, *Sociometry* 35: 270–9.

Ciolek, T. M. and Kendon, A. (1980) 'Environment and the spatial arrangement of conversational interaction', *Sociological Inquiry* 50: 237, 271.

Goffman, E. (1961a) 'Fun in games', in his *Encounters*, Indianapolis: Bobbs-Merrill, 17–81.

—— (1961b) 'Role distance', in his *Encounters*, Indianapolis: Bobbs-Merrill, 85–152.

—— (1963) *Behavior in Public Places*, New York: The Free Press of Glencoe.

—— (1974) *Frame Analysis*, Cambridge, MA: Harvard University Press.

Goodwin, C. (1981) *Conversational Organization: Interaction between Speakers and Hearers*, New York: Academic Press.

Hall, E. T. (1966) *The Hidden Dimension*, Garden City, New York: Doubleday.

Kendon, A. (1970) 'Movement coordination in social interaction: some examples described', *Acta Psychologica* 32: 1–25.

—— (1973) 'The role of visible behaviour in the organization of face-to-face interaction', in von Cranach, M. and Vine, I. (eds), *Social Communication and Movement: Studies of Interaction and Expression in Man and Chimpanzee*, London: Academic Press, 29–74.

—— (1976) 'Some functions of the face in a kissing round', *Semiotica* 15: 299–334.

—— (1977) 'Spatial organization in social encounters: the F-formation system, chapter 5 in Kendon, A., *Studies in the Behavior of Social Interaction*, Lisse: Peter de Ridder Press.

—— (1985) 'The behavioural foundations for the process of frame attunement in face-to-face interaction', in Ginsburg, G. P., Brenner, M. and von Cranach, M. (eds) *Discovery Strategies in the Psychology of Action*, London and New York: Academic Press, 229–53.

Kendon, A. and Ferber, A. (1973) 'A description of some human greetings', in Michael, R. P. and Cook, J. H. (eds), *Comparative Ecology and Behaviour of Primates*, London: Academic Press.

Lockard, J., Allen, D., Schiele, B. and Wierner, M. (1978) 'Human postural signals: stance, weight shifts and social distance as intention movements to depart', *Animal Behaviour* 26: 219–24.

McDermott, R., Gospodinoff, K. and Aron, J. (1978) 'Criteria for an ethnographically adequate description of concerted activities', *Semiotica* 24: 245–75.

Pelose, G. C. (1987) 'The functions of behavioral synchrony and speech rhythm in conversation', *Research on Language and Social Interaction* 20: 171–220.

Scheflen, A. E. (1964) 'The significance of posture in communication systems', *Psychiatry* 27: 315–31.

Scheflen, A. E. and Ashcraft, N. (1976) *Human Territories: How We Behave in Space–Time*, Englewood Cliffs, NJ: Prentice-Hall.

Streeck, J. (1984) 'Embodied contexts, transcontextuals and the timing of speech acts', *Journal of Pragmatics* 8: 113–37.

Chapter 23

Gunther Kress and
Theo van Leeuwen

REPRESENTATION AND INTERACTION: DESIGNING THE POSITION OF THE VIEWER

[. . .] IMAGES INVOLVE two kinds of participants, *represented participants* (the people, the places and things depicted in images), and *interactive participants* (the people who communicate with each other *through* images, the producers and viewers of images), and three kinds of relations: (1) relations between represented participants; (2) relations between interactive and represented participants (the interactive participants' attitudes towards the represented participants); and (3) relations between interactive participants (the things interactive participants *do* to or for each other through images).

Interactive participants are therefore real people who produce and make sense of images in the context of social institutions which, to different degrees and in different ways, regulate what may be 'said' with images, and how it should be said, and how images should be interpreted. In some cases the interaction is direct and immediate. Producer and viewer know each other and are involved in face-to-face interaction, as when we make photographs of each other to keep in wallets or pin on pinboards, or draw maps to give each other directions, or diagrams to explain ideas to each other. But in many cases there is no immediate and direct involvement. The producer is absent for the viewer, and the viewer is absent for the producer. Think of photographs in magazines. Who is the producer? The photographer who took the shot? The assistant who processed and printed it? The agency who selected and distributed it? The picture editor who chose it? The layout artist who

Source: Gunther Kress and Theo van Leeuwen, *Reading Images: The Grammar of Visual Design*, London: Routledge, 1996.

cropped it and determined its size and position on the page? Most viewers will not only never meet all these contributors to the production process face to face, but also have only a hazy, and perhaps distorted and glamourized idea of the production processes behind the image. All they have is the picture itself, as it appears in the magazine. And producers, similarly, can never really know their vast and absent audiences, and must, instead, create a mental image of 'the' viewers and 'the' way viewers make sense of their pictures. In everyday face-to-face communication it is easy enough to distinguish interactive participants from represented participants: there is always an image-producer and a viewer (who, depending on the situation, may swap roles with the producer, add to the scribbled floorplan or diagram, for instance), and then there are the represented participants (for instance, the people on the quick sketch of the dinner table arrangement, or the landmarks on the hand-drawn map), and these may, of course, include the producer and/or the viewer themselves. Producer and viewer are physically present. The participants they represent need not be. But when there is a disjunction between the context of production and the context of reception, the producer is not physically present, and the viewer is alone with the image and cannot reciprocate – an illuminating exception is the case of the 'defacement' of billboard advertisements, when graffiti artists 'respond' to the initial 'turn' or statement of the image.

Something similar occurs in writing. Writers, too, are not usually physically present when their words are read, and must address their readers in the guise of represented participants, even when they write in the first person. Readers, too, are alone with the written word, and cannot usually become writers in turn. Literary theorists (e.g. Booth 1961; Chatman 1978) have addressed this problem by distinguishing between 'real' and 'implied' authors, and between 'real' and 'implied' readers. The 'implied author' is a disembodied voice, or even 'a set of implicit norms rather than a speaker or a voice' (Rimmon-Kenan 1983: 87): 'he, or better, *it* has no voice, no direct means of communicating, but instructs us silently, through the design of the whole, with all the voices, by all the means it has chosen to let us learn' (Chatman 1978: 148). The 'implied reader', 'preferred reading position', etc., similarly, is 'an image of a certain competence brought to the text and a structuring of such competence within the text' (Rimmon-Kenan 1983: 118): the text selects a 'model reader' through its 'choice of a specific linguistic code, a certain literary style' and by presupposing 'a specific encyclopedic competence' on the part of the reader (Eco 1979: 7). This we can know. Of this we have evidence in the text itself. Real authors and real readers we cannot ultimately know. This bracketing out of real authors and real readers carries the risk of forgetting that texts, literary and artistic texts

as much as mass-media texts, are produced in the context of real social institutions, in order to play a very real role in social life – in order to do certain
things to or for their readers, and in order to communicate attitudes towards
aspects of social life and towards people who participate in them, whether
authors and readers are consciously aware of this or not. Producers, if they
want to see their work disseminated, must work within more or less rigidly
defined conventions, and adhere to the more or less rigidly defined values
and beliefs of the social institution within which their work is produced and
circulated. Readers will at least recognize these communicative intentions
and these values and attitudes for what they are, even if they do not ultimately accept them as their own values and beliefs. They can 'recognize the
substance of what is meant while refusing the speaker's interpretations and
assessments' (Scannell 1994: 11).

However important and real this disjunction between the context of
production and the context of reception, the two do have elements in
common: the image itself, and a knowledge of the communicative resources
that allow its articulation and understanding, a knowledge of the way social
interactions and social relations can be encoded in images. It is often said
that the knowledge of the producer and the knowledge of the viewer differ
in a fundamental respect: the former is active, allowing the 'sending' as well
as the 'receiving' of 'messages'; the latter is passive, allowing only the
'receiving' of 'messages'. Producers are able to 'write' as well as 'read',
viewers are only able to 'read'. Up to a point this is true, at least in the
sense that the production of images is still a specialized activity, so that
producers 'write' more fluently and eloquently, and more frequently, than
viewers. But we hope our attempts to make that knowledge explicit will
show that the interactive meanings are visually encoded in ways that rest on
competencies shared by producers and viewers. The articulation and understanding of social meanings in images derives from the visual articulation of
social meanings in face-to-face interaction, the spatial positions allocated to
different kinds of social actors in interaction (whether they are seated or
standing, side by side or facing each other frontally, etc.). In this sense the
interactive dimension of images is the 'writing' of what is usually called 'nonverbal communication', a 'language' shared by producers and viewers alike.

The disjunction between the context of production and the context of
reception has yet another effect: it causes social relations to be *represented
rather than enacted*. Because the producers are absent from the place where
the actual communicative transaction is completed, from the locus of reception, they cannot say 'I' other than through a substitute 'I'. Even when the
viewer receives an image of the 'real author' or a contributor to the production process, the presenter in a television programme, the painter in a

self-portrait, the owner of the company (or the worker in the centuries-old distillery) in an advertisement, that image is only an image, a double of the 'real author', a representation, detached from his or her actual body. And the 'real authors' may also speak in the guise of someone else, of a 'character', as when, instead of the owner of a company, it is Uncle Sam, or a larger than life walking and talking teddy bear, who addresses us in an advertisement. This dimension of representation is another one which has been studied extensively in literary theory (e.g., Genette 1972). The relation between producer and viewer, too, is represented rather than enacted. In face-to-face communication we must respond to a friendly smile with a friendly smile, to an arrogant stare with a deferential lowering of the eyes, and such obligations cannot easily be avoided without appearing impolite, unfriendly or impudent. When images confront us with friendly smiles or arrogant stares, we are not obliged to respond, even though we do recognize how we are addressed. The relation is only represented. We are *imaginarily* rather than really put in the position of the friend, the customer, the lay person who must defer to the expert. And whether or not we identify with that position will depend on other factors – on our real relation to the producer or the institution he or she represents, and on our real relation to the others who form part of the context of reception. All the same, whether or not we identify with the way we are addressed, we do understand how we are addressed, because we do understand the way images represent social interactions and social relations. It is the business of this chapter to try and make those understandings explicit.

The image act and the gaze

In Figure 23.1 on the left we see photographs from which the Australian Antarctic explorer Sir Douglas Mawson looks directly at the viewer. The somewhat schematic drawing of a 'generalized' explorer is on the right, and this explorer does not look at the viewer. The photos and the drawing serve different communicative functions: the photos (especially the close-up) seek above all to bring about an imaginary relation between the represented explorer and the children for whom the book is written, a relation perhaps of admiration for, and identification with, a national hero. And this means also that the producer of the images (the institution of educational publishing) addresses the children in the voice of the national hero and makes that national hero an 'educational' voice. The drawing, on the other hand, seeks, first of all, to be read as a piece of objective, factual information, and in this way aims to set into motion the actual process of learning.

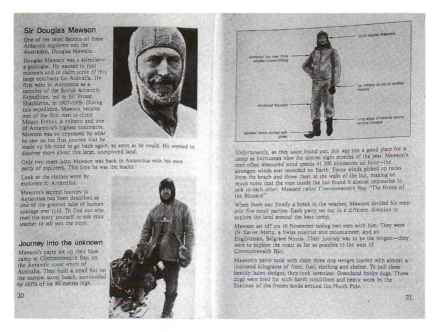

Figure 23.1 Antarctic explorer
Source: Oakley 1985

There is then, a fundamental difference between pictures from which represented participants look directly at the viewer's eyes, and pictures in which this is not the case. When represented participants look at the viewer, vectors, formed by participants' eyelines, connect the participants with the viewer. Contact is established, even if it is only on an imaginary level. In addition there may be a further vector, formed by a gesture in the same direction, as in Figure 23.2.

This visual configuration has two related functions. In the first place it creates a visual form of direct address. It acknowledges the viewers explicitly, addressing them with a visual 'you'. In the second place it constitutes an 'image act'. The producer uses the image to *do* something to the viewer. It is for this reason that we have called this kind of image a 'demand': the participant's gaze (and the gesture, if present) demands something from the viewer, demands that the viewer enter into some kind of imaginary relation with him or her. Exactly what kind of relation is then signified by other means, for instance by the facial expression of the represented participants. They may smile, in which case the viewer is asked to enter into a relation

Figure 23.2 Recruitment poster
Source: Alfred Leete 1914, Imperial War Museum

of social affinity with them; they may stare at the viewer with cold disdain, in which case the viewer is asked to relate to them, perhaps, as an inferior relates to a superior; they may seductively pout at the viewer, in which case the viewer is asked to desire them. The same applies to gestures. A hand can point at the viewer, in a visual 'Hey, you there, I mean you', or invite the viewer to come closer, or hold the viewer at bay with a defensive gesture, as if to say: stay away from me. In each case the image wants something from the viewers – wants them to do something (come closer, stay at a

distance) or to form a pseudo-social bond of a particular kind with the represented participant. And in doing this, images define to some extent who the
viewer is (e.g., male, inferior to the represented participant, etc.), and in
that way exclude other viewers.

[. . .]

According to Belting (1990) 'the suggestion of reciprocity between the
viewer and the person depicted in the image' had a devotional purpose. By
the thirteenth century, monks in their cells 'had before their eyes images of
the Virgin and her crucified son, so that while reading, praying and sleeping,
they could look upon them and *be looked upon* with the eyes of compassion'
(p. 57, our italics).

[. . .]

Other pictures address us indirectly. Here the viewer is not object, but
subject of the look, and the represented participant is the object of the viewer's
dispassionate scrutiny. No contact is made. The viewer's role is that of an invisible onlooker. All images which do not contain human or quasi-human participants looking directly at the viewer are of this kind. For this reason we have
called this kind of image an 'offer' — it 'offers' the represented participants to
the viewer as items of information, objects of contemplation, impersonally, as
though they were specimens in a display case.

It is always interesting to study which kinds of represented participants
are, in a given context, depicted as demanding an imaginary social response of
some kind from the viewer, and which are not. In the Australian primary
school social studies textbook *Our Society and Others*, for instance, immigrant
families smile at the viewer. However, the human participants in pictures from
these immigrants' countries of origin do *not* look at the viewer, not even in
close-up portraits, as, for instance, in the portrait of an Italian grandmother
who stayed behind. In the chapter on Aborigines, by contrast, hardly any of
the Aboriginal participants look at the viewer. The Aboriginal poet Oodgeroo
Noonuccal, referred to in the book as Kath Walker, and depicted in close up
in the last illustration of that chapter, is the only exception (see Figure 23.3
below). Her expression, her make-up, her hair style and dress hardly distinguish her from non-Aboriginal women of her age. At most her skin is somewhat darker, but even that is not very pronounced in the black-and-white shot.
Other Aboriginal people in the chapter are much more clearly depicted as
'other', and even if they do, occasionally, look directly at the viewer, they do
so from a long distance, which greatly diminishes the impact of their look, or
are figures in the background, looking blankly and more or less accidentally
in the direction of the camera. Aboriginal people, in this primary school

textbook, are depicted as objects of contemplation, not as subjects for the pupil to enter into an imaginary social relation with. Immigrants, by contrast, at least once they are in Australia, are portrayed as people with whom the pupils should engage more directly, and in a friendly way, as equals.

The choice between 'offer' and 'demand', which must be made whenever people are depicted, is not only used to suggest different relations with different 'others', to make viewers engage with some and remain detached from others; it can also characterize pictorial genres. In some contexts, for instance television newsreading and the posed magazine photograph, the 'demand' picture is preferred: these contexts require a sense of connection between the viewers and the authority figures, celebrities and role models they depict. In other contexts, for example feature film and television drama and scientific illustration, the 'offer' is preferred: here a real or imaginary barrier is erected between the represented participants and the viewers, a sense of disengagement, in which the viewer must have the illusion that the represented participants do not know they are being looked at, and in which the represented participants must pretend that they are not being watched. And what in one context is accepted convention may in another be a startling mistake or an innovative experiment. Film theorists (e.g., Allen 1977; Wollen 1982) have hailed the look at the camera as a daring, Brechtian, 'self-reflexive' style figure, but in television newsreading the look at the camera is commonplace and, we would think, not exactly 'self-reflexive' – at least for the presenters: an interviewee who looks at the camera in a television news programme breaks the rules in an unacceptable way. Not everyone may address the viewer directly. Some may only be looked *at*, others may themselves be the bearers of the look. There is an issue of communicative power or 'entitlement' (Sacks 1992) involved in this, not only in pictures, but also in everyday face-to-face communication, for instance in interactions between men and women:

> As he answers the girl's last statement he begins talking and reaches the point where normally he would look away, but instead he is still staring at her. This makes her uncomfortable, because she is forced either to lock eyes with him, or to look away from him while *he* is talking. If he continues to talk and stare while she deflects her eyes, it puts her into the 'shy' category, which she resents. If she boldly locks eyes with him, he has forced her into a 'lover's gaze', which she also resents.
>
> (Morris 1977: 76)

Diagrams, maps and charts are most often found in contexts that offer the kind of knowledge which, in our culture, is most highly valued – objective, dispassionate knowledge, ostensibly free of emotive involvement and subjectivity. Hence the 'demand' is rare in these visual genres. But there are contexts in which the two forms of address are combined. School textbooks, for instance, may construct a progression from 'demand' to 'offer' pictures, and this not only in the course of a chapter, as in the chapter on Antarctic exploration, but also in the course of a whole book or series of books, and indeed, in the course of education as a whole: illustrations that serve to involve students emotively in the subject matter gradually drop out as higher levels of education are reached. In senior highschool textbooks we find 'demand' pictures at most in the cartoons which, in almost apologetic fashion, seek to alleviate the seriousness of the text from time to time, as in a cartoon in a geography textbook (Bindon and Williams 1988) where a girl looks despondently at the viewer, with the words 'What does hypothesis mean?' in a dialogue balloon emanating from her mouth. In the context of education, the 'demand' picture plays an ambivalent role. On the one hand, it is not a highly valued form, but a form deemed suitable only for beginners, a form one grows out of as one climbs the educational ladder; on the other hand, it plays an indispensable role in educational strategy: objective knowledge must, apparently, be built upon a foundation of emotive involvement, of identification with celebratory mythologies, for instance. This foundation must then, gradually, be repressed, for if it is not repressed, the knowledge built on it cannot be seen to be objective. Outside the sphere of education, the value of the 'demand' picture will depend on the assumed educational level of the reader. When, for instance, the mass media (or automatic teller machines) begin to use 'demand' pictures, those educated in the linguistic and visual genres of objective knowledge and impersonal address may feel patronized, 'addressed below their class'. Those not so educated (or those who contest the value of such an education) may feel that communication has become more effective (and more fun) than was the case in the era of more formal and impersonal public communication.

The meanings conveyed by 'demands' and 'offers' can be related to the grammatical system of person. As we have seen, 'demand' pictures address the viewer directly, realizing a visual 'you'. But this is not matched by a visual 'I'. The 'I' is absent in pictures, or rather, objectified, hiding behind a he/she/they. The 'demand' picture therefore recalls more the language of, for instance, advertisements and instructions, where 'you's' abound but 'I's' are rare, than say, of the language of personal letters where 'I's' and 'you's' are likely to be equally common. 'Real producers' cannot refer to themselves directly. They must speak impersonally, as in bureaucratic and scientific language, where 'I's' are also repressed. The public, on the other hand, is addressed directly. And yet, as we have seen, the distinction between 'offers' and 'demands' derives historically from attempts of Renaissance painters to find ways of saying 'I', in the self-portraits which expressed their new found self-confidence and status of independent artists rather than humble craftsmen.

[. . .]

Size of frame and social distance

There is a second dimension to the interactive meanings of images, related to the 'size of frame', to the choice between close-up, medium shot and long shot, and so on. Just as image-producers, in depicting human or quasi-human participants, must choose to make them look at the viewer or not, so they must also, and at the same time, choose to depict them as close to or far away from the viewer – and this applies to the depiction of objects also. And like the choice between the 'offer' and the 'demand', the choice of distance can suggest different relations between represented participants and viewers. In handbooks about film and television production size of frame is invariably defined in relation to the human body. Even though distance is, strictly speaking, a continuum, the 'language of film and television' has imposed a set of distinct cut-off points on this continuum, in the same way as languages impose cut-off points on the continuum of vowels we can produce. Thus the close shot (or 'close-up') shows head and shoulders of the subject, and the very close shot ('extreme close-up', 'big close-up') anything less than that. The medium close shot cuts off the subject approximately at the waist, the medium shot approximately at the knees. The medium long shot shows the full figure. In the long shot the human figure occupies about half the height of the frame, and the very long shot is anything 'wider' than that. Stylistic variants are possible, but they are always seen and talked about in terms of this system, as when film and television people talk of 'tight close shots' or 'tight framing', or about the amount of 'headroom' in a picture (i.e., space between the top of the head and the upper frame line).

In everyday interaction, social relations determine the distance (literally and figuratively) we keep from one another. Edward Hall (e.g., 1966: 110–20) has shown that we carry with us a set of invisible boundaries beyond which we allow only certain kinds of people to come. The location of these invisible boundaries is determined by configurations of sensory potentialities – by whether or not a certain distance allows us to smell or touch the other person, for instance, and by how much of the other person we can see with our peripheral (60°) vision. 'Close personal distance' is the distance at which 'one can hold or grasp the other person' and therefore also the distance between people who have an intimate relation with each other. Non-intimates cannot come this close, and if they do so, it will be experienced as an act of aggression.

'Far personal distance' is the distance that 'extends from a point that is just outside easy touching distance by one person to a point where two people can touch fingers if they both extend their arms', the distance at which 'subjects of personal interests and involvements are discussed'. 'Close social distance' begins just outside this range and is the distance at which 'impersonal business occurs'. 'Far social distance' is 'the distance to which people move when some-body says "Stand away so I can look at you" ' – 'business and social interaction conducted at this distance a more formal and impersonal character than in the close phase'. 'Public distance', finally, is anything further than that, 'the dis-tance between people who are and are to remain strangers'. These judgements apply, of course, within a particular culture, and Hall cites many examples of the misunderstandings which can arise from intercultural differences in the interpretation of distance.

With these differences correspond different fields of vision. At intimate distance, says Hall (1964), we see the face or head only. At close personal distance we take in the head and the shoulders. At far personal distance we see the other person from the waist up. At close social distance we see the whole figure. At far social distance we see the whole figures 'with space around it'. And at public distance we can see the torso of at least four or five people. It is clear that these fields of vision correspond closely to the traditional definitions of size of frame in film and television, in other words, that the visual system of size of frame derives from the 'proxemics', as Hall calls it, of everyday face-to-face interaction. Hall is aware of this and in fact acknowledges the influence of the work of Grosser, a portrait painter, on his ideas. According to Grosser (quoted in Hall 1966: 71–2), at a distance of more than 13 feet, people are seen 'as having little connection with ourselves', and hence 'the painter can look at his model as if he were a tree in a landscape or an apple in a still life'. Four to eight feet, on the other hand, is the 'portrait distance':

> the painter is near enough so that his eyes have no trouble in understanding the sitter's solid forms, yet he is far enough away so that the foreshortening of the forms presents no real problem. Here at the normal distance of social intimacy and easy conver-sation, the sitter's soul begins to appear. . . . Nearer than three feet, within touching distance, the soul is far too much in evidence for any sort of disinterested observation.

The distances people keep, then, depend on their social relation – whether this is the more permanent kind of social relation on which Hall mainly concentrates (the distinction between intimates, friends, acquaintances,

strangers, etc.) or the kind of social relation that lasts for the duration of a
social interaction and is determined by the context (someone in the audience
of a speech given by an acquaintance or relative would nevertheless stay at
public distance, the distance of the 'stranger'). But these distances also, and
at the same time, determine how much of the other person is in our field
of vision – just as does the framing of a person in a portrait or film shot.

Like the 'demand' picture, the close-up came to the fore in the
Renaissance. Ringbom (1965) argues that it has its origin in devotional
pictures, where it served to provide 'the "near-ness" so dear to the God-
seeking devout' (p. 48). In Italian and Dutch paintings of the early sixteenth
century it acquired a 'dramatic' function, allowing 'the subtlest of emotional
relationships with a minimum of dramatic scenery' (*ibid.*).

The people we see in images are for the most part strangers. It is true
that we see some of them (politicians, film and television stars, sports heroes,
etc.) a good deal more than others, but this kind of familiarity does not of
itself determine whether they will be shown in close shot or medium shot
or long shot. The relation between the human participants represented in
images and the viewer is once again an imaginary relation. People are
portrayed *as though* they are friends, or *as though* they are strangers. Images
allow us to imaginarily come as close to public figures as if they were our
friends and neighbours – or to look at people like ourselves as strangers,
'others'. In the primary school social studies textbook from which we have
quoted several examples, three Aboriginal boys are shown in long shot, occupying only about a quarter of the height of the 'portrait' format frame. The
caption reads 'These people live at Redfern, a suburb of Sydney.' They are
shown impersonally, as strangers with whom we do not need to become
acquaintances, as 'trees in a landscape'. Although they do look at the viewer,
they do so from such a distance that it barely affects us. Indeed, they are so
small that we can hardly distinguish their facial features. 'Their soul does not
yet begin to appear', to coin Grosser's words. The caption, significantly,
gives them no name; in fact, where the more friendly 'boys' could have
been, the quite formal 'people' has been used.

The portrait of the Aboriginal poet Oodgeroo Noonuccal (Figure 23.3)
is a right close shot. *She* is depicted in a personal way. If this was all we
could see of her reality, we would be close enough to touch her. As
mentioned, the section in which the photo occurs concludes a chapter on
Aborigines in which no other Aborigine smiles at the viewer in this way.
One of her poems is quoted: 'Dark and white upon common ground/ In
club and office and social round/ Yours the feel of a friendly land/ The grip
of the hand' (Oakley *et al.* 1985: 164). But Noonuccal's message is not borne
out by the way 'dark and white' are portrayed in the chapter.

Figure 23.3   Oodgeroo Noonuccal
Source: Oakley 1985

Patterns of distance can become conventional in visual genres. In current affairs television, for example, 'voices' of different status are habitually framed differently: the camera 'moves in for bigger close-ups of subjects who are revealing their feelings, whereas the set-up for the "expert" is usually the same as that for the interviewer – the breast pocket shot'. Both kinds of 'statused participants' tend to be 'nominated' (their names appear on the screen in superimposed captions) and 'have their contributions framed and summed up' (Brunsdon and Morley 1978: 65). In other words, distance is used to signify respect for authorities of various kinds, on television as in face-to-face interaction.

In diagrams the human figure is almost always shown in medium long or long shot – objectively, 'as if he were a tree in a landscape'. The pictures in Figures 23.4 illustrated a front-page newspaper story about a murder case in Sydney. The diagrams show exactly what happened, from an objectifying and impersonal distance (and from a high angle). The close-up photos accompany testimonies by former patients of the victim, but are represented as also 'friends' of us readers of the *Sydney Morning Herald*, and therefore as

HIS PATIENTS

Figure 23.4   The murder of Dr Chang
Source: Sydney Morning Herald, 5 July 1991

people whose relation with the victim we should identify with. The personal and the impersonal, the emotive and the detached, are combined.

[. . .]

Involvement and the horizontal angle

When we prolong the converging parallels formed by the walls of the houses in Figure 23.5 they come together in two vanishing points. Both points are located outside the vertical boundaries of the image, as shown in Figure 23.6. These vanishing points allow us to reconstruct what we can see even without the aid of geometrical projection: the scene has been photographed from an oblique angle. The photographer has not situated her/himself in front of the Aborigines, but has photographed them from the side.

Figure 23.7 shows how the position from which the photo was taken can be reconstructed by dropping lines from the vanishing points in such a way that they meet to form a 90° angle on the line drawn through the closest corner of the cottages. Figure 23.8 shows the scene from above. The line

Figure 23.5   Aborigines
Source: Oakley 1985

(ab) represents the frontal plane of the subject of the photograph: the line formed by the front of the cottages, which, as it happens, is also the line along which the Aborigines are lined up. The line (cd) represents the frontal plane of the photographer (and hence of the viewer). Had these two lines been parallel to one another, the horizontal angle would have been frontal, in other words, the photographer would have been positioned in front of the Aborigines and their cottages, facing them. Instead, the two lines diverge: the angle is oblique. The photographer has not aligned her/himself with the subject, not faced the Aborigines, but viewed them 'from the sidelines'.

Horizontal angle, then, is a function of the relation between the frontal plane of the image-producer and the frontal plane of the represented participants. The two can either be parallel, aligned with one another, or form an angle, diverge from one another. The image can have either a frontal or an oblique point of view. It should be noted that this is not strictly an either/or distinction. There are degrees of obliqueness, and we will, in fact, speak of a frontal angle so long as the vanishing point(s) still fall(s) within the vertical boundaries of the image (they may fall outside the horizontal boundaries).

Figure 23.8 has a frontal angle. As shown in Figure 23.9, there is only one major vanishing point, and it lies inside the vertical boundaries of the

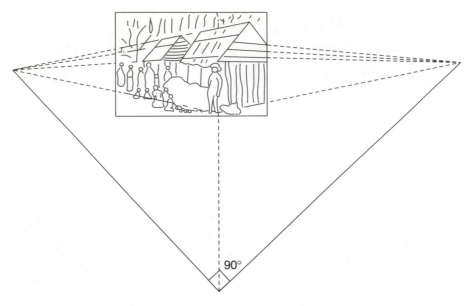

Figure 23.6   Schematic drawing: vanishing points of 'Aborigines' (Figure 23.5)

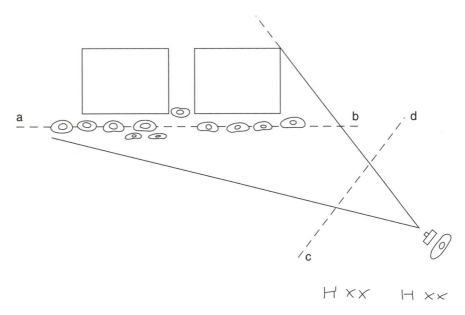

Figure 23.7   Schematic drawing: top view of 'Aborigines' (Figure 23.5)

Figure 23.8   Aboriginal children at school
Source: Oakley 1985

Figure 23.9   Schematic drawing: vanishing point of 'Aboriginal children at school' (Figure 23.8)

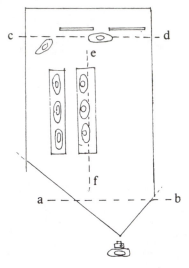

Figure 23.10   Schematic drawing: top view of 'Aboriginal children at school'
(Figure 23.8)

image. Figure 23.10 shows how the frontal plane of the photographer (line
ab) and the frontal plane of the represented participants (line cd) run parallel
– that is, *if one only considers one set of represented participants*, the teachers, the
blackboard and the reading chart. The frontal plane of the Aboriginal children
(line ef) makes an angle of 90° with the frontal plane of the teachers and
with the frontal plane of the photographer. The Aboriginal children have
been photographed from a very oblique angle!

The difference between the oblique and the frontal angle is the difference
between detachment and involvement. The horizontal angle encodes whether
or not the image-producer (and hence, willy-nilly, the viewer) is 'involved'
with the represented participants or not. The frontal angle says, as it were:
'what you see here is part of our world, something we are involved with.'
The oblique angle says: 'what you see here is *not* part of our world, it is
their world, something *we* are not involved with.' The producers of these
two photographs have, perhaps unconsciously, aligned themselves with the
white teachers and their teaching tools, but *not* with the Aborigines. The
teachers are shown as 'part of our world', the Aborigines as 'other'. And as
viewers we have no choice but to see these represented participants as they
have been depicted. We are addressed as viewers for whom 'involvement'
takes these particular values. In reality, they might not – we might be
Aboriginal viewers, for example. It is one thing for the viewer to be limited

by what the photograph shows (and to understand what this means, for example exclusion, in the case of an Aboriginal viewer); it is another thing to actually identify with the viewpoint encoded in the photo. We can accept or reject, but either way we first need to understand what is meant.

[. . .]

In the depiction of humans (and animals) 'involvement' and 'detachment' can interact with 'demand' and 'offer' in complex ways. The body of a represented participant may be angled away from the plane of the viewer, while his or her head and/or gaze may be turned towards it (see e.g., Figure 23.12 below) – or vice versa. The result is a double message: 'although I am not a part of your world, I nevertheless make contact with you, from my own, different world'; or 'although this person is part of our world, someone like you and me, we nevertheless offer his or her image to you as an object for dispassionate reflection.' The latter is the case, for example, in an illustration from a Dutch junior highschool geography textbook (Bols *et al.* 1986: 21). In a section entitled 'De Derde Wereld in onze straat' ('The Third World in our street'), two pictures are shown side by side. On the left we see three older women, their headscarves an emblem of their status as immigrants. They are photographed from an oblique angle, hence as 'not part of our world' and in long shot, hence as 'others', 'strangers'. On the right we see, left in the foreground, a blonde girl, clearly meant to be taken as Dutch, with a black friend, who has his arm around her. The angle is a good deal more frontal than that of the shot of the three women, and the shot is a close-up: she is shown as like 'us', Dutch highschool students, and from 'close personal' distance. But she does not make contact with the viewers. She does not invite the viewers to identify with her, and with her relationship to a black man. Instead, the viewer is invited to contemplate her relationship detachedly, to ponder the fact that some people like 'us' have relationships with black people, but not, it is implicitly suggested, 'we' viewers ourselves. She is a phenomenon to be observed, not a person addressing the viewer.

Equally complex and ambivalent is the back view. One of the authors, at age 21, photographed his parents in a snow-covered park, just outside Brussels (Figure 23.11), and, perhaps more importantly, it was this picture he chose to pin on the pinboard of his student room in Amsterdam, rather than one of the other, more frontal pictures he had taken on the same day. At the time, his feelings for his parents were complex. Deep attachment was mixed with only half-understood desire to distance himself from the world in which he was brought up. Perhaps the picture crystallized these confused emotions for him. On the one hand, it showed his parents turning their back on him,

Figure 23.11   Photograph of author's parents, 1968

walking away from him (a reversal, of course, of the actual situation); on the other hand, it showed this gesture of 'turning one's back', in a sense, 'frontally', in a maximally 'confronting' way. But to expose one's back to someone is also to make oneself vulnerable, and this implies a measure of trust, despite the abandonment which the gesture also signifies. Perhaps the picture reminded him of a passage from a Dutch novel he liked at the time:

> Through the window he sees them walk away. 'How much I love that man', he thinks, and how impossible he has made it for me to express that. . . . His mother has linked arms with him. With hesitant steps she walks beside him on the frozen pavement. He keeps looking at them until they turn the corner, near the tall feathered poplars.
>
> (Wolkers 1965: 61)

How is 'involvement' realized in language? Perhaps the system of possessive pronouns comes closest to realizing the kinds of meanings we have discussed here. But the two systems, the visual system of horizontal angle and the linguistic system of possessive pronouns, differ in many ways. Involvement, as we have seen, is always plural, a matter of 'mine' and 'his/her/its'; a matter of distinguishing between what belongs to 'us' and what to 'them'. And while in language one cannot easily have *degrees* of 'ourness' and 'theirness', in images such gradation is an intrinsic part of the system of involvement. Finally, there is no 'yours' in the system of horizontal angle. The visual 'you-relation' is, as we have seen, realized by the system of 'offer' and 'demand'. Perspective puts a barrier between the viewer and the represented participants, even in the case of a frontal angle: the viewer looks *at* the represented participants and has an attitude towards them, but does not imaginarily engage with them.

Power and vertical angle

Textbooks of film appreciation never fail to mention camera height as an important means of expression in cinematography. A high angle, it is said, makes the subject look small and insignificant, a low angle makes it look imposing and awesome: 'Low angles generally give an impression of superiority, exaltation and triumph . . . high angles tend to diminish the individual, to flatten him morally by reducing him to ground level, to render him as caught in an insurmountable determinism' (Martin 1968: 37–8). But this leaves the viewer out of the picture. We would rather say it in a somewhat different way: if a represented participant is seen from a high angle, then the relation between the interactive participants (the producer of the image, and hence also the viewer) and the represented participants is depicted as one in which the interactive participant has power over the represented participant – the represented participant is seen from the point of view of power. If the represented participant is seen from a low angle, then the relation between the interactive and represented participants is depicted as one in which the represented participant has power over the interactive participant. If, finally, the picture is at eye level, then the point of view is one of equality and there is no power difference involved.

This is, again, a matter of degree. A represented participant can tower high above us or look down on us ever so slightly. In many of the illustrations in school textbooks we look down rather steeply on people – workers in the hall; children in a school yard. In such books the social world lies at the feet of the viewer, so to speak: knowledge is power. The models in magazine advertisements and features, and newsworthy people and celebrities in magazine articles, on the other hand, generally look down on the viewer: these models are depicted as exercising symbolic power over us. It is different, again, with pictures of the products advertised in the advertisements: these are usually photographed from a high angle, depicted as within reach, and at the command of the viewer.

How is power realized in language? Here we need, again, to remember the difference between face-to-face communication and mediated communication. In the classroom, for example, power will manifest itself first of all in the relation between teacher and pupil. This, as Cate Poynton has shown (1985), is in the main realized through the *difference* between the linguistic forms that may be used by the teachers and the linguistic forms that may be used by the pupils; in other words, through a lack of reciprocity between the choices available to each party in the interaction. The teacher may use first names in addressing the pupils; the pupils may not use first names in addressing teachers. The teacher may use imperatives to 'demand goods-and-services'; the pupils would have to use polite forms, for instance, questions. This lack of reciprocity has its effect on every level of language: phonology, grammar, vocabulary, discourse, and on ideational, interpersonal, as well as textual meanings. If there is, in face-to-face communication, any question of power relation between represented participants and the pupils, then this results from the power relation between the teacher and the pupils.

[. . .]

Two portraits and two children's drawings

Rembrandt's famous *Self-portrait with Saskia* dates from 1634 (Figure 23.12). John Berger (1972: 111) calls it 'an advertisement of the sitter's good fortune, prestige and wealth', and he adds, 'like all such advertisements it is heartless'. Yet, from the point of view of the interactive meanings we have discussed in this chapter, the painting is perhaps a little more complex than Berger's remarks suggest. On the one hand, it is a 'demand' picture – Rembrandt and Saskia smile at the viewer, Rembrandt perhaps a little more effusively and invitingly than Saskia: he even raises his glass in a gesture directed at the viewer. On the other hand, he has shown himself and Saskia from behind, and from what Hall would call 'close social' distance, with Saskia a little further away from the viewer than Rembrandt – her head is considerably smaller than Rembrandt's even though she is sitting on his lap and should therefore, strictly speaking, be closer to the viewer than Rembrandt (the angle at which her head is turned to acknowledge the viewer also seems unnatural). Is Rembrandt distancing himself (and Saskia even more) from the viewer, excluding the viewer from involvement and intimacy with his new-found (and Saskia's already established) social status, thus contradicting the invitation? Perhaps, but the portrait is also a self-portrait. Rembrandt, the miller's son, now

Figure 23.12   Self-portrait with Saskia (Rembrandt, 1634)
Source: Pinakotek, Dresden

married into a wealthy and respectable family and living in grand style, also distances *himself* from his new self (and to some extent from Saskia), as if he cannot feel fully involved and intimate with his new environment. As a self-portrait the picture may be self-congratulatory and smug, 'heartless', but it also betrays a degree of alienation, positioning the represented Rembrandt in a complex and contradictory social class position, between the world of his

Figure 23.13   Self-portrait (Rembrandt, 1661)
Source: Kunsthistorisches Museum, Vienna

origins, which is also the point of view of the picture, and the world of Saskia
into which he has moved. This, we think, makes it a little less smug, and a
little more touching than Berger gave it credit for.

Figure 23.13 shows a later self-portrait, painted in 1661. By this time,
Saskia has died and Rembrandt has gone bankrupt. He now lives with his

former housekeeper, Hendrickje, in a more downmarket neighbourhood, and in much reduced circumstances. In this portrait he is able to come to face to face with himself, to confront himself (and the viewer) squarely and intimately with himself 'He is an old man now. All has gone, except a sense of the question of existence, of existence as a question' (Berger 1972: 112).

The picture on the cover of 'My Adventure', the story by an eight-year-old boy (Figure 23.14) constitutes a 'demand': the little boy is looking at us; and smiling. He seeks our recognition. He wants to be acknowledged. On the other hand, the angle is oblique, and high, and the boy is shown from a great distance. Not only does the writer of this story show himself in the role of being shipwrecked, he also shows himself as 'other' (the oblique angle), as someone over whom the viewer has power (the high angle) and as socially distant, a 'stranger' (the long shot). In other words, he uses the interactive resources of the subjective image (quite precociously, we feel) to

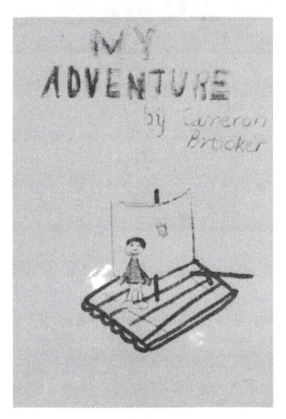

Figure 23.14   Cover illustration of 'My adventure'

show himself as small, insignificant and alienated, yet demanding recognition from the viewer. At the same time the act of drawing himself like this affords him, as the producer of the image, some power over that image of himself, an outlet for his feelings. In support of this interpretation it can be noted that the boy does not exactly play a heroic role in the story. After creating the raft, and just as the raft 'started to be good fun', everything goes wrong for him: he loses his money and never finds it again, the raft collapses and is lost irretrievably, and the hero has to walk all the way home, wet and cold. It is an unhappy ending for a hero unable to control the unpleasant events that happen to him.

Figure 23.15 is the front cover of a 'story' on sailing boats by a child from the same class as the author of 'My Adventure'. Its subject is similar:

Figure 23.15   Cover illustration of 'Sailing boats'

people on a boat. But the systems of 'image act', 'social distance' and 'attitude' take on very different values. The characters do not look at us: the picture is an 'offer'. The angle is frontal and eye level, and the two figures in the boat are neither particularly distant, nor particularly close. There is no setting, no texture, no colour, no light and shade. The sailing boat is drawn with geometrical accuracy. But for the two figures, simply drawn, and more or less identical, except for their size (a father and son?), this could be a technical drawing. As such it suits the objective, generic, title, 'Sailing Boats', just as the cover illustration of 'My Adventure' suits that story's subjective, specific title. In most of the illustrations inside the essay, no human figures are seen, as though the child already understands that the 'learning' of technical matters should be preceded by a 'human element' to attract non-initiates to the subject.

Clearly, children actively experiment both with the interactive resources of language and with the interactive resources of visual communication. They are active sign-makers. And the different ways in which these two children represent boats show two different subjectivities at work.

References

Allen, J. (1977) 'Self-reflexivity in documentary', *Cinetracts* 2: 37–44.

Belting, H. (1990) *The Image and its Public in the Middle Ages*, New Rochelle, NY: Aristide D. Caratzay.

Berger, J. (1972) *Ways of Seeing*, Harmondsworth: Penguin.

Bindon, H. and Williams, H. (1988) *Geography Research Project: A Senior Student's Handbook*, Melbourne: Edward Arnold.

Bols, P., Houppermans, M., Krijger, C., Lentjes, W., Savelkouls, T., Terlingen, M. and Teune, P. (1986) *Werk aan de Wereld*, Ben Bosch: Malmberg.

Booth, W. C. (1961) *The Rhetoric of Fiction*, Chicago: Chicago University Press.

Brunsden, C. and Morley, D. (1978) *Everyday Television: Nationwide*, London: BFI.

Chatman, S. (1978) *Story and Discourse*, Ithaca, NY: Cornell University Press.

Eco, U. (1976a) 'Articulations of the cinematic code', in B. Nichols (ed) *Movies and Methods*, vol. 1, Berkeley and Los Angeles: University of California Press.

Genette, G. (1972) *Narrative Discourse*, Oxford: Blackwell.

Hall, E. (1964) 'Silent assumptions in social communication', *Disorders of Communication* 42: 41–55.

—— (1966) *The Hidden Dimension*, New York: Doubleday.

Martin, M. (1968) *Le Langage cinématographique*, Paris: Éditions du Cerf.

Morris, D. (1977) *Manwatching*, London: Cape.

Oakley, M. *et al.* (1985) *Our Society and Others*, Sydney: McGraw-Hill.

Poynton, C. (1985) *Language and Gender: Making the Difference*, Geelong: Deakin University Press.

Rimmon-Kenan, S. (1983) *Narrative Fiction: Contemporary Poetics*, London: Methuen.

Ringbom, S. (1965) *Icon to Narrative: The Rise of the Dramatic Close-Up in Fifteenth-Century Painting*, Abo: Abo Akademie.

Sacks, H. (1992) *Lectures on Conversation*, Oxford: Blackwell.

Scannell, P. (1994) 'Communicative intentionality in broadcasting', unpublished paper.

Wolkers, J. (1965) *Een Roos van Vlees*, Amsterdam: Meulenhoff.

Wollen, P. (1982) 'Godard and counter-cinema: *Vent d'est*', in Nichols, B. (ed) *Movies and Methods*, vol. 2, Berkeley and Los Angeles: University of California Press.

Identity and subjectivity

Editors' Introduction to Part Five

W E BEGIN THIS PART by referring, again, to Goffman, who describes
the participants in a communicative event as engaging in a form of
social action. Extending his theatrical metaphor (see the Introduction to Part
Three), and at certain points actually referring to how social actors create
a specific 'dramatic effect' (Goffman 1959), he analyses how people manage
their *self-presentation*. Communication is, then, a ritualised process which
allows the participants to construct and project desirable versions of their
identities, in a succession of performances targeted at specific audiences.
Owing to the interdependence of social actors in conversation, the behaviour
of one participant defines and constructs social relations and identities for
the other members of the group. This is one clear way in which social and
interactional meaning can be shown to be *emergent*, which allows for the
identities of social actors to be multiple and dynamic – flexible and change-
able in the course of interaction.

The conceptualisation of interaction as theatre with (social) actors playing out different roles is especially resonant in the study of narratives. Indeed,
as Katharine Young in her chapter on personal narratives indicates, Goffman's
approach allows her to dissociate the speaker from the subject of the story:

> Erving Goffman argues that persons are in the way of presenting
> themselves, guiding controlled impressions, not necessarily to

deceive, but to sustain a reality, an event, a self. Structurally, the
self is divided into two aspects: (1) the performer who fabricates
these impressions, and (2) the character who is in the immersion
fabricated by the ongoing performance which entails them both.

(pp. 429–30)

More recent sociological work on selfhood echoes these sentiments that
we have to deal with a multiplicity of personal and social identities in
discourse. For example, Anthony Giddens, whose chapter opens this Part,
refers to 'the reflexive project of the self' (1990; 1991; see also discussion
in Coupland, Nussbaum and Grossman 1993). He conceptualises identity as
a process, not as a state, and as a series of choices one continually makes
about one's self and one's lifestyle rather than a set of personal attributes,
and as emerging from one's relationships with others. Although Giddens does
not offer an empirically orientated programme for the analysis of how these
processes are generated or mediated discursively, he puts discourse at the
centre of his theory of selfhood by adopting a discursive metaphor of identities construed as 'biographical narratives':

The reflexive project of the self, which consists in the sustaining of
coherent, yet continuously revised, biographical narratives, takes
place in the context of multiple choice as filtered through abstract
systems. In modern social life, the notion of lifestyle takes on a
particular significance. The more tradition loses its hold, and the
more daily life is reconstituted in terms of the dialectical interplay
of the local and the global, the more individuals are forced to
negotiate lifestyle choices among a diversity of options.

(Giddens 1991: 5)

However, as Giddens points out in the chapter we have reproduced here
(Chapter 24), the new conditions of life which have contributed to this
'dynamisation' of selfhood have generated restlessness and anxiety.
Traditional systems of belief based on faith have given way to secularisation
and the emergence of a multitude of competing ideologies (of which religious
faith is only one). The versions of self which people can choose for themselves come from an increasing pool of options which are often unfamiliar
to them, bringing new risks and conflicting interests. Consumerist discourse/
lifestyle propagated by advertising, for example, stands in conflict with the
discourse/lifestyle of prudence dominating the discussions of the welfare-

system reforms. Giddens refers to these problems as 'tribulations of the self', and discusses them in terms of four pairs of oppositions: unification versus fragmentation, powerlessness versus appropriation, authority versus uncertainty, personalised versus commodified experience.

These dilemmas are ongoing and can only be resolved temporarily by engaging in a particular type of ideology, relationship or activity, in which an individual may manifest his/her stance or allegiance towards a particular orientation. The sites for such position-taking are to be found in interaction between the self and the contexts in which he/she operates, whether we think of other human agents, mediated communication, or more abstract notions such as ideologies. In all these processes discourse can be seen as constitutive not only of identities but also of social relations and categories, and other aspects of people's social lives (cf. Shotter 1993; Coupland, Nussbaum and Grossman 1993).

The social constructionist approach to identity (e.g., Gergen 1985; Potter and Wetherell 1987; papers in Coupland and Nussbaum 1993; Potter 1996) is echoed more or less explicitly in all the chapters included in Part Five. Katharine Young's chapter ('Narrative embodiments') presents a link between identity viewed as the embodied self and a discursive enactment of this identity through narrative. Her case-study deals with a patient in a medical consultation. This is a situation in which the self is typically displaced from the body (p. 429); an anxiety-provoking experience which may be likened to Giddens's notion of fragmentation resulting from having to cope with a relatively unfamiliar realm of medicine. The patient, a seventy-year-old man, professor of Jewish history and literature, is first asked by the doctor about different parts of his body. Then, he is asked to take off his clothes, and he undergoes a thorough medical examination. Both verbal interview and physical examination fragment the self of the patient even further by attending to only one part of his body at a time.

In the course of the interview and the examination, the patient tells several narratives which reconstruct his displaced self. He manages to establish a link between the realm of medicine and the *storyrealm* by recounting his experiences from the Second World War, as a prisoner of Auschwitz, refugee, patient of American army doctors, and so on. Although he is careful to maintain a thematic link with the frame of medical consultation, the *taleworld* which he creates lies outside of the medical frame and allows him to be seen as a legitimate actor and a fully-fledged individual. The narratives become enclaves in which the patient's self finds refuge while being fragmented and displaced by the discourse of medicine.

Deborah Cameron's chapter focuses on the discursive construction of heterosexual male identity in an informal conversation among five American college students. In a manner which is not dissimilar to Giddens's 'reflexive project of the self', Cameron views gender identity as social performances (cf. Austin, Chapter 2; Goffman, see above and the Introduction to Part Three). She repeats after Judith Butler that 'Gender is the repeated stylization of the body' (p. 444), which results in certain actions or effects conventionally read to enact masculinity or femininity. Thus, gender roles are not given, static attributes but recursive, dynamic patterns of *being* and *doing*.

One resource available to social actors in manifesting their gender is *gendered speech*. Cameron examines how the students enact their male, heterosexual identity by engaging in a disparaging exchange of opinions about other men as 'gays'. In this specific instance and frame of talk, references to 'gayness' are largely a ritualistic, boundary-marking activity, as the classification of people as 'gay' in their conversation has little to do with the known or suspected sexuality of the objects of their gossip. However, displaying hostility to gays is a way for these conversationalists to establish their preferred version of masculinity in this particular context of an all-male peer group. In other contexts, for example at a party with their girlfriends present, the heterosexual masculine identity of the same men could be enacted in totally different, possibly non-verbal means.

Another interesting aspect of Cameron's chapter is the role of stereotypes and expectations in attributing meaning to the communicative strategies when used by males and females. The five men engage in an act of asserting their solidarity and in-groupness through a stereotypically female verbal activity: gossip. However, their competent gossip is precisely used to allow them to dissociate themselves from the stereotypically non-masculine concerns (e.g. alleged preoccupation of females and gays with their bodies). Besides, the men display certain conversational features (joint discourse production through interruptions and overlapping talk), which in female talk is associated with conversational cooperativity. In male talk, it seems more like competitiveness. Cameron demonstrates how both these interpretations (cooperativity and competitiveness) may suit her data and warns against 'gender-stereotyping that causes us to miss or minimize the status-seeking element in women friends' talk, and the connection-making dimension in men's' (pp. 453–54).

Deborah Tannen's chapter, 'New York Jewish conversational style' is firmly rooted in the tradition of interactional sociolinguistics (see the general Introduction). The data come from a Thanksgiving dinner conversation in 1978, which brought together three New Yorkers of Jewish background and three non-New Yorkers from different parts of the English-speaking world. Tannen focuses on the notion of conversational style characteristic of the former group. New York Jewish conversational style is described as displaying the following features: fast rate of speech; fast rate of turn-taking; persistence – if a turn is not acknowledged, try, try again; marked shifts in pitch; marked shifts in amplitude; preference for story-telling; preference for personal stories; tolerance of, preference for simultaneous speech; abrupt topic shifting (this list is in fact based on Tannen 1985: 102). In Chapter 27, Tannen demonstrates how the sharing of these features creates *involvement* between members of the same ethnic group, while non-New Yorkers react to some of these features with unease or downright opposition by intensifying opposing behaviour.

Again, it is possible to notice how the participants are (or are not) doing being 'New York Jews', how they rejoice in the shared construction of discourse and, consequently, their shared ethnic identity. On the other hand, the anxiety with which the non-members of the in-group react to this discourse reminds us of Giddens's observation that one of the sources of the 'tribulation of the self' comes from the tension brought about by globalisation. Note that this conversation was recorded in the home of one of the 'New York Jews' in his home in . . . Oakland, California, and that the other participants came from other parts of the USA and from the UK. This situation seems to provide a good illustration of Shotter's (1993: 5–6) observation that

> as Gergen (1991) has described in detail, due to the way that our technologies of communication and travel have advanced, there is a quantum leap in our exposure to each other; we have become 'saturated' with the voices of others. We have become embroiled in (what Giddens 1991 calls) the dialectic of local and the global: Events distant from us in both space *and time*, transmitted to us through communication media, play an intimate part in who we feel we want or ought to be. No wonder that *identity* has become the watchword of the times; for it provides the much needed vocabulary in terms of which we now define our loyalties and our commitments.

Last but not least, Charles Goodwin's chapter brings a multi-modal perspective into his micro-analysis of video-taped interaction between two archaeology students engaged in the task of classifying the colour of dirt at an archaeological site. The methodology of this study successfully combines elements from different strands of discourse analysis (conversation analysis, ethnography) and cognitive science. Goodwin demonstrates how the superficially simple act of deciding on the colour of a sample of soil depends on a complex network of semiotic systems used in a negotiated act of meaning making. The interaction is an interplay between spoken language, movements and orientations of the participants' bodies, their use of tools (e.g., a trowel) and the mediating role of the Munsell colour chart, which in itself is a multimodal 'cognitive artefact'. Despite these complexities, the task of colour classification within a situated activity system that links a range of apparently disparate phenomena is shown to result in a coherent course of action.

The students operate under a number of social, cultural and historical constraints which are shown to be as significant in their classificatory work as the perceptual qualities of their brains in identifying colours and their referential (linguistic) abilities to label them. Additionally, by attending carefully to their task and engaging in its linguistic and bodily realisation, they reassert their identity as members of a professional group. This fascinating study also makes a contribution to our understanding of the ethnography of science. As the archaeologists' task is to 'translate' a fragment of a continuous field (of colour) to a discrete category, we see how the interaction between them becomes a site of 'science making':

> The encounter between coding scheme and the world that occurs as the archaeologist in the field holds a sample of dirt under the Munsell page, is one example of a key locus for scientific practice. This is the place where the multifaceted complexity of 'nature' is transformed into the phenomenal categories that make up the work environment of a scientific discipline. It is precisely here that nature is transformed into culture.
>
> (p. 481)

As we have argued in this Introduction, the emergence and re-emergence of the self is a process which is a function of a number of situational, social, cultural and historical factors. The role of discourse (in its various multimodal guises) and its meaning-making capacity is paramount. Thus, the ways we speak (as males, females, doctors, patients, Jews, non-Jews, archaeologists, and so on), and the way we speak to and about others (the 'narrated self' in Young's chapter, or the 'gays' in Cameron's data) turns individuals into *subjective* selves. Even though we mistakenly treat our descriptive categories as 'natural' (cf. our general Introduction), and our descriptions of self and other may be meant 'objectively', various private and institutional discourses are constitutive of us (and others) as *social subjects*; in other words – these discourses fabricate our subjectivities (Foucault 1972; see also Potter 1996; Mills 1997).

Cameron (1992: 161–2) gives one compelling example of how our gendered social subjectivities are fabricated discursively from the day we are born:

> Recently a woman who had just had a baby told me that in the hospital nursery, each newborn's crib bore a label announcing its sex. The label said either 'I'm a boy' or 'It's a girl'. Obviously none of the infants was yet capable of speech. But on the day they were born, the culture hailed them differently: boys were hailed as active 'speaking subjects', unproblematically 'I'; girls were not. This is the order which, as they grow older, these children will be forced to enter.

Subjectivity is the site of our consciousness, but far from being a fully independent entity, it is bound up by the structures and discourses of institutional and interpersonal order, power and ideology.

References

Cameron, D. (1992) *Feminism & Linguistic Theory*, 2nd edn, London: Macmillan.

Coupland, N. and Nussbaum, J. F. (eds) (1993) *Discourse and Lifespan Identity*, Newbury Park, CA.: Sage.

Coupland, N., Nussbaum, J. F. and Grossman, A. (1993) 'Introduction: discourse, selfhood and the lifespan', in Coupland, N. and Nussbaum, J. F. (eds) *Discourse and Lifespan Identity*, Newbury Park, CA.: Sage, x–xxviii.

Foucault, M. (1972) *The Archaeology of Knowledge*, trans. Smith, S., London: Tavistock.

Gergen, K. J. (1985) 'Social constructionist inquiry: context and implications', in Gergen, K. J. and Davis, K. E. (eds) *The Social Construction of the Person*, New York: Springer-Verlag.

Giddens, A. (1990) *The Consequences of Modernity*, Cambridge: Polity Press (in assoc. with Blackwell).

—— (1991) *Modernity and Self-Identity: Self and Society in the Late Modern Age*, Cambridge: Polity Press (in assoc. with Blackwell).

Goffman, E. (1959) *The Presentation of Self in Everyday Life*, New York: Anchor Books.

Mills, S. (1997) *Discourse*, London: Routledge.

Potter, J. (1996). *Representing Reality: Discourse, Rhetoric and Social Construction*, London: Sage.

Potter, J. and Wetherell, M. (1987) *Discourse and Social Psychology: Beyond Attitudes and Behaviour*, London: Sage.

Shotter, J. (1993) 'Becoming someone', in Coupland, N. and Nussbaum, J. F. (eds) *Discourse and Lifespan Identity*, Newbury Park, CA: Sage. 5–27.

Shotter, J. and Gergen, K. J. (eds) (1989) *Texts of Identity*, London: Sage.

Tannen, D. (1985) 'Silence: anything but', in Tannen, D. and Saville-Troike, M. (eds) *Perspectives on Silence*, Norwood, NJ: Ablex, 93–111.

Anthony Giddens

MODERNITY AND SELF-IDENTITY: TRIBULATIONS OF THE SELF

[. . .]

'Living in the world': dilemmas of the self

In conditions of late modernity, we live 'in the world' in a different sense from previous eras of history. Everyone still continues to live a local life, and the constraints of the body ensure that all individuals, at every moment, are contextually situated in time and space. Yet the transformations of place, and the intrusion of distance into local activities, combined with the centrality of mediated experience, radically change what 'the world' actually is. This is so both on the level of the 'phenomenal world' of the individual and the general universe of social activity within which collective social life is enacted. Although everyone lives a local life, phenomenal worlds for the most part are truly global.

Characterising individuals' phenomenal worlds is difficult, certainly in the abstract. Every person reacts selectively to the diverse sources of direct and mediated experience which compose the *Umwelt*. One thing we can say with some certainty is that in very few instances does the phenomenal world any longer correspond to the habitual settings through which an individual physically moves. Localities are thoroughly penetrated by distanciated influences, whether this be regarded as a cause for concern or simply accepted

Source: Anthony Giddens, *Modernity and Self-identity: Self and Society in the Late Modern Age*, Cambridge: Polity Press in association with Blackwell, 1991.

as a routine part of social life. All individuals actively, although by no means always in a conscious way, selectively incorporate many elements of mediated experience into their day-to-day conduct. This is never a random or a passive process, contrary to what the image of the *collage* effect might suggest. A newspaper, for example, presents a collage of information, as does, on a wider scale, the whole bevy of newspapers which may be on sale in a particular area or country. Yet each reader imposes his own order on this diversity, by selecting which newspaper to read – if any – and by making an active selection of its contents.

In some part the appropriation of mediated information follows pre-established habits and obeys the principle of the avoidance of cognitive dissonance. That is to say, the plethora of available information is reduced via routinised attitudes which exclude, or reinterpret, potentially disturbing knowledge. From a negative point of view, such closure might be regarded as prejudice, the refusal seriously to entertain views and ideas divergent from those an individual already holds; yet, from another angle, avoidance of dissonance forms part of the protective cocoon which helps maintain ontological security. For even the most prejudiced or narrow-minded person, the regularised contact with mediated information inherent in day-to-day life today is a positive appropriation: a mode of interpreting information within the routines of daily life. Obviously there are wide variations in terms of how open a given individual is to new forms of knowledge, and how far that person is able to tolerate certain levels of dissonance. But all phenomenal worlds are active accomplishments, and all follow the same basic psychodynamics, from the most local of ways of life to the most cosmopolitan.

'Living in the world', where the world is that of late modernity, involves various distinctive tensions and difficulties on the level of the self. We can analyse these most easily by understanding them as dilemmas which, on one level or another, have to be resolved in order to preserve a coherent narrative of self-identity.

Unification versus fragmentation

The first dilemma is that of *unification* versus *fragmentation*. Modernity fragments; it also unites. On the level of the individual right up to that of planetary systems as a whole, tendencies towards dispersal vie with those promoting integration. So far as the self is concerned, the problem of unification concerns protecting and reconstructing the narrative of self-identity in the face of the massive intensional and extensional changes which modernity sets into being. In most pre-modern contexts, the fragmentation of experience was not a prime source of anxiety. Trust relations were localised and focused through personal ties, even if intimacy in the modern sense was generally lacking. In a post-traditional order, however, an indefinite range of possibilities present themselves, not just in respect of options for behaviour, but in respect also of the 'openness of the world' to the individual. 'The world', as indicated above, is not a seamless order of time and space stretching away from the individual; it intrudes into presence via an array of varying channels and sources.

Yet it is wrong to see the world 'out there' as intrinsically alienating and oppressive to the degree to which social systems are either large in scale or spatially distant from the individual. Such phenomena may often be drawn on to supply unifying influences; they are not just fragmenting in their impact on the self. Distant events may become as familiar, or more so, than proximate influences, and integrated into the frameworks of personal experience. Situations 'at hand' may in fact be more opaque than large-scale happenings affecting many millions of people. Consider some examples. A person may be on the telephone to someone twelve thousand miles away and for the duration of the conversation be more closely bound up with the responses of that distant individual than with others sitting in the same room. The appearance, personality and policies of a world political leader may be better known to a given individual than those of his next-door neighbour. A person may be more familiar with the debate over global warming than with why the tap in the kitchen leaks. Nor are remote or large-scale phenomena necessarily factors only vaguely 'in the background' of an individual's psychological make-up and identity. A concern with global warming, for example, might form part of a distinctive lifestyle adopted by a person, even if she is not an ecological scientist. Thus she might keep in close contact with scientific debates and adjust various aspects of her lifestyle in relation to the practical measures they suggest.

Fragmentation clearly tends to be promoted by the influences emphasised by Berger and others: the diversifying of contexts of interaction. In many modern settings, individuals are caught up in a variety of differing encounters and milieux, each of which may call for different forms of 'appropriate' behaviour. Goffman [Chapter 18] is normally taken to be the theorist *par excellence* of this phenomenon. As the individual leaves one encounter and enters another, he sensitively adjusts the 'presentation of self' in relation to whatever is demanded of a particular situation. Such a view is often thought to imply that an individual has as many selves as there are divergent contexts of interaction, an idea which somewhat resembles poststructuralist interpretations of the self, albeit from a differing theoretical perspective. Yet again it would not be correct to see contextual diversity as simply and inevitably promoting the fragmentation of the self, let alone its disintegration into multiple 'selves'. It can just as well, at least in many circumstances, promote an integration of self. The situation is rather like the contrast between rural and urban life. A person may make use of diversity in order to create a distinctive self-identity which positively incorporates elements from different settings into an integrated narrative. Thus a cosmopolitan person is one precisely who draws strength from being at home in a variety of contexts.

The dilemma of unification versus fragmentation, like the others to be mentioned below, has its pathologies. On the one hand we find the type of person who constructs his identity around a set of fixed commitments, which act as a filter through which numerous different social environments are reacted to or interpreted. Such a person is a rigid traditionalist, in a compulsive sense, and refuses any relativism of context. On the other hand, in the case of a self which evaporates into the variegated contexts of action, we find the adaptive response which Erich Fromm has characterised as 'authoritarian conformity'. Fromm (1960: 160) expresses this in the following way:

> The individual ceases to be himself; he adopts entirely the kind of personality offered to him by cultural patterns; and he therefore becomes exactly as all others are and as they expect him to be . . . this mechanism can be compared with the protective colouring some animals assume. They look so similar to their surroundings that they are hardly distinguishable from them.

In such circumstances, we might argue, the false self overrides and blankets out the original acts of thinking, feeling and willing which represent the true motivations of the individual. What remains of the true self is experienced as empty and inauthentic; yet this vacuum cannot be filled by the 'pseudo-selves' brought into play by the individual in different contexts, because these are as much stimulated by the responses of others as drawn from the person's inner convictions. Ontological security in this situation is as weakly founded as in the case of the rigid traditionalist. The individual only feels psychologically secure in his self-identity in so far as others recognise his behaviour as appropriate or reasonable.

Powerlessness versus appropriation

A second dilemma is that of *powerlessness* versus *appropriation*. If there is one theme which unites nearly all authors who have written on the self in modern society, it is the assertion that the individual experiences feelings of power-lessness in relation to a diverse and large-scale social universe. In contrast to the traditional world, it is supposed, where the individual was substantially in control of many of the influences shaping his life, in modern societies that control has passed to external agencies. As specified by Marx, the concept of alienation has served as the centre-point for analyses of this issue. As the forces of production develop, particularly under the aegis of capitalistic production, the individual cedes control of his life circumstances to the domi-nating influences of machines and markets. What is originally human becomes alien; human powers are experienced as forces emanating from an objecti-fied social environment. Not only have the followers of Marx expressed such a view; it is also found, in somewhat different guise, in the works of the theorists of 'mass society'. The more extensive modern social systems become, according to this position, the more each particular individual feels shorn of all autonomy. Each, as it were, is merely an atom in a vast agglom-eration of other individuals.

The ideas I seek to develop in this chapter are distinctively different from such a standpoint. In many pre-modern contexts, individuals (and humanity as a whole) were more powerless than they are in modern settings. People typically lived in smaller groups and communities; but smallness is not the same as power. In many small-group settings individuals were relatively powerless to alter or escape from their surrounding social circumstances. The hold of tradition, for example, was often more or less unchallengeable. There are many other illustrations. Pre-modern kinship systems, for example, were often quite rigid, and offered the individual little scope for independent action. We would be hard pressed to substantiate an overall generalisation that, with the coming of modern institutions, most individuals either are (or feel) more powerless than in preceding times.

Modernity expropriates – that is undeniable. Time-space distanciation and the deskilling effects of abstract systems are the two most important influences. Even if distance and powerlessness do not inevitably go together, the emergence of globalised connections, together with high consequence risks, represent parameters of social life over which the situated individual has relatively little control. Similarly, expropriation processes are part and parcel of the maturation of modern institutions and reach not only spheres of day-to-day life but the heart of the self.

If we understand such processes in dialectical fashion, however, and if we see that globalisation produces not just extensional but intensional change, a complex picture emerges. We cannot say that all forms of expropriation necessarily provide the possibility of reappropriation, certainly on the level of individual conduct. Many of the processes transformed by disembedding, or reorganised in the light of the intrusion of abstract systems, move beyond the purview of the situated actor. On the other hand, others make possible forms of mastery over life circumstances unavailable in pre-modern situations.

Powerlessness and reappropriation intertwine variously in different contexts and at varying times: given the dynamism of modernity, there is little stability in the relations between them. An individual who vests trust in others, or in a given abstract system, normally thereby recognises that she lacks the power to influence them significantly. Yet the vesting of trust can also generate new capacities. Consider the example of money. In order to utilise money, an individual must participate in systems of economic exchange, banking and investment and so forth, over which she has little direct control. On the other hand, this process allows the individual – given sufficient resources – a diversity of opportunities which would otherwise be absent.

The experience of powerlessness, considered as a psychic phenomenon, naturally always relates to aims, projects or aspirations held by the individual, as well as to the composition of the phenomenal world. Powerlessness experienced in a personal relationship may be psychologically more damaging and consequential than powerlessness felt in relation to more encompassing social systems. Of course, these may feed into one another in various ways. Diffuse anxieties about high-consequence risks, for instance, might contribute in a general fashion to feelings of powerlessness experienced by an individual in more local contexts. Conversely, feelings of personal impotence may become diffused 'upwards' towards more global concerns. It seems reasonable to posit that connections of this kind are likely to underlie a 'survival' mentality. A 'survivor' is someone who feels deprived of adequate social mastery in a threatening series of personal and social environments. Yet a survivalist outlook carries connotations of appropriation as well as of powerlessness. Someone who concentrates on surviving in personal relations, as in other spheres of life, cannot be said to have abandoned all autonomy over his or her life's circumstances. Even if only in a somewhat negative sense, the individual clearly seeks active mastery: to survive is to be able in a determined way to ride out the trials life presents and overcome them.

Once again, the dilemma of powerlessness versus appropriation has its pathologies. Where an individual feels overwhelmed by a sense of power-lessness in the major domains of his phenomenal world, we may speak of a process of *engulfment*. The individual feels dominated by encroaching forces from the outside, which he is unable to resist or transcend. He feels either haunted by implacable forces robbing him of all autonomy of action, or caught up in a maelstrom of events in which he swirls around in a helpless fashion. At the other pole of the powerlessness/appropriation divide is *omnipotence*.

Like all personality pathologies, it is a fantasy state. The individual's sense of ontological security is achieved through a fantasy of dominance: the phenomenal world feels as if it is orchestrated by that person as a puppeteer. Since omnipotence is a defence it is brittle, and often links psychologically to the other pole of the powerlessness/appropriation composition: in other words, under pressure it can dissolve into its contrary, engulfment.

Authority versus uncertainty

A *third* dilemma is that of *authority* versus *uncertainty*. In conditions of high modernity, in many areas of social life – including the domain of the self – there are no determinant authorities. There exist plenty of claimants to authority – far more than was true of pre-modern cultures. Tradition was itself a prime source of authority, not located within any particular institution, but pervading many aspects of social life. Diffuse though it may have been, tradition was in an important sense a single authority. Although in the larger pre-modern cultures there may quite often have been clashes between rival traditions, for the most part traditional outlooks and ways of doing things precluded other alternatives. Even where there were vying traditions, involvement in a traditional framework was normally quite exclusive: the others were thereby rejected.

When we speak of specific institutions of authority, religion obviously has a leading place. In virtually all smaller pre-modern cultures there was only one main religious order – although such cultures have had their share of sceptics, and magicians and sorcerers were available to those diverging from religious orthodoxy. Yet these alternatives were scarcely substitutes for the overarching authoritative reach of the dominant religious system. In larger traditional societies, where religious orders sometimes were more diversified, there was little pluralism in the modern sense: orthodoxy confronted various heresies. The local community and the kinship system were two further sources of stabilising authority, directly relevant to the sustaining of trust relations in traditional contexts. Both were the source of 'binding doctrines' as well as of forms of behaviour endowed with strong normative compulsion.

Submission to traditional authorities, no matter how deep, did not move uncertainty from day-to-day life in traditional cultures. The strength of pre-modern forms of authority could almost be understood as a response to the very unpredictability of daily life and to the number of influences felt to be outside human control. Religious authorities in particular quite often cultivated the feeling that individuals were surrounded by threats and dangers –

since only the religious official was in a position to be able either to under-stand or to seek successfully to control these. Religious authority created mysteries while simultaneously claiming to have privileged access to them (Wagar 1982).

In modern times some forms of traditional authority continue to exist, including, of course, religion. Indeed, for reasons that are to do precisely with the connections between modernity and doubt, religion not only refuses to disappear but undergoes a resurgence. Yet there is now a basic contrast with the past. Forms of traditional authority become only 'authorities' among others, part of an indefinite pluralism of expertise. The expert, or the specialist, is quite different from the 'authority', where this term is under-stood in the traditional sense. Except where authority is sanctioned by the use of force (the 'authorities' of the state and legal authority), it becomes essentially equivalent to specialist advice. There are no authorities which span the diverse fields within which expertise is claimed – another way of repeating the point that everyone in modern systems is a lay person in virtually all aspects of social activity. Authority in this situation is no longer an alterna-tive to doubt. On the contrary, modes of expertise are fuelled by the very principle of doubt; in assessing the claims of rival authorities, the lay indi-vidual tends to utilise that principle in the sceptical outlook which pluralistic circumstances almost inevitably presuppose.

Of course, day-to-day life is not ordinarily experienced as perennially 'in doubt'. The reorganisation of daily life through abstract systems creates many routine forms of activity having a higher level of predictability than most contexts in pre-modern cultures. Through the protective cocoon, most people are buffered most of the time from the experience of radical doubt as a serious challenge either to the routines of daily activity or to more far-reaching ambitions. The dilemma of authority versus doubt is ordinarily resolved through a mixture of routine and commitment to a certain form of lifestyle, plus the vesting of trust in a given series of abstract systems. Yet this 'compromise package', under pressure, can begin to disintegrate.

Some individuals find it psychologically difficult or impossible to accept the existence of diverse, mutually conflicting authorities. They find that the freedom to choose is a burden and they seek solace in more overarching systems of authority. A predilection for *dogmatic authoritarianism* is the patho-logical tendency at this pole. A person in this situation is not necessarily a traditionalist, but essentially gives up faculties of critical judgement in exchange for the convictions supplied by an authority whose rules and provi-sions cover most aspects of his life. We should distinguish this attitude from faith, even faith in fundamentalist religious codes. For faith almost by defi-nition rests on trust. Taking refuge in a dominant authority, however, is essentially an act of submission. The individual, as it were, no longer needs to engage in the problematic gamble which all trust relations presume. Instead, he or she identifies with a dominant authority on the basis of projection. The psychology of leadership plays an important role here. Submission to authority normally takes the form of a slavish adherence to an authority figure, taken to be all-knowing.

At the other pole, we find pathological states in which individuals are virtually immobilised through a tendency towards universal doubt. In its most marked versions, this outlook takes the form of paranoia or a paralysis of the will so complete that the individual effectively withdraws altogether from ordinary social intercourse.

Personalised versus commodified experience

A fourth dilemma is that between *personalised* versus *commodified* experience. Modernity opens up the project of the self, but under conditions strongly influenced by standardising effects of commodity capitalism. Here I do not seek to trace out in a detailed fashion the impact of capitalistic production on modern social life. Suffice to affirm that capitalism is one of the main institutional dimensions of modernity, and that the capitalist accumulation process represents one of the prime driving forces behind modern institutions as a whole. Capitalism commodifies in various senses. The creation of the abstract commodity, as Marx pointed out, is perhaps the most basic element in the expansion of capitalism as an overall production system. Exchange-value is only created when use-values become irrelevant to the mechanisms whereby the production, sale and distribution of goods and services are carried on. Exchange-value thus allows for the disembedding of economic relations across indeterminate spans of time-space.

Commodification further, crucially, affects labour power: in fact labour power as such only comes into existence when separated as a commodity from 'labour' as a whole. Finally, commodification directly affects consumption processes, particularly with the maturation of the capitalistic order. The establishing of standardised consumption patterns, promoted through advertising and other methods, becomes central to economic growth. In all of these senses, commodification influences the project of the self and the establishing of lifestyles.

We can detail the impact of commodification in the following ways. The capitalistic market, with its 'imperatives' of continuous expansion, attacks tradition. The spread of capitalism places large sectors (although by no means all) of social reproduction in the hands of markets for products and labour.

Markets operate without regard to pre-established forms of behaviour, which for the most part represent obstacles to the creation of unfettered exchange. In the period of high modernity, capitalistic enterprise increasingly seeks to shape consumption as well as monopolise the conditions of production. From the beginning, markets promote individualism in the sense that they stress individual rights and responsibilities, but at first this phenomenon mainly concerns the freedom of contract and mobility intrinsic to capitalistic employment. Later, however, individualism becomes extended to the sphere of consumption, the designation of individual wants becoming basic to the continuity of the system. Market-governed freedom of individual choice becomes an enveloping framework of individual self-expression.

The very corruption of the notion of 'lifestyle', reflexively drawn into the sphere of advertising, epitomises these processes. Advertisers orient themselves to sociological classifications of consumer categories and at the same time foster specific consumption 'packages'. To a greater or lesser degree, the project of the self becomes translated into one of the possession of desired goods and the pursuit of artificially framed styles of life. The consequences of this situation have often been noted. The consumption of ever-novel goods becomes in some part a substitute for the genuine development of self; appearance replaces essence as the visible signs of successful consumption come actually to outweigh the use-values of the goods and services in question themselves. Bauman (1989: 189) expresses this well:

> Individual needs of personal autonomy, self-definition, authentic life or personal perfection are all translated into the need to possess, and consume, market-offered goods. This translation, however, pertains to the appearance of use value of such goods, rather than to the use value itself; as such, it is intrinsically inadequate and ultimately self-defeating, leading to momentary assuagement of desires and lasting frustration of needs. . . . The gap between human needs and individual desires is produced by market domination; this gap is, at the same time, a condition of its reproduction. The market feeds on the unhappiness it generates: the fears, anxieties and the sufferings of personal inadequacy it induces release the consumer behaviour indispensable to its continuation.

Commodification is in some ways even more insidious than this characterisation suggests. For the project of the self as such may become heavily commodified. Not just lifestyles, but self-actualisation is packaged and distributed according to market criteria. Self-help books, like *Self Therapy*, stand in a precarious position with regard to the commodified production of self-actualisation. In some ways such works break away from standardised, packaged consumption. Yet in so far as they become marketed as prepackaged theorems about how to 'get on' in life, they become caught up in the very processes they nominally oppose.

The commodifying of consumption, it should be made clear, like other phenomena discussed earlier, is not just a matter of the reordering of existing behaviour patterns or spheres of life. Rather, consumption under the domination of mass markets is essentially a novel phenomenon, which participates directly in processes of the continuous reshaping of the conditions of day-to-day life. Mediated experience is centrally involved here. The mass media routinely present modes of life to which, it is implied, everyone should aspire; the lifestyles of the affluent are, in one form or another, made open to view and portrayed as worthy of emulation. More important, however, and more subtle, is the impact of the narratives the media convey. Here there is not necessarily the suggestion of a lifestyle to be aspired to; instead, stories are developed in such a way as to create narrative coherence with which the reader or viewer can identify.

No doubt soap operas, and other forms of media entertainment too, are escapes – substitutes for real satisfactions unobtainable in normal social conditions. Yet perhaps more important is the very narrative form they offer, suggesting models for the construction of narratives of the self. Soap operas mix predictability and contingency by means of formulae which, because they are well known to the audience, are slightly disturbing but at the same time reassuring. They offer mixtures of contingency, reflexivity and fate. The form is what matters rather than the content; in these stories one gains a sense of reflexive control over life circumstances, a feeling of a coherent narrative which is a reassuring balance to difficulties in sustaining the narrative of the self in actual social situations.

Yet commodification does not carry the day unopposed on either an individual or collective level. Even the most oppressed of individuals – perhaps in some ways particularly the most oppressed – react creatively and interpretatively to processes of commodification which impinge on their lives. This is true both within the realm of mediated experience and of direct consumption. Response to mediated experience cannot be assessed purely in terms of the content of what is disseminated: individuals actively discriminate among types of available information as well as interpreting it in their own terms. Even young children evaluate television programmes in terms of their degree of realism, recognising that some are wholly fictional, and treat programmes as objects of scepticism, derision or humour (see Hodge and Tripp 1989; Fiske 1989). The fact that commodification is not all-triumphant at a collective level is also important for realms of individual experience. Space, for example, becomes commodified as a fundamental part of disembedding processes. However, space does not thereby become fully commercialised or subject to the standardising impact of commodity production. Many aspects of the built environment, and other spatial forms too, reassert themselves (through the active engagements of agents) in decommodified modes. [. . .]

It is against this complicated backdrop that we should understand processes of individuation. The reflexive project of the self is in some part necessarily a struggle against commodified influences, although not all aspects of commodification are inimical to it. A market system, almost by definition, generates a variety of available choices in the consumption of goods and services. Plurality of choice is in some substantial part the very outcome of commodified processes. Nor is commodification merely the same as standardisation. Where mass markets are at issue, it is clearly in the interests of producers to ensure the large-scale consumption of relatively standardised products. Yet standardisation can often be turned into a mode of creating individual qualities – as in the previously quoted example of clothing. Mass-produced clothing still allows individuals to decide selectively on styles of dress, however much the standardising influence of fashion and other forces affect those individual decisions.

A prime type of behaviour pathology associated with commodifying influences is narcissism – in this respect Lasch's thesis is valid, if over-generalised.

Unification versus fragmentation: the reflexive project of the self incorporates numerous contextual happenings and forms of mediated experience, through which a course must be charted.

Powerlessness versus appropriation: the lifestyle options made available by modernity offer many opportunities for appropriation, but also generate feelings of powerlessness.

Authority versus uncertainty: in circumstances in which there are no final authorities, the reflexive project of the self must steer a way between commitment and uncertainty.

Personalised versus commodified experience: the narrative of the self must be constructed in circumstances in which personal appropriation is influenced by standardised influences on consumption.

Figure 24.1 Dilemmas of the self

Of course, narcissism springs from other sources too, especially as a deepseated phenomenon of personality development. But in so far as commodification, in the context of consumerism, promotes appearance as the prime arbiter of value, and sees self-development above all in terms of display, narcissistic traits are likely to become prominent. Individuation, however, also has its pathological aspects. All self-development depends on the mastering of appropriate responses to others; an individual who has to be 'different' from all others has no chance of reflexively developing a coherent self-identity. Excessive individuation has connections to conceptions of grandiosity. The individual is unable to discover a self-identity 'sober' enough to conform to the expectations of others in his social milieux.

[. . .]

References

Bauman, Z. (1989) *Legislators and Interpreters*, Cambridge: Polity.
Fiske, J. (1989) *Understanding Popular Culture*, London: Unwin Hyman.
Fromm, E. (1960) *The Fear of Freedom*, London: Routledge.
Hodge, R. and Tripp, D. (1989) *Children and Television*, Cambridge: Polity.
Wagar, W. W. (1982) *Terminal Visions*, Bloomington: University of Indiana Press.

Chapter 25

Katharine Young

NARRATIVE EMBODIMENTS: ENCLAVES OF THE SELF IN THE REALM OF MEDICINE

To write the body.
Neither the skin, nor the muscles, nor the bones,
nor the nerves, but the rest: an awkward, fibrous,
shaggy, raveled thing, a clown's coat.

Roland Barthes

Persons are tender of their bodies as if their selves inhered in its organs, vessels, tissues, bones and blood, as if they were embodied. For us, the body is the locus of the self, indistinguishable from it and expressive of it. As the phenomenologist, Maurice Natanson, writes,

> The immediacy of my experience of corporeality should be under-
> stood as an indication of the interior perspective I occupy with
> respect of 'my body'. I am neither 'in' my body nor 'attached to'
> it, it does not belong to me or go along with me. *I am my body*.
>
> (Natanson 1970: 12)

I experience myself as embodied, incorporated, incarnated in my body. To appear in my own person is to evidence this implication of my self in my body.

Medical examinations threaten this embodied self with untoward intimacies. The accoutrements of propriety are stripped away: I appear in nothing but my body. What follows has the structure of a transgression, an infringement,

Source: Katharine Young, 'Narrative embodiments: enclaves of the self in the realm of medicine', in John Schotter and Kenneth J. Gergen (eds) *Texts of Identity*, London: Sage, 1989, 152–65.

but one in which I am complicit. I disclose my body to the other, the stranger, the physician (see Berger and Mohr 1976: 68). To deflect this threat to the embodied self, medicine constitutes a separate realm in which the body as lodgement of the self is transformed into the body as object of scrutiny: persons become patients. This transformation is intended to protect the sensibilities of the social self from the trespasses of the examination. Whatever the medical business of the examination, its phenomenological business is to displace the self from the body. However, persons can perceive rendering the body an object as depersonalizing, dehumanizing or otherwise slighting to the self.[1] The disparity between the physician's intention and the patient's perception establishes the context for 'gaps', 'distortions' and 'misunderstandings' between patients and physicians (Mishler 1984: 171).

Because of their sense of the loss of self – a well-founded sense if also a well-intentioned loss – patients can have some impulse to reconstitute a self during medical examinations. This reconstitution can be undertaken by the patient in one of two moves: either by breaking the framework of the realm of medicine by disattending, misunderstanding or flouting its conventions or by maintaining the framework but inserting into the realm of medicine an enclave of another ontological status, specifically, a narrative enclave.

Rules for producing narratives on ordinary occasions require that they be set off by their frames from the discourses in which they are embedded (see Young 1982). Narrative frames – prefaces, openings, beginnings, endings, closings, codas – create an enclosure for stories within medical discourse. The discourse within the frames is understood to be of a different ontological status from the discourse without. In particular, the *storyrealm*, the realm of narrative discourse, conjures up another realm of events, or *taleworld*, in which the events the story recounts are understood to transpire (see Young 1987: 15–18). It is in this alternate reality that the patient reappears as a person. This move depends on the existence of what Alfred Schutz calls 'multiple realities' (1967: 245–62), the different realms of being, each with its own 'metaphysical constants' (Natanson 1970: 198), which individuals conjure up and enter into by turning their attention to them.

Embodying the self in a narrative enclave respects the conventions of the realm of medicine and at the same time manages the presentation of a self, but of one who is sealed inside a story. An inverse relationship develops between the uniquely constituted narrative enclosure in which a patient presents a self and the jointly constituted enclosing realm in which the patient undergoes a loss of self. Stories become enclaves of self over the course of an occasion on which medicine inhabits the realm of the body.

Erving Goffman argues that persons are in the way of presenting themselves, guiding controlled impressions, not necessarily to deceive, but to sustain a reality, an event, a self. Structurally, the self is divided into two aspects: (1) the performer who fabricates these impressions, and (2) the character who is the impression fabricated by an ongoing performance which entails them both (Goffman 1959: 252). On ordinary occasions, then, persons do not provide information to recipients but present dramas to an audience (Goffman 1974: 508). It is here that the theatrical metaphor for which Goffman is famous takes hold: talk about the self is not so far removed from enactment. We do not have behaviours and descriptions of them but a modulation from embodied to disembodied performances. Storytelling is a special instance of the social construction of the self in which 'what the individual presents is not himself but a story containing a protagonist who may happen also to be himself' (Goffman 1974: 541). On the occasion investigated here, embodying the self in stories occurs in circumstances in which the self is being disembodied, a complication of the matter Goffman has called 'multiple selfing', that is, the evolving or exuding of a second self or several selves over the course of an occasion on which the self is being presented (Goffman 1974: 521 fn.).

The natural occurrence of these 'texts of identity' in the course of a medical examination suggests implications about the uses of narrativity in social scientific discourse. Kenneth and Mary Gergen write that 'rules for narrative construction guide our attempt to account for human actions across time', both in making ourselves intelligible informally and in social scientific discourse (Gergen and Gergen 1986: 6). Individuals use narratives, they argue, to reflexively reconstruct a sense of self. 'The fact that people believe they possess identities fundamentally depends on their capacity to relate fragmentary occurrences across temporal boundaries' (Gergen and Gergen 1983: 255). What the Gergens call 'self-narratives' then 'refer to the individual's account of the relationship among self-relevant events across time' (p. 255). Kenneth Gergen's speculation that 'lives are constructed around pervading literary figures or tropes' (Gergen 1986: 3) is an instance of his more general claim 'that scientific theory is governed in substantial degree by what are essentially aesthetic forms' (Gergen and Gergen 1986: 20).

Note that two claims are being made here: that individuals use stories to make sense of events, and that so, in the same vein, do social scientists. The narrativity of social scientific discourse, then, takes its legitimation from storytelling in everyday life. This in turn warrants the application of narrative theory to social scientific discourse. However, discovering the structures of narrative in discourses about the self must be distinguished from imputing narrative structures to discourses about the self. The first is an ethnographic enterprise; the second an analytic one. To regard social scientific discourse as narrative is to treat it under a metaphor, in the same way that it is to regard cultures as texts or minds as cybernetic systems or reality as mechanistic. Analysts' uses of the devices of narrative to structure their approaches to discourses about the self render problematic the conventions that narrativity imports into the social sciences. My concern as a narratologist is to distinguish these approaches from persons' presentations of self in narrative modes. It is crucial to return to the social disposition of stories, to their linguistic coding, their contexts of use, to see how they illuminate the way individuals construe their lives. Doing so lays the groundwork for pursuing enquiries into narrativity as an interpretive structure for social scientific discourses about the self.

This is an analysis of a medical examination in the course of which the patient tells three stories in which he appears as a character. The links and splits between the realm of medicine and the realm of narrative illuminate the nature of narrative, the nature of medicine, and the nature of the self.

Medical examinations are divided into two parts: the history-taking, and the physical examination. These internal constituents of the realm of medicine are bounded by greetings and farewells which mark the transition between the realm of the ordinary and the realm of medicine. The shift from greetings, in which the physician emerges from his professional role to speak to his patient as a social person, to history-taking, in which the physician elicits information from the patient about his body, is the first move towards dislodging the self from the body. The patient's social person is set aside to attend to his physical body.

The patient on this occasion is Dr Michael Malinowski, a seventy-eight-year-old professor of Jewish history and literature. He has come to University Hospital to consult an internist, Dr Mathew Silverberg. Dr Silverberg shakes hands with the professor and his son in the waiting room, escorts them to his office, and there begins to take the patient's history. The shift from the waiting room to the office reifies the transition between realms. The history-taking reorientates the person's attitude towards his body in two respects: it invites him to regard his body from outside instead of from inside, and it invites him to see it in parts instead of as a whole. Dr Silverberg's enquiries direct the patient to attend to his body as an object with its own vicissitudes which he recounts with the detachment of an outsider. In so doing, Dr Malinowski suffers a slight estrangement from his own body. In making these enquiries, Dr Silverberg asks about the parts of the body separately, disarticulating it into segments. So Dr Malinowski's body undergoes a fragmentation. Since the self is felt to inhere in the body as a whole from the inside, these shifts of perspective tend to separate the self from the body. It is against the thrust of this ongoing estrangement and fragmentation that the professor sets his first story, the story of the liberation. Dr Silverberg has shifted from general enquiries about the whole body – height, weight, age, health – to specific enquiries about the eyes, the throat and the blood. He continues:

Story 1
The liberation

    Dr S: Have you ever had any problems with your heart?
    Dr M: No.
    Dr S: No heart attacks?
    Dr M: Pardon me?
    Dr S: Heart attacks?
    Dr M: No.
    Dr S: No pain in the chest?
    Dr M: No pain in the chest.
    Dr S: I
             noticed that =
    Dr M: I am a graduate from Auschwitz.
    Dr S: I know— I heard already =
    Dr M: Yeah.
             I went there when— I tell Dr Young about this
             and
             after Auschwitz
             I went through a lot of— I lost this
    Dr S: Umhm.
    Dr M: top finger there
             and
             I was in a—
             after the liberation we were under supervision of
             American doctors.
    Dr S: Yeah?
    Dr M: American doctors.
    Dr S: Right.
    Dr M: And it uh
             I was sick of course after two years in Auschwitz I was
                quite uh uh exhausted.
             And later I went through
             medical examination
             in the American Consul
             in Munich
    Dr S: Yeah?
    Dr M: and I came to the United States.

Dr S: Right?
Dr M: In nineteen hundred forty-seven.
        Nineteen forty-six—
        about nineteen forty-seven.
        One day—
        I lived on Fairfield Avenue
        I started to spit
        blood.
Dr S: Right?
Dr M: Yeah?
        And I called the doctor
        and he found that something here ((*gestures to his chest*))
Dr S: Tuberculosis?
Dr M: Somethin— yeah.
        And I was in the Deborah
        Sanitorium for a year.
Dr S: In nineteen forty-seven.
Dr M: I would say forty-seven and about
        month of forty-eight.
          . . .
Dr S: Back
        to your heart.

The story conjures up a *taleworld*, the realm of Auschwitz, which is juxtaposed to the ongoing history-taking. The preface, 'I am a graduate from Auschwitz', opens onto the other realm. Prefaces are a conventional way of eliciting permission to take an extended turn at talk in order to tell a story (Sacks 1970: II: 10). In response to what he perceives as a divagation from the realm of medicine, Dr Silverberg says, 'I know – I heard already.' Having heard a story is grounds for refusing permission to tell it again (Goffman 1974: 508). Dr Malinowski persists in spite of this refusal, thus overriding one of the devices available to physicians for controlling the course of an examination, namely, a relevancy rule: that the discourse stay within the realm of medicine. To insert the realm of narrative into the realm of medicine, the professor initially breaks its frame. But in so doing, he substitutes another relevancy rule: topical continuity. Like the history-taking, the *taleworld* focuses on a part of the body, the chest. It is this part of the body that the professor uses to produce topical continuity between the history-taking and the story. However, it is not the chest but the heart on which the physician is focusing. When he returns talk to the realm of medicine with the remark, 'Back to your heart', he is at the same time protesting the irrelevance of the excursion. As is apparent from this, the rule for topical continuity, the selection of a next discourse event which shares at least one element with a previous discourse event, permits trivial connections between discourses and, by extension, between realms. But there is a deeper continuity here. Both the realm of Auschwitz and the realm of medicine address the body.

In the realm of medicine, the dismantling of the body continues with Dr Silverberg's enquiries about the heart, breath, ankles and back; he recurs to whole body concerns with enquiries about allergies, habits and relatives; then he goes on to segment the body into the skin, head, eyes again, nose, throat again, excretory organs, stomach again, muscles, bones and joints. Into this discourse, the professor inserts his second story, the story of the torture. This story is also about a part of the body, the finger, and so again maintains a parallel with the realm in which it is embedded, although not the strict tie of topical continuity. Having created an enclosure in medical discourse for the Auschwitz stories earlier on, Dr Malinowski now feels entitled to extend or elaborate that Taleworld (see Young, 1987, pp. 80–99). This story is tied not to the discourse that preceded it but to the previous story in which he mentions his finger. As if in acknowledgement of the establishment of this enclosure, Dr Malinowski's preface, 'I was not sick except this finger', elicits an invitation from Dr Silverberg to tell the story: 'What happened to that finger.' The Taleworld is becoming a realm of its own.

Story 2
The torture

    Dr M: No.

              I don't know.

              I tell you— I told you Dr ((*to me*)) I don't—

              during the twenty-three months in Auschwitz

    Dr S: Yeah?

    Dr M: I was not sick except this finger.

    Dr S: What happened to that finger?

    Dr M: I wa—

              I tell Dr Young

              I was sitting

              ((*coughs*)) you have something to drink

    Dr S: Yeah.

              I have for you.

    Dr M: Yeah.

              I was sitting at the press—

              the machine

> I don't know how to say in English
> [— a machine or]
>
> Dr S: [I understand.]
>
> Dr M: Anyway I had to put in this was
> iron
> and I had to put in— in here with the right hand to put
>   this which made a hole or whatever it did.
>
> Dr S: Made a hole in your finger.
>
> Dr M: No.
> Made a hole here. ((*in the piece of iron*))
> My finger got it.
> And behind me was an SS man.
> And he stood behind me
> and at one moment he pushed me.
> Just— this was a— a— a—
> daily sport.
> And instead to put the iron in I put my finger in.
> /
> But otherwise I wasn't sick.

The shift from taking the history to giving the physical examination involves moving to another space, the examining room, which is an even more narrowly medical realm. Dr Silverberg closes the history-taking by saying:

> Dr S: I would like to examine you.
>
> Dr M: For this I came.
>
> Dr S: I will lead you into the examining room?
>
> Dr M: All right.
>
> Dr S: I would like you to
> take everything off
> Down to your undershorts.
> And have a seat on the table.

Dr Silverberg then takes his patient to the examining room down the hall and leaves him to take off his clothes. Clothes are the insignia of the social self. Their removal separates the body from its social accoutrements. This reduction of the social self along with the enhancement of the medical realm completes the dislodgement of the self. What remains is the dispirited, unpersoned, or dehumanized body.

During the physical examination, the body is handled as an object. When Dr Silverberg returns he finds the professor lying on the examining table in old-fashioned long white shorts that button at the top, with his arms folded across his chest. They speak to each other and then Dr Silverberg comes up to the examining table, picks the patient's right hand up off his chest, holds it in his right hand, and feels the pulse with his left fingertips. Here is the inversion of the initial handshake which enacted a symmetry between social selves; the physician touches the patient's hand as if it were inanimate. The examination is the rendering in a physical medium of the estrangement of the self and the fragmentation of the body. The external perspective is substituted for the internal perspective and the whole is disarticulated into parts. Of course, there is still talk – questions, comments, instructions; but now such remarks are inserted into interstices between the acts, the investigations, the physical manipulations that structure the examination. Henceforth, for the course of the physical examination, the patient's body is touched, lifted, probed, burned, bent, tapped, disarranged and recomposed by the physician. It is here that the absence of the self from the body can be intended as a protection: the social self is thereby preserved from the trespasses of the examination. These are committed only on an object.

The physical examination proceeds from the hands up the arms; then Dr Silverberg sits the patient up, looks at his head, ears, eyes, nose, mouth, throat, back, chest and heart; then he lays the patient back down on the table, tucks down the top of his shorts, examines his genitals, and folds the shorts back together at the top. He continues down the legs to the feet, then sits him up again and returns to the arms and hands. At this point, Dr Silverberg asks the patient to touch his nose with the tips of his fingers and as he does so the patient alludes to a bump on his skull: 'I have to tell you how I got that.' And the physician responds, 'How.' Despite this invitation, Dr Malinowski appears uncertain about the propriety of inserting a story into this realm.

Story 3
The capture

    Dr M: I have to tell you how I got that. ((*the bump*))
    Dr S: How.
    Dr M: Should I talk here?
    Dr S: You
    Dr M: Can I talk here?
    Dr S: Sure.
            /
    Dr M: You already know. ((*to me*))
            When I (s— try) to go the border
            between Poland and Germany

Dr S: Yeah?

Dr M: I wanted to escape
        to the border over Switzerland=

Dr S: Umhm.

Dr M: as a Gentile.

Dr S: Yeah?

Dr M: When they caught me
        they wanted investigation.
        /

Dr S: That it?

Dr M: (At)
        the table was (sitting) near me
        and (his arm) was extending behind me
        with— how the police ha— how do you call it.
        A police club?

Dr S: Nightstick.

Dr M: Nightstick.

Dr S: Umhm.

Dr M: And they—
        I had to count
        and they hit me twenty
        times over the head.
        And er— he told me zählen
        zähle means you count.
        And after the war—
        after the liberation shortly about two three days
        American Jewish doctors came
        they (examined us)
        and he told me
        that I have
        a nerve splint here?

Dr S: Yeah.

Dr M: And this made me be deaf.

The physician then examines the patient's ears, and finally his prostate and rectum. So here, suspended between the genital and rectal examinations, the two procedures towards which the displacement of the self from the body are primarily orientated, is the professor's third and last story. Once again, the story is about a part of the body, the ears, which maintains a continuity with the realm of medicine. But it is also about another part of the body, the genitals. As he mentions. Dr Malinowski has already told me this story when I talked to him in the waiting room to get his permission to observe and tape-record his examination. He told me that he and a friend had decided, boldly, to cross the border out of Poland into Germany and work their way across Germany to the Swiss border. They carried forged papers. He himself got through the border and was already on the other side when something about his friend aroused the border guard's suspicion and they called him back. To check their suspicions, the guards pulled down his pants and exposed his genitals. Jews were circumcised. This story is concealed as a subtext directed to me within a text directed to the physician. On this understanding, the positioning of the story between the genital and rectal examinations has a tighter topical continuity than is apparent on the surface.

Stories are sealed off from the occasions on which they occur – here, the realm of medicine – as events of a different ontological status. For that reason they can be used to reinsert into that realm an alternate reality in which the patient can reappear in his own person without disrupting the ontological conditions of the realm of medicine. Stories about the realm in which he appears, the world of Auschwitz, might be supposed to be inherently theatrical, on the order of high tragedy. But the boundary between realms insulates medicine in some measure from the tragic passion. The apertures along the boundary through which the realms are connected are here restricted to parts of the body. In telling these stories, Michael Malinowski is not intending to play on his hearers' emotions. He is rather reconstituting for them the ontological conditions of his world and, having done so, inserting himself into that realm as a character. Besides creating a separate reality, telling stories during a medical examination creates a continuity between the two realms which converts the ontological conditions of the realm of medicine precisely along the dimensions of the body.

The stories are tokens of the man, talismans of the salient and defining history which has shaped him. They are not, on that account, unique to this occasion, but are invoked as touchstones of his presence (as they were, for instance, for me when we talked before the examination). They present a person whose life is wrought around an event of existential proportions. Auschwitz was a life-pivoting, world-splitting event: time is reckoned before-Auschwitz and after-Auschwitz; space is divided by it. Not only has he lost a country, a language and a childhood, but he has also lost a life-form. Before Auschwitz, he had a wife and child in Poland; the son who has brought him today is the only child of a second marriage made in the USA after the war. Dr Malinowski mentions once that he had two sisters: one perished, the other died a few years ago of cancer.

The sequential order of events in a story replicates the temporal unfolding of events in the realm it represents (Labov 1972: 359–60; [see Chapter 12]).

This replication is supposed by social scientists to extend to the sets of stories which are strung together to make a life history. In this instance, the sequential order in which these stories are told does not replicate the temporal order in which the events they recount occurred. He tells about the liberation first, then the torture, and finally the capture. There are of course clear contextual reasons for this which have been detailed here in terms of topical continuity. But I would like to suggest a deeper reason for their array. These stories cluster around Michael Malinowski's sense of self. Auschwitz provides what I would like to call centration: life is anchored here, everything else unfolds around this. The set of stories that make up the Auschwitz experience could be told in any order. There is an implication here for the use of narrativity in the social sciences. In insisting either on the notion that temporally ordered events are presented sequentially in stories or on re-ordering stories to present them so, social scientists have misunderstood the shape of experience: a life is not always grasped as a linear pattern. Serious attention to narrativity in stories of the self will not force the sense of self into the pattern of narrative, but will deploy narrative to discover the sense of self.

In so presenting the man and reconstituting the ontological conditions of his world, these stories attain the status of moral fables and lend the medical examination a delineation which renders the etiquette of touch an ethical condition. Not that the stories are warnings to the physician against similar transgressions. Rather, in the existential context of these stories, what might otherwise be seen as indignities to the body are transmuted into honours: the physician is a man whose touch preserves just those proprieties of the body that are infringed at Auschwitz.

The body in the *taleworld* is the analogue of the body in the realm of the examination, connected to it part for part, but inverted. The stories spin out existential situations in which the self is constrained to the body. In the first story, 'The liberation', the part of the body is the chest and the mode of insertion of the self in the body is sickness. The self cannot transcend its absorption in its bodily discomforts: its sensibilities are sealed in its skin. In the second story, 'The torture', the part of the body is the finger and the mode of insertion of the self in the body is pain. The self is jolted into the body, its sensibilities concentrated in its minutest part, the tip of a finger. In the third story, 'The capture', the parts of the body are the head and the genitals, and the mode of insertion is humiliation. Here the body is emblematic of the man, literally inscribed with his identity. Its degradations are his.

The phenomenological cast of the *taleworld* is set against the phenomenological cast of the realm of the examination in which the self is extricated from the body. The medical history of the tuberculosis, the severed fingertip, the deafness, which could be detached, is instead enfolded in the personal history of the concentration camp and recounted as a story. So Auschwitz is invoked not as the cause of these dissolutions of the flesh, but as the frame in terms of which we are to understand what has befallen the body and, it transpires, the frame in terms of which we are to understand what has become of the man. To see the fact that both the realm of medicine and the realm of narrative are about the body as topical continuity is a trivial rendering. The stories are transforms of the ontological problem that is central to the examination: the fragile, stubborn, precarious, insistent insertion of a self in the body.

Transcription conventions

Line-ends	Pauses
From Tedlock, 1978:	
=	Absence of obligatory end-pause
/	One turn pause
Capital letters	Start of utterance
.	Down intonation at end of utterance
?	Up intonation at end of utterance
——	Correction phenomena
( )	Doubtful hearings
(( ))	Editorial comments
[[	Simultaneous speech
[ ]	Extent of simultaneity

Adapted by Malcah Yeager from Schenkein, 1972:
. . .   Elisions
Initials before turns are abbreviations of speakers
English spelling indicates English speaking

Note

This paper was first given in 1985 at the American Folklore Society Meetings in Cincinnati, Ohio. The present version was clarified by a critical reading by Kenneth Gergen. The data were collected in 1984 during my research on the phenomenology of the body in medicine.

1   This sense of dehumanization is well attested to in both popular and social
     scientific literature. Elliot Mishler locates dehumanization in the discourse

of medicine, where he describes it as the conflict between the voice of
medicine, which is understood to dominate during medical examinations,
and the voice of the life-world, which is suppressed in a way, he argues, that
leads to an 'objectification of the patient, to a stripping away of the life-world
contexts of patient problems' (Mishler 1984: 128). To protect confidential-
ity, the names of the patient, the physician and the hospital are fictitious.

References

Barthes, R. (1977) *Roland Barthes*, New York: Hill and Way.
Berger, J. and Mohr, J. (1976) *A Fortunate Man: The Story of a Country Doctor*,
    New York: Pantheon.
Gergen, K. (1986) *If Persons are Texts*, New Brunswick, NJ: Rutgers University Press.
Gergen, K. and Gergen, M. (1983) 'Narratives of the self', in Sarbin, T. R.
    and Scheibe, K. E. (eds) *Studies in Social identity*, New York: Praeger.
—— (1986) 'Narrative form and the construction of psychological theory',
    unpublished paper, Swarthmore College/Pennsylvania State University.
Goffman, E. (1959) *The Presentation of Self in Everyday Life*, New York: Doubleday.
—— (1974) *Frame Analysis*, New York: Harper & Row.
Labov, W. (1972) 'The transformation of experience in narrative syntax', in
    Language in the Inner City, Philadelphia: University of Pennsylvania Press.
Mishler, E. G. (1984) *The Discourse of Medicine: Dialectics of Medical Interviews*,
    Norwood, NJ: Ablex.
Natanson, M. (1970) *The Journeying Self: A Study in Philosophy and Social Role*,
    Reading, MA: Addison Wesley.
Sacks, H. (1968) Unpublished lecture notes, University of California, Irvine,
    17 April 1968.
—— (1970) Unpublished lecture notes, University of California, Irvine, 17 April
    1970.
Schenkein, J. (1972) *Foundations in Sociolinguistics*, Philadelphia: University of
    Pennsylvania Press.
Schutz, A. (1967) *On Phenomenology and Social Relations*, Chicago and London:
    University of Chicago Press.
Tedlock, D. (1978) *Finding the Center: Narrative Poetry of the Zuni Indians*, Lincoln
    and London: University of Nebraska Press.
Young, K. (1982) 'Edgework: frame and boundary in the phenomenology of
    narrative communication', *Semiotica* 41(1.4): 277–315.
—— (1987) *Taleworlds and Storyrealms: The Phenomenology of Narrative*, Dordrecht:
    Martinus Nijhoff.

Chapter 26

Deborah Cameron

PERFORMING GENDER IDENTITY: YOUNG MEN'S TALK AND THE CONSTRUCTION OF HETEROSEXUAL MASCULINITY

Introduction

In 1990, a 21-year-old student in a language and gender class I was teaching at a college in the southern USA tape-recorded a sequence of casual conversation among five men; himself and four friends. This young man, whom I will call 'Danny',[1] had decided to investigate whether the informal talk of male friends would bear out generalizations about 'men's talk' that are often encountered in discussions of gender differences in conversational style – for example that it is competitive, hierarchically organized, centres on 'impersonal' topics and the exchange of information, and foregrounds speech genres such as joking, trading insults and sports statistics [cf. Holmes, Chapter 20].

Danny reported that the stereotype of all-male interaction was borne out by the data he recorded. He gave his paper the title 'Wine, women, and sports'. Yet although I could agree that the data did contain the stereotypical features he reported, the more I looked at it, the more I saw other things in it too. Danny's analysis was not inaccurate, his conclusions were not unwarranted, but his description of the data was (in both senses) *partial*: it was shaped by expectations that caused some things to leap out of the record as 'significant', while other things went unremarked.

Source: Deborah Cameron, 'Performing gender identity: young men's talk and the construction of heterosexual identity', in Sally Johnson and Ulrike Hanna Meinhof (eds) *Language and Masculinity*, Oxford: Blackwell, 1997, 47–64.

I am interested in the possibility that Danny's selective reading of his data was not just the understandable error of an inexperienced analyst. Analysis is never done without preconceptions, we can never be absolutely non-selective in our observations, and where the object of observation and analysis has to do with gender it is extraordinarily difficult to subdue certain expectations.

One might speculate, for example, on why the vignettes of 'typical' masculine and feminine behaviour presented in popular books like Deborah Tannen's *You Just Don't Understand* (1990) are so often apprehended as immediately *recognizable*.[2] Is it because we have actually witnessed these scenarios occurring in real life, or is it because we can so readily supply the cultural script that makes them meaningful and 'typical'? One argument for the latter possibility is that if you *reverse* the genders in Tannen's anecdotes, it is still possible to supply a script which makes sense of the alleged gender difference. For example, Tannen remarks on men's reluctance to ask for directions while driving, and attributes it to men's greater concern for status (asking for help suggests helplessness). But if, as an experiment, you tell people it is women rather than men who are more reluctant to ask for directions, they will have no difficulty coming up with a different and equally plausible explanation – for instance that the reluctance reflects a typically feminine desire to avoid imposing on others, or perhaps a well-founded fear of stopping to talk to strangers.[3]

What this suggests is that the behaviour of men and women, whatever its substance may happen to be in any specific instance, is invariably read through a more general discourse on gender difference itself. That discourse is subsequently invoked to *explain* the pattern of gender differentiation in people's behaviour; whereas it might be more enlightening to say the discourse *constructs* the differentiation, makes it visible *as* differentiation.

I want to propose that conversationalists themselves often do the same thing I have just suggested analysts do. Analysts construct stories about other people's behaviour, with a view to making it exemplify certain patterns of gender difference; conversationalists construct stories about themselves and others, with a view to performing certain kinds of gender identity.

Identity and performativity

In 1990, the philosopher Judith Butler published an influential book called *Gender Trouble: Feminism and the Subversion of Identity*. Butler's essay is a postmodernist reconceptualization of gender, and it makes use of a concept familiar to linguists and discourse analysts from speech-act theory: *performativity*.

For Butler, gender is *performative* – in her suggestive phrase 'constituting the identity it is purported to be'. Just as J. L. Austin [Chapter 2] maintained that illocutions like 'I promise' do not describe a pre-existing state of affairs but actually bring one into being, so Butler claims that 'feminine' and 'masculine' are not what we are, nor traits we *have*, but effects we produce by way of particular things we *do*: 'Gender is the repeated stylization of the body, a set of repeated acts within a rigid regulatory frame which congeal over time to produce the appearance of substance, of a "natural" kind of being' (p. 33).

This extends the traditional feminist account whereby gender is socially constructed rather than 'natural;', famously expressed in Simone de Beauvoir's dictum that 'one is not born, but rather becomes a woman'. Butler is saying that 'becoming a woman' (or a man) is not something you accomplish once and for all at an early stage of life. Gender has constantly to be reaffirmed and publicly displayed by repeatedly performing particular acts in accordance with the cultural norms (themselves historically and socially constructed, and consequently variable) which define 'masculinity' and 'femininity'.

This 'peformative' model sheds an interesting light on the phenomenon of gendered *speech*. Speech too is a 'repeated stylization of the body'; the 'masculine' and 'feminine' styles of talking identified by researchers might be thought of as the 'congealed' result of repeated acts by social actors who are striving to constitute themselves as 'proper' men and women. Whereas sociolinguistics traditionally assumes that people talk the way they do because of who they (already) are, the postmodernist approach suggests that people are who they are because of (among other things) the way they talk. This shifts the focus away from a simple cataloguing of differences between men and women to a subtler and more complex inquiry into how people use linguistic resources to produce gender differentiation. It also obliges us to attend to the 'rigid regulatory frame' within which people must make their choices – the norms that define what kinds of language are possible, intelligible and appropriate resources for performing masculinity or femininity.

A further advantage of this approach is that it acknowledges the instability and variability of gender identities, and therefore of the behaviour in which those identities are performed. While Judith Butler rightly insists that gender is regulated and policed by rather rigid social norms, she does not reduce men and women to automata, programmed by their early socialization to repeat forever the appropriate gendered behaviour, but treats them as conscious agents who may – albeit often at some social cost – engage in acts of transgression, subversion and resistance. As active producers rather than passive reproducers of gendered behaviour, men and women may use their awareness of the gendered meanings that attach to particular ways of speaking and acting to produce a variety of effects. This is important, because few, if any, analysts of data on men's and women's speech would maintain that the differences are as clear-cut and invariant as one might gather from such oft-cited dichotomies as 'competitive/cooperative' and 'report talk/rapport talk'. People *do* perform gender differently in different contexts, and do sometimes behave in ways we would normally associate with the 'other' gender. The conversation to which we now turn is a notable case in point.

The conversation: wine, women, sports . . . and other men

The five men who took part in the conversation, and to whom I will give the pseudonyms Al, Bryan, Carl, Danny and Ed, were demographically a homogeneous group: white, middle-class American suburbanites aged 21, who attended the same university and belonged to the same social network on campus. This particular conversation occurred in the context of one of their commonest shared leisure activities: watching sports at home on television.

Throughout the period covered by the tape-recording there is a basketball game on screen, and participants regularly make reference to what is going on in the game. Sometimes these references are just brief interpolated comments, which do not disrupt the flow of ongoing talk on some other topic; sometimes they lead to extended discussion. At all times, however, it is a legitimate conversational move to comment on the basketball game. The student who collected the data drew attention to the status of sport as a resource for talk available to North American men of all classes and racial/ethnic groups, to strangers as well as friends, suggesting that 'sports talk' is a typically 'masculine' conversational genre in the US, something all culturally competent males know how to do.

But 'sports talk' is by no means the only kind of talk being done. The men also recount the events of their day – what classes they had and how these went; they discuss mundane details of their domestic arrangements, such as who is going to pick up groceries; there is a debate about the merits of a certain kind of wine; there are a couple of longer narratives, notably one about an incident when two men sharing a room each invited a girl-friend back without their room-mate's knowledge – and discovered this at the most embarrassing moment possible. Danny's title 'Wine, women and sports' is accurate insofar as all these subjects are discussed at some length.

When one examines the data, however, it becomes clear there is one very significant omission in Danny's title. Apart from basketball, the single most prominent theme in the recorded conversation, as measured by the amount of time devoted to it, is 'gossip': discussion of several persons not present but known to the participants, with a strong focus on critically examining these individuals' appearance, dress, social behaviour and sexual mores. Like the conversationalists themselves, the individuals under discussion are all men. Unlike the conversationalists, however, the individuals under discussion are identified as 'gay'.

The topic of 'gays' is raised by Ed, only a few seconds in to the tape-recorded conversation:

> ED: Mugsy Bogues (.) my name is Lloyd Gompers I am a
>   homosexual (.) you know what the (.) I saw the new
>   Remnant I should have grabbed you know the title? Like
>   the head thing?

'Mugsy Bogues' (the name of a basketball player) is an acknowledgement of the previous turn, which concerned the on-screen game. Ed's next comment appears off-topic, but he immediately supplies a rationale for it, explaining that he 'saw the new Remnant' – *The Remnant* being a deliberately provocative right-wing campus newspaper whose main story that week had been an attack on the 'Gay Ball', a dance sponsored by the college's Gay Society.

The next few turns are devoted to establishing a shared view of the Gay Ball and of homosexuality generally. Three of the men, Al, Bryan and Ed, are actively involved in this exchange. A typical sequence is the following:

> AL: gays=
> ED: =gays w[hy? that's what it should read [gays why?
> BRYAN: [gays]   [I know]

What is being established as 'shared' here is a view of gays as alien (that is, the group defines itself as heterosexual and puzzled by homosexuality ('gays, why?'), and also to some extent comical. Danny comments at one point, 'it's hilarious', and Ed caps the sequence discussing the Gay Ball with the witticism:

> ED: the question is who wears the boutonnière and who wears
>   the corsage, flip for it? or do they both just wear flowers
>   coz they're fruits

It is at this point that Danny introduces the theme that will dominate the conversation for some time: gossip about individual men who are said to be gay. Referring to the only other man in his language and gender glass, Danny begins

> DANNY: My boy Ronnie was uh speaking up on the male perspec-
> tive today (.) way too much

The section following this contribution is structured around a series of refer-ences to other 'gay' individuals known to the participants as classmates. Bryan mentions 'the most effeminate guy I've ever met' and 'that really gay guy in our Age of Revolution class'. Ed remarks that 'you have never seen more homos than we have in our class. Homos, dykes, homos, dykes, everybody is a homo or a dyke'. He then focuses on a 'fat, queer, goofy guy . . . [who's] as gay as night' [sic], and on a 'blond hair, snide little queer weird shit', who is further described as a 'butt pirate'. Some of these references, but not all, initiate an extended discussion of the individual concerned. The content of these discussions will bear closer examination.

'The antithesis of man'

One of the things I initially found most puzzling about the whole 'gays' sequence was that the group's criteria for categorizing people as gay appeared to have little to do with those people's known or suspected sexual prefer-ences or practices. The terms 'butt pirate' and 'butt cutter' were used, but surprisingly seldom; it was unclear to me that the individuals referred to really were homosexual, and in one case where I actually knew the subject of discussion, I seriously doubted it.

Most puzzling is an exchange between Bryan and Ed about the class where 'everybody is a homo or a dyke', in which they complain that 'four homos' are continually 'hitting on' [making sexual overtures to] one of the women, described as 'the ugliest-ass bitch in the history of the world'. One might have thought that a defining feature of a 'homo' would be his lack of interest in 'hit-ting on' women. Yet no one seems aware of any contradiction in this exchange.

I think this is because the deviance indicated for this group by the term 'gay' is not so much *sexual* deviance as *gender* deviance. Being 'gay' means failing to measure up to the group's standards of masculinity or femininity. This is why it makes sense to call someone '*really* gay': unlike same- versus other-sex preference, conformity to gender norms can be a matter of degree. It is also why hitting on an 'ugly-ass bitch' can be classed as 'homosexual' behaviour – proper masculinity requires that the object of public sexual interest be not just female, but minimally attractive.

Applied by the group to men, 'gay' refers in particular to insufficiently masculine appearance, clothing and speech. To illustrate this I will reproduce a longer sequence of conversation about the 'really gay guy in our Age of Revolution class', which ends with Ed declaring: 'he's the antithesis of man'.

BRYAN: uh you know that really gay guy in our Age of Revolution class who sits in front of us? he wore shorts again, by the way, it's like 42 degrees out he wore shorts again [laughter] [Ed: That guy] it's like a speedo, he wears a speedo to class (.) he's got incredibly skinny legs [Ed: it's worse] you know=

ED: =you know like those shorts women volleyball players wear? it's like those (.) it's l[ike

BRYAN: [you know what's even more ridicu[lous? When
ED: [French cut spandex]

BRYAN: you wear those shorts and like a parka on . . .
(5 lines omitted)

BRYAN: he's either got some condition that he's got to like have his legs exposed at all times or else he's got really good legs=
ED: =he's probably he'[s like
CARL: [he really likes

BRYAN: =he
ED: =he's like at home combing his leg hairs=
CARL: his legs=

BRYAN: he doesn't have any leg hair though=   [yes and oh
ED: =he real[ly likes

ED: his legs=
AL: =very long very white and very skinny

BRYAN: those ridiculous Reeboks that are always (indeciph) and goofy white socks always striped=   [tube socks
ED: =that's [right

ED: he's the antithesis of man

In order to demonstrate that certain individuals are 'the antithesis of man', the group engages in a kind of conversation that might well strike us as the

antithesis of 'men's talk'. It is unlike the 'wine, women, and sports' stereotype of men's talk – indeed, rather closer to the stereotype of 'women's
talk' – in various ways, some obvious, and some less so.

The obvious ways in which this sequence resembles conventional notions
of 'women's talk' concern its purpose and subject-matter. This is talk about
people, not things, and 'rapport talk' rather than 'report talk' – the main
point is clearly not to exchange information. It is 'gossip', and serves one
of the most common purposes of gossip, namely affirming the solidarity of
an in-group by constructing absent others as an out-group, whose behaviour
is minutely examined and found wanting.

The specific subjects on which the talk dwells are conventionally 'feminine' ones: clothing and bodily appearance. The men are caught up in a
contradiction: their criticism of the 'gays' centres on their unmanly interest
in displaying their bodies, and the inappropriate garments they choose for
this purpose (bathing costumes worn to class, shorts worn in cold weather
with parkas which render the effect ludicrous, clothing which resembles the
outfits of 'women volleyball players'). The implication is that real men just
pull on their jeans and leave it at that. But in order to pursue this line of
criticism, the conversationalists themselves must show an acute awareness
of such 'unmanly' concerns as styles and materials. ('French cut spandex',
'tube socks'), what kind of clothes go together, and which men have 'good
legs'. They are impelled, paradoxically, to talk about men's bodies as a way
of demonstrating their own total lack of sexual interest in those bodies.

The less obvious ways in which this conversation departs from stereotypical notions of 'men's talk' concern its *formal* features. Analyses of men's
and women's speech style are commonly organized around a series of global
oppositions, e.g. men's talk is 'competitive', whereas women's is 'cooperative'; men talk to gain 'status', whereas women talk to forge 'intimacy' and
'connection'; men do 'report talk' and women 'rapport talk'. Analysts
working with these oppositions typically identify certain formal or organizational features of talk as markers of 'competition' and 'cooperation' etc. The
analyst then examines which kinds of features predominate in a set of conversational data, and how they are being used.

In the following discussion, I too will make use of the conventional oppositions as tools for describing data, but I will be trying to build up an argument
that their use is problematic. The problem is not merely that the men in my
data fail to fit their gender stereotype perfectly. More importantly, I think it
is often the stereotype itself that underpins analytic judgements that a certain
form is cooperative rather than competitive, or that people are seeking status
rather than connection in their talk. As I observed about Deborah Tannen's
vignettes, many instances of behaviour will support either interpretation, or

both; we use the speaker's gender, and our beliefs about what sort of behaviour makes sense for members of that gender, to rule some interpretations in and others out.

Cooperation

Various scholars, notably Jennifer Coates (1989), have remarked on the 'cooperative' nature of informal talk among female friends, drawing attention to a number of linguistic features which are prominent in data on all-female groups. Some of these, like hedging and the use of epistemic modals, are signs of attention to others' face, aimed at minimizing conflict and securing agreement [cf. Chapter 20]. Others, such as latching of turns, simultaneous speech where this is not interpreted by participants as a violation of turn-taking rights (cf. Edelsky 1981), and the repetition or recycling of lexical items and phrases across turns, are signals that a conversation is a 'joint production': that participants are building on one another's contributions so that ideas are felt to be group property rather than the property of a single speaker.

On these criteria, the conversation here must be judged as highly cooperative. For example, in the extract reproduced above, a strikingly large number of turns (around half) begin with 'you know' and/or contain the marker 'like' ('you know like those shorts women volleyball players wear?'). The functions of these items (especially 'like') in younger Americans' English are complex and multiple, and may include the cooperative, mitigating/face-protecting functions that Coates and Janet Holmes (1984) associate with hedging. Even where they are not clearly hedges, however, in this interaction they function in ways that relate to the building of group involvement and consensus. They often seem to mark information as 'given' within the group's discourse (that is, 'you know', 'like', 'X' presupposes that the addressee is indeed familiar with X); 'you know' has the kind of hearer-orientated affective function (taking others into account or inviting their agreement) which Holmes attributes to certain tag-questions; while 'like' in addition seems to function for these speakers as a marker of high involvement. It appears most frequently at moments when the interactants are, by other criteria such as intonation, pitch, loudness, speech rate, incidence of simultaneous speech, and of 'strong' or taboo language, noticeably excited, such as the following:

> ED: he's I mean he **like** a real artsy fartsy fag he's **like** (indeciph) he's so gay he's got this **like** really high voice and

wire rim glasses and he sits next to the ugliest-ass bitch
in the history of the world

ED: [and
BRYAN: [and they're all hitting on her too, **like** four

ED: [I know it's **like** four homos hitting on her
BRYAN: guys [hitting on her

It is also noticeable throughout the long extract reproduced earlier how much
latching and simultaneous speech there is, as compared to other forms of
turn transition involving either short or long pauses and gaps, or interruptions which silence the interruptee. Latching – turn transition without pause
or overlap – is often taken as a mark of cooperation because in order to
latch a turn so precisely onto the preceding turn, the speaker has to attend
closely to others' contributions.

The last part of the reproduced extract, discussing the 'really gay' guy's
legs, is an excellent example of jointly produced discourse, as the speakers
cooperate to build a detailed picture of the legs and what is worn on them,
a picture which overall could not be attributed to any single speaker. This
sequence contains many instances of latching, repetition of one speaker's
words by another speaker (Ed recycles Carl's whole turn, 'he really likes his
legs', with added emphasis), and it also contains something that is relatively
rare in the conversation as a whole, repeated tokens of hearer support like
'yes' and 'that's right'.[4]

There are, then, points of resemblance worth remarking on between
these men's talk and similar talk among women as reported by previous
studies. The question does arise, however, whether this male conversation
has the other important hallmark of women's gossip, namely an egalitarian
or non-hierarchical organization of the floor.

Competition

In purely quantitative terms, this conversation cannot be said to be egalitarian.
The extracts reproduced so far are representative of the whole insofar as
they show Ed and Bryan as the dominant speakers, while Al and Carl
contribute fewer and shorter turns (Danny is variable; there are sequences
where he contributes very little, but when he talks he often contributes turns
as long as Ed's and Bryan's, and he also initiates topics). Evidence thus exists
to support an argument that there is a hierarchy in this conversation, and
there is competition, particularly between the two dominant speakers, Bryan

and Ed (and to a lesser extent Ed and Danny). Let us pursue this by looking more closely at Ed's behaviour.

Ed introduces the topic of homosexuality, and initially attempts to keep 'ownership' of it. He cuts off Danny's first remark on the subject with a reference to *The Remnant*: 'what was the article? cause you know they bashed them they were like'. At this point Danny interrupts: it is clearly an interruption because in this context the preferred interpretation of 'like' is quotative – Ed is about to repeat what the gay-bashing article in *The Remnant* said. In addition to interrupting so that Ed falls silent, Danny contradicts Ed, saying 'they didn't actually (.) cut into them big'. A little later on during the discussion of the Gay Ball, Ed makes use of a common competitive strategy, the joke or witty remark which 'caps' other contributions (the 'flowers and fruits' joke quoted above). This, however, elicits no laughter, no matching jokes and indeed no take-up of any kind. It is followed by a pause and a change of direction if not of subject, as Danny begins the gossip that will dominate talk for several minutes.

This immediately elicits a matching contribution from Bryan. As he and Danny talk, Ed makes two unsuccessful attempts to regain the floor. One, where he utters the prefatory remark 'I'm gonna be very honest', is simply ignored. His second strategy is to ask (about the person Bryan and Danny are discussing) 'what's this guy's last name?'. First Bryan asks him to repeat the question, then Danny replies 'I don't know what the hell it is'.

A similar pattern is seen in the long extract reproduced above, where Ed makes two attempts to interrupt Bryan's first turn ('That guy' and 'it's worse'), neither of which succeeds. He gets the floor eventually by using the 'you know, like' strategy. And from that point, Ed does orient more to the norms of joint production; he overlaps others to produce simultaneous speech but does not interrupt; he produces more latched turns, recyclings and support tokens.

So far I have been arguing that even if the speakers, or some of them, compete, they are basically engaged in a collaborative and solidary enterprise (reinforcing the bonds within the group by denigrating people outside it), an activity in which all speakers participate, even if some are more active than others. Therefore I have drawn attention to the presence of 'cooperative' features, and have argued that more extreme forms of hierarchical and competitive behaviour are not rewarded by the group. I could, indeed, have argued that by the end, Ed and Bryan are not so much 'competing' – after all, their contributions are not antagonistic to one another but tend to reinforce one another – as engaging in a version of the 'joint production of discourse'.

Yet the data might also support a different analysis in which Ed and Bryan are simply *using* the collaborative enterprise of putting down gay men as an occasion to engage in verbal duelling where points are scored – against fellow group members rather than against the absent gay men – by dominating the floor and coming up with more and more extravagant put-downs. In this alternative analysis, Ed does not so much modify his behaviour as 'lose' his duel with Bryan. 'Joint production' or 'verbal duelling' – how do we decide?

Deconstructing oppositions

One response to the problem of competing interpretations raised above might be that the opposition I have been working with – 'competitive' versus 'cooperative' behaviour – is inherently problematic, particularly if one is taken to exclude the other. Conversation can and usually does contain both cooperative and competitive elements: one could argue (along with Grice [Chapter 3]) that talk must by definition involve a certain minimum of cooperation, and also that there will usually be some degree of competition among speakers, if not for the floor itself then for the attention or the approval of others (see also Hewitt 1997).

The global competitive/cooperative opposition also encourages the lumping together under one heading or the other of things that could in principle be distinguished. 'Cooperation' might refer to agreement on the aims of talk, respect for other speakers' rights or support for their contributions; but there is not always perfect co-occurrence among these aspects, and the presence of any one of them need not rule out a 'competitive' element. Participants in a conversation or other speech event may compete with each other and at the same time be pursuing a shared project or common agenda (as in ritual insult sessions); they may be in severe disagreement but punctiliously observant of one another's speaking rights (as in a formal debate, say); they may be overtly supportive, and at the same time covertly hoping to score points for their supportiveness.

This last point is strangely overlooked in some discussions of women's talk. Women who pay solicitous attention to one another's face are often said to be seeking connection or good social relations *rather than* status; yet one could surely argue that attending to others' face and attending to one's own are not mutually exclusive here. The 'egalitarian' norms of female friendship groups are, like all norms, to some degree coercive: the rewards and punishments precisely concern one's status within the group (among women, however, this status is called 'popularity' rather than 'dominance'). A woman may gain status by displaying the correct degree of concern for others, and lose status by displaying too little concern for others and too much for herself. Arguably, it is gender-stereotyping that causes us to miss or minimize the status-seeking element in women friends' talk, and the connection-making dimension of men's.

How to do gender with language

I hope it will be clear by now that my intention in analysing male gossip is not to suggest that the young men involved have adopted a 'feminine' conversational style. On the contrary, the main theoretical point I want to make concerns the folly of making any such claim. To characterize the conversation I have been considering as 'feminine' on the basis that it bears a significant resemblance to conversations among women friends would be to miss the most important point about it, that it is not only *about* masculinity, it is a sustained performance *of* masculinity. What is important in gendering talk is the 'performative gender work' the talk is doing; its role in constituting people as gendered subjects.

To put matters in these terms is not to deny that there may be an empirically observable association between a certain genre or style of speech and speakers of a particular gender. In practice this is undeniable. But we do need to ask: in virtue of what does the association hold? Can we give an account that will not be vitiated by cases where it does *not* hold? For it seems to me that conversations like the one I have analysed leave, say, Deborah Tannen's contention that men do not do 'women's talk', because they simply *do not know how*, looking lame and unconvincing. If men rarely engage in a certain kind of talk, an explanation is called for; but if they do engage in it even very occasionally, an explanation in terms of pure ignorance will not do.

I suggest the following explanation. Men and women do not live on different planets, but are members of cultures in which a large amount of discourse about gender is constantly circulating. They do not only learn, and then mechanically reproduce, ways of speaking 'appropriate' to their own sex; they learn a much broader set of gendered meanings that attach in rather complex ways to different ways of speaking, and they produce their own behaviour in the light of those meanings.

This behaviour will vary. Even the individual who is most unambiguously committed to traditional notions of gender has a range of possible gender identities to draw on. Performing masculinity or femininity 'appropriately' cannot mean giving exactly the same performance regardless of the circumstances. It may involve different strategies in mixed and single-sex company, in private and in public settings, in the various social positions (parent, lover, professional, friend) that someone might regularly occupy in the course of everyday life.

Since gender is a relational term, and the minimal requirement for 'being a man' is 'not being a woman', we may find that in many circumstances, men are under pressure to constitute themselves as masculine linguistically by avoiding forms of talk whose primary association is with women/ femininity. But this is not invariant, which begs the question: under what circumstances does the contrast with women lose its salience as a constraint on men's behaviour? When can men do so-called 'feminine' talk without threatening their constitution as men? Are there cases when it might actually be to their advantage to do this?

When and why do men gossip?

Many researchers have reported that both sexes engage in gossip, since its social functions (like affirming group solidarity and serving as an unofficial conduit for information) are of universal relevance, but its cultural meaning (for us) is undeniably 'feminine'. Therefore we might expect to find most men avoiding it, or disguising it as something else, especially in mixed settings where they are concerned to mark their difference from women (see Johnson and Finlay 1997). In the conversation discussed above, however, there are no women for the men to differentiate themselves from; whereas *there is* the perceived danger that so often accompanies western male homosociality: homosexuality. Under these circumstances perhaps it becomes acceptable to transgress one gender norm ('men don't gossip, gossip is for girls') in order to affirm what in this context is a more important norm ('men in all-male groups must unambiguously display their heterosexual orientation').

In these speakers' understanding of gender, gay men, like women, provide a contrast group again whom masculinity can be defined. This principle of contrast seems to set limits on the permissibility of gossip for these young men. Although they discuss other men besides the 'gays' – professional basketball players – they could not be said to gossip about them. They talk about the players' skills and their records, not their appearance, personal lives or sexual activities. Since the men admire the basketball players, identifying *with* them rather than *against* them, such talk would border dangerously on what for them is obviously taboo: desire for other men.

Ironically, it seems likely that the despised gay men are the *only* men about whom these male friends can legitimately talk among themselves in such intimate terms without compromising the heterosexual masculinity they are so anxious to display – though in a different context, say with their girlfriends, they might be able to discuss the basketball players differently. The presence of a woman, especially a heterosexual partner, displaces the dread spectre of homosexuality, and makes other kinds of talk possible; though by the same token her presence might make certain kinds of talk that take place among men *impossible*. What counts as acceptable talk for men is a complex matter in which all kinds of contextual variables play a part.

In this context – a private conversation among male friends – it could be argued that to gossip, either about your sexual exploits with women or about the repulsiveness of gay men (these speakers do both), is not just one way, but the most appropriate way to display heterosexual masculinity. In another context (in public, or with a larger and less close-knit group of men), the same objective might well be pursued through explicitly agonistic strategies, such as yelling abuse at women or gays in the street, or exchanging sexist and homophobic jokes. *Both* strategies could be said to do performative gender work: in terms of what they do for the speakers involved, one is not more 'masculine' than the other, they simply belong to different settings in which heterosexual masculinity may (or must) be put on display.

Conclusion

I hope that my discussion of the conversation I have analysed makes the point that it is unhelpful for linguists to continue to use models of gendered speech which imply that masculinity and femininity are monolithic constructs, automatically giving rise to predictable (and utterly different) patterns of verbal interaction. At the same time, I hope it might make us think twice about the sort of analysis that implicitly seeks the meaning (and sometimes the *value*) of an interaction among men or women primarily in the style, rather than the substance, of what is said. For although, as I noted earlier in relation to Judith Butler's work, it is possible for men and women to performatively subvert or resist the prevailing codes of gender, there can surely be no convincing argument that this is what Danny and his friends are doing. Their conversation is animated by entirely traditional anxieties about being seen at all times as red-blooded heterosexual males: not women and not queers. Their skill as performers does not alter the fact that what they perform is the same old gendered script.

Transcription conventions

=	latching
[	turn onset overlaps previous turn

[]	turn is completely contained within another speaker's turn
?	rising intonation on utterance
(.)	short pause
(indeciph)	indecipherable speech
italics	emphatic stress on italicized item

Notes

1   Because the student concerned is one of the speakers in the conversation I analyse, and the nature of the conversation makes it desirable to conceal participants' identities (indeed, this was one of the conditions on which the data were collected and subsequently passed on to me), I will not give his real name here, but I want to acknowledge his generosity in making his recording and transcript available to me, and to thank him for a number of insights I gained by discussing the data with him as well as by reading his paper. I am also grateful to the other young men who participated. All their names, and the names of other people they mention, have been changed, and all pseudonyms used are (I hope) entirely fictitious.

2   I base this assessment of reader response on my own research with readers of Tannen's book (see Cameron 1995: Chapter 5), on non-scholarly reviews of the book, and on reader studies of popular self-help generally (e.g., Lichterman 1992; Simonds 1992).

3   I am indebted to Penelope Eckert for describing this 'thought experiment', which she has used in her own teaching (though the specific details of the example are not an exact rendition of Eckert's observations).

4   It is a rather consistent research finding that men use such minimal responses significantly less often than women, and in this respect the present data conform to expectations – there are very few minimal responses of any kind. I would argue, however, that active listenership, involvement and support are not *absent* in the talk of this group; they are marked by other means such as high levels of latching/simultaneous speech, lexical recycling and the use of *like*.

References

Butler, J. (1990) *Gender Trouble: Feminism and the Subversion of Identity*, New York: Routledge.

Cameron, D. (1995) *Verbal Hygiene*, London: Routledge.

Coates, J. (1989) 'Gossip revisited: language in all-female groups' in Coates, J. and Cameron, D. (eds) *Women in their Speech Communities*, Harlow: Longman, 94–121.

Edelsky, C. (1981) 'Who's got the floor?' *Language in Society* 10 (3): 383–422.

Hewitt, R. (1997) ' "Box-out" and "Taxing" ', in Johnson, S. and Meinhof, U. H. (eds) *Language and Masculinity*, Oxford: Blackwell, 27–46.

Holmes, J. (1984) 'Hedging your bets and sitting on the fence: some evidence for hedges as support structures', *Te Reo* 27: 47–62.

Johnson, S. and Finlay, F. (1997) 'Do men gossip? An analysis of football talk on television', in Johnson, S. and Meinhof, U. H. (eds) *Language and Masculinity*, Oxford: Blackwell, 130–43.

Lichterman, P. (1992) 'Self-help reading as a thin culture', *Media, Culture and Society* 14: 421–47.

Simonds, W. (1992) *Women and Self-help Culture: Reading Between the Lines*, New Brunswick, NJ: Rutgers University Press.

Tannen, D. (1990) *You Just Don't Understand: Women and Men in Conversation*, New York: Ballantine Books.

Chapter 27

Deborah Tannen

NEW YORK JEWISH CONVERSATIONAL STYLE[1]

A pause in the wrong place, an intonation misunderstood, and a
whole conversation went awry.

E. M. Forster, A Passage to India

Conversation, New York's biggest cottage industry, doesn't exist
in San Francisco in the sense of sustained discourse and friendly
contentiousness.

Edmund White, States of Desire[2]

Take for example, the following conversation.[3]

F: How often does your acting group work?
M: Do you mean how often we rehearse or how often we
      perform.⌐
F: ⌐Both.
M: [Laughs uneasily.]
F: Why are you laughing?
M: Because of the way you said that. It was like a bullet. Is
      that why your marriage broke?
F: What?
M: Because of your aggressiveness.

Source: Deborah Tannen, 'New York Jewish conversational style', *International Journal of Sociology of Language* 30: 133–49, 1981.

Of the many observations that could be made based on this interchange, I would like to focus on two: the general tendency to extrapolate personality from conversational style, and the specific attribution of aggressiveness to a speaker who uses fast pacing in conversation. In the discussion that follows, I will suggest that the stereotype of the 'pushy New York Jew' may result in part from discourse conventions practiced by some native New Yorkers of East European Jewish background. After examining some evidence for the existence of such a stereotype, I will (1) briefly present my notion of conversational style, (2) outline the linguistic and paralinguistic features that make up New York Jewish style and (3) demonstrate their use in cross-stylistic and co-stylistic interaction. In conclusion, I will (4) discuss the personal and social uses of conversational style.

The negative stereotype

Evidence abounds of the negative stereotype of New York speech in general and New York Jewish speech in particular. The most widely recognized component of this speech is, of course, phonology. An Associated Press release (Boyer 1979) reports on California therapists who help cure New York accents. One such therapist is quoted: 'It's really a drag listening to people from New York talk. It upsets me when I hear a New York accent. . . . We're here to offer a service to newcomers, they alienate everyone. We're here to help them adjust to life in Marin County.'

A third-grade teacher in Brooklyn wrote to Ann Landers complaining of native-born children who say, for example, 'Vot's the kvestion?', 'It's vorm ottside', and 'heppy as a boid'. Ann Landers advised the teacher, 'With consistent effort, bad speech habits can be unlearned. I hope you will have the patience to work with these students. It's a real challenge.'

Teachers in New York City have been rising to the challenge for a long time. Not so long ago one of the requirements for a license to teach in the New York City public schools was passing a speech exam, which entailed proving that one did not speak with the indigenous 'accent'. I myself recall being given a shockingly low midterm grade by a speech teacher in a Manhattan high school who promised that it would not be raised until I stopped 'dentalizing'. I am not aware of any other group whose members feel that their pronunciation is wrong, even when they are comfortably surrounded by others from the same group and have never lived anywhere else. Labov (1970) has documented the hypercorrection that results from the linguistic insecurity of middle-class Jewish New York women. I confronted this myself each time I recognized a fellow New Yorker in California by her

or his accent. The most common response was, 'Oh is it THAT obvious?'
or 'Gee, I thought I'd gotten rid of that'.

[. . .]

Background of the study

My own findings on New York Jewish conversational style were in a way
serendipitous as well. I had begun with the goal of discovering the features
that made up the styles of each participant in two-and-a-half hours of naturally occurring conversation at dinner on Thanksgiving 1978. Analysis
revealed, however, that three of the participants, all natives of New York of
East European Jewish background, shared many stylistic features which could
be seen to have a positive effect when used with each other and a negative
effect when used with the three others. Moreover, the evening's interaction
was later characterized by three of the participants (independently) as 'New
York Jewish' or 'New York'. Finally, whereas the tapes contained many
examples of interchanges between two or three of the New Yorkers, it had
no examples of talk among non-New Yorkers in which the New Yorkers
did not participate. Thus, what began as a general study of conversation
style ended by becoming an analysis of New York Jewish conversational style
(Tannen 1984).

The dinner at which this conversation was taped took place in the home
of Kurt, a native New Yorker living in Oakland, California. The guests, who
were also New Yorkers living in California, were Kurt's brother, Peter, and
myself.[4] The three other guests were Kurt's friend David, a native of Los
Angeles of Irish, Scotch and English parents from Iowa and North Dakota;
David's friend Chad, a native and resident of Los Angeles whose father was
of Scotch/English extraction and whose mother was from New York, of
Italian background; and Sally, born and raised in England, of a Jewish father
and American mother.[5] Complex as these ethnic backgrounds are, the group
split into two when looked at on the basis of conversational style.

Theoretical background

My notion of conversational style grows out of R. Lakoff's (1973; 1979)
work on communicative style and Gumperz's (1982 [Chapter 5]) on conversational inference. 'Style' is not something extra, added on like frosting on
a cake. It is the stuff of which the linguistic cake is made: pitch, amplitude,
intonation, voice quality, lexical and syntactic choice, rate of speech and

turntaking, as well as what is said and how discourse cohesion is achieved. In other words, style refers to all the ways speakers encode meaning in language and convey how they intend their talk to be understood. Insofar as speakers from similar speech communities share such linguistic conventions, style is a social phenomenon. Insofar as speakers use particular features in particular combinations and in various settings, to that extent style is an individual phenomenon. (See Gumperz and Tannen 1979, for a discussion of individual vs. social differences.)

Lakoff (1973) observes that speakers regularly avoid saying precisely what they mean in the interest of social goals which they pursue by adhering to one of three *rules of politeness*, later renamed *rules of rapport* (Lakoff 1979). Each rule is associated with a communicative style growing out of habitual application of that rule:

1   Don't impose (distance).
2   Give options (deference).
3   Be friendly (camaraderie).

To illustrate (with my own examples), if a guest responds to an offer of something to drink by saying, 'No thank you; I'm not thirsty', s/he is applying R1. Is s/he says, 'Oh, I'll have whatever you're having', s/he is applying R2. If s/he marches into the kitchen, throws open the refrigerator, and says, 'I'm thirsty. Got any juice?' s/he is applying R3. Individuals differ with regard to which sense of politeness they tend to observe, and cultural differences are reflected by the tendency of members of a group to observe one or the other sense of politeness in conventionalized ways.

[. . .]

Another deeply related strand of research in sociology is brilliantly elaborated by Goffman, building on the work of Durkheim. Durkheim (1915) distinguished between negative and positive religious rites. Negative rites are 'a system of abstentions' which prepares one for 'access to the positive cult'. Goffman (1967: 72–3) builds upon this dichotomy in his notion of *deference*, 'the appreciation an individual shows of another to that other, whether through avoidance rituals or presentational rituals'. Presentational rituals include 'salutations, invitations, compliments, and minor services. Through all of these the recipient is told that he is not an island unto himself and that others are, or seek to be, involved with him [. . .]'. Avoidance rituals 'lead the actor to keep at a distance from the recipient' (Goffman 1967: 62) and include 'rules regarding privacy and separateness' (Goffman 1967: 67). Following Lakoff and Goffman, Brown and Levinson (1987 [Chapter 19]) refer to two overriding goals motivating linguistic forms of politeness: negative face, 'the want of every adult member that his actions be unimpeded by others', and positive face, 'the want of every adult member that his actions be desirable to at least some others'.

All these schemata for understanding human interaction recognize two basic but conflicting needs: to be involved with others and to be left alone. Linguistic systems, like other cultural systems, represent conventionalized ways of honoring these needs. I would like to suggest that the conversational style of the New Yorkers at Thanksgiving dinner can be seen as conventionalized strategies serving the need for involvement, whereas the non-New York participants expected strategies serving the need for independence.

Features of New York Jewish conversational style

Following are the main features found in the talk of three of the six Thanksgiving celebrants.

1   *Topic* (a) prefer personal topics, (b) shift topics abruptly, (c) introduce topics without hesitance, (d) persistence (if a new topic is not immediately picked up, reintroduce it, repeatedly if necessary).
2   *Genre* (a) tell more stories, (b) tell stories in rounds, (c) internal evaluation (Labov 1970 [Chapter 12]) is preferred over external (i.e., the point of a story is dramatized rather than lexicalized), (d) preferred point of a story is teller's emotional experience.
3   *Pacing* (a) faster rate of speech, (b) inter-turn pauses avoided (silence is evidence of lack of rapport), (c) faster turntaking, (d) cooperative overlap and participatory listenership.
4   *Expressive paralinguistics* (a) expressive phonology, (b) pitch and amplitude shifts, (c) marked voice quality, (d) strategic within-turn pauses.

All of these marked features were combined to create linguistic devices which enhanced conversational flow when used among the New Yorkers, but they had an obstructive effect on conversation with those who were not from New York. Comments by all participants upon listening to the tape indicated that they misunderstood the intentions of members of the other group.

Perhaps the most easily perceived and characteristic feature of this style is the fast rate of speech and tendency to overlap (speak simultaneously) and latch (Sacks's term for allowing no pause before turntaking). Overlap is used cooperatively by the New Yorkers, as a way of showing enthusiasm and interest, but it is interpreted by non-New Yorkers as just the opposite:

evidence of lack of attention. The tendency to use fast pace and overlap often combines, moreover, with preference for personal topics, focusing attention on another in a personal way. Both the pacing and the personal focus can be seen repeatedly to cause Sally, Chad and David to become more hesitant in their speech as they respond in classic complementary schismogenetic fashion (Bateson 1972). That is, the verbal devices used by one group cause speakers of the other group to react by intensifying the opposing behavior, and vice versa.

Cross-stylistic interchange

The following conversation illustrates how both Peter and I use fast pacing and personal focus to show interest in David's discourse, with the result that he feels 'caught off guard' and 'on the spot'. (This is only one of many such examples.) David, a professional sign interpreter, has been talking about American Sign Language.

(1) D: So: and thís is the one that's Bėrkeley. This is the Bėrkeley
          . . . sign for . . . for ⌐Christmas
                                    ∟ p
(2) T: ∟Do yòu figure oút those . . those
                                      f
          um correspòndences?
          Or do? when you learn the signs, /does/ somebody télls
          you.
(3) D: Oh you mean ⌐watching it? like
(4) T: ∟Cause I can imagine knówing that sìgn,
          . . . and not . . figuring out that it had anything to do with
          the decorations.
          . . . .
(5) D: No. Y You knów that it has to do with the
          decorátions.⌐
(6) T: ∟ Cause somebody télls you? Or you figure⌐ it oút.
     D: ∟No⌏
(7) D: Oh. [. . .] You you talking about mé, or a deáf person.⌐
(8) T: ∟Yeah.⌋   ∟You.
          You.
(9) D: Me? uh: someone télls me, ùsually. . . . . But a lót of em I
          can tèll. I mean they're òbvious. . . . . . the bétter I get the
          mòre I can tell. The lónger I do it the mòre I can tell what
          they're talking about.

..... Without knowing what the sign is.⌉(10)   T:
[Huh.] [That's interesting.]
(11)   P: ⌊ But   how   do
you learn a new sign.
(12)   D: How do I learn a new sign?⌉
(13)   P: ⌊Yeah. I mean supposing [. . .]
Victor's talking and all of a sudden he uses a sign for
Thanksgiving, and you've never seen it before.

My questions (2) (4) and (6) and Peter's Questions (11) and (13) overlap
or latch onto David's preceding comments. In contrast, David's comments
follow out questions after 'normal' or even noticeable (5, 12) pauses.

My question (2) about how David learns about the symbolism behind
the signs not only is latched onto David's fading comment (1) but is spoken
loudly and shifts the focus from a general discourse about signs to focus on
David personally. The abrupt question catches him off guard, and he hesitates by rephrasing the question. I then interrupt David's rephrasing to supply
more information (4), interpreting his hesitation as indication that I had been
unclear. The real trouble, however, was the suddenness of my question and
its shift from general to personal. Thus, I hoped to make David comfortable
by acknowledging the fault had been mine and rectifying the matter by
supplying more information right away, but the second interruption could
only make him more uncomfortable; hence, the pause.

David answers my question (4) by commenting (5) 'You know that it
has to do with the decorations', but he avoids the more personal focus of
my question (2) and *how* he knows. I therefore become more specific (6)
and again latch my question. David stalls again, this time by asking (7) for
clarification. His question comes after a filler, a pause, a slight stutter: 'Oh.
. . . You you talking about me . . .'. He expresses his surprise at the shift
in focus. Yet again, I clarify in machine-gun fashion: (8) 'Yeah. You. You.'
David then answers the question and my response (10) overlaps his answer.

Just as this interchange between David and me is settled, Peter uses precisely the strategy that I was using, with the same results. Latching onto
David's answer (9), Peter asks another question focusing on David (11); David
hesitates by rephrasing the question after a pause (12); Peter barely waits for
the rephrasing to finish before he makes his question more specific (13).

The rhythm of this segment is most peculiar. Normally, a question–
answer are seen as an 'adjacency pair' (Sacks, Schegloff and Jefferson 1974),
and in a smooth conversation they are rhythmically paired as well. The differences in David's pacing on the one hand and Peter's and mine on the other,
however, create pauses between our questions and his delayed answers, so that

the resultant rhythmic pairs are made up of an answer and the next question. This is typical of how stylistic differences obstruct conversational rhythm. While participants in this conversation were friends and disposed to think well of each other, the operation of such differences in other settings can leave participants with the conviction that the other was uncooperative or odd.

Co-stylistic interchange

In the previous example, Peter and I directed similar questions to David, with unexpected results. The following segment shows how the same device serves to enhance conversational flow when used with each other. This segment begins when I turn to Peter suddenly and address a question to him.

(1)   T: Do you réad?

 . . . .

(2)   P: Do I |réad?

 . . .

(3)   T: Do you reàd things just for fún?

 . . . .

(4)   P: Yeah. . . . . . Right now I'm reading Norma Jean the Térmite Queen.

 [Laughs]

(5)   T: ⌈Whàt's thát? . . . . Norma Jean like uh: . . . . Marilyn
 f
 Mon|róe?

(6)   P: It's . . |No: It's a book about . . . . . . a housewife /??/
(7)   T: Is it a ⌈nóvel ^dec or whàt.
(8)   P: |It's a |nóvel.
(9)   T: |Yeah?
(10) P: Before that . . . I read the French Lieutenant's Woman?
 ⌈Have you ⌈ read that?
(11) T: ⌊⌈Oh yeah? No. Whó wrote that?
(12) P: John Fowles.
(13) T: Yeah I've heárd that he's good.
(14) P: |He's a ⌊gréat writer. |Í think he's one of the ⌊bést writers.
 T: hm
(15) T: /?/
(16) P: |Hé's really |goòd.
(17) T: /?/

 . . . .

(18) P: But Í get very bùsy. . . . ⌈Yknow?
(19) T: ⌊Yeah. I? . . hàrdly éver read.

 . . . .

(20) P: What I've been dòing is cutting down on my sléep.
(21) T: Oy! ⌉ [sighs]
(22) P: ⌊ And I've been   . . . . . and I ⌈ s

             [K laughs]   ⌊
(23) T: Lí do that tòo

     but it's páinful.⌉
(24) P: ⌊ Yeah, Fi:ve, six hours a ǀníght, and⌉
(25) T: ⌊ Oh

     Gód, hòw can you dó it. You survíve?

     . . . .

(26) P: Yeah làte afternoon méetings are hàrd. . . . . But outside
     of thát I

                                        T: mmm
     can keep ⌈ gòing pretty well.
(27) T: ⌊ Not sleeping enough is térrible. . . . . I'd múch
     rather not eàt ţhan not sleèp.
                  P
                 [S laughs]
(28) P: I próbably should not eàt so much, it would . . it would
     uh . . . sáve a lot of time.
(29) T: If I'm /like really/ busy I don't I don't I don't eat. I don't
     yeah I just don't eat but ⌈I
(30) P: ⌊I ?I tend to spend a lòt of time
     eáting and prepáring and ⌈/?/
(31) T: ⌊Oh: I néver prepare foòd. . . .
     . . . I eat whatéver I can get my hánds on.⌉
(32) P: ⌊ Yeah.

This interchange exhibits many features of New York Jewish conversational style. In addition to the characteristic use of overlap, fast pacing and
personal focus, it exhibits devises I have called (Tannen 1984) persistence,
mutual revelation and expressive paralinguistics.

Both Peter and I use overlap and latching in this segment: Peter's (22)
(24) and (30) and my (19) (23) (25) (27) and (31). The interchange begins
with a sudden focus of attention on him by my question (1). Like David,
Peter is initially 'caught off guard', so he repeats the question after a pause.
But then he not only answers the question but supplies specific information
(4) about the book he is reading. A common feature of participatory listenership is seen in (5) and (6). While (6) is ostensibly an answer to my question

(5), it is clear that Peter would have gone to give that information in any case. He begins, 'It's . . .', has to stop in order to answer my question with 'No', and then repeats the beginning and continues, 'It's a book about a housewife'.

Persistence refers to the pattern by which speakers continue trying to say something despite lack of attention or interruption. In this example it can be seen in (22) and (24), in which Peter makes three attempts to say that he sleeps only five or six hours a night. Persistence is a necessary concomitant to overlap. It reflects a conversational economy in which it is not the business of a listener to make room for another speaker to speak. Rather, it is the business of the listener to show enthusiasm; the speaker, in this system, can be counted on to find room to speak. The conversational burden, in other words, is to serve the need for involvement at the risk of violating independence.

The mutual revelation device can be seen in the series of observations Peter and I make about our own habits. In (19) I state that I hardly ever read as a way of showing understanding of Peter's tight schedule (18). (23) is a similar response to his statement that he cuts down on sleep. (27) is a statement of my preference to balance his statement (26) about sleeping. In (28) Peter makes a statement about his eating habits; in (29) I describe mine; in (30) he reiterates his, and in (31) I reiterate mine. It might seem to some observers that we are not 'communicating' at all, since we both talk only about ourselves. But the juxtaposition of comments and the relationship of topics constitutes thematic cohesion and establishes rapport. In this system, the offer of personal information is encouragement to the other to volunteer the same, and volunteered information is highly valued.

Throughout the Thanksgiving conversation, Peter, Kurt and I use exaggerated phonological and paralinguistic cues. For example, my question (5) 'What's that?' is loud and high pitched. When any of the New Yorkers uses such features with Chad or David, the result is that they stop talking in surprise, wondering what caused the outburst. When used in talk among the New Yorkers, introduction of exaggerated paralinguistics spurs the others to follow suit, in a mutually escalating way such as Bateson (1972) has characterized as symmetrical. In the present segment, many of the words and phrases are uttered with extra high or low pitch as well as heavily colored voice quality.

It seems likely that my use of high pitch on 'What's that?' as well as on the last syllable of 'Monroe' in (5) was triggered by Peter's laughter while uttering the book title. In any case, Peter's response (6) uses sharp contrasts in pitch and pacing to signal the message, 'I know this is a silly book'. The pitch on 'No' is very low, the vowel is drawn out, the sentence is uttered slowly, and it contains a very long pause before the key work 'housewife' is uttered. Similar sharp shifts from high to low pitch can be seen repeatedly:

(8) P: |It's a |novel.
(14) P: |He's a ⌊great writer. |I think he's one of the ⌊best writers.
(16) P: |He's really |good.

These pitch shifts, together with voice quality, signal in (8) denigration of the book discussed and in (14) and (16) great earnestness.

Exaggerated paralinguistics can be seen as well in my expressions of concern for Peter's loss of sleep in (23) (25) and (27). These are all uttered with marked stress and breathy voice quality that demonstrate exaggerated and stylized concern.

Yet another stylized response to Peter's assertion that he doesn't sleep enough is a Yiddish non-verbal 'response cry' (Goffman 1978), 'Oy!'. This utterance is rapport-building in a number of ways. Obviously, the choice of a Yiddish expression signals our shared ethnic background. At the same time, the exaggerated nature of my response – the utterance of a great sigh along with 'oy' – is a way of mocking my own usage, making the exclamation ironic in much the way Peter was mocking his own reading material while telling about it. (In a similar way, Kurt often mocks his own hosting behavior by offering food in an exaggerated Yiddish accent.) Finally, I utter this cry as if it were an expression of my own feeling, thus taking Peter's point of view as a show of empathy.

The interchange between Peter and me ends with another cooperative use of overlap and repetition. The conversation has turned to dating, and it has continued to be characterized by the features seen in the earlier segment. It ends this way:

(1) P: And you just cán't get to know . . . . ten   people really well.

                                                [breathy]

          ⌈ You can't dó it.
          | P
(2) T: ⌊ Yeah right. Y'have to there's no? Yeah there's ⌈no time.
(3) P: ⌊There's
          not tíme.
(4) T: Yeah . . . . 'strue.

Peter's statements (1) and (3) flow in a continuous stream, ending with 'You can't do it. There's not time'. However the last phrase echoes my words in

(2). The end of the talk is signaled by a quieting down of voices as well as the pattern of blended voices and phrases.

The coherence of conversational style

As Reisman (1974: 110) points out, 'The conventions which order speech interaction are meaningful not only in that they order and mediate verbal expression, but in that they participate in and express larger meanings in the society which uses them'. Becker (1979a: 18) explains, 'The figure a sentence makes is a strategy of interpretation' which 'helps the people it is used by understand and feel coherent in their worlds'. The structure and habits of language which seem self-evidently natural, serve not only as a way to communicate meaning but also to reestablish and ratify one's way of being in the world. In another paper, Becker (1979b: 241) explains:

> The universal source of language pathology is that people appear to say one thing and 'mean' another. It drives people mad (the closer it gets to home). An aesthetic response is quite simply the opposite of this pathology. . . . Schizophrenia, foreign language learning, and artistic expression in language all operate under the same set of linguistic variables – constraints on coherence, invention, intentionality, and reference. The difference is that in madness (and in the temporary madness of learning a new language or a new text) these constraints are misunderstood and often appear contradictory, while in an aesthetic response they are understood as a coherent integrated whole. . . . The integration of communication (art) is, hence, as essential to a sane community as clean air, good food, and, to cure errors, medicine.

The emotional/aesthetic experience of a perfectly tuned conversation is as ecstatic as an artistic experience. The satisfaction of having communicated successfully goes beyond the pleasure of being understood in the narrow sense. It is a ratification of one's place in the world and one's way of being human. It is, as Becker calls a well-performed shadow play, 'a vision of sanity'.

To some extent there is for everyone a discontinuity between the private code, i.e., communicative habits learned at home and on the block (or in the fields) around one's home, and the public code, i.e., the form of language used in formal settings. Hence the anxiety most people feel about communicating with strangers. But the degree of discontinuity may be greater or lesser. Those who learned and have reinforced at home norms of interaction which are relatively similar to those which are widely accepted in society at large have a certainty about their linguistic convictions. If they proclaim that it is rude to interrupt or that one ought to state the point of a story outright, it is without ambivalence. But those who have grown up hearing and using norms of interaction which differ significantly from more widely accepted ones may feel ambivalent about their own styles. Thus New Yorkers of Jewish background cannot complain 'Why don't you interrupt?'. On hearing a taperecording of a conversation they thoroughly enjoyed in the process, they often feel critical of themselves and slightly embarrassed. They, too, believe that it is rude to interrupt, to talk loudly, to talk too much. The 'interruption' may actually be the creation of the interlocutor who stopped when s/he was expected to continue talking over the overlap, but the cooperative overlapper is no more likely to realize this than the overlap-resistant speaker.

The greater the discontinuity between ingroup style and public expectations, the more difficult it is for one to feel sane in both worlds. Hence it is not surprising that many speakers reject one or the other style, and New York Jews who have moved away from New York may be heard to proclaim that they hate New York accents, hate to go back to New York or hate to go home, because 'no one listens to anyone else' to 'it's so loud' or 'people are so rude'. There are probably few speakers of this background who have not at times felt uncomfortable upon seeing through public eyes someone from their own background talking in a way that is attracting attention in an alien setting, just as American travelers may feel embarrassed on seeing another American tourist who fits too neatly the stereotype of the ugly American abroad. In contrast, the comfort of interaction in a setting in which one's home style predominates goes far to explain what often appears as clannishness – the preference for the company of those of similar ethnic background. The coherence principles (to borrow a term from Becker) that create conversational style operate on every level of discourse and contribute to, at the same time that they grow out of, people's attempts to achieve coherence in the world.

Notes

1   My thanks to Stephen Murray for this reference.
2   This conversation was reconstructed from memory. Other presented are transcribed from tape recordings. The following transcription conventions are used, as gleaned from Schenkein (1978) and from those developed at the University of California, Berkeley, by Gumperz and Chafe and their respective collaborators.

. . . half second pause. Each extra dot represents another half second of pause.

´ marks primary stress

ˋ marks secondary stress

underline indicates emphatic stress

| marks high pitch on word

⌐ marks high pitch on phrase, continuing until punctuation

| marks low pitch on word

. sentence-final falling intonation

, clause-final intonation (more to come)

? yes/no question rising intonation

ʔ glottal stop

: lengthened vowel sound

p spoken softly (piano)

f spoken loudly (forte)

dec spoken slowly

/?/ inaudible segment

⌐ Brackets connecting lines show overlapping speech.
[Two people talking at the same time.

Brackets with reversed flaps ⌐
                          └ indicate latching (no intraturn pause)

3   Thus I was both perpetrator and object of my analysis, making me not a participant observer (an observer who becomes a participant) but a participant who is also an observer. At the time of taping, I was in the habit of taping many interactions and had not decided to use this one, let alone what I would look for in analysis. Nonetheless there is a problem of objectivity which I have tried to correct for by painstaking review of the analysis with participants as well as others. I believe that the loss of objectivity is a disadvantage outweighed by the advantage of insight into what was going on which is impossible for a nonparticipant to recover, and that only by taping an event in which one is a natural participant can one gather data not distorted by the presence of an alien observer.

4   With the exception of my own, names have been changed. Now, as always, I want to express my gratitude to these friends who became my data, for their willingness and insight during taping and later during playback. The transcripts will reflect initials of these pseudonyms, except for my own, which is rendered 'T' to avoid confusion with 'D' (David).

References

Bateson, Gregory (1972) *Steps to an Ecology of Mind*, New York: Ballantine.

Becker, A. (1979a) 'The figure a sentence makes', in Givon, T. (ed.) *Discourse and Syntax*, New York: Academic Press.

—— (1979b) 'Text-building, epistemology and aesthetics in Javanese Shadow Theatre', in Becker, A. L. and Yengoyan, A. A. (eds) *The Imagination of Reality: Essays in Southeast Asian Coherence Systems*, Norwood, New Jersey: Ablex.

Boyer, P. J. (1979) 'Therapists cure New York accents', *The Tribune*, 4 February: 6E.

Brown, P. and Levinson, S. C. (1987) *Politeness: Some Universals in Language Usage*, Cambridge: Cambridge University Press.

Durkheim, E. (1915) *The Elementary Forms of the Religious Life*, New York: The Free Press.

Forster, E. M. (1924) *A Passage to India*, New York: Harcourt Brace Jovanovich.

Goffman, E. (1967) *Interaction Ritual: Essays on Face-to-Face Behavior*, Garden City: Doubleday.

—— (1978) 'Response cries', *Language* 54(4): 787–815.

Gumperz, J. (1982) *Discourse Strategies*, Cambridge: Cambridge University Press.

Gumperz, J. and Tannen, D. (1979) 'Individual and social differences in language use', in Fillmore, C. J., Kempler, D. and Wang, W. S.-Y. (eds) *Individual Differences in Language Ability and Language Behavior*, New York: Academic Press.

Labov, W. (1970) 'The study of language in its social context', *Studium Generale* 23: 30–87.

Lakoff, R. (1973) 'The logic of politeness; or, minding your p's and q's', *Papers from the Ninth Regional Meeting of the Chicago Linguistics Society*, Chicago: University of Chicago Department of Linguistics.

—— (1979) 'Stylistic strategies within a grammar of style', in Oransanu, J., Slater, M. and Adler, L. (eds) *Language, Sex and Gender*, Annals of the New York Academy of Sciences.

Reisman, K. (1974) 'Contrapuntal conversations in an Antiguan village', in Bauman, R. and Sherzer, J. (eds) *Explorations in the Ethnography of Speaking*, Cambridge: Cambridge University Press, 110–24.

Sacks, H., Schegloff, E. and Gail, J. (1974) 'A simplest systematics for the organization of turn-taking for conversation', *Language* 50(4): 696–735.

Schenkein, J. (1978) *Studies in the Organization of Conversational Interaction*, New York: Academic Press.

Tannen, D. (1984) *Conversational Style*, Norwood, NJ: Ablex.

White, E. (1980) *States of Desire: Travels in Gay America*, New York: Dutton.

Chapter 28

Charles Goodwin

PRACTICES OF COLOR CLASSIFICATION IN PROFESSIONAL DISCOURSE[1]

[. . .]

One of the most enduring topics in the study of cognition is the analysis of categories. This paper will use video-tapes of archaeologists in the field of classifying color to investigate how categories are socially organized as situated practices.

At times, categorization has constituted the major agenda of entire fields, such as cognitive anthropology. The classic work of Berlin and Kay (1967; 1969), on color categories provides an excellent example of one major approach to the study of human cognition. Different languages classify the color spectrum in different ways.

[. . .]

However, Berlin and Kay (1969) demonstrated that the diversity of human color systems was built on a universal infrastructure, one almost certainly linked to structures in the brain. To show this Berlin and Kay first located a basic set of color terms in a number of different languages. Then they had speakers of those languages show which color patches on a Munsell color chart fell within the boundaries of each basic color term. The Munsell chart, consisting of carefully prepared samples of precisely defined colors arranged in a grid, is the accepted reference standard for color description. When Berlin

Source: Charles Goodwin, 'Practices of color classification', *Cognitive Studies: Bulletin of the Japanese Cognitive Society* 3(2): 1996, 62–82.

and Kay compared the Munsell maps for different languages they found that all languages locate the foci of their basic color labels at roughly the same place in the color spectrum and, moreover, that a universal pattern exists for adding basic color terms to a language. If a language has only two color names they will be black and white, if it has three the third will be red, the fourth will be either green or yellow, blue will be added next, etc. This work remains one of the central accomplishments of cognitive anthropology.

The theories and methods used to analyze how human beings build and use categories are themselves shaped by deep assumptions about what counts as human cognition, where it is located, and what constitutes an interesting and important finding. Clearly visible in the work of Berlin and Kay are a number of quite pervasive assumptions about the underlying organization of both language and cognition. First, the structures that provide universal mechanisms for human cognition reside in two interrelated places: the human brain and a linguistic system. Cognition is a psychological process and its crucial machinery is found within the human skull. Second, meaning is defined in terms of reference, e.g., the range of color patches that a speaker of a particular language identifies as falling within the scope of a specific color term. Third, the basic units being samples are human languages such as English, Japanese or Tzeltal. The color systems of different languages are systematically compared with each other. Fourth, this vision of where the crucial phenomena relevant to the organization of cognition were to be found had important methodological consequences. Berlin and Kay never looked at how people use color categories to pursue a relevant course of action in the consequential scenes that make up their lifeworld. Instead, all of their informants were performing exactly the same experimental task, and, with the exception of Tzeltal speakers, all the speakers resided in the San Francisco Bay area. The notion of a community of competent practitioners was completely irrelevant to Berlin and Kay's analysis; indeed for many languages, only a single speaker was used.

It is however possible to conceptualize human cognition in ways that challenge these assumptions. Thus, with respect to the second assumption in which meaning is analyzed in terms of reference, Wittgenstein (1958; see also Baker and Hacker 1980) argued that the meaning of a term is not its bearer, the entities it refers to (e.g., shades of color). Instead the study of meaning should focus on description of the practices required to use a term appropriately within a relevant language game.

[. . .]

We will begin by looking at how archaeologists classify color as one component of the work of competently excavating a site. Rather than being lodged entirely in the world of mental representations, the perceptual task of assessing color as an archaeologist requires systematic use of specific tools, indeed the very tool used by Berlin and Kay: a Munsell color chart. As a coding framework, the chart both mediates perceptual access to the dirt being classified, and provides a color reference standard. This tool does not stand alone as a self-explicating artifact; instead its proper use is embedded within a set of systematic work practices. Moreover, these practices vary from community to community. Though the chart is used by both archaeologists and linguistic anthropologists (as well as other professions concerned with color), each discipline situates the chart within different sets of work procedures. In brief, it will be suggested that an appropriate unit for the cognitive processes involved in color discrimination is not the brain in isolation, or the categories provided by semantic systems of languages as self-contained entities, but instead the situated activity systems used by endogenous work groups to properly constitute the categories that are relevant to the work they are engaged in. Rather than sustaining an opposition between the "mental" and the "material" such activity systems seamlessly link phenomena such as the embodied actions of participants, physical tools, language use, work relevant writing practices, etc., into the patterns of coordinated action that make up the lifeworld of a workgroup.

Central to the cognitive processes that constitute science are writing practices quite unlike those typically studied by social scientists investigating literacy. In order to generate a data set – collections of observations that can be compared with each other – scientists use coding schemes to transform the world that they scrutinize into the categories and events that are relevant to the work of their profession (Cicourel 1964; 1968). When disparate events are viewed through a single coding scheme, equivalent observations become possible. The process of systematically making relevant observations about the color of the materials being examined, and then writing them on a coding form (see Figure 28.1), located a small activity system. Within it the categorization of color is mediated by both material artifacts and specific work-relevant practices. Moreover, the vision required to see color in this activity has strong temporal, historical and spatial dimensions as well; to competently perform the task the technician(s) coding the data must use a tool to look at a specific space, at a particular point in the process.

[. . .]

The form contains slots for describing the color, consistency, and texture of the dirt being examined. Those filling in the form are faced with the task of systematically examining the dirt and making appropriate entries in each slot.

The use of coding forms such as this to organize the perception of nature, events, or people within the discourse of a profession carries with it an array of perceptual and cognitive operations that have far-reaching impact. First, by

SOIL DESCRIPTION: A ZONE upper plow zone	D 1985 backdirt	B lower p
Color (Wet) 10YR 3/4	10YR 4/3 brown to dk brown	10YR 3/6 yellowish
Texture dk yellowish brown sandy clay loam	sandy loam	loamy sa
Consistency somewhat sticky somewhat plastic	fairly sticky fairly plastic	sticky somewhat
Mottles scattered light	heavily w/ 10YR 5/4 sand and areas of 10YR3/3	lightly w soil.
Cultural/Natural cultural		
Comments	silty loam. Scattered charcoal and	
	burnt earth.	

Figure 28.1

using such a system, a worker views the world from the perspective it establishes. Of all the possible ways that the earth could be looked at, the perceptual work of students using this form is focused on determining the exact color of a minute sample of dirt. They engage in active cognitive work, but the parameters of that work have been established by the system that is organizing their perception. In so far as the coding scheme established an orientation toward the world, it constitutes a structure of intentionality whose proper locus is not the isolated, Cartesian mind, but a much larger organizational system, one that is characteristically mediated through mundane bureaucratic documents such as forms.

[. . .]

Rather than standing alone as self-explicating textual objects, forms are embedded within webs of socially organized, situated practices. In order to make an entry in the slot provided for color an archaeologist must make use of another tool, the set to standard color samples provided by a Munsell chart. This chart incorporates into a portable physical object the results of a long history of scientific investigation of the properties of color. The version of this chart that archaeologists bring into the field has been tailored to the distinctive requirements of their work situation. First, the color samples are organized as pages that fit into a small loose leaf book that can be easily carried to the field. Second, since dirt typically contains only a limited range of color, only a subset of the color samples that would be found in a complete chart (approximately one fifth of the total) are necessary for the work that archaeologists do. Issues of cost also figure into this calculation. Even the reduced sample book costs $80. While this is inexpensive enough to risk taking into harsh field conditions, it is still considered a costly, valuable tool to be carefully protected. By being adapted to the specific requirements of their work the Munsell book used by archaeologists is as small, portable and inexpensive as possible. Third, circular holes are cut next to each color patch. The archaeologist holds a sample of the dirt being coded on a trowel held under the page. The trowel is moved from hole to hole until the best fit between the color of the dirt on the trowel and an adjacent patch of the chart is found.

Foucault (1970; 1986) uses the term heterotopia to mark "a relatively segregated place in which several spatial settings coexist, each being both concrete and symbolically loaded" (Ophir and Shapin 1991: 13). With elegant simplicity the Munsell page with its holes for viewing the sample of dirt on the trowel juxtaposes in a single visual field two quite different kinds of spaces: (1) actual dirt from the site at the archaeologists' feet is framed by (2) a theoretical space for the rigorous, replicable, classification of color. The

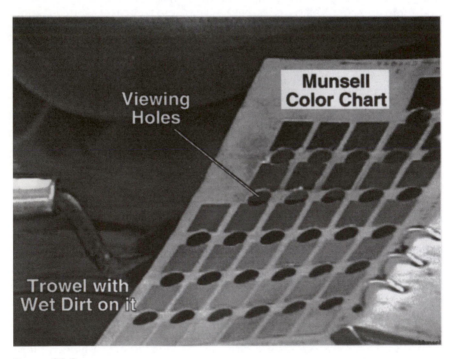

Figure 28.2

latter is both a conceptual space, the product of considerable research into properties of color, and an actual physical space instantiated in the orderly modification of variables arranged in a grid on the Munsell page. Ophir and Shapin (1991: 13) propose that in the modern West the sites where science is done are fundamentally heterotopic spaces. This notion is applicable not only to tools such as the Munsell book, but also to the excavation site itself, with its specialized personnel making visible the phenomena that define their discipline in limited, carefully organized places, such as the pits they system-atically dig. Though segregated from the everyday world just outside its borders, the site and its tools are systematically linked to the work and activ-ities of other archaeologists. Thus the Munsell book encapsulates in a material object theory and solutions developed by earlier workers at other sites faced with the task of color classification. The pages juxtaposing color patches and viewing holes that allow the dirt to be seen right next to the color sample provide an historically constituted architecture for perception.

The Munsell system organizes color description by using three variables: hue, chroma and value. Each page in the book (Figure 28.3) is organized as a

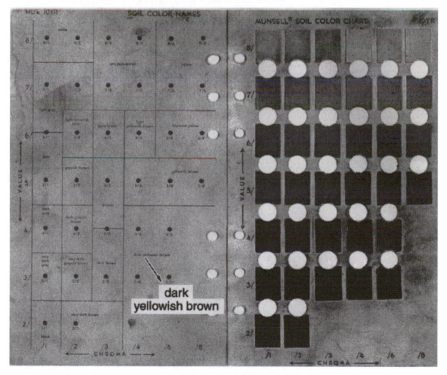

Figure 28.3

grid of chroma and value samples for a single hue. In addition to the samples and viewing holes, each Munsell page also contains several different kinds of written text: (1) numbers; (2) labels for the two axes, with value from bottom to top, and chroma from left to right; and (3) standard color names, such as "dark yellowish brown", which are found on the facing page to the left of the actual sample page (because of the reduced size and degradation of the small print on the original page I've rewritten the bottom right color name in larger type).

The page thus provides not one, but three complementary systems for identifying a reference color: (1) the actual color patch; (2) numeric coordinates specifying its position in the grid (e.g. "3/4"); and (3) color names. Moreover, these systems are not precisely equivalent to each other. For example, a single color name may include several different color patches and grid descriptions. Thus, on the page reproduced above the color name "dark yellowish brown" in the bottom right quadrant of the grid, refers to four patches/sets of coordinates: 4/4, 4/6, 3/4 and 3/6. Similarly, "yellow brown" just above it includes 5/4, 5/6 and 5/8.

Why does the Munsell page contain multiple, overlapping representations of what is apparently the same entity (e.g. a particular choice within a larger set of color categories)? The answer seems to lie in the way that each representation makes possible alternative operations and actions, and thus fits into different kinds of activities. Both the names and numbered grid coordinates can be written, and thus easily transported from the actual excavation to the other work site, such as laboratories and journals, that constitute archaeology as a profession. Unlike the names, the numbers can be used in statistical analysis (the patches are carefully constructed to represent equal intervals). Moreover, as noted in the preface to the Munsell soil color book that archaeologists use, numbers are "especially useful for international correlation, since no translation of color names is needed." However, despite its greater precision, the number system has its own distinct liabilities. In order to grasp the color being referred to as "10 YR 3/4" a reader needs access to a Munsell book. Color names, such as "dark yellowish brown" are thus more appropriate than the numbers for general journal publication, since they can be recognized and compared, at least roughly but adequately for the purposes of the moment, by any speaker of the language. The outcome of the activity of color classification initiated by the empty square on the coding form is thus a set of portable linguistic objects that can easily be incorporated into the unfolding chains of inscription that lead step by step from the dirt at the site to reports in the archaeological literature (see also Hutchins 1995: 123). However, as arbitrary linguistic signs produced in a medium that does not actually make visible color, neither the color names nor the numbers allow direct visual comparison between a sample of dirt and a reference color. This is precisely what the color patches and viewing holes make possible. Moreover, as discrete, bounded places on the surface of the page they can be identified not only through language, but also by pointing. In brief, rather than simply specifying unique points in a larger color space, the Munsell chart is used in multiple overlapping activities (comparing a reference color and a patch of dirt as part of the work of classification, transporting those results back to the lab, comparing samples, publishing reports, etc.), and thus represents the "same" entity, a particular color, in multiple ways, each of which makes possible different kinds of operations because of the unique properties of each representational system. [. . .]

The chart does not stand alone as an isolated tool; instead, its proper, appropriate use is situated within a larger set of work-relevant practices. First, a place for taking a sample of dirt from the site has to be chosen. In its original location in the ground itself the dirt to be sampled is embedded within a dense, complex visual environment. A trowel is used to lift the sample from this dense perceptual field so that it can be scrutinized in isolation. A figure constituted as the object of current work-relevant attention, the dirt on the tip of the trowel, is quite literally extracted from an amorphous ground. This process of *positioning for perception* is one particular type of *highlighting* (Goodwin 1994), one of the most general practices used to reshape phenomena in the domain being scrutinized by a workgroup so that just those events which are relevant to the tasks they are engaged in are made salient.

Archaeologists know from experience that the apparent color of a bit of dirt can be modified by many factors. After the dirt has been placed on the trowel it is sprayed with water. By squirting all samples with water some of the variables relevant to the perception of its color can be controlled by creating a consistent environment for viewing. The moment where the archaeologist gazes at the dirt through the Munsell chart is thus but one stage within a larger sequence of temporally unfolding practices. Mundane, routine work with the Munsell chart seems quite distant from the abstract world of archaeological theory, and the debates that are currently animating the discipline. However, the encounter between coding scheme and the world that occurs as the archaeologist in the field holds a sample of dirt under the Munsell page, is one example of a key locus for scientific practice. This is the place where the multifaceted complexity of "nature" is transformed into the phenomenal categories that make up the work environment of a scientific discipline. It is precisely here that nature is transformed into culture.

Despite the rigorous way in which the combination of a tool such as the Munsell color chart, and the practices developed by archaeologists for its relevant and appropriate use, structure perception of the dirt being scrutinized, finding the correct category for the classification of a bit of dirt is not

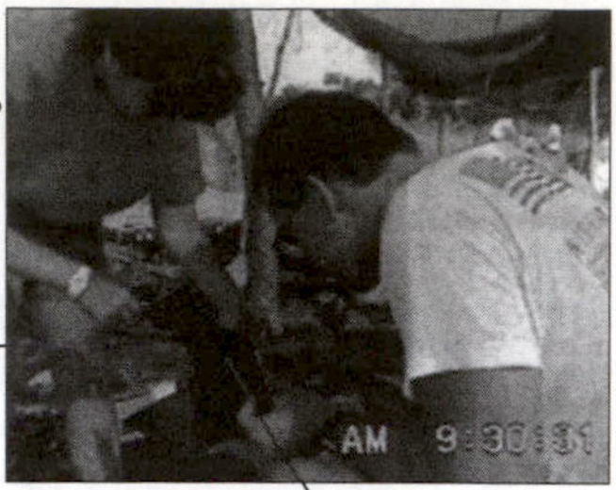

```
 1  Pam:    Okay that should be, wet enough.
 2              (1.5)
 3  Pam:    ° Hmph  (0.7) ((holding trowel))
 4  Jeff:   We're lookin at that right there?
 5              (0.3)
 6  Pam:    Mmm,
 7              (0.4)
 8  Jeff:   Much darker than tha:t.────────
 9            ┌there.
10  Pam:    └Yeah. I'm not-
11          I'm just tryin ta put it in the:re.=
12          =eh hih an(h)ywhere. °hih heh huh
13  Jeff:   I'll take it. ((takes trowel))
14              (2.0)
15  Pam:    Down.
16              (1.2)
17  Pam:    En this one. ((Points))────────
18              (0.4) ((Moves Trowel))
19  Jeff:   yuhhh?
20              (1.8)
21  Pam:    °Try that one? ((Points))
22              (0.8)
23  Pam:    Fou:r.
24              (0.8)
25  Pam:    Is it that?
26          Na: That's- not-
27          ↑What was the browness of that?
28  Jeff:   °mmhh,
```

Munsell Book

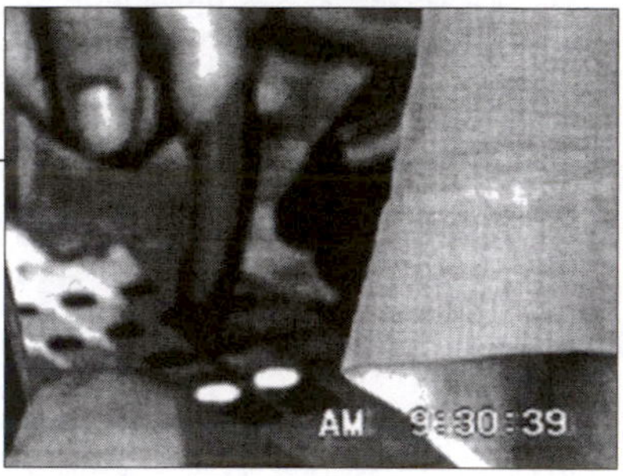

Figure 28.4a

an automatic, or even easy task. According to the instructions at the beginning of the Munsell book:

> Rarely will the color of the sample be perfectly matched by any color in the chart. The probability of having a perfect matching of the sample color is less than one in one hundred.

Rather than automatic matching, the person doing the coding is charged with making a competent judgement, deciding which of the chart's colors the sample falls between, and which reference color provides the closest, but by no means exact, match. Moreover, the very way in which the Munsell chart provides a context-free reference standard creates problems of its own.

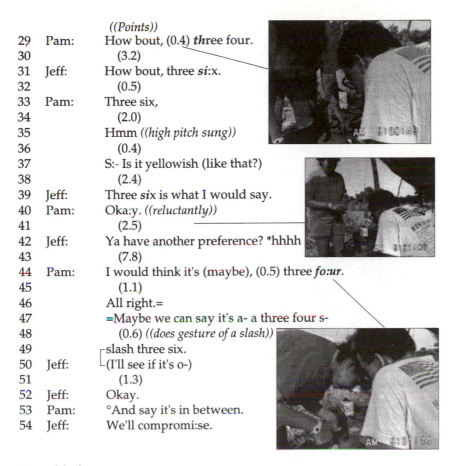

```
                  ((Points))
29   Pam:    How bout, (0.4) three four.
30                 (3.2)
31   Jeff:   How bout, three si:x.
32                 (0.5)
33   Pam:    Three six,
34                 (2.0)
35           Hmm ((high pitch sung))
36                 (0.4)
37           S:- Is it yellowish (like that?)
38                 (2.4)
39   Jeff:   Three six is what I would say.
40   Pam:    Oka:y. ((reluctantly))
41                 (2.5)
42   Jeff:   Ya have another preference? *hhhh
43                 (7.8)
44   Pam:    I would think it's (maybe), (0.5) three fo:ur.
45                 (1.1)
46           All right.=
47           =Maybe we can say it's a- a three four s-
48                 (0.6) ((does gesture of a slash))
49          ┌slash three six.
50   Jeff:  └(I'll see if it's o-)
51                 (1.3)
52   Jeff:   Okay.
53   Pam:    °And say it's in between.
54   Jeff:   We'll compromi:se.
```

Figure 28.4b

The color patches on the chart are glossy, while dirt never is, so that the chart color and the sample color never look exactly the same. In Figure 28.4 two students at the field school looking at exactly the same dirt and reference colors disagree as to how it should be classified.

In this sequence the task of color classification is organized within a situated activity system that links a range of apparently disparate phenomena, including talk, the bodies of the participants, the dirt they are examining, and the tools being used to scrutinize that dirt, into a coherent course of action. It is useful to begin with consideration of the participation framework visible in the orientation of their bodies. For Goffman (1961: 7) "focused interaction occurs when people effectively agree to sustain for a time a single focus of cognitive and visual attention." Orientation to such a common focus

organizes the bodies of participants in an encounter into visible patterns of
mutual orientation which frame the talk and other interaction which occurs
within them (Kendon 1990; [Chapter 22]). Goodwin (1981) has demonstrated the central importance of mutual gaze between speakers and hearers
in the organization of turns-at-talk in conversation. However, here the parties
are gazing not at each other, but instead at the Munsell page with the dirt
sample beneath it. This chart with its viewing holes organizes not only the
color spectrum represented on its surface, but also the embodied actions of
those who use it. Its proper use proposes a particular orientation of the body
and focus of attention. The participation framework necessary for the analysis
of what is happening here thus includes not only the bodies of the participants, but also the tools they are using. Color classification could be done,
indeed characteristically is done, by a single archaeologist peering through
the Munsell book alone. In light of this it is possible to see the defining
feature noted in Goffman's definition, a focus of cognitive and visual attention, as applying not only to focused multi-party interaction, but also the
engagement of a single party with a relevant tool that organizes a visible
focus of attention (though quite properly this situation would fall outside the
scope of Goffman's focus on multi-party interaction). In brief, rather than
drawing an analytic bubble that ends at the actors' bodies, it is useful to
extend the notion of participation framework to encompass as well the tools
that participants are working with.

Let us now look more closely at how action is organized within this
framework. Use of the Munsell chart structures the activity of color classification in a quite specific way. To locate the proper color category the sample
is moved from color patch to color patch under the ordered grid provided
by the page until the best match is found. Through use of the chart the
process of color classification has been reorganized as a spatial task. Consider
for a moment some of the issues posed in the analysis of action that includes
an intrinsic spatial component. A goal in American football occurs when a
player carrying a ball crosses a particular line drawn on the field where the
game is played. The action can be neither defined nor analyzed by looking
at the body of the running player alone. Instead, the playing field as a visible
arrangement in space that carries specific kinds of meaning as defined by the
rules of the game, makes possible forms of action (balls going out of bounds,
touchdowns, etc.) that could not exist without it. The Munsell chart, the
place where the archaeologists performing this classification are looking so
intently, provides a similar arena for the constitution of meaningful action.
At line 17 Pam moves her hand to the space above the page and points at a
particular color patch while saying "En this one." Within the field of action
created by the activity in progress this is not simply an indexical gesture,

but a proposal that the indicated color might be the one they are searching for. It creates a new context in which a reply from Jeff is the expected next action.

In line 19 Jeff rejects the proposed color. His move occurs after a noticeable silence in line 18. Dispreferred actions in conversation, such as this rejection, are frequently preceded by gaps (Pomerantz 1984). However, when the tape is examined something else seems to be going on. The silence is not an empty space, but a place occupied by its own relevant activity (Goodwin 1980). Before a competent answer to Pam's proposal in line 17 can be made, the dirt being evaluated has to be placed under the viewing hole next the color sample she indicated, so that the two can be compared. During line 18 Jeff moves the trowel to this position. Because of the spatial organization of this activity, specific actions have to be performed before a relevant task, a color comparison, can be competently performed. In brief, in this activity the spatial organization of the tools being worked with, and the sequential organization of talk in interaction interact with each other in the production of relevant action (e.g., getting to a place where one can make an expected answer requires rearrangement of the visual field being scrutinized so that the judgement being requested can be competently performed).

This has a number of additional consequences. First, Pam's own ability to evaluate the appropriateness of the color she proposed changes when Jeff moves the sample to the correct viewing hole. Only then is she in a position to rigorously compare the dirt with the Munsell color. Pam's action of pointing to a particular color patch at line 17 could be heard as a request to perform this action, to put them both in a position where that patch might be evaluated, rather than a definitive judgement that is subsequently disagreed with. Indeed, a moment later, in line 23, Pam suggests another possible color. However when the trowel is moved to the appropriate viewing hole she herself rejects the match, saying in lines 25–26 "Is it that? Na: That's- not-".

This process of color classification involves a sequence of movements through space and time. What can be seen and evaluated changes as each step in this process. The relevant unit for analyzing the problematic status of a specific proposal is not primarily the mental state of a particular actor, but instead the different possibilities for seeing relevant phenomena that alternative positions in this sequence provide.

Second, it is sometimes argued that abstract, context-free language is not only superior to context-bound talk (the latter argued to constitute a restricted linguistic code), but a defining characteristic of rational discourse in institutions such as science (see for example Bernstein 1964). Here we see people who are actually doing scientific classification making extensive use of indexical language ("this one" line 17, "that one" line 21, etc.) tied to pointing gestures. Moreover the very instrument they are looking at and pointing to contains both (relatively) context free numbers for describing these entities, and a set of color names that their community has explicitly agreed to treat as a common standard. However, there are very good reasons for use of indexical language here. First, the task posed at this point in the process is visual comparison of the reference color with the sample of dirt. Locating the scientific name or number for that sample requires an extra step, a look away from the color of the sample to the borders of the chart or even the facing page. By way of contrast, pointing right at the sample heightens focus on its relevant visual properties, which is precisely the task of the moment. Reading off the correct name from the chart can be done later, after a particular patch has been located as the best match. Second, this gesture is lodged within multiple spatial frameworks that are relevant to the organization of the activity in progress. In addition to the way that the pointing finger locates a particular patch within the larger array, which we can gloss as the *reference space*, the hand carrying the gesture also constitutes a relevant action within the *participation space* being sustained through the orientation of the participants' bodies toward the materials (chart and dirt sample) that are the focus of their attention; Pam's hand moves right into Jeff's line of sight as he gazes toward the chart. Rather than telling him what color to look at, she shows him. Third, as noted above, Pam's proposal constitutes a request that he move the sample to the viewing hole for this patch. By pointing at the patch she makes a relevant move within the *local action space* by showing him where to position the sample next. In brief, the proposed advantages of apparently abstract, context-free descriptions, such as the standard names or coordinates, pertain to use of the Munsell system in a quite different domain, such as publishing findings in journal articles (which is of course contextually organized in its own right). Within the activity of color classification that is occurring here Pam's gestures are not only appropriate, but rich, multi-functional actions.

Indeed the data suggest that there might be a systematic ordering of representations throughout this sequence, with pointing being the first choice, and numerical coordinates the second. At line 19 Pam starts to move her extended index finger to a particular color patch. What she says while making this movement "How bout," explicitly classifies what her hand is doing as a next proposal. She then delays the onward progression of her talk until her moving finger actually lands on the appropriate patch. Her action of proposing a particular color category as the best match is done through the integrated coordination of talk, body movement, and the representational field provided by the Munsell chart. Only as her finger is leaving the chart does she state vocally the grid coordinates that name this patch "*three* four." In a very real

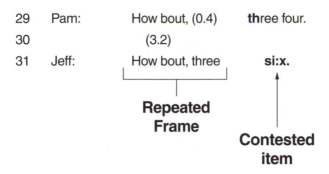

Figure 28.5

sense the syntactic construction initiated by "How bout" has two comple-
ments, first a visible reference color specified by the pointing finger, and
second a verbal name for that color, spoken as the gesturing finger departs.
Pam's finger on the patch, in addition to showing Jeff the color she wants
him to evaluate, might also help her read the coordinates. Her raised finger
provides a prominent, fixed reference point as she moves her eyes to each
of the chart's borders to find the correct numbers. The third representational system provided by the chart, the standard set of color names, is never
used in this sequence. These color names do not uniquely identify reference
colors, and they are written on the page facing the color samples. This page
is being held in a position that makes it difficult to see.

Jeff never points to a color patch. He can't, since one of his hands is
holding the Munsell book and the other the trowel with the dirt sample.
However he does perform an action that is structurally similar to Pam's
points by moving the dirt sample to specific viewing holes.

At line 31 (see Figure 28.5) Jeff uses the resources provided by the organization of talk in interaction to make visible explicit disagreement with Pam's
position. Rather than simply proposing a new color, he reuses the structure of
her utterance, the "How bout" frame, but replaces her proposal with his own,
giving "**si:x**", the syllable that marks the difference, enhanced contrastive
stress.

[. . .]

Recently renewed attention has been focused on the body, and the nature
of embodied experience, by scholars in a number of different disciplines.
The situated activity system of doing color classification, with its tools and
distinctive tasks, creates a framework within which the bodies of the participants are seen to be doing specific things. This visible meaningfulness arises

not from the body in isolation, but rather from the way actors can be seen to be using particular tools to perform relevant tasks. The conclusion to this sequence provides one example. Pam does not acquiesce to Jeff's "Three six" (see lines 33–37) but finally agrees reluctantly to let it stand. As she says "Oka:y" at line 40 she stands up so that she is no longer gazing intently at the Munsell chart with its dirt sample (see the fourth picture from the top in Figure 28.4). The end of the classification activity is thus marked by the removal of her body from a position required to perform that task.

However, recognizing her reluctance, Jeff reopens the task, asking at line 42 if she has "another preference." A quite long silence ensues before she offers "**th**ree four" as an alternative to his "three **si:x**." Research in conversation analysis (Pomerantz 1984; Sacks [1973] 1987; 1995) has demonstrated that, as part of a structural preference for agreement, disagreements are frequently preceded by long silences (which can do a number of different jobs, such as giving the party whose talk is being disagreed with an opportunity to revise it before overt disagreement becomes explicit). While upcoming disagreement is certainly relevant, the silence here is occupied by Pam visibly putting herself in a position to produce a careful, competent answer. Just after Jeff asks if she has another preference Pam walks around to the side of the Munsell book, leans down and grasps it with her hands while putting her head as close to its surface as Jeff's is (see the picture attached to line 44 in the transcript), and then stares intently at the page with the dirt sample under it for several seconds before offering her alternative category. People are sometimes described producing a "thoughtful" answer. Here through a display of her body intensely scrutinizing the materials required for a competent judgement Pam visibly demonstrates that the answer she eventually produces is the product of the systematic practices required to make such a judgement in this activity.

[. . .]

Finally, the visible structure of the Munsell chart interacts with talk in more subtle ways as well. In a paper investigating how intricate pun-like processes organize some aspects of talk Sacks (1973) has described how the selection of words and images by a speaker can be influenced by quite diverse properties of the talk that preceded it, e.g. not only its explicit, topic-relevant semantic structure but also its sound structure, the scenes it represents, etc. In the present data, when offering the compromise that ends the activity Pam uses both the word slash ("we ca say it's a- a three four s- slash three six") and a gesture depicting a slash. To determine the grid coordinates of her proposed category she has just been looking at the borders of the chart where row and column labels are written as numbers next to slashes ("3/" or "4/").

The graphic organization of the Munsell page shapes not only her task of color classification, but also her talk in many complex ways.

With respect to the scope of the disagreement that occurs here it should be noted that the 3/4 and 3/6 colors patches on the 10YR page are extremely similar to each other. I can barely tell the difference between them. Both fall within the boundaries of a single color name "dark yellowish brown." For all practical purposes, including subsequent analysis of the data being coded here, whether the color of the dirt is a 3/4 or a 3/6 will not matter at all. The carefulness of the students here, and their unwillingness to acquiesce to an answer that one does not think is quite right, in no way undermines the scientific work being done here. Instead, the trustworthy, objective character of the descriptions they enter on the coding sheet emerges precisely from their detailed attention to the systematic practices used to constitute the categories of their profession, and their recognition of the real difficulties involved in unambiguously classifying complex continuous phenomena into discrete categories.

The definitiveness provided by a coding scheme typically erases from subsequent documentation the cognitive and perceptual uncertainties that these students are grappling with, as well as the work practices within which they are embedded, leading to what Shapin (1989) has called "the invisible technician."

This paper has not attempted to challenge the findings of Berlin and Kay (e.g. to propose a different sequence of color universals, or even to suggest that theirs is wrong), but instead to explore the possibilities provided by an alternative geography of cognition, one in which the crucial phenomena relevant to color classification are not located exclusively in the human brain, but instead in the situated activity systems that make up the lifeworld of a work group. Within such systems human cognition is embedded not only in biology and linguistic structure, but also history, culture and the details of local, situated interaction. By using historically constituted tools new archaeologists, such as the students examined here, are able to build on the work of their ancestors in not only archaeology but also other fields faced with the task of systematically describing color. The solutions these predecessors have found, and built into material artifacts such as the Munsell color chart, shape in fine detail the processes of cognition implicated in work-relevant classification of color. However these tools cannot be analyzed as self-contained objects in themselves. They only become meaningful when used to accomplish relevant tasks within local activity systems. As a particular kind of hetrotopia that juxtaposes in a single visual field the world being classified and an artfully crafted system of classification (one that contains multiple representations of the same category, each suited to alternative tasks), the Munsell page provides an example of an historically shaped, locally constituted architecture for perception. The analytic unit required for describing how a competent member of this social group, an archaeologist, understands an expression such as "dark yellowish brown" when used in the context of her work, is not the English language as a homogeneous, autonomous structural system, but instead a situated activity system that includes not only semantic categories, but also specific tools, such as the Munsell book, and the practices required to use these tools appropriately. When multiple parties work on this task together the full resources provided by the organization of talk-in-interaction for shaping intersubjectivity within process of coordinated action are mobilized. The objectivity of the work of coding is provided for by the in-situ articulation of a dense web of local, accountable practice, built through the actual spatio-temporal arrangement of talk, gestures and relevant tools. The products of this process are trustworthy classifications that can be transported as written inscriptions to other work sites (excavations, offices, journals, etc.) that constitute the field of archaeology. The outcome of the activity of color classification initiated by the empty space on the coding form is a fully realized world of space, cognition and lived action embedded within the worklife of a particular scientific discipline.

Note

1.   I am deeply indebted to Dr. Gail Wagner and the students at her archaeological field school for allowing us to videotape their work, and to Candy Goodwin and Aug Nishizaka for insightful comments on this analysis.

References

Baker, G. P. and P. M. S. Hacker (1980) *Wittgenstein: Understanding and Meaning*, Chicago: The University of Chicago Press.
Berlin, B. and P. Kay (1967) 'Universality and evolution of basic color terms', working paper no. 1, Berkeley, CA: Laboratory for Language Behavior Research.
—— (1969) *Basic Color Terms: Their Universality and Evolution*, Berkeley, CA: University of California Press.
Bernstein, B. (1964) 'Elaborated and restricted codes: their social origins and some consequences', in Gumperz, J. J. and Hymes, D. (eds) *The Ethnography of Communication*, *American Anthropologist*, 66(6) Petronio. II: 55–69.
Cicourel, A. V. (1964) *Method and Measurement in Sociology*, New York: Free Press.
—— (1968) *The Social Organization of Juvenile Justice*, New York: Wiley.

Foucault, M. (1970) *The Order of Things: An Archaeology of Human Sciences*, New York: Vintage Books.

—— (1986) 'Of other spaces', *Diacritics*, 16: 22–27.

Goodwin, C. (1981) *Conversational Organization: Interaction Between Speakers and Hearers*, New York: Academic Press.

—— (1994) Professional Vision, *American Anthropologist*, 96(3), 606–633.

Hutchins, E. (1995) *Cognition in the Wild*, Cambridge, MA: MIT Press.

Kendon, A. (1990) *Conducting Interaction: Patterns of Behavior in Focused Encounters*, Cambridge: Cambridge University Press.

Ophir, A. and Shapin, S. (1991) 'The place of knowledge: a methodological survey', *Science in Context*, 4(1): 3–21.

Pomerantz, A. (1984) 'Agreeing and disagreeing with assessments: some features of preferred/dispreferred turn shapes', in Atkinson, J. M. and Heritage, J. (eds) *Structures of Social Action: Studies in Conversation Analysis*, Cambridge: Cambridge University Press, 57–101.

Sacks, H. (1973) 'On some puns with some intimations', in Shuy, R. W. (ed.) *Report of the Twenty-Third Annual Round Table Meeting on Linguistics and Language Studies*, Washington, DC: Georgetown University Press, 135–44.

—— ([1973] 1987) 'On the preferences for agreement and contiguity in sequences in conversation', in Button G. and Lee, J. R. E. (eds) *Talk and Social Organisation*, Clevedon, England: Multilingual Matters, 54–69.

—— (1995) *Lectures on Conversation: Volumes 1 and 2*. Edited by Jefferson, G. Oxford: Blackwell.

Shapin, S. (1989), 'The invisible technician', *American Scientist*, 77, 554–63.

Wittgenstein, L. (1958), *Philosophical Investigations*, Anscombe, G. E. M. and Rhees, R. (eds) translated Anscombe, G. E. M., 2nd edn, Oxford: Blackwell.

PART SIX

Power, ideology and control

Editors' Introduction to Part Six

EVER SINCE THE WORK of Roger Brown and his associates (Brown and Gilman [1960] 1972; Brown and Ford 1964) on pronouns and other forms of address, *power*, and its relational counterpart *solidarity*, have remained firmly at the centre of discourse analytic and sociolinguistic research into interpersonal and intergroup relations. In this Part we have included six chapters representing different approaches to the study of discourse and power, while most chapters in Parts Three and Four deal more expressly with intimacy, involvement, detachment and other manifestations of inter-personal distance.

A related concept which these chapters explore is the belief systems or *ideologies* underlying different power relations. Following the work of Billig (e.g., 1990) in rhetoric and van Dijk (e.g., 1998) in discourse analysis, it is demon-strably the case that ideology, not unlike social categories in general (see the Editors' Introduction to Part Five) is intimately related to situated practices of day-to-day interaction. In fact, van Dijk argues that it is through discourse and other semiotic practices that ideologies are formulated, reproduced and reinforced. Accomplishing ideology is an important end in political (both with capital and small 'p') discourse because its acceptance by the audience, espe-cially mass media audiences, ensures the establishment of group rapport. As Fowler (1985: 66) puts it, through the emergence of a 'community of ideology, a shared system of beliefs about reality' creates group identity.

We understand the term *ideology* as social (general and abstract) representations shared by members of a group and used by them to accomplish everyday social practices: acting and communicating (e.g., van Dijk 1998; Billig *et al*. 1988; Fowler 1985). These representations are organised into systems which are deployed by social classes and other groups 'in order to make sense of, figure out and render intelligible the way society works' (Hall 1996: 26).

Billig *et al*. (1988) make a distinction between 'lived' and 'intellectual' ideology. The former term is close to the way ideology was defined in the preceding paragraph. The latter term is understood as an overall, coherent system of thought: political programmes or manifestos, philosophical orientations or religious codifications. This distinction is useful as it reflects the working of ideology on two levels: the participants' coherent, formal systems of belief (i.e., their intellectual ideologies), and their objectives in self- and other-presentation, expression of opinions which represent and satisfy their and their groups' preferred views of reality constructed to suit local goals of interaction (see Jaworski and Galasiński 1998). One of the ideologically relevant discourse structures pointed to by van Dijk (1988: 209) is interaction, and, more specifically, the realm of interactional control or legitimisation of ideologies (see Jaworski and Galasiński 2000). Who starts the exchange, who ends it, who initiates new topics, who interrupts whom, and which address forms are used in the course of interaction, may all be indicative of the interlocutor's power and as such is ideologically charged, or to use van Dijk's (1988: 209) term, has an 'ideological dimension'.

Teun van Dijk's contribution to this Part (Chapter 32) is an example of the sinister and twisted working of discursive processes which are involved in the legitimising of racist ideology in face-to-face conversation (interview) and in newspaper articles. The practices are 'sinister' and 'twisted' because they depend on the overt denial of the underlying ideology. It takes a fine-grained textual analysis of discourse for van Dijk to demonstrate how the socially unacceptable positions are overtly denied but covertly present in the speakers'/writers' accounts of race and ethnic relations.

The original article, too long for us to be able to reproduce here in its entirety, offers a simple taxonomy of *denials of racism*:

1   act–denial ('I did not do/say that at all').
2   control–denial ('I did not do/say that on purpose', 'It was an accident').
3   intention–denial ('I did not mean that', 'You got me wrong').
4   goal–denial ('I did not do/say that, in order to [. . .]').

(van Dijk 1992: 92)

Why do white people put so much effort into disguising their racism with such regularity? Racism is an ideology, which officially does not find social approval. Therefore, denying racism (despite one's beliefs, or one's 'lived' ideology) is an important aspect of positive self-presentation, whether it is a private individual, journalist, or MP (one part of the original article which is not reproduced here examines denials of racism in parliamentary debates). On the other hand, maintaining racist ideology is an expression and reinforcement of white, middle-class power over ethnic minorities.

Much of the research on power, ideology and control in discourse falls under the aegis of critical discourse analysis (CDA – see the general Introduction), which has adopted the social constructionist view of language (see the Editors' Introduction to Part Five), rather than one of language as a 'mirror' of social relations. Thus, CDA examines the structure of spoken and written texts in search of politically and ideologically salient features, which are constitutive of the (re)produced power relations without often being evident to participants.

Some of the linguistic features discussed in the critical linguistic framework include: nominalisation, passivisation, and sequencing. They are used for ideological control as 'masking devices' (Ng and Bradac 1993) as they allow speakers or writers to withhold the identity of the actors and causality of events. For example, nominalisation: **Failure** to display this notice will result in **prosecution**, and passivisation: John was murdered (Fowler 1985: 71) remove the element of agency and, consequently, responsibility (compare: John was murdered by the police). Exploitation of sequencing as in: Fords I find particularly reliable (Fowler 1985: 72), is a rhetorical device serving the purpose of manipulating the addressee's attention. The seemingly semantically equivalent sentences: Employers always quarrel with unions, and Unions always quarrel with employers (Ng and Bradac 1993: 156) give varying impressions of importance as to who quarrels the most.

Another area of discourse analysis in which power, dominance and control have been major agenda-setting issues is one we have discussed briefly already – language and gender. Women have been shown to be linguistically dominated by men, whose assertive and aggressive communication strategies are not 'mere' cultural differences between the sexes but manifestations of male dominance over females (Henley and Kramarae 1991). However, as Tannen (1993) argues, different discourse strategies do not uniformly create dominance or powerlessness. One has to look at their 'meaning' in relation to context, the conversational styles of the participants and the interaction between different speakers' styles and strategies. Only then might it be possible to interpret such strategies as silence, interruption or indirectness as expressions of power, powerlessness, assertion, aggressiveness or co-operation (see also Holmes, Chapter 20; Cameron, Chapter 26).

The first two chapters of this Part represent the work on discourse and power from two major social theorists: Pierre Bourdieu and Michel Foucault. As we have pointed out in the general Introduction, their interest in discourse is not so much in empirical examination of actual, interactional data, but, as in the case of Giddens (Chapter 24), in discourse as an abstract vehicle for social and political processes. Language in Bourdieu's (1986; 1991; 1993; Chapter 29) theory of social practice is related to his notion of *habitus*, i.e., internalised group norms or dispositions whose task is to regulate and generate the actions (practices), perceptions and representations of individuals, and to mediate the social structures which they inhabit. Two important and interrelated aspects of habitus are that it reflects the social structures in which it was acquired and also reproduces these structures. Thus, a person who was brought up in a working-class background will manifest a set of dispositions which are different from those acquired by a person from a middle-class background and these differences will, in turn, reproduce the class divisions between both individuals (and their groups).

For Bourdieu, language is a locus of struggle for power and authority in that some types of language (styles, accents, dialects, codes, and so on) are presupposed to be 'correct', 'distinguished' or 'legitimate' in opposition to those which are 'incorrect' or 'vulgar'. Those who use (in speaking or writing) the varieties ranked as acceptable, exert a degree of control over those with the dominated linguistic habitus (Bourdieu 1991: 60). The field of linguistic production, however, can be manipulated in that the symbolic capital claimed by the authority of 'legitimate' language may be reclaimed in the process of negotiation 'by a metadiscourse concerning the conditions of use of discourse' (p. 505). In sum,

> The habitus . . . provides individuals with a sense of how to act and respond in the course of their daily lives. It 'orients' their actions and inclinations without strictly determining them. It gives them a 'feel for the game', a sense of what is appropriate in the circumstances and what is not, a 'practical sense'.
>
> (Thompson 1991: 13)

Foucault's model of power is 'productive' (Mills 1997). For him, power is dispersed throughout all of social relations and as a force which prevents some actions but enables others. However, power is not confined to large-scale, macro processes of politics and society. It is a *potential* present in all everyday exchanges and social encounters. This point is taken up by Ian Hutchby (Chapter 34) in his analysis of locally produced patterns of power and resistance in argumentative talk of phone-in radio programmes. His methodology is conversation analytic (see the general Introduction; Schegloff, Chapter 6; Schegloff and Sacks, Chapter 15). But like Foucault, he defines power not as a set of attributes characterising any one person, but 'as a set of potentials which, while always present, can be variably exercised, resisted, shifted around and struggled over by social agents' (p. 586). In Foucault's system, one of the significant influences of power is in constituting different versions of individuals' subjectivity (see Editors' Introduction to Part Five). For example, in the extract from *The History of Sexuality* (Chapter 30) it transpires that in the Victorian era, children's sexuality (especially male masturbation) was not 'simply' suppressed, but that a certain version of acceptable sexuality was constructed for children.

This constitutive aspect of discourse with regard to the subjective individual selves is very clear in Caldas-Coulthard's chapter on women's sex stories in women's magazines. Far from repressing *all* talk about (illegitimate) sex of women, women's magazines publish highly formulaic texts, which reproduce traditional, dominant ideologies of women's sexuality as a taboo; these stories in which women 'speak' (in a voice mediated by the editor) about sex they have had with male prostitutes is framed as 'transgression', a deviation from the desired and accepted norm of married life and sex within marriage. In this way, conservative patterns of power and patriarchal dominance reinforce women's traditional subjectivities as defined by and dependent on men.

Another important aspect of Foucault's (1997) view of power is that it is explicitly linked to *knowledge*. Let us take Mills's (1997: 21) illustration of this issue:

> [W]hat is studied in schools and universities is the result of struggles over whose version of events is sanctioned. Knowledge is often the product of the subjugation of objects, or perhaps it can be seen as the process through which subjects are constituted as subjugated; for example, when consulting a university library catalogue, if you search under the term 'women', you will find a vast selection of books and articles discussing the oppression of women, the psychology of women, the physical ailments that women suffer

from, and so on. If you search under the term 'men' you will not find the same wealth of information.

Mehan's chapter (Chapter 33) 'Oracular reasoning in a psychiatric exam' is another, excellent example of the power/knowledge interface. In his study, a panel of psychiatrists and a patient diagnosed as schizophrenic put forward their arguments to each other in order (for the panel) to decide whether the patient can be released from the mental hospital (a kind of negative gate-keeping exercise). As Mehan demonstrates, both sides come to the examination totally unprepared to accept the opposite (and conflicting) views of the other party; the patient claims he is ready to be released from the hospital and the panel sees him as totally unfit to be released. Both sides engage in an argument trying to sanction their version of reality but in the end it is the party which can command greater power, i.e., the panel, whose version of the 'truth' about the patient becomes dominant. As Mehan (p. 573) aptly puts it:

> All people define situations as real; but when powerful people define situations as real, then they are real *for everybody involved* in their consequences.

In sum, Part Six offers a selection of readings which discuss power from a number of different positions and in several different contexts. Principally, we see these chapters as conceptualising power in two basic ways: as an attribute of 'unequal' relations, defined so pre-discursively in institutional or otherwise contexts (e.g., parent–child, teacher–pupil, officer–private, employer–employee), and/or as an emergent interactional quality (between 'equals' or 'non-equals') through the strategic deployment of strategies of language and other symbolic systems (see Grimshaw 1990; Fowler *et al.* 1979; Fairclough 1989; Sarangi and Slembrouck 1996).

References

Billig, M. (1990) 'Stacking the cards of ideology: the history of the *Sun Royal Album*', *Discourse & Society* 1: 17–37.

Billig, M., Condor, S., Edwards, D., Gane, M., Middleton, D. and Radley, A. R. (1988) *Ideological Dilemmas*, London: Sage.

Bourdieu, P. (1986) *Distinction: A Social Critique of the Judgement of Taste*, London: Routledge.

—— (1991) *Language and Symbolic Power*, Cambridge: Polity Press.

—— (1993) *The Field of Cultural Production: Essays on Art and Literature*, Cambridge: Polity Press.

Brown, R. and Ford, M. (1964) 'Address in American English', in Hymes, D. (ed.) *Language in Culture and Society*, New York: Harper & Row, 234–44.

Brown, R. and Gilman, A. (1972) 'The pronouns of power and solidarity', in Giglioli, P. P. (ed.) *Language and Social Context*, Harmondsworth: Penguin, 256–82. [First published in: Sebeok, T. A. (ed.) *Style in Language*, Cambridge, MA: MIT Press, 253–77.]

Fairclough, N. (1989) *Language and Power*, London: Longman.

Foucault, M. (1997) *Power/Knowledge*, Hemel Hempstead: Harvester.

Fowler, R. (1985) 'Power', in van Dijk, T. (ed.) *Handbook of Discourse Analysis*, vol. 4, London: Academic Press, 61–82.

Fowler, R., Hodge, R., Kress, G. R. and Trew, T. (1979) *Language and Control*, London: Routledge & Kegan Paul.

Grimshaw, A. (1990) 'Research on conflict talk: antecedents, resources, findings, directions', in Grimshaw, A. (ed.) *Conflict Talk*, Cambridge: Cambridge University Press, 280–324.

Hall, S. (1996) 'The problem of ideology: Marxism without guarantees', in Morley, D. and Chen, K. H. (eds) *Stuart Hall: Critical Dialogues in Cultural Studies*, London: Routledge, 25–46.

Henley, N. and Kramarae, C. (1991) 'Miscommunication, gender, and power', in Coupland, N., Wiemann, J. M. and Giles, H. (eds) *'Miscommunication' and Problematic Talk*, Newbury Park, CA: Sage, 18–43.

Jaworski, A. and Galasiński. D. (1998) 'The last Romantic hero: Lech Wałęsa's image-building in TV presidential debates', *Text* 18.

—— (2000) 'Vocative address forms and ideological legitimisation in political debates', *Discourse & Society* 11.

Mills, S. (1997) *Discourse*, London: Routledge.

Ng, S. H. and Bradac, J. J. (1993) *Power in Language: Verbal Communication and Social Influence*, Newbury Park, CA: Sage.

Sarangi, S. and Slembrouck, S. (1996) *Language, Bureaucracy and Social Control*, London: Longman.

Tannen, D. (1993) 'The relativity of linguistic strategies: rethinking power and solidarity in gender and dominance', in Tannen, D. (ed.) *Gender and Conversational Interaction*, New York: Oxford University Press, 165–88.

Van Dijk, T. A. (1992) 'Discourse and the denial of racism', *Discourse & Society* 3/1: 87–118.

—— (1998) *Ideology*, London: Sage.

Chapter 29

Pierre Bourdieu

LANGUAGE AND SYMBOLIC POWER

[. . .]

Linguistic exchange – a relation of communication between a sender and a receiver, based on enciphering and deciphering, and therefore on the implementation of a code or a generative competence – is also an economic exchange which is established within a particular symbolic relation of power between a producer, endowed with a certain linguistic capital, and a consumer (or a market), and which is capable of procuring a certain material or symbolic profit. In other words, utterances are not only (save in exceptional circumstances) signs to be understood and deciphered; they are also *signs of wealth*, intended to be evaluated and appreciated, and *signs of authority*, intended to be believed and obeyed. Quite apart from the literary (and especially poetic) uses of language, it is rare in everyday life for language to function as a pure instrument of communication. The pursuit of maximum informative efficiency is only exceptionally the exclusive goal of linguistic production and the distinctly instrumental use of language which it implies generally clashes with the often unconscious pursuit of symbolic profit. For in addition to the information expressly declared, linguistic practice inevitably communicates information about the (differential) manner of communicating, i.e., about the *expressive style*, which, being perceived and appreciated with reference to the universe of theoretically or practically competing styles, takes on a social value and a symbolic efficacy.

Source: Pierre Bourdieu, *Language and Symbolic Power*, Translated by Gino Raymond and Matthew Adamson. Edited by John B. Thompson. Cambridge: Polity Press in association with Blackwell, 1991.

Capital, market and price

Utterances receive their value (and their sense) only in their relation to a market, characterized by a particular law of price formation. The value of the utterance depends on the relation of power that is concretely established between the speakers' linguistic competences, understood both as their capacity for production and as their capacity for appropriation and appreciation; it depends, in other words, on the capacity of the various agents involved in the exchange to impose the criteria of appreciation most favourable to their own products. This capacity is not determined in linguistic terms alone. It is certain that the relation between linguistic competences – which, as socially classified productive capacities, characterize socially classified linguistic units of production and, as capacities of appropriation and appreciation, define markets that are themselves socially classified – helps to determine the law of price formation that obtains in a particular exchange. But the linguistic relation of power is not completely determined by the prevailing linguistic forces alone: by virtue of the languages spoken, the speakers who use them and the groups defined by possession of the corresponding competence, the whole social structure is present in each interaction (and thereby in the discourse uttered). That is what is ignored by the interactionist perspective, which treats interaction as a closed world, forgetting that what happens between two persons – between an employer and an employee or, in a colonial situation, between a French speaker and an Arabic speaker or, in the post-colonial situation, between two members of the formerly colonized nation, one Arabic-speaking, one French-speaking – derives its particular form from the objective relation between the corresponding languages or usages, that is, between the groups who speak those languages.

The concern to return to the things themselves and to get a firmer grip on 'reality', a concern which often inspires the projects of 'micro-sociology', can lead one purely and simply to miss a 'reality' that does not yield to immediate intuition because it lies in structures transcending the interaction which they inform. There is no better example of this than that provided by *strategies of condescension*. Thus a French-language newspaper published in Béarn (a province of south-west France) wrote of the mayor of Pau who, in the course of a ceremony in honour of a Béarnais poet, had addressed the assembled company in Béarnais: 'The audience was greatly moved by this thoughtful gesture' [*La République des Pyrénées*, 9 September 1974]. In order for an audience of people whose mother tongue is Béarnais to perceive as a 'thoughtful gesture' the fact that a Béarnais mayor should speak to them in Béarnais, they must tacitly recognize the unwritten law which prescribes French as the only acceptable language for formal speeches in formal situations. The strategy of condescension consists in deriving *profit* from the objective relation of power between the languages that confront one another in practice (even and especially when French is absent) in the very act of symbolically negating that relation, namely, the hierarchy of the languages and of those who speak them. Such a strategy is possible whenever the objective disparity between the persons present (that is, between their social properties) is sufficiently known and recognized by everyone (particularly those involved in the interaction, as agents or spectators) so that the symbolic negation of the hierarchy (by using the 'common touch', for instance) enables the speaker to combine the profits linked to the undiminished hierarchy with those derived from the distinctly symbolic negation of the hierarchy – not the least of which is the strengthening of the hierarchy implied by the recognition accorded to the way of using the hierarchical relation. In reality, the Béarnais mayor can create this condescension effect only because, as mayor of a large town, attesting to his urbanity, he also possesses all the titles (he is a qualified professor) which guarantee his rightful participation in the 'superiority' of the 'superior' language (no one, and especially not a provincial journalist, would think of praising the mayor's French in the same way as his Béarnais, since he is a qualified, licensed speaker who speaks 'good quality' French by definition, *ex officio*). What is praised as 'good quality Béarnais', coming from the mouth of the legitimate speaker of the legitimate language, would be totally devoid of value – and furthermore would be sociologically impossible in a formal situation – coming from the mouth of a peasant, such as the man who, in order to explain why he did not dream of becoming mayor of his village even though he had obtained the biggest share of the vote, said (in French) that he 'didn't know how to speak' (meaning French), implying a definition of linguistic competence that is entirely sociological. One can see in passing that strategies for the subversion of objective hierarchies in the sphere of language, as in the sphere of culture, are *also* likely to be strategies of condescension, reserved for those who are sufficiently confident of their position in the objective hierarchies to be able to deny them without appearing to be ignorant or incapable of satisfying their demands. If Béarnais (or, elsewhere, Creole) is one day spoken on formal occasions, this will be by virtue of its takeover by speakers of the dominant language, who have enough claims to linguistic legitimacy (at least in the eyes of their interlocutors) to avoid being suspected of resorting to the stigmatized language *faute de mieux*.

The relations of power that obtain in the linguistic market, and whose variations determine the variations in the price that the same discourse may receive on different markets, are manifested and realized in the fact that certain agents are incapable of applying to the linguistic products offered, either by themselves or others, the criteria that are most favourable to their own products. This effect of the imposition of legitimacy is greater – and the laws of the market are more favourable to the products offered by the holders of the greatest linguistic competence – when the use of the legitimate language is more imperative, that is, when the situation is more formal (and when it is more favourable, therefore, to those who are more or less formally delegated to speak), and when consumers grant more complete recognition to the legitimate language and legitimate competence (but a recognition which is relatively independent of their knowledge of that language). In other words, the more formal the market is, the more practically congruent with the norms of the legitimate language, the more it is dominated by the dominant, i.e., by the holders of the legitimate competence, authorized to speak with authority.

[. . .]

It is true that the definition of the symbolic relation of power which is constitutive of the market can be the subject of *negotiation* and that the market can be manipulated, within certain limits, by a metadiscourse concerning the conditions of use of discourse. This includes, for example, the expressions which are used to introduce or excuse speech which is too free or shocking ('with your permission', 'if I may say so', 'if you'll pardon the expression', 'with all due respect', etc.) or those which reinforce, through explicit articulation, the candour enjoyed on a particular market ('off the record', 'strictly between ourselves', etc.). But it goes without saying that the capacity to manipulate is greater the more capital one possesses, as is shown by the strategies of condescension. It is also true that the unification of the market is never so complete as to prevent dominated individuals from finding, in the space provided by private life, among friends, markets where the laws of price formation which apply to more formal markets are suspended. In these private exchanges between homogeneous partners, the 'illegitimate' linguistic products are judged according to criteria which, since they are adjusted to their principles of production, free them from the necessarily comparative logic of distinction and of value. Despite this, the formal law, which is thus provisionally suspended rather than truly transgressed, remains valid, and it re-imposes itself on dominated individuals once they leave the unregulated areas where they can be outspoken (and where they can spend all their lives), as is shown by the fact that it governs the production of their spokespersons as soon as they are placed in a formal situation.

[. . .]

The anticipation of profits

Since a discourse can only exist, in the form in which it exists, so long as it is not simply grammatically correct but also, and above all, socially accept-able, i.e., heard, believed, and therefore effective within a given state of relations of production and circulation, it follows that the scientific analysis of discourse must take into account the laws of price formation which char-acterize the market concerned or, in other words, the laws defining the social conditions of acceptability (which include the specifically linguistic laws of grammaticality). In reality, the conditions of reception envisaged are part of the conditions of production, and anticipation of the sanctions of the market helps to determine the production of the discourse. This anticipation, which bears no resemblance to a conscious calculation, is an aspect of the linguistic habitus which, being the product of a prolonged and primordial relation to the laws of a certain market, tends to function as a practical sense of the acceptability and the probable value of one's own linguistic productions and those of others on different markets. It is this sense of acceptability, and not some form of rational calculation oriented towards the maximization of symbolic profits, which, by encouraging one to take account of the probable value of discourse during the process of production, determines corrections and all forms of self-censorship – the concessions one makes to a social world by accepting to make oneself acceptable in it.

Since linguistic signs are also goods destined to be given a price by pow-ers capable of providing credit (varying according to the laws of the market on which they are placed), linguistic production is inevitably affected by the anticipation of market sanctions: all verbal expressions – whether words exchanged between friends, the bureaucratic discourse of an authorized spokesperson or the academic discourse of a scientific paper – are marked by their conditions of reception and owe some of their properties (even at a gram-matical level) to the fact that, on the basis of a practical anticipation of the laws of the market concerned, their authors, most often unwittingly, and without expressly seeking to do so, try to maximize the symbolic profit they can obtain – from practices which are, inseparably, oriented towards communication and exposed to evaluation. This means that the market fixes the price for a lin-guistic product, the nature, and therefore the objective value, of which the practical anticipation of this price helped to determine; and it means that the practical relation to the market (ease, timidity, tension, embarrassment, silence, etc.), which helps to establish the market sanction, thus provides an apparent justification for the sanction by which it is partly produced.

In the case of symbolic production, the constraint exercised by the market via the anticipation of possible profit naturally takes the form of an anticipated *censorship*, of a self-censorship which determines not only the manner of saying, that is, the choice of language – 'code switching' in situations of bilingualism – or the 'level' of language, but also what it will be possible or not possible to say.

[. . .]

What our social sense detects in a form which is a kind of symbolic expression of all the sociologically pertinent features of the market situation is precisely that which oriented the production of the discourse, namely, the entire set of characteristics of the social relation obtaining between the interlocutors and the expressive capacities which the speaker was able to invest in the process of euphemization. The interdependence between linguistic forms and the structure of the social relation within and for which it is produced can be seen clearly, in French, in the oscillations between the forms of address, *vous* and *tu*, which sometimes occur when the objective structure of the relation between two speakers (e.g., disparity in age or social status) conflicts with the length and continuity of their acquaintance, and therefore with the intimacy and familiarity of their interaction. It then seems as if they are feeling their way towards a readjustment of the mode of expression and of the social relation through spontaneous or calculated slips of the tongue and progressive lapses, which often culminate in a sort of linguistic contract designed to establish the new expressive order on an official basis: 'Let's use *tu*.' But the subordination of the form of discourse to the form of the social relationship in which it is used is most strikingly apparent in situations of *stylistic collision*, when the speaker is confronted with a socially heterogeneous audience or simply with two interlocutors socially and culturally so far apart that the sociologically exclusive modes of expression called for, which are normally produced through more or less conscious adjustment in separate social spaces, cannot be produced simultaneously.

What guides linguistic production is not the degree of tension of the market or, more precisely, its degree of formality, defined in the abstract, for any speaker, but rather the relation between a degree of 'average' objective tension and a linguistic habitus itself characterized by a particular degree of sensitivity to the tension of the market; or, in other words, it is the anticipation of profits, which can scarcely be called a subjective anticipation since it is the product of the encounter between an objective circumstance, that is, the average probability of success, and an incorporated objectivity, that is, the disposition towards a more or less rigorous evaluation of that probability. The practical anticipation of the potential rewards or penalties is a practical quasi-corporeal sense of the reality of the objective relation between a certain linguistic and social competence and a certain market, through which this relation is accomplished. It can range from the certainty of a positive sanction, which is the basis of *certitudo sui*, of *self-assurance*, to the certainty of a negative sanction, which induces surrender and silence, through all the intermediate forms of insecurity and timidity.

The linguistic habitus and bodily hexis

The definition of acceptability is found not in the situation but in the relationship between a market and a habitus, which itself is the product of the whole history of its relations with markets. The habitus is, indeed, linked to the market no less through its conditions of acquisition than through its conditions of use. We have not learned to speak simply by hearing a certain kind of speech spoken but also by speaking, thus by offering a determinate form of speech on a determinate market. This occurs through exchanges within a family occupying a particular position in the social space and thus presenting the child's imitative propensity with models and sanctions that diverge more or less from legitimate usage. And we have learned the value that the products offered on this primary market, together with the authority which it provides, receive on other markets (like that of the school). The system of successive reinforcements or refutations has thus constituted in each one of us a certain sense of the social value of linguistic usages and of the relation between the different usages and the different markets, which organizes all subsequent perceptions of linguistic products, tending to endow it with considerable stability. (We know, in general terms, that the effects that a new experience can have on the habitus depend on the relation of practical 'compatibility' between this experience and the experiences that have already been assimilated by the habitus, in the form of schemes of production and evaluation, and that, in the process of selective re-interpretation which results from this dialectic, the informative efficacy of all new experiences tends to diminish continuously.) This linguistic 'sense of place' governs the degree of constraint which a given field will bring to bear on the production of discourse, imposing silence or a hyper-controlled language on some people while allowing others the liberties of a language that is securely established. This means that competence, which is acquired in a social context and through practice, is inseparable from the practical mastery of a usage of language and the practical mastery of situations in which this usage of language is *socially acceptable*. The sense of the value of one's own linguistic products is a fundamental dimension of the sense of knowing the place which one occupies in the social space. One's original relation with different markets and the experience of the sanctions applied to one's own productions, together with the experience of the price attributed to one's own body, are doubtless some of the mediations which help to constitute that *sense of one's own social worth* which governs the practical relation to different markets (shyness, confidence, etc.) and, more generally, one's whole physical posture in the social world.

While every speaker is both a producer and a consumer of his own linguistic productions, not all speakers, as we have seen, are able to apply to their own products the schemes according to which they were produced. The unhappy relation which the petits bourgeois have to their own productions (and especially with regard to their pronunciation, which, as Labov shows, they judge with particular severity); their especially keen sensitivity to the tension of the market and, by the same token, to linguistic correction in themselves and in others, which pushes them to hyper-correction; their insecurity, which reaches a state of paroxysm on formal occasions, creating 'incorrectness' through hyper-correction or the embarrassingly rash utterances prompted by an artificial confidence – are all things that result from a divorce between the schemes of production and the schemes of evaluation. Divided against themselves, so to speak, the petits bourgeois are those who are both the most 'conscious' of the objective truth of their products (the one defined in the academic hypothesis of the perfectly unified market) and the most determined to reject it, deny it, and contradict it by their efforts. As is very evident in this case, what expresses itself through the linguistic habitus is the whole class habitus of which it is one dimension, which means in fact, the position that is occupied, synchronically and diachronically, in the social structure.

As we have seen, hyper-correction is inscribed in the logic of pretension which leads the petits bourgeois to attempt to appropriate prematurely, at the cost of constant tension, the properties of those who are dominant. The particular intensity of the insecurity and anxiety felt by women of the petite bourgeoisie with regard to language (and equally with regard to cosmetics or personal appearance) can be understood in the framework of the same logic: destined, by the division of labour between the sexes, to seek social mobility through their capacity for symbolic production and consumption, they are even more inclined to invest in the acquisition of legitimate competences. The linguistic practices of the petite bourgeoisie could not fail to strike those who, like Labov, observed them on the particularly tense markets created by linguistic investigation. Situated at the maximum point of subjective tension through their particular sensitivity to objective tension (which is the effect of an especially marked disparity between recognition and cognition), the petits bourgeois are distinct from members of the lower classes who, lacking the means to exercise the liberties of plain speaking, which they reserve for private usage, have no choice but to opt for the broken forms of a borrowed and clumsy language or to escape into abstention and silence. But the petits bourgeois are no less distinct from the members of the dominant class, whose linguistic habitus (especially if they were born in that class) is the *realization of the norm* and who can express all the self-confidence that is associated with a situation where the principles of evaluation and the principles of production coincide perfectly.

In this case, as, at the other extreme, in the case of popular outspoken-ness on the popular market, the demands of the market and the dispositions of the habitus are perfectly attuned; the law of the market does not need to be imposed by means of constraint or external censorship since it is accomplished through the relation to the market which is its incorporated form. When the objective structures which it confronts coincide with those which have produced it, the habitus anticipates the objective demands of the field. Such is the basis of the most frequent and best concealed form of censorship, the kind which is applied by placing, in positions which imply the right to speak, those agents who are endowed with expressive dispositions that are 'censored' in advance, since they coincide with the exigencies inscribed in those positions. As the principle underlying all the distinctive features of the dominant mode of expression, *relaxation in tension* is the expression of a relation to the market which can only be acquired through prolonged and precocious familiarity with markets that are characterized, even under ordinary circumstances, by a high level of control and by that constantly sustained attention to forms and formalities which defines the 'stylization of life'.

[. . .]

It is no coincidence that bourgeois distinction invests the same intention in its relation to language as it invests in its relation to the body. The sense of acceptability which orients linguistic practices is inscribed in the most deep-rooted of bodily dispositions: it is the whole body which responds by its posture, but also by its inner reactions or, more specifically, the articulatory ones, to the tension of the market. Language is a body technique, and specifically linguistic, especially phonetic, competence is a dimension of bodily hexis in which one's whole relation to the social world, and one's whole socially informed relation to the world, are expressed. There is every reason to think that, through the mediation of what Pierre Guiraud calls 'articulatory style', the bodily hexis characteristic of a social class determines the system of phonological features which characterizes a class pronunciation. The most frequent articulatory position is an element in an *overall way of using the mouth* (in talking but also in eating, drinking, laughing, etc.) and therefore a component of the bodily hexis, which implies a *systematic informing* of the whole phonological aspect of speech. This 'articulatory style', a life-style 'made flesh', like the whole bodily hexis, welds phonological features – which are often studied in isolation, each one (the phoneme 'r', for example) being compared with its equivalent in other class pronunciations – into an indivisible totality which must be treated as such.

Thus, in the case of the lower classes, articulatory style is quite clearly part of a relation to the body that is dominated by the refusal of 'airs and graces' (i.e., the refusal of stylization and the imposition of form) and by the valorization of virility – one aspect of a more general disposition to appreciate what is 'natural'. Labov is no doubt right when he ascribes the resistance of male speakers in New York to the imposition of the legitimate language to the fact that they associate the idea of virility with their way of speaking or, more precisely, their way of using the mouth and throat when speaking. In France, it is surely no accident that popular usage condenses the opposition between the bourgeois relation and the popular relation to language in the sexually over-determined opposition between two words for the mouth: *la bouche*, which is more closed, pinched, i.e., tense and censored, and therefore feminine, and *la gueule*, unashamedly wide open, as in 'split' (*fendue, se fendre la gueule*, 'split oneself laughing'), i.e., relaxed and free, and therefore masculine. Bourgeois dispositions, as they are envisaged in the popular mind, and in their most caricatured, petit-bourgeois form, convey in their physical postures of tension and exertion (*bouche fine, pincée, lèvres pincées, serrées, du bout des lèvres, bouche en cul-de-poule* – to be fastidious, supercilious, 'tight-lipped') the bodily indices of quite general dispositions towards the world and other people (and particularly, in the case of the mouth, towards food), such as haughtiness and disdain (*fare la fine bouche, la petite bouche* – to be fussy about food, difficult to please), and the conspicuous distance from the things of the body and those who are unable to mark that distance. *La gueule*, by contrast, is associated with the manly dispositions which, according to the popular ideal, are rooted in the calm certainty of strength which rules out censorships – prudence and deviousness as well as 'airs and graces' – and which make it possible to be 'natural' (*la gueule* is on the side of nature), to be 'open' and 'outspoken' (*jouer franc-jeu, avoir son franc-parler*) or simply to sulk (*faire la gueule*). It designates a capacity for verbal violence, identified with the sheer strength of the voice (*fort en gueule, coup de gueule, grande gueule, engueuler, s'engueuler, gueuler, aller gueuler* – 'loud-mouthed', a 'dressing-down', 'bawl', 'have a slanging match', 'mouth-off'). It also designates a capacity for the physical violence to which it alludes, especially in insults (*casser la gueule, mon poing sur la gueule, ferme ta gueule* – 'smash your face in', 'a punch in the mouth', 'shut your face'), which, through the *gueule*, regarded both as the 'seat' of personal identity (*bonne gueule, sale gueule* – 'nice guy', 'ugly mug') and as its main means of expression (consider the meaning of *ouvrir sa gueule*, or *l'ouvrir*, as opposed to *la fermer, la boucler, taire sa gueule, s'écraser* – 'say one's piece', as opposed to 'shut it', 'belt up', 'shut your mouth', 'pipe down'), aims at the very essence of the interlocutor's social identity and self-image. Applying the same 'intention' to the site of food intake and the site of speech output, the popular vision, which has a clear grasp of the unity of habitus and bodily hexis, also associates *la gueule* with the frank acceptance (*s'en foutre plein la gueule, se rincer la gueule* – stuffing oneself with food and drink) and frank manifestation (*se fendre la gueule*) of elementary pleasure.

On the one hand, domesticated language, censorship made natural, which proscribes 'gross' remarks, 'coarse' jokes and 'thick' accents, goes hand in hand with the domestication of the body which excludes all excessive manifestations of appetites or feelings (exclamations as much as tears or sweeping gestures), and which subjects the body to all kinds of discipline and censorship aimed at denaturalizing it. On the other hand, the 'relaxation of articulatory tension', which leads, as Bernard Laks has pointed out, to the dropping of the final 'r' and 'l' (and which is probably not so much an effect of *laisser-aller* as the expression of a refusal to 'overdo it' to conform too strictly on the points most strictly demanded by the dominant code, even if the effort is made in other areas), is associated with rejection of the censorship which propriety imposes, particularly on the tabooed body, and with the outspokenness whose daring is less innocent than it seems since, in reducing humanity to its common nature – belly, bum, bollocks, grub, guts and shit – it tends to turn the social world upside down, arse over head. Popular festivity as described by Bakhtin and especially revolutionary crisis highlight, through the verbal explosion which they facilitate, the pressure and repression which the everyday order imposes, particularly on the dominated class, through the seemingly insignificant constraints and controls of politeness which, by means of the stylistic variations in ways of talking (the formulae of politeness) or of bodily deportment in relation to the degree of objective tension of the market, exacts recognition of the hierarchical differences between the classes, the sexes and the generations.

It is not surprising that, from the standpoint of the dominated classes, the adoption of the dominant style is seen as a denial of social and sexual identity, a repudiation of the virile values which constitute class membership. That is why women can identify with the dominant culture without cutting themselves off from their class as radically as men. 'Opening one's big mouth' (*ouvrir sa grande gueule*) means refusing to submit, refusing to 'shut it' (*la fermer*) and to manifest the signs of docility that are the precondition of mobility. To adopt the dominant style, especially a feature as marked as the legitimate pronunciation, is in a sense doubly to negate one's virility because the very fact of acquiring it requires docility, a disposition imposed on women by the traditional sexual division of labour (and the traditional division of sexual labour), and because this docility leads one towards dispositions that are themselves perceived as effeminate.

In drawing attention to the articulatory features which, like the degree of 'aperture', sonority or rhythm, best express, in their own logic, the deep-rooted dispositions of the habitus and, more precisely, of the bodily hexis, spontaneous sociolinguistics demonstrates that a differential phonology should never fail to select and interpret the articulatory features characteristic of a class or class fraction in relation not only to the other systems with reference to which they take on their distinctive value, and therefore their social value, but also in relation to the synthetic unity of the bodily hexis from which they spring, and by virtue of which they represent the ethical or aesthetic expression of the necessity inscribed in a social condition.

> The linguist, who has developed an abnormally acute perception (particularly at the phonological level), may notice differences where ordinary speakers hear none. Moreover, because he has to concentrate on discrete criteria (such as the dropping of the final 'r' or 'l') for the purposes of statistical measurement, he is inclined towards an analytical perception very different in its logic from the ordinary perception which underlies the classificatory judgements and the delimitation of homogeneous groups in everyday life. Not only are linguistic features never clearly separated from the speaker's whole set of social properties (bodily hexis, physiognomy, cosmetics, clothing), but phonological (or lexical, or any other) features are never clearly separated from other levels of language; and the judgement which classifies a speech form as 'popular' or a person as 'vulgar' is based, like all practical predication, on sets of indices which never impinge on consciousness in that form, even if those which are designated by stereotypes (such as the 'peasant' 'r' or the southern *ceusse*) have greater weight.

The close correspondence between the uses of the body, of language and no doubt also of time is due to the fact that it is essentially through bodily and linguistic disciplines and censorships, which often imply a temporal rule, that groups inculcate the virtues which are the transfigured form of their necessity, and to the fact that the 'choices' constitutive of a relationship with the economic and social world are incorporated in the form of durable frames that are partly beyond the grasp of consciousness and will.

Chapter 30

Michel Foucault

THE INCITEMENT TO DISCOURSE

T HE SEVENTEENTH CENTURY was the beginning of an age of repression emblematic of what we call the bourgeois societies, an age which perhaps we still have not completely left behind. Calling sex by its name thereafter became more difficult and more costly. As if in order to gain mastery over it in reality, it had first been necessary to subjugate it at the level of language, control its free circulation in speech, expunge it from the things that were said, and extinguish the words that rendered it too visibly present. And even these prohibitions, it seems, were afraid to name it. Without even having to pronounce the word, modern prudishness was able to ensure that one did not speak of sex, merely through the interplay of prohibitions that referred back to one another: instances of muteness which, by dint of saying nothing, imposed silence. Censorship.

Yet when one looks back over these last three centuries with their continual transformations, things appear in a very different light: around and apropos of sex, one sees a veritable discursive explosion. We must be clear on this point, however. It is quite possible that there was an expurgation – and a very rigorous one – of the authorized vocabulary. It may indeed be true that a whole rhetoric of allusion and metaphor was codified. Without question, new rules of propriety screened out some words: there was a policing of statements. A control over enunciations as well: where and when it was not possible to talk about such things became much more strictly defined; in which circumstances, among which speakers, and within which social relationships.

Source: Michel Foucault, *The History of Sexuality: An Introduction*, Translated by Robert Huxley, London: Penguin, 1978.

Areas were thus established, if not of utter silence, at least of tact and discretion: between parents and children, for instance, or teachers and pupils, or masters and domestic servants. This almost certainly constituted a whole restrictive economy, one that was incorporated into that politics of language and speech – spontaneous on the one hand, concerted on the other – which accompanied the social redistributions of the classical period.

At the level of discourses and their domains, however, practically the opposite phenomenon occurred. There was a steady proliferation of discourses concerned with sex – specific discourses, different from one another both by their form and by their object: a discursive ferment that gathered momentum from the eighteenth century onward. Here I am thinking not so much of the probable increase in "illicit" discourses, that is, discourses of infraction that crudely named sex by way of insult or mockery of the new code of decency; the tightening up of the rules of decorum likely did produce, as a countereffect, a valorization and intensification of indecent speech. But more important was the multiplication of discourses concerning sex in the field of exercise of power itself: an institutional incitement to speak about it, and to do so more and more; a determination on the part of the agencies of power to hear it spoken about, and to cause it to speak through explicit articulation and endlessly accumulated detail.

[. . .]

It was here, perhaps, that the injunction, so peculiar to the West, was laid down for the first time, in the form of a general constraint. I am not talking about the obligation to admit to violations of the laws of sex, as required by traditional penance; but of the nearly infinite task of telling – telling oneself and another, as often as possible, everything that might concern the interplay of innumerable pleasures, sensations, and thoughts which, through the body and the soul, had some affinity with sex. This scheme for transforming sex into discourse had been devised long before in an ascetic and monastic setting. The seventeenth century made it into a rule for everyone. It would seem in actual fact that it could scarcely have applied to any but a tiny elite; the great majority of the faithful who only went to confession on rare occasions in the course of the year escaped such complex prescriptions. But the important point no doubt is that this obligation was decreed, as an ideal at least, for every good Christian. An imperative was established: not only will you confess to acts contravening the law, but you will seek to transform your desire, your every desire, into discourse. Insofar as possible, nothing was meant to elude this dictum, even if the words it employed had to be carefully neutralized. The Christian pastoral prescribed as a fundamental duty the task of passing everything having to do with sex through the endless mill of speech. The forbidding of certain words, the decency of expressions, all the censorings of vocabulary, might well have been only secondary devices compared to that great subjugation: ways of rendering it morally acceptable and technically useful.

One could plot a line going straight from the seventeenth-century pastoral to what became its projection in literature, "scandalous" literature at that. "Tell everything," the directors would say time and again: "not only consummated acts, but sensual touchings, all impure gazes, all obscene remarks . . . all consenting thoughts" (de'Liguori 1835: 5). Sade takes up the injunction in words that seem to have been retranscribed from the treatises of spiritual direction: "Your narrations must be decorated with the most numerous and searching details; the precise way and extent to which we may judge how the passion you describe relates to human manners and man's character is determined by your willingness to disguise no circumstance; and what is more, the least circumstance is apt to have an immense influence upon the procuring of that kind of sensory irritation we expect from your stories" (de Sade 1966: 271).

[. . .]

Toward the beginning of the eighteenth century, there emerged a political, economic, and technical incitement to talk about sex. And not so much in the form of sexuality as in the form of analysis, stocktaking, classification, and specification, of quantitative or causal studies. This need to take sex "into account," to pronounce a discourse on sex that would not derive from morality alone but from rationality as well, was sufficiently new that at first it wondered at itself and sought apologies for its own existence. How could a discourse based on reason speak of *that*? "Rarely have philosophers directed a steady gaze to these objects situated between disgust and ridicule, where one must avoid both hypocrisy and scandal" (Flandrin 1976). And nearly a century later, the medical establishments which one might have expected to be less surprised by what it was about to formulate, still stumbled at the moment of speaking: "The darkness that envelops these facts, the shame and disgust they inspire, have always repelled the observer's gaze. . . . For a long time I hesitated to introduce the loathsome picture into this study" (Tardieu 1857: 114). What is essential is not in all these scruples, in the "moralism" they betray, or in the hypocrisy one can suspect them of, but in the recognized necessity of overcoming this hesitation. One had to speak of sex; one had to speak publicly and in a manner that was not determined by the division between licit and illicit, even if the speaker maintained the distinction for himself (which is what these solemn and preliminary declarations were intended to show): one had to speak of it as of a thing to be not simply condemned or tolerated but managed, inserted into systems of utility, regulated for the greater good of all, made to function according to an optimum. Sex was not something one simply judged; it was a thing one administered. It was in the nature of a public potential; it called for management procedures; it had to be taken charge of by analytical discourses. In the eighteenth century, sex became a "police" matter – in the full and strict sense given the term at the time: not the repression of disorder, but an ordered maximization of collective and individual forces.

[. . .]

A policing of sex: that is, not the rigor of a taboo, but the necessity of regulating sex through useful and public discourses.

A few examples will suffice. One of the great innovations in the techniques of power in the eighteenth century was the emergence of "population" as an economic and political problem: population as wealth, population as manpower or labor capacity, population balanced between its own growth and the resources it commanded. Governments perceived that they were not dealing simply with subjects, or even with a "people," but with a "population," with its specific phenomena and its peculiar variables: birth and death rates, life expectancy, fertility, state of health, frequency of illnesses, patterns of diet and habitation. All these variables were situated at the point where the characteristic movements of life and the specific effects of institutions intersected.

[. . .]

At the heart of this economic and political problem of population was sex: it was necessary to analyze the birthrate, the age of marriage, the legitimate and illegitimate births, the precocity and frequency of sexual relations, the ways of making them fertile or sterile, the effects of unmarried life or of the prohibitions, the impact of contraceptive practices – of those notorious "deadly secrets" which demographers on the eve of the Revolution knew were already familiar to the inhabitants of the countryside.

Of course, it had long been asserted that a country had to be populated if it hoped to be rich and powerful; but this was the first time that a society had affirmed, in a constant way, that its future and its fortune were tied not only to the number and the uprightness of its citizens, to their marriage rules and family organization, but to the manner in which each individual made use of his sex. Things went from ritual lamenting over the unfruitful debauchery of the rich, bachelors, and libertines to a discourse in which the sexual conduct of the population was taken both as an object of analysis and as a target of intervention; there was a progression from the crudely populationist arguments of the mercantilist epoch to the much more subtle and

calculated attempts at regulation that tended to favor or discourage –
according to the objectives and exigencies of the moment – an increasing
birthrate. Through the political economy of population there was formed
a whole grid of observations regarding sex. There emerged the analysis of
the modes of sexual conduct, their determinations and their effects, at the
boundary line of the biological and the economic domains. There also
appeared those systematic campaigns which, going beyond the traditional
means – moral and religious exhortations, fiscal measures – tried to transform the sexual conduct of couples into a concerted economic and political
behavior. In time these new measures would become anchorage points for
the different varieties of racism of the nineteenth and twentieth centuries. It
was essential that the state know what was happening with its citizens' sex,
and the use they made of it, but also that each individual be capable of
controlling the use he made of it. Between the state and the individual, sex
became an issue, and a public issue no less; a whole web of discourses, special
knowledges, analyses, and injunctions settled upon it.

The situation was similar in the case of children's sex. It is often said that
the classical period consigned it to an obscurity from which it scarcely emerged
before the *Three Essays* or the beneficent anxieties of Little Hans. It is true that
a long-standing "freedom" of language between children and adults, or pupils
and teachers, may have disappeared. No seventeenth-century pedagogue
would have publicly advised his disciple, as did Erasmus in his *Dialogues*, on
the choice of a good prostitute. And the boisterous laughter that had accompanied the precocious sexuality of children for so long – and in all social classes,
it seems – was gradually stifled. But this was not a plain and simple imposition
of silence. Rather, it was a new regime of discourses. Not any less was said
about it; on the contrary. But things were said in a different way; it was
different people who said them, from different points of view, and in order to
obtain different results. Silence itself – the things one declines to say, or is
forbidden to name, the discretion that is required between different speakers
– is less the absolute limit of discourse, the other side from which it is separated by a strict boundary, than an element that functions alongside the things
said, with them and in relation to them within over-all strategies. There is no
binary division to be made between what one says and what one does not say;
we must try to determine the different ways of not saying such things, how
those who can and those who cannot speak of them are distributed, which type
of discourse is authorized, or which form of discretion is required in either
case. There is not one but many silences, and they are an integral part of the
strategies that underlie and permeate discourses.

Take the secondary schools of the eighteenth century, for example. On
the whole, one can have the impression that sex was hardly spoken of at all

in these institutions. But one only has to glance over the architectural layout, the rules of discipline, and their whole internal organization: the question of sex was a constant preoccupation. The builders considered it explicitly. The organizers took it permanently into account. All who held a measure of authority were placed in a state of perpetual alert, which the fixtures, the precautions taken, the interplay of punishments and responsibilities, never ceased to reiterate. The space for classes, the shape of the tables, the planning of the recreation lessons, the distribution of the dormitories (with or without partitions, with or without curtains), the rules for monitoring bedtime and sleep periods – all this referred, in the most prolix manner, to the sexuality of children. What one might call the internal discourse of the institution – the one it employed to address itself, and which circulated among those who made it function – was largely based on the assumption that this sexuality existed, that it was precocious, active, and ever present. But this was not all: the sex of the schoolboy became in the course of the eighteenth century – and quite apart from that of adolescents in general – a public problem. Doctors counseled the directors and professors of educational establishments, but they also gave their opinions to families; educators designed projects which they submitted to the authorities; schoolmasters turned to students, made recommendations to them, and drafted for their benefit books of exhortation, full of moral and medical examples. Around the schoolboy and his sex there proliferated a whole literature of precepts, opinions, observations, medical advice, clinical cases, outlines for reform, and plans for ideal institutions. With Basedow and the German "philanthropic" movement, this transformation of adolescent sex into discourse grew to considerable dimensions.

[. . .]

It would be less than exact to say that the pedagogical institution has imposed a ponderous silence on the sex of children and adolescents. On the contrary, since the eighteenth century it has multiplied the forms of discourse on the subject; it has established various points of implantation for sex; it has coded contents and qualified speakers. Speaking about children's sex, inducing educators, physicians, administrators, and parents to speak of it, or speaking to them about it, causing children themselves to talk about it, and enclosing them in a web of discourses which sometimes address them, sometimes speak about them, or impose canonical bits of knowledge on them, or use them as a basis for constructing a science that is beyond their grasp – all this together enables us to link an intensification of the interventions of power to a multiplication of discourse. The sex of children and adolescents has become, since the eighteenth century, an important area of contention around which innumerable institutional devices and discursive strategies have been deployed. It may well be true that adults and children themselves were deprived of a certain way of speaking about sex, a mode that was disallowed as being too direct, crude, or coarse. But this was only the counterpart of other discourses, and perhaps the condition necessary in order for them to function, discourses that were interlocking, hierarchized, and all highly articulated around a cluster of power relations.

One could mention many other centers which in the eighteenth or nineteenth century began to produce discourses on sex. First there was medicine, via the "nervous disorders"; next psychiatry, when it set out to discover the etiology of mental illnesses, focusing its gaze first on "excess," then onanism, then frustration, then "frauds against procreation," but especially when it annexed the whole of the sexual perversions as its own province; criminal justice, too, which had long been concerned with sexuality, particularly in the form of "heinous" crimes and crimes against nature, but which, toward the middle of the nineteenth century, broadened its jurisdiction to include petty offenses, minor indecencies, insignificant perversions; and lastly, all those social controls, cropping up at the end of the last century, which screened the sexuality of couples, parents and children, dangerous and endangered adolescents undertaking to protect, separate, and forewarn, signaling perils everywhere, awakening people's attention, calling for diagnoses, piling up reports, organizing therapies. These sites radiated discourses aimed at sex, intensifying people's awareness of it as a constant danger, and this in turn created a further incentive to talk about it.

[. . .]

Since the eighteenth century, sex has not ceased to provoke a kind of generalized discursive erethism. And these discourses on sex did not multiply apart from or against power, but in the very space and as the means of its exercise. Incitements to speak were orchestrated from all quarters, apparatuses everywhere for listening and recording, procedures for observing, questioning, and formulating. Sex was driven out of hiding and constrained to lead a discursive existence. From the singular imperialism that compels everyone to transform their sexuality into a perpetual discourse, to the manifold mechanisms which, in the areas of economy, pedagogy, medicine, and justice, incite, extract, distribute, and institutionalize the sexual discourse, an immense verbosity is what our civilization has required and organized. Surely no other type of society has ever accumulated – and in such a relatively short span of time – a similar quantity of discourses concerned with sex. It may well be that we talk about sex more than anything else; we set our minds to the task; we convince ourselves that we have never said enough on the subject, that, through inertia or submissiveness, we conceal from ourselves the blinding evidence, and that what is essential always eludes us, so that we must always start out once again in search of it. It is possible that where sex is concerned, the most long-winded, the most impatient of societies is our own.

But as this overview shows, we are dealing less with *a* discourse on sex than with a multiplicity of discourses produced by a whole series of mechanisms operating in different institutions. The Middle Ages had organized around the theme of the flesh and the practice of penance a discourse that was markedly unitary. In the course of recent centuries, this relative uniformity was broken apart, scattered, and multiplied in an explosion of distinct discursivities which took form in demography, biology, medicine, psychiatry, psychology, ethics, pedagogy, and political criticism. More precisely, the secure bond that held together the moral theology of concupiscence and the obligation of confession (equivalent to the theoretical discourse on sex and its first-person formulation) was, if not broken, at least loosened and diversified: between the objectification of sex in rational discourses, and the movement by which each individual was set to the task of recounting his own sex, there has occurred, since the eighteenth century, a whole series of tensions, conflicts, efforts at adjustment, and attempts at retranscription. So it is not simply in terms of a continual extension that we must speak of this discursive growth; it should be seen rather as a dispersion of centers from which discourses emanated, a diversification of their forms, and the complex deployment of the network connecting them. Rather than the uniform concern to hide sex, rather than a general prudishness of language, what distinguishes these last three centuries is the variety, the wide dispersion of devices that were invented for speaking about it, for having it be spoken about, for inducing it to speak of itself, for listening, recording, transcribing, and redistributing what is said about it: around sex, a whole network of varying, specific, and coercive transpositions into discourse. Rather than a massive censorship, beginning with the verbal proprieties imposed by the Age of Reason, what was involved was a regulated and polymorphous incitement to discourse.

The objection will doubtless be raised that if so many stimulations and constraining mechanisms were necessary in order to speak of sex, this was because there reigned over everyone a certain fundamental prohibition; only definite necessities – economic pressures, political requirements – were able to lift this prohibition and open a few approaches to the discourse on sex, but these were limited and carefully coded; so much talk about sex, so many insistent devices contrived for causing it to be talked about – but under strict conditions: does this not prove that it was an object of secrecy, and more important, that there is still an attempt to keep it that way? But this often-stated theme, that sex is outside of discourse and that only the removing of an obstacle, the breaking of a secret, can clear the way leading to it, is precisely what needs to be examined. Does it not partake of the injunction by which discourse is provoked? Is it not with the aim of inciting people to speak of sex that it is made to mirror, at the outer limit of every actual discourse, something akin to a secret whose discovery is imperative, a thing abusively reduced to silence, and at the same time difficult and necessary, dangerous and precious to divulge? We must not forget that by making sex into that which, above all else, had to be confessed, the Christian pastoral always presented it as the disquieting enigma: not a thing which stubbornly shows itself, but one which always hides, the insidious presence that speaks in a voice so muted and often disguised that one risks remaining deaf to it. Doubtless the secret does not reside in that basic reality in relation to which all the incitements to speak of sex are situated – whether they try to force the secret, or whether in some obscure way they reinforce it by the manner in which they speak of it. It is a question rather of a theme that forms part of the very mechanics of these incitements: a way of giving shape to the requirement to speak about the matter, a fable that is indispensable to the endlessly proliferating economy of the discourse on sex. What is peculiar to modern societies, in fact, is not that they consigned sex to a shadow existence, but that they dedicated themselves to speaking of it *ad infinitum*, while exploiting it as *the* secret.

References

Flandrin, J.-L. (1976) *Familles: parenté, maison, sexualité dans l'ancienne société*, Paris: Hachette.

De' Ligouri, A. (1835) *Préceptes sur le sixième commandement*, Trans., 5.

De Sade, D.-A. ([1931–5] 1966) *The 120 Days of Sodom*, Trans. Wainhouse, A. and Seaver, R., New York: Grove Press, 271.

Tardieu, A. (1857) *Étude médico-légale sur les attentats aux mœurs*, 114.

Chapter 31

Carmen Rosa Caldas-Coulthard

'WOMEN WHO PAY FOR SEX. AND ENJOY IT': TRANSGRESSION VERSUS MORALITY IN WOMEN'S MAGAZINES

WOMEN'S MAGAZINES ARE INCREASINGLY the object of critical sociological and cultural analysis (Ballaster *et al.* 1991; Ferguson 1983; McCracken 1993; Winship 1987). As mass-culture texts they are pervasive in modern societies, and, as the studies prove, are a continuing presence in many women's lives. They have a highly important role in the maintenance of cultural values, since they construct an 'ideal' reader who is at the same time both produced and in a sense imprisoned by the text.

I examine here, from a textual perspective, a very popular genre in women's magazines: first-person narratives concerned with one of the most private parts of the private life – sex. Giddens argues that sexuality is essential to the 'regime of truth', and texts about sexuality are seen as a form of access to the truth: 'since women are historically linked to the private world, sexuality as a topic is directly connected to women's "truth"' (Giddens 1992: 30). The real self is the self revealed in personal intimacy and in modern women's magazines this real self is understood as sexual behaviour.

Source: Carmen Rosa Caldas-Coulthard, ' "Women who pay for sex. And enjoy it" ': Transgression versus morality in women's magazines, in Carmen Rosa Caldas-Coulthard and Malcolm Coulthard (eds) *Texts and Practices: Readings in Critical Discourse Analysis*, London: Routledge, 1996, 250–70.

The personal narratives I concentrate on provide an entrance point to the lives of others, exactly because they deal with sex. They are there to provoke a vicarious participation, since most of them are about transgression. Voyeurism is an opportunity to see the 'truth' of someone else's life.

I want to argue that writers create, through first-person testimonies, a fictionalised world that helps to construct and maintain a contradictory ideology of femininity and sexuality. First-person narratives project a fallacious idea of modernity, which as McCracken suggests, 'covers up a system of domination and praises tradition and accepted values' (1993: 37). In mass culture, as Jameson (1981) points out, there is a compensatory exchange process, where people are offered a series of gratifications in return for their passivity. The cultural forms touch on, but at the same time neutralise, social problems.

I also argue, by focusing on the narrative analysis categories of orientation and evaluation that the narrator although apparently transgressive, in fact reinforces moral values in the report of her sexual practices. Women's magazines ultimately reaffirm traditional views of the role of women in society. Through evaluative structures that link positive images to ideas of inadequate and insecure women, these texts put an emphasis on themes of social asymmetries. Transgressive pleasure and social punishment are closely associated.

[. . .]

The first-person narratives (from now on the 'sex narratives') I want to discuss here contagiously provide for the reader vicarious and transgressive pleasures linked to the prohibited and the utopian. That is why they are so exciting. Who would stop reading, for instance, after this beginning?

> JANE, 51, HOUSEWIFE
> For the past two years, I've been seeing young men in the afternoons.

These pleasures offer fantasy and an escape from routine and daily life. The sad part, however, is that a deeper discussion of gender politics and power relations is totally absent from these magazines and the oppositions of masculine and feminine, public and private, production and consumption continue to structure the magazine text. Sexuality is merely an object of consumption.

Narratives of transgression: the 'fresh approach'

Narratives about sexual encounters or experiences, especially of a transgressive kind, are the modern version of the romance stories. Sex narratives are small reports retold by different voices and put together under a general heading ('Why Women Go to Male Prostitutes', 'Men Talk about their Mistresses', 'Women Who Pay for Sex. And Enjoy It').

Although popular magazines have changed in their visual representations over time, they preserve a basic macro-narrative which is an articulation of the world centred on the woman and retold supposedly from a woman's perspective. Constructed from an explicit point of view (the voice who tells the story), sex narratives are a crucial sub-genre in the articulation of sexuality and femininity.

In organisational terms, each text is voiced by a supposedly real person who, prior to the recounting act, has undergone some kind of personal experience. Labov [Chapter 12] refers to the concept of 'reportability'. For any narrative to be successfully encoded by the participants of the interaction, it needs to have a 'point' and a reason to be told. The sexual component makes the report exciting, but the transgressive is the reason for the story to be told.

Because narrative or storytelling is one of the most attractive and vivid representations of experience through language, first-person narratives are, as I pointed out above, one of the preferred organisational patterns found in female magazines. In *Marie Claire*, for instance, there is a massive concentration on narrative – from the eight sections that together constitute the magazine, five consist of narratives – reportage, emotional issues, first person, life stories, fashion story.

[. . .]

Labov [Chapter 12, p. 227; see also Chapter 13] suggests that narratives of personal experience are of the following structural categories:

1   abstract
2   orientation
3   complicating action
4   evaluation
5   result
6   coda

[. . .]

In the particular sex narratives from *Marie Claire* chosen for analysis (ten from the February 1994 issue – **'I pay men for sex'** – **Ten women explain why**), the headlines function as the abstract or the summary of what is yet to come. The abstract summarises the central action and it is used to answer the questions: what is this about, why is this story being told. Orientation sets the scene: the who, when, where and what of the story. It establishes the 'situation' of the narrative.

In newspapers the *headline* and the *lead* (the first paragraph of the text), in most cases, fulfil the dual function of the abstract and the orientation. The lead is the most important paragraph of the story. It establishes the main theme and gives information about the basic facts and people involved in the event. Orientation, on the other hand, can also continue through the story, and characters can be introduced as the events develop.

By contrast, in other written narratives the title, which corresponds to the headline in the written media, does not necessarily give the listener/reader a clue to the topic to be developed. The title of a film, for example, *Best Intentions* (directed by Bille August, winner of the 1992 Cannes Film Festival and about the early married life of Ingmar Bergman's parents) tells us nothing about the theme of the narrative. In magazines the headline is crucial: it not only contains basic information about the topic but also has to be catchy and sometimes poetic.

Headlines are the most powerful persuasive and auto-promotional tool used to attract magazine readers. Just as in the newspapers, they have the purpose of selling the magazine and attracting readers. In fact, many readers choose to read a story only if the headline attracts their attention.

Headlines appear three times: on the cover, on the feature page and framing the actual text, where they are rearticulated and expanded. This is an interesting feature of this kind of text and differs from newspaper news, where the headline only appears once and then is followed by a summary of the story, the lead paragraph. The following headline, for example, appears on the cover of the February issue of *Marie Claire:*

'I pay men for sex' – Ten women explain why

It is rewritten on the feature page as:

Why Women Go to Male Prostitutes – Ten women talk to Clare Campbell about hiring men for sex

and, once again, inside the magazine heading the actual narrative:

> Why women go to Male Prostitutes.
> Men who charge for sex can be found in hotel bars, or through escort agencies, personal columns and ads in newsagent's windows. Clare Campbell talks to ten women who have hired male prostitutes.

The transformations are meaningful in terms of the fictionalisation of the events and also in terms of power relations. In the examples above, a series of linguistic strategies are used. In the cover headline voice is given to a supposedly 'real' person who will reveal her sexual activities. This narrator is a persona created to be exactly like you and me, through the device of reported speech which dramatises the recounting and supposedly gives veracity to it. Quote is the final layer in a hierarchy of narrative levels, since it is the introduction of one text into another.

[. . .]

The recursive potentiality of the syntactic structure of report allows speakers and writers to create different layers of narration. This is the case in the example

First layer narration:	**I** (person/writer in the real world) tell **you** (reader in the real world) *that*
Second layer narration:	**someone** (identified only as an 'I') told **me** *that*
Third layer narration:	QUOTE

The use of the quote on the cover is a strategy of authorial detachment and approximation of reader and character. Although quoted material represents interaction, the represented speech is always mediated and indirect, since it is produced by someone (in this case the writer of the article, who interprets the speech acts represented according to her point of view (see Caldas-Coulthard 1987; 1994)). The apparent 'factuality' is a fiction.

The problem (why women pay for sex) is only suggested in the headline and raises expectations. The explanation will be given inside the magazine – 'Ten women explain why'. This is a powerful strategy used to make readers continue reading. It is the basic technique used by all episodic narrative: the action is suspended to be continued later on.

The feature page introduces a new headline where the problem is now mediated through an omniscient voice, thereby establishing distance between text and reader and changing the perspective of the telling. It also introduces a very important participant in the creation of the story – Clare Campbell, the receiver of the verbal process. In fact, she is the explicit name through whose point of view the events will be retold. The clauses are constructed in such a way, however, that Clare is in the receiving position and the women narrators are the *sayers*. The feature page headline also reclassifies the 'men' of the cover as 'male prostitutes'.

Finally, inside the magazine, the headline is expanded to an orientative section – 'men can be found in certain places or through certain agents'.

The male participants, who are given theme position in the sentences, are once again reclassified as 'men who charge for sex'. They are now the actors in charge of the action, and Clare Campbell from receiver of the message in the previous headline becomes the sayer of the process. In this last headline, the meaning of the text has changed. Power is attributed to men. The writer of supposedly 'real' events is given voice.

Another interesting fact is that the quote reported in the cover headline never reappears in the ten short narratives that make up the section *Emotional Issues*. This is another of the signs of the fictionalisation of the supposedly factual tellings.

[. . .]

In the text itself, the macro-narrative is framed by the reporter, whose name appears in the headline and who introduces the subnarratives and describes the narrators by first name plus age. The age information is ideo-logically interesting – Irene, 37, Yasmin, 44, Louise, 47, Ann, 64, Jane, 51 – because age here is attached to transgression. The implicit message is that these middle-aged women should not be doing what we are about to read. The macro-narrative is subsequently layered, and the women are given voice to recount their personal experiences.

All the sex narratives follow basically the same structures as the one below:

IRENE, 37, HOUSEWIFE AND MOTHER
Richard, my husband, hasn't made love to me for ten years. We have a lovely twelve-year-old son called Liam, so I wouldn't dream of breaking up my marriage by having an affair or leaving Richard for another man. I have tried to get him to go for marriage guidance or some sort of sex therapy, but he absolutely refuses. I ended up going on my own and I realised afterwards that I either had to learn to live without sex or find an alternative way of living.

Then I read an article about gigolos in a women's magazine. I didn't do anything about it immediately, but I began to think about it and eventually even told Richard what I was considering. Even at that stage, I think I was still hoping that he would be so outraged that it would make him do something. But it didn't.

He said that as long as I didn't do it in the house and Liam never found out, it was all right by him. He justified this by saying that he didn't want to lose me, and that maybe this was the only way of finding a compromise. He also said he never, never wanted me to tell him the details.

I have now been going with paid men for over a year. It isn't that expensive – about £100 a time – and I only do it about once a month at the most. The agency regard me as a regular now and have been very good about finding us a place to go each time. The only aspect that worries Richard is when I see the same man too often. Otherwise I think he has got quite used to it. I felt guilty about the expense at first, but I now look on it as an extended mortgage – certainly cheaper and less upsetting than a divorce.

All texts examined follow the same formulaic pattern: there which indicates a problem:

Richard, my husband, hasn't made love to me for ten years.

(Irene)

I'm twice divorced . . . I don't want any more relationships with men especially gold diggers. The only thing lacking in my life is regular and uncomplicated sex.

(Yasmin)

Until about two years ago . . . I had never questioned whether my husband and I were happy. It was only then that I began to recognise the huge gap between us.

(Louise)

Two years ago I had a hysterectomy. I am not married and have no children, but until that time I had been in an eleven-year relationship I believed to be a happy one. Then my partner left me – just like that, a fortnight after my operation.

(Nicole)

My husband went off with another woman six years ago.

(Jean)

In the orientation (discussed in more detail below), the woman narrators are classified through the representation of family actors – husbands, daughters and sons.

I have a beautiful and successful daughter of 24. . . . My daughter, who is terribly Sloane these days, despite her Asian origins . . .

(Yasmin)

[My husband] has got a demanding job as a sales director, and he
has hobbies like gardening and model making.

(Louise)

My husband Leo died four years ago.

(Ann)

My husband Derek is the managing director of a large chemical
company.

(Jane)

The idea of going to a gigolo horrified me at first. But I love my
husband, Gary, very much and he *wanted me to do it*.

(Julie)

After the problem is introduced, responses are proposed but are negatively
evaluated by the narrators:

I have tried to get him to go for marriage guidance or some sort
of sex therapy, but he absolutely refuses.

(Irene)

I do still love [my husband] and we make love at least twice a
month. But he never talks to me like he used to and sex is no
fun without the pillow talk.

(Louise)

I am terribly fond of Derek [my husband] but he is often away
and never really listens to anything I say when he is here.

(Jane)

Because the responses to the problems are negatively evaluated, further
responses are sought:

I realised afterwards that I either had to learn to live without sex
or find an alternative way of living.

(Irene)

Hiring a man for sex was my equivalent of finding a hobby.

(Nicole)

> For the past two years, I've been seeing young men in the after-noons. I don't really know why I do it – the most obvious reason is sheer boredom.
>
> (Jane)

Then a series of dynamic actions make up the complicating action, which is the essence of the narrative. For Labov [Chapter 12] complicating action answers the question 'what happened'. Complicating action brings in the elements which disrupt the equilibrium which will be finally restored by the resolution: in our case, the narrator becomes attracted to the idea of hiring a male prostitute, then finds one and reports on the sometimes ludicrous details. It is interesting to note that in the narrative quoted above, this section is introduced by self-referentiality:

> Then I read an article about gigolos in a *women's magazine*.
>
> (Irene; my emphasis)

This points to the fact that the autopromotional discourse is subtly inserted in the different sections of the text.

The actions are extensively evaluated (discussed below) through the text, and we come to the end of the stories with some odd/funny/cynical reso-lutions (finally what happened?) and codas (explicit signal of the end of the report):

> I felt guilty about the expense at first, but I now look on it as an extended mortgage – certainly cheaper and less upsetting than a divorce.
>
> (Irene)

> I can't say there isn't a certain satisfaction in knowing that the money I pay comes out of my husband's pocket.
>
> (Jane)

> After all, you only get one life, don't you?
>
> (Louise)

All these sex narratives have not only the main components that Labov refers to, but also some structural variations. Source attributions, actors, time and place are also important features of all sex narratives. In fact, according to Bell (1991: 175 [see also Chapter 13]), journalists have a short list of what should go in a story, 'the five Ws and a H' – who, when, where, what, why and how. In the sex narratives the emphasis, however, falls on orientation and evaluation, which I shall discuss below.

Another important characteristic of sex narratives is that women readers are addressed as a large group undefined by political, or ideological allegiance and undifferentiated at personal level. There is an assumption that 'all' women are interested in the sexual activities reported.

I want now to concentrate on how social actors are constructed through voice, orientation and evaluation.

Whose voice?

Facts and fictions

The question of voice is an interesting one in sex narratives. First-person accounts in media discourse make pretensions to factuality. 'I' narrators are put forward as real people. The Brazilian *Marie Claire*, for instance, introduces first-person narratives with:

> This space belongs to *Marie Claire* readers. If you have an unusual story write to . . .

and ends with

> Report collected by Aida Veiga.
> (Brazilian *Marie Claire*, March 1994, my translation)

Another formula used by both the Brazilian and the English *Marie Claires* is

> Clare Campbell *talks* to ten women who have hired male prostitutes.

Or

> Marie Claire *listened* to married and single men, who told her why they continue to pay for sex.

These statements make the authorship very problematic. In the written press in general, narratives are not produced by a single source. According to Bell (1991) a factual newspaper report for instance is a text produced by multiple parties: principal sources of information, agencies, institutions, other media and authors, editors, copy editors, reporters, and others.

The 'copy' – the actual written text – is handled by many people and undergoes transformations as it follows its way to printing. Bell (1991) also points out that the copy follows a path which is itself a narrative of changes: from chief reporter to journalist (the first writer), to sub-editor and finally to the editor. Thus the number of people involved in the production of a newspaper text is quite large. This naturally accounts for one of the major characteristics of media narrative texts – embedding. Version 1 is embedded in version 2 which is embedded in version 3 and so on. The text therefore undergoes many modifications, and authorship and responsibility for the text is diluted in the process. Ultimately, the magazine editor is responsible for what is said, although all the versions are based on other authors, including the unknown ones who write for the agencies.

In classical narratives, by contrast, there are tellers who are somehow identifiable and who can choose to *aver*, in other words, to be responsible for what they recount or to detach themselves from the responsibility of what is being uttered by transferring the averral to other tellers and creating other narrators.

The sex narratives are a composite of these two sub-genres: the appearance of factuality is due to the fact that there seems to be a person out there in the world who is recounting events from her/his life. However, if we start examining the textualisations of this narrator, we find many traces of fictionality. The narrators are presented by their first name; age and some kind of 'occupation' are attached to it:

> Irene, 37, housewife and mother
> Yasmin, 44, charity fund-raiser
> Louise, 47, housing officer
> Ann, 64, housewife
> Jane, 51, housewife
> Jean, 39, teacher

First names do not in fact identify real people, and most of the professional glossing attached to the names fails to place the women in any recognisable space. There are no addresses or further indications of where the activities are being developed. Naturally, the activity of being a housewife and mother does not need any other development – women are attached here to the domestic space.

By contrast, when men are described, particularly in the press (see Caldas-Coulthard 1993), they are glossed by their professional designations or positions in the government or in some kind of public institution:

Keith Wafter, medical director of Cilag
Sir Charles Tidbury, former chairman of Whitbread brewers
        (examples taken from the COBUILD newspaper corpora)

By contrast, the sex narrators cannot be factually identified. Although the magazine wants the readers to believe that the stories are real the texts are not produced by the 'I' narrator that appears in the text, but by a series of people that put the text together, ultimately Clare Campbell or Aida Veiga. Even if there were a primary report by a Yasmin or a Louise, the media writers are in charge of selecting, ordering and organising the sequence in which events will be recounted. There is always a choice and a construction since events are interpreted and then recounted by tellers who live in a particular society at a given time and have possibly different ideological values for the supposed women who 'recount' their sad stories.

[. . .]

Orientation, evaluation and guilt

As I have indicated, the orientation section of the narrative specifies the participants and the circumstances – place and time. In a linear narrative, orientation is generally placed after the abstract and before the complicating action. However, very commonly, orientative clauses can be found embedded throughout the text. The most interesting uses of orientation are when parts of it are strategically delayed, and surprising effects are created because important information is recounted later in the telling. This is the case in the sex narratives. One of their major characteristics is that the women narrators have to describe their family links in order to define their own identities. So we have descriptions like:

> [My husband] has got a demanding job as a sales director, and he has hobbies like gardening and model making.
>
> (Louise)

> My husband Leo died four years ago. We had been married for nearly 40 years and his death was a terrible shock. I recently moved next door to my daughter and I have lots of women friends and have a very good pension from my husband's company.
>
> (Ann)

My husband Derek is the managing director of a large chemical company. We own a lovely house with a swimming-pool, as well as holiday homes both in France and the US.

(Jane)

I'm twice divorced. I have a beautiful and successful daughter of 24, plenty of money in my own right and many women friends.

(Yasmin)

We have a lovely twelve-year-old son called Liam.

(Irene)

The identities of the narrators are constructed through their relationships with husbands and children and through the money that they spend on their lovers:

It isn't that expensive – about £100 a time.

(Irene, 37)

I paid him £150 for the afternoon – which was much more than I expected, and also more than I had in cash in the house. I was worried about writing a cheque for so much in case Colin [my husband] questioned it.

(Louise, 47)

We went back to my cabin together and he told me it would cost £300 for him to stay all night. I agreed.

(Ann, 64)

The older the woman, the more expensive the encounter becomes! Ann, 64, in fact says:

I wouldn't expect a man to want to do it with a woman of my age for nothing.

The lovers, by contrast with the husbands and family, are unnamed. They are labelled as 'lovers', 'gigolos', 'men' or by reference to their youth or physical attributes:

He looked like one of the Chippendales – he was a young Australian with huge muscles and lovely blond hair.

(Jane, 51)

Suddenly I noticed a very handsome young man staring hard in my direction. At first I tried to ignore him. Then he came over.

(Yasmin, 44)

I have now been going with paid men for over a year.

(Irene, 37)

I rang [an escort agency] and asked them to send a young man round to see if I liked him.

(Jane, 51)

I have only had sex with three men in my life — one of whom is Colin [my husband], one I met after answering an advertisement in the personal column, and the other one was from an escort agency.

(Louise, 47)

Van Leeuwen (1996) suggests, in his discussion of how social practices are transformed into discourses, that there is an 'array of choices' or a system network that people choose from for representing other social actors. If we analyse the choices found in the examples above according to his categories, we notice that husbands and children are *included*, *personalised*, *determined* and *nominalised* (husband + name, children + name). The narrator's identity is shaped by the ways these other actors appear in the text. Lovers, on the other hand, are included in the discourse, but are sometimes *undetermined* (the one, the other one), explicitly differentiated from the family group and they are not *nominated*. In terms of functionalisation (the activities or roles people have in society) husbands are classified in terms of their professional status whereas lovers are classified by their looks.

Husbands and children are classified in the text to establish relational identification, while lovers are classified according to their physical identification. Van Leeuwen (1996) observes that physical identification is always overdetermined since physical attributes have special connotations. We can see that in the sex narratives, lovers are reduced to bodies, while husbands and children are integral parts of the narrator's identification.

Finally, I want to examine the question of how the narrators evaluate their actions and how they contribute to reinforcing moral and traditional values and practices.

Evaluation is a very important category in all kinds of narratives. It can appear at any point in a story. It is through evaluation that narrators reveal their degree of involvement in the action and show their recognition of the audience's expectation of reportability. It is also through evaluation that ideological values are conveyed. In media discourse in general, evaluation is a crucial entrance point to the hidden discourse. In the sex narratives under analysis, the women narrators always evaluate their transgression negatively:

I felt *guilty* about the expense at first.

(Irene)

It made me feel good about myself for a short time, but *very bad* later. I am deeply *ashamed* of doing it.

(Louise)

Maybe if Derek and I had had children of our own *I wouldn't be doing* this. I am sure Derek would leave me if he ever found out. Yet part of me blames him for leaving me on my own.

(Jane)

The sex was very good, but I felt *miserable* about it afterwards. Whenever I have paid other men for sex, I have always been left with that same *feeling of loss*.

(Barbara)

These utterances are examples of what Labov [Chapter 12] calls external evaluation. The narrator breaks the frame of the report to address the reader directly and interrupts the actions to express her general evaluation of the distant events. The lexical items chosen in all the narratives are part of the same lexical field: guilt, shame, misery, loss. The actions are therefore evaluated negatively with obvious connotations. The women transgressors regret and repent afterwards. The ambiguous message, based on the contradictory nature of the narratives, is either 'don't do it' or 'if you do it you will feel guilty afterwards'. The transgressive pleasure leads to social punishment.

Conclusions

I have tried to show that narrative structures and subjects are like working apparatuses of ideology, repositories for the meanings by which we live. Without any doubts, the sex narratives I have analysed here testify to 'the pervasive power of narrative and in particular romance narrative as the structuring agent or generic continuity of the women's magazines' (Ballaster *et al.* 1991: 172).

The paradox to be noted, however, is that the sex narratives provide readers with forms of sexual deviance and prohibited love affairs but maintain a moral attitude of condemnation towards the facts portrayed. The combination of reporting and condemning is a commercial formula adopted by the press to attract more readers. All texts code the ideological position of their producers. 'The everyday, innocent and innocuous, mundane text is as ideologically saturated as a text which wears its ideological constitution overtly' (Kress 1993: 174). Consumerism and traditional values are the underlining ideology of these texts.

The first-person narratives that are supposedly transgressive are transgressive only in terms of a traditional view of human sexuality and sexual relationships: to be happy a woman should be in a long-term heterosexual relationship. The analysis of how the social actors are included and named in the sex narratives proves this point. The women are identified by their family links and the most important actors are the husbands. The report of the deviations in the heterosexual marriage is a spectacle which may be glimpsed without any reader involvement. As Chibnall (1977: 32) suggests, 'the reader can sit over her cornflakes in mild moral indignation while today's shock horror probe into yesterday's sex, drugs/orgy unfolds its unseemly content'. The topic of 'sexual practices' examined here shows women who are apparently liberated, but are intrinsically subordinated to kinship evaluation. This evaluation, however, implies social punishment.

In constructing a fictionalised world, sex narratives do not challenge the hegemonic power of middle-class values. The texts analysed prove that women's magazines cannot offer political resolutions to what they consistently define as personal problems. There is a pervasive 'personalised politics' structuring the magazines.

Women's magazines are an institution produced for profit sold all over the world and consequently they are potent cultural forms. It is sad to acknowledge that many women read them, not for intellectual or political challenge, but only for relaxation and 'easy' pleasure. It is also sad to notice the misappropriation of the feminist discourse of sexual liberation. The transgressive woman of *Marie Claire* is not very different from the first readers of the early women's magazines.

Sex narratives as cultural texts and discourses are responsible for maintaining a state of affairs which feminism has fought hard to change: inadequate and insecure women who, to have a voice, have to tell of their secret affairs even though they feel guilty.

Acknowledgement

I am grateful to Susana Funck, Philippe Humblé and Luiz Paulo Moita Lopes for their valuable comments on earlier versions of this chapter, needless to say any remaining deficiencies are my own.

References

Ballaster, R., Beetham, E., Fraser, E. and Hebron, S. (1991) *Women's Worlds: Ideology, Femininity and the Woman's Magazine*, London: Macmillan.

Bell, A. (1991) *The Language of the News Media*, Oxford: Blackwell.

Caldas-Coulthard, C. R. (1987) 'Reporting speech in narrative written texts', in Coulthard, R. M. (ed.) *Discussing Discourse*, Discourse Analysis Monographs, 14, English Language Research, University of Birmingham, 149–67.

Caldas-Coulthard, C. R. (1992) *News as Social Practice*, Florianópolis, Brazil: Universidade Federal de Santa Catarina.

Caldas-Coulthard, C. R. (1993) 'From discourse analysis to critical discourse analysis: the differential representation of women and men speaking in written news', in Sinclair, J. McH., Hoey, M. and Fox, G. (eds) *Techniques of Description: Spoken and Written Discourse*, London: Routledge, 196–208.

Caldas-Coulthard, C. R. (1994) 'On reporting reporting: the representation of speech in factual and factional narratives', in Coulthard, R. M. (ed.) *Advances in Written Text Analysis*, London: Routledge, 295–308.

Chibnall, S. (1977) *Law and Order News: An Analysis of Crime Reporting in the British Press*, London: Tavistock.

Ferguson, M. (1983) *Forever Feminine: Women's Magazines and the Cult of Femininity*, London: Heinemann.

Fowler, R. (1991) *Language in the News: Discourse and Ideology in the Press*, London: Routledge.

Giddens, A. (1992) *A Transformação da Sociedade; Sexualidade, Amor e Erotismo nas Sociedades Modernas* (Portuguese trans.), São Paulo: Editora da UNESP.

Jameson, F. (1981) *The Political Unconscious: Narrative as a Socially Symbolic Act*, London: Methuen.

Kress, G. (1993) 'Against arbitrariness: the social production of the sign as a foundational issue in critical discourse analysis', *Discourse and Society* 4(2): 169–91.

McCracken, E. (1993) *Decoding Women's Magazines: From Mademoiselle to MS*, London: Macmillan.

Van Leeuwen, T. (1996) 'The representation of social actors', in Coulthard, M. and Caldas-Coulthard C. R. (eds) *Texts and Practices: Readings in Critical Discourse Analysis*, London: Routledge, 32–70.
Winship, J. (1987) *Inside Women's Magazines*, London: Pandora.

Chapter 32

Teun A. van Dijk

DISCOURSE AND THE DENIAL OF RACISM

[. . .]

Discourse and racism

One of the crucial properties of contemporary racism is its denial, typically illustrated in such well-known disclaimers as 'I have nothing against blacks, but . . . '. This article examines the discursive strategies, as well as the cognitive and social functions, of such and other forms of denial in different genres of text and talk about ethnic or racial affairs.

[. . .]

The guiding idea behind this research is that ethnic and racial prejudices are prominently acquired and shared within the white dominant group through everyday conversation and institutional text and talk. Such discourse serves to express, convey, legitimate or indeed to conceal or deny such negative ethnic attitudes. Therefore, a systematic and subtle discourse analytical approach should be able to reconstruct such social cognitions about other groups.

It is further assumed in this research programme that talk and text about minorities, immigrants, refugees or, more generally, about people of colour or Third World peoples and nations, also have broader societal, political and

Source: Teun A. van Dijk, 'Discourse and the denial of racism', *Discourse & Society* 3(1), 1992, 87–118.

cultural functions. Besides positive self-presentation and negative other-presentation, such discourse signals group membership, white ingroup allegiances and, more generally, the various conditions for the reproduction of the white group and their dominance in virtually all social, political and cultural domains.

[. . .]

Political, media, academic, corporate and other elites play an important role in the reproduction of racism. They are the ones who control or have access to many types of public discourse, have the largest stake in maintaining white group dominance, and are usually also most proficient in persuasively formulating their ethnic opinions. Although there is of course a continuous interplay between elite and popular forms of racism, analysis of many forms of discourse suggests that the elites in many respects 'preformulate' the kind of ethnic beliefs of which, sometimes more blatant, versions may then get popular currency. Indeed, many of the more 'subtle', 'modern', 'everyday' or 'new' forms of cultural racism, or ethnicism, studied below, are taken from elite discourse. This hypothesis is not inconsistent with the possibility that (smaller, oppositional) elite groups also play a prominent role in the preformulation of anti-racist ideologies.

[. . .]

The denial of racism

The denial of racism is one of the moves that is part of the latter strategy of positive in-group presentation. General norms and values, if not the law, prohibit (blatant) forms of ethnic prejudice and discrimination, and many if not most white group members are both aware of such social constraints and, up to a point, even share and acknowledge them (Billig 1988). Therefore, even the most blatantly racist discourse in our data routinely features denials or at least mitigations of racism. Interestingly, we have found that precisely the more racist discourse tends to have disclaimers and other denials. This suggests that language users who say negative things about minorities are well aware of the fact that they may be understood as breaking the social norm of tolerance or acceptance.

Denials of racism, and similar forms of positive self-presentation, have both an *individual* and a *social* dimension. Not only do most white speakers individually resent being perceived as racists, also, and even more importantly, such strategies may at the same time aim at defending the in-group as a whole: 'We are not racists', 'We are not a racist society'.

Whereas the first, individual, form of denial is characteristic of informal everyday conversations, the second is typical for public discourse, for instance in politics, the media, education, corporations and other organizations. Since public discourse potentially reaches a large audience, it is this latter, social form of denial that is most influential and, therefore, also most damaging: it is the social discourse of denial that persuasively helps construct the dominant white consensus. Few white group members would have reason or interest, to doubt let alone to oppose such a claim.

[. . .]

Conversation

Everyday conversation is at the heart of social life. Whether in informal situations, with family members or friends, or on the job with colleagues or clients or within a multitude of institutions, informal talk constitutes a crucial mode of social interaction. At the same time, conversations are a major conduit of social 'information-processing', and provide the context for the expression and persuasive conveyance of shared knowledge and beliefs.

In ethnically mixed societies, minority groups and ethnic relations are a major topic of everyday conversation. Whether through direct personal experience, or indirectly through the mass media, white people in Europe and North America learn about minorities or immigrants, formulate their own opinions and thus informally reproduce – and occasionally challenge – the dominant consensus on ethnic affairs through informal everyday talk.

Our extensive discourse analytical research into the nature of such everyday talk about ethnic affairs, based on some 170 interviews conducted in the Netherlands and California, shows that such informal talk has a number of rather consistent properties:

1   Topics are selected from a rather small range of subjects, and focus on sociocultural differences, deviance and competition. Most topics explicitly or implicitly deal with interpersonal, social, cultural or economic 'threats' of the dominant white group, society or culture.
2   Storytelling is not, as would be usual, focused on entertaining, but takes place within an argumentative framework. Stories serve as the strong, while personally experienced, premises of a generally negative conclusion, such as 'We are not used to that here', 'They should learn the language' or 'The government should do something about that.'
3   Style, rhetoric and conversational interaction generally denote critical distance, if not negative attitudes towards minorities or immigration.

However, current norms of tolerance control expressions of evaluations in such a way that discourse with strangers (such as interviewers)
is generally rather mitigated. Strong verbal aggression tends to be
avoided.

4   Overall, speakers follow a double strategy of positive self-presentation
and negative other-presentation.

It is within this latter strategy also that disclaimers, such as 'I have nothing
against Arabs, *but* . . .' have their specific functions. Such a denial may be
called 'apparent', because the denial is not supported by evidence that the
speaker does not have anything against 'them'. On the contrary, the denial
often serves as the face-keeping move introducing a generally negative assertion, following the invariable *but*, sometimes stressed, as in the following
example from a Dutch woman:

(1)   uhh . . . how they are and that is mostly just fine, people
have their own religion have their own way of life, and
I have abso*lutely* nothing against that, *but*, it *is* a fact that
if their way of life begins to differ from mine to an *extent*
that. . . .

Talking about the main topic of cultural difference, the denial here focuses
on relative tolerance for such cultural differences, which, however, is clearly
constrained. The differences should not be too great. So, on the one hand,
the woman follows the norm of tolerance, but on the other hand, she feels
justified to reject others when they 'go too far'. In other words, the denial
here presupposes a form of limited social acceptance.

Speakers who are more aware of discrimination and racism, as is the
case in California, are even more explicit about the possible inferences of
their talk:

(2)   It sounds prejudiced, but I think if students only use
English. . . .

The use of English, a prominent topic for 'ethnic' conversations in the
USA, may be required for many practical reasons, but the speaker realizes
that whatever the good arguments he or she may have, it may be heard as
a form of prejudice against immigrants. Of course the use of 'It sounds'
implies that the speaker does not think he is really prejudiced.

One major form of denial in everyday conversation is the denial of discrimination. Indeed, as also happens in the right-wing media (see below), we

also find reversal in this case: we are the real victims of immigration and minorities. Here are some of the ways people in Amsterdam formulate their denials:

(3) Yes, they have exploited them, that's what they say at least, you know, but well, I don't believe that either. . . .

(4) Big cars, they are better off than we are. If anybody is being discriminated against, our children are. That's what I make of it.

(5) And the only thing that came from her mouth was I am being discriminated against and the Dutch all have good housing, well it is a big lie, it is not true.

(6) And they say that they are being dismi discri discriminated against. That is not true.

(7) Listen, they always say that foreigners are being discriminated against here. No, *we* are being discriminated against. It is exactly the reverse.

In all these situations, the speakers talk about what they see as threats or lies by immigrants: a murder in (3), cheating on welfare in (4), a radio programme where a black woman says she is discriminated against in (5), and neighbourhood services in (6) and (7). In conversations such reversals may typically be heard in working-class neighbourhoods where crime is attributed to minorities, or where alleged favouritism (e.g., in housing) is resented. Poor whites thus feel that they are victims of inadequate social and urban policies, but instead of blaming the authorities or the politicians, they tend to blame the newcomers who, in their eyes, are so closely related to the changing, i.e., deteriorating, life in the inner city. And if *they* are defined as those who are responsible, such a role is inconsistent with the claim that *they* are discriminated against (Phizacklea and Miles 1979).

Note that this consensus is not universal. Negative behaviour may be observed, but without generalization and with relevant comparisons to Dutch youths:

(8) And that was also, well I am sorry, but they were foreigners, they were apparently Moroccans who did that. But God, all young people are aggressive, whether it is Turkish youth, or Dutch youth, or Surinamese youth, is aggressive. Particularly because of discrimination uhh that we have here . . .

Here discrimination is not reversed, and the young immigrants are represented as victims of discrimination, which is used to explain and hence to excuse some of their 'aggressiveness'. Such talk, however, is rather exceptional.

The press

Many of the 'ethnic events' people talk about in everyday life are not known from personal experiences, but from the media. At least until recently, in many parts of Western Europe and even in some regions of North America, most white people had few face-to-face dealings with members of minority groups. Arguments in everyday talk, thus, may be about crime or cultural differences they read about in the press, and such reports are taken as 'proof' of the negative attitudes the speakers have about minorities.

Our analyses of thousands of reports in the press in Britain and the Netherlands (van Dijk 1991), largely confirm the common-sense interpretations of the readers: a topical analysis shows that crime, cultural differences, violence ('riots'), social welfare and problematic immigration are among the major recurrent topics of ethnic affairs reporting. In other words, there are marked parallels between topics of talk and media topics.

Overall, with some changes over the last decade, the dominant picture of minorities and immigrants is that of *problems* (Hartmann and Husband 1974). Thus the conservative and right-wing press tends to focus on the problems minorities and immigrants are seen to create (in housing, schooling, unemployment, crime, etc.), whereas the more liberal press (also) focuses on the problems minorities have (poverty, discrimination), but which *we* (white liberals) do something about. On the other hand, many topics that are routine in the coverage of white people, groups or institutions tend to be ignored, such as their contribution to the economy, political organization, culture and in general all topics that characterize the everyday lives of minorities, and their own, active contributions to the society as a whole. Thus, in many respects, except when involved in conflicts or problems, minorities tend to be 'denied' by the press (Boskin 1980).

Practices of newsgathering as well as patterns of quotation also show that minorities and their institutions have literally little to say in the press. First of all, especially in Europe, there are virtually no minority journalists, so that the perspective, inside knowledge and experience, prevailing attitudes and necessary sources of journalists tend to be all white, as are also the government agencies, police and other institutions that are the main sources of news in the press (van Dijk 1988a; 1988b). Even on ethnic events, minority spokespersons are less quoted, less credibly quoted, and if they are quoted their opinions are often 'balanced' by the more 'neutral' comments of white spokespersons. Especially on delicate topics, such as discrimination, prejudice and racism, minority representatives or experts are very seldom heard in a credible, authoritative way. If at all, such quotes are often presented as unwarranted or even ridiculous accusations.

It is at this point where the overall strategy of denial has one of its discursive manifestations in press reports. Of course, as may be expected, there is a difference between liberal, conservative and right-wing newspapers in this respect. Note, however, that there are virtually no explicitly anti-racist newspapers in Europe and North America. The official norm, even on the right, is that 'we are all against racism', and the overall message is, therefore, that serious accusations of racism are a figment of the imagination.

Liberal newspapers, however, do pay attention to stories of explicit discrimination, e.g., in employment (though *rarely* in their own newsrooms or news reports), whereas right-wing extremism is usually dealt with in critical terms, although such coverage may focus on violent or otherwise newsworthy incidents rather than on racist attitudes *per se*. By such means ethnic or racial inequality is redefined as marginal, that is, as individualized or outside the consensus. Thus, the Dutch liberal press extensively reports cases (accusations) of discrimination, and the same is true in the USA. In the right-wing press, discrimination is also covered, but from a different perspective. Here, it is usually covered as a preposterous accusation, preferably against 'ordinary' people, or embedded in explanations or excuses (the act was provoked).

Whereas discrimination gets rather wide attention in the press, racism does not. Indeed, discrimination is seldom qualified as a manifestation of racism. One of the reasons is that racism is still often understood as an ideology of white supremacy, or as the kind of practices of the extreme right. Since the large majority of the press does not identify with the extreme right, any qualification of everyday discriminatory practices as 'racism' is resolutely rejected.

For large sections of the press, only anti-racists see such everyday racism as racism, which results in the marginalization of anti-racists as a radical, 'loony' group. For much of the press, at least in Britain, the real enemies, therefore, are the anti-racists: they are intolerant, anti-British, busybodies, who see racism everywhere, even in 'innocent' children's books, and even in the press.

It is not surprising, therefore, that reports on general aspects of racism in one's own society or group tend to be rare, even in the liberal press. Anti-racist writers, researchers or action groups have less access to the media, and their activities or opinions tend to be more or less harshly scorned, if not ridiculed. For the right-wing press, moreover, they are the real source of the 'problems' attributed to a multicultural society, because they not only attack venerable institutions (such as the police, government or business), but also provide a competing but fully incompatible definition of the ethnic situation. It is this symbolic competition for the definition of the situation and the intellectual struggle over the definition of society's morals, that pitches the right-wing press against left-wing, anti-racist intellectuals, teachers, writers and action groups.

Let us examine in more detail how exactly the press engages in this denial of racism. Most of our examples are taken from the British press, but it would not be difficult to find similar examples in the Dutch, German and French press. Because of its long history of slavery and segregation, the notion of white racism is more broadly accepted in the USA, even when today's prevailing ideology is that, now minorities have equal rights, racism is largely a thing of the past.

Racism and the press

The denial of racism in and by the press is of course most vehement when the press itself is the target of accusations. Reflecting similar reactions by other editors of Dutch newspapers to our own research on racism in the press, the editor-in-chief of a major elite weekly, *Intermediair*, catering especially for social scientists and the business community, writes the following in a letter:

> (9)   In particular, what you state about the coverage of minorities remains unproven and an unacceptable caricature of reality. Your thesis 'that the tendency of most reports is that ethnic minorities cause problems for us' is in my opinion not only not proven, but simply incorrect.
>
> *(Translated from the Dutch)*

This reaction was inspired by a brief summary of mostly international research on the representation of minorities in the press. The editor's denial is not based on (other) research, but simply stated as a 'fact'.

[. . .]

Other editors take an even more furious stand, and challenge the very academic credentials of the researcher and the university, as is the case by the editor of the major conservative popular daily in the Netherlands, *De Telegraaf*, well known for its biased reporting on minorities, immigrants and refugees:

> (10)   Your so-called scientific research does not in any sense prove your slanderous insinuations regarding the contents of our newspaper, is completely irrelevant and raises doubt

about the prevailing norms of scientific research and social
prudence at the University of Amsterdam.

(Translated from the Dutch)

We see that whatever 'proof' may be brought in one's painstaking
analyses of news reports, the reaction is one of flat denial and counter-attack
by discrediting the researcher. Examples like these may be multiplied at
random. No newspaper, including (or especially) the more liberal ones, will
accept even a moderate charge of being biased, while allegations of racism
are rejected violently. Recall that these newspapers, especially in Europe,
generally employ no, or only one or two token, minority journalists.

With such an editorial attitude towards racism, there is a general reluctance to identify racist events as such in society at large. Let us examine the
principal modes of such denials in the press. Examples are taken from the
British press coverage of ethnic affairs in 1985 (for analysis of other properties of these examples, see van Dijk 1991). Brief summaries of the context
of each fragment of news discourse are given between parentheses.

Positive self-presentation

The semantic basis of denial is 'truth' as the writer sees it. The denial of
racism in the press, therefore, presupposes that the journalist or columnist
believes that his or her own group or country is essentially 'tolerant' towards
minorities or immigrants. Positive self-presentation, thus, is an important
move in journalistic discourse, and should be seen as the argumentative denial
of the accusations of anti-racists:

(11)   [Handsworth] Contrary to much doctrine, and acknowl-
       edging a small malevolent fascist fringe, this is a remarkably
       tolerant society. But tolerance would be stretched were it
       to be seen that enforcement of law adopted the principle
       of reverse discrimination.

(Daily Telegraph, editorial, 11 September)

(12)   [Racial attacks and policing] If the ordinary British taste for
       decency and tolerance is to come through, it will need posi-
       tive and unmistakable action.

(Daily Telegraph, editorial, 13 August)

(13)   [Racial attacks against Asians] . . . Britain's record for
       absorbing people from different backgrounds, peacefully

and with tolerance, is second to none. The descendants of
Irish and Jewish immigrants will testify to that. It would
be tragic to see that splendid reputation tarnished now.

(Sun, editorial, 14 August)

(14)   [Immigration] Our traditions of fairness and tolerance are
being exploited by every terrorist, crook, screwball and
scrounger who wants a free ride at our expense. . . . Then
there are the criminals who sneak in as political refugees
or as family members visiting a distant relative.

(Mail, 28 November)

(15)   We have racism too – and that is what is behind the plot.
It is not white racism. It is black racism. . . . But who is
there to protect the white majority? . . . Our tolerance is
our strength, but we will not allow anyone to turn it into
our weakness.

(Sun, 24 October)

These examples not only assert or presuppose white British 'tolerance'
but at the same time define its boundaries. Tolerance might be interpreted
as a position of weakness and, therefore, it should not be 'stretched' too far,
lest 'every terrorist', 'criminal' or other immigrant, takes advantage of it.
Affirmative action or liberal immigration laws, thus, can only be seen as a
form of reverse discrimination, and hence as a form of self-destruction of
white Britain. Ironically, therefore, these examples are self-defeating because
of their internal contradictions. It is not tolerance *per se* that is aimed at, but
rather the limitations preventing its 'excesses'. Note that in example (15)
positive self-presentation is at the same time combined with the well-known
move of reversal. 'They are the real racists', 'We are the real victims.' We
shall come back to such reversal moves below.

Denial and counter-attack

Having constructed a positive self-image of white Britain, the conservative
and tabloid press especially engages in attacks against those who hold a
different view, at the same time defending those who agree with its position,
as was the case during the notorious Honeyford affair (Honeyford was headmaster of a Bradford school who was suspended, then reinstated and finally
let go with a golden handshake, after having written articles on multicultural

education which most of the parents of his mostly Asian students found racist). The attacks on the anti-racists often embody denials of racism:

(16)   [Reaction of 'race lobby' against Honeyford] Why is it that this lobby have chosen to persecute this man. . . . It is not because he is a racist; it is precisely because he is not a racist, yet has dared to challenge the attitudes, behaviour and approach of the ethnic minority professionals.
(*Daily Telegraph*, 6 September)

(17)   [Honeyford and other cases] Nobody is less able to face the truth than the hysterical 'anti-racist' brigade. Their intolerance is such that they try to silence or sack anyone who doesn't toe their party-line.
(*Sun*, 13 October, column by John Vincent)

(18)   [Honeyford] For speaking commonsense he's been vilified; for being courageous he's been damned, for refusing to concede defeat his enemies can't forgive him. . . . I have interviewed him and I am utterly convinced that he hasn't an ounce of racism in his entire being.
(*Mail*, 18 September, column by Lynda Lee-Potter)

(19)   [Honeyford quits] Now we know who the true racists are.
(*Sun* editorial, 30 November)

These examples illustrate several strategic moves in the press campaign against anti-racists. First, as we have seen above, denial is closely linked to the presupposition of 'truth': Honeyford is presented as defending the 'truth', namely the failure and the anti-British nature of multiculturalism. Second, consequent denials often lead to the strategic move of reversal: *we* are not the racists, *they* are the 'true racists'. This reversal also implies, thirdly, a reversal of the charges: Honeyford, and those who sympathize with him, are the victims, not his Asian students and their parents. Consequently, the anti-racists are the enemy: *they* are the ones who persecute innocent, ordinary British citizens, *they* are the ones who are intolerant. Therefore, victims who resist their attackers may be defined as folk heroes, who 'dare' the 'anti-racist brigade'.

Note also, in example (17), that the 'truth', as the supporters of Honeyford see it, is self-evident, and based on common sense. Truth and common sense are closely related notions in such counter-attacks, and reflect the power of the consensus, as well as the mobilization of popular support by 'ordinary' (white) British people. Apart from marginalizing Asian parents and other anti-racists by locating them outside of the consensus, and beyond the community of ordinary people like 'us', such appeals to common sense also have powerful ideological implications: self-evident truth is seen as 'natural', and hence the position of the others as 'unnatural' or even as 'crazy'. The anti-racist left, therefore, is often called 'crazy' or 'loony' in the right-wing British press.

Moral blackmail

One element that was very prominent in the Honeyford affair, as well as in similar cases, was the pretence of censorship: the anti-racists not only ignore the 'truth' about multicultural society, they also prevent others (us) from telling the truth. Repeatedly, thus, journalists and columnists argue that this 'taboo' and this 'censorship' must be broken in order to be able to tell the 'truth', as was the case after the disturbances in Tottenham:

> (20) [Tottenham] The time has come to state the truth without cant and without hypocrisy . . . the strength to face the facts without being silenced by the fear of being called racist.
> (*Mail*, 9 October, column by Lynda Lee-Potter)

Such examples also show that the authors feel morally blackmailed, while at the same time realizing that to 'state the truth', meaning 'to say negative things about minorities', may well be against the prevalent norms of toler-ance and understanding. Clamouring for the 'truth', thus, expresses a dilemma, even if the dilemma is only apparent: the apparent dilemma is a rhetorical strategy to accuse the opponent of censorship or blackmail, not the result of moral soul-searching and a difficult decision. After all, the same newspapers extensively *do* write negative things about young blacks, and never hesitate to write what they see as the 'truth'. Nobody 'silences' them, and the taboo is only imaginary. On the contrary, the right-wing press in Britain reaches many millions of readers.

Thus, this strategic play of denial and reversal at the same time involves the construction of social roles in the world of ethnic strife, such as allies and enemies, victims, heroes and oppressors. In many respects, such discourse mimics the discourse of anti-racists by simply reversing the major roles: victims become oppressors, those who are in power become victims.

Subtle denials

Denials are not always explicit. There are many ways to express doubt, distance or non-acceptance of statements or accusations by others. When the official Commission for Racial Equality (CRE) in 1985 published a report on discrimination in the UK, outright denial of the facts would hardly be credible. Other discursive means, such as quotation marks, and the use of words like 'claim' or 'allege', presupposing doubt on the part of the writer, may be employed in accounting for the facts, as is the case in the following editorial from the *Daily Telegraph*:

> (21) In its report which follows a detailed review of the oper-
> ation of the 1976 Race Relations Act, the Commission
> claims that ethnic minorities continue to suffer high levels
> of discrimination and disadvantage.
> *(Daily Telegraph*, 1 August)

Such linguistic tricks do not go unnoticed, as we may see in the following reaction to this passage in a letter from Peter Newsam, then Director of the CRE.

> (22) Of the Commission you say 'it claims that ethnic minori-
> ties continue to suffer high levels of discrimination and
> disadvantage'. This is like saying that someone 'claims' that
> July was wet. It was. And it is also a fact supported by the
> weight of independent research evidence that discrimina-
> tion on racial grounds, in employment, housing and
> services, remains at a disconcertingly high level.
> *(Daily Telegraph*, 7 August)

Denials, thus, may be subtly conveyed by expressing doubt or distance. Therefore, the very notion of 'racism' usually appears between quotation marks, especially also in the headlines. Such scare quotes are not merely a journalistic device of reporting opinions or controversial points of view. If that were the case, also the opinions with which the newspaper happens to agree would have to be put between quotes, which is not always the case. Rather, apart from signalling journalistic doubt and distance, the quotes also connote 'unfounded accusation'. The use of quotes around the notion of 'racism' has become so much routine, that even in cases where the police or the courts themselves established that racism was involved in a particular case, the conservative press may maintain the quotes out of sheer habit.

Mitigation

Our conceptual analysis of denial already showed that denial may also be implied by various forms of mitigation, such as downtoning, using euphemisms or other circumlocutions that minimize the act itself or the responsibility of the accused. In the same editorial of the *Daily Telegraph* we quoted above, we find the following statement:

> (23)   [CRE report] No one would deny the fragile nature of race relations in Britain today or that there is misunderstanding and distrust between parts of the community.
> (*Daily Telegraph*, editorial, 1 August)

Thus, instead of inequality or racism, race relations are assumed to be 'fragile', whereas 'misunderstanding and distrust' is also characteristic of these relations. Interestingly, this passage also explicitly denies the prevalence of denials and, therefore, might be read as a concession: there *are* problems. However, the way this concession is rhetorically presented by way of various forms of mitigation, suggests, in the context of the rest of the same editorial, that the concession is apparent. Such apparent concessions are another major form of disclaimer in discourse about ethnic relations, as we also have them in statements like: 'There are also intelligent blacks, but . . .', or 'I know that minorities sometimes have problems, but . . .'. Note also that in the example from the *Daily Telegraph* the mitigation not only appears in the use of euphemisms, but also in the *redistribution of responsibility*, and hence in the denial of blame. Not we (whites) are mainly responsible for the tensions between the communities, but everybody is, as is suggested by the use of the impersonal existential phrase: '*There is* misunderstanding . . .'. Apparently, one effective move of denial is to either dispute responsible agency, or to conceal agency.

Defence and offence

On the other hand, in its attacks against the anti-racists, the right-wing press is not always that subtle. On the contrary, they may engage precisely in the 'diatribes' they direct at their opponents:

> (24)   [Anti-fascist rally] The evening combined emotive reminders of the rise of Nazism with diatribes against racial discrimination and prejudice today.
> (*Daily Telegraph*, 1 October)

(25)   [Black sections] In the more ideologically-blinkered sections
of his [Kinnock's] party . . . they seem to gain pleasure from
identifying all difficulties experienced by immigrant groups,
particularly Afro-Caribbeans, as the result of racism . . .
(*Daily Telegraph*, editorial, 14 September)

(26)   [Worker accused of racism] . . . The really alarming thing is
that some of these pocket Hitlers of local government are
moving into national politics. It's time we set about exposing their antics while we can. Forewarned is forearmed.
(*Mail*, editorial, 26 October)

These examples further illustrate that denial of discrimination, prejudice
and racism is not merely a form of self-defence or positive self-presentation.
Rather, it is at the same time an element of attack against what they define
as 'ideologically blinkered' opponents, as we also have seen in the move of
reversal in other examples. Anti-racism is associated with the 'loony left',
and attacking it therefore also has important ideological and political implications, and not just moral ones.

'Difficulties' of the Afro-Caribbean community may be presupposed,
though not spelled out forcefully and in detail, but such presuppositions rather
take the form of an apparent concession. That is, whatever the causes of
these 'difficulties', as they are euphemistically called, they can not be the
result of racism. Implicitly, by attributing 'pleasure' to those who explain
the situation of the blacks, the newspaper also suggests that the left has an
interest in such explanations and, therefore, even welcomes racism. This
strategy is familiar in many other attacks against anti-racists: 'If there were
no racism, they would invent it'. It hardly needs to be spelled out that such
a claim again implies a denial of racism.

The amalgamation of comparisons and metaphors used in these attacks is
quite interesting. That is, in one example an ironic reference is made to the
'emotive reminders' of Nazism, and in another these same opponents of Nazism
are qualified as 'pocket Hitlers'. Yet, this apparent inconsistency in socio-
political labelling has a very precise function. By referring to their opponents in
terms of 'pocket Hitlers' the newspapers obviously distance themselves from
the fascist opinions and practices that are often part of the more radical accusations against the right. At the same time, by way of the usual reversal, they
categorize their opponents precisely in terms of their own accusations, and thus
put them in a role these opponents most clearly would abhor.

Thus, the anti-racist left is associated with fascist practices, ideological
blinkers and antics. Apart from their anti-racist stance, it is, however, their

(modest) political influence which particularly enrages the right-wing press —
although virtually powerless at the national level, and even within their own
(Labour) party, some of the anti-racists have made it into local councils, and
therefore control (some) money, funding and other forms of political influence.
That is, they have at least some counter-power, and it is this power and its
underlying ideology that is challenged by a press which itself controls the news
supply of millions of readers. What the denial of racism and the concomitant
attacks against the anti-racists in education or politics is all about, therefore, is
a struggle over the definition of the ethnic situation. Thus, their ideological and
political opponents are seen as symbolic competitors in the realm of moral influence. Whether directed at a headmaster or against other ordinary white British
or not, what the right-wing press is particularly concerned about is its own
image: by attacking the anti-racists, it is in fact defending itself.

[. . .]

Conclusions

Whether in the streets of the inner city, in the press or in parliament, dominant group members are often engaged in discourse about 'them': ethnic
minority groups, immigrants or refugees, who have come to live in the
country. Such discourses, as well as the social cognitions underlying them,
are complex and full of contradictions. They may be inspired by general
norms of tolerance and acceptance, but also, and sometimes at the same
time, by feelings of distrust, resentment or frustration about those 'others'.

Topics, stories and argumentation may thus construct a largely negative
picture of minorities or immigrants, e.g., in terms of cultural differences,
deviance or competition, as a problem or as a threat to 'our' country, territory, space, housing, employment, education, norms, values, habits or
language. Such talk and text, therefore, is not a form of individual discourse,
but social, group discourse, and expresses not only individual opinions, but
rather socially shared representations.

However, negative talk about minority groups or immigrants may be
heard as biased, prejudiced or racist, and as inconsistent with general values
of tolerance. This means that such discourse needs to be hedged, mitigated,
excused, explained or otherwise managed in such a way that it will not
'count' against the speaker or writer. Face-keeping, positive self-presentation
and impression management are the usual strategies that language users have
recourse to in such a situation of possible 'loss of face': they have to make
sure that they are not misunderstood and that no unwanted inferences are
made from what they say.

One of the major strategic ways white speakers and writers engage in such a form of impression management is the denial of racism. They may simply claim they did not say anything negative, or focus on their intentions: it may have sounded negative, but was not intended that way. Similarly, they may mitigate their negative characterization of the others by using euphemisms, implications or vague allusions. They may make apparent concessions, on the one hand, and on the other hand support their negative discourse by arguments, stories or other supporting 'facts'.

Also, speakers and writers may abandon their position of positive self-presentation and self-defence and take a more active, aggressive counter-attack: the ones who levelled the accusations of racism are the real problem, if not the real racists. They are the ones who are intolerant, and they are against 'our' own people. We are the victims of immigration, and we are discriminated against.

It is interesting to note that despite the differences in style for different social groups, such discourse may be found at any social level, and in any social context. That is, both the 'ordinary' white citizens as well as the white elites need to protect their social self-image, and at the same time they have to manage the interpretation and the practices in an increasingly variegated social and cultural world. For the dominant group, this means that dominance relations must be reproduced, at the macro- as well as at the micro-level, both in action as well as in mind.

Negative representations of the dominated group are essential in such a reproduction process. However, such attitudes and ideologies are inconsistent with dominant democratic and humanitarian norms and ideals. This means that the dominant group must protect itself, cognitively and discursively, against the damaging charge of intolerance and racism. Cognitive balance may be restored only by actually being or becoming anti-racist, by accepting minorities and immigrants as equals, or else by denying racism. It is this choice that white groups in Europe and North America are facing. So far they have largely chosen the latter option.

References

Billig, M. (1988) 'The notion of "prejudice": some rhetorical and ideological aspects', *Text* 8: 91–110.

Boskin, J. (1980) 'Denials: the media view of dark skins and the city', in Rubin, B. (ed.) *Small Voices and Great Trumpets: Minorities and the Media*, New York: Praeger, 141–7.

Hartmann, P. and Husband, C. (1974) *Racism and the Mass Media*, London: Davis-Poynter.

Phizacklea, A. and Miles, R. (1979) 'Working-class racist beliefs in the inner city', in Miles, R. and Phizacklea, A. (eds) *Racism and Political Action in Britain*, London: Routledge & Kegan Paul, 93–123.

Van Dijk, T. A. (1988a) *News Analysis: Case Studies of International and National News in the Press*, Hillsdale, NJ: Erlbaum.

Van Dijk, T. A. (1988b) *News as Discourse*, Hillsdale, NJ: Erlbaum.

Van Dijk, T. A. (1991) *Racism and the Press*, London: Routledge.

Chapter 33

Hugh Mehan

ORACULAR REASONING IN A PSYCHIATRIC EXAM: THE RESOLUTION OF CONFLICT IN LANGUAGE

> Men define situations as real and they are real in their consequences.
>
> (W. I. Thomas[1])

The two major purposes of this chapter are (1) to show how competing definitions of the situation are constructed and revealed in ongoing interaction within an institutionalized setting (a mental hospital), and (2) to show how institutionalized power is displayed and used to resolve disputes over conflicting definitions of the situation. In so doing, I will be commenting on the famous "Thomas Theorem." Parts of what I say will provide support for Thomas's idea that people define situations as real in and through their interaction. Other parts will stretch the limits of the theorem. Not all definitions of situations have equal authority. Competing definitions are resolved by imposing institutional definitions on lay persons' definitions. This "ironicizing of experience" (Pollner 1975) requires a modification in Thomas's consensual world view, which I have reformulated as follows:

> All people define situations as real; but when powerful people define situations as real, then they are real *for everybody involved* in their consequences.

Source: Hugh Mehan, 'Oracular reasoning in a psychiatric exam: the resolution of conflict in language', in Allen D. Grimshaw (ed.) *Conflict Talk: Sociolinguistic Investigations of Arguments in Conversation*, Cambridge: Cambridge University Press, 160–77.

My presentation will take a circuitous route. Before showing how institutionalized power is used to impose a certain definition on the situation, I
will place the discussion in the context of debates about the thinking of "primitive" and "advanced" peoples. After introducing the notion of "oracular
reasoning" (a concept which is central to the understanding of the events
which follow), I will examine closely the interaction between a board of
examining psychiatrists and a mental patient.

The thinking of primitive and advanced peoples

[. . .]

Oracular reasoning in a "primitive" society

The quintessential example of oracular reasoning is found in Evans-Pritchard's
(1973) account of the Azande of Africa. When the Azande are faced with
important decisions – decisions about where to build their homes, or whom
to marry, or whether the sick will live, for example – they consult an oracle.
They prepare for these consultations by following a strictly prescribed ritual.
First, a substance is gathered from the bark of a certain type of tree. Then
this substance is prepared in a special way in a séance-like ceremony. The
Azande then poses a question to the oracle in a way that permits a simple
yes or no answer and feeds the substance to a small chicken. The person
consulting the oracle decides beforehand whether the death of the chicken
will signal an affirmative or negative response, and so they always receive an
unequivocal answer to their questions.

For monumental decisions, the Azande add a second step. They feed the
substance to a second chicken, asking the same question, but reversing
the importance of the chicken's death. If in the first consultation sparing the
chicken's life meant the oracle said "yes," in the second reading, the oracle
must now kill the chicken to once more reply in the affirmative and be
consistent with the first response.

Seemingly, insuperable difficulties accrue to people who hold such beliefs,
because the oracle could contradict itself. What if, for example, the first
consultation of the oracle produces a positive answer and then the second
produces a negative reply? Or, suppose that someone else consults the oracle
about the same question, and contradictory answers occur? What if the oracle
is contradicted by later events – the house site approved by the oracle, for
example, is promptly flooded; or the wife the oracle selected dies or turns

out to be infertile? How is it possible for the Azande to continue to believe in their oracle in the face of so many evident contradictions of their faith?

The answers to these questions are both simple and complex. Simple, because the Azande do not see the events just listed as contradictions, as threats to the oracle. Complex, because of the reasoning practices that are invoked to keep the efficacy of the oracle intact. The Azande know that an oracle exists. That is their beginning premise. All that subsequently happens is interpreted in terms of that "incorrigible proposition" – a proposition that one never admits to be false whatever happens; one that is compatible with any and every conceivable state of affairs (Gasking 1955: 432 as quoted in Pollner 1975). The Azande employ what Evans-Pritchard (1973: 330) calls "secondary elaborations of belief," practices which explain the failure of the oracle by retaining the unquestioned faith in oracles.

The culture provides the Azande with a number of ready-made explanations of the oracle's seeming contradictions. The secondary elaborations of belief that explain the failure of the oracle attribute the failure to other circumstances, some of this world, some of the spirit world – the wrong variety of poison being gathered, breach of taboo, witchcraft, the anger of the owners of the place where the poison plants grow, the age of the poison, the anger of ghosts, or sorcery.

By explaining away contradictions through these secondary elaborations of the belief in oracles, the reality of a world in which oracles are a basic feature is reaffirmed. Failures do not challenge the oracle. They are elaborated in such a way that they provide evidence for the constant success, the marvel, of oracles. Beginning with the incorrigible belief in oracles, all events reflexively become evidence for that belief.

Recent research suggests that maintaining belief by denying or repelling contradictory evidence is not limited to so-called primitives. Well-educated "modern" people also give evidence of oracular reasoning.

Oracular reasoning in modern form

Everyday reasoning
Wason (1977) reviewed a set of delightful experiments that he and Johnson-Laird have conducted, with the same problems presented to subjects alternatively in abstract and concrete form. Again and again, the subjects of these ingenious experiments seemed to be influenced by the context and the content of the problems. When information was presented in semantically coherent form, such as stories, or with real-life manifestations, subjects performed consistently better than when information was presented in

algebraic or symbolic form. When the totality of these studies is considered, we find that people do not employ problem-solving procedures that would challenge or falsify the hypothesis being tested nearly as often as they employ problem-solving procedures that confirm the hypothesis under consideration.

Pollner and McDonald-Wikler (1985) examined the routine transactions of a family with their severely mentally retarded child. They reported that the family employed practices which sustained the family's belief in the competence of the child in the face of overwhelming evidence to the contrary, i.e., a team of medical practitioners had diagnosed the child as severely mentally retarded. The authors' observations of video-taped family interaction revealed that family members pre-structured the child's environment to maximize the likelihood that whatever the child did could be seen as meaningful, intentional activity. The child's family would establish a definition of the situation and use it as a frame of reference for interpreting and describing any and all of the child's subsequent behavior. They also tracked the child's ongoing behavior and developed physical or verbal contexts that could render the behavior intelligent and interactionally responsive.

Religious reasoning
Millennial groups are organized around the prediction of some future events, for example, the second coming of Christ and the beginning of Christ's reign on earth, the destruction of the earth through a cataclysm – usually with a select group, the believers, slated for rescue from the disaster.

[. . .]

No millennial group is more fascinating than the Millerites. William Miller was a New England farmer who believed in literal fulfillment of biblical prophecy. In 1818, after a two-year study of the Bible, Miller reached the conclusion that the end of the world would occur in 1843. He slowly developed a following. The faithful took all the necessary precautions including dissolving relationships, settling debts, selling possessions – and waited together for the second coming of Christ. When the fateful day came – and went – the faithful were confronted with a devastating contradiction to their belief (and lives which were in total disrepair). Their response to this devastation was amazing: instead of turning away from their religious beliefs and spiritual leaders, they used the failure of prophecy as further proof of the wonder and mystery of God. The leaders, far from doubting their basic belief in the second coming, elaborated their belief by citing errors in calculation and weakness in faith as reasons why God did not reveal Himself at the time they predicted. Group leaders retreated to their texts and emerged some time later with new calculations. The number of believers increased – as if conviction was deepened by evidence which contradicted their beliefs. Alas, after three more specific predictions failed, the group disbanded in disbelief.

Scientific reasoning

Oracular reasoning appears among scientists as well as among religious zealots, as Gould's (1981) chronicle of a long history of research conducted in defense of Caucasian racial superiority shows. Morton's craniology, Lombroso's criminal anthropology and Burt's intelligence testing start from the premise that whites are superior to blacks, native Americans and other racial or ethnic groups. Gould describes the methodological errors and outright fraud which arose, often unintentionally, when researchers held too dearly to that basic belief. For example, Gould's meticulous re-analysis of Morton's data uncovered a systematic pattern of distortion in the direction of the preferred hypothesis. Statistics were summed inappropriately across groups and groups which seemed to counter the argument were excluded from statistical analysis. The overall effect of these practices was the production of data that confirmed the hypothesis of racial superiority, but did so by systematically manipulating or excluding potentially contradictory evidence.

Gould says that the recurrence of racist uses of IQ tests and other measurement techniques is aided by "unconscious bias." This concept liberates us from the suspicion that all racists are cynical plotters against the truth and it implies the existence of a coherent structure of expectations about the phenomena of the world which guides the thoughts of scientists and non-scientists alike. But "unconscious bias" is too limited an idea for such a pervasive intellectual practice (Greenwood 1984: 21). To the extent that unconscious biases are shared widely and perpetuated despite the use of empirical data and sound analytical procedures, they are not biases at all; they are collective conceptions about the structures and operation of the natural world.

Oracular reasoning in a psychiatric exam

These discussions have identified oracular reasoning in general terms. I want to show its practice concretely, in the detail of on-going discourse. To do so, I will discuss a "gatekeeping encounter" (Erickson 1975) between a board of psychiatrists and a mental patient. Unlike most gatekeeping encounters (in which the gatekeeper is judging whether the applicant is worthy of *entering* an institution – a place of business, a college, a medical care center) in this encounter the gatekeepers are deciding whether the applicant can *leave* the institution (the mental hospital).

The materials used in this analysis come from an unusual source, which requires some comment. During the course of making his documentary film on a mental hospital in the State of Massachusetts, *Titicut Follies*, Frederick Wiseman filmed a "psychiatric out-take interview." The edited version of this interview appearing in the film is the one I use for the analysis which follows. The use of edited documentary film for discourse analysis, of course, places me at a disadvantage: I neither have the background knowledge of the setting normally available to ethnographers nor am I privy to the film-editing process. Nevertheless, the language in the interview is so provocative that I can not resist analyzing it. It is my hope that readers of the analysis will forgive problems associated with the data in exchange for the heuristics with the analysis.

I approached the analysis of this film as I have others: I have watched the film numerous times – both in private viewings and in courses I teach. I constructed a transcript of the interview. The transcript and my memory of the audio and visual record served as the basis of my interpretation. After I completed the analysis which follows, I watched the film again, and made minor modifications – mostly concerning seating arrangements and the physical movements of the participants.[2]

The basis of the conflict

The interview starts with the patient, Vladimir, being led into the examining room. He stands before a table, behind which are seated four members of the examining board. The head psychiatrist begins questioning the patient, but the interrogation quickly breaks down into an argument about the quantity and quality of the patient's treatment. After a number of exchanges, the head psychiatrist abruptly orders the patient to be taken away. At this point, the film is edited; we see the members of the examining board give their interpretation of the case, and reach a conclusion about the patient's status.

The status of a patient's "career" in a hospital (Goffman 1959), indeed, about the patient's life, was established during the course of this gatekeeping encounter. He will remain in the hospital, diagnosed as a paranoid schizophrenic, and receive increased dosages of medicine.

At the outset, it is important to comment on the *social* nature of the outcome. The state of the patient's mental health was not the automatic result of a machine or a meter reading; the patient's mental state was determined by people, who participated in the assembly of an outcome. Here then we have a quintessential example of social construction (Berger 1968; Garfinkel 1967; Scheff 1966; Cicourel 1973; Mehan 1983a; 1983b): the medical fact of mental illness is constructed in social circumstances.

While this event is social in that a medical fact is assembled in interaction, it is not social in another sense. The event is not social in the sense that the participants failed to reach a mutually agreed-upon definition of the situation. Here we have a set of circumstances in which people, a group of doctors and a patient, have interacted with each other for a stretch of time; each has arrived at a definition of the situation, but the definitions are considerably different, indeed, in conflict with each other.

By looking at the interaction which takes place among the participants in this meeting closely, I will try to determine how it is that the doctors and the patient come to conflicting definitions of the situation. Putting the punch line up front, I will try to demonstrate that both the doctors and the patient were engaged in "oracular reasoning." Normally associated with the procedures used by so-called primitive, or poorly educated peoples when making decisions about life, both the psychiatrists (a presumably well-educated group of people in an "advanced" Western society) and a mental patient (not as well educated, nonetheless a member of an industrialized society) are engaged in this mode of discourse.

The practices of oracular reasoning which are visible in the out-take interview include the following:

> A basic premise or a fundamental proposition is presented which forms the basis of an argument.
>
> When confronted with evidence which is potentially contradictory to a basic position, the evidence is ignored, repelled, or denied.
>
> The presence of evidence which opposes a basic position is used reflexively as further support of the efficacy of the basic position.

I will now go through the transcript of the out-patient interview and show the presence of these features in both the doctors' *and* the patient's discourse. Doing so will enable us to understand how multiple and conflicting definitions of the situation were arrived at. The location of these features in the doctors' and not just the patient's discourse will illustrate the further point that oracular reasoning practices are not limited or confined to primitives or the uneducated; they make their appearance in the reasoning of highly educated thinkers. The persistent presence of oracular reasoning in a wide variety of domains recommends that we consider the possibility that oracular reasoning is a more widespread practice than often acknowledged.

The basic propositions

The basic premise or proposition which underlies the psychiatrists' definition of the situation concerns the health or rather, ill-health of the patient. From the doctors' point of view, the patient is mentally ill. The conclusion about this particular case is founded in even a more basic premise about a physician's expertise: the psychiatrist has access to a body of knowledge which is inaccessible to lay people. This premise gains ready empirical support: the patient is, after all, in a mental hospital. People who are in mental hospitals are presumed to be mentally ill (Scheff 1966). The psychiatrists' commitment to this assumption is voiced by the head psychiatrist, who begins the hearing by saying:

> okay, now Vladimir, as I've promised you before, if I see enough improvement in you . . .

Although the patient, Vladimir, interrupts the psychiatrist before he finishes his introductory statement, the syntax of the psychiatrist's utterance enables us to infer the concluding phrase: (if you show improvement, then we will release you). The "need to show improvement" presupposes a prior mental state which is in need of improvement, i.e., mental illness. The fact of incarceration presupposes that same damaged mental state.

The psychiatrists' commitment to this assumption is reinforced throughout the hearing, especially as the head psychiatrist challenges the patient's arguments. He parries the patient's assertions of his mental health with questions about how he came to be a patient in the hospital ("what got you down here?") and his strange beliefs ("you felt the coffee was poison . . . you felt that people were mixing you up in your thinking").

The patient also has a basic premise from which he argues his definition of the situation. It is the exact opposite of the psychiatrists' definition: he is mentally healthy and does not deserve to be hospitalized. The patient's assertion of his mental health, argued in the face of underlying belief in psychiatric expertise, is to be found in virtually every one of his utterances during the hearing. Here are some quotes which give a sense of belief in his health and the depth of his commitment to this belief:

> my mind's perfect . . . I'm obviously logical, I know what I'm talking about. . . . everytime I come in here you call me I am crazy. Now, what's, if, if it's something you don't like about my face, that's I mean, that's another story. But that has nothing to do with my mental stability.

The incorrigibility of the propositions

The reasoning of the psychiatrists and of the patient share another feature: they both retain their belief in their basic premises and do so despite evidence which is presented to the contrary. The psychiatrists and the patient maintain the incorrigibility of their propositions by deflecting, ignoring, or reinterpreting evidence which is contrary to their basic beliefs.

The incorrigibility feature of oracular reasoning is present in virtually every exchange between the psychiatrists and the patient. I include some of these exchanges here to show how each uses the evidence presented by the other to retain their commitment to their original belief.

The head psychiatrist asks the patient about his participation in hospital activities, including work, sports, and therapy. The assumption underlying the doctor's line of questioning is that affirmative answers to these questions indicate a positive approach on the part of the patient – a patient who is making an effort to improve himself. The following exchanges indicate that the patient has a different attitude about these issues:

(1) HP: Are you working here Vladimir?

(2) Pt: No, there is no suitable work for me here. All I've got is, all I got is

(3)   the kitchen and all they do is throw cup cups around. In fact,

(4)   they got two television sets which are blaring, machines which

(5)   are going, everything which is against the mind. There is one

(6)   thing uh uh uh that a patient does need, and this is what I do

(7)   know, absolutely, is is quiet, if I have a mental problem or even

(8)   an emotional problem. I'm thrown in with over a hundred of

(9)   them and all they do is yell, walk around, televisions are blaring,

(10)   so that's doing my mind harm!

(11) HP: Are you involved in any sports here?

(12) Pt: There are no sports here. All I've got is a baseball and – and–a a

(13)   glove, and that's it! There's nothing else. Hum. There's nothing

(14)   else . . .

(15) HP: Are you in any group therapy here?

(16) Pt: No! There is no group, obviously I do not need group therapy, I

(17)   need peace and quiet. See me. This place is disturbing me! It's

(18)   harming me . . . I'm losing weight. Every, everything that's been

(19)   happening to me is bad. And all I got, all I get is: "well, why don't

(20)   you take medication?" Medication is disagreeable to me. There

(21)   are people to whom you may not give medication. Obviously,

(22)   and the medication that I got is hurting me, it's harming me!

The doctor has phrased his questions (1), (11), (15) in such a way that a "yes" or "no" is the expected reply. Instead of providing the canonical yes or no response to the doctor's questions about work, sports, and therapy, the patient denies the premise underlying the doctor's questioning (and by extension his professional expertise). There *is no* work, there *are no* sports, there *is no* therapy:

> I was supposed to only come down here for observation. What observation did I get? You called me up a couple of times.

In denying the doctor's fundamental assumption, the patient articulates his commitment to his own belief — his health:

> I do not need group therapy, I need peace and quiet. . . . This place is disturbing me.

The doctors do not respond immediately to the patient. We must wait until the patient is removed from the room to hear them articulate their reaction to his position. In general, they do not accept the patient's assertion of his health; in fact, they maintain the opposite — that "he's now falling apart", "reverting". "So he's not looking ready to be able to make it back to prison". The patient's assertions on his behalf contribute to the doctors' conclusion. By his own admission, he doesn't participate in hospital activities, sports, work and therapy. These are the very activities which have been established to help to rehabilitate the patient. The patient's calculated avoidance of these rehabilitative activities becomes further proof of his recalcitrance and contribute to his regression to a prior, unhealthy state of mind.

The attitude that the doctors and patient adopt toward medicine is a particularly telling example of how the same evidence can be used to support diametrically opposed positions. For the patient, medicine is for sick people; since he is healthy, he doesn't need it. In fact, to take medicine would be to admit that he *is* sick. Since he is healthy, he doesn't need the medicine. For the doctors, medicine is a part of a rehabilitation process; the patient's admitted reticence to take medicine is taken as a sign that the patient is both sick and unwilling to help in his own rehabilitation:

> Well I think what we have to do with him is, uh, put him on a higher dose of tranquilizers and see if we can bring the paranoid element under a little bit better control and see if we can get him back on medication. If he's taking it now, and I'm not even sure that he is.

Coulter (1979: 101) discusses how psychiatrists may engage in "strategic contextualization" to make sense out of what is manifestly disorderly or contradictory. In this instance, we seem to have the opposite set of circumstances: a strategic contextualization which undermines the ostensive rationality or logic of the patient's presentation. The patient's very logic becomes an expression of disorder. This strategic decontextualization through the selective invocation of background knowledge and the demand for literal (yes/no) answers to questions, simultaneously frames and undercuts the speaker and the power of his discourse. From the psychiatrists' point of view, even the patient's expressed emotion is symptomatic of his disorder (cf. Rosenhan 1973):

> the louder he shouts about going back the more frightened he indicates that he probably is.

The patient has presented himself to the doctors as agitated and unreasonable, which is further proof that he is mentally ill.

Of course, there is another perspective on the patient's presentation of himself. He feels unjustly treated, confined against his will. Given this one, brief opportunity to present his case, he does so forcefully, energetically. Anticipating the prospect of leaving the hospital, he is excited, which is an understandable emotion for a person who sees himself languishing in a cell:

> I have a perfect right to be excited. I've been here for a year and a half, hum, and this place is doing me harm.

With the patient's presentation of himself, as with the medicine and hospital activities, then, we have an instance in which the same state of affairs is interpreted differently from different perspectives. This perspectively induced perception contributes to the maintenance of belief on the part of the physicians and on the part of the patient. Both cling to their basic assertions, denying the information presented which has the potential of undermining those basic beliefs.

One member of the board of examiners makes this belief-validating process visible for us during her contribution to the board's interpretation of the case:

> Dr 2: He argues in a perfectly paranoid pattern. If you accept his basic premise the rest of it is logical. But, the basic premise is not true.

She admits to the possibility of the patient's interpretation ("If you accept his basic premise"), entertains the viability of the patient's conclusions and the evidence he has presented in defense of his conclusions ("the rest is logical"), yet she does not change her opinion. She rejects the patient's line of reasoning and remains committed to her belief that the patient is mentally ill.

Competing languages of expression: the medical and the sociological

Two competing languages about the nature of mental illness have developed in the recent history of medicine. One, called the "medical model," treats the issue in biological terms. Because the body is an organism, its various parts are subject to pathologies. Mental illness has developed as an extension of this way of thinking. The mind is treated by analogy to an organ of the body; it, like the heart, liver or pancreas, is subject to disease. As an organ, it can be treated in the same way as disease to other organs, i.e., by medicine, confinement, operations to remove diseased tissues. The cause and the cure of mental illness, like physical illness, is to be found in the biological realm, a state or trait of the individual person.

The second, called the "sociological" or "deviance" model, treats the issue of mental illness in social and contextual terms. Denying the analogy between the mind and organs of the body, mental illness is talked about in terms of actions and rules. Mental illness is the label attached to people who break a certain set of society's rules. Its origins are to be found, therefore, not in biological pathologies, but in the social context of relationships between people, people who identify rule breakers, people who apply labels and in extreme cases, institutionalize the rule breakers (Scheff 1966; Kitsuse 1963; Becker 1963; Goffman 1959; Laing 1967; Szasz and Hollender 1956). Mental illness is eliminated by rearranging social contexts such that bizarre behavior is no longer necessary.

The participants in the meeting use these two languages during the course of their interaction. The medical language appears in most pronounced form during the discussion among the doctors after the patient was removed from the room. The cause of the patient's difficulties are talked about in terms of the patient's personal states. He is "paranoid," "schizophrenic", "depressed". That is, the cause of the problem is located within the patient. Increased doses of medicine are prescribed in order to gain better control of his paranoid state.

The patient voices the sociological model in virtually every one of his pronouncements. He blames the circumstances, focusing particular attention on the hospital and the treatment he has been getting (or rather, has not been getting) but *not* his mental state for his problems:

> I've been trying to tell you. I can tell you, day by day, I'm getting worse, because of the circumstances, because of the situation.

> So, it's obviously the treatment I'm getting or it's the situation or the place or or or the patients or the inmates or either of them. I don't know which.

His denial of the equation of mind to body, internal causes of illness, and the proposition that medicine can cure the mind, could have come from any of Thomas Szasz's or R. D. Laing's books:

> You say "well, take some medication." Medication for the mind? I am supposed to take medication for, if I have some bodily injury. Not for the mind. My mind's perfect.

A crucial exchange between the head psychiatrist and the patient highlights the patient's articulation of the sociological theory of mental illness with its emphasis on contextual causes:

> Pt: if you leave me here, that means that YOU want me to get harmed. Which is an absolute fact. That's plain logic. That goes without saying. Obviously.
> HP: That's interesting logic.
> Pt: Yes. It's absolutely perfect, because if I am, if I am at a point, it's as if I were in some kind of a hole or something, right, and if you keep me there, obviously you intend to do me harm.

By blaming the hospital and the doctors, the patient gives us a perfect rendition of the iatrogenic theory of illness; the locus of the patient's trouble is in the social context, not his own mental state.

Conclusions

We can draw the following conclusions from the doctor–patient exchange:

1   The psychiatrists and the patient differ in their definitions of the situation.
2   These differences are assembled because an array of behavioral particulars

are bestowed with different meaning by participants operating from different theoretical perspectives and in different common sense systems of belief.

3   Within each system of belief, the participants marshal evidence to support a basic proposition and deflect evidence which has the potential to challenge the basic proposition.

If left here, the conclusion would be a (potentially interesting) demonstration of the Thomas theorem and would point to relativism played out in face-to-face interaction, i.e., that each perspective – that of doctor and patient – is equivalent.

While we can see that differences in perspective were visible in the interaction and maintained by a belief-validating process, there is another, important, dimension to the interaction that can not be overlooked. That dimension has to do with conflict and its resolution in language.

Conflict resolution in language: the politics of experience

While the physicians and the patient have conflicting definitions of the situation, these definitions are not equal. The patient's definition of his sanity is not on a par with the psychiatrists' definition of his insanity. The doctors' definition prevails. Despite the vehemence of his protestations and the admitted logic of his presentation, at the end of the meeting the patient is led from the examining room and returned to his lodgings, still convinced that he is healthy, there to await the decision and subsequent treatment recommended by the examining board.

So, although there is evidence of the socially negotiated construction of a medical fact here, the constituent negotiation is not evenly balanced. Instead, we have an example of what R.D. Laing (1967) has called "the politics of experience." Some persons, by virtue of their institutional authority, have the power to impose their definitions of the situation on others, thereby negating the others' experience. Speaking with the authority of the medical profession, in particular psychiatry, and, by extension, the legal institution, the definition voiced by members of the board is imposed on the definition voiced by the patient. The conflict between the patient and the psychiatrists is resolved by the imposition of an institutional definition of the situation on top of an everyday or lay definition of the situation. This imposition negates the patient's definition, relegating his experience to an inferior status.

The process by which the patient's experience is ironicized demonstrates how institutionalized power is manifested in language, making it necessary to fashion the corollary of the Thomas theorem that I proposed at the outset of this chapter.

> All people define situations as real; but when powerful people define situations as real, then they are real *for everybody involved* in their consequences.

The logical status of oracular reasoning

In closing, I'd like to make some final comments on the status of the logic of oracular reasoning. These comments are admittedly speculative, requiring further specification.

The parties in the conflict that I examined each operated within a certain frame of knowledge. They adhered to statements about the world whose validity could neither be confirmed nor disconfirmed (Shweder 1984: 39–40). The doctors maintained the absoluteness of their belief in the patient's mental illness by denying, repelling and transforming evidence which was contrary to their basic belief. The patient, too, used evidence presented in opposition to his argument as further support for the efficacy of his position. Thus, both a poorly educated, hospitalized patient and professionally educated physicians engaged in similar reasoning process. They admit to no universal standard (i.e., one that is outside both frames or in some frame acceptable by the people in the two frames) for judging the adequacy of ideas. As a result, no evidence or experience was allowed to count as disproof by either party.

[. . .]

The widespread appearance of belief-validating practices should lead us to realize that oracular reasoning is not limited to primitives, ancients, children or the uneducated, and to consider the possibility that it is a more extensive feature of reasoning. Since the appearance of oracular reasoning is not universal but variable, a productive next step would be to investigate how belief-validating practices operate in detail. If such practices can be found in any group, in any belief system, then it becomes important to determine when protection against discrediting evidence becomes so extensive that disconfirmation becomes virtually impossible and how potentially contradictory evidence is sufficient to change the structure and practice of belief.

Acknowledgements

This chapter was prepared for presentation at the Eleventh World Congress of the International Sociological Association, New Delhi, India, 18–24 August 1986.

A number of colleagues have commented on earlier drafts of the chapter. I wish to thank Dede Boden, Aaron Cicourel, Roy D'Andrade, Allen Grimshaw, Ed Hutchins, Jean Lave, Jim Levin, Tom Scheff, Ron Ryno, Alexandra Todd, Jim Wertsch – and especially Mell Pollner for penetrating criticisms and helpful suggestions.

Permission to quote from Frederick Wiseman's film, *Titicut Follies*, was kindly granted by *Zipporah Films*, Cambridge, Mass.

Notes

1   Thomas, W. I. and Thomas, D. S. (1928) *The Child In America*, New York: Alfred Knopf, 81.
2   [Excerpts from the transcript are used as examples in the text of the article. Pt is Patient (Vladimir), HP is head psychiatrist and Dr 2 is the Second doctor.]

References

Becker, H. (1963) *Outsiders*, New York: The Free Press.
Berger, P. (1968) *The Sacred Canopy*, Garden City, NY: Doubleday.
Cicourel, A. V. (1973) *Cognitive Sociology: Language and Meaning in Social Interaction*, New York: The Free Press.
Coulter, J. (1979) *Social Construction of Mind: Studies in Ethnomethodology and Linguistic Philosophy*, London: Macmillan.
Erickson, F. (1975) 'Gatekeeping and the melting pot: interaction in counseling encounters', *Harvard Educational Review* 45: 44–70.
Evans-Pritchard, E. E. (1937) *Witchcraft, Oracles and Magic Among the Azande*, Oxford: Clarendon Press.
Garfinkel, H. (1967) *Studies in Ethnomethodology*, Englewood Cliffs, NJ: Prentice-Hall.
Gasking, D. (1955) 'Mathematics: another world', in Flew, A. (ed.) *Logic and Language*, Garden City, NY: Anchor Books.
Goffman, E. (1959) 'The moral career of the mental patient', *Psychiatry* 22: 123–42.
Gould, S. J. (1981) *The Mismeasure of Man*, New York: W. W. Norton.

Greenwood, D. J. (1984) *The Taming of Evolution*, Ithaca: Cornell University Press.

Kitsuse, J. (1963) 'Societal reaction to deviant behavior', in Becker, H. S. (ed.) *The Other Side: Perspective on Deviance*, New York: Free Press.

Laing, R. D. (1967) *The Politics of Experience*, New York: Pantheon.

Mehan, H. (1983a) 'Le constructivism social en psychologie et sociologie', *Sociologie et Sociétés* XIV (2): 77–96.

—— (1983b) 'The role of language and the language of role in practical decision making', *Language in Society* 12: 1–39.

Pollner, M. (1975) '"The very coinage of your brain": the anatomy of reality disjunctures', *Philosophy of Social Science* 5: 411–30.

Pollner, M. and McDonald-Wikler, L. (1985) 'The social construction of unreality', *Family Process* 24: 241–54.

Rosenhan, D. L. (1973) 'On being sane in insane places', *Science* 179: 250–8.

Scheff, T. J. (1966) *Being Mentally Ill: A Sociological Theory*, Chicago: Aldine Publishing Company.

Shweder, R. A. (1984) 'Anthropology's romantic rebellion against the enlightenment, as there's more to thinking than reasoning and evidence', in Shweder, R. A. and LeVine, R. A. (eds) *Cultural Theory, Essays on Mind, Self and Emotion*, Cambridge: Cambridge University Press, 27–66.

Szasz, T. and Hollender, M. H. (1956) 'A contribution to the philosophy of medicine: the basic models of doctor–patient relationship', *AMA Archives of Internal Medicine* 97: 585–92.

Wason, P. C. (1977) 'The theory of formal operations: a critique', in Gerber, B. A. (ed.) *Piaget and Knowing*, London: Routledge and Kegan Paul, 119–35.

Chapter 34

Ian Hutchby

POWER IN DISCOURSE: THE CASE OF ARGUMENTS ON A BRITISH TALK RADIO SHOW

[. . .]

In this article, I show how an approach informed by conversation analysis (CA) can provide an account of power as an integral feature of talk-in-interaction. CA has placed great emphasis on examining how participants in interaction display their orientation to phenomena that analysts claim are relevant (Schegloff 1991). This has proved a highly successful platform for analysing talk in institutional settings (e.g., Drew and Heritage 1992). What I show is that this approach, through focusing on such issues as how participants orient to features of a setting by designing their turns in specialized ways (e.g., restricting themselves either to asking questions or to giving answers), can be used to address how power is produced through oriented-to features of talk. One way in which this might be shown is by looking for occasions when participants actually topicalize or *formulate* the power relations between themselves (in the sense intended in Garfinkel and Sacks 1970). However, this clearly does not happen very often. An alternative possibility is this: the very ways in which participants design their interaction can have the effect of placing them in a relationship where discourse strategies of greater or lesser power are differentially available to each of them. In this sense, power can be viewed as an 'emergent feature' of oriented-to discourse practices in given settings. It is that possibility that I want to explore in the case of calls to a British talk radio show.

Source: Ian Hutchby, 'Power in discourse: the case of arguments on a British talk radio show', *Discourse & Society* 7: 481–97.

The data come from a collection of approximately 100 recorded calls to a British talk radio show. I began to study interaction on talk radio out of an interest in analysing argument and conflictual talk, and a recognition that this was a common occurrence on open-line talk radio shows. Observing the data, my interests rapidly turned to the question of how participation in talk radio disputes can be asymmetrical. In institutionalized settings for dispute, one of the things that may be of interest is the relationship between verbal patterns and resources used and the asymmetric social identities associated with the setting. In this article, I go further and argue that some of the asymmetrics we identify can be conceptualized in terms of the power of certain participants to engage in communicative actions not available (or not available in the same way) to others. This argument is based on a CA account of the ways in which arguments on talk radio articulate with, and are shaped and constrained by, the organizational and interactional parameters of the talk radio setting itself.

[. . .]

Analysing power: 'first' and 'second' positions

Talk radio represents a public context in which private citizens can articulate their opinions on social issues. In different shows, the space allotted to callers to forward their views is mapped out in different ways. For instance, some shows expressly address themselves to one issue per broadcast and the caller's role is to have a say on that issue while the host acts as a moderator, relating contributions together and drawing out differences and similarities between them. But in other shows, known as open-line, callers select their own issue to talk about and are given the floor at the beginning of calls in order to introduce their issue and express an opinion on it. In this sense, open-line talk radio shows enable callers to set the agenda for a discussion with the host.

However, agendas are not fixed things, nor are they established from one perspective only. In fact, agendas can become the contested arena for disputes focusing on what can relevantly be said within their terms. This leads to a paradox in talk radio disputes. While it may seem that the caller is in a position to control what will count as an acceptable or relevant contribution to his or her topic, in fact it is the host who tends to end up in that position. The very fact that introducing an agenda is the caller's prerogative on talk radio leads to a situation in which the argumentative initiative can rest with the host and the caller can relatively easily be put on the defensive.

How does this situation emerge? I suggest that it is an outcome of two factors. First, the way that arguments are sequentially organized and second, the way in which calls on talk radio themselves are organized. The principal sequential unit in an argument is the 'action–opposition' sequence (Hutchby 1996: 22–4), in which actions that can be construed as arguable are opposed, with the opposition itself subsequently open to being construed as arguable (Eisenberg and Garvey 1981; Maynard 1985). Within the organization of calls on talk radio, callers are required to begin by setting out their position (Hutchby 1991). This in turn situates the caller's opening turn as a possible first action in a potential action–opposition sequence. To put it another way, it is the host who has the first opportunity for opposition within each call. This turns out to be a powerful argumentative resource, which is not only linked to a particular kind of asymmetry between hosts and callers, but also has consequences for the shape and trajectory of disputes in the talk radio setting.

The asymmetry between first and second positions in arguments was first remarked on by Sacks in one of his lectures on conversation (1992: 2: 348–53). Sacks proposed that those who go first are in a weaker position than those who get to go second, since the latter can argue with the former's position simply by taking it apart. Going first means having to set your opinion on the line, whereas going second means being able to argue merely by challenging your opponent to expand on or account for his or her claims.

In many situations, first and second positions are open to strategic competition between participants. In such situations we can find speakers using systematic means to try and avoid first position, or to try and prompt or manoeuvre another into taking first position. For instance, Sacks (1992: 2: 344–7) discusses the following fragment of data:

Extract (1) GTS [From a conversation among teenagers]

```
1   Jim:    Isn't the New Pike depressing?
2   Mike:   hhh The Pike?
3   Jim:    Yeah. Oh the place is disgusting. Any day of
4           the week.
```

In line 1, Jim indicates a position on the 'New Pike', a local amusement park. The way he states this position is designed to invite Mike's agreement that the New Pike is in fact 'depressing'.

In the next turn, however, Mike neither agrees nor disagrees with Jim. Rather, he produces a turn which on one level looks like an 'understanding check': a turn in which he initiates repair on Jim's prior turn, perhaps because he isn't sure he properly heard what Jim said. But there are features of Mike's turn which militate against that interpretation. For instance, he doesn't say: 'The what?' – which would be a straightforward way of indicating a possible mishearing or misunderstanding (Schegloff *et al.* 1977). Neither does he repeat Jim's naming of the place in full (i.e., 'The New Pike?'), which again might suggest a difficulty in locating the referent in his own stock of knowledge (Clark and Schaefer 1989). Rather, Mike 're-references' the amusement park, calling it 'The Pike' – an abbreviation which suggests he is in fact familiar with the place. Finally, Jim himself exhibits in his next turn that he does not take Mike's utterance to be initiating repair, by carrying on with and expanding his assessment (lines 3–4) instead of repairing his first turn by saying, for example: 'Yeah. You know, the amusement park?'.

Instead of an understanding check, Mike's turn can be treated as a move in an incipient argument: a manoeuvre by which the floor is thrown back to Jim with an invitation to go on and develop his position on the ways in which the New Pike is depressing. In other words, it is a manoeuvre which seeks to place Mike in second position with respect to Jim's opinion of the Pike. If he can succeed in manoeuvring Jim into first position, Mike would then be in a position to attack Jim's opinion by using what Jim said as a resource for disagreeing, rather than immediately focusing on building a defence for his own opinion.

In fact, this is precisely what happens as the conversation proceeds. Jim goes on to elaborate on his view of the Pike, which then places Mike in a position to attack that view merely by undermining its weaknesses rather than arguing for a particular counter-position:

Extract (2) GTS

```
1  Jim:    But you go down- dow- down to the New Pike
2          there's a buncha people, oh:: an' they're old,
3          an' they're pretending they're having fun, but
4          they're really not.
5  Mike:   How can you tell. Hm?
6  Jim:    They're- they're tryina make a living, but the
7          place is on the decline, 's like a degenerate
8          place . . .
```

In line 5 here, Mike takes up a critical stance *vis-à-vis* Jim's argument, not by putting forward a counter-position, but by undermining Jim's competence to make the claims he is making. This is done by using 'How can you tell' (line 5) to challenge Jim's grounds for the claim that people at the New Pike are 'really not' having fun. This turn does not give Jim much in the way of resources that will allow him to take up the offensive and challenge Mike. Rather, his options are either to account for how he can tell, or to attempt to change tack.

It is this situation which is at the root of the asymmetry between first and second positions in argument. While first-position arguers are required to build a defence for their stance, those in second position are able to choose if and when they will set out their own argument, as opposed to simply attacking the other's.

The point I want to make is that on talk radio, this asymmetry is one that is 'built into' the overall structure of calls. Callers are expected, and may be constrained, to go first with their line, while the host systematically gets to go second, and thus to contest the caller's line by picking at its weaknesses. The fact that hosts systematically have the first opportunity for opposition within calls opens to them a collection of argumentative resources which are not available in the same way to callers.

In the following sections, I explore some of the uses and consequences of these second-position resources. In order to do this, I concentrate on episodes in which the participants argue about the dispute's agenda itself.

Agenda contests

One of the things that argument may be about is the struggle between participants over what can and cannot legitimately be said in a dispute: in other words, defining the boundaries of the dispute's agenda. I have already remarked that on talk radio, callers' agendas have an interesting status. While it is the role of the caller to set up an agenda for discussion, the agenda is not something that the caller necessarily maintains subsequent control of. By being in second position, the host is able to challenge the 'agenda-relatedness' of the caller's remarks: to question whether what the caller says is actually relevant within the terms of his or her own agenda.

One way in which this may be done is through the use of a class of utterances, including 'So?' and 'What's that got to do with it?' which challenge a claim on the grounds of its validity or relevance to the matter in question. However, a significant aspect of such turns is that they need not make clear precisely on what terms the claim is being challenged. They may function purely as second position moves by which the first speaker is required to expand on or account for the challenged claim.

In the following extract the caller is complaining about the number of mailed requests for charitable donations she receives. Note that in line 7, the host responds simply by saying 'So?'

Extract (3) H:21.11.88:6:1

```
1   Caller:  I: have got three appeals letters here this
2            week.(0.4) All a:skin' for donations. (0.2) .hh
3            Two: from tho:se that I: always contribute to
4            anywa:y.
5   Host:    Yes?
6   Caller:  .hh But I expect to get a lot mo:re.
7   Host:    So?
8   Caller:  .h Now the point is there is a limi⌈t to (    )
9   Host:                                        ⌊What's that
10           got to do- what's that got to do with telethons
11           though.
12  Caller:  hh Because telethons . . . ((Continues))
```

As an argumentative move, this 'So?' achieves two things. First, it challenges the validity or relevance of the caller's complaint within the terms of
her own agenda, which in this case is that charities represent a form of
'psychological blackmail'. Second, because it stands alone as a complete turn,
'So?' requires the caller to take the floor again and account for the relevance
of her remark.

[. . .]

Another way in which the host may attempt to establish control over the
agenda is by selectively *formulating* the gist or upshot of the caller's remarks.
Heritage (1985: 100) describes the practice of formulating as: 'summarising,
glossing, or developing the gist of an informant's earlier statements'. He adds:
'Although it is relatively rare in conversation, it is common in institutionalised,
audience-directed interaction', that is, settings such as courtrooms, classrooms
and news interviews, as well as other forms of broadcast talk.

Heritage also notes that in these institutional settings, formulating 'is
most commonly undertaken by questioners' (1985: 100). This accords with
the common finding in studies of institutional discourse that '[i]nstitutional
incumbents (doctors, teachers, interviewers, family social workers, etc.) may
strategically direct the talk through such means as their capacity to change
topics and their selective formulations, in their "next questions," of the salient
plants in the prior answers' (Drew and Heritage 1992: 49).

In Extract 4, we see a particular kind of strategic direction of talk, that
is related to the argumentative uses of formulations in a setting such as talk
radio. The host here uses two closely linked proposals of upshot to con-
tentiously reconstruct the position being advanced by the caller. The caller

has criticized the 'contradictions' of telethons, claiming that their rhetoric of concern in fact promotes a passive altruism which exacerbates the 'separateness' between donors and recipients. He goes on:

Extract (4) H:21.11.88:11:3

```
 1   Caller:  . . . but e:r, I- I think we should be working at
 2            breaking down that separateness I ⌜think ⌝ these
 3   Host:                                      ⌊Ho:w?⌋
 4            (.)
 5   Caller:  these telethons actually increase it.
 6   Host:    Well, what you're saying is that charity does.
 7   Caller:  .h Charity do::es, ye⌜ ::s I mean-       ⌝
 8   Host:                        ⌊Okay we- so you're⌋ (.) so
 9            you're going back to that original argument we
10            shouldn't have charity.
11   Caller:  Well, no I um: I wouldn't go that fa:r, what I
12            would like to ⌜see is-
13   Host:                  ⌊Well how far are you going then.
14   Caller:  Well I: would- What I would like to see is . . .
```

In line 6, the host proposes that the caller's argument in fact embraces charities in general and not just telethons as one sort of charitable endeavour. This is similar to the 'inferentially elaborative' formulations that Heritage (1985) discusses. Note that although the caller has not made any such generalization himself in his prior talk, he assents to this in the next turn (line 7).

However, it turns out that the caller, by agreeing, provides the host with a resource for *reformulating* the agenda in play here. By linking a second formulation to the first, this time describing the 'upshot' of the caller's position, it is proposed that the caller is going back to an argument which the host had with a previous caller ('that earlier argument'), whose view had been that 'we shouldn't have charity' (lines 8–10).

The caller in fact rejects this further formulation (line 11). But the point is that the host is able to use the fact that the call is based on what the caller thinks about an issue to construct an argument without having to defend his own view. By relying on his ability to formulate the gist or upshot of the caller's remarks, the host can argumentatively define – and challenge – an underlying agenda in the caller's remarks.

In this sense, the 'agenda contests' which occur within calls begin to reveal significant aspects of the play of power in talk radio disputes. The fact that callers must begin by setting out a topical agenda means that argumentative resources are distributed asymmetrically between host and callers. The host

is able to build opposition using basic second-position resources. The characteristic feature of these resources is that they require callers to defend or
account for their claims, while enabling hosts to argue without constructing a
defence for an alternative view. At the same time, as long as the host refrains
from setting out his own position, such second-position resources are not available to the caller. Distinctive interactional prerogatives are thereby available
to the host, by which he can exert a degree of control over the boundaries of
an agenda which is ostensibly set by the caller.

Strategies for resistance

The implication so far has been that the way calls are set up provides the
host with a natural incumbency in second position. This does not mean,
however, that callers are incapable of offering resistance to the host's challenges. One way of doing this is to adopt the use of second-position resources
on their own part. But as I have suggested, particular sequential environments are necessary for this. In particular, the host must have moved or been
manoeuvred into adopting first position (that is, indicating an opinion in his
or her own right). On talk radio, the host is able to choose when, or if, to
express a view on the caller's issue: technically, the host is able to conduct
a whole call simply by challenging and demanding justifications for the caller's
claims. This, however, is very rare. And once the host has abandoned second
position, that position then becomes available for the caller.

Extract 5 shows how a caller may succeed in turning the tables in this
way. In this case the tables are turned only briefly because the host subsequently adopts a strategy for re-establishing himself in second position:

Extract (5) H:2.2.89:3:3

```
 1   Caller: But I still think a thousand pounds a night at a
 2           hotel:, .hhh a:nd the fact that she's going on
 3           to visit homeless peop┌le,
 4   Host:                          └Where should sh- Where
 5           should she be staying in New York.
 6           (0.2)
 7   Caller: We:ll u-th- at a cheaper place I don't think the
 8           money-=.h WE'RE paying that money for her to
 9           stay there and I think it's ob°scene.
10   Host:   Well we're not actually paying the ┌-e the money,
11   Caller:                                     └Well
12           who:'s paying for it.
```

```
13   Host:   Well thee:: e:rm I imagine the the:r the money
14           the Royal Family has .h er is paying for it, .h
15           or indeed it may be paid for by somebody else, .h
16           erm but .h y'know if the Princess of Wales lives
17           in: (.) a palace in this country, w-w-why do
18           you think she should not live in something which
19           is comparable, .hh when she's visiting New York?
20   Caller: Well I should think that she could find
21           something comparable that- that- or- e-it could
22           be found for her that doesn't cost that money.
```

One thing to notice is the way the caller responds to the host's hostile questioning (which has been going on for some while) by suddenly attempting to shift the topical focus of her agenda (line 8). From the question of the price of the hotel suite, she shifts, by means of a self-interruption, to the more emotive issue of the ultimate responsibility of the tax-payer for footing the bill: '.h WE'RE paying that money for her to stay there' (lines 8–9).

The host's response to this, in line 10, is significant. By opposing the caller's assertion, he abandons his series of questioning challenges and instead asserts an opinion in his own right. It is this turn which allows the caller to move onto the offensive and produce a challenge of her own which, in a way characteristic of the second-position moves I have been discussing, requires the host to account for his assertion (lines 11–12).

At this stage, then, the local roles of challenger and defender of a position have been inverted. The host, from being in his customary challenger role, has suddenly been swung around into the role of defender. However, this inversion turns out to be only temporary. In the very next turn, the host manages to re-establish the prior state of affairs. He does this by not simply responding to the caller's challenge but also going on to produce a next challenge-bearing question of his own (lines 16–19). With this move, the host succeeds in doing two things. First, he re-establishes the agenda to which his earlier question, in the second turn of the extract, had been addressed and which the caller had attempted to shift away from. Second, he resituates the caller as the respondent to his challenging initiatives, rather than as the initiator of challenge-bearing moves herself.

The asymmetry between first and second positions is not, then, a straightforward, one-way feature of talk radio disputes. Although the organizational structure of calls situates callers in first position initially, they may subsequently find themselves with opportunities to move into the stronger second position. As the previous extract shows, the sequential space for this arises once the host has abandoned the second-position strategy of issuing challenges and made an assertion in his own right. However, the extract also shows that there are strategies available for turning the tables back again; and this suggests that the second position itself can become actively contested over a series of turns.

To illustrate this, finally, we can continue with this call and find that the caller subsequently adopts the host's strategy in order to retake the initiative in the argument. The following extract takes up towards the end of Extract 5:

Extract (6) H: 2.2.89:3:3

```
20  Caller: Well I should think that she could find
21          something comparable that- that- or- e-it could
22          be found for her that doesn't cost that money.
23          A ┌nd ┐ you're only imagining that she's paying=
24  Host:    └But┘
25  Caller: =for herself you don't know ei:ther do you.
26  Host:   E:rm, well . . .
```

The feature of interest here is in lines 22–5. In a similar way to the host in Extract 5, the caller moves from responding to a challenge to issuing a question. This requires the host in turn to respond and further account for his own position that 'she's paying for herself'. In part, the basis for this second challenge lies in the host's long turn in lines 13–19 of Extract 5, where he responded to the caller's first challenge. That is, the caller is not simply revisiting or revamping the earlier challenge, but developing a new line of attack which relies on the fact that the host's earlier response had been quite vague (see especially lines 13–15 of Extract 5).

To summarize: the call's initial stages situate the caller in first position and furnish the host with the power of second position. But that asymmetry is not an unchanging feature of the context. The more powerful argumentative resources attached to second position may also become available to the caller. Yet this is dependent upon the host expressing an opinion in his own right. Nonetheless, once the opportunity arises, determined and resourceful callers may challenge the host using second position tactics; although second position itself can then become the focus of a discursive struggle.

Discussion

In this article I have used the idea of a relationship between interactional activities and organizational structures as the basis for developing an account of the play of power in calls to a British talk radio show. In doing so, I have illustrated how power is a phenomenon brought into play through discourse. I focused on relatively small sequential details of arguments in order to show this. The upshot is that the sequential approach developed within CA has been applied to a question which has concerned critical linguists and discourse analysts – i.e., how power operates in and through language – by viewing power in terms of the relationships between turns (as actions) in sequences.

The analysis has detailed the relationship between the organization of activities within calls and the asymmetrical distribution of argument resources. On talk radio, the opening of the call is not only designed to set up an environment in which callers introduce the topic, but by virtue of that it also places the participants on significantly asymmetrical footings with respect to those topics. The fact that callers are required to go first by expressing a point of view on some issue means that hosts systematically get to go second. Going second, I have argued, represents a more powerful position in argumentative discourse than first position. Principally, the host is able to critique or attack the caller's line simply by exhibiting skepticism about its claims, challenging the agenda relevance of assertions, or taking the argument apart by identifying minor inaccuracies in its details (see also Hutchby 1992).

However, the fact that hosts may conduct arguments without expressing a counter-opinion or providing explanations and accounts for their own positions does not mean that they never do the latter. The asymmetry that I have noted is simply this: hosts are in a position to do this whereas callers, by virtue of the organization of the call, are not. At the same time, there are resources available for callers to resist the host's powerful strategies and sometimes to exercise powerful strategies themselves. Thus, power is not a monolithic feature of talk radio, with the corresponding simplistic claim that the host exercises power over the caller by virtue of his or her 'control of the mechanics of the radio program' (Moss and Higgins 1984: 373). Rather, in a detailed way, the power dynamics at work within calls are variable and shifting.

This argument results in a model of power which comes close to the theoretical conception outlined by Foucault (1977). Like Foucault, a CA approach seeks to view power not as a zero–sum game but as a set of potentials which, while always present, can be variably exercised, resisted, shifted around and struggled over by social agents. Foucault argued that power is not something that is possessed by one agent or collectivity and lacked by another, but a potential that has to be instantiated within a network equally including those who exercise power and those who accept or resist it. The network itself is viewed as a structure of possibilities and not as a concrete relationship between determinate social entities.

While Foucault's work is often pitched at the broadest theoretical level, the empirical analysis in this article goes some way towards demonstrating how two of his central ideas can be located in the analysis of power in the details of talk-in-interaction. These ideas are, first, that wherever there is power, there is resistance; and second, that power operates in the most mundane contexts of everyday life, not just at the macro-level of large processes (Foucault 1977).

On the first point, I have stressed that although hosts have a 'natural' incumbency in second position, and thereby have a set of powerful resources available for dealing skeptically with callers' contributions, there are ways in which callers may resist those strategies. They may do this by recognizing and attempting to forestall the effects of the powerful strategy being used by the host (as discussed, for example, by Hutchby 1992). Or they may resist by attempting to adopt the powerful strategies available to the host for themselves, by taking opportunities to move into second position.

The second point is perhaps the one with which this article resonates most strongly. There is a tendency in both mundane and social scientific discourse to conceive of power as a 'big' phenomenon, operating at the largest scale within social formations. Foucault, on the other hand, suggests that power is pervasive even at the smallest level of interpersonal relationships. The kind of power with which Foucault is mainly concerned exists in the form of the manifold 'discourses' by which we make sense of ourselves, others and the world in which we are situated. This tends to lead Foucault's analyses away from the detailed character of social interaction and towards the larger-scale historical trajectories of discursive formations that can be traced in archive documents. I have focused on a different kind of power, traced in a different level of discourse. By power, I have meant the interactional power that threads through the course and trajectory of an argument. But in line with the conversation analytic approach, I have located that form of power in some of the smallest details of social life: the relationship between turns at talk-in-interaction.

References

Clark, H. and Schaefer, E. (1989) 'Contributing to discourse', *Cognitive Science* 13: 259–94.

Drew, P. and Heritage, J. (1992) *Talk at Work: Interaction in Institutional Settings*, Cambridge: Cambridge University Press.

Eisenberg, A. and Garvey, C. (1981) 'Children's use of verbal strategies in resolving conflicts', *Discourse Processes* 4: 149–70.

Foucault, M. (1977) *Power/Knowledge*, Hemel Hempstead: Harvester.

Garfinkel, H. and Sacks, H. (1970) 'On formal structures of practical actions', in McKinney, J. C. and Tiryakian, E. A. (eds) *Theoretical Sociology*, New York: Appleton Century Croft, 338–66.

Heritage, J. (1985) 'Analysing news interviews: aspects of the production of talk for an overhearing audience', in van Dijk, T. (ed.) *Handbook of Discourse Analysis*, vol. 3, London: Academic Press, 95–119.

Hutchby, I. (1991) 'The organisation of talk on talk radio', in Scannell, P. (ed.) *Broadcast Talk*, London: Sage, 119–37.

—— (1992) 'The pursuit of controversy: routine skepticism in talk on talk radio', *Sociology* 26: 673–94.

—— (1996) *Confrontation Talk: Arguments, Asymmetries and Power on Talk Radio*, Hillsdale, NJ: Erlbaum.

Maynard, D. W. (1985) 'How children start arguments', *Language in Society* 14: 1–30.

Moss, P. and Higgins, C. (1984) 'Radio voices', *Media, Culture & Society* 6: 353–75.

Sacks, H. (1992) *Lectures on Conversation*, vols 1 and 2, Oxford: Blackwell.

Schegloff, E. A. (1991) 'Reflections on talk and social structure', in Boden, D. and Zimmerman, D. (eds) *Talk and Social Structure*, Cambridge: Polity Press, 44–70.

Schegloff, E. A., Jefferson, G. and Sacks, H. (1977) 'The preference for self-correction in the organisation of repair in conversation', *Language* 53: 361–82.

INDEX